Britain since 1688

D0217562

Now in its second edition, *Britain since 1688* is an accessible and comprehensive introduction to British history from 1688 to the present day that assumes no prior knowledge of the subject.

Chronological in structure yet thematic in approach, the book guides the reader through major events in British history from the Glorious Revolution of 1688, offering extensive coverage of the British Empire and continuing through to recent events such as Britain's exit from the European Union. Fully revised and updated using the most recent historical scholarship, this edition includes discussion of the Brexit referendum and Britain's subsequent exit from the European Union, along with increased coverage of Britain's imperial past and its legacy in the present. New sidebars on themes such as race, immigration, religion, sexuality, the presence of empire and the experience of warfare are carried across chapters to offer students current and relevant interpretations of British history.

Written by a team of expert North American university professors and supported by textboxes, timelines, bibliographies, glossaries and a fully integrated companion website, this textbook provides students with a strong grounding in the rich tapestry of events, characters and themes that encompass the history of Britain since 1688.

Stephanie Barczewski is Professor of History at Clemson University, USA.

John Eglin is Professor of History at University of Montana, USA.

Stephen Heathorn is Professor of History at McMaster University, Canada.

Michael Silvestri is Professor of History at Clemson University, USA.

Michelle Tusan is Professor of History at University of Nevada, Las Vegas, USA.

"An effective four-nation focus is provided in a narrative that North American students will find particularly engaging. *Britain since 1688: A Nation in the World* is a balanced, historiographically astute, and compelling account."

Timothy Jenks, *East Carolina University*

"This engaging and accessible new edition uses recent developments in Britain and the world – Brexit, Black Lives Matter, the Queen's death – to reframe and reconsider the more traditional moments, events, and themes that have defined Britain's modern history. I appreciate the humility of the authors, who make clear from the outset that theirs is an interpretation, open to debate and revision. I look forward to assigning this edition to my undergraduates."

Arianne Chernock, *Associate Dean of the Faculty for the Social Sciences, Boston University*

"The updates to the second edition strengthen the text, increasing the coverage of empire and Britain's relationship with Europe and the wider world. The extension of coverage to 2020 is vital in bringing in discussions around democracy and the current state of the UK. Overall, this text does well in its goal of introducing North American students to Britain's global role."

Kyle Thompson, *Associate Professor of History, Pittsburg State University*

Britain since 1688

A Nation in the World

Second edition

Stephanie Barczewski, John Eglin, Stephen Heathorn, Michael Silvestri and Michelle Tusan

Routledge
Taylor & Francis Group

LONDON AND NEW YORK

Designed cover image: Loop Images Ltd / Alamy Stock Photo

Second edition published 2023
by Routledge
4 Park Square, Milton Park, Abingdon, Oxon, OX14 4RN

and by Routledge
605 Third Avenue, New York, NY 10158

Routledge is an imprint of the Taylor & Francis Group, an informa business

© 2023 Stephanie Barczewski, John Eglin, Stephen Heathorn, Michael Silvestri, Michelle Tusan

The right of Stephanie Barczewski, John Eglin, Stephen Heathorn, Michael Silvestri, Michelle Tusan to be identified as authors of this work has been asserted in accordance with sections 77 and 78 of the Copyright, Designs and Patents Act 1988.

All rights reserved. No part of this book may be reprinted or reproduced or utilised in any form or by any electronic, mechanical, or other means, now known or hereafter invented, including photocopying and recording, or in any information storage or retrieval system, without permission in writing from the publishers.

Trademark notice: Product or corporate names may be trademarks or registered trademarks, and are used only for identification and explanation without intent to infringe.

First edition published by Routledge 2015

British Library Cataloguing-in-Publication Data
A catalogue record for this book is available from the British Library

Library of Congress Cataloging-in-Publication Data
Names: Barczewski, Stephanie L., author. | Eglin, John, 1962– author. |
  Heathorn, Stephen J., 1965– author. | Silvestri, Michael, 1966– author. |
  Tusan, Michelle Elizabeth, 1971– author.
Title: Britain since 1688 : a nation in the world / Stephanie Barczewski, John Eglin,
  Stephen Heathorn, Michael Silvestri, Michelle Tusan.
Other titles: Britain since sixteen eighty eight
Description: 2nd edition. | New York : Routledge, 2023. | Includes bibliographical
  references and index.
Identifiers: LCCN 2022048300 (print) | LCCN 2022048301 (ebook) |
  ISBN 9781032257365 (hardback) | ISBN 9781032257174 (paperback) |
  ISBN 9781003284758 (ebook) | ISBN 9781000859225 (adobe pdf) |
  ISBN 9781000859331 (epub)
Subjects: LCSH: Great Britain—History.
Classification: LCC DA460 .B27 2023 (print) | LCC DA460 (ebook) |
  DDC 941—dc23/eng/20221011
LC record available at https://lccn.loc.gov/2022048300
LC ebook record available at https://lccn.loc.gov/2022048301

ISBN: 978-1-032-25736-5 (hbk)
ISBN: 978-1-032-25717-4 (pbk)
ISBN: 978-1-003-28475-8 (ebk)

DOI: 10.4324/9781003284758

Typeset in Goudy
by Apex CoVantage, LLC

Visual Tour (How to Use This Book)

Listed next are the various pedagogical features that can be found within the text, with visual examples of the boxes to look out for, and descriptions of what you can expect them to contain.

Topics covered

Each chapter begins with an outline of the wider topics covered in the study of the era in question.

<table>
<tr><td colspan="2">Topics covered</td></tr>
<tr><td>•</td><td>Glorious Revolution</td></tr>
<tr><td>•</td><td>The Revolution's impact on Scotland and Ireland</td></tr>
<tr><td>•</td><td>The Revolution's international and imperial consequences</td></tr>
<tr><td>•</td><td>Emergence of the fiscal – military state</td></tr>
<tr><td>•</td><td>Hanoverian Succession</td></tr>
<tr><td>•</td><td>Act of Union with Scotland</td></tr>
</table>

Timelines

There follows a chronological timeline of the key events that occurred during the period covered by the chapter, such as important royal and political developments. Events from the timelines appear in italics the first time that they are mentioned in the text.

Timeline

1715	Jacobite rebellion
1720	South Sea Bubble
1721	Robert Walpole becomes Lord Treasurer, effectively first Prime Minister
1726	Jonathan Swift, Gulliver's Travels
1727	Accession of George II
1731	William Hogarth, The Harlot's Progress
1733	Excise Crisis
1739	War of Jenkins' Ear begins, expands into War of Austrian Succession
1745	Last major Jacobite rebellion
1755	Samuel Johnson's Dictionary

Boxed features

Integrated throughout the text are numbered boxes (Box 1, Box 2, etc.) highlighting a specific point of detail, providing illustrative background to one of the wider topics covered.

Sexuality and Gender 1

Mother Clapp's Molly House

Male homosexuality was illegal in Britain until 1967, and in the eighteenth century a man caught in the act could be sentenced to a fine, imprisonment, transportation to an overseas colony or even death. Gay men thus had to meet in secret, and the clubs, taverns and coffee houses in London where they did so became known as "molly houses," as "molly" was a term for an effeminate man. Originally a derogatory term, it was reclaimed by gay men as a positive self-description, much as "queer" has been in more recent years. Molly houses provided a safe space in which gay men could interact and in some cases served as places of sexual assignation or brothels. In the 1720s, the most famous molly house was Mother Clapp's in London. It was owned by John Clapp, but run by his wife Margaret, who let gay men lodge there for extended periods and provided false alibis for them when they were arrested. In February 1726, the police raided Mother Clapp's; Margaret was fined, forced to stand in the pillory and then imprisoned for two years. Forty men were arrested along with her; some were sentenced to harsher punishments, including in three cases death. Although molly houses appear to be a new phenomenon in the early eighteenth century, in fact they had likely been around for decades or even centuries. The development of organized

Online documents

Whenever this symbol appears in the text, you will find a related document on the book's companion website at **www.routledge.com/cw/barczewski**.

See document "A Vision for the Welfare State" at www.routledge.com/cw/barczewski

Bibliographies

Each chapter concludes with the list of scholarly publications covered in the writing of the chapter, which also serve as useful suggestions for further reading.

Bibliography

Brewer, John, *The Sinews* ... *Power: War, Money, and the English State 1688–1783* (1989)
Fry, Michael, *The Union* ... *England, Scotland, and the Treaty of 1707* (2013)
Harris, Tim, *Revolution: The Great Crisis of the British Monarchy, 1685–1720* (2008)
Israel, Jonathan I., ed., *The Anglo-Dutch Moment: Essays on the Glorious Revolution and Its World Impact* (2003)
Kishlansky, Mark, *A Monarchy Transformed: Britain 1630–1714* (1997)
Pettigrew, William, *Freedom's Debt: The Royal African Company and the Politics of the Atlantic Slave Trade, 1672–1752* (2013)
Pincus, Steve, *1688: The First Modern Revolution* (2011)
Rose, Craig, *England in the 1690s: Revolution, Religion, and War* (1999)
Southcombe, George and Grant Tapsell, *Restoration Politics, Religion, and Culture: Britain and Ireland,*

Glossary

Key terms that are highlighted in bold within the text can be found in the comprehensive glossary at the end of the book.

apartheid: South African government policy, enforced through legislation, from 1948 to 1994 which mandated racial separation between whites and those of other races (defined as "black," "coloured," and "Indian"). The policy, derived from an Afrikaans word meaning "separateness," discriminated against the African minority and was used to maintain white minority rule.

Ascendancy: the Protestant elite in eighteenth-century Ireland. The Ascendancy controlled both the Irish Parliament in Dublin and the vast majority of Irish land. The height of the Ascendancy's power came between 1782 and 1800, when the Irish Parliament had legislative independence. Also known as the "Protestant Ascendancy" or the "Anglo-Irish Ascendancy."

Contents

Preface to the 2nd Edition

Days before the manuscript for the second edition of this textbook was submitted to the publisher, Queen Elizabeth II died. This compelled the authors, like so many other historians, journalists, politicians, pundits and ordinary people, to assess the meaning of her passing for the British nation. Many of the assessments of her long reign that appeared in the first days were laudatory, some attempted to take a more detached view, and a handful were condemnatory. This latter group predominantly focused on Elizabeth's role as the titular head of the British Empire and the Commonwealth. Three days after her death, British novelist Hari Kunzru wrote in the *New York Times*:

> Elizabeth was queen when British officers tortured Kenyans during the Mau Mau uprising. She was queen when troops fired on civilians in Northern Ireland. She spent a lifetime smiling and waving at cheering native people around the world, a sort of living ghost of a system of rapacious and bloodthirsty extraction. Throughout that lifetime, the British media enthusiastically reported on royal tours of the newly independent countries of the Commonwealth, dwelling on exotic dances for the white queen and cargo cults devoted to her consort.

It is not the role of a textbook to laud or to condemn, but rather to describe and explain. That Kunzru could even write such a piece reveals how much Britain's place as a "nation in the world" has changed. In fact, a case could be made that it changed as much between the start of Elizabeth's reign in 1952 and the present as it did between 1688, when this textbook begins, and 1952. In 1688, Britain was a second-tier European power about to embark on its rise to global dominance. It would then spend most of the period that this textbook covers as the world's most powerful nation, and even at the time of Elizabeth's accession Malaya, large swathes of Africa and a clutch of Caribbean and Pacific islands remained British possessions. There is no doubt that she took her responsibilities as an imperial monarch seriously, famously pledging on her twenty-first birthday to devote her life to the "service of our great imperial family to which we all belong." This quotation has appeared repeatedly in appraisals of Elizabeth's reign, but never as something for which she is praised. Rather, it is seen as at best archaic or at worst, to Kunzru and other critics of the Empire in its last, violent days, worthy of condemnation.

Whatever one's feelings about the passing of the "second Elizabethan age," there is no doubt that Elizabeth's "great imperial family" is no more. Although a few fragments of the Empire remain, Britain is now clearly a post-imperial rather than an imperial nation, even if it still experiences aftershocks of decolonization and its attendant loss of power and prestige such as Brexit. This means that its place in the world is now very different from what it was when Elizabeth acceded to the throne. Even if the dismantling of the Empire had already begun with the independence of India five years earlier, few envisioned how swiftly most of the remaining colonies would follow. In 1952, Britain still had pretensions of great-power status, which its leaders, no doubt including its queen, thought attainable. In 2022, these are all but gone, although some politicians try to convince voters that they can "make Britain great again." From the authors' perspective, it has been a fascinating journey, in which the world has been changed by the nation, but the nation has also been changed by the world.

We have sought to capture these changes in the chapters that follow. Regarding how this second edition differs from, and we hope improves upon, its predecessor, we have focused our efforts in three main areas. First, we have revised the pre-1945 chapters in order to reflect recent historiography. This includes a significantly expanded section on the American Revolution that incorporates new scholarship on the role of slavery; greater emphasis on Ireland's multifaceted relationship to the British Empire; and increased attention to the presence of black, Asian and Afro-Caribbean populations in Britain. More generally, we have made substantial revisions to the chapters and sections within chapters on the British Empire, in order to reflect interpretative changes and historiographical developments in this dynamic field and to take into account the impact of current events on our view of Britain's imperial past. Second, we have revised the chapters after 1945 to take into account the context and impact of recent events. This includes expanded coverage of topics such as the impact of immigration on British society and culture since the Second World War; social and cultural change in the 1960s and 1970s; and Britain's evolving relationship with the European Economic Community and European Union, up through the Brexit referendum of 2016 and beyond. We have added a new final chapter (Chapter 16) that covers post-Brexit politics; the COVID-19 pandemic; and the Black Lives Matter movement. Third, we have added themed sidebars that run across the chapters. Their themes, which we have chosen for their contemporary relevance, are race, immigrants and refugees, religion and difference, the press and the media, sexuality and gender, the experience of warfare, the presence of empire, the unity of the United Kingdom, Britain and America, and Britain and Europe. And finally, we have substantially revised the companion website in order to make it more useful as a faculty and student resource.

Preface

In November 2012, as this textbook was being written, the co-authors presented a round-table discussion on the process at the North American Conference on British Studies in Portland. We wondered how large a crowd we would attract, as we were up against what might be perceived as more exciting panels at which new ideas and research were being offered. We were pleasantly surprised, however, by both the size of the audience and the number of prominent scholars of British history from both sides of the Atlantic who chose to attend. After we each made brief presentations of our experience as fledgling textbook authors, a flurry of hands went up and a lively discussion ensued.

The main topic of that discussion was what the main theme or central narrative of our text would be. The audience was well aware that many of the traditional narratives of British history no longer seemed useful. A triumphalist story that focused on Britain's emergence as the most powerful nation in the world in the late eighteenth and nineteenth centuries was clearly both out of date and morally problematic, as assertions of the greatness of the British Empire have given way to newer interpretations that acknowledge the often negative impact it had on colonial peoples. And the old "Whig interpretation," which emphasized the rise of constitutional democracy and individual freedom, now appears to be, in the words of Sir David Cannadine, "an extremely biased view of the past: eager to hand out moral judgments, and distorted by teleology, anachronism, and present-mindedness."

But what, then, is the story of British history now? When our audience in Portland asked us that question, we resisted offering a definitive answer. All five authors are from a generation that attended graduate school in the 1990s, an age in which postmodernism reigned supreme. We were taught to be suspicious of dominant – or "meta" – narratives, which all too often are so powerful that they shut out alternative perspectives and voices that do not support their view of the past. But the discussion also helped us to recognize that there was a need to ensure that we were clear about our own views of what British history was and about what story we wanted to tell. Or stories, as we believed that a single narrative could not present the complexity of the British past with any hope of accuracy or without excluding too many things.

This textbook thus emphasizes two main themes and a number of sub-themes. First, we have focused on Britain's history of interaction with the world. This entails a thorough treatment of the British Empire, including its impact on both the colonies and the British metropolis. The Empire is treated in three chapters that deal with it exclusively, as well as in parts of numerous others. Our global focus, however, also means taking into account the influence of Britain's engagement with the non-imperial world. We have tried to show throughout this textbook the extent of the impact that the external world, in its colonial and non-colonial forms, had on not only Britain's foreign but also its domestic affairs. The second major theme is a treatment of Britain, or more accurately the United Kingdom, as a multinational state. We have endeavored throughout to avoid Anglocentrism and to include substantial material on Scotland, Wales and Ireland. In some places, we treat these nations as parts of a whole; in others, we recognize their separate and distinctive histories and identities.

We have selected these two major themes because we think they, more than anything else, have defined Britain as a nation over the last three centuries. We also, however, think that they help to show why the history of Britain remains relevant to students who do not live there. The long and complex story of Britain's interaction with the rest of the world illustrates that, even if "globalization" as we use the term today carries a meaning that is specific to our own time, living in a world that was in some ways globalized is not new. The heavy dependence of the British economy on foreign and colonial trade helps us to understand the global spread of capitalism, a process that is very much still ongoing today. The contacts with other peoples that occurred as Britons explored, settled and visited virtually every corner of the globe helps us to understand how cultural exchange takes place, and that it is almost always in two directions, rather than only one. The military and naval forces, as well other means of coercion, that Britain used to impose its will upon the world help to illustrate that globalization is often about power and violence.

The United Kingdom's existence as a multinational state, meanwhile, helps us to understand the nature of "nationhood." In recent decades, thanks to the work of Benedict Anderson and others, we have come to see nations not as ethnic or geographical entities but rather as cultural constructs, or as Anderson puts it, "imagined communities." In the United Kingdom, that imagination has operated both within its constituent nations and among them, as it has worked to bring them together as a single state and to keep alive the distinctive identities of each one. The period that this textbook covers encompasses the union with Scotland in 1707 and the union with Ireland in 1800, as well as the dissolution of the latter union and the creation of Northern Ireland in 1921. The question of how united the nations of the British Isles were and should be, or how separate, constantly recurred over the eighteenth, nineteenth and twentieth centuries, and it is far from resolved today. By the time this textbook appears, Scotland will have voted on its future within the United Kingdom; at present, with the vote only months away, the result is anybody's guess.

Our two primary themes overlay a number of sub-themes. First, because this book has been written predominantly for North American students, we have emphasized Britain's relationship with the United States. More space than British history textbooks usually provide has been given to topics such as the War of 1812 and Britain's role in the American Civil War. Second, we have retained what some scholars might think of as a traditional narrative of Britain's political history. Though we do not wish to privilege political events as the "spine" or "backbone" of history, as they are sometimes characterized, we do acknowledge that they are important and that they help to provide a clear sense of chronology that is useful for students. Third, we have attempted to incorporate newer approaches derived from cultural history, gender history and postcolonial history. We recognize that half of the British population was female and that colonial peoples had their own perspective on the British Empire that differed from that of the metropolitan elite.

We make no claim that our approach to British history is the only one possible, or even that it is comprehensive in covering the things we have chosen to emphasize. The clarity and brevity that is necessary for undergraduate students to understand Britain's past as they learn about it for the first time means that many things have to be left out or massively simplified. But we do claim to have provided an interpretation of British history that is distinctive without entirely abandoning tradition, and that is relevant to the world in which we live today. We have tried to write a textbook that explains Britain in 2014, not 1880 or 1945. For that latter reason, we have brought the textbook as close to the present as possible. The thirty-year rule has recently permitted the release of documents relating to key events of the early 1980s, including the hunger strikes in Northern Ireland and the Falklands War; we have incorporated the new revelations they contain. We have also devoted two chapters to the period after 1980, because we think it is important for students to understand recent British history as well as the more distant past.

This textbook was written to provide a learning experience for students, but, inevitably, it became one for the authors. We learned that it is easy to criticize other textbooks for being Anglocentric and difficult to avoid doing the same thing in your own. We learned that it is easy to say that you do not want a narrative of high politics to dominate and difficult to fit the other aspects of British history into the text after we had used up most of our allotted word length explaining the Glorious Revolution or the Great Reform Act. We learned, most of all, how much we are still learning about a subject that all of us are well into our second decade of teaching. We encourage all of our colleagues to attempt the writing of a textbook at some point in their careers. It will force you to think of the history that you teach both more broadly and more precisely. It will remind you of why you fell in love with that history in the first place. And most of all, it will humble you.

Author Biographies

Stephanie Barczewski, Professor of History at Clemson University, is the author of, most recently, *Heroic Failure and the British* (2016) and *Country Houses and the British Empire, 1700–1930* (2014). Her next project is an Anthropocene history of British national parks.

John Eglin, Professor of History at the University of Montana, specializes in the culture and politics of Britain in the long eighteenth century. His publications include *Venice Transfigured* (2001), *The Imaginary Autocrat* (2005) and *The Gambling Century* (2023).

Stephen Heathorn, Professor of History at McMaster University, researches popular uses of the past in Britain and has published a number of books, including *For Home, Country and Race* (2000) and *Haig and Kitchener in 20th Century Britain* (2013).

Michael Silvestri, Professor of History at Clemson University, is the author of *Ireland and India: Nationalism, Empire and Memory* (2009) and *Policing "Bengali Terrorism" in India and the World: Imperial Intelligence and Revolutionary Nationalism, 1905–1939* (2019). His current research focuses on the Irish role in British imperial policing.

Michelle Tusan, Professor of History at the University of Nevada, Las Vegas, teaches and writes about humanitarianism, world war and human rights. She has authored numerous articles and books, including *The British Empire and the Armenian Genocide* (2019) and *Smyrna's Ashes* (2012). *The Last Treaty: Lausanne and the End of the First World War in the Middle East* is due out with Cambridge.

Acknowledgments

Because there are five authors of this textbook, each with their own set of people who require thanks, we will keep the acknowledgments brief and for the most part collective rather than individual. We each would like to thank our academic institutions (Clemson University, the University of Montana, McMaster University, and the University of Nevada, Las Vegas) for their support. We all have family and friends who have contributed significantly to this textbook with their love, advice and toleration of the time it has taken us to write it (now twice), and we all thank our co-contributors to this book for their patience and comradeship in its composition. Eve Setch at Routledge has shown faith in this project from the beginning and has been a model of professional editorial assistance; she remained confident that we would produce something worthwhile even when we doubted it ourselves. Our original panel of readers suffered through our early drafts; we thank them for not giving up on us. The image credits can be found within the text, but we would like to thank Yale University, the Metropolitan Museum of Art, the Getty Museum, the Library of Congress and the Wellcome Collection for particular generosity in this regard.

Finally, all five authors feel that our greatest debt is owed to our undergraduate students, who have served as both our real audience as we have developed our ideas about British history in the past and as our imagined audience as we wrote this textbook. Their interest and curiosity has been a constant source of inspiration. We are all well into our second decade of teaching British history in North America. The story that this textbook tells about that history is very different today from what it was even fifteen years ago. That, to us, is the beauty of British history – it remains a living thing that continues to evolve before our eyes. We look forward to many more years of trying to tell its story.

1 The Making of a Modern State

Topics covered

- Glorious Revolution
- The Revolution's impact on Scotland and Ireland
- The Revolution's international and imperial consequences
- Emergence of the fiscal–military state
- Hanoverian Succession
- Act of Union with Scotland

Timeline

1688	Glorious Revolution
1689	Bill of Rights
1690	Battle of the Boyne
1692	Glencoe Massacre
1694	Death of Queen Mary
1694	Triennial Act passed
1694	Bank of England founded
1698	First Darien expedition
1701	Act of Settlement
1702	Death of William III
1702	War of the Spanish Succession begins
1707	Act of Union with Scotland
1709	Sacheverell Riots
1713	Treaty of Utrecht
1714	Accession of George I

Introduction

Why begin a course on modern Britain with the Revolution of 1688? For generations of scholars and students of British history, the *Glorious Revolution* was seen as a major step in the shift away from a powerful monarchy and towards a more democratic system in which Parliament was the dominant institution. This shift, so the conventional story goes, occurred in a constitutional, bloodless transfer that confirmed the capacity of the British state to evolve gradually, in contrast to the violent change that occurred in France's revolution a

DOI: 10.4324/9781003284758-1

century later. In this view, the Revolution of 1688 was significant not so much for what it did but rather for what it did not do, or in other words for what it confirmed rather than what it created. It confirmed the uniqueness of the British political system, which instead of alternating between the extremes of tyranny and revolution as occurred on the European continent evolved gradually and peacefully, all the while protecting the rights and liberties of the people. It also confirmed that the British state would remain Protestant-dominated. From this perspective, 1688 was *anti-revolutionary*, as it had preserved the state in the face of King James II's efforts to fundamentally alter its political and religious balance; James wanted to impose absolute monarchy and return Britain to the Catholic fold, and the "Glorious" Revolution prevented him from doing so.

In recent years, however, historians have come to interpret the events of 1688 differently. In these new views, the Glorious Revolution was *truly* revolutionary, as it led to the creation of the modern British state. Historian Steven Pincus describes 1688 as "the first modern revolution." What does this mean? When we speak of a modern society, we mean one that is urbanized, industrialized and bureaucratized; when we speak of a modern constitutional democracy, we mean one in which political participation is offered to, and even expected of, all adult citizens. At the beginning of 1688, the three kingdoms that made up the British state were far from modern according to these definitions. Over the course of the next year, however, decisive steps were taken that, without anyone intending or foreseeing it, put Britain on a path to modernity. Moreover, in these new interpretations, the Glorious Revolution is no longer a uniquely English event, but a British and global one. The traditional claim that the Revolution was "bloodless" is based on the course of events in England. In Scotland and Ireland, however, the political settlement was contested and had to be imposed by force, leading to significant violence and loss of life. The Glorious Revolution was also a global event, in two ways. First, the events of 1688 furthered the development of a large-scale **fiscal–military state** that could undertake long and expensive wars. Second, the Glorious Revolution was closely tied to the increasingly international orientation of the British economy, and in particular to the expansion of the British Empire.

This textbook begins with the Glorious Revolution for reasons related to both the traditional and new interpretations. The authors believe that there is sufficient merit to the traditional interpretation to warrant its being used as a jumping-off point for our discussion of British political developments thereafter. In addition, the Glorious Revolution provides a way to put British history in a context that encompasses all of the nations that are or have been part of the United Kingdom, as well as the global world with which Britain has long been engaged. Until recently, few events were more entrenched in an insular version of national history that barely recognized the importance of the non-English nations of the United Kingdom, much less the Empire and the rest of the world. Recasting the Glorious Revolution to encompass a broader, more global view shows how interpretations of British history have changed in recent years to include a more global perspective.

The Political Environment

In order to understand the Glorious Revolution, the forces that gave rise to it, and those that emerged from it, we must first understand the basic contours of British political life in the decades around 1700. It is often said that Britain possesses an "unwritten constitution." This characterization is not really accurate, as Britain's form of government *is* "written" into the statute law. It is not, however, *codified* in the way that the constitution of the United States is, that is, separate from and above statute, requiring special and extraordinary procedures to amend it. Britain's constitution can be and has been altered by ordinary legislation enacted through simple majority votes in Parliament. It was fundamentally altered, and in fact ultimately transformed, by statutes that Parliament passed in the wake of the events of 1688 and 1689. Consequently, legislation such as the Bill of Rights (1689), the Triennial Act (1694), the Act of Settlement (1701), and the Reform Acts of 1832 and 1867 are components of Britain's constitution in the same way that the first and fourteenth amendments are of the United States constitution.

Another crucial difference from the US constitution is the absence of what Americans think of as a "separation of powers" between the executive and legislative branches. Unlike their US equivalents, the British prime minister and her/his cabinet are and always have been members of the legislature, holding seats in Parliament, usually the House of Commons. Today, the British political party that controls the majority of seats in Parliament also controls the executive branch. This circumstance held from the time of the earliest recognizable political parties in England, which formed in the decade before 1688. The chief executive was understood to be the monarch and the cabinet the officers of state (the lord treasurer, the secretaries of state, the attorney general, etc.) that the monarch appointed. While the "royal prerogative" allowed the ruler to appoint whomever he/she wished, monarchs generally recognized that there was no point in delegating authority to those whose initiatives would be routinely voted down in Parliament. Correspondingly, cabinet ministers who lost Parliamentary support, usually indicated by the loss of key legislation, had to be replaced. This reality still holds true in Britain, where national elections occur at what would seem to Americans to be irregular intervals.

In addition to statutes passed by Parliament, there was another body of "unwritten" law, the English common law, that was determined by and encoded in judicial rulings dating in some cases from the Middle Ages. Common law was at the foundation of what is thought of as the Anglo-American legal tradition, and an important source of what Britons, and later Americans, thought of as their "liberty." To give a twentieth-century example of the importance of the common law, in 1944 the Trinidadian cricketer Learie Constantine successfully sued for breach of contract when a London hotel refused him a room on the grounds of his race. There was no statute in force against racial discrimination in the UK until 1965; Constantine instead won his case on the basis of a common law ruling of 1558 that an innkeeper could not refuse to lodge a bona fide traveler if accommodation were available.

"Citizenship" was a concept that did not exist in the way that it does today. No one was a citizen merely by virtue of being British, for neither Britain nor the concept of a nation in their modern senses existed. In contemporary usage, the term "citizen" referred to a politically privileged resident of a city or town, especially of "*the* City," as the central business district of London is still known. Nor did anyone have an automatic right to vote based on their citizenship. Instead, to be able to vote, a person generally had to be male and Protestant, and he had to own a certain amount of property, measured in value rather than acreage. The property restrictions on the right to vote were removed only incrementally, a process that did not begin until well into the nineteenth century and was not complete until the early twentieth. Prior to that, the ownership of property conferred membership in the community of the realm precisely because a property owner literally owned a piece of that realm. This meant that the unpropertied lower classes, and even the minimally propertied middle classes, were not entitled to direct political participation. The proportion of adult males who could vote in England and Wales was no more than one in four. In Scotland, the **franchise** was even narrower: there, a voter had to own land worth at least £2 "of old extent," which meant that it had to have been worth that much since the creation of the Scottish

Parliament in the seventeenth century. Only a handful of wealthy landowners qualified, and in most constituencies there were fewer than a hundred voters. As late as 1830, there were only 4,500 Scottish voters out of a total population of 2.6 million.

Most people, however, would not have considered this a hardship, because before 1689, Parliament was not a permanent legislative body but an ad hoc assembly that met only when, and only for as long as, a monarch wished it to. Contemporaries spoke of "Parliaments" as periodic events, not "Parliament" as a legislative assembly that met regularly. Technically, a *Triennial Act* had been in force since 1641 that obliged the monarch to call a Parliament every three years, but there was no mechanism for enforcement. A Parliament had to be summoned at the beginning of a reign in order to supply a portion of the funds that went into the royal purse, but at other times people understood that an English Parliament was at the beck and call of the ruler. The Scottish Parliament was even more so, as it lacked even the power of the purse strings over the monarch. The summoning of the Parliament of Ireland, meanwhile, could be vetoed by the **Privy Council** in **Whitehall**.

The English and Irish Parliaments were bicameral, with an "upper" **House of Lords** and a "lower" **House of Commons**. (The Scottish Parliament was unicameral, meaning that all its members sat in a single house.) In the Lords, the titled nobility – in descending order Dukes, Marquesses, Earls, Viscounts and Barons, collectively known as "peers of the realm" – made up the "lords temporal." All English and Welsh peers sat in the House of Lords in London, but later when first Scotland (1707) and then Ireland (1800) were amalgamated into the United Kingdom, those two nations were permitted to elect only a small portion of their titled aristocracy as "representative peers." Otherwise, the 180 or so English and Welsh peers would have been outnumbered by the 150 peers each from Scotland and Ireland, who existed in greater numbers relative to the populations of their countries than did their English and Welsh counterparts. The Scots and Irish should, however, have been allotted significantly more seats in the Lords than they were: only sixteen for Scottish representative peers and, after 1800, twenty-eight for their Irish counterparts. The House of Lords also included around two dozen of the most senior bishops of the **Church of England**, the "lords spiritual." As peers were notorious for lax attendance, the bishops, who appeared more regularly, were a formidable voting bloc, despite their small numbers.

The Lords' main power derived from its right to veto any legislation passed by the Commons. Despite its status as the "lower" house, however, the Commons was always more important, as all legislation originated there. The members of the House of Commons were known as members of Parliament, or "MPs." Each of the forty counties of England and Wales elected two at-large MPs. The remaining 405 members of the House of Commons were elected for borough constituencies, which were usually, but not always, towns that had grown sufficiently large to merit their own representation. Any adult male with freehold property worth at least £2 per year in rents or other income (the "forty **shilling** franchise") was eligible to vote in the county constituencies, effectively qualifying any man who owned any real estate at all. (This was still a small percentage of the population as a whole.) In the boroughs, eligibility requirements varied but were generally much more stringent than in the counties.

Moreover, there was no standard for what constituted a borough. Bristol, which emerged in this period as England's "second city" thanks to its role as the nation's second largest port after London, had a population of 50,000 and an electorate of 5000, while the nearby resort town of Bath had an off-season population of only a few thousand and an electorate of only twenty-five. Both elected two MPs to Parliament. In other cases, monarchs had created boroughs in places with small populations in order to create seats in the Commons for their loyal supporters while some places had lost substantial numbers of people since the creation of the borough centuries earlier. Other places that had gained significantly in population, meanwhile, did not possess status as a borough.

The small size of some boroughs made them easy prey for wealthy and powerful people who were looking to increase their parliamentary influence, especially in an age where ballots were open rather than secret. "**Rotten boroughs**," or places with only a handful of eligible voters who could thus be easily bribed, came to be notorious for their electoral corruption, as were "**pocket boroughs**," or constituencies that were dominated by powerful electoral patrons. Prior to 1688, it was possible to ignore such glaring inequities because of the essentially medieval conception of Parliaments. But once Parliament became a permanent legislative assembly, as occurred in the eighteenth century, these anomalies became more and more conspicuous. This was one of the most important outcomes of the Glorious Revolution.

Another key aspect of the political and legal world of the eighteenth century was the strong presence of religion. In contrast to the principles that would later be established in the American Constitution, in Britain church and state were not separate. Instead, the monarchy, the head of the executive branch of government, was also the head of the Church of England, which was the state, or "established," church. This did not mean that everyone was compelled to worship in it, but it did mean that the rights of those who chose not to were diminished. Catholics suffered from the worst prejudice. In the second half of the seventeenth century, they were unfairly blamed for the Great Fire of London of 1666 and for fictitious conspiracies such as the Popish Plot of the late 1670s, in which they supposedly planned to assassinate King Charles I. Anti-Catholic prejudice led to the passage of a series of **penal laws**, which, variably according to time and place, subjected Catholics to punitive taxation, restrictions on the ownership or inheritance of land, and disqualification from holding office, and effectively from voting, among other things. Their numbers declined sharply, as many people opted to convert in the face of such crippling discrimination. By 1700, less than 2 percent of the population of Great Britain (excluding Ireland) was Catholic.

Religion and Difference 1

The Sacheverell Riots

Doctor Henry Sacheverell was a "**high church**" Anglican clergyman who staunchly opposed toleration for Catholics and Dissenters. On the 5th of November 1709, the anniversary of the Gunpowder Plot, an attempt in 1605 by Roman Catholics to blow up the Houses of Parliament, Sacheverell delivered a sermon at St. Paul's Cathedral in London in which he strongly denounced Dissenters. After he gave a similar sermon a few weeks later, the **Whig** government felt that it had to take action. Sacheverell was brought before the House of Commons and found guilty of promoting sedition; he was banned from preaching for three years. The public response, however, was not what the government desired, as many people saw Sacheverell as an heroic martyr and defender of the true faith. Chanting "High Church and Sacheverell," angry crowds attacked Dissenters' meetinghouses and burned their contents in the street. The sentiments that had been unleashed played a major role in a landslide victory by the **Tories** in the election that was held later that year. The Sacheverell Riots showed that the debate over the toleration of other religious faiths in England besides Anglicanism was far from settled.

Figure 1.1   A Staffordshire pottery figurine of Doctor Henry Sacheverell from the 1740s, showing that his reputation as an heroic defender of the Church of England lingered for decades after his controversial speeches in 1709.

Reproduced courtesy of the Metropolitan Museum of Art, Gift of Carleton Macy, 1934.

Another group who saw their rights constrained due to their religion were **Dissenters** (also referred to as **Nonconformists**), who were non-Anglican Protestants such as Baptists, Presbyterians, Congregationalists, Quakers, Unitarians, and (later) Methodists. Dissenters comprised between 5 and 8 percent of the population. Before 1689, they suffered under a series of discriminatory statutes that outlawed their religious services and penalized their clergy. While the 1689 Act of Toleration allowed them freedom of worship, they were still prevented from holding even the humblest public office. However, a dissenter with a sufficiently flexible conscience was able to evade these proscriptions through "occasional conformity," taking Anglican communion once a year for the purpose of holding office, a practice common enough that it was briefly outlawed. It was well into the nineteenth century before the political restrictions that were imposed upon Catholics and Dissenters were entirely removed.

The Tumultuous Seventeenth Century

To understand the Glorious Revolution, we must think about Britain very differently than how we typically do in most western or European history courses. In that context, Britain is usually presented as extremely politically stable, a country in which the nature of government changed gradually, peacefully and constitutionally, in contrast to the abrupt and violent revolutions that shook other European countries like France and Russia. But in the seventeenth century, Britain was a very different place. It was unstable and violent, particularly in the two decades between 1640 and 1660, when it was torn apart by civil war. This conflict was over two issues: what would be the dominant institution in the political system, the monarchy or Parliament, and what form of Christianity would prevail.

Regarding the former issue, the question was whether Britain would follow other European nations, France in particular, down the path to absolute monarchy, as the Stuart kings from 1603 onwards desired, or whether it would move in a more republican direction, like the Netherlands. In the end, Britain would create its own hybrid form of constitutional monarchy. Regarding the second issue, that of religion, the most pressing questions surrounded the issue of what kind of Protestantism would prevail within the Church of England. The supporters of the King tended to favor a "high church" establishment governed by bishops, with a fixed liturgy focused on the sacraments, and those of Parliament, a "**low church**" form that curtailed the power of bishops, eschewed music and ceremony, and emphasized preaching. This meant that high-church Anglicanism, which more closely resembled and was thus linked to Catholicism, was associated with absolutism, and the most extreme versions of low-church Protestantism, often referred to as puritanism, with republicanism. Both were unpopular with – and threatening to – the majority of British people, who favored a political and religious settlement that was somewhere in the middle.

These political and religious conflicts were brought to the forefront when Elizabeth I died without issue in 1603 and passed the thrones of England, Wales and Ireland to her cousin, King James VI of Scotland, who became James I of England, Wales and Ireland. (Though Scotland was now governed by the same king as England, Wales and Ireland, it remained politically separate for another century.) James I and his son Charles I were chronically short of revenue, as Parliaments were reluctant to supply them with money in light of fears that they would move the Church of England closer to Catholicism and Britain towards absolute monarchy. These fears may have been exaggerated, but they were not entirely unfounded. In the early 1640s, the political and religious conflict between king and Parliament erupted into a civil war that embroiled England, Wales, Scotland and Ireland. In 1646, the parliamentarian New Model Army defeated the king's forces. Three years later, Charles I was beheaded for high treason, and the monarchy, along with the Church of England, was abolished. England and Wales became a republic, while rebellions in Scotland and Ireland were put down and both nations subjected to military occupations.

It proved easier, however, to dismantle the old government than to construct a new one. The death of the King gave rise to a series of constitutional experiments, culminating in the ascension of Oliver Cromwell, the parliamentarian commander, to the position of lord protector. But following his death in 1658, the government dissolved into factions, and there were fears among the political elite that Britain was descending into chaos once again. A solution was found in tradition, and in 1660 Charles Stuart, son of Charles I, was called back from exile in France and restored as King Charles II. The restoration, however, did not put an end to the turmoil, as important social and economic changes made a return to a traditional monarchy impossible. After 1650, commerce, mining and manufacturing began to challenge the monopoly that had long been held by agriculture as the linchpin of the British economy. In addition, the country was much more urban than it had been under the Tudors, as the proportion of the population living in cities and towns tripled between

1500 and 1700. These socioeconomic changes contributed to the emergence of a mercantile and manufacturing class, or "middling sort," that was gaining rapidly in wealth and status. In consequence, British society became increasingly mobile; if it was still extremely difficult for a man to rise from the bottom to the top of the social ladder, at least he could reasonably hope to ascend a few rungs. The emergence of this "middling sort" had an effect on politics, because people who had a larger economic stake in the nation tended to be more politically engaged. They were also better educated and more literate, making it possible for them to read about, discuss and debate political events, even if many of them could not vote because they did not own sufficient property.

Such was the "Restoration Settlement" that settled nothing. Initially, the political elite so wanted stability that a precarious balance was achieved, but the political and religious conflicts were too deep and too unresolved, and by the end of Charles II's reign they had flared up with renewed vigor. The tensions were exacerbated by the issue of the royal succession, as Charles failed to produce a legitimate heir, though he had over a dozen illegitimate children with his various mistresses. This meant that his younger brother James, Duke of York, was in line for the throne, but this posed a serious problem, as James was Catholic.

The crisis that ensued gave rise to the political parties that dominated British governments into the early twentieth century. On one side were the traditionalists who believed that the balance of political power should reside with the monarchy. This group also supported the ecclesiastical, political and cultural dominance of the Church of England, and they sought to protect the economic interests of the large landowners. Because they opposed James's exclusion from the royal succession, their enemies viewed them as overly tolerant of Catholicism and labeled them as "Tories," Irish slang for horse thieves. The opposing party located the balance of political power with Parliament, favored a broader religious establishment that tolerated a wide variety of practices (so long as they were Protestant), and advanced the interests of newer sectors of the economy such as trade, commerce and manufacturing. The Tories viewed them as partisans of what they saw as the more aggressive sects of Protestant Nonconformists, such as Scottish Presbyterians, and thus nicknamed them the "Whigs," after Scottish highwaymen called "whiggamores."

For his part, Charles tried to steer a middle path through the competing factions, but he fiercely resisted Whig pressure to exclude his brother from the succession. The intense discussions over James's legitimacy, referred to as the Exclusion Crisis, proved that the old questions about religion, royal prerogative and the balance of power between Parliament and the monarchy were far from resolved. To be sure, there was little support for further radical experiments with republicanism – no one wanted a return of Cromwell's Commonwealth – but there were many people who believed that monarchs had to adhere to the rules that Parliament set for them. To make matters worse, James had neither the political acumen nor the common sense to take advantage of the innate loyalty to the monarchy felt by many members of the political elite. An unfortunate combination of stubbornness and insecurity, he vacillated when he needed to be resolute and dug in his heels when he needed to be flexible.

Following his accession to the throne in 1685, James progressively alienated virtually the entire political nation. His inflated notion of his prerogative and his heavy-handed recourse to it placed even his supporters in an impossible position. As the head of the Church of England, James had discretionary power to suspend the enforcement of religious statutes. It was generally agreed, however, that this power was limited to clearly specified periods of time or to specific individuals. But in order to reintegrate Catholics into public life, James adopted a much broader conception of this power, as he issued comprehensive and indefinite suspensions of and dispensations from the Test Act of 1673, which required all holders of public office to swear an oath to the Church of England. In 1687, he announced his intention to have the Test Act repealed entirely, and issued a Declaration of Indulgence that suspended the civil disabilities against Catholics and Dissenters. Judges who ruled that his power did not extend that far were simply removed from the bench; as many were removed between 1685 and 1688 as had been under the previous three Stuarts combined. James also expanded the size of the army, staffed it with Irish Catholic officers and stationed it ominously close to the capital. This gave rise to fears that he would use military power to reimpose Catholicism upon the British people by force. He removed justices of the peace who would not pledge to support a repeal of the Test Act, replacing them, it was claimed, with men who could barely write their own names. Events on the European continent, meanwhile, deepened people's suspicions. In 1685, King Louis XIV's revocation of the Edict of Nantes, which had allowed freedom of worship for French Protestants, aroused fears that another zealous Catholic king would attempt to reimpose Catholicism in Britain, fears that were exacerbated when James refused to accept Protestant Huguenot refugees.

Historians continue to debate James II's intentions. Some see him as a zealot who was blinded by his faith and refused to listen to reason and as a tyrant who ignored the rule of law and the desires of his subjects with equal disdain. Others see him as an enlightened exponent of religious tolerance who sought to expand the political nation beyond the Church of England to Catholics and Dissenters. His contemporaries, however, saw him only in the first light. If he had been willing to practice his faith quietly and not assert his prerogative boldly, he might have survived. But whether it was the cause of tyranny or toleration, he did neither of these things, and in consequence his reign was destined to be short-lived.

1688: A Coup d'Etat

In the first two years of James's reign, Tories and Whigs alike feared a return to the political turmoil of the mid-seventeenth century, and so they both took comfort in the fact that the aging monarch had, by his late first wife Anne Hyde, two daughters who were safely and firmly Protestant. With James now well into his fifties, an old age by the standards of the time, there seemed to be little prospect of this changing. The hope for a smooth Protestant succession was shattered in June of 1688, however, when James's second wife Mary of Modena gave birth to a healthy infant son. (Until 2011, males took precedence over females in the British royal line of succession.) Rumors swirled that the baby had been smuggled into the birthing chamber in a warming pan, but this did not change the reality that Britain now faced an endless succession of Catholic monarchs, rather than a brief and isolated interruption in the Protestant line.

This unanticipated – and to most people unwelcome – development changed the political discussions about the future. Faced with a monarch with an overexpansive conception of his powers, with a military establishment to back it up, and with a new prospect of the secure succession of a like-minded heir, Whigs and Tories alike agreed that they had to act. The strategy they chose was bold, and potentially treasonous: in short, a *coup d'etat* in the form of an invitation to a foreign power to invade and overthrow a legitimate king. Their chosen liberator was William of Orange, *Stadtholder* (Head of State) of the Netherlands. William came equipped with impeccable Protestant credentials and a strong record of military success against the French. He also had a viable claim to the throne: he was both James II's nephew – he was the son of the king's sister Mary – and married to James's elder daughter, also named Mary. (His choice of wife had been a deliberate one to move him closer to the English throne.) Moreover, he appeared to be well suited to the limited form of monarchy envisioned by most English political leaders, as he was accustomed to deferring to a legislative body. In the Netherlands, the *Stadtholder* was merely a presiding executive, while sovereignty rested with the seven provinces that comprised the country.

In November 1688, William landed with 20,000 troops on the southwest coast of England. An invasion on such a massive scale by a foreign power would ordinarily have roused a call to arms. Instead of mustering militias, however, the English people watched and waited behind closed doors to see who would emerge victorious. It was not that they were particularly enthusiastic about William's arrival, for they were unsure of his exact intentions and almost as afraid of the potential threat he posed as they were of James's absolutism and Catholicism. But they were sufficiently threatened by the latter to wait and see what happened rather than rallying to James's side. William thus met no resistance as he marched east towards London. Along the way, the first sign appeared of which way the wind was blowing: he was joined by some of James's highest-ranking officers, most significantly his most trusted commander, John Churchill. As they neared London, a panicked James promised a flurry of concessions, but it was too late to rally any significant support. On the 2nd of December, a disguised Queen and infant Prince of Wales fled to France. Nine days later James attempted to follow. He was quickly captured but allowed to escape, as William did not want the blood of another Stuart martyr on his hands. William had gained the thrones of all four nations of the British Isles without having to fight so much as a skirmish.

The events of 1688 were quickly termed the "Glorious Revolution" because they were supposedly nonviolent. British Catholics, who were subjected to weeks of terror as their houses and chapels were ransacked and burnt, would have disagreed. Outside of England, meanwhile, the settlement was contentious and bloody. In Scotland, three factors complicated the situation. First, most Scottish Protestants were not members of the Church of England or Episcopalians, but rather were members of the Church of Scotland or Presbyterians. This was because in Scotland the Protestant Reformation had taken a different path, following the lead of John Knox rather than Henry VIII. Second, though James was not popular among the Presbyterian-dominated **Lowland** Scottish elite, who fiercely opposed his pro-Catholic policies, there was greater loyalty to him among Episcopalians and in the **Highlands**. Third, there was the issue that James had not actually fled from Scottish territory, and so the argument that he had abdicated the throne could not be used to justify a change of king.

The Scots called a Convention to discuss the best course. Most Episcopalians boycotted it, and so it was dominated by anti-James Presbyterians. In April 1689, they issued a Claim of Right, which justified James's removal on the basis that he had violated a number of Scottish laws. The Claim also barred Catholics from the Scottish throne in the future. The Claim was intended to demonstrate that it was the Scottish Parliament, not the monarchy, that now held the most power. The Convention also dictated religious policy, sweeping aside royal supremacy and establishing a Presbyterian "**Kirk**" that was free from royal control. Many of the now-marginalized Episcopalians were in consequence nudged into **Jacobitism**, or support for James II, a term that derived from "Jacobus," the Latin form of James.

Faced with a divided religious nation and such entrenched recalcitrance to bend to his will, William found Scotland's political terrain more difficult to negotiate than England's. In the years that followed 1688, Lowland Scots, who had mostly welcomed the Glorious

Revolution, felt that they had earned greater independence and were frustrated by William's refusal to grant it. Those Scots who continued to favor James, meanwhile, constantly sought opportunities to restore him to the throne. In April 1689, James Graham, Viscount Dundee, launched a rebellion. The rebels won a key battle at Killiecrankie in July, in which 2000 of William's troops were killed. Dundee perished as well, however, and afterwards the rebels' fortunes declined. But even though overtly rebellious Jacobitism had – temporarily – been suppressed, William faced continuous demands for concessions from the Scottish Parliament. Eventually, in exasperation he declared that he would "yield no more . . ., and if the Parliament in Scotland did not like it, he would dissolve it and get another." Gradually, a compromise was reached, in which royal power remained reasonably secure and the supremacy of the Church of Scotland was confirmed.

In the Highlands, however, William badly botched gaining the allegiance of the **clans**, who were the primary sources of authority in the region. In 1691, William offered to pardon the clans who had supported James, so long as they swore an oath of allegiance to him by the 1st of January 1692. Traveling in the harsh Scottish winter, the MacDonald clan arrived five days late. They duly swore the oath and thought they had met William's conditions, but John Dalrymple, secretary of state for Scotland, saw an opportunity to break the power of the clans once and for all. He dispatched a regiment of the army that was full of men from the estate of the Earl of Argyll, head of the MacDonalds' bitter enemies the Campbell clan, to visit the MacDonalds in their homes at Glencoe in the western Highlands, ostensibly for the purpose of collecting tax. For two weeks, the regiment enjoyed the hospitality that Highland custom required, but on the morning of the 13th of February they turned on their hosts and murdered them in their beds. In all, thirty-eight MacDonald men were killed, and forty women and children died of exposure after their homes were destroyed. Under Scottish law, "murder under trust" was a particularly heinous crime, and the *Glencoe Massacre*, as it became known, ensured that sympathy for the Jacobite cause remained strong in the Highlands for decades to come.

In Ireland, where three-quarters of the population was Catholic, the Glorious Revolution was even bloodier. While seventeenth-century Ireland had the constitutional status of a kingdom, most historians contend that Ireland is best understood as both a kingdom and a colony in this era. The predominantly Gaelic-speaking Irish, whose language, religion, culture and society differed sharply from contemporary England's, were considered to be a "barbarous" and "savage" people and compared to both ancient Britons and indigenous Americans. During the Reformation, Catholic Ireland came to pose a security threat to the English crown, which feared Irish alliances with continental Catholic powers. As a result, the English state made repeated efforts to subjugate Ireland. Many of the strategies used in the conquest of Ireland would serve as models for British overseas expansion. These included not only military force, but also large-scale colonization projects (referred to as "plantations"), and, in what would later be termed the imperial "civilizing mission," an effort to compel the Irish to adopt the English language, law, customs and economic practices.

Following a failed uprising in the mid-seventeenth century, most Irish Catholics lost their ownership of land. James II's accession to the throne raised the hopes of Catholics, particularly the Irish gentry, that their land and political power would be restored under the new monarch. Under the leadership of the Catholic Earl of Tyrconnell, whom James had appointed as his lord deputy or chief representative in Ireland, thousands of Irish Catholics rebelled against William and declared for James. The exiled king landed with 6000 French troops to defend his throne. His forces enjoyed considerable initial success, but in July of 1690, they were decisively defeated by William at the *Battle of the Boyne*.

Religion and Difference 2

Battle of the Boyne

On the 1st of July 1690, William of Orange and James II faced each other across the River Boyne, thirty miles north of Dublin. James, who hoped to use Ireland as a staging ground for an invasion of England, landed at Kinsale on Ireland's southwestern coast in March 1689 with 6000 French troops. As he marched north, 20,000 Irish Catholics rallied to his side; they quickly seized control of Ireland apart from the Protestant-dominated northern province of Ulster. William knew that he had to meet the threat forcefully; as one English Member of Parliament stated, "If Ireland be lost, England will follow." He arrived in June 1690 with an army of 35,000 English, Dutch, German, Danish, French Huguenot and Irish Protestant troops. On the day of the battle, William used aggressive tactics to cross the river and drive James's troops back. James's army suffered 1500 casualties, as compared to 750 for William's. Though his army was largely intact, James opted to return to exile in France. His Irish supporters fought on for another year, but in the summer of 1691 the Treaty of Limerick ended the war and James's hopes of regaining his throne.

Today, the Battle of the Boyne is surrounded by myth. Each year on the 12th of July, Unionist organizations in Northern Ireland hold marches and parades to commemorate William's victory. (The date is the 12th rather than the 1st of July

Figure 1.2 A mural in the Protestant neighborhood of Shankill in Belfast, Northern Ireland. The mural shows how William of Orange remains a symbol of Ulster loyalists' commitment to the Union today, over three centuries after the Battle of the Boyne.

Reproduced courtesy of Supermac 1961.

because in 1752 Britain switched from the Julian to the Gregorian calendar, resulting in the addition of eleven days to the "old style" dates.) But although Unionists celebrate William as a Protestant hero, he rather than the Catholic James was supported by Pope Alexander VIII, who had joined the "Grand Alliance" against Louis XIV's efforts to dominate Europe. The nationalist interpretation of the Boyne is equally shrouded in myth. The battle was not a clear-cut struggle between Protestant English conquerors who sought to dominate Ireland and Catholic Irish patriots who resisted them. In fact, it was not about Ireland at all. The island was merely a pawn in James's and William's struggle for the throne, and in the broader European conflict between Britain and the Netherlands on the one side and France on the other. Even so, the Boyne had a tremendous impact upon Ireland's future. The power and wealth of the Catholic elite was all but destroyed, while Protestants gained in confidence that God was on their side. This was to have major ramifications for Irish history for centuries to come.

Though the terms of the ensuing Treaty of Limerick (1691) were relatively generous, the victorious Irish Protestants often ignored them as they tightened their grip on political power and the ownership of the vast majority of the island's land. Thousands of James II's Irish supporters, the "Wild Geese," fled to the continent. The Catholic Irish left behind were subjected to harsh punishments: almost 2 million acres of their land were confiscated, and they were subsequently prohibited from purchasing land, from intermarrying with Protestants, from holding parliamentary seats and from voting in parliamentary elections. By the mid-eighteenth century, only 5 percent of Irish land was owned by Catholics. For centuries, Ireland had been at times a semi-independent kingdom and at others a conquered territory. Now, the balance shifted decisively in favor of the latter. This was confirmed in 1720, when the British Parliament passed the Declaratory Act, clarifying its right to impose legislation upon Ireland.

In both Scotland and Ireland, writes David Hayton, William's victory was thus "a crucial moment in the expansion of English control over the other parts of the British Isles." The violence in those two places, however, was downplayed in England, as the promulgators of the regime change seized control of the interpretation of events. First, they ensured that James's removal from the throne was seen as legal. A Convention Parliament – meaning that it had been called without a royal summons – declared that James had abdicated the throne when he fled from London. In February 1689, it was offered jointly to William and Mary, she by right of descent and he by right of conquest. The prospective monarchs were also presented with the Declaration of Rights, which placed limits on the power of the monarchy to levy taxes, to maintain a standing army in peacetime, to interfere with the right of Britons to bear arms, to deny their freedom of speech, to imprison them without trial and to subject them to cruel and unusual punishments. When the Declaration was approved by Parliament the following year, it became the *Bill of Rights*. It is often assumed that its provisions were conditions placed on the offer of the throne, but this was not the case. Instead, William and Mary assumed that they would enjoy the same prerogatives that James had inherited in 1685.

Immigrants and Refugees 1

Huguenots

Another consequence of the Glorious Revolution was the arrival of a significant number of Calvinist Protestant refugees, known as "Huguenots," from France. From the time of the English Reformation onwards, Britain was a popular destination for Protestants fleeing persecution in Catholic countries. The steady trickle, however, became a flood after 1685, when King Louis XIV revoked the Edict of Nantes, which had protected the rights and civil liberties of France's Protestants. Although Britain was ruled by a Catholic monarch at the time, James II promised the Huguenots toleration in his Declaration of Indulgence of 1687, and a year later the Glorious Revolution ensured that Britain would remain a Protestant country. In addition to freedom from persecution, the Huguenots were drawn across the English Channel by the prospect of employment. Many Huguenots were skilled artisans and craftsmen such as weavers, silversmiths and watchmakers, and were attracted to the booming consumer markets in London and other cities. Although they met with some hostility from British people who disliked the French or feared they would take their jobs, for the most part the Huguenots received a warm welcome as fellow Protestants. Numbering around 50,000, or 1 percent of the country's population at the time, the Huguenots were the largest single group of immigrants to arrive in Britain before the modern era; another 10,000 settled in Ireland. The word "refugee," from the French *réfugié*, entered the English language in the 1680s as a result of the arrival of so many Huguenots.

Figure 1.3 Huguenot silk merchants' and weavers' houses from the early eighteenth century in Spitalfields in East London.

Reproduced courtesy of Amanda Slater.

What exactly had happened in 1688? That question was as puzzling for contemporaries as it is for historians today. Differing interpretations of the Revolution lay at the root of British politics for the next quarter-century. Even if most people were able to accept the new settlement, a significant number continued to be disturbed by the removal of a legitimate king. As a stable, committed group, the Jacobites were never large in number, but a substantial number of people flirted with Jacobitism in the ensuing decades. The Stuarts existed as an idealized shadow government, with an appeal that increased in times when the current regime was unpopular. In an age in which monarchs were personally unappealing and politically ineffective and other politicians corrupt and venal, it was easy to romanticize them as national saviors. They would haunt the political scene until the mid-eighteenth century, and at times would present a viable threat in the form of French-backed military invasions. At the end of the day, however, too few people were willing to risk the disruption and chaos that another alteration of the royal succession would bring.

There were other consequences of the Glorious Revolution besides a change of monarch. English Dissenters had resisted James's efforts to enlist them in his cause by including them in the Declaration of Indulgence of 1687, which had suspended the penal laws compelling conformity to the Church of England. They were rewarded with an Act of Toleration in 1689 that did not include Catholics. Dissenters would no longer be prosecuted for nonattendance at the services of the established church or for holding "conventicles" (unofficial meetings that were not formally identified as religious services), so long as their chapels and meeting-houses were registered with the authorities and kept unlocked. Over the long term, the Act of Toleration contributed significantly to the gradual unraveling of the cultural hegemony of the Church of England. While church attendance remained compulsory for conforming Anglicans, it became virtually impossible to enforce. Within a few decades, religious reformers like the Wesleys found it necessary to bring the church to the people, since the latter no longer had to – and increasingly chose not to – bring themselves to the church.

The years after 1688 witnessed a steady erosion of not only the power of the Church of England, but also of the monarchy. Although, as we have seen, no conditions had been placed on William and Mary's accession to the throne, a series of measures that constrained their power was imposed in the decade after 1688. In 1694, a renewed Triennial Act required Parliament to meet every three years, while the emergence of a large-scale fiscal–military state made a perennially sitting Parliament a permanent feature of the political landscape. The monarchy had effectively lost one of its main prerogatives: the ability to call, or not call, Parliament into session. Parliament also gained additional powers over taxation and political appointments. Much of the bargaining power that Parliament used to extract concessions, however, derived not from the Glorious Revolution itself, but rather from William III's desire to wage war with France, which required him to negotiate for the necessary resources.

In some ways, then, the conventional interpretation of the Glorious Revolution as having fundamentally altered the balance of power in the British constitution is inaccurate. It is also misleading in another way: proponents argued that the Revolution was essentially conservative, in the sense that it had defended the existing constitutional settlement from a tyrant who wanted to destroy it. This was initially a rhetorical strategy of expedience that was intended to convince the Tories to accept the disruption of the legitimate royal succession. Over the next century, however, the view that 1688 had been restorative rather than innovative became the prevailing interpretation. In the late eighteenth century, the Whig philosopher and politician Edmund Burke contrasted the Glorious Revolution to the violence and radicalism of the French Revolution. In his *Reflections on the Revolution in France* (1790), Burke wrote that the former Revolution had been carried out in order "to preserve our ancient indisputable laws and liberties."

See document "The Glorious Revolution as Restoration" at www.routledge.com/cw/ barczewski.

Recent scholars, however, have viewed the Glorious Revolution in a more radical light. Steven Pincus sees it as a clash not between two different versions of political tradition (absolute versus constitutional monarchy) but between two competing visions of a modern political state. Both James II and Parliament, Pincus argues, agreed that a modern state required a large government bureaucracy and a large army and navy. They disagreed, however, on what government institution was best equipped to control them, the monarchy or Parliament. It is somewhat surprising for James to be identified as a modernizer, but many Britons besides him in the 1680s saw the future as lying in continental absolutist states like France or Spain. In these states, the executive authority of monarchs was unchallenged and government highly centralized, while Catholicism strongly supported monarchical ambitions. **Mercantilist** economic policy, employed in captive colonial markets, guaranteed that vast cash reserves accumulated in royal treasuries. In Pincus's view, James II was trying to take Britain in a similar direction.

His efforts were resisted, however. Over the next century, Britain followed a different, quasi-Dutch model, with a semi-representative government under an increasingly symbolic monarch, a national church with ever-expanding latitude for nonadherents and a maritime empire in which free trade flourished. There was, however, a vein of irony in subsequent political developments. The Glorious Revolution had been undertaken to resist the centralization of executive authority, the growth of government bureaucracy and the increasing size of the military and naval establishment. Instead, it resulted in the dramatic expansion of all these areas, thanks largely to William of Orange's wars. These wars required a new system of finance, which led to the founding of the *Bank of England* in 1694, as well as an expanded government bureaucracy to oversee and manage the more complex budgets that resulted.

 See document "A Writer Reflects on the New World of High Finance" at www. routledge.com/cw/barczewski.

Britain's new financial capacity played a major role in setting it on the road to becoming a major European power. In the late seventeenth century, overseas trade surged, as traditional European markets remained strong and commerce with America and Asia expanded significantly. Commodities such as pepper and brightly printed cotton textiles (known as "**calicoes**") from India, tobacco from North America and sugar from the West Indies were imported in increasing amounts. Many of these items were re-exported to the European continent, thereby generating profits for the capital's merchants. At the same time, a vast array of British-manufactured goods were exported to colonial markets in America. But for these commercial enterprises to succeed, they needed a sound financial system that could supply capital and credit. The Glorious Revolution created the context for this by leading to a more efficient, more reliable and more orderly system of public finance. In this view, it was not subsequent political events, but rather the desire of a new commercial class to see their interests protected, that ensured that the settlement of 1688 endured.

The Glorious Revolution and Empire

As a struggle between rival conceptions of empire, the Glorious Revolution had a significant impact upon Britain's overseas colonies. James II wanted the monarchy to exercise control over – and reap the profits of – Britain's colonies, whereas his Whig opponents believed that trade should be free in order to benefit the nation's commercial interests more broadly. The inhabitants of Britain's colonies, meanwhile, had their own opinions. In North America, the colonists saw their interest as lying in a decentralized government, under which they would enjoy greater autonomy. Prior to 1688, they objected to James II's efforts to impose greater royal control, such as his creation of the Dominion of New England, a union of the colonies stretching from Maine to New Jersey, which attempted to create a centralized colonial government similar to that of the French and Spanish empires.

The colonists thus sympathized with William's cause, which they saw as offering the best chance of protecting their autonomy. There was also a fierce strain of anti-Catholicism in North America, which was both religious-based and anti-French, as they feared Louis XIV's ambitions to expand New France and therefore cut off their prospects of westward expansion. It was thus not surprising that when rumors of a French–Indian conspiracy combined with news of the Glorious Revolution, several colonies staged revolts in the spring and summer of 1689. The governor of the Dominion of New England, Sir Edmund Andros, was deposed, as were the governors of New York and Maryland. These were not, to be sure, anti-imperial revolts. As in England, the rebellious colonists asserted that they were acting to restore a legitimate government and that they were merely defending their rights and liberties. But although it did not have revolutionary consequences in 1688, the emergence of arguments that the political rights of the "free-born Englishman" extended across the Atlantic was to have significant consequences in the 1770s.

The Glorious Revolution also had repercussions for what was ultimately to become the most important part of the British Empire: India. At the beginning of the seventeenth century, England had challenged the dominant trading position of the Portuguese in Asia by establishing the East India Company, whose royal charter granted it a monopoly over Britain's Asian trade. In order to establish a commercial foothold in India, however, the English had to deal with the Mughal Empire, which ruled the Indian subcontinent. At its height in the seventeenth century, the Mughal Empire encompassed 1 million square miles and 150 million subjects, approximately one-fourth of the world's population at the time.

In 1613, the Mughal emperor granted the East India Company the right to build their first "factory," or trading station, at Surat on the western coast of India. From there, the Company gradually established a series of fortified trading posts. Madras was founded in 1639, followed by Calcutta in 1690, while Bombay was given to King Charles II as part of the dowry of his Portuguese bride Catherine of Braganza in 1661. These places ultimately grew into major cities as well as centers of British power and influence. The Glorious Revolution, however, had a significant impact on the East India Company's political fortunes back in Britain. James II was a strong supporter of the monopoly that the Company had been granted over trade with India, but the majority of England's merchant community resented the Company's exclusive privileges and backed William of Orange in 1688. After the Revolution, the Company was seen as closely associated with James's discredited regime, and as a result in 1698 it lost its charter and a New East India Company, with Whig support, was established. Even without its monopoly, however, the "Old Company" continued to operate much as before, and in 1709 the two entities were merged. Despite the fact that its monopoly and its centralized, independent way of operating were contrary to the prevailing spirit of free trade and greater parliamentary control, the East India Company thus emerged from the Glorious Revolution with its privileges and power not only intact but also enhanced.

See document "The Growing Importance of East Indian Trade" at www.routledge. com/cw/barczewski.

A final imperial consequence of the Glorious Revolution was its impact on the slave trade. In 1662, Charles II had granted a monopoly on the slave trade in West Africa to the Company of Royal Adventurers Trading to Africa, which evolved into the Royal African Company in 1672. By the 1680s, the Company had brought over 150,000 enslaved people to the Americas, but private traders who wished to gain a share of the lucrative business demanded that its monopoly be revoked. By removing the ruling monarch, who was the Company's head, the Glorious Revolution also removed the monopoly. By 1710, there were three times as many non-Company slave-trading ships traveling across the Atlantic as there were Company vessels. With free competition now permitted, the British became the leading slave-trading nation, importing over 20,000 enslaved people annually to North America and the West Indies by 1700. The newly increased availability of enslaved people marked a final shift away from **indentured servitude** as the primary source of plantation labor in the Americas and towards enslaved Africans.

War and the Fiscal–Military State

Another key outcome of the Glorious Revolution was the development of what historian John Brewer has called the "fiscal–military state," which funded a newly bellicose foreign policy focusing on an intensified rivalry with France. This was to play a major role in Britain's emergence as the dominant power in the western world over the next two centuries. Within two decades of 1688, Britain had come to rival France as Europe's leading military power. The Glorious Revolution influenced this development in two ways. First, it led to the emergence of Parliament as the branch of government that controlled the Royal Navy, at a time when sea power was the bulwark of British strength. This allowed the Navy to become a national, rather than royal, possession. Second, it installed the first in a succession of continental monarchs on the throne, which dramatically increased Britain's engagement in continental wars.

Britain's new military capacity was first demonstrated in the Nine Years' War of 1689–97, which became the first phase of the series of wars that have been called "the Second Hundred Years' War" between Britain and France. The biggest question surrounding Britain's expanding military ambitions was how to pay for them. Britain's population was a fourth of that of France; competition with so much larger a rival therefore necessitated massive changes in government finance. To be sure, many of the institutions and practices associated with this "financial revolution" existed earlier, but it took a Dutch ruler with Dutch advisors who were familiar with Dutch financial practices, together with a pressing military and naval agenda, to transform these elements into an integrated system.

Wars had traditionally been funded and fought by the ruling monarch. After 1688, however, it was recognized that this was not only politically undesirable, as it increased the power of the monarchy, but inefficient. Parliament thus took over the responsibility of meeting all military and naval expenditure in both peace and wartime. To bring in more revenue, the land tax was increased by 5 percent, and **excise** duties were imposed on more consumer goods. Annual tax revenue now exceeded £4,000,000, enough to cover much of the cost of war. The remaining bill was paid for on credit, much of it supplied by the new Bank of England. A secondary benefit of the new tax revenue stream was that it allowed the government to borrow large sums of money and service the debt that resulted, without endangering the fiscal health of the realm. Of all the innovations of this era, the creation of a national debt may have been the most significant. The growth in government debt contributed to the stability of the post-1688 monarchy, since the holders of government debt and shareholders in the Bank of England did not want further political upheaval that might threaten their investments.

This latter factor became particularly important after William's direct hereditary link to the throne was severed by *Mary's death* from smallpox in 1694. Eight years later, William suffered a broken collarbone after being thrown from his horse and *died* two weeks later. He was succeeded by Mary's sister Anne, whose reign was dominated by the *War of the Spanish Succession*, which began in 1702, after the last of the Spanish Habsburg kings, Charles II, died without heir. There were two claimants: Charles, son of the Austrian Habsburg emperor, and Philip, the son of Louis XIV of France. A French Bourbon on the Spanish throne opened up the possibility of the Spanish Netherlands (now Belgium) being ceded to France, therefore putting French forces in striking distance of both the Dutch Republic and Britain. Britain allied with Austria in order to prevent this from occurring.

The first years of the war saw a series of spectacular allied victories. British forces were commanded by John Churchill, who had been rewarded for his support of William in 1688 with the title of Earl of Marlborough. In 1704, Marlborough won a key victory at the Battle of Blenheim, which won him promotion to a dukedom, the highest rank of the peerage. Subsequent victories drove the French from the Spanish Netherlands. But the British and their allies were fighting the largest nation in Europe, ruled by an absolute and determined monarch. Even Britain's financial revolution could not compensate for the disparity in wealth of the two nations: the annual revenues of the French government totaled £12 million, while Britain's were only £3 million. The war, meanwhile, cost £10 million annually.

By 1711, British merchants were weary of the disruption of trade and landowners of the increased land tax that had been imposed to pay for it. Many people had come to believe that wars were expensive and wasteful and that the financial machinations required to fund them promoted corruption. When the Tories returned to power in 1710, they began winding down Britain's involvement and secretly negotiating with France to end the war. The *Treaty of Utrecht* formally ended British participation in 1713. The Dutch and Austrians attempted to fight on, but without British support their capacity was limited, and by 1714 all combatants had signed peace treaties.

New Rules, New Ruling Dynasty: The Hanoverian Succession

The political disagreements that occurred over the war show that this period saw an intensification of party strife. In a general sense, the Whigs wanted Britain to have the capability to fight large land wars, which necessitated a large number of ground troops. The Tories, on the other hand, preferred a "blue water" strategy focusing on naval warfare. Religion also remained a divisive issue. The Tories pushed for bills to outlaw occasional conformity – and succeeded in passing one in 1711 – while the Whigs pressed for greater toleration and the naturalization of foreign Protestants, in particular the Huguenots who sought refuge from persecution by Louis XIV. The political elite had spent a half-century fighting over issues of conscience and the principles by which Britain would be governed. Both Whigs and Tories had to learn to move from the kind of bitter division that led to civil war to airing their differences within the existing political framework. They had to learn, in other words, how to become political parties rather than enemies ready to draw swords against each other.

There was plenty of opportunity for these conflicts to be aired in public, for the Triennial Act of 1694 required the election of a new Parliament every three years. During the twenty-two years that it was in force, elections took place on average every two years; there were twelve elections in the 1690s alone. This meant that politicians had to pay some attention to "public opinion," which was now recognized as a factor in the political world. Though the parliamentary electorate comprised only between 5 and 10 percent of the population, it was one of the largest in Europe at the time, and the voters who comprised it were not shy about expressing their views. The trouble was, they, too, were unsure what the events of 1688 meant, and unsure what they wanted them to mean. This electoral volatility sharpened the contention between the Whigs and the Tories. The Tories were more popular with the electorate; the Whigs commanded majorities in the House of Commons for only five of the twenty years between 1690 and 1710.

Both parties, however, struggled to adapt to the new political universe. The Whigs had been the most concerned about the expansion of government during the reign of James II. Now, however, they increasingly found themselves sustaining and even championing the instruments of government power under his successors. Moreover, though the Whigs had been the primary architects of the Glorious Revolution that had brought them to the throne, both William and Anne favored the Tories as the main defenders of the monarchy. But the Tories, too, were confused. They had been forced in 1688 to choose between their two main pillars, the Church of England and the King. They had opted for the former, but they remained solicitous of the prerogatives of the monarchy and worried that the Whigs wanted to overturn it entirely and return to the Commonwealth. Their ambivalence about the way in which the royal succession had been altered made them vulnerable to charges of disloyalty and Jacobitism. Indeed, in the ensuing decades many prominent Tories would make overtures to the exiled Stuarts, albeit with the proviso that they would have to convert to the Church of England.

In 1714, Queen Anne, whose health had never been strong, died. During her lifetime, she had become pregnant at least seventeen times and had given birth six times. Only one of these children, a boy named William, survived past infancy, and he died of a fever at the age of eleven in 1700. In the absence of a direct heir, the next fifty-one people in the line for the throne were Catholic Stuarts, beginning with James II's son, James Edward Stuart. As soon as it became apparent that Anne was unlikely to produce an heir, efforts were made to convince him to convert to Protestantism, and had he been willing to do so, he might have regained his father's crown. But he was not, and so in 1701 an *Act of Settlement* was passed, declaring that all future monarchs had to be Protestants sworn to uphold the Church of England. The succession was bestowed upon Sophia, Electress of Hanover, who was the granddaughter of King James I on her mother's side. Fifty-second in line for the throne, she was the first Protestant in the queue, which was enough to vault her over her rivals. She died six months before Queen Anne, however, and so in 1714 her son became King George I, in what was called the *Hanoverian Succession*.

These repeated alterations of the hereditary line of succession did not mean that Parliament's power was now absolute. To the contrary, though the Bill of Rights and other limits had been imposed upon the royal prerogative, in some ways the emergence of the fiscal–military state, which provided vast resources that were available to the Crown as well as to Parliament, gave the monarchy new capabilities. But if Parliament did not yet have total control over what monarchs did, it had established its right to determine who sat on the throne, or at least its right to determine who could not sit there. Nothing made this clearer than the fact that Parliament would never intervene again in altering the line of succession;

every monarch since 1714 is a direct descendant of George I. They did not intervene because they did not need to: they had established the rules by which monarchs could come to the throne, and those rules would never again be challenged.

The Act of Union of 1707

Since 1689, Scotland had been a point of vulnerability for England, especially with regard to the royal succession. As successive monarchs failed to produce natural heirs, anxiety reigned over whether the union of crowns would disintegrate, and worse, whether the Scots would enthrone one of the exiled Stuarts. For their part, the Scots had long disliked being subjected to policies passed in England that they saw as not being in their interest. Things became even more problematic as Parliament gained ascendancy over the monarchy, as Scotland had a Parliament of its own that they did not wish to see subordinated to its English counterpart. These tensions meant that the political relationship between England and Scotland required clarification. The situation was exacerbated when the former James II died in 1701, and his thirteen-year-old heir James Edward Stuart, known as the "**Old Pretender,**" asserted his claim to the Scottish as well as the English throne. The Scottish Parliament deeply resented being pressed to concur with the Act of Settlement without having been consulted on its provisions. In reprisal, the Scottish Parliament passed its own act, making it clear that they would not automatically accept the English choice.

Scotland's desire to remain independent, however, was complicated by its disastrous foray into colonization in the Americas. The Company of Scotland, established in 1695, was Scotland's bid to establish a stake in the expanding Atlantic economy. Its signature venture was a colony, *Darien*, near what is today the Isthmus of Panama; the intent was to establish a settlement that would charge a fee to carry goods from merchant vessels that arrived on the Atlantic side of the isthmus to boats on the Pacific side, thereby avoiding the long journey around Cape Horn at the southern tip of South America. "The time and expense of navigation to China, Japan, the Spice Islands, and the far greatest part of the East Indies will be lessened more than half," declared William Paterson, the scheme's leading visionary. "Trade will increase trade, and money will beget money . . . Thus this door to the seas, and the key of the universe . . . will of course enable its proprietors to give laws to both oceans, and to become arbitrators to the commercial world."

This was a creative idea, but its success was rendered problematic by a number of obstacles. Darien was located in territory claimed by Spain, one of William III's allies against Louis XIV. William's intervention prevented the Company from raising money outside of Scotland and cut off any prospect of aid from nearby English colonies. For their part, the Scots were extremely naïve about the obstacles they faced, notably the torrid Central American climate and hostility from both the local indigenous peoples and the Spanish. The Darien colony was a catastrophic failure, in which 2000 people died and as much as a quarter of all Scottish capital was lost.

The essentially bankrupt Scottish elite now faced an impossible dilemma: remain an impoverished independent nation and sink into the economic and political backwater of Europe, or join with their wealthy and increasingly powerful southern neighbor. Unification would allow Scottish merchants to trade freely with England's expanding overseas empire and with England itself. The English also offered a payment of £398,000, referred to as "the Equivalent," to compensate Scotland for its massive losses. Though many Scots harbored bitter feelings towards England for their role in the Darien disaster, at the end of the day commercial considerations won out. An *Act of Union* was passed by the Scottish Parliament in January 1707; the English Parliament followed suit two months later. The union of crowns was now a union of countries, "one kingdom by the name of Great Britain."

As controversial as the Union was in Scotland, there were many English observers who thought that the Scots had gotten the better end of the deal. Scottish goods that crossed into England would no longer be subject to customs duties, and Scottish merchants would no longer be barred from trade with the colonies of the English Atlantic. The Scots preserved their distinctive legal code and its separate court system, rather than being made to adopt English common law. Scotland's Presbyterian religious establishment also survived. Scotland was, however, short-changed in political terms, receiving only forty-five seats in the House of Commons, while England and Wales elected 513. (England's population was five times that of Scotland's, so there should have been around a hundred Scottish MPs.) Inevitably, unification failed to end tensions between the English and the Scots. Scottish Jacobites revolted twice before mid-century, and it would be decades before Scotland learned how to turn the union to its advantage.

Conclusion

The first generation after the Revolution of 1688 is sometimes called the "Augustan Age," recalling the flourishing of arts and literature in classical Rome under Augustus Caesar that put an end to a century of political strife in the Roman world. This label, however, also evoked the increasingly global nature of the British state. Just as Augustus promoted the notion that he was restoring the virtue of the old Roman Republic after decades of corruption, many people in Britain believed that their constitution had been restored and that they had undergone a "revolution" in the sense of revolving back to an earlier position. In reality, however, they had instituted a far more dramatic, if slower and less immediately perceptible, alteration of the British polity into a powerful, increasingly centralized nation-state at the center of a widening international and imperial world. The consequences of that alteration would resonate for decades, and even centuries, to come.

Bibliography

Brewer, John, *The Sinews of Power: War, Money, and the English State 1688–1783* (1989)

Fry, Michael, *The Union: England, Scotland, and the Treaty of 1707* (2013)

Harris, Tim, *Revolution: The Great Crisis of the British Monarchy, 1685–1720* (2008)

Israel, Jonathan I., ed., *The Anglo-Dutch Moment: Essays on the Glorious Revolution and Its World Impact* (2003)

Kishlansky, Mark, *A Monarchy Transformed: Britain 1630–1714* (1997)

Pettigrew, William, *Freedom's Debt: The Royal African Company and the Politics of the Atlantic Slave Trade, 1672–1752* (2013)

Pincus, Steve, *1688: The First Modern Revolution* (2011)

Rose, Craig, *England in the 1690s: Revolution, Religion, and War* (1999)

Southcombe, George and Grant Tapsell, *Restoration Politics, Religion, and Culture: Britain and Ireland, 1660–1714* (2009)

Stern, Philip J., *The Company-State: Corporate Sovereignty and the Early Modern Foundations of the British Empire in India* (2011)

2 The Whig World

Topics covered

- British society in the eighteenth century
- Poverty
- Women in Georgian society
- Emergence of the public sphere
- First two Hanoverian monarchs
- Jacobite rebellions
- Whig dominance, 1720–60
- Sir Robert Walpole as Britain's first prime minister

Timeline

1715	Jacobite rebellion
1720	South Sea Bubble
1721	Robert Walpole becomes lord treasurer, effectively first prime minister
1726	Jonathan Swift, *Gulliver's Travels*
1727	Accession of George II
1731	William Hogarth, *The Harlot's Progress*
1733	Excise Crisis
1739	War of Jenkins's Ear begins, expands into War of Austrian Succession
1745	Last major Jacobite rebellion
1755	Samuel Johnson's *Dictionary*

Introduction

In September 1714, George Ernest, the Elector of Hanover, arrived in Britain to become King George I of Great Britain (i.e., England, Wales and Scotland) and Ireland. Sir James Thornhill, recently appointed "Sergeant Painter" to the royal household, commemorated the event by incorporating a portrait of the new king into the decorative scheme of the new naval hospital at Greenwich. In Thornhill's painting, the new king sits armored and crowned, surrounded by members of his family, including his eldest son George Augustus.

DOI: 10.4324/9781003284758-2

Figure 2.1 Detail from Sir James Thornhill's painting of King George I in the Painted Hall of the Royal
Hospital for Seamen (now the Royal Naval College) in Greenwich. Executed between 1714
and 1727, the painting shows the new king surrounded by his family, an early example of a
shift away from images of royal power and towards a more domestic image as the monarchy's
role in British politics gradually declined after the Glorious Revolution.

Reproduced courtesy of Graham Mulrooney/Alamy Stock Photo.

Showing how much the political world had changed since 1688, the painting contrasts
markedly with Thornhill's earlier treatment of William and Mary on an adjacent ceiling,
which showed them enthroned in heaven, surrounded by the Virtues, as William's foot
rested triumphantly on the neck of Louis XIV. Unlike William's glorious apotheosis, George
I was brought decisively down to earth by being placed in a cozy domestic context that
did not even have the advantage of being accurate. Thornhill's image of George's happy
grandchildren sitting at his feet disguised his familial difficulties. On the king's right was his
wife Sophia Dorothea, whom he had divorced in 1694 after she was accused of infidelity –
something of which both spouses were probably guilty. He subsequently imprisoned her in
Ahlden Castle in Hanover, where she remained for thirty-two years until her death in 1726.
Nor did George get along with his eldest son, George Augustus, as he was jealous of the latter's popularity and was barely on speaking terms with him. This is perhaps why the son's
gaze in the painting is turned firmly away from his father.

The grounded nature of Thornhill's vision of the new dynasty was entirely appropriate
for the Hanoverian Succession. It had been legislated by Parliament, where the balance
of political power increasingly resided. Soon after the Hanoverian Succession, the **Whigs**,
the promoters of parliamentary dominance, gained an unbreakable lock on power. For

much of this period of "Whig Ascendancy," the reins of power were tightly gripped by one man, Robert Walpole. Though he never held the title in any official sense, Walpole is now recognized as Britain's first **prime minister**, because he established the system of cabinet government that still exists today. As the power of the monarchy waned, it was supplanted not only by Parliament but also by a growth in the power of the cabinet, or the most senior government ministers. Americans might think of the cabinet as replacing the monarchy as the executive branch of the British government, but in America cabinet secretaries (i.e., the heads of the various government departments) cannot sit in the House of Representatives or the Senate. In Britain, however, where there is no "separation of powers" enshrined in a written constitution, most cabinet ministers hold (and historically have held) seats in Parliament. It was thus appropriate that Thornhill depicted the royals sitting placidly and passively as various forces swirled around them, forces that were rapidly escalating beyond their control.

A Changing Society?

The political developments of the first half of the eighteenth century occurred against the backdrop of a society that was at once stable and in flux. Rank was precisely defined, but although birth determined much, it was not everything. At the top of the hierarchy was the aristocracy, or the peers who passed their titles to their heirs. These heirs were almost always defined by law as male, though there were a handful of peerages that were permitted to pass through the female line if there were no male heirs. The number of peers fluctuated slightly as occasionally a peerage died out due to a lack of an heir or a new one was created by the ruling monarch. But the peerage remained a very small group, as primogeniture, in which only the eldest son inherited his father's estate and title, preventing it from expanding significantly. In the eighteenth century, there were around 180 English and Welsh peerages and 150 Scottish ones. (After Ireland joined the United Kingdom in 1800, the peerage expanded to include 150 Irish peers, though Irish peerages were considered to be less prestigious.) Even including their families, the peerage thus numbered only a few thousand people, out of a total British population of 6.5 million in 1750.

Below the peers, but still included in the ranks of the upper class, were the baronets. Baronetcies were the only hereditary honor – meaning they could be inherited – that were not peerages. (Thus they did not sit in the House of Lords.) The oldest baronetcies dated to the thirteenth century, but their creation was expanded in the early 1600s by King James I, who sold them for cash as he sought ways to raise money without calling Parliament into session. When James revived baronetcies in 1611, no more than 200 were supposed to be created, but by the eighteenth century there were considerably more than that. Next in line behind the baronets were knights. Like baronets, knights were referred to by the title of "Sir" and also like them they did not sit in the House of Lords, but knighthoods were not hereditary, meaning that they could not be passed to one's heirs. The last members of the upper class were the gentry, who had lifestyles and levels of wealth similar to those of the aristocracy, baronetcy and knights, but who did not have titles of any sort. If the upper ranks of the aristocracy were on average wealthier than the lower ranks of the gentry, both of them, as well as everyone in between, were by any measure rich.

Together, these people comprised the upper class of British society. Historians often refer to them as the "landed class," both because they owned a huge percentage of all the land in Britain and because their wealth and lifestyles were based on land. The peerage alone owned about 20 percent of all the land in Britain, while comprising only 0.02 percent of the population. This land was used primarily for agriculture, which until the end of the nineteenth century remained the most important sector of the British economy. The upper classes lived in grand houses on large estates, ranging from hundreds to tens of thousands of acres, but they did not farm most of this land themselves. Instead, they earned the bulk of their incomes from renting out their land to tenant farmers. This was a lucrative source of revenue in the eighteenth century, because agricultural prices were rising, allowing landlords to charge higher rents. In England between 1750 and 1800, rents rose by 70 percent, with similar gains in the other parts of the British Isles.

Agricultural rents were not the only source of elite incomes, however. They also made money from mining the natural resources beneath their land, particularly in the second half of the century as the Industrial Revolution increased demand for coal and iron. Most members of the elite also owned land in cities. As the British population doubled from 5.5 million in 1700 to 11 million a hundred years later, more and more housing was needed in urban areas. Through rents and real estate development, the ownership of land in London in particular provided significant earnings for many members of the elite. Today, some of London's most famous squares, such as Bedford and Grosvenor, recall the names of the eighteenth-century aristocrats who were responsible for, and who profited immensely from, their development.

Below the elite were those people who were comfortably off but lacked the wealth and social prestige of the aristocracy and gentry. They worked for a living rather than being able to live off the income from land and other investments. A growing group in the eighteenth century, they included merchants and manufacturers as well as professionals such as physicians, lawyers and clergymen. Today, we would describe them collectively as the "middle class," but historians continue to debate whether this term is appropriate to the eighteenth century, and some prefer to refer to them as the "middling ranks" or "middling sort." One reason for this preference is that in some ways this group had not yet established an independent set of values and attitudes. Instead, they attempted to emulate the behavior and lifestyles of the upper classes by wearing cheaper versions of their fashions and by sinking their wealth into land as soon as they could afford it. These efforts at emulation were enhanced by what historians have termed a "consumer revolution" that made a new range of products available for the growing number of people who could afford them.

In recent years, however, social historians have argued that emulation of the landed elite was not the sole preoccupation of the middling ranks. Rather than dreaming of moving in a higher sphere, they were instead busily developing their own social networks. This was particularly true after 1770, when changes in the British economy that marked the early stages of industrialization began to increase non-landed wealth. This is when we can see the definite emergence of a "middle class." In this new economic world, there were very sound reasons for people to avoid the appearance of emulating the elite, for the maintenance of good credit could be undermined by extravagant spending. Moreover, the middling ranks wielded growing power as consumers, as political activists and as philanthropists. By the end of the eighteenth century, they were a sufficiently large and defined group that they were beginning to pose a challenge to the economic and political dominance of the upper classes.

Sexuality and Gender 1

Mother Clapp's Molly House

Male homosexuality was illegal in Britain until 1967, and in the eighteenth century a man caught in the act could be sentenced to a fine, imprisonment, transportation to an overseas colony or even death. Gay men thus had to meet in secret, and the clubs, taverns and coffee houses in London where they did so became known as "molly houses," as "molly" was a term for an effeminate man. Originally a derogatory term, it was reclaimed by gay men as a positive self-description, much as "queer" has been in more recent years. Molly houses provided a safe space in which gay men could interact and in some cases served as places of sexual assignation or brothels. In the 1720s, the most famous molly house was Mother Clapp's in London. It was owned by John Clapp but run by his wife Margaret, who let gay men lodge there for extended periods and provided false alibis for them when they were arrested. In February 1726, the police raided Mother Clapp's; Margaret was fined, forced to stand in the pillory and then imprisoned for two years. Forty men were arrested along with her; some were sentenced to harsher punishments, including in three cases death. Although molly houses appear to be a new phenomenon in the early eighteenth century, in fact they had likely been around for decades or even centuries. The development of organized police forces around 1700 led to them being surveilled and targeted for the first time, while the rapidly increasing number of newspapers published stories about the raids and thus brought the molly houses further into the public eye. These efforts to stamp out the molly houses confirm that there was flourishing gay male subculture in London. Some historians estimate that there were more molly houses in London in the 1720s than there were gay bars in the 1950s.

Women, meanwhile, enjoyed less freedom, as their legal status in this period ensured that their opportunities for economic independence were limited. "Husband and wife are one person in law," wrote the jurist William Blackstone in 1765, "and the husband is that one." As Blackstone observed, a married woman was a *femme covert*, meaning that she lacked legal rights and that any property she held at her marriage became the property of her husband. For elite women, **coverture** could be circumvented through pre-arranged settlements that were negotiated by a bride's parents or through legal mechanisms such as trusts that established sources of independent income for their betrothed daughters. As a result, many of them were able to carve out independent roles for themselves. Women who outlived their husbands, for example, frequently ran estates for their children until they came of age. And even while her husband lived, the mistress of an estate had an important role to play. Running a great household was like running a business, with as many as a hundred or more servants to be supervised. Although upper-class women did not have the right to vote or hold political office, they could play important political roles. Politicians often made and consolidated connections through their wives, and wealthy women could also act as political patrons.

None of this, however, should cause us to forget that women's roles in society were almost always defined by their male relations. This was particularly true for married women. For members of the elite, not only material wealth but also important social and political connections were at stake in the choice of a spouse. Similar considerations often applied to couples from the middling ranks as well. Both elite and middling families regarded "love matches" based on mutual attraction to be sentimental, silly and unwise, although it was thought that couples should at least be compatible. Lower-class couples had more latitude and were freer to marry for "love," although economic factors played a role in those cases as well.

Women from the upper and middle ranks of society did not generally work for pay outside the home. Among the lower orders, however, the division of labor between the sexes was not as stark, as many women had to work for long hours to support their families or themselves. In the manufacture of woolen cloth, for example, women had always dominated certain phases of the process, especially spinning, so much so that the term "spinster," used to indicate an unmarried woman, derived from the number of single women who relied on this means of support. In agriculture, women worked alongside men in the fields, while in towns and cities, women were prominent in the retail sector of the economy, either independently or as surrogates in their husbands' business endeavors.

The Problem of Poverty

In the eighteenth century, the bottom rungs of society encompassed, at the upper end, artisans and small farmers and, at the lower, itinerant agricultural laborers and workers in the urban "pauper trades" such as costermongers (mobile fruit and vegetable vendors), street sweepers and porters. In between were a wide range of occupations that shared the common characteristic of being poorly paid. Until well into the nineteenth century, most people in Britain were employed in agriculture, which accounted for at least 60 percent of gross domestic product throughout the century. (It was the middle of the next century before manufacturing supplied the same proportion.) Unfortunately for them, large landholders increasingly sought to enhance their profit margin by reducing costs, starting with labor. Agricultural workers were hired for shorter terms, by the week or even the day, rather than the traditional one- or two-year period. For many people, it thus became more difficult to make a living from the land.

Although agriculture remained the largest sector of the economy, manufacturing came to be increasingly important, as it supplied a growing number of middle-income households with consumer goods. Although it was not yet conducted on an industrial scale, it witnessed a transition away from manufacture by workers in their own homes to "outwork" that was carried out in small workshops. This change meant that women in the labor force were increasingly marginalized, as they were excluded from many skilled trades and earned progressively lower wages in the unskilled occupations that remained open to them. Many lower-class men, as well, were forced to join a permanent underclass of journeymen and day laborers. For them, employment was irregular, determined by season and by cycles of boom and bust.

 See document "Bound Out: The Life of an Apprentice" at www.routledge.com/cw/ barczewski.

For the lower classes as a whole, the limited data that exists is too piecemeal to allow precise calculations as to whether standards of living were rising or falling, but a general picture can be painted of improvements prior to 1750 and increasing pressure thereafter. In the first four decades of the eighteenth century, burgeoning export trade and flat population growth meant ample employment for skilled and semi-skilled labor. By the middle of the eighteenth century, however, population increases were beginning to make life harder for the poor, though there was considerable variance from region to region. In the North of England, incomes rose over the course of the eighteenth century, as the introduction of larger-scale manufacturing after 1760 provided men with more lucrative forms of employment and offered new opportunities for women and children for wage work. But in the South, earnings were outpaced by the same rising food prices that benefited the elite. Lowland Scotland and South Wales, where the early stirrings of industrialization were also felt, did better than the remote Highlands and rugged North Wales. In general, then, a poor family's relative degree of comfort depended on whether the increase in food prices – driven by population growth – was offset by new employment opportunities provided by economic changes.

To be sure, eighteenth-century Britain was no longer threatened by mass starvation, but that did not mean that everyone could afford even basic necessities. Many people earned far less than the minimum required for subsistence. Working families thus depended on the labor of both parents and all children capable of remunerative work. At the same time, what today would be called the "social safety net" was minimal. In England and Wales, the system of what was called "poor relief" was based on the Poor Law of 1601, which identified the parish as responsible for providing assistance to those deemed to be legitimately in need, or "deserving." The funds for relief came from a levy, or "poor rate," imposed on the wealthier inhabitants of the parish. Local authorities assessed claims for poor relief on a case-by-case basis and determined how much, if any, aid the claimant would receive. The "deserving poor" typically included orphaned children, the elderly, the mentally and physically handicapped and the infirm, but able-bodied adults who did not work, whether by choice or not, were usually considered to be "idle" and therefore not eligible for relief. The Poor Law provided for "outdoor relief," which meant that the recipients were allowed to remain in their own homes. In rural areas, it was reasonably effective until demographic pressures overtaxed its capacities after 1780. In more densely populated urban areas, however, it was woefully inadequate. Moreover, it prevented people from moving elsewhere in order to find work, as only those persons who could prove their right of "settlement" in a particular parish – which required a person to have been born there, to have married someone who was born there, or to have served an apprenticeship there – were eligible for relief.

Scotland had its own Poor Law, which dated from 1579. There, poor relief was funded not by poor rates, but by voluntary contributions that were collected by the Church of Scotland. This meant that impoverished Scots were not entitled to relief as they were in England and Wales (so long as they were deemed deserving), but rather they were forced to rely on the charitableness of their neighbors. By the mid-eighteenth century, elite Scottish landlords had come to assume a high degree of control over the administration of relief, as they were the principal contributors to it. More compassionate Scots pointed to the English system as a model that might better alleviate the sufferings of the Scottish poor, while English observers looking to decrease the number of applicants for poor relief pointed to the Scottish system as a means of accomplishing their objective. In Ireland, meanwhile, there was no system of statutory poor relief at all, which meant that the Irish poor were forced to rely on private charity in an even more haphazard manner than was the case in Scotland. This system left Ireland extremely vulnerable to agricultural failure, as was painfully demonstrated by the famine of 1740–1. The "Great Frost" that struck Europe for several winters from 1739 onwards froze potato crops in the ground. As Ireland depended heavily on the potato as a source of food, the effect was devastating; historians estimate that 400,000 people died, out of a total Irish population at the time of 3 million.

Some people believed that the system of outdoor relief was ineffectual because it did not sufficiently discourage idleness. They believed that poor relief had to be made so unpleasant that the vast majority of people would not choose it over gainful employment. This attitude led to the creation of workhouses, in which as a price for accepting relief poor people were forced to live in single-sex dormitories where they were employed in menial labor, with few comforts or freedoms. Workhouses are often thought of as a nineteenth-century invention, but by the 1770s there were 2000 in Britain, with a total of 100,000 inhabitants. Some workhouses were reasonably comfortable places that were administered with compassion and charity, but many, particularly in urban areas, were grim and overcrowded. In London in the 1750s, the death rate for children in the city's workhouses exceeded 90 percent.

Most eighteenth-century Britons, however, would have seen little reason to do more to help the poor. They regarded poverty as a "natural" and inevitable condition that arose from erratic harvests and disruptions to the food supply such as wars, and felt that there was nothing that could be done to eradicate it permanently. Poverty was little understood: a government inquiry into its causes that began in 1796 was abandoned a few years later due to the "complicated nature and extent of the misery." It would be several more decades before changes would be made to a system of poor relief that had existed for over 200 years.

The Public Sphere and the Global World

In 1695, the lapse of the Licensing Act led to a rapid expansion of the periodical press, particularly newspapers. Britain boasted one of the highest literacy rates in Europe, with almost half the population able to read by 1715. By then, London featured a dozen newspapers, including four dailies, circulating over 40,000 copies a week. As each copy was read by as many as twenty individuals, this meant that almost all literate Londoners read a newspaper at least once a week. Soon, provincial cities also had newspapers. Much like social media today, eighteenth-century newspapers and periodicals recirculated items that surfaced in other publications, a process facilitated by the absence of effective copyright legislation. A single item might be repeated in several different publications, the Augustan equivalent of "going viral."

In addition to helping to widen the public sphere, the periodical press also played a role in shaping and reflecting the increasingly global world in which contemporary Britons lived. This was a world in which connections with far-flung places were being made; in which new ideas and commodities were traveling faster and over greater distances; and in which, as the historian Miles Ogborn has written, "The lives of many people were increasingly shaped by the decisions made by others who lived far away." Decisions that Britons made in this period had an enormous impact on the lives of other people, as the next chapter, which covers the British Empire, will illustrate. But Britons, too, lived increasingly what Ogborn terms "global lives," even if they never left the shores of their island.

This could be measured in a variety of ways. A bevy of new products, including tea, coffee, sugar and tobacco – became available. These were initially affordable only to the elite, but later, as imports increased and costs came down, they spread to the masses. The growing popularity of these new consumables meant that a variety of people saw the Empire and international trade as relevant to their lives, and as a result they closely followed the news of battles and imperial events. In this way, views that were favorable to trade and empire became an important component of the emerging middle-class identity that was described earlier, and increasingly became a part of British identity as a whole.

The Presence of Empire 1

Tea

Tea first arrived in Britain in the seventeenth century via Charles II's queen, Catherine of Braganza, who had grown up drinking it at the royal court in her native Portugal. The fashion quickly spread to urban coffee houses, where men gathered to relax and discuss the issues of the day. In order to make tea available to women, the proprietors of coffee houses began selling it in loose-leaf form so that it could brewed at home. It was very expensive, however, and so only wealthy women could afford to purchase it. They would serve the tea at fancy parties, using porcelain cups, saucers and teapots that had been imported by the East India Company from China. It was not until the middle of the eighteenth century that British manufacturers such as Royal Crown Derby, Royal Worcester and Wedgwood learned to produce fine porcelain. As the demand for tea rose, smuggling became increasingly prevalent; by the late eighteenth century, more tea was being smuggled into Britain than was being

THE SPOIL'D CHILD

Figure 2.2 Dating from around 1802, the first in a series of six watercolor images entitled *The Spoiled Child* by Lewis Vaslet. The painting depicts what is termed in the inscription "the fatal effects of unbounded Parental fondness" as a female child sits on the lap of her doting father. Her mother pours sugar into a pot of tea, showing the association of the beverage with luxury and indulgence. On the left, a servant from Africa or the West Indies carries a pot of coffee and a cake on a tray; it was an indication of fashion and wealth in eighteenth-century Britain to employ black domestic servants.

Reproduced courtesy of the Yale Center for British Art.

legally imported. This drove the price down significantly, making tea available to a broader range of people. As an ever-higher proportion of their profits was eroded by smuggling, tea merchants began pressuring the government to lower the tax. In 1785, the government gave in and significantly reduced the tax, which had the effect of further expanding the market for tea. Tea was now cheap enough that employers provided cups to their employees and masters to their servants, doubtless in the hope that its stimulant properties would increase their productivity. There were those who objected to the democratization of tea: in 1757, philanthropist Jonas Hanway claimed that it was "impoverishing the nation," because poor people "will have tea who have not bread." Others feared that the control of tea-drinking rituals by women threatened to undermine traditional gender roles. These warnings fell on deaf ears, however, and by the end of the eighteenth century tea was well on its way to becoming the symbol of British identity that it is today.

This marked a key shift in the British political universe. Previously, Britain's strength and standing in the world had been measured relative to its European neighbors. After the mid-eighteenth century, however, Britons came to view the defense and expansion of the Empire as more important. It was widely assumed that colonies were both economically valuable as sources of raw materials and markets for finished goods and strategically significant as indicators of global dominance. Less pragmatically but equally significant in contemporary perceptions, they also were seen as aiding the spread of liberty around the world via the superiority of the British constitution. That this gift of "liberty" required the conquest of many parts of the world by the British and in the West Indian and North American colonies depended on the enslavement of millions of Africans was not seen as contradictory. Instead, the Empire was widely seen as beneficial both to the colonies and to Britain, and as a result it was an increasingly important part of the British domestic realm.

A New Dynasty, and a New Dynamic

King George I brought with him from Hanover a retinue of nearly a hundred, including his consort Madam Schulenburg, by whom he had three daughters. The King's efforts to impress his new subjects, however, were hindered by his age – he was fifty-four when he arrived in Britain – and physical infirmities, by his reclusive personality, by his inability to speak English, and by the absence of any grand royal spaces in London in which royal majesty could be effectively displayed. But even if George I had been a younger and more forceful character, even if he had spoken English well, and even if London had contained the kinds of ceremonial spaces found in capital cities on the continent, it would have made little difference, as he was dependent on his ministers to a degree that no previous monarch had ever been. This situation was exacerbated, to be sure, by his frequent absences in Hanover, during which a regency council was established so that government business could go forward. These arrangements further increased the maneuvering and intrigue that characterized high politics in this period, and created a perception that George I was less interested in Britain than he was in Hanover. His son and successor George II did little to improve the situation. In 1743, when he led British troops into battle at Dettingen during the War of the Austrian Succession, he wore the Guelphic Order of Hanover rather than the English Order of the Garter.

On the other hand, we must be careful about dismissing the first two Hanoverians, for their reigns were crucial in securing the political settlement that had originated in 1688 and continued through the Hanoverian Succession in 1714. At the end of the day, they might not have done much to increase the popularity of the monarchy, but nor did they seriously undermine it by pushing too hard for their own agenda at a time when the rival Stuart dynasty was still waiting eagerly in the wings for a chance to regain the throne. History tends to favor monarchs who effect change, but the greatest achievement of the Hanoverians was stability.

This stability provided a political environment in which Britain could turn outwards. By the time George II's reign ended in 1760, Britain had become the leading European global power. He and his predecessor had done little directly to bring this about, but they had created the preconditions for it by not aggressively challenging a political settlement that had reduced the power of the monarchy. Had any of the Jacobite rebellions succeeded and the pro-French Stuarts returned to the throne, it is unlikely that the British would have challenged France for global hegemony, and the history of the British Empire would thus have been very different. It is also unlikely that the United Kingdom would have developed in the way that it did, as the increase of English dominance over Scotland and Ireland might well have been diminished.

But the Jacobites did not succeed, and the Hanoverians remained. They still remain, in fact, as George I's descendants are on the throne today. At the time of his accession, however, it would have been clear to contemporary observers neither that the new dynasty was going to last, nor that the Tories were to be exiled to the political wilderness for almost half a century. What happened to cause the latter situation? In 1715, the Jacobite supporters of the exiled Stuarts staged a rebellion, led by the Earl of Mar and known in popular memory as "the Fifteen." As in 1689, much of the support came from the Scottish Highlands, though Jacobitism was not an exclusively Highland phenomenon, as there were a significant number of Jacobites in the Lowlands and even in England as well. In retrospect, the 1715 uprising may have been Jacobitism's greatest chance for success, as a significant number of people in both England and Scotland were dissatisfied with the 1707 union and with the potential consequences of the Hanoverian Succession, which promised to increase British involvement in unpopular and expensive wars on the European continent. The Jacobites, however, were hampered by two serious disadvantages. First, Louis XIV had banished the Stuart court to Lorraine under the terms of the Treaty of Utrecht that had ended the War of the Spanish Succession, and thus no French aid to the Jacobite cause was forthcoming. Second, the Earl of Mar was a poor military commander. At Sheriffmuir, his forces outnumbered the Hanoverian government's, under the command of the Duke of Argyll, by two to one, but Mar refused to commit the full strength of his army, which allowed Argyll's troops to escape and effectively halted the Jacobite advance. The rebellion was over by February 1716.

As disorganized as "the Fifteen" was, and as relatively easily as it was put down, it was still seen as a viable threat to the new Hanoverian dynasty. In an effort to prevent future uprisings, the government garrisoned the Highlands by building a network of barracks linked by 250 miles of new roads and bridges. The massive expenditure this required showed just how seriously the government took the Jacobite threat. South of the Scottish border, the Fifteen had lasting political consequences, as it provided the Whigs with the political ammunition to label the Tories as disloyal. The aftermath of the rebellion saw a purge of Tories from public offices, including the armed forces, the civil service, the judicial system, local government and the church. The following year, the Whig-dominated Parliament prolonged its majority by passing the Septennial Act, which extended the term between mandatory general elections from three years to seven. The effect of this legislation was dramatic. During the previous twenty years, elections had taken place on average once every two years. Such frequent elections generated high voter participation and interest in politics; during Anne's reign, nearly the entire eligible electorate went to the polls. In the decades following the Septennial Act, however, Parliament generally sat for its full seven-year term. By the middle of the century, voter participation had declined to one-third of its level at the beginning of the century. This contributed to a Whig monopoly on power that lasted for the next four decades.

The Rise of Robert Walpole

The main architect of this era of Whig dominance was Robert Walpole. From a family of Norfolk gentry, he inherited an indebted estate and married an extravagant wife. He also harbored his own tastes for the finer things in life. He thus needed money, and turned to politics in order to get it. Walpole was elected to Parliament for the borough of King's Lynn in 1701, when he was twenty-two, which seems very young by modern standards but was not particularly unusual for men from elite families at the time. His talents, in particular his financial acumen, were quickly recognized, and in 1708 he was made secretary at war. He was among the Whigs imprisoned in the Tower of London for malfeasance after the Tory victory in 1710, a humiliation that Walpole never forgot nor forgave. In 1714, he was rewarded for his loyalty to the Hanoverian Succession with the lucrative post of Paymaster of the Forces, which netted him over £100,000, a vast sum at the time. Even so, the King disliked Walpole, and his obvious ambition led many of his fellow Whigs to distrust him as well. The feeling was mutual: in 1717, Walpole resigned from the ministry and joined other disaffected Whigs in opposition. But he proved dangerous in this role, as he helped to defeat the Peerage Bill, an attempt to prevent the creation of "occasional peerages" to get stalled legislation through the House of Lords. His nuisance value proven, Walpole was brought back into the ministry as **chancellor of the Exchequer**.

Back in office, Walpole had a chance to prove his usefulness. In 1719, a private **joint stock company**, the South Sea Company, offered to take over the national debt, mostly accumulated during the War of the Spanish Succession, from the Bank of England. Shares of Company stock skyrocketed, rising tenfold in a single year, until the share price was ludicrously inflated to over £1000 by the middle of 1720. In September, however, the bubble burst and stock prices crashed, ruining most of the investors. The public outcry over the *South Sea Bubble* brought down the Whig government, but Walpole came to the rescue. He had opposed the South Sea scheme from the beginning, which allowed him to act as a disinterested crisis manager. (His criticism of the scheme did not prevent him from amassing a huge profit on South Sea stock, which he prudently sold before the crash.) Walpole brokered an agreement between the company and its shareholders, obliging each to cut some of their losses. He prevented panic from spreading to other financial institutions, and – controversially – limited the scope of the subsequent investigation, earning him the nickname "Screenmaster General." A grateful George I named him lord treasurer in April of 1721; he used this as a springboard to remain in power for the next twenty-one years.

It was not clear at the time, however, that things would work out this way. An election was scheduled for 1722, and it seemed likely that the Tories would make significant gains at the polls over the discredited Whigs. Walpole, however, had an ace up his sleeve. Unbeknownst to the general public, letters arriving in England from France had been opened and inspected for a number of years. By this means, Walpole discovered that Francis Atterbury, the Tory

Bishop of Rochester, had been corresponding with the exiled Stuart court. Atterbury's arrest on the eve of the election reinforced the view of the Tories as a Jacobite party who were disloyal to the King and to the Protestant religion. The "Atterbury plot" ensured that the Tories remained in the political wilderness for decades to come.

Another reason why Walpole held on to office for so long was his recognition that the chaotic politics of the previous two reigns had largely stemmed from opposition to unpopular wars. He realized that peace took away the main source of popular discontentment. The quarter-century from 1714 to 1739, the longest period of peace Britain was to enjoy in the eighteenth century, is often called the "Pax Walpoliana." It helped that Louis XIV had died in 1715 and that thereafter France was ruled by regents for the young Louis XV, who was only five when he became king. The Regent, Philippe II, Duke of Orleans, was extravagant and perennially short of cash, which the Walpole ministry was more than happy to provide, surreptitiously, provided that he steered French foreign policy in the direction that Walpole wanted.

Peace meant that prices remained stable and taxes low, which gave Britons an economic interest in preserving it. It also helped that Walpole was adept at fiscal policy, establishing, for example, a "**sinking fund**" to pay off the national debt, and transferring duties on tea, coffee and chocolate from the jurisdiction of the complacent and inefficient Customs Office to the Excise Office, resulting in additional revenue of £120,000 annually. Sir Robert Walpole, as he was titled after receiving a knighthood in 1725, also made changes in the structure of the cabinet. Previously the cabinet had been a loose assembly of semi-autonomous ministers, of which the lord treasurer was simply first among equals. Walpole, however, demanded that every other minister in the cabinet report to him rather than the King. Anyone suspected of going behind his back was ruthlessly shut out of office. The tight control that Walpole exerted over the cabinet is why he is regarded as the first prime minister in British history. Ironically, "prime minister" was not initially a positive term, but rather was a criticism made by Walpole's enemies, who resented his ever-tightening vise grip on power.

Some of Walpole's opposition came from within his own party. A group known as the "Patriot Whigs" believed that in his quest for personal power, Walpole had betrayed key Whig principles. For example, Whigs were the party of religious tolerance and opposed the civil disabilities that **Dissenters** still labored under. Walpole, however, placated the predominantly Tory clergy of the Church of England by agreeing not to seek broader toleration for Dissenters, in exchange for the clergy not using their pulpits for partisan purposes and for their acceptance of Whig bishops. Whigs also historically championed the power of Parliament over the Crown, but Walpole undermined the independence of Parliament by buying off MPs with the many forms of largesse that the government had at its disposal, including lucrative government offices and outright bribes. And all the while he lined his own pockets with the profits from various **sinecures** and government offices.

Today, this all seems highly corrupt. But the exploitation of power for private gain and the use of money and other enticements to influence the votes of MPs was an accepted part of the eighteenth-century political world. After the heated ideological conflicts of the seventeenth century, politics in this era was less about principle than about profit. Civil servants were not paid salaries, but instead earned large incomes from activities such as making loans with public funds and keeping the interest for themselves. This widespread use of bribes and other financial incentives to influence politics is known as "Old Corruption." It was not until the end of the eighteenth century that attitudes began to alter, and not until well into the nineteenth that many of the worst abuses were eliminated.

Contemporary authors were a prominent part of this world. This was an era in which politics spilled over into culture, due largely to the role of **patronage**. In the early eighteenth century, the number of people who had the means and desire to purchase books was small, making it impossible for writers to earn a living through sales alone. Writers who lacked independent means thus needed patrons, in other words wealthy, powerful and well-connected individuals who could either support them out of their own pockets or get them government sinecures. Walpole wielded personal control over many such positions; the price of getting a sinecure was thus less a matter of literary merit than of obtaining his support. Control of literary patronage made Walpole a master of propaganda, as he bankrolled journalists and authors and used them to manipulate public opinion. Consequently, talented authors who were Tories, such as Alexander Pope and Jonathan Swift, resented Walpole bitterly, while less distinguished but more pro-Walpole writers like the poet laureate Colley Cibber benefited from government patronage.

Much of the literary opposition to Walpole took the form of satire. A new degree of freedom of the press after the lapse of the Licensing Act in 1695 allowed the creation of a political culture that was far less reverential towards those in authority. Swift's *Gulliver's Travels* (1726) contained a series of thinly veiled attacks on powerful institutions and individuals, most famously in his depiction of George I's court and Walpole's ministry as tiny Lilliputians. Other contemporary satirists were more direct. The anonymous cartoon "Idol Worship, or the Way to Preferment" (1740), depicted Walpole's bare hindquarters from the rear, suggesting that kissing that part of his anatomy was necessary for preferment. These cartoons and caricatures did not appear in newspapers or periodicals but were instead printed separately and sold as prints that were suitable for framing. Those who could not afford to purchase them could still view them, as they were displayed in shop windows; to be "hung up in the shops" was to be a target of satire.

A master of both Old Corruption and the satirical cultural propaganda that helped to maintain it, Walpole was highly successful as Britain's first prime minister. He even survived the "reversion" – the transition from one monarch to another – when George I died and was succeeded by George II in 1727. This was a rare feat for a politician in the eighteenth century, because royal dynasties were often severely dysfunctional families. As a monarch aged, disaffected politicians would gravitate to the heir, hoping to acquire an advantage "on the reversion." To thwart them, Walpole cultivated the affections of Caroline, the Princess of Wales, who was the most influential voice in her husband's household. Walpole also secured for George II an unprecedentedly large income from the **Civil List** (£800,000 annually, plus another £100,000 a year for the queen), thereby bringing the new king firmly into his camp.

Walpole's Decline, Fall and Legacy

After the reversion, Walpole appeared to be unassailable. Opposition and tension within and without his administration, however, gradually took a toll on his power. The Tories and Patriot Whigs finally found an opening in 1733, when Walpole embarked on a major restructuring of the tax system. He sought to lower the land tax, which he believed would win him support from landowners, by shifting the tax burden to **excise taxes**, essentially sales taxes. In 1724, he had already introduced an excise tax on chocolate, tea and coffee, but in 1733 he sought to extend it to tobacco and wine. Walpole's opponents pounced, attacking the expanded excise as regressive taxation that hurt the poor and as a cynical attempt on Walpole's part to create new sources of patronage in the form of the additional collectors it would require. Their successful orchestration of public opinion ensured that the new taxes were extremely unpopular. Walpole was forced to withdraw the legislation; had the bill been

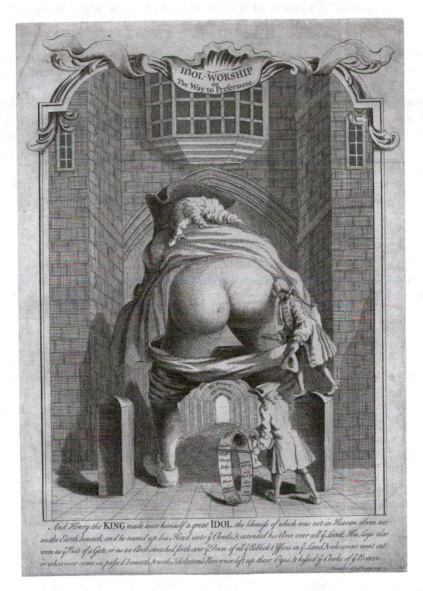

Figure 2.3 A broadside image from 1740 that satirizes Britain's first prime minister, Sir Robert Walpole. It shows him as being of gargantuan size, an indication of his political dominance. By an unknown artist, it shows an eager supplicant climbing on a block to kiss Walpole's bare backside in order to gain his patronage.

Reproduced courtesy of the Lewis Walpole Library, Yale University.

defeated, he would have been forced to resign. Thanks to the continuing support of George II and his queen, he survived what became known as the *Excise Crisis*, but his position was seriously weakened.

The crisis came in 1739, as British merchants, who were disappointed with the meager profits from the South American slave trade, agitated for war with Spain.

See document "A Critique of Walpole's Conduct of the War with Spain" at www.routledge.com/cw/barczewski.

They were frustrated in particular by Spain's insistence on boarding British ships to ensure that the terms of the *asiento*, the permission granted by the Spanish government to sell enslaved people to Spain's colonies, were not being violated. Popular hostility to Spain increased significantly after the Patriot Whigs began making much of the case of Captain Robert Jenkins, who in 1731 had allegedly lost his ear in an altercation with Spanish officers after they had intercepted the merchant vessel under his command. William Pitt, the rising young star of the Patriot Whigs, brandished what was supposedly Jenkins's severed ear, pickled in spirits, in a jar on the floor of the House of Commons. Walpole, as ever, was extremely reluctant to go to war, but he had little choice. "You have your war," Walpole coldly told his ministers. "I wish you joy of it." He had been right to recognize that war was a threat to his political survival. By early 1742, his position had so deteriorated that he resigned, accepting promotion into the House of Lords as the Earl of Orford. But politics had been his lifeblood, and within three years, he was dead. Walpole's demise illustrated the growing importance of global trade and empire to the British economy and therefore to British politics as well. His Patriot Whig opponents believed that a "blue water" strategy of relying on a strong navy to defend the nation's colonial interests was necessary for continued prosperity. This view dominated British attitudes for the remainder of the eighteenth century and beyond.

Walpole's fall engendered high expectations for reform of the political system. But the hoped-for changes did not occur; instead, one group of Whigs was exchanged for another. But although the Whigs remained in power, Walpole's demise significantly altered the course of British foreign policy, as the steadfast opposition to war diminished and the conflict with Spain metastasized into the pan-European War of the Austrian Succession. The war was fought over the right of a woman, Maria Theresa, to succeed to the Habsburg throne. It ended in 1748 with the Peace of Aix-la-Chapelle, observed in London with a magnificent pyrotechnic display accompanied by music specially commissioned from Georg Friedrich Handel. The fireworks halted abruptly when the great ornamental centerpiece caught fire, but this was a minor negative note to the conclusion of a successful war: Britain had preserved the balance of power on the European continent and established its command of the seas.

Nor was this the only Hanoverian success on the battlefield in the 1740s. In 1745, a major *Jacobite rebellion* broke out in Scotland. The rebellion later became later known as "the Forty-Five," linking it in popular memory with its predecessor of thirty years earlier. This time, hopes were high: France and Britain were at war, and the French promised to land a force of 10,000 men on the south coast of England in support of the Jacobites. "Bonnie Prince Charlie" – Charles Edward Stuart, the Old Pretender's twenty-five-year-old heir and James II's grandson – landed in Scotland to rally the Highland clans. The rebels quickly seized Edinburgh and defeated the British Army at Prestonpans in September 1745. Their support growing, they marched over the border into England, taking the northwestern city of Carlisle in November. Strategic miscalculations on the part of the British commanders left the Jacobites with an unimpeded route to London.

 See document "The Jacobite Threat" at www.routledge.com/cw/barczewski.

But at the same time, the Jacobites faced an increasing number of obstacles. The French ultimately delivered only money, weapons and a mere dozen artillerymen, not the promised 10,000 troops. The Jacobites in the North of England did not, contrary to expectations, rally to Bonnie Prince Charlie's standard. Not trusting their strength, the Jacobite commanders debated what to do at Derby, in north central England, and then decided to retreat back to Scotland rather than advance on London. With that reversal of course went their last chance of victory. A force under the command of George II's second son, William, Duke of Cumberland, moved to intercept the rebels. In April 1746, at Culloden Moor near Inverness in the Scottish Highlands, a vastly superior force of 9000 English, Scottish and Hanoverian troops made short work of the Jacobites, slaughtering 2000 of them and earning Cumberland the sobriquet the "Butcher of Culloden." Afterwards, the Jacobite movement faded into permanent irrelevance, and Bonnie Prince Charlie became an alcoholic recluse. The Highlands, meanwhile, suffered harsh retribution for their support of the rebellion, as legislation eviscerated the cultural traditions of the Highland clans. The speaking of **Gaelic**, the wearing of tartans and the playing of bagpipes were banned, and the Highland chieftains were stripped of their power and autonomy.

The Experience of Warfare 1

The Aftermath of the Battle of Culloden

The defeat of Bonnie Prince Charlie's army at Culloden in 1746 is typically viewed as marking the end of the **Jacobite** threat. Afterwards, the Duke of Cumberland, who commanded the British forces in the battle, carried out a brutal campaign of repression that sought to destroy the Highland culture from which Jacobitism had drawn much of its support. Built on the shore of Moray Firth, Fort George was a base for what was essentially the military occupation of Scotland. The British army marched through Scottish towns and villages, looting, vandalizing and burning whatever lay in its path. In Aberdeen, they ordered the local inhabitants to burn candles in their windows to celebrate the birthday of George II. When few people complied, the troops damaged over 200 houses. Over 20,000 head of livestock were confiscated and sold, with the profits divided among the soldiers. The government then turned to a longer-term effort to undermine the authority of the Highland clan chieftains once and for all. The Heritable Jurisdictions Act (1746) ended the judicial and military power that the chieftains had over their followers. The lairds and chieftains who had supported the rebellion were stripped of their estates, and the wearing of traditional Highland dress, specifically tartan plaid, was banned for ordinary people, though the Highland regiments of the British army, the upper classes and women could still wear it. The British government depicted Culloden as a victory of the forces of civilization and order over the primitive, savage Jacobites. Artistic renditions of the battle typically showed British troops armed with muskets fighting against Jacobites using medieval-style swords, shields and clubs. (In reality, both sides had been armed with muskets.) These views not only helped to justify the harsh treatment of the Scottish Highlanders afterwards, but they created a template for the juxtaposition of a civilized British "us" against a savage "them." This template would be used in numerous imperial wars over the next century-and-a-half.

Figure 2.4 Built as a stronghold for Clan Forbes, Corgarff Castle in northeastern Scotland was abandoned in the seventeenth century. After the Battle of Culloden, however, it was used as a barracks by the British army; the star-shaped wall surrounding it dates from this time.

Reproduced courtesy of Shutterstock/inspi_ml.

Jacobitism is often dismissed as having been doomed from the start, because in the first half of the eighteenth century England was stable and prosperous, and too many people had a vested interest in keeping it so to be in favor of a major political upheaval. But the Forty-Five, like the Fifteen, was a real threat to the government. As the rebellion gathered momentum, the French attempted to send 6000 men to the Jacobites' aid, but storms prevented them from crossing the English Channel in time. At a time when the bulk of the English army was fighting on the continent, such a force might well have been sufficient to turn the tide in Bonnie Prince Charlie's favor. But the weather prevented this from happening, and the defeat of the Forty-Five marked the end of Jacobitism as a serious challenge to the Hanoverian state. In assessing its meaning from a modern perspective, it is important to understand that it cannot be reduced to a simple conflict between English Hanoverians and Scottish Jacobites. There were many Scots who opposed the Jacobites, and there were numerous English people – predominantly Catholics and Tories who believed in the immutability of the royal succession – who supported them. In 1714, there were over eighty riots in England and Wales against the Hanoverian Succession. The decision to support the Jacobite cause was less a matter of national allegiance than of religious belief, political principle and economic self-interest; if a higher percentage of Scots saw these latter factors as aligned in favor of the Jacobites, this was because in Scotland these issues were perceived differently than in England. Recent scholarship shows that even the chiefs of the Highland clans, who are often seen as the leaders of archaic communities with archaic ways of life, considered their options very carefully as they weighed their allegiances to their clans, to the deposed Stuarts and to Scottish independence from England against the advantages of increased integration with the British state. It is thus important not to dismiss Jacobitism as a romantic lost cause; this *"Braveheart"* view of tartan-clad, bagpipe-playing Highlanders waging a futile campaign against far superior English forces was a later invention that concealed a far more complex reality.

The defeat of the Jacobite threat and the return of peace in Europe in 1748 saw the Whig administration secure in its power, but war was once again to propel a switch from one Whig ministry to another. By the mid-1750s, Anglo-French relations were becoming fractious over the North American frontier and competing interests in the Indian subcontinent. The current prime minister, the Duke of Newcastle, was a consummate administrator, but he lacked the charisma to lead a government, and he was subjected to blistering attacks after war broke out in 1756. Newcastle was compelled to resign, making way for the most outspoken of his critics, William Pitt, the Patriot Whig who had made his name in 1739 by bringing Captain Jenkins's ear onto the floor of the House of Commons. In the Seven Years' War, Pitt led Britain to victory and to a new pinnacle of global and imperial power, as we will see in the chapters that follow.

Conclusion

The decades after the Hanoverian Succession of 1714 saw the chaos that had characterized British politics for much of the seventeenth century at long last give way to greater stability. This stability was enhanced by the dominance of the Whig party under the leadership of Sir Robert Walpole. Stability did not mean stasis, however, as a number of dynamic forces continued to operate. Jacobitism remained a viable threat to the Hanoverian settlement, even if Britain's economic prosperity made the path to a Stuart restoration difficult. At the same time, the wider imperial and international world was a growing presence in British politics, society and culture. Neither the narrowly continental perspectives of the first two Georges nor Sir Robert Walpole's staunch determination to keep Britain out of foreign entanglements could prevent that wider world from intruding. Instead, it was now a permanent part of the British universe, abroad and at home.

Bibliography

Earle, Peter, *The Making of the English Middle Class: Business, Society and Family Life in London 1660–1730* (1989)

Hay, Douglas and Nicholas Rogers, *Eighteenth-Century English Society: Shuttles and Swords* (1997)

Hunt, Margaret R., *The Middling Sort: Commerce, Gender, and the Family in England 1680–1780* (1996)

Monod, Paul Kléber, *Jacobitism and the English People,1688–1788* (1989)

Plumb, J.H., *The Growth of Political Stability in England, 1675–1725* (1967)

Porter, Roy, *English Society in the Eighteenth Century*, 2nd edn (1990)

Rosenheim, James, *The Emergence of a Ruling Order: English Landed Society 1650–1750* (1998)

Smith, Hannah, *Georgian Monarchy: Politics and Culture 1714–1760* (2006)

Szechi, Daniel, *The Jacobites: Britain and Europe,1688–1788* (1994)

Vickery, Amanda, *Behind Closed Doors: At Home in Georgian England* (2010)

3 The British Empire in the Eighteenth Century

Topics covered

- Transatlantic slave trade
- Slavery in the Caribbean
- Slavery's impact on Britain
- Seven Years' War
- Growth of British territorial empire in India
- Scotland and empire
- American Revolution
- Discovery and conquest in the Pacific
- Abolition of the slave trade and slavery in the British Empire

Timeline

1690	Calcutta founded
1756	Seven Years' War begins
1757	Battle of Plassey
1759	"Year of Victories," including capture of Quebec
1765	East India Company gains right of revenue collection in Bengal
1766	Repeal of the Stamp Act
1768–70	Captain Cook's first voyage to the Pacific
1773	Tea Act and Boston Tea Party
1775	American Revolution begins
1781	*Zong* case
1787	Society for Effecting the Abolition of the Slave Trade established
1787	Warren Hastings impeached
1788	First British settlement in Australia
1789	*The Interesting Narrative of the Life of Olaudah Equiano* published
1799	Defeat and death of Tipu Sultan of Mysore
1807	Slave trade abolished
1834	Abolition of slavery within most British colonies

DOI: 10.4324/9781003284758-3

Introduction

By the beginning of the eighteenth century, the mercantile character of British society was well established. Ports on the west coast of England such as Liverpool and Bristol, which were oriented towards Atlantic trade, had emerged as major centers of commerce. Following the Act of Union in 1707, the Scottish port of Glasgow began to play a major role in this commerce as well. By the mid-eighteenth century, Glasgow's "tobacco lords" dominated the tobacco trade with the North American colonies. Across the Atlantic, the American ports of Boston, New York and Philadelphia enjoyed similar growth. By 1700, 30 percent of English exports went to North America and the West Indies, while 15 percent of imports came from India. The French philosopher Voltaire, who lived in England from 1726 to 1728, was struck by the importance of the nation's commercial interests. In his *Letters Concerning the English Nation* (1733), he observed that in Britain "the merchant, who enriches his country" was more important than the "powdered lord."

Empire of Liberty?

The British conceived of their empire as not only one of trade but also one of liberty. In this view, a Protestant British Empire would not subject indigenous peoples to oppression and rapacity as Catholic colonial powers such as Spain had done. Eighteenth-century Britons took pride in the fact that colonial settlers enjoyed the benefits of representative government both by the British Parliament in London and by local assemblies, rather than being subjected to the autocratic rule of absolute monarchs. This ideal was embodied in one of the most popular patriotic songs of the age, "Rule Britannia" (1740). Written by two Scots, James Thomson and David Mallet, the song was originally from a stage production about the life of the Saxon king Alfred the Great, whose resistance to Danish Viking invaders contemporary Britons equated with Britain's imperial rivalry with Spain. The song appears at the end of the performance, as a prophet predicts the future glory of England:

> *Rule*, Britannia, *rule the waves*;
> Britons *never will be slaves*.

For the white settler population in Britain's colonies, there was considerable truth to this statement. The British Empire was not only diverse, but also decentralized. The East India Company received only minimal oversight from Parliament for much of the eighteenth century, while the North American colonies were governed largely by their colonial legislatures with little interference from Britain. For Britons, and other European settlers of Britain's colonies, the idea of an "Empire of Liberty" had considerable force.

Race 1

The Earliest Afro-Britons

The presence of people of black African origins in Britain dates from long before the colonization of Africa in the nineteenth century, as African soldiers in the Roman army were stationed along Hadrian's Wall in the second and third century AD. In the early sixteenth century, a black trumpeter named John Blanke played on several occasions at the courts of Henry VII and Henry VIII. London's first black African resident, a man named Cornelius, was recorded in 1593. The success of British privateers led to the release of African enslaved people freed from captured Spanish ships in London and other port cities. But with an increased black presence came racist laws: in 1601 Elizabeth I deemed the number of "blackamoors which are crept into this realm" to be excessive and ordered steps to be taken to remove them, although it is unclear whether anything was actually done. The number of Afro-Britons continued to grow during the seventeenth century, but it was the massive expansion of the slave trade that took place in the eighteenth that led to the emergence of a significant black population – likely numbering in the tens of thousands – in Britain for the first time.

The experience of non-white peoples, however, was often starkly different. Most obviously, millions of Africans were subjected to slavery under British rule. The transatlantic trade that made Liverpool, Bristol and Glasgow such flourishing ports depended heavily on slavery, as did the production of many of the consumables, such as sugar and tobacco, that transformed the everyday lives of Britons. The institution of slavery was fundamental to both the eighteenth-century British Empire and the British economy. The British were responsible for bringing over 3 million enslaved people to North America and the West Indies, or around half of the total number transported from Africa between the late sixteenth and early nineteenth centuries. The slave trade was an extremely lucrative business: though the most recent scholarly assessments have revised downwards earlier claims that annual profits were as high as 50 percent, the current consensus still allows for a healthy rate of return of over 7 percent.

The British slave trade arose because white indentured servants, who served a period (normally five years) in bondage in return for passage across the Atlantic, proved inadequate for the labor required to produce crops in tropical and semitropical climates. Increasingly, plantation owners in the West Indies and North America turned to African slave labor. The British, like other Europeans of the day, accepted slavery as an institution that had been prevalent in human societies since antiquity and that had biblical sanction. In addition, the dark skin color of Africans and the differences in their religion, culture and customs marked them in European eyes as an inferior people. Until the last quarter of the eighteenth century, few Britons displayed concern about the enslavement of Africans.

In this period, the plantation islands of the Caribbean were Britain's most valuable colonial possessions. When they were established in the early seventeenth century, colonies such as Barbados produced a variety of crops for export, including tobacco, cotton and indigo. By mid-century, however, the Caribbean colonies had begun to focus on sugar. In 1700, over 22,000 tons of sugar were exported to England and Wales; by 1748, that total had almost doubled to more than 41,000 tons. In 1751, it was reported that on the island of Antigua, there was "hardly one Acre of ground, even to the Top of the Mountains, fit for Sugar Canes and other necessary Produce, but what is taken in and cultivated."

This shift was made possible by increased reliance on the labor of African enslaved people. From the middle of the seventeenth century, British **joint stock** companies like the Guinea Company were formed to enter the slave trade, and it was partly over the trade that the English went to war with the Dutch three times in this period. The real boon to the slave trade, however, came in 1713 with the Treaty of Utrecht, which granted the *asiento* giving British merchants the right to supply enslaved people to Spanish colonies in Latin America. British ambitions to increase their share of this trade were a major incentive for war with Spain in 1739. By 1780, there were close to half a million enslaved people in Britain's Caribbean colonies, as compared to only 48,000 whites.

The commerce that evolved is often termed the "triangular trade": durable goods made of iron, copper and cloth, together with luxury items such as glass beads, were manufactured in England and traded in Africa for enslaved people and for gold. (Hence the term "guinea" for a gold coin valued at twenty-one shillings.) The enslaved people were sent to the West Indies, while the sugar, molasses and rum that they produced were exported to England. The slave trade, to be sure, required the active cooperation of Africans. By the middle of the eighteenth century, the King of Dahomey, in present-day Benin, was reaping £250,000 a year from the trade. There were important differences, however, as an African enslaved in Africa could hold on to the hope of being released if their families amassed the sum needed to purchase them out of slavery. Across the Atlantic, their slavery was a permanent condition. Increasingly, enslaved people were captives from wars fought specifically to further the slave trade, which turned West Africa into a combat zone as the populations of entire villages were captured and sold.

Figure 3.1   Halse Hall, a plantation in Jamaica that was owned by the Halse family, shown in a watercolor painting from c. 1780. The image depicts the plantation in pastoral style, almost as if it were a farm in rural England. A female slave is visible in the lower right, but she is not shown performing onerous labor or being supervised by a white overseer. The painting is typical of eighteenth-century depictions of West Indian plantations, which rarely illustrated slavery in a realistic manner.

Reproduced courtesy of the Yale Center for British Art, Paul Mellon Collection.

For these captives, the horrors of slavery were only beginning. One in five of them would die on the four- to six-week-long journey across the Atlantic, which was called the "Middle Passage" because it was the middle leg of the triangular trade. Those who survived the Middle Passage faced a brutal life on the sugar plantations of the British Caribbean islands, where existence was a constant struggle for survival. The reliance on slave labor was driven by the difficulty of producing sugar. In order to prevent the crop from spoiling, ripe sugar cane had to be crushed immediately after it was harvested. The resulting liquid had to be boiled to prevent it from fermenting or solidifying, or else the harvest would be ruined. All of this labor-intensive work required a diligent and compliant workforce. John Pinney, a merchant from Bristol, observed, "It is as impossible for a man to make sugar without the assistance of Negroes, as to make bricks without straw." Enslaved people spent almost all of their waking hours working for their masters; malnutrition was common, and punishments for resistance were harsh, reflecting the fears of British colonists that they would be overwhelmed by the black majority. Over 100 enslaved people were executed in Jamaica for their role in Tacky's War in 1760; some were gibbeted in iron cages and others burned alive.

Race 2

Tacky's War

Historians have for some time considered the Haitian Revolution of 1791–1804 as part of the "age of revolutions" that includes its American and French predecessors, but they have only very recently begun to include the slave revolts in the British Empire in the same category. One of the most important of these was Tacky's War, a large-scale uprising of enslaved people in Jamaica in 1760–1. The rebellion took its name from its leader Tayki, or "Tacky." His goal was to seize control of Jamaica and establish an independent, majority-black nation. The rebels killed white owners and overseers on several plantations before taking the town of Port Maria, where they found weapons and gunpowder. But they were defeated in the Battle of Rocky Valley, in which Tacky was killed. Many of those who survived, knowing that harsh punishments awaited them, committed mass suicide in a nearby cave. Of those who were captured, over a hundred were executed and 600 were sent as slave labor to the Bay of Honduras. Tacky's War showed that black people were determined to be the agents of their own fate, rather than passively accepting the circumstances of their enslavement or waiting for white abolitionists to come to their rescue.

The sugar plantations of the West Indies generated enormous wealth for their owners; in the 1780s, at a time when the average wealth of a British person was £42, it was £2000 in Jamaica, which ranked, after French Hispaniola (the island that today contains Haiti and the Dominican Republic), as the second richest colony in the world. Plantation owners tended not to reside permanently in the West Indies, where tropical disease and slave rebellions were constant threats; instead, they left their plantations to be managed by agents and returned to Britain, where they purchased landed estates and acquired seats in Parliament. An early example of their influence was the passage of the Molasses Act in 1731, which placed high customs duties on all foreign sugar, as well as rum and molasses, that entered the American colonies. Later, planters lobbied effectively against legislation abolishing the transatlantic slave trade; only when they saw public opinion turning decisively against the trade in the late eighteenth century did they begin to diversify their investments.

Profits from the slave trade had a massive impact on the British metropolis. The city of Bristol in southwestern England provides a case in point. By the 1720s, Bristol had surpassed London as Britain's primary slave-trading port. Between 1698 and 1807, over 2000 slaving voyages embarked from Bristol, carrying almost 500,000 Africans to North America and the West Indies. Bristol's population tripled during the eighteenth century, and the wealth of the slave trade helped to fund public buildings such as the city's theatre and library. One contemporary observer commented that there was "not a brick in the city but what is cemented with the blood of a slave." Bristol's example illustrates how empire affected everyday life in eighteenth-century Britain. Once an expensive luxury product, sugar now became widely available and was particularly popular in what became the iconic British national drink: tea, another imperial commodity that the East India Company imported from China. By the 1780s, the average Briton consumed twelve pounds of sugar annually.

Not only commodities produced by slave labor, but also enslaved men, women and children were a feature of eighteenth-century British society. Both free and enslaved black people came to Britain during these years. The distinction between servant and slave was often blurred, however, and the conditions of both waged and enslaved servants varied considerably. Historians have located more than eight hundred advertisements in the eighteenth-century British press placed by owners seeking runaway enslaved people or bound servants. Some enslaved people were treated more as household servants and were able to purchase or were granted their freedom. These men and women benefitted from the patronage of their owners, who provided them with educations and apprenticeships that enabled them to forge independent careers. Cesar Picton was born into a Muslim family in what is today Senegal around 1755 and was brought to England as a servant. The family of the Anglican minister who baptized Picton granted him several large inheritances, which enabled him to establish himself as a successful coal merchant in Kingston-upon-Thames. Although Picton never became involved in the emerging abolitionist cause, other prominent members of the black community in Britain played an important role in the campaign against slavery later in the century.

By the late eighteenth century, as many as 10,000 people of African descent lived in London, as well as thousands more in other locales in Britain and Ireland. Most eighteenth-century black Britons were domestic servants who, dressed in elaborate uniforms, served as fashionable accessories for their masters or employers as pageboys or coachmen. Yet black people were also employed as craftsmen, dock workers, laborers and seamen on merchant ships. Some gained prominence as preachers or ran public houses. Although emerging racial theory branded Africans as an inferior race, black people in London and other cities tended not to live apart from their white neighbors. Members of the free black community frequently intermarried with white English men and women of their social class, and words of African origin entered the English spoken in London. Although black people appear as objects of commentary in travelers' accounts, they were a far from uncommon sight on the streets of London.

Figure 3.2 William Hogarth's painting *Uvedale Tomkyns Price and Members of His Family* (early 1730s)
includes a black servant in the center background. Hogarth depicted over twenty-five
black people in his paintings, showing that they were an increasing presence in eighteenth-
century London.

Reproduced courtesy of the Rogers Fund, 1920, Metropolitan Museum of Art.

India and the Seven Years' War

The East India Company had a well-established economic presence in the Indian subcontinent by the end of the seventeenth century. Historians have recently argued, however, that
from the early years of its existence, the Company aspired not simply to trade but to exercise
sovereignty. By the eighteenth century, the political situation had begun to shift in ways that
facilitated the growth of a territorial British Empire in Asia. A key factor was the declining
power of the Mughal Empire. The prolonged military campaigns of the emperor Aurangzeb,
who died in 1707, had strained the resources of the imperial government and weakened its
control. Mughal vulnerability was demonstrated by the shah of Persia's invasion in 1739, in
which troops sacked the capital of Delhi, slaughtered thousands of its residents and carried
off the famous Peacock Throne.

Imperial historians of an earlier age saw India as falling into chaos and anarchy in this
period, a situation from which Britain "rescued" India and established order and stability.
Modern historians discredit this view and instead emphasize the dynamism of Indian political and economic life. New political and commercial elites emerged, and many Mughal governors established what were essentially independent kingdoms. This was the case in Bengal
in northeastern India, which was the richest province in India. By the 1740s, the *nawab*, or
governor, ruled as an independent sovereign over Bengal, which produced fine cotton and

silk textiles, indigo, opium, and saltpeter, commodities for which there was high demand in Europe. By the mid-eighteenth century, three-quarters of the goods that the East India Company obtained in India came from the province.

The British already had a base from which to expand in Bengal: *Calcutta*, which had been founded on swampy ground along the Hooghly River in 1690. By the end of the eighteenth century, Calcutta was one of the largest cities in Asia. The city's 5000 white-stuccoed mansions, which were occupied almost exclusively by Europeans, earned it a reputation as the "city of palaces." Elsewhere in India, Bombay and Madras were also important British settlements. Outside of these large cities, the East India Company had a prominent commercial presence through its "factories," or trading settlements. By the mid-eighteenth century, the Company maintained large armies of European and Indian troops (known as "sepoys," from the Persian word for soldier).

As the political picture in India shifted, the East India Company took advantage of opportunities to become rulers of a large territorial empire. The British fought not only other Indian rulers, but also their great European rival, the French. In the 1740s, at a time when both powers were at war in Europe during the War of the Austrian Succession, the French and British fought in India as well. Less than a decade later, the two sides renewed their conflict in the greatest imperial struggle of the eighteenth century: the *Seven Years' War*. At the Battle of Wandiwash in south India in 1760, the East India Company's victory brought an end to French territorial power in India.

The Company not only defeated their French rivals during the Seven Years' War, but also established their own territorial empire in India with a series of victories over Indian rulers. In 1756, the new nawab of Bengal, Siraj ud-Daula, had ordered Europeans in the province to disarm. The French and Dutch complied, but the British resisted. When the nawab's forces occupied Calcutta, 146 Europeans were imprisoned overnight in a crowded, airless cell. One hundred twenty-three of them died, an incident that became infamous to subsequent generations of Britons as "the Black Hole of Calcutta." In January 1757, British forces retook Calcutta, and later that year a British commander named Robert Clive won a decisive victory over the nawab's forces at the *Battle of Plassey*. The battle's date, June 23, 1757, has often been interpreted as the foundation of the British territorial empire in India. In the aftermath of Plassey, the British emerged as the dominant power in Bengal, winning victories against the armies of both rival nawabs and the Mughal emperor. The Treaty of Allahabad in 1765 marked a new phase in the East India Company's transition from trading company to ruler. In return for a fixed payment to the emperor, the Company gained the *diwani* of Bengal, or the right to impose and collect taxes in the province.

The global imperial struggle with the French extended far beyond India. Historians have with good reason referred to the Seven Years' War as the first "world war." While the French and British had clashed repeatedly since the accession of William and Mary, this was the first time that their most important battles took place outside of Europe. The early part of the war was disastrous for the British. An effort to take the French fortress of Louisbourg in Canada failed, while a raid on the French coast cost vast amounts of money and achieved nothing. French troops advanced southwards from Canada and threatened the Hudson River Valley in New York. They also overran the kingdom of Hanover, the home of the reigning British monarchs.

The leadership of the Whig politician William Pitt was crucial to changing the tide of British fortunes. Pitt, who assumed charge of the government in coalition with the Duke of Newcastle in 1757, helped to build support for an ambitious and costly foreign policy, which aimed to counter the French both in Europe and around the world. Under Pitt, the size of the

British Army doubled to 140,000 men, while the navy increased to 70,000, huge numbers by the standards of the time. In addition, 50,000 troops of Britain's ally Frederick the Great of Prussia were funded by the British government. This intensive commitment of resources achieved impressive results, and 1759 became the "*Year of Victories*," beginning with a joint Anglo-Hanoverian triumph at the Battle of Minden in Prussia. British naval forces won a series of victories, most notably at Quiberon Bay off the coast of Brittany, where Admiral Edward Hawke destroyed a French fleet. The British also conquered Guadeloupe, one of the richest sugar-producing islands of the Caribbean, and occupied a number of French forts in North America. The most dramatic victory, however, was that won by General James Wolfe, whose troops scaled the cliffs along the St. Lawrence River to capture the city of *Quebec* in Canada. The Peace of Paris in 1763 confirmed Britain's dominant global imperial position. Although Guadeloupe was returned to France, all French territory east of the Mississippi River was incorporated into the British Empire. British annexation of Florida established a buffer between its North American colonies and French and Spanish territory further south.

The British emerged from the war flush with confidence. The young Whig politician Charles James Fox declared, "Look around. Observe the magnificence of our metropolis, the extent of our empire, the immensity of our commerce and the opulence of our people." The victory was emphatically a British, rather than an English, triumph. The eighteenth-century British Empire depended on the participation of not only English, but also Scottish, Welsh and, by the end of the century, Irish people in its defense, administration and trade. Peoples from the parts of the British Isles with lesser economic prospects were especially attracted to the potential for opportunity and wealth within the Empire. Of these groups, Scotland's contribution was the most prominent. We have already seen how Glasgow's merchants came to dominate the transatlantic tobacco trade. The Hudson's Bay Company, which dominated the fur trade in Canada, was staffed predominantly by Scots, in particular by men from the Orkney Islands off the north coast of the mainland.

The British Empire also increasingly depended on Scottish military manpower. From the mid-eighteenth century onwards, new Scottish traditions of military service within the British Empire developed. The formerly Jacobite areas of the Highlands, which had fiercely resisted Hanoverian rule as recently as 1745, now became the foci of recruitment efforts to the British Army. Six Scottish Highland regiments were raised during the Seven Years' War and ten during the American Revolution. Scotland's highly educated population also bolstered the administrative ranks of empire, in particular the civil service of the East India Company. Between 1774 and 1785, almost half of the writers (entry-level administrators) in Bengal were Scots. Yet in spite of Scotland's increasingly prominent role in the British Empire, the English equation of Scotland with Jacobitism was slow to change. The young Scottish writer James Boswell was attending the theater in London in 1762 when two Scottish army officers in Highland dress entered. The crowd erupted in rage, shouted out "No Scots! No Scots! Out with them!" and pelted the men with apples from the upper gallery. The officers told Boswell that they had just returned from wartime service in the Caribbean. "And this," they said, "is the thanks that we get – to be hissed when we come home."

A British Civil War? The American Revolution

The scale of the victory in the Seven Years' War created a new set of issues, as the composition of the Empire over which Britain ruled changed markedly. "There was a palpable and broadly shared sense," writes the historian Joseph Ellis, "that Great Britain was entering a chapter in its history that was simultaneously glorious and ominous." This feeling of triumph and trepidation was in large measure due to the acquisition of the former French Empire in North America, which meant that the British now possessed all the land from the Appalachian Mountains to the Mississippi River between Canada and "the Floridas." It was a mixed blessing. The massive size of Britain's North American territory meant that the authorities in London could no longer administer it with what Edmund Burke, one of the most important political thinkers of the late eighteenth century, would later term "salutary neglect." But how to govern it, especially when the colonists were unaccustomed to close supervision from London?

This was a particularly fraught question because this new empire was not only bigger but also much more diverse in its inhabitants. Prior to the war, the British Empire had consisted largely of two types of peoples: white European settlers and enslaved Africans. After 1763, however, in addition to the East India Company's new political sovereignty over millions of Indians, the Empire also had to absorb 70,000 French-speaking, predominantly Roman Catholic settlers in Quebec. Securing this diverse empire was costly. During the Seven Years' War, the British national debt doubled to £133 million, and by the end of the war, £5 million of the government's £8 million annual budget went to paying interest on the debt. Britain's sophisticated financial system, which had enabled the government to borrow vast amounts of money to fund the war effort, allowed it to win the war but also caused serious budget problems in the decades that followed. In the short term, the debt led to higher taxes and popular unrest in Britain, where people paid twenty-six times the amount of annual taxes as the American colonists did, and to a serious debate over the desirability of maintaining colonies by military means. The defense of the newly acquired North American empire required troops and forts, which colonial legislatures were reluctant to fund.

These soldiers and fortifications were necessary because the colonists were eager to continue expanding westwards in search of more land as America's population doubled every twenty-five years, causing land prices to soar. This brought them into conflict, at times violent, with indigenous Americans. Between 1763 and 1766, the indigenous peoples of the Great Lakes and Ohio Valley captured most of the British forts in the region; the British named the uprising "Pontiac's Rebellion" after the Ottawa chief who had been one of its leaders. Around 900 white soldiers and civilians were killed along with over 200 indigenous combatants. Wishing to avoid more such episodes, the British government tried to limit westward expansion. In 1763, King George III issued a proclamation that prohibited American settlements west of a line running from the Great Lakes to the Gulf of Mexico. Ten thousand troops were deployed to enforce this proclamation, five times the number that had been stationed in America before the Seven Years' War. But it was already too late: thousands of settlers each year continued to move across the Appalachians. In 1768 the British abandoned most of their forts west of the Appalachians and let colonial governments assume responsibility for regulating the interactions of settlers and indigenous Americans. The result was a free-for-all of land-grabbing and speculation. When indigenous peoples tried to resist, they were massacred or driven from their land.

The Experience of Warfare 2

Indigenous Americans and the American Revolution

The American Revolution was in some ways a product of indigenous American resistance to the attempts of white settlers and speculators to seize their land. If they had not resisted, the British would not have needed to station so many troops in

America, which would have meant that there was no need for the Stamp Act and the other efforts to get the colonists to pay for their upkeep. When the Revolution began, indigenous peoples were forced to choose sides between the patriots and loyalists or try to remain neutral, as they sought to prevent further encroachment upon their land and to maintain the trade networks they had developed with European settlers. In the Declaration of Independence, Thomas Jefferson claimed that the British had "endeavoured to bring on the inhabitants of our frontiers, the merciless Indian Savages whose known rule of warfare, is an undistinguished destruction of all ages, sexes and conditions." Jefferson's words painted indigenous Americans as opponents to the patriot cause, but although it was true that most fought on the British side, their choice had nothing to do with political ideology. Rather, they hoped that a British victory would slow the westward expansion of colonial settlement. In the southern colonies, the Cherokee, whose land had shrunk dramatically in the 1760s

Figure 3.3 Depicted by the painter Benjamin West in 1776, the British colonel Guy Johnson, who served as the main diplomatic liaison to the six nations of the Iroquois Confederacy during the American Revolution, sits in front of the Mohawk chief Karonghyontye. Johnson wears moccasins and a wampum belt and holds a Mohawk cap in his right hand; a Mohawk blanket is draped over his left shoulder. Karonghyontye points to a peace pipe. In these ways, West symbolizes the alliance between the British and the Iroquois.

Reproduced courtesy of the Andrew W. Mellon Collection, National Gallery of Art.

and 1770s, attacked the colonists without waiting for British support, but they were quickly defeated and forced to cede over 5 million acres to Virginia, the Carolinas and Georgia. The Iroquois Confederacy was rewarded by the British on a per-scalp basis for raiding American settlements in western Pennsylvania and upstate New York. In early 1779, George Washington detached 5000 troops from the Continental Army to carry out a violent campaign of retribution. Twenty Iroquois villages were destroyed, and the power of the Iroquois Confederacy was permanently diminished; Washington was given the nickname "Town Destroyer" by the Iroquois in consequence. At the end of the war, the British abandoned their indigenous American allies and ceded all land east of the Mississippi River to the new United States. The new American government treated indigenous Americans as a conquered people, seizing their land to raise cash or to give to Continental Army veterans as a promised reward. In response, some indigenous peoples migrated to Canada, while others continued armed resistance and still others attempted to negotiate a place for themselves in a newly independent United States that had little regard for their cultures or right to exist.

Ten thousand British troops, however, remained in North America, at a cost of £360,000 a year. The obvious solution was to tax the colonies to pay for their own defense. Britain could not directly tax the thirteen colonies – only colonial legislatures had that authority – so the government turned to indirect taxes such as customs duties. Successive ministries in Whitehall could not be blamed for thinking of the North American colonies as a vast untapped source of revenue. When the American Revolution broke out, colonial householders on average possessed a net worth 50 percent greater than their English counterparts and enjoyed the highest standard of living anywhere in the world at that time. The taxes proposed for the colonies were of the sort that had been collected in Britain for decades.

The colonists, however, rejected the argument that Parliament had the authority to impose taxes. They believed that the French no longer posed a threat and feared that a standing army stationed in the colonies would be used to dominate them and block further westward expansion. Colonists increasingly felt that a British government located thousands of miles away could not possibly understand their perspective or problems. And finally, they chafed at the system of colonial commerce, which due to the Navigation Acts required them to sell their exports to and to purchase their imports from Britain.

The situation was further exacerbated because the British government was in the process of completing the transfer of power from monarchy to Parliament, which had been confirmed by the Glorious Revolution of 1688. Parliament therefore asserted its sovereignty with particular vehemence, over the king and the American colonists alike. The colonists, however, saw their legislatures as equal rather than subordinate to Parliament; they envisioned a federal system of imperial governance with the monarch at its head. A vicious cycle ensued in which the British met every expression of American resistance as a move towards independence, which led to further repression as Parliament tried to impose its will, which in turn led to further acts of resistance. British policy quickly escalated from imposing taxes on the colonies to raise revenue to imposing taxes on the colonies to assert the sovereignty of Parliament. Most of the taxes and duties that the British imposed actually cost more to administer than they raised in revenue. By 1770, the colonies were costing the British £5 million a year to govern.

In America, meanwhile, outrage over the new taxes and customs duties grew. The colonists were not angry about the amount of tax they had to pay; rather, they believed that Parliament had no right to tax them at all. They therefore argued that it was Parliament that was being revolutionary, because it was attempting to make fundamental changes to the nature of colonial governance. These arguments came to a head over the *Stamp Act* (1765), which required colonists to purchase stamps for many printed documents and publications. The Stamp Act angered wealthy and influential colonists, such as merchants and lawyers, as well as the press, and provoked not only resolutions in colonial legislatures condemning it, but also riots in Boston, New York and other cities. It was impossible for the small number of British troops stationed in any one place to enforce British authority in the face of mass resistance; officials who tried quickly backed down when their homes were surrounded by mobs numbering in the thousands. By the time the Stamp Act was repealed in 1766, tremendous damage had been done to the relationship between Britain and the American colonies. Even so, the British made further efforts to extract revenue from and impose their will on the colonies, in the form of the Declaratory Act (1766), which emphatically stated that Parliament had sovereign power over the American colonies, and the Townshend Acts (1767), which taxed glass, lead, paper, paint and tea. The colonists boycotted British goods and engaged in other acts of resistance, and in 1769 the British repealed the Townshend taxes, except for the one on tea, as well. But the episode had exacerbated tensions, and in March 1770 a confrontation between British redcoats and Bostonian civilians on the streets of Boston led to the deaths of five colonists. After the "Boston Massacre," however, tensions diminished. Wishing to avoid such episodes, the British pulled most of their troops out of Boston, and their efforts to impose additional taxes on the colonists were largely abandoned. For the next few years, it seemed as if a larger-scale confrontation between Britain and America might be avoided.

From an American perspective, then and now, Britain's actions in the period immediately after the Seven Years' War can seem almost deliberately provocative. It must be borne in mind, however, that officials in London were trying to determine how to govern an entire empire, not just America. Their actions show just how interconnected the British Empire had become. In this era, the British government embarked upon a thorough program of reforming the way that its colonies were administered. It was the authorities in London who were initially dissatisfied with the way the Empire was being run and sought to change it, not the colonists in America. In the early 1760s, Tacky's War had frightened not only the island's white planters but also politicians in London, who feared for the loss of Jamaica and the other British sugar islands. The British were determined to exercise tighter control of the slave population in order to prevent such uprisings in the future. The Sugar Act (1764), meanwhile, was intended to benefit British West Indian planters by imposing a tariff on imported French sugar, which was otherwise cheaper. But it angered Americans who in consequence had to pay more for their sugar.

There were concerns, too, about the future of Canada. In order to secure the loyalty of Quebec's Catholic, Francophone population, in 1774 the British government enacted the Quebec Act, which permitted civil disputes in Quebec to be settled using French-style law, under which cases were heard by judges rather than juries. In addition, both Catholic and Protestant churches in Quebec were permitted to pay their priests by imposing a tax on their parishioners, and, in another attempt to halt the westward expansion of the American colonies, the border of Quebec was shifted south to the Ohio River and west to the Mississippi River. These measures aggrieved the Protestant-dominated American colonists, many of whom had inherited the virulent anti-Catholicism that was prevalent in Britain. They feared that the British government was trying to use French Canadian "papists" as a means of imposing a tyrannous system of imperial governance upon them.

British policies intended to support the East India Company also alienated the American colonists. In the early 1770s, the Company was facing bankruptcy as a result of its costly wars in India, the high dividends paid to its shareholders, and a large surplus of tea imported from China that the Company was unable to sell. The British government believed that the development of a robust tea trade with America would help the East India Company to solve its financial problems, and the Company was allowed to begin exporting tea directly to the thirteen colonies without first paying a 25 percent tax in Britain first. This would, the government estimated, triple the Company's American sales to around £1.5 million a year and simultaneously cut the rug out from under the Dutch smugglers from whom the Americans were currently illegally buying much of their tea.

Although this policy lowered the price of tea for the colonists, the American merchants who were cut out of markets were aggrieved, and they were able to present it to the public as a further demonstration of Parliament's tyranny. On the 16th of December 1773, around fifty colonists disguised as Mohawk indigenous peoples boarded three East India Company ships in Boston Harbor and dumped 90,000 pounds of *tea*, worth around £10,000 – or between $1 and $2 million today – overboard. The British government responded to what George III termed "the violent and outrageous proceedings of the Town and Port of Boston" with a series of coercive measures, which the colonists quickly dubbed "the Intolerable Acts." The Acts closed the port of Boston to commerce, which disrupted trade throughout the colonies, and allowed for the construction of military barracks and the stationing of troops in Boston. Four regiments of troops were transferred to the city to enforce the Acts. The colonists responded with a display of unity, sending delegates from twelve of the thirteen colonies – all except Georgia – to the First Continental Congress in Philadelphia in September 1774. Britain's attempt to solve a problem in one part of the British Empire had thus created a crisis in another and had revived the conflict between Britain and its American colonists.

Despite the growing tensions with the American colonies, in some ways British efforts to secure the loyalty of its colonies succeeded. Fourteen other colonies in North America rejected any notion of rebellion. The Caribbean colonies, meanwhile, had populations that were only 10 percent white, which meant their planters and political leaders were very worried about slave rebellions. They also relied on British consumers to purchase the sugar, rum and molasses they produced. With their larger populations and smaller proportion of enslaved people – even the southern colonies were almost two-thirds white – the thirteen colonies were less dependent on Britain for defense and markets. Southern planters saw the British government as a bigger threat to the continuation of slavery than slave revolts, a view that was exacerbated as British officials began to make noises about freeing enslaved people to win their loyalty against the upstart Americans. These threats were initially a bluff, but in November 1775 the governor of Virginia, Lord Dunmore, issued a proclamation offering freedom to enslaved people who would help to suppress the growing rebellion. Within a few months, more than 800 enslaved people had taken up Dunmore's offer; they were formed into a special unit called the "Ethiopian Regiment," which was led by white officers. Virginia's planters were furious: George Washington denounced Dunmore as an "arch traitor to the rights of humanity."

The British government's decision to double down on the imposition of imperial sovereignty meant that, as George III wrote to his prime minister Lord North, "the die is now cast, and the colonies must either submit or triumph." For the British, their right to rule their colonial possessions as they saw fit was at stake, as was the sovereignty of Parliament. For the leaders of the patriot cause in America, the Intolerable Acts were clearly tyrannous and therefore had to be resisted. But for the majority of both Britons and Americans, the issue was more complicated. On both sides of the Atlantic, opinion was split. American "patriots" and their British supporters saw the struggle as an echo of the "Glorious Revolution"; loyalists, on the other hand, saw in the colonial rebellion a replay of the disastrous civil wars of the 1640s. The conflict divided families; most famously, the American patriot Benjamin Franklin and his son William, the last British governor of New Jersey, took opposite sides, and their relationship was destroyed as a result. Loyalists who felt a strong attachment to Britain were very much a minority – probably around a fifth – of the American population, but there was a larger number of people who wished to remain neutral in order to protect themselves and their property or who resented the increasing demands that the patriot cause made on their incomes, service and allegiance. In Britain, meanwhile, the parts of the country, such as East Anglia and Wales, from which large numbers of migrants to America had originated, generally sympathized with the colonists. The Welsh Dissenting clergyman Richard Price, for example, argued that the increased executive power that the British government was exercising over the colonists would later be used in Britain itself. Scotland, meanwhile, displayed firm support for the war; in the wake of the Jacobite uprisings, many Scots viewed the conflict as a way to demonstrate their loyalty to Britain.

THE PRESENT STATE OF GREAT BRITAIN.

Figure 3.4 A broadside entitled "The Present State of Great Britain," by James Phillips, from 1779. In the center, John Bull, representing England, dozes while a female indigenous American steals his cap of liberty. A Dutchman crawls forward to pick John Bull's pocket, while a fierce-looking Scottish Highlander holds off a scrawny Frenchman. The image shows the alliance of other European nations against the British in the American Revolution, as well as the increasingly important role of Highland troops in defending the British Empire.

Reproduced courtesy of the Library of Congress OR Gift of William H. Huntington, 1883, Metropolitan Museum of Art.

But even though many people remained ambivalent about an open conflict, the momentum towards war continued to build. British troops and colonial militias began seizing arms in preparation for battle, while the rhetoric on both sides escalated. In April 1775, the military governor of Massachusetts and commander-in-chief of British forces in North America General Thomas Gage was ordered to arrest the leaders of the Massachusetts provincial congress, but, knowing that this would inflame anti-British sentiment, he refused. But in an effort to appease his superiors in London, he attempted to seize the weapons that the colonists had stored in the town of Concord. Warned – not by Paul Revere as legend has it (he was arrested in the nearby town of Lexington) but by Samuel Prescott – that the British were marching their way, the local militia mustered about 130 men to oppose them. When the two forces met at Lexington, someone – both sides claimed later that it was the other side – discharged his musket, and the British regulars opened fire. When the shooting stopped, seven militiamen lay dead, and nine others were wounded, two of whom died later. The British marched on to Concord, where there was a second confrontation in which two militiamen and three British redcoats were killed. On the sixteen-mile march back to Boston, the British faced constant fire from behind trees and walls. When they limped, shell-shocked, into Charlestown, just across the Charles River from Boston, they had suffered 272 casualties, and the colonists ninety-four. The Battle of Lexington and Concord was a warning to the British: their professional army in fact had little battlefield experience, whereas many of the American colonists had fought in local conflicts against indigenous peoples or at the very least were experienced huntsmen.

Once the war started, it quickly became apparent that politicians in London had little sense of the realities on the ground in America. Gage informed his superiors in London that he needed 20,000 rather than 3000 troops to defend Boston. In response, Gage was relieved of his duties, but he was soon proved right. At the Battle of Bunker Hill in June 1775, three frontal assaults up Breed's Hill (the actual site of the battle) led to over a thousand casualties among 2200 British troops.

The colonists possessed some serious advantages in the war: they could remain on the defensive and force the British to try to take territory. Every tree and building became what one British general described as a "temporary fortress." This in a sense made the British the underdogs throughout the conflict. The patriot commanders, however, were slow to recognize this and continued to seek direct confrontations with the British. Moreover, there were limits to what untrained and undisciplined troops could accomplish, even if they significantly outnumbered their opponents. After George Washington was appointed commander-in-chief of the 19,000 militiamen, now rechristened the "Continental Army," surrounding Boston in June 1775, his first task was to transform them into a proper army. When the Continental Army forced the British to evacuate nine months later, it seemed that his mission had been achieved, but in fact it was only just beginning.

The British had assembled a massive force of 32,000 soldiers, the largest army ever to cross the Atlantic prior to the departure of the American Expeditionary Force in 1917, with the intention of crushing American resistance swiftly and decisively. Its destination was New York, a city of islands where Britain could take advantage of its naval prowess. Washington thought the city indefensible, but he was ordered to defend it nonetheless. The British quickly forced the Continental troops back to their redoubts on Brooklyn Heights and should have been able to smash the rebellion then and there, but General William Howe was slow to exploit the victory. Some historians argue that this was because Howe was ambivalent about the war and keener to reconcile with the rebel Americans than defeat them. Others, however, claim that it was because Howe was an excellent battlefield commander but a poor strategist. Whatever the reason, Howe's inaction allowed Washington to evacuate his troops to Manhattan and ultimately retreat across the Hudson River to New Jersey and, after a twelve-day march, across the Delaware to Pennsylvania. The British had missed a huge, perhaps their only, opportunity to end the revolution quickly.

If the Continental Army had avoided a catastrophic defeat in New York, it was still a long way from victory. Washington now had only 5400 demoralized men under his command, while the Continental Congress fled from Philadelphia to Baltimore as the British advanced to the south. But on the day after Christmas 1776, Washington made a daring recrossing of the Delaware River and attacked a force of British-paid Hessian mercenaries at Trenton, capturing 900 of them while losing only a few men. The Americans gained a major boost in morale, while it was now clear that British hopes for a swift victory would not be realized.

The fundamental problem for the British was that while they could win battles, there were not enough loyalists to allow them to hold territory once they had conquered it. In upstate New York, a British army commanded by General John Burgoyne marched south from Quebec, hoping to seize control of the Hudson River Valley by converging with two other British forces as part of a broader plan to wall off New England from the rest of the colonies. In two battles in late September and early October, however, Burgoyne's men were halted by General Horatio Gates's Continentals, supplemented by thousands of militiamen. Badly outnumbered, Burgoyne attempted to retreat back to Canada but was cut off and forced to surrender his entire army of 7000 men – one-sixth of British troops in North America – at Saratoga on the 17th of October.

Saratoga was the turning point of the American Revolution, because it convinced the French that the American rebels could win, and they entered the war on their side the following year. France's entry meant that the British could no longer devote such massive military and naval resources to America, because they now had to defend their other imperial possessions from French attacks. Eight thousand British troops were pulled out of America and sent to protect their colonies in the Caribbean, which would be Britain's first priority for the remainder of the war. This forced the British to evacuate Philadelphia and concentrate on New York. British slave-trading bases in West Africa were threatened by the French, and the British were also forced to defend their Mediterranean possessions of Gibraltar and Minorca and the East India Company's holdings in India. The French even attacked the Isle of Jersey in the English Channel and threatened to invade both England and Ireland in 1779. By the end of the war, the British were fighting against the Spanish and Dutch as well as the French, without any European allies to counterbalance this alliance.

Even with French help, however, it would still take five more years for the British to decide that the cost of the war in men and money was too great, because the alternative – acknowledging American independence and shocking military failure – was too awful to contemplate. The war evolved into a stalemate, with the British unable to bring sufficient resources to bear and forced increasingly to focus on defending their colonies elsewhere from the French, while the Americans, in spite of the increasing effectiveness of the Continental Army, were as yet not powerful enough to confront the British.

As a stopgap more than a strategy, the British began shifting their operations in North America to the southern colonies, initially because they needed to secure safe harbors in Charleston and Savannah for their West Indian fleet during hurricane season. But after they were able to take all of Georgia and the port of Charleston with relative ease in early 1780, thanks to a combination of weak American resistance and a surge in loyalist sentiment, the mission expanded into a full-blown "southern strategy." The strategy was founded on the belief that there were tens of thousands of loyalists in the southern colonies who would rally to the British cause, as well as the fact that around 40 percent of the population of Virginia, the Carolinas and Georgia was comprised of African-American enslaved people – around 360,000 in total – whom the British hoped to convince to fight in exchange for giving them their freedom. The British also expected that the large number of indigenous Americans – Cherokees, Choctaws and Chickasaws – would fight for them.

In August 1780, a British victory over American troops who outnumbered them nearly two-to-one at Camden, South Carolina, seemingly confirmed that the strategy was sound. But the British could only put 3000 men in the field as they marched further inland into the South Carolina backcountry. They failed to exploit fully the enslaved people who did join them, relegating them to menial duties rather than training them to fight. Their presence among the British, meanwhile, outraged southern whites and increased support for the patriot cause. Weakened by heat and disease, British forces were sharply rebuffed at King's Mountain in October 1780 and Cowpens the following January. By the summer of 1781, the British had lost or abandoned all of their posts in the Carolina backcountry, and the southern strategy was in tatters. The viciousness of the campaign, in which neither side typically took prisoners, had alienated even many former loyalists, as had the British reliance on enslaved people and indigenous Americans. Colonists increasingly believed that the best route to ensure an end to the violence and the continuation of white supremacy was a patriot victory.

In what turned out to be their final campaign in America, the British turned to the Chesapeake, hoping to use it as a gateway to Virginia. Through a series of misunderstood and misguided orders, however, the British commander General Charles Cornwallis positioned his army on the bluffs at the end of a peninsula near the settlement of Yorktown, ostensibly for the purpose of providing a safe anchorage for the Royal Navy. There, they were bottled up by the French from the sea and a combined Continental and French force on land. Forty thousand French and Continental soldiers and sailors besieged Cornwallis's 7200 men, a fourth of British forces in North America. When a British naval squadron dispatched from New York failed to break them out, Cornwallis knew that his situation was hopeless. On the 17th of October, he surrendered. Yorktown was the last large-scale military engagement of the war. In February 1782, Parliament voted to cease offensive operations in North America, although the Treaty of Paris formally ending the hostilities was not signed until the end of the year.

The British viewed their defeat with disbelief. In his portrait of the peace negotiations at Paris, the artist Benjamin West was forced to leave one side of the painting blank because the British diplomatic team refused to pose for him. Politicians blamed the generals; the generals blamed the politicians. The British were able, however, to prevent even more disastrous consequences for their Caribbean colonies when Admiral George Rodney convincingly defeated the French Admiral de Grasse at the Battle of the Saintes in April 1782. The British Empire would soon recover. It also became more centralized and hierarchical, as the authorities in London, convinced that their lax supervision of the thirteen colonies had been responsible for the revolution, tightened their grip on their overseas possessions.

For non-white Americans, the consequences of the American Revolution were profound. Before the war, abolitionist sentiment in parts of America, particularly the northern colonies where there were relatively few enslaved people, had been growing: some people felt it was inhumane, while others argued that it depressed wages for white workers and kept prices for tobacco and other agricultural commodities low. The British had, in contrast, defended slavery as a mainstay of the system of colonial commerce; they saw no contradiction between the claim that theirs was an "empire of liberty" because its white subjects were permitted considerable political independence and a modicum of democracy and the enslavement of

Africans. But during the war the dynamic had shifted: the British had offered freedom to enslaved Americans as a means of bolstering their forces with additional recruits, while the Americans had opposed such efforts. (In the end about the same number – around 9000 – of African-Americans fought on each side.)

Indeed, few Americans thought that the fight for liberty extended to the 500,000 African-Americans (out of a total American population of 2.5 million) who remained enslaved at the war's end. It is not only with hindsight that the contradiction between patriotic American claims that the revolution was being fought for freedom and mass enslavement is obvious. After the Declaration of Independence was published, Lemuel Hayes, a free African-American in the Continental Army, wrote an essay entitled "Liberty Further Extended" in which he argued that the Declaration's assertion that "all men are created equal" applied to black as well as white people. Some white Americans, too, felt that liberty should extend to all. The British, meanwhile, argued that Americans were hypocrites for proclaiming they were fighting for liberty while enslaving hundreds of thousands of people. "How is it that we hear the loudest yelps for liberty among the drivers of negroes?" asked the writer Samuel Johnson. A clause in the Treaty of Paris required the British to return all enslaved people who had been seized by the British army. Some were, but around 15,000 others managed to escape to or were evacuated to Canada, Britain and other locales where they could remain free. The British commander at the end of the war, General Guy Carleton, refused to deliver enslaved people who had served the British to their former masters. But the now free African-Americans who immigrated to other parts of the Empire faced a difficult time adapting to their new lives. The British government denied them full political rights or the economic compensation that it granted to white loyalists.

Imperial Resurgence: The Second British Empire in India

The end of the American Revolution in 1783 marks a divide in the history of British imperial expansion between what historians have termed the First and the Second British Empires. Fears that the loss of the American colonies would result in a collapse of the rest of the Empire quickly proved unfounded. In the decades following the American Revolution, Britain's overseas empire expanded dramatically in Asia and the Pacific, in the latter case into regions that were unknown to Europeans prior to the final quarter of the eighteenth century. In 1750, the population of the British Empire had been around 12.5 million people. By 1820, it had reached 200 million, approximately one-quarter of the earth's population.

This "new" empire was not entirely new, however, and historians caution against regarding 1783 as a sharp dividing line. In India, as we have seen, the transformation of the East India Company into a territorial power was already well underway prior to the American Revolution. Yet it is the case that the Second British Empire encompassed new lands and engendered new ideas about how the British ought to govern their overseas territories. In general, the lesson that Britain's political leaders drew from the American Revolution was that their governance of the North American colonies had been too lenient. More authoritarian forms of government were thus developed. In Canada, for example, when colonial legislatures were established for Upper (Anglophone) and Lower (Francophone) Canada, they were made subordinate to a colonial governor appointed by Britain.

In India, the military conquests of the East India Company continued into the early decades of the nineteenth century. The conquest of India raised major questions about the conflict between colonial expansion and British pride in the nation's commitment to liberty for all its subjects, at home and overseas. "Plantation colonies" like those in North America and, later, Australia and New Zealand, were based upon the premise that British settlers would assume authority over a small, primitive and therefore insignificant indigenous population and were therefore easily envisioned as replica Britains in miniature. The British used the legal doctrine of *terra nullius*, which claimed that human beings had a right to territory that was not being properly utilized, to justify their encroachment upon these lands. Imperial expansion into Asia, however, required Britons to confront large populations and civilizations with very different social, cultural and political attitudes and institutions from their own. In India, territorial control required conquest of the alien but obviously sophisticated Mughal Empire, which occupied a land that was far from "empty." This reality was difficult to reconcile with the contemporary belief that empires won by way of conquest would lead to a loss of political liberty not just for the conquered but also for the conqueror.

Much effort, therefore, had to be expended in order to explain why the expansion of British power in India was not setting the nation on the road to Roman-style despotism. The primary argument that was deployed was the contention that the failings of the Mughal Empire necessitated British intervention in order to prevent India from descending into political chaos. The Indians, it was claimed, had proven incapable of governing themselves through their degeneracy, indolence and willingness to submit to tyranny; it was therefore up to the British to intervene and rule in benevolent fashion. This argument had previously been used in Ireland, where the English had viewed themselves as the civilizers of a "barbarous" people who lacked a governing structure that would enable them to progress to the highest levels of civilization. But it also possessed elements that were specific to British conceptions of Asian modes of governance. Derived in part from the French philosopher Baron de Montesquieu's concept of "oriental despotism" in his *Spirit of Laws* (1748), these conceptions were based upon notions that the warm Asian climate created a torpid political environment that was uniquely susceptible to despotic rule. Islamic despotism aroused particularly intense fears in eighteenth-century Europeans because of the ever-present threat of the continued expansion of the Ottoman Empire. But in India, it was the collapse rather than growth of Islamic power that was used to justify British intervention. The Company had no choice, it was argued, but to step in as Mughal authority disintegrated on a local level.

Further questions about the nature of Indian administration were raised by the numerous civil and military officials who returned home with large fortunes. They became notorious for their conspicuous display of their new wealth, which was widely suspected to have been acquired by corrupt and unsavory means. In the mid-eighteenth century, the term "nabob," a corruption of the Hindi word "nawab" referring to a Muslim nobleman, began to be applied to these men. The nabobs aroused envy and resentment, as they were accused of inflating the prices of everything from country houses to soap and sullying the nation's moral fiber with their decadent ways. To make matters worse, they threatened to use their ill-gotten gains to buy their way into Parliament, thereby acquiring undue influence and political power. "Without connections, without any natural interest in the soil, the importers of foreign gold forced their way into Parliament by such a torrent of corruption, as no private hereditary fortune can resist," thundered William Pitt in the 1760s.

 See document "Nabobs" at www.routledge.com/cw/barczewski.

Pitt was an unlikely source of such righteous indignation, as his grandfather, Thomas Pitt, had made his fortune in India. But even so he had a point, for the combination of nabob wealth and the irregularities of the eighteenth-century British political system made it a fairly simple matter for a wealthy Company servant to purchase parliamentary influence in the form of the "rotten boroughs" that supplied many representatives to the House of Commons. In 1770, the auction of New Shoreham's parliamentary seat among a group of nabobs, with an opening bid of £3000, intensified fears that the nation's most sacred political institutions were threatened by Asiatic corruption. Three years later, Samuel Foote's play *The Nabob* premiered in London. It featured a protagonist named Sir Matthew Mite, who fulfilled every stereotype of the vulgar, grasping returnee from India. "With the wealth of the East," declared one of the play's characters, "we have too imported the worst of its vices." Foote's message was echoed by contemporary political cartoonists, as well as by numerous novelists, poets and satirists.

Why did nabobs receive so much negative attention? They threatened the British character in two different ways. First, they threatened to upset the social order, as the infusion of so much cash from men of relatively humble origins was perceived as posing a danger to the traditional supremacy of landed wealth. Second, their corrupt practices threatened to undermine the nation's deeply held belief that it must exercise its imperial power in a morally upright manner. The British, as we have seen, had long prided themselves on being benevolent colonizers, particularly in comparison to supposedly tyrannous and oppressive Catholic countries like Spain and France. To be sure, the actual administration of the British Empire rarely lived up to these expectations, but the nabobs seemed to represent such a blatant case of self-interest that they made even the continued belief in the ideal difficult. The British public worried that a territorial empire acquired for the purpose of private profit would prove a moral albatross as well as a financial burden to the nation. A bevy of contemporary authors contended that the British had become corrupted by the same "oriental despotism" that they had supposedly intervened to rescue India from.

In addition to returning nabobs, Indian men and women traveled to Britain during the seventeenth and eighteenth centuries. They were typically sailors known as lascars, servants, ayahs (housemaids), or the wives or mistresses of Britons. Although British domestic servants were readily available, returning nabobs often preferred to bring Indians who could attend to them on the sea voyage home and who served as exotic symbols of nabobs' wealth and status. Governor-General Warren Hastings and wife brought four maids and two boys from India to England when they returned to England in 1785. The East India Company, which was financially responsible for the repatriation of Indian men and women, required Britons to post a bond of £50 for every Indian servant traveling to Britain. Despite these restrictions, however, some Indian men and women did manage to settle permanently in Britain. Their condition varied widely and their legal status as free servants or chattel was also ambiguous. Some were abandoned by their nabob employers; many impoverished servants desperately sought employment with Britons traveling to India in the hopes of returning home. Others ran away in search of better opportunities. Advertisements, similar to those for escaped African enslaved people, were posted in newspapers for their return, such as a 1743 notice offering a reward for a "Runaway Bengal Boy." Many were able to find employment in Britain, however, suggesting that the negative reputation of the nabobs did not affect the employability of their Indian servants.

Religion and Difference 3

Britain's First Muslims

In 2018, there were over 3.4 million Muslims living in the United Kingdom, comprising 5.1 percent of the population. Although their numbers have grown more rapidly since the Second World War, they have been a presence for centuries. Due to the Crusades,

Muslims were seen by most British people as their enemies throughout the Middle Ages. Those views began to change in the late sixteenth century, however. After Elizabeth I was excommunicated by Pope Pius V in 1570, she could ignore papal edicts prohibiting trade with Muslims. She actively sought commercial engagement with the Ottoman Empire, the Sa'adian dynasty in Morocco and the Shi'a Persian Empire. As a result, Muslims began coming to London, where they appear in the archival records as "Turks" and "Moors"; they are recorded as being brewers, weavers, tailors and metalsmiths. But after some of Elizabeth's subjects chose or were forced to convert to Islam, anti-Muslim sentiment increased. The activity of the Barbary pirates, who captured hundreds of British ships and sold their crews and passengers into slavery in the early seventeenth

Figure 3.5　Thomas Mann Baynes's portrait of Sake Dean Mahomed from around 1810.
Reproduced courtesy of Royal Pavilion and Museums, Brighton and Hove.

century, further stoked anti-Islamic sentiment. Even so, the growing awareness of and interest in Islam resulted in the founding of the first chair of Arabic studies at Oxford in 1636. It was in this period that the words "Islam" and "Muslim" entered the English language, replacing "Saracens," a disparaging term derived from the Crusades. A century later in 1734, the first English translation of the Quran was published. The expansion of the British Empire in India in the second half of the eighteenth century brought an increasing number of Muslims to Britain, although the numbers remained small in absolute terms. One of the most prominent was Sake Dean Mahomed, who was born in the city of Patna in Bengal and served as a trainee surgeon in the East India Company's army before he migrated to Ireland in 1784, where he converted to Christianity and married an Irish woman. Mahomed subsequently migrated to London, where he opened the Hindoostane Coffee House, London's first Indian restaurant, in 1810. He then moved to Brighton on the south coast of England, where he opened a precursor to a modern spa offering massages, vapor baths and shampoos with Indian oils. Mahomed became sufficiently prominent that he was appointed "Shampooing Surgeon" to King George IV. In the words of historian Michael Fisher, Mahomed's Baths became "the epitome of fashion in Brighton for nearly two decades." Although Mahomed's experiences were unique, his success demonstrates the how India occupied an increasing presence in British culture by the early nineteenth century.

There was some truth to the accusations that the East India Company had become almost entirely focused on the extraction of profit, at the expense of good governance. The Company's newly enhanced power, particularly that of tax collection, brought increased revenues to both the Company and its servants, but it also brought increased expenditures. The need to identify further sources of revenue led to continual pressure to expand the territory under the Company's control. The Company's army contained 18,000 soldiers at the end of the Seven Years' War; by 1820, it numbered 300,000 – the vast majority of whom were Indian sepoys – making it one of the largest military forces in the world. (It was more than three times the size of the British army.) It is no wonder that historians have referred to the Company's empire in this era as a "military despotism."

One of the foremost rivals of the British in India in this era was the warrior kingdom of Mysore in southern India, which was founded in 1761. From 1789 to 1792 and again in 1799, the British fought against Tipu Sultan, the "Tiger of Mysore," one of the most powerful and capable Indian rulers of the era. Tipu's army, which utilized European military advisors, rivaled that of the East India Company. While heir to the kingdom, Tipu had, with his French allies, won an important victory over the British at the Battle of Pollilur in 1780. Later, his donning of the "liberty cap" of the French Revolution and his continued allegiance with France made Tipu one of the greatest imperial villains of the age. In 1799, however, *Tipu was killed* and his fortress capital of Seringapatam taken; items from his rich treasury became fashionable items to display in British royal palaces and country houses. (Items from Tipu's collection are still on display at Windsor Castle, the British monarchy's primary residence.) The governor general of India, Richard Wellesley, declared, "the glorious termination of the late war in Mysore . . . [has] established the ascendancy of British power over all the states of India."

At the same time as the East India Company was expanding its territorial empire in India, the British government established greater control over the Company. In response to the Company's mounting debt and concerns about misgovernment, a series of reforms were passed. In 1773, the office of governor-general was established, which together with a council of four government appointees ruled the Company's territories in India from a base in Calcutta. Eleven years later, a Board of Control was established in London to supervise the operations of the Company. These administrative changes meant that the powers of war and peace in British India were now vested in the state rather than the Company.

The first governor-general, Warren Hastings (1773–85), was a scholar of Indian languages who promoted learning about India. To be sure, this scholarship was also an important tool of imperial rule; Hastings believed that the British in Bengal were the successors to the Mughal state, and by understanding the "true" laws of India in their ancient and uncorrupted form, they could more effectively rule over their Indian subjects.

The Presence of Empire 2

The Impeachment of Warren Hastings

Warren Hastings, the first governor-general of British India from 1773 to 1785, held this new and important imperial office at a time when India was assuming greater importance within the British Empire. Hastings had a strong knowledge of Indian culture and spoke several Indian languages, but he also firmly believed that British rule in India must be absolute, and he involved the Company in unpopular and expensive wars against the

Figure 3.6 A contemporary engraving of Warren Hastings's impeachment trial in 1789. It depicts Westminster Hall as packed with people, showing the intense public interest in the proceedings.

Reproduced courtesy of the British Library.

Maratha states in western India. After his return to Britain, Hastings became the focal point of growing criticism of the East India Company. Many MPs were concerned that Company officials were more focused on personal profit than good governance. In 1787, Hastings was formally impeached and placed on trial before the House of Lords. The Whig MP Edmund Burke argued that the Company, in attempting to preserve India from despotism, had become despotic itself. The trial dragged on for nine years; Hastings was acquitted, but his legal bills left him massively in debt. The negative publicity garnered by the Hastings trial did not slow the expansion of British power in India, however. It may, in fact, have enhanced it. Nicholas Dirks argues that the Hastings trial led to the transfer of power over India from the "rogue" East India Company to the British state, thereby removing the taint of corruption by giving the governance of India official sanction. Even Burke never suggested that the answer to this problem was for Britain to abandon India. Instead, his rhetoric about the need to purge the corruption of the nabobs and exercise responsible rule over the nation's colonial possessions played a significant part in constructing a framework in which the military conquest of India could be reconciled to the moral imperatives of good governance.

Later governors-general tended to strongly favor British forms of governance. Hastings's successor Lord Cornwallis reserved the highest ranks of the civil service for Britons, excluding both Indians and the children of mixed British–Indian background. While Cornwallis did not seek to add territories to Britain's empire in India, Richard Wellesley, governor-general from 1799 to 1805, embodied a newly aggressive spirit of imperial expansion at the end of the eighteenth century. Wellesley argued that British conquest had saved the province of Bengal and that the British had a right to depose regional rulers such as Tipu Sultan, whom they regarded as tyrants and usurpers of the emperor's authority. At the Battle of Assaye in 1803, Wellesley's younger brother Arthur, the future Duke of Wellington and conqueror of Napoleon, won a major victory over the Marathas, another successor state to the Mughals. By 1820, the British were the dominant land power in India.

In the nineteenth century, a "civilizing mission" was to become an important rationale for British imperial expansion. Yet historians have recently called attention to the fact that Indian culture, society and religion also exerted a powerful influence on Britons in India in this period. British funeral memorials in Calcutta incorporated Islamic architectural features such as Mughal-style domes. William Jones, a leading British scholar in India, stressed the common roots of European and Indian languages; Jones recognized India as a land of ancient civilization and learning that compared favorably to Britain. On a more personal level, many British men had Indian mistresses and sometimes wives, and occasionally they converted to Islam in order to marry elite Muslim women. At the beginning of the nineteenth century, James Achilles Kirkpatrick, the British resident in the kingdom of Hyderabad in south India, converted to Islam and married Khair un-Nissa, a member of one of Hyderabad's leading noble families and a descendent of the Prophet Mohammed.

By this time, however, Kirkpatrick's behavior was highly exceptional, as the late-eighteenth-century impulse to understand India gave way in the early nineteenth to a desire to control and subordinate it. Prior to 1800, many of the wills of British men in Bengal mentioned Indian *bibis*, or mistresses, but afterwards few did. The Indian clothing known as "pajamas" became something that British men slept in, rather than something they wore during the day. British colonial buildings, such as Government House in Calcutta, were typically **neoclassical** structures that were inspired by architecture in Britain – in the case of Government House the model was a country house called Kedleston Hall in Derbyshire – rather than by Indian styles.

Imperial Expansion in the Pacific

In addition to consolidating its authority over existing parts of the empire, the British Empire also expanded into the Pacific, territory previously unmapped by Europeans. Here, exploration formed another facet of the Anglo-French rivalry, as both nations launched expeditions to map and claim territories. These expeditions were undertaken for scientific as well as strategic and geographical purposes. In response to a request from the **Royal Society**, in 1768 the naval ship *Endeavour* under *Captain James Cook* traveled to the South Pacific to observe an astronomical event known as the Transit of Venus. Cook was also charged with searching for an uncharted continent that was believed to be located in the southern hemisphere, *Terra Australis Incognita*. During the three-year-long voyage, Cook charted more than 5000 miles of territory previously unknown to Europeans, including the coastlines of New Zealand and eastern Australia. Cook's two further Pacific voyages added immensely to European knowledge of geography, astronomy, botany and other branches of science. He was acclaimed as one of the greatest British heroes of the age, an Enlightenment figure who in spite of his status as a naval officer stood for peace and knowledge, not war. Cook's popularity was increased not only by his death in Hawaii on his final voyage, but also by a British desire for a new hero in the wake of their defeat in the American Revolution.

 See document "Captain Cook in Australia" at www.routledge.com/cw/barczewski.

Cook's voyages also, however, demonstrated the complexities of cultural encounters with peoples so different from the British. A Pacific islander known as Mai, or Omai, returned to Britain with Cook on his second voyage. He was received warmly by London society, enjoyed an audience with King George III and posed for portraits by prominent artists. The attention proved fleeting, however, and Omai returned home, laden with gifts including a horse and a suit of armor, on Cook's third and final voyage in 1777. Omai's visit occurred at a moment of transition for British attitudes towards the external world. He was regarded by many people not as a primitive savage but as a representative of a purer form of humanity uncorrupted by the decadence and immorality bred by civilization. Britons thus looked for similarities, not differences, between him and his European counterparts. This sensibility is reflected in his portrait by the noted artist Sir Joshua Reynolds, which depicts him in romanticized but not alien form, in flowing robes that hearkened back to Greek or Roman classical garb and with dark skin but anglicized features.

Cook was to be less fortunate in his reception by the peoples of the Pacific. In February 1779, he was killed by native Hawaiians while attempting to kidnap their king in retribution for the theft of some of his ship's boats. For decades afterwards, books and visual images presented Cook as a brilliant navigator who showed uncommon care for his men and treated the peoples whom he encountered with unprecedented humanity and kindness. In keeping with the values of the Enlightenment, his peaceful intentions were repeatedly lauded, as was his role as the deliverer of the bounties of European technology, commerce and agriculture. His death was a tragedy that he had in no way provoked; he was the innocent victim of the barbarous Hawaiians, who had savagely and irrationally turned on their benevolent "discoverer."

Figures 3.7 and 3.8   Two images related to Captain James Cook's voyages. Figure 3.7 is an engraving
from 1777 based on Sir Joshua Reynolds's painting of Omai, who had returned
to England with Cook from the island of Ra'ia-tea four years earlier. Reynolds
depicted Omai not as a primitive savage, but as a romantic figure with dark skin
but European-style features. Figure 3.8 is Francis Bartolozzi's mezzotint of Cook's
death, dating from 1783. The scene shows Cook attempting to stop his men from
shooting at the indigenous Hawaiians; the image of Cook as a man of peace was
central to his status as an Enlightenment hero.

Both figures reproduced courtesy of the Yale Center for British Art, Paul Mellon Collection.

Beneath this hagiographic surface, however, lurked other, less positive interpretations of
Cook's death and the actions that had prompted it. Almost immediately upon the *Resolution's* return to England, rumors circulated of his uncharacteristically violent and impulsive
behavior on his final voyage. Accounts by officers and seamen from the *Resolution* suggested
that Cook, rather than the Hawaiians, had been the aggressor in the final, fatal confrontation. More disturbingly, reports surfaced that he had permitted and even encouraged the
Hawaiians to worship him as if he were a deity.

Indeed, all three of Cook's voyages occasioned complex responses from contemporary
Britons. In the eyes of the British public, the geographic and scientific discoveries of his
first voyage from 1768 to 1771 had been overshadowed by the sexual nature of the Tahitian
rituals that were circumspectly described in John Hawkesworth's official account of the voyage and by the stories of the ribald activities of Cook's botanist Joseph Banks that circulated
widely in contemporary periodicals. The defining event of the second voyage, meanwhile,
became the violent encounter that took place at Grass Cove in New Zealand, in which
several members of Cook's crew were killed and possibly eaten by the indigenous Maori as
they gathered fodder for the expedition's livestock. Cook's voyages were therefore associated
not only with heroism and discovery but with sexual promiscuity, violent death and cross-
cultural misunderstanding.

Shadowed by this complex legacy, British whalers, settlers and missionaries followed Cook
into the Pacific. In January 1788, the *first British settlement* in the region was established at
Botany Bay in southeastern Australia, where Cook had landed two decades earlier. The

settlement, which quickly moved to Sydney Harbor, was intended primarily as a penal colony, although historians have pointed to the importance of strategic elements in its foundation as well. The colony was to serve as a basis for further British expansion in the Pacific. After encountering a French expedition off the south coast of Australia in 1802, the British occupied Van Diemen's Land (the modern island of Tasmania), which also became a penal settlement. The British presence in Australia gradually extended inland, and by the turn of the nineteenth century, there were 5000 British settlers in the colony of New South Wales. Early convicts were mostly guilty of property offenses, and after having served out their sentence or being pardoned, they were freed and given grants of land. In 1800, two-thirds of the settler population consisted of former convicts. Australia also served as a place of transportation for Irish rebels, particularly those from the rebellion of the United Irishmen in 1798. Although convict discipline was harsh, with flogging a common punishment, the new colony was marked in its early years by frequent outbreaks of disorder. Three hundred men staged an uprising in 1804 that was brutally suppressed by government troops.

The Presence of Empire 3

Transportation

In the eighteenth century, what to do with convicted criminals was a complex question. Relative to today, large numbers were sentenced to death. The number of capital offenses increased from around fifty in 1688 to 220 by century's end. People were hanged for what we would consider very petty crimes today. There remained, however, many crimes that were not punishable by death. There was insufficient prison capacity for large numbers of people to be incarcerated for long periods of time, and so an alternative was found in the form of the penal colony. The idea was to deter crime by imposing a penalty that involved sending the convicted criminal thousands of miles from home and making him perform hard labor when he got there. In 1717, the first Transportation Act was passed, allowing convicts to be transported to Britain's colonies, where they served as indentured labor. On arrival, they were auctioned off to the highest bidder, for whom they would work for a seven-year term. An estimated 50,000 convicts were sent to the American colonies. The American Revolution meant, however, that America was no longer available as a destination for transported prisoners. Between 1776 and 1787, convicted criminals who were not sentenced to death were incarcerated in prison hulks, or stationary ships, anchored off Britain's south coast. These hulks soon became dangerously overcrowded, however, and so another solution had to be found. In 1787, the "First Fleet" of eleven ships carrying around a thousand convicts departed for New South Wales in Australia. The intention was for them to establish an agricultural colony there, but few possessed any farming experience or skills. They were treated harshly by their guards, who doled out minimal food and frequent harsh punishments, including flogging, being put in leg irons or solitary confinement. Between 1787 and 1868, around 162,000 convicts were transported to Australia; the numbers peaked in the 1830s when industrialization meant that many British workers in traditional nonmechanized occupations were put out of work and forced to turn to crime to support themselves. About 20 percent of transportees to Australia were female. After they had served their sentences, most transported convicts decided to remain. Today, Australia's origin as a penal colony is a badge of pride, as it contributes to a picture of the earliest white settlers overcoming severe hardship to establish a new country. This picture, however, ignores the devastating impact of this history on Australia's aboriginal population, who were almost eradicated by the combined effect of imported diseases and theft of their land.

Figure 3.9 Completed in 1836, the Great North Road Convict Trail in Sydney, Australia, was built using the labor of around 720 convicts. 165 miles long, it connected Sydney to settlements in the Hunter Valley. Around twenty-seven miles remains intact today, when it serves as a recreational walking trail and a reminder of Australia's past as a penal colony.

Reproduced courtesy of Shutterstock/Destinations Journey.

The transportation of prisoners to Australia slowed due to the urgent need for manpower during the Napoleonic Wars, but it increased again after 1815. By 1820, the settler population of Australia was 26,000, bringing the colony increasingly into conflict with the indigenous Aborigines. In the 1780s, the commander of the Botany Bay expedition had been ordered to "open an intercourse with the natives, and to conciliate their affections, enjoining all our subjects to live in amity and kindness with them," but relations quickly deteriorated. In British eyes, the Aborigines ranked as a lower order of humanity – the *Times* in 1793 compared them to "beasts of the field" – who were increasingly seen as uncivilizable. By 1800, the interactions between the settlers and the Aborigines were marked more by hostility and violence than by "amity and kindness."

Believing that the Aborigines were nomadic hunter-gatherers who had no fixed ties to the land, the British took possession of territory in Australia under the legal doctrine known as *terra nullius* or "empty land." It soon became clear, however, that Aboriginal peoples did in fact have deep ties to the landscape and were willing to fight to defend their territory. The British refusal to recognize Aboriginal land rights, combined with Aboriginal peoples' lack of interest in abruptly abandoning a way of life that they had followed for millennia, sharply limited opportunities for peaceful interchange. Sexual abuse of Aboriginal women by convicts and soldiers added to tensions. There is also evidence that British officers or convicts may have deliberately spread smallpox among the indigenous population in the early years of the colony. Relations between Aboriginal peoples and the British were never marked exclusively by conflict, however. After efforts to drive out the invaders failed, many Aborigines around Sydney Harbor saw accommodation with the British as a way to retain access to their land, and traded food and other goods with the colonists. Some served as intermediaries between the British and the Aboriginal population. Early nineteenth-century governors especially valued a man of the Kuring-gai people named Bungaree, who assisted in the mapping of the Australian coastline and served as a mediator with other Aboriginal peoples. In return for his service, Governor Lachlan Macquarie awarded him a breastplate that read "King of the Blacks."

Yet sporadic attempts at "civilizing" the Aborigines and incorporating them into the lower ranks of colonial society were always mixed with episodes of violence. On the colonial frontier, first on the coastal plain surrounding Sydney and after 1815 in the interior of southeastern Australia, settlers and military forces carried out a brutal campaign of terror against Aboriginal resistance. By 1824, over 1200 European ranchers were grazing more than 100,000 livestock on the same number of acres. No recognition was made for the land rights of the local Wiradjuri people, who began to carry out guerilla attacks on settlers. Retaliatory attacks by settlers and military forces killed thousands of Aborigines (in only two instances were Britons brought to trial for Aboriginal killings); in one episode the skulls of forty-five massacred Aborigines were sent to England as souvenirs.

Some British observers lamented that the coming of western civilization to Australia had brought nothing but death and misery to the Aborigines, yet none called for the halt of British expansion on the continent. Emigration from Britain mainly to white settler colonies more than doubled from the 1830s to the 1840s and continued to grow, steadily outpacing immigration to Britain during the same period. While reports of violent conflicts with the Aborigines, along with the vast distance and Australia's reputation as a penal colony, may have deterred free migrants in the early nineteenth century, migration increased markedly after government-assisted passage began in 1831. Australia came to be a seen as a land of opportunity, and many white emigrants took part in Australia's new pastoral economy, which offered the prospect of success for those with limited resources. New South Wales's population more than doubled to 187,000 from 1836 to 1851. Migration surged further during the 1850s, when gold was discovered in New South Wales, and 230,000 migrants arrived with government assistance in the decade.

The Abolition of Slavery

For much of the eighteenth century, Britons had few qualms about enslaving and transporting Africans for plantation labor in the Americas. Shifts in the intellectual and cultural climate, however, led more people to question slavery in the decades after 1750. Enlightenment philosophers objected to the denial of political and civil liberty to the enslaved. In the Somerset case of 1772, a British judge ruled that an enslaved person brought to England by a West Indian planter was free because slavery was not sanctioned by English law. The ruling left the question of emancipation ambiguous but provided the legal basis for keeping slavery as practiced in the colonies out of the "free air" of England. The growing religious revival of the late eighteenth century also contributed to the rise of the antislavery movement. Many abolitionists were Quakers or evangelical members of the Anglican Church. The latter group included William Wilberforce, MP for Yorkshire and a passionate and committed antislavery activist for over thirty years. Wilberforce is often credited as the man most responsible for the abolition of the slave trade and slavery.

The abolition of the slave trade was not due solely to arguments made by Wilberforce and other members of Parliament, however. Extraparliamentary organization and activity also formed a major part of the campaign, as the antislavery movement united British men and women from across the political spectrum. Women played a prominent role by circulating petitions, speaking at public meetings, boycotting sugar and other products of slave labor, and writing antislavery poetry. Abolitionists also created effective propaganda to illustrate the brutality of slavery and the ways it reduced African people to commodities. Created in 1787, an image of the slave ship *Brookes* packed with 454 Africans was used by abolitionists to show the horrors of the Middle Passage; it appeared widely in newspapers, pamphlets and books, and Wilberforce carried a wooden model of it into Parliament to aid his arguments. The Quaker Thomas Clarkson later observed that the "print seemed to make an instantaneous impression of horror upon all who saw it, and was therefore instrumental, in consequence of the wide circulation given it, in serving the cause of the injured Africans." Clarkson toured Britain carrying shackles and other implements of slavery; he also visited slave ports in West Africa and interviewed sailors and others involved with the slave trade in order to bring firsthand knowledge of its horrors before the public. The pottery maker Josiah Wedgwood produced a medallion inscribed with a depiction of an enslaved man kneeling under the legend "Am I not a man and a brother?" There was also a strong market for abolitionist books, driven in part by evangelicals' emphasis on literacy, which members of the black community helped to satisfy. Ottaboh Cugoano and Olaudah Equiano, friends and former enslaved people, both published autobiographies which reached wide audiences; George III reportedly received a copy of Cugoano's 1787 *Thoughts and Sentiments on the Evils of Slavery*, which offered the strongest condemnation of slavery to date by an author of African descent.

A notorious incident, known as the *Zong* case, drew particular attention to the appalling treatment of enslaved Africans on the "Middle Passage" to the West Indies. In 1781, the *Zong*, a ship owned by Liverpool slave-traders, had sailed from West Africa with a cargo of 450 enslaved people, far more than it could safely carry. Dozens of them had already perished from malnutrition, dehydration and disease when the crew made a navigational error that caused the ship to sail 300 miles past its destination of Jamaica. With their provisions dwindling, the crew decided to throw some of the "cargo" overboard, as any who died at sea would be covered by the voyage's insurers, whereas those who died on land were not. Over the next few days, over 130 people were cast overboard alive. The *Zong* finally arrived in Jamaica with 208 enslaved individuals in the hold, less than half the number that had been boarded in Africa. In England, the ship's owners submitted a claim for the "lost cargo." They argued that it had been necessary to throw some overboard in order to save the rest, because there was not sufficient water to sustain all of them for the extra length of the voyage due to the navigational error. The insurer refused to pay, but the courts upheld the claim. Influenced by the abolitionist Granville Sharp, the insurers appealed. In the retrial, it was determined that the crew had passed up opportunities to obtain more water and that the *Zong* had arrived in Jamaica with over 400 gallons. The judge, Lord Mansfield (who had also decided the Somerset case), found that, because there

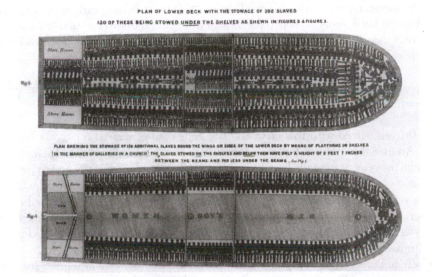

Figures 3.10 and 3.11   Two examples of the kinds of materials abolitionists used to bolster their case. Originally produced in 1787, Figure 3.10 shows the slave ship *Brookes* with its decks crammed with kidnapped Africans; this image became one of the most powerful pieces of abolitionist propaganda. Figure 3.11 is a mezzotint from 1791 by John Raphael Smith of George Morland's painting *The Slave Trade*. The image shows an African family being torn apart as different purchasers buy the father and the mother and child. The inscription at the bottom reads, "Lo! the poor Captive with distraction wild/Views his dear Partner torn from his embrace!/A diff'rent Captain buys his Wife and Child/What time can from his Soul such ills erase?"

Figure 3.10 reproduced courtesy of Shutterstock/Everett Collection; Figure 3.11 reproduced courtesy of the Yale Center for British Art.

had been no need to "jettison" any of the human cargo, the insurers were not liable. He did not, however, recognize the drowned victims as human beings; rather, he continued to define them in legal terms as property. The solicitor general bluntly stated, "this is a case of chattels or goods. Blacks are goods and property; it is madness to accuse these well-serving honorable men of murder."

 See document "The Zong Incident and the Abolitionist Movement" at www. routledge.com/cw/barczewski.

Most Britons agreed with this view, and the *Zong* case generated relatively little public outrage. Among abolitionists, however, it brought a new sense of energy to their cause. The abolitionist movement formally began in 1787 with the foundation of the *Society for Effecting the Abolition of the Slave Trade*. Abolitionists were also involved in efforts to alleviate widespread poverty among London's black community, which had rapidly increased following the American Revolution. An estimated 9,000 of the 60,000 loyalists who departed North America at the war's conclusion were former enslaved people. Thousands arrived in Britain with minimal possessions and soon found themselves destitute. Former enslaved people were rarely able to earn a living in a labor market flooded with demobilized soldiers and sailors and were unable to receive poor relief, since their parish of origin typically lay outside Britain. The Committee for the Relief of the Black Poor, established by British abolitionists and philanthropists, supplied food and assistance and also worked with the Treasury on a plan to resettle former enslaved people on the Sierra Leone peninsula on the west coast of Africa. The prominent abolitionist Granville Sharpe hoped that the settlement, under the protection of the Crown and the Royal Navy, would be a "Province of Freedom," based on ideals of British liberty and Christian values, that would serve as a new model for British relations with Africa, one based on trade rather than enslavement. Despite the efforts of abolitionists such as Sharpe, who donated funds for trade goods and wrote a plan for the colony's government, the initial settlement was poorly planned. Most of the original 411 settlers died of disease or in conflicts with local African peoples. The colony nearly failed, but in 1792 1200 black loyalists from Nova Scotia, who had struggled to support themselves on the marginal land they had been allocated in Canada, migrated to Sierra Leone and helped to establish the new settlement of Freetown. In 1808 Sierra Leone became a crown colony. Although the colony failed to achieve the promises of racial equality and self-government that had been offered to black settlers, tens of thousands of former enslaved people settled there in the following decades.

Abolitionists' main focus in the late eighteenth and early nineteenth centuries was the cessation of the transatlantic slave trade. While they quickly succeeded in making the slave trade an issue for public debate, it would be another two decades before they managed to end it. Britain's wars with revolutionary France bolstered the abolitionist cause. A third of the Africans transported on British ships were supplied to the colonies of other European nations, and the abolitionists argued convincingly that it was a patriotic duty to deny the French enslaved labor as long as the war continued. The slave trade to foreign nations was abolished in 1806, and the *slave trade* the following year. The Royal Navy stationed a squadron of ships at Freetown to enforce the ban and freed an estimated 175,000 captives in the years after 1807. Although this only represented a fraction of the total trade – Spain, Portugal and later Brazil continued for decades to transport enslaved people across the Atlantic – British abolition of the slave trade represented an important milestone in the antislavery campaign.

Sugar planting in the West Indies remained a source of substantial profits, however, and it would be another three decades before slavery itself was abolished. Their zeal in condemning the slave trade notwithstanding, Wilberforce and other influential abolitionists were conservatives who argued that the end of slavery must be a gradual process, giving both the enslaved and enslavers time to adjust. In addition, the Tory governments of the early nineteenth century had little interest in reform. It was not until the Whig movement for parliamentary reform gained momentum in the late 1820s that the cause gained any real vigor. A series of rebellions by the enslaved in the Caribbean also provided impetus; the largest and most prolonged of these, the Baptist War in Jamaica, began on Christmas Day 1831 and involved around 60,000 enslaved people. The rebellion acquired its name because it was led by the black Baptist deacon Samuel Sharpe.

Race 3

The West Indies After Emancipation

On the 1st of August 1834, approximately 750,000 enslaved people in Britain's West Indian colonies became free. Many aspects of their lives, however, did not change. In many cases, they could only find jobs on the same sugar plantations on which they had been enslaved, where they now worked for low wages and were forced to pay high rents. Little land was available for purchase, and those former enslaved people who did attempt to strike out on their own were confronted with strict laws against vagrancy and squatting. Although colonial assemblies were now elected by majority-black populations, property ownership and other requirements for candidates meant that they remained under white control, as only a few of the very wealthiest black or mixed-race citizens qualified. Black West Indians did not accept this situation passively, however. In 1865, workers from St. Ann parish in Jamaica sent Queen Victoria a petition listing their grievances and declaring their "great want at this moment from the bad state of our island soon after we became free subjects." When the British government responded by telling black Jamaicans to work harder, a resident of St. Thomas parish named Paul Bogle led a march on the courthouse in Morant Bay; hundreds were killed in the ensuing violence and by the harsh measures of retaliation that were imposed by the colony's governor, Edward Eyre. Gradually, however, conditions in the West Indian colonies began to improve as judicial systems, education and health care were slowly reformed. Numbering tens of thousands of people by the mid-nineteenth century, a new class of black artisans and tradesmen emerged. Even so, the West Indian colonies struggled economically in the post-emancipation era, as their productivity and profitability had depended upon the free labor supplied by enslaved Africans.

Parliament voted to *end slavery* in most British colonies in 1833, and the law came into effect the following year, freeing close to over 750,000 people in the West Indies. Legislation provided £20 million to planters as compensation, and the formerly enslaved were forced to enter a system of apprenticeship to their former masters that ended in 1838. To perform the work that the enslaved had previously done, indentured laborers were brought from India.

Over 400,000 Indians came to the British Caribbean, mostly to the island of Trinidad, until the system was ended during the First World War.

Slavery was not abolished in India and other East India Company territories or in Ceylon (modern Sri Lanka) until 1843. Even after abolition, forms of unfree labor persisted under the imperial economic system. Although legal emancipation delegitimized the institution of slavery, it opened the door for new exploitative labor systems. Often, these post-emancipation labor systems ended up looking much like slavery, with workers forced to toil far from home and under harsh conditions that they had little recourse to challenge. As scholars such as Catherine Hall have shown, empire continued to have a deep and profound effect on Britain itself. An imperial economic web bound Britain to colonies in Africa and Asia that provided raw materials, using a system that kept workers tied to the plantations where they worked. Ceylon was the site of large coffee and later tea plantations that produced much of the colony's wealth. The labor for these plantations came from tens of thousands of Tamil laborers from India who were recruited by the British government. This mass migration forever changed the face of the island and contributed to the present-day unrest between the Tamil and Sinhalese populations.

Conclusion

The use of Indian indentured labor in the West Indies and Ceylon following the abolition of slavery demonstrates a prominent facet of the British Empire in the early nineteenth century: its interconnections. In the first half of the nineteenth century, Indian sepoys fought in imperial campaigns in Egypt, Burma, China and Afghanistan. The migration of Indian men and women to work in the sugar cane fields of Caribbean islands also demonstrates how the focus of the Empire shifted over the course of the period discussed in this chapter. In the second half of the eighteenth century, the British Empire was transformed from an empire whose population consisted primarily of white European settlers and African enslaved people into a multiethnic, multiracial and multireligious empire, whose subjects included French-speaking Canadians, Indian Hindus and Muslims, and the descendants of Dutch settlers in southern Africa. The political and economic focus of the British Empire shifted as well, away from the Atlantic World and towards Asia. By the early nineteenth century, the British had displaced the Mughals and their successors to become the dominant political, economic and military power in India. Territories in the Pacific such as Australia, which at the beginning of the eighteenth century had never been glimpsed by Europeans, now formed an important part of Britain's expanding empire.

By 1800, Britain's overseas empire was also manifestly a British Empire rather than an English one, in which Scottish, Welsh and Irish people contributed to its trade, defense and administration. Empire's impact was never solely limited to Britain's overseas territories, however; in these years it affected the everyday lives of men and women in the British Isles and brought black and Asian peoples to Britain in larger numbers than ever before. Finally, while the late eighteenth and early nineteenth century witnessed the development of a humanitarian campaign to end Britain's involvement in the slave trade and the institution of slavery, the British Empire had become more authoritarian. While the different colonies of Britain's empire were not governed in a uniform fashion, a common theme was that Britain sought to maintain greater control over imperial governance. The Empire's growth would continue in the nineteenth century, and its influence on British society and culture would continue to grow as well.

Bibliography

Bayly, C. A., *Imperial Meridian: The British Empire and the World 1780–1830* (1989)

Blaufarb, Rafe and Liz Clarke, *Inhuman Traffick: The International Struggle against the Transatlantic Slave Trade* (2015)

Brown, Christopher Leslie, *Moral Capital: Foundations of British Abolitionism* (2007)

Dalrymple, William, *The Anarchy: The Relentless Rise of the East India Company* (2019)

Day, David, *Claiming a Continent: A New History of Australia* (2001)

Devine, T. M., *To the Ends of the Earth: Scotland's Global Diaspora 1750–2000* (2011)

Ellis, Joseph J., *The Cause: The American Revolution and its Discontents, 1773–1783* (2021)

Flavell, Julie, *When London Was the Capital of America* (2010)

Hackforth-Jones, Jocelyn, et al., *Between Worlds: Voyagers to Britain 1700–1850* (2007)

Holton, Woody, *Liberty Is Sweet: The Hidden History of the American Revolution* (2021)

Jasanoff, Maya, *Liberty's Exiles: American Loyalists in the Revolutionary World* (2011)

Lawson, Philip, *The East India Company: A History* (1993)

Midgeley, Clare, *Women Against Slavery: The British Campaigns, 1780–1870* (1992)

Olusoga, David, *Black and British: A Forgotten History* (2016)

Taylor, Alan, *American Revolutions: A Continental History, 1750–1804* (2017)

4 A United Kingdom? 1760–1820

Topics covered

- John Wilkes and calls for political reform
- Greater integration of Scotland into the United Kingdom
- United Irish Rebellion and the Act of Union with Ireland
- Religious pluralism
- Agricultural revolution and improvements in transportation
- Revolutionary and Napoleonic Wars
- War of 1812
- Congress of Vienna
- Response to the French Revolution in the United Kingdom

Timeline

1760	Accession of George III
1761	Bridgewater Canal opens
1763	Issue 45 of the *North Briton* published
1776	Adam Smith, *The Wealth of Nations*
1780	Gordon Riots
1782	Irish Parliament granted legislative independence
1783	William Pitt the Younger becomes prime minister
1790	Edmund Burke, *Reflections on the Revolution in France*
1791	Thomas Paine, *The Rights of Man*
1792	Mary Wollstonecraft, *A Vindication of the Rights of Women*
1793	Britain goes to war with France
1794	*Habeas Corpus* Suspension Act
1798	Rebellion by United Irishmen
1798	Battle of the Nile
1800	Act of Union with Ireland
1805	Battle of Trafalgar
1811	Regency declared
1812	War of 1812 begins
1815	Napoleon defeated at Waterloo; Congress of Vienna
1819	Peterloo Massacre; Six Acts passed

DOI: 10.4324/9781003284758-4

Introduction

Why was there no British Revolution in 1789 as there was in France? While France erupted into dramatic political and social upheaval, no similar cataclysmic event occurred across the English Channel. This chapter will show that, although between 1760 and 1820 there was strong pressure for change in Britain to address some of the anomalies and archaisms of the political system, the forces of unity were ultimately greater than those of revolution. The history of this period is often presented as a debate between those who supported revolution and those who wished to repress it, with the latter ultimately prevailing. Traditionally, historians have offered two explanations for this. First, they argue that the British political system proved sufficiently flexible to adapt gradually to a changing society and economy, thereby avoiding having pressure build to a breaking point as it did in France. Second, they argue that the elite, or what in France was called the *ancien régime*, were so powerful that they could resist more radical change, though they did have to make some concessions. In more recent years, however, some historians have argued that a key force in overcoming demands for dramatic upheaval was the underlying unity of the British nation that developed in this period. This unity allowed Britain to establish itself as the leading global and imperial power in Europe. That power was not secure, however, as a major war with France that began in 1793 threatened the very survival of the British nation. Though victory was ultimately achieved, it required the rebuilding of a Europe that had been forever altered.

Wilkes and Liberty

As we have seen, the Glorious Revolution was seen as having given the leading role in the British political system to Parliament. The *accession of George III* in 1760, however, threatened to overturn this consensus. Predeceased by his father, Frederick, Prince of Wales, he was George II's grandson and only twenty-two years of age when he came to the throne. His youthful vitality, and the absence of a serious Jacobite rival, led him to attempt to restore some of the power that had slipped away from the monarchy. The vulnerability of a political settlement that relied more on mutual agreement than written law soon became apparent. As there was no legislation to prevent him from choosing his own ministers, George III installed his former tutor, the Earl of Bute, as his prime minister. Bute's main qualifications for the job were his close relationship with the King and his good looks; otherwise, he was inexperienced (having spent only three years in Parliament) and, in the eyes of his numerous critics, incompetent. To make matters worse, he was Scottish, at a time when memories of the Jacobite Rebellion of 1745 were still fresh and the Scots were still widely distrusted in England.

The fear that Bute's installation was the thin end of a wedge of resurgent royal power opened up key questions about the nature of British governance. The political upheavals of the seventeenth and early eighteenth centuries had left two questions unresolved. First, there was the issue of how wide the parliamentary franchise should be. Full participation in the British political system continued to be based on property ownership, but the dramatic growth in the British population from 6 million to 16 million between 1700 and 1800 meant that an ever-smaller proportion of Britons met the qualification, even if the number of eligible voters had increased in absolute terms. Whereas as many as 23 percent of all adult males could vote in the early eighteenth century, only 17 percent could by century's end. Outside of England, the situation was worse. As few as 3000 men in all of Scotland could vote, as opposed to as many as 300,000 in England and Wales. In Ireland, the majority of the population was excluded on religious grounds, as Catholics were banned from voting until 1793. There was a growing sense that this electoral situation was inadequate, though only a handful of radicals wished to dispense with the property qualification altogether.

The second question that faced the British political system in the second half of the eighteenth century involved the rotten and pocket boroughs that were such a key component of a political system that depended heavily upon bribes, patronage and sinecures. A system in which almost three-quarters of the 405 members of the House of Commons were elected by constituencies of less than 500 voters was ripe for, and rife with, corruption, or at least the undue application of influence by the rich and powerful. The economic and demographic change that occurred over the course of the eighteenth century meant that rotten and pocket boroughs were no longer merely archaic relics of an outmoded demographic map; they were now preventing other parts of Britain from gaining proper representation. By the last quarter of the century, the early stirrings of industrialization caused people to move in significant numbers to manufacturing centers such as Manchester, Birmingham, Leeds and Sheffield, none of which were represented except as part of the county in which it was located. The comparison of Manchester, which by 1800 had a population of over 200,000 and no representation as a borough, to Old Sarum in Wiltshire, which had less than ten eligible voters and was a borough constituency, was a frequent tactic for those wishing to point out the absurdity of maintaining constituencies that had not changed since the fourteenth century. Cornwall, with a population of 100,000, had twenty-one borough constituencies, whereas rapidly industrializing Lancashire, with a population of 150,000, had only six. Middlesex, where London was located, was even worse off, with a million inhabitants and only eight boroughs.

Sexuality and Gender 2

The Trial of Captain Robert Jones

Robert Jones was a captain in the Royal Artillery regiment of the British army; although he actually held the rank of lieutenant, he was referred to in the press as "Captain Jones." Well known in London social circles for flamboyant acts such as attending parties dressed as the puppet-show character Mr. Punch, he had written popular books promoting figure skating and fireworks. In 1772, Jones was convicted of having committed a sexual act with a twelve-year-old boy. (We would of course consider this a case of pedophilia today, but at the time the victim's age was not a relevant factor.) He was initially sentenced to death but was pardoned by King George III on the condition that he leave the country. He duly departed for the south of France. The decision led to a fierce debate in the press about whether Jones should have been shown such leniency relative to others accused of similar crimes. Jones had influential friends, including the chief justice Lord Mansfield and the foreign secretary Henry Howard, 12th Earl of Suffolk, and some people, like the political reformer John Wilkes, claimed that his reprieve was an example of government corruption. Others asserted Jones should have received the death sentence because they believed that homosexuality was a mortal sin. But he had his defenders as well: some people thought that homosexuality was a natural trait that could not be altered. After the trial, much more negative attention came to be focused on the men known as "macaronis," who were known for their androgynous clothes, extravagant hairstyles and affected mannerisms, as the kinds of bigoted attitudes that would later lead to modern homophobia started to emerge. Formerly seen as effete but fashionable, from the 1770s onward macaronis were perceived as threats to conventional masculinity.

A MACARONI DRESSING ROOM.

Figure 4.1 This engraving from 1772 by an unknown artist shows a group of macaronis fussing over their dress and hairstyles. It illustrates how the image of the macaroni had become more negative by the 1770s.

Reproduced courtesy of the Yale Center for British Art, Paul Mellon Collection.

The first political movement that raised serious questions about this situation centered on an unlikely figure. Known as the ugliest man in Britain because of a squint in one eye and a protruding jaw, John Wilkes was a disreputable rake with a penchant for drinking and debauchery. First elected to Parliament in 1757, he spent his first five years as an undistinguished and unnoticed Whig **backbencher**. But when George III appointed Bute as his **prime minister**, Wilkes sprang to life as a critic of the new government. His opposition was sparked by deep-rooted anti-Scottish prejudice that had been inflamed by what he saw as Bute's undeserved elevation. Wilkes began publishing a newspaper called the *North Briton*; the title was a derogatory reference to Scotland. In it, he relentlessly attacked the government and spread rumors of disloyalty and immorality on the part of its ministers. Bute, Wilkes's primary target, was satirized as a tartan-clad Jacobite and accused of having a romantic liaison with the King's mother, Princess Augusta. The strategy was effective: Bute became the most hated politician in Britain, leading him to resign in April 1763.

Even after vanquishing Bute, Wilkes was enjoying his role as the government's archenemy too much to abandon it. In the *forty-fifth issue* of the *North Briton*, he criticized the King's speech at the opening of Parliament in 1763, which defended the terms of the peace with France. The King was considered to be immune from direct political attacks, and Wilkes was arrested for seditious libel. At the ensuing trial, he transformed himself into a popular hero whose liberty was being infringed upon by a tyrannous government. He declared that his case would show the government that "the liberty of an English subject is not to be sported away with impunity, in this cruel and despotic manner." Commemorating the now-famous issue of the *North Briton*, the number "45" appeared on a variety of souvenirs, ranging from buttons to snuffboxes to teacups.

When the judge dismissed the charges against him, on the ground that MPs were protected from prosecution for libel, Wilkes's victory was complete. From the government's perspective, there was only one way to get rid of this vexing problem: remove Wilkes's immunity by removing him from Parliament. This was accomplished via a pornographic poem published in the *North Briton* that had listed a bishop as one of its "authors," making Wilkes vulnerable to a charge of blasphemy. He was expelled from Parliament and found guilty, and he fled to France in order to escape a prison sentence. Upon his return to England three years later, he immediately stood for Parliament for the county of Middlesex. Because of its highly urbanized nature, Middlesex was a unique constituency, full of small businessmen and early industrial laborers who met the property qualification because of London's inflated real estate prices. Wilkes won, but while he waited to take his seat he was arrested and imprisoned. Daily, a crowd gathered outside his cell, chanting, "Wilkes and Liberty!" He was found guilty of libel and expelled from Parliament. Undaunted, Wilkes stood a second time for Middlesex, and won again. The cycle was repeated two more times before the government intervened and declared his opponent to be the winner. In the eyes of Wilkes's sympathizers, this only confirmed the tyranny of the King and his ministers.

There was an element of farce to all of this. Wilkes was primarily seeking to draw attention to himself and to raise money to pay off his mounting debts, rather than trying to bring about significant political change. But his supporters, known as "Wilkites," saw the issue as one of liberty versus tyranny. They formed a group called the Society for the Supporters of the Bill of Rights (SSBR), which was comprised largely of middle-class lawyers and merchants and which conducted an organized campaign for political reform that called for more frequent elections and for the exclusion from Parliament of "placemen," or men who held appointments in the government and were thus beholden to it. Though none of their goals were achieved, the SSBR demonstrated that there was a political nation beyond Parliament and the enfranchised electorate.

 See document "Boston's Sons of Liberty Write to John Wilkes" at www.routledge. com/cw/barczewski.

Another approach to political reform was taken by Christopher Wyvill, a clergyman from Yorkshire. No radical, Wyvill owned a landed estate and enjoyed a comfortable income. But in the late 1770s, he became concerned that corruption was rife in the British political system. Wyvill believed that the monarchy and the aristocracy exercised too much control over Parliament, and that only by a reduction in the role of patronage and the introduction of a degree of parliamentary reform could a proper balance be restored. He called for more frequent elections and the addition of 100 MPs for the county constituencies, as they were larger and therefore less susceptible to bribery and influence than the boroughs. Wyvill was

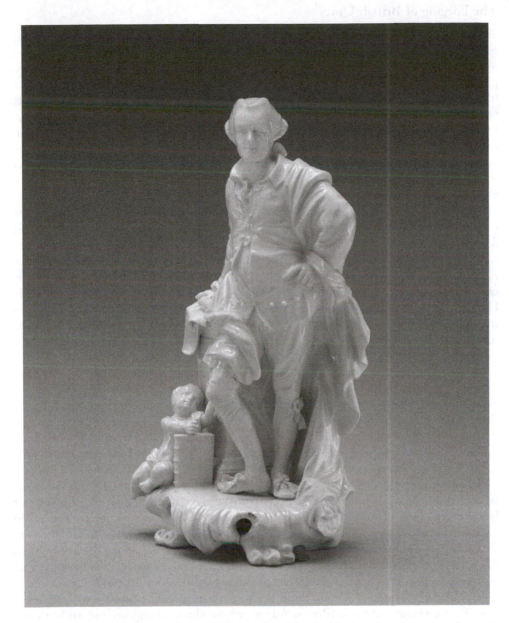

Figure 4.2 A ceramic figurine of John Wilkes produced by the Chelsea Porcelain Manufactory in London in the mid-1760s. Because Chelsea wares were intended for a luxury market, the figurine shows that Wilkes had support from middle- and upper-class Britons.

Reproduced courtesy of the Rogers Fund, 1927, Metropolitan Museum of Art.

very much a moderate voice for reform: he remained committed to the property qualification for the parliamentary franchise. But he did believe that the franchise needed to be extended in order to restore the rightful independence of Parliament. Though neither the Wilkites nor Wyvill's supporters achieved any of their goals in the short term, they set the agenda for reform for the next half-century.

The Forging of British Unity

Traditionally, John Wilkes is discussed almost exclusively in terms of his contribution to the growing movement for political reform. This view, however, overlooks a central component of his political rhetoric: his anti-Scottishness. Wilkes saw the English as the defenders of political liberty, whereas Scotland was the breeding ground of Stuart absolutism. This was blatant prejudice, but Wilkes's antipathy for the Scots was based in one way on reality: their presence and influence south of the border was indeed increasing. As we have seen, one English response to the Jacobite Rebellion of 1745 had been punitive. Highland traditions such as the wearing of tartan had been banned, and the power of the clan chieftains severely curtailed. But there was another response as well, as English politicians became more conscious of the need to incorporate the Scots fully into the Union, and the Scots themselves eagerly sought new opportunities to build their fortunes and influence.

There were three main lines along which this integration took place. First, Scots were recruited into government office. This trend was exemplified by men like Alexander Wedderburn, who became attorney general in 1780, and Henry Dundas, who became home secretary in 1791, as well as by the aforementioned Lord Bute. Second, Scots joined the British Army in increasing numbers. Between 1740 and 1815, eighty-six Highland regiments were created; they quickly came to be regarded as some of the British Army's best troops. The Highland traditions that had so recently been symbols of rebellion against the Union were thus within a generation transformed into symbols of British military might. Third, Scots served the British Empire. By 1800, two-thirds of the East India Company's civilian ranks were Scottish.

Scotland's transformation from bastion of rebellion to loyal partner in the United Kingdom was remarkably rapid. In the eyes of some Scottish people, the participation of so many Scots in British affairs exacted a high cost in terms of the loss of national independence. But there is no doubt that the gains for Scotland were substantial. The expansion of colonial trade sparked significant economic growth, transforming Scotland from an impoverished backwater on the northern fringes of Europe. Now, its cities and towns were some of the most elegant in Britain, as was exemplified by Edinburgh's New Town, developed from the 1760s onwards. Its rival Glasgow, meanwhile, boomed on the back of the tobacco and sugar trades, which embedded Scotland's economy in the slave trade that provided plantation labor in this period. Late-eighteenth-century Scotland also became famous for the quality of its intellectual talent, which collectively is referred to as the "Scottish Enlightenment." The emergence of more moderate and free-thinking Presbyterians among the leadership of the Church of Scotland played a key role in laying the foundation for this newly vibrant intellectual climate, as did the emergence of some of the best universities in Europe. Scotland produced economists (Adam Smith), philosophers (David Hume), engineers (Matthew Boulton) and architects (Robert Adam), whose ideas, inventions and works we still admire today. Ten thousand doctors graduated from Scottish medical schools annually, as compared to only 500 from their English counterparts. This stunning array of talent clustered in Edinburgh, which was rivaled by only the much-larger London and Paris as a European intellectual center.

Not only in Scotland but also throughout Britain, the Enlightenment operated differently than it did on the European continent, promoting unity rather than revolution. Instead of directly challenging the established political, social and religious order, British Enlightenment thinkers worked within it; their ideas were innovative, but not radical. Whereas in other parts of Europe the Enlightenment focused on political change and the replacement of religion with rational thought, in Britain it focused primarily on what the historian Joel Mokyr has termed "useful knowledge," or the improvement of the economy's capacity to produce goods and wealth. The political critiques of British Enlightenment thinkers, meanwhile, were limited to the placing of boundaries on royal power and ensuring that private property was protected, not overturning the entire system of government.

The ideas of Scottish economist Adam Smith provide an example of the nature of the Enlightenment in Britain. In his *treatise The Wealth of Nations* (1776), Smith argued against the mercantilist economic policies that had prevailed for much of the eighteenth century. Mercantilism called for the government to regulate foreign trade by maintaining a closed network of colonies that could trade only with the mother country. Smith challenged mercantilism by advancing free trade as the best system, asserting that the "invisible hand" of the market would allow it to correct itself without government regulation. Smith believed that self-interest was the strongest economic motivator. He did not think that greed was good, only that it was inevitable, and that government policies that failed to recognize this were doomed to failure. Smith found slavery personally abhorrent, but his arguments against it in his writings were not based on moral grounds. He argued that maximum productivity and efficiency would happen under conditions that promoted competition rather than closed mercantilist practices. He did not support the cries of West Indian planters for protection from slave revolts. His arguments, however, were not based on the "rights of man" but on his efforts to make markets operate more efficiently. Here, then, was a classic example of Enlightenment ideas being used not to overturn political and social institutions, as they were in France, but to support British imperialism and economic advancement.

Other social and cultural forces promoted unity in this period as well. The historian Linda Colley has written of an "invention of Britishness" that took place in the eighteenth century, driven predominantly by the rivalry with France. Colley argues that the constant wars between the two nations led to France's being defined as the "Other," in other words as something that the British defined themselves against. There were two specific points of contrast. The first was political: the British saw the French as being under the thumb of a tyrannous, arbitrary government in which there was no restraint on the power of the monarchy. The second was religious: the British view of Protestantism as being under constant threat from the Catholic powers in Europe had altered little since the sixteenth century. It was in the crucible of war that these contrasts were highlighted. "Time and time again," Colley writes, "war with France brought Britons, whether they hailed from Wales or Scotland or England, into confrontation with an obviously hostile Other and encouraged them to define themselves collectively against it."

An example of this newly developing unity was the evolving institution of the monarchy. By the late 1780s, the formerly divisive King George III was becoming an important symbol of the new Britishness. One cause of this, ironically, was his deteriorating mental stability. George III probably suffered from a hereditary disease called porphyria, which caused abdominal pain as well as hallucinations and other neurological problems. Though his declining health, which first became apparent in the late 1780s, caused political problems, as we will see later, it also engendered sympathy and, more importantly, prevented him from continuing to interfere in politics. No longer regarded with suspicion for trying to reassert the power of the monarchy, he was now seen as a family man who was devoted to his wife and thirteen children and as "Farmer George," a nickname he earned for his interest in agriculture and animal husbandry. This was a key step in the British monarchy's transformation from political institution to an important symbol of national unity.

Figure 4.3 In this political cartoon by James Gillray from 1807, George III appears as a farmer using a pitchfork to drive Whig politicians, who are here being accused of greed in their pursuit of government office, over a cliff. Gillray uses the King's nickname of "Farmer George" to depict him as protecting the British people from avaricious politicians.

Reproduced courtesy of the Harris Brisbane Dick Fund, 1917, Metropolitan Museum of Art.

Ireland

If Scotland was becoming more integrated into the Union in the second half of the eighteenth century, Ireland presented a more complex case. While the Glorious Revolution and penal laws had confirmed their pre-eminent position in legal terms, the Protestant Anglo-Irish elite, or **"Ascendancy,"** were frustrated by their political subordination. All legislation had to be approved in London before it could even be discussed by the Irish Parliament in Dublin. In the 1770s, a loose association of members of the Irish Parliament known as the "Patriot Party" pressed for an independent Irish parliament. The American Revolution also contributed indirectly to rising nationalism in Ireland. The 4000 British troops normally stationed there were sent to North America, and France and Spain's entry into the war left Ireland vulnerable to invasion. In response, local militias known as "Volunteer Companies" were formed, and by 1782 there were 80,000 men under arms in Ireland. The Volunteers spent much of their time debating political issues, arguing for parliamentary independence and free trade for Ireland. Some even argued that Ireland should be independent of Britain.

The threat that armed rebellion might break out in Ireland in a time of imperial crisis led to substantial political change there for the first time in almost a century. In 1782, the *Irish Parliament gained the right to legislate for Ireland*. Henry Grattan, the leader of the Patriot Party, proudly proclaimed to the Irish Parliament, "Ireland is now a nation." The "nation" that was represented in the Irish Parliament, however, was still that of the Protestant Anglo-Irish elite. This changed only gradually. Beginning in the 1770s, the penal laws began to be modified, and by the end of the decade Catholics could bequeath and inherit land on the same terms as Irish Protestants. More significant changes came in the 1790s, when the British government, fearing the impact of the French Revolution on Irish Catholics, pressured the Irish Parliament to repeal almost all of the remaining penal laws. Catholics were now allowed to vote if they met the property qualification, as well as to practice law and to bear arms. Other discriminatory measures remained in place, however. The right of Catholics to sit in Parliament continued to be denied until 1829.

British fears that the Irish would be inspired by the French Revolution were not unfounded. In the 1790s, many Irish people came to see a secular, independent republic as the solution to Ireland's continuing religious inequalities and subordination to British authority. In 1791, the Society of United Irishmen was founded. Its leader, Theobald Wolfe Tone, a Protestant from Dublin, was deeply interested in the ideology of the French Revolution. The United Irishmen initially sought political change through constitutional means, but frustration with the slow pace of reform led them to enlist the aid of the revolutionary French government and plan an uprising in Ireland in 1798. As many as 50,000 Irish people participated, but the rebels' actions were uncoordinated and their troops poorly trained. Moreover, the British authorities were well prepared. In consequence, the rebellion was brief and its repression brutal, leading to the deaths of 30,000 Irish people.

 See document "A Plea for Irish Independence" at www.routledge.com/cw/barczewski.

Over the long term, the 1798 rebellion saw the introduction of **republican** ideology into Irish politics, though it would be over a century before the rebels' objective was attained. In the short term, however, the British government's response represented a typical solution to imperial issues in this period: the imposition of tighter control from **Westminster**. Prime minister William Pitt saw the insurrection as an opportunity to bring Ireland into a closer legislative union, which was achieved through the passage of an *Act of Union* that brought Ireland into the United Kingdom in 1800. At a time of global war with France, union with Ireland was seen as crucial to the security of Britain, as it would eliminate the prospect of an independent Ireland, located on Britain's doorstep, forming an alliance with revolutionary France.

Although the Union had far-reaching consequences, its logistics were relatively simple. The Irish Parliament in Dublin ceased to exist; instead, MPs now represented Ireland in the House of Commons in London alongside representatives from England, Scotland and Wales. Four Church of Ireland bishops and twenty-eight representative Irish peers sat in the House of Lords. For the Union to take effect, however, the Irish Parliament, like the Scottish Parliament almost a century before, had to vote itself out of existence. Irish nationalists later claimed that the Irish Parliament was "bribed and bullied" to vote in favor of its dissolution, a powerful argument for those who argued that the Union was illegitimate. The British government did spend £32,000 (over $3 million today) to ensure the election of pro-Union members to the Irish Parliament prior to the crucial vote. The Irish Parliament, however, was too large for any government to buy complete control of it, and the British expended tremendous effort on cultivating public opinion, with considerable success. They often found a receptive audience for their arguments: many of Ireland's landed and commercial elite favored the Union, as did many Irish Catholics, who believed that entrance into the United Kingdom would mark the end of the Protestant Anglo-Irish Ascendancy's grip on political power.

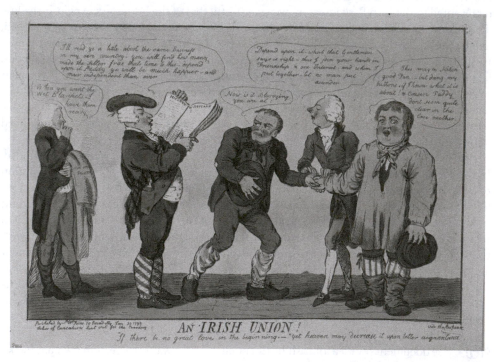

Figure 4.4 In this broadside from 1799 expressing skepticism about the Act of Union with Ireland, William Pitt joins the hands "in friendship" of a reluctant John Bull, representing England, and "Paddy," representing Ireland. The Scotsman Henry Dundas, who was war secretary at the time and one of the architects of the Act of Union, reads from a "History of Scotland." He assures Paddy that he will be "much happier" within the Union, as well as "mair [i.e., more] independent than ever." On the left, however, a figure informs the group, "when you want the wet blankets I have them ready."

Reproduced courtesy of the Library of Congress.

While Ireland was given representation in the British Parliament, it was less than was warranted by its respective population. Irish representatives made up only 100 of 658 MPs in the post-Union Parliament, at a time when Ireland's population was almost half that of England, Scotland and Wales combined. This underrepresentation was similar to what had occurred when Scotland had been brought into the Union in 1707, but the differences between Scotland's and Ireland's entry into the Union were more striking than the similarities. While the Union of 1707 was the product of negotiations between representatives of the Parliaments of two independent nations, that of 1800 was a settlement imposed by Britain upon Ireland. The issue of religion was also treated differently. Whereas the Union of 1707 guaranteed the established status of the (Presbyterian) Church of Scotland, the Union of 1800 ensured that the (Anglican) Church of Ireland remained the established church in Ireland, a church in which few Irish people worshipped. The Union also left unresolved the question of the political rights of the Catholic majority of Ireland. In William Pitt's original vision, Ireland's integration within the British Empire was to be guaranteed in part by the extension of the final political right that had been denied to Irish Catholics: the right to sit in Parliament. Pitt's desire for what became known as "Catholic Emancipation," however, foundered on the opposition of King George III, who viewed the law as a violation of his coronation oath to uphold the Church of England. Opposition to Catholic Emancipation was not limited to the King. In England, patriotism and a sense of Protestant "Britishness" were pronounced in the midst of the war against Napoleonic France. This created serious problems for the stability of the new Union. Instead of securing the support of almost three-quarters of the Irish population, the lack of Catholic Emancipation embedded inequality within the United Kingdom, stiffened Irish Catholic opposition to the Union, and created the major political issue of early nineteenth-century Anglo-Irish relations.

Religion

The situation in Ireland demonstrates that, although Protestantism was central to British identity in the eighteenth century, religious belief and worship was far from uniform throughout the United Kingdom. In England, some scholars contend that the Anglican Church dominated to such a degree that it could be termed a "confessional state." In this view, England had much in common with continental absolute monarchies such as France and Austria, in which religion – in those cases Catholicism rather than Protestantism – was a key source of not only national unity but also political stability. Other historians, however, contend that the dominance of the Church of England was never total. They point out that the Anglican Church did not have nearly the same degree of legal monopoly as the Catholic Church did in France and Austria. The Church's hegemony was also challenged by a changing social environment. The upper ranks of its clergy were almost exclusively men from the elite classes, while the parish clergy were either well-educated middle-class men or younger sons of the aristocracy and gentry. They were generally conscientious and well meaning, but they had little in common with their parishioners. To make matters worse, the Church had failed to keep pace with the rapid increase in Britain's population, leaving many people, particularly in urban areas, without access to Anglican services on Sundays. In 1800, for example, rural Norfolk had 700 parishes, while industrializing Lancashire had a mere seventy.

In this changing world, the Church struggled to keep its message relevant. In the first half of the eighteenth century, a sense that religious overzealousness had contributed to the political chaos of the Civil War and Interregnum led to a retreat from overtly spiritual forms of worship. More restrained and less dogmatic forms of faith emerged, as denominations such as Unitarianism and Deism gained adherents. Unitarians rejected the concept of original sin and believed in a single God rather than a trinity, thereby rejecting the divinity of Christ. Deists believed that reason demanded the existence of a God who had set the universe in motion, but that afterwards his role had been minimal.

Many people, however, missed the more emotional and inspirational side of religion. Into this void stepped two new forms of Christian worship. First, there was an increase in evangelicalism within the Church of England, which was manifested in the campaign to abolish slavery. Second, there was significant growth in Nonconformism. Here, the emergence of Methodism, which accounted for half of the 3 million British Nonconformists by the end of the eighteenth century, was the most significant development. Methodism was founded in 1738 by the Anglican clergyman John Wesley, after he became convinced of the necessity of bringing the Gospel directly to ordinary people. Focusing on Wales and the North of England, Wesley soon attracted a rapidly growing number of adherents, who were drawn to his call for thrift, abstinence and hard work. Wesley did not desire to break away from the Church of England and always staunchly maintained his allegiance to it. Only when the Church began refusing to ordain his ministers in the 1780s did he begin ordaining them himself, but even then he never formally split from Anglicanism. It was only after his death in 1791 that his followers seceded.

Methodism became particularly popular among industrial workers such as coal miners in South Wales. Though oriented towards the lower classes, it was expressly apolitical, and as such provided an alternative to the radicalism and socialism that would later develop among early industrial workers on the continent. John Wesley and other Methodist leaders fiercely opposed revolution and even moderate political reform. Some scholars therefore argue that the religious developments of the second half of the eighteenth century further help to explain the lack of revolution or radical change in Britain in this period. But on the other hand, Methodist and other religious leaders did not entirely control the hearts and minds of their flocks, and there is little evidence that working-class people turned to new faiths as an alternative to revolutionary politics. On the contrary, many turned to them in response to the economic difficulties they faced in their daily lives, a situation that could also lead them to embrace radical politics. The frequency with which Wesley preached against radicalism might have been because he recognized its prevalence among his adherents.

The prevalence of Methodism in Wales demonstrates the diversity of religious belief in Britain in this period. By 1750, there were over 400 *seiadau*, or fellowships, of Welsh Methodists. Other Nonconformist denominations, including Baptism, Congregationalism, and Presbyterianism, also made significant inroads in Wales, and by 1851, four out of five Welsh people were Nonconformists. In Scotland, meanwhile, the established Presbyterian Church of Scotland enjoyed the allegiance of the majority of the population. In Ireland, around four-fifths of the population was Catholic, but, as we have seen, they were still subject to a variety of legal restrictions. The established church in Ireland was the Anglican Church of Ireland, in which only about 10 percent of the population worshipped. Another 10 percent was Presbyterian, showing that there were divisions among Protestants as well as between Protestants and Catholics. Almost all the Presbyterians, and over half the Anglicans, lived in northeastern Ireland in the province of Ulster, while Catholics dominated the west and south of the country.

Even if Britain and Ireland were pluralistic religious states, Protestantism did serve as a force of unity, sometimes in not very attractive ways. Deep-rooted religious prejudice, much of which continued to focus on Catholics, was very much a part of British society in this period. Catholics were subjected to abuse and physical violence, especially when Britain was at war with France or Spain. The worst episode occurred in 1780, when Lord George Gordon, a younger son of the Duke of Gordon, convinced a group of his virulently anti-Catholic friends to protest what they claimed was increasing Catholic influence. The immediate cause of their anger was the Catholic Relief Act of 1778, which removed the prohibition of the purchase of property by Catholics and reduced some of the sanctions against Catholic priests. This played to the baser instincts of the masses, and when Gordon's supporters presented their petition to Parliament, five days of rioting began that escalated into looting, burning and other forms of destruction, directed in particular against the homes of London's Catholic population. Around 300 people were killed in the violence. The *Gordon Riots* demonstrated that religious prejudice was still prevalent in late-eighteenth-century Britain.

Religion and Difference 4

The Gordon Riots and Anti-Catholicism

In late-eighteenth-century Britain, popular anti-Catholicism remained prevalent even as some of the most discriminatory penal laws limiting the rights of British Catholics were being repealed. In 1778, the House of Commons passed the Catholic Relief Act, which allowed Catholics to join the army, to operate Catholic schools and

NO POPERY or NEWGATE REFORMER.

The He Says he's a Protestant; look at the Print.
The Face and the Bludgeon will give you a hint.
Religion he cries, in hopes to deceive,
While his practice is only to burn and to thieve.

Figure 4.5 In this cartoon attributed to James Gillray, a Gordon rioter carries a cudgel and has a cockade reading "No Popery" in his hat. The inscription below casts doubt on the sincerity of his claims to be acting out from religious motives: "Religion he cries, in hopes to deceive/While his practice is only to burn and to thieve." Etching attributed to J. Gillray.

Reproduced courtesy of the Wellcome Collection.

to purchase and inherit land, so long as they swore an oath of allegiance to the monarch. In response, the act's opponents formed the Protestant Association to press for its repeal and invited the eccentric and possibly mentally unstable Scottish nobleman and Member of Parliament Lord George Gordon to become its leader. On the 2nd of June 1780, Gordon led 60,000 supporters on a march on the House of Commons to present a petition demanding repeal. His action sparked several days of anti-Catholic riots across London in which Catholic homes and chapels were attacked. As many as 700 people were killed and 12,000 troops from the British army had to be deployed to restore order. In recent years, historians have argued that the Gordon Riots were motivated as much by social discontentment as by anti-Catholicism. Frequent wars with France led to high taxes, inflationary prices for basic necessities and the threat of impressment into the army and navy; many ordinary Britons felt that the upper classes were profiteering from the wars while they suffered. In the riots, prisons and the Bank of England were targeted, showing that the crowds were expressing their dissatisfaction with the broader state of the country as well as hostility to Catholics.

Changes in Agriculture and Transportation

The second half of the eighteenth century saw far-reaching changes in the British economy that had profound social consequences, bringing, like the religious developments detailed earlier, both unity and disunity. What historians call the "agricultural revolution" began gradually, as a handful of innovative farmers began to practice a more scientific type of agriculture that employed new technology and techniques of cultivation. As early as 1701, Jethro Tull's horse-drawn drill allowed seeds to be planted in straight rows, producing a higher crop yield. Two decades later, Viscount Townshend promoted the cultivation of turnips as a winter crop. Turnips, which could be used to feed livestock, returned nitrogen to the soil, so they could be planted on land that formerly would have been left fallow. It was subsequently discovered that clover, another source of fodder for livestock, also returned nitrogen to the soil. Clover and turnips increased the amount of land that was available for cultivation by as much as 50 percent.

The changes did not stop there, however. For centuries, there had been a gradual trend towards the "**enclosure**" of rural land, which meant that instead of being left open for the shared use of the community, land was hedged or fenced for private use. This trend accelerated dramatically after 1750 due to improved drainage and fertilizers and the introduction of better systems of crop rotation. These methods, however, worked better for large farms; thus "smallholdings," or small farms that provided subsistence for the farmer and his family, virtually disappeared. They were replaced by the distinctive system of large, rectangular fields broken up by hedgerows that characterizes much of rural Britain today. Between 1760 and 1815, more than 7 million acres were enclosed in England and Wales.

Enclosure led to increased agricultural efficiency and is almost certainly a major reason why the rapidly growing British population was never in serious danger of famine after 1750. At the same time, however, there were detrimental social and environmental consequences of enclosure. Smallholders clearly lost out, as land was concentrated in fewer and fewer hands, forcing displaced farmers to work as laborers on someone else's land or to find alternative occupations. There were scattered riots and protests against enclosure, but the power of the landed elite was too great for there to be any serious resistance. The surplus labor helped to supply the human resources for industrialization: by 1800, only three out of five British workers were required for agricultural employment, whereas on the European continent four out of five were. Enclosure also had a dramatic effect on Britain's environment. Whereas forests and wetlands had previously been commonly owned, they were now in the possession of a single owner, who had an interest in extracting profits from them. The process of clearing Britain's land had been going on for centuries, but enclosure accelerated the deforestation of the country's few remaining woodlands, as owners sought to sell the timber. The draining and filling of marshy areas, meanwhile, altered drainage patterns and led to flooding and the silting up of rivers across the countryside.

In Scotland, where the population was smaller relative to the size of the country, there was less pressure for enclosure. There, only half a million acres were enclosed between 1720 and 1850. But there were still far-reaching agricultural changes in this era. After the chiefs of the Highland clans were stripped of much of their power following the 1745 rebellion, they began searching for ways to make their land more profitable. They began evicting their tenant farmers and using the land for the grazing of sheep and cattle. By the nineteenth century, this was having a major effect on the demographics of the Highlands. In Ireland, where there was little industry to take up the surplus population, rapid population growth meant that agricultural land was divided into smaller and smaller plots. By the early nineteenth century, most farmers had barely enough land to feed their families, and they avoided starvation only through heavy reliance on the potato. This was to have dire consequences in the 1840s.

Enclosure was one of the few areas in which the government directly intervened in the economy. When smallholders, who stood to lose the most, resisted, large landowners sought private Acts of Parliament to force the issue. Over 4000 enclosure acts were passed between 1750 and 1830, affecting one out of every five acres in England. The former owners were either given an allotted portion of the enclosed land or paid compensation. Most of the development of Britain's infrastructure, however, continued to be supported by private initiatives. Enclosure often required roads to be moved so that they did not cross the new property boundaries, and they also needed to be improved in order to transport the larger crops that were produced to market efficiently. In 1700, maintenance of most roads was the responsibility of parishes, which had limited resources to repair or maintain them. As the eighteenth century wore on, however, private companies called "turnpike trusts" began to take control of some roads, financing improvements through issuing shares and collecting tolls. By 1770, there were over 15,000 miles of turnpiked roads in Britain. The quality of these roads gradually improved. In the early nineteenth century, Scottish engineer James Loudon McAdam developed a method, which became known as "macadamization," for building smoother and more durable roads by creating a surface of crushed stone and gravel atop a bed of larger stones.

There were limits, however, to the weight that even turnpiked roads could carry, particularly after the beginnings of industrialization created a demand for heavy commodities such as coal and iron. Fortunately, Britain's geography, in which few places were more than 60 miles from the coast or more than a few miles from a navigable waterway, offered another option: transport by water. All that was needed was a network of canals to connect the abundant natural waterways. There was a ready-made source of capital for canal-building projects, as most of the land under which the coal and iron was located was owned by the upper classes, who were eager to get their mineral and ore wealth to market. The most enthusiastic canal builder was the Duke of Bridgewater, who in 1761 constructed a *canal* from his coal mines in Lancashire to Manchester and then another from Manchester to the port of Liverpool. Over the next half-century, 2500 miles of canals were constructed, most of them financed by private investors like Bridgewater. This improved transportation network was another important factor in unifying the nation, as it led to faster connections between London, other large cities, and the provinces, helping to bring people, ideas, and points of view together.

Politics: Pitt Versus Fox

Even as various forces pushed Britain towards greater unity, oppositional rivalries re-emerged after almost a half-century of single-party dominance. For a long time, it was conventionally argued that George III's appointment of the third Earl of Bute as prime minister in 1762 signaled the return of the Tories as a major political presence for the first time since the Hanoverian Succession in 1714, but this is not really what happened. Lord North and William Pitt the Younger, prime ministers often identified with the supposed "second Tory party," were both from established Whig families. Once again, it was opposi-tional opprobrium that served to apply this nomenclature to the members and supporters of the ministries in power during the American and French revolutions. American "patriots" who thought of themselves as "Whigs" naturally applied the term "Tory" to colonists loyal to the Crown. The Whigs, meanwhile, splintered into factions, limiting their ability to acquire and retain power for the remainder of the century. The most prominent Whig leader of the time was Charles James Fox, whose views were extremely radical for a mainstream politician. He supported major parliamentary reform, the abolition of the slave trade, the American Revolution and increased rights for Catholics and Dissenters. Fox became a hero to later generations of British liberals and radicals, but he was only able to reach the apex of power for a brief period in 1783, when he agreed to serve as one of the leaders of a short-lived coalition.

   It was instead William Pitt the Younger, the son of the former Patriot Whig prime minis-ter, who became the dominant political figure of the late eighteenth century. *Pitt first became prime minister in 1783* at the age of only twenty-four; one critic jeered that Britain had been "entrusted to a schoolboy's care." Despite his youth, however, he brought to high office a single-minded devotion to duty – he never married and had few friends – and a coolness of temperament that served him well in the tempestuous years ahead. Pitt was above all a pragmatist who did not like political partisanship. He spent the next decade rebuilding the government's finances from the dire state into which they had fallen as a result of the expense of the American Revolution. By the early 1790s, he had transformed the large debt into a surplus. He also sought to end the worst forms of corruption. He conducted frequent and detailed audits of government funds to root out abuses; opened government contracts to open bidding; and refused to accept the usual array of sinecures that went to high-ranking ministers. He even introduced a reform bill to eliminate some of the worst rotten boroughs but was forced to abandon it in the face of overwhelming hostility in the House of Commons. Pitt's arrival at Westminster set the tone for a new political style, in which sobriety, diligence and morality replaced the lax ways of the past. Suddenly, politicians felt a need to abandon, or at least hide, their mistresses and to be seen going to church rather than to the racetrack or the tavern. This was not only an attempt to make the British government more moral, but also served as a bulwark against the gale-force winds that were blowing from France by demonstrating the worthiness of the elite to continue to rule. Pitt believed that the men who had the greatest stake in the nation – those who owned substantial property – should continue to direct its political affairs.

The challenges faced by Pitt from within, however, were less threatening than those from without. In 1789, revolution erupted in France. Initially, British observers were, as the Whig politician Edmund Burke put it, unsure "whether to blame or to applaud." It was hoped that political change would lead to an English-style constitutional monarchy in France. But as the Revolution became more radical and as French armies began launching attacks on their European neighbors, it became apparent that it might spread to Britain, and that a war might be required to prevent it from doing so.

The Revolutionary and Napoleonic Wars

In 1792, France attacked Austria. Much of Europe, including Prussia, Holland, Spain, and the German and Italian states, was quickly dragged in. Pitt initially attempted to keep Britain out of the conflict. But when the French Army took the Austrian Netherlands (covering most of modern-day Belgium and Luxembourg), he felt that the danger posed by the Channel ports falling into French hands was too great. In 1793, *Britain went to war*, a state in which it would remain for the next twenty-two years, with only a brief respite in 1802 and 1803. In the first decade of the conflict, called the French Revolutionary Wars, Pitt fought using the traditional British method of paying mercenaries and funding allies, while relying on the Royal Navy to win victories at sea. Soldiers fighting for pay proved no match for soldiers motivated by revolutionary fervor, however, and by 1797 Britain found itself fighting alone against not only France but Spain as well. The following year, the British managed to assemble a second coalition, with Austria and Russia as the main partners. But this alliance, too, rapidly crumbled before a French Army that was now brilliantly led by the Corsican-born general Napoleon Bonaparte.

The Royal Navy fared better. It kept the French bottled up in their home ports, preventing an invasion of Britain. British crews were consistently able to maneuver their ships more skillfully and fire their guns more rapidly than the French. This allowed the British to use more sophisticated tactics. In engagements, European navies had traditionally fought broadside-to-broadside in a single-file row called a "line of battle." This rarely resulted in decisive victories, as engagements were broken off before significant damage occurred to either fleet. But in the 1780s, the British introduced new tactics in which they sent ships through the enemy line, so that they could attack the vulnerable bows and sterns of enemy vessels. This resulted in a far greater number of casualties, in terms of both ships and men, and it enabled the British to win a series of decisive victories, often against superior forces. In 1798, Napoleon launched an invasion of Egypt, with the intention of threatening the route to India. But Admiral Horatio Nelson, who emerged as the war's greatest naval hero, caught the French fleet unawares in Aboukir Bay and destroyed it in the *Battle of the Nile*. The British lost only 450 men, while the French lost 5500, with an additional 3000 taken prisoner. Of the thirteen ships of the line and four smaller frigates with which the French began the battle, one was sunk, two were burned, and nine were captured. No British ships were lost.

The Revolutionary and Napoleonic Wars required the British to mobilize manpower on an unprecedented scale. At the outbreak of the war in 1793, the British Army numbered 40,000 men, but by 1813 it had grown to 250,000. £30 million of the total annual government expenditure of £72 million was spent on the army. Even so, it was still less than half the size of Napoleon's Grand Armée. There was no official system of **conscription**: the army recruited many of its men by offering bounties (i.e., cash bonuses), and in some cases by getting men so drunk that they did not know that they were signing up. The vast majority of recruits were from the lowest ranks of society; the Duke of Wellington referred to them as "the scum of the earth." This has given rise to the myth that the army was filled with criminals, but in reality most were laborers who joined because they could not find work. Like the army, the navy grew significantly during the war, from 40,000 in 1793 to 130,000 in 1800. The navy required more skilled men than the army; about a third of its sailors had to have significant experience at sea. This need gave rise to the press gang, a group of recruiters who were permitted to "press" any man who "used the sea" (i.e., had maritime experience) into naval service.

The Experience of Warfare 3

Press Gangs and the Napoleonic Navy

Press gangs were a notorious and much-feared means of recruiting men to serve in the Royal Navy in the late eighteenth and early nineteenth centuries. As the size of the navy quadrupled from around 250 ships in 1700 to around 1000 in 1800, there was an increased demand for sailors. During the Napoleonic Wars, the navy required a staggering 150,000 men on board its ships; by the end of the war in 1815, almost three-quarters of those on active duty had been impressed into service. As this latter figure illustrates, getting men to volunteer for service was not easy, as naval life was characterized by hard work, low pay, poor living conditions and harsh discipline, with the added danger of being killed in battle during wartime. Press gangs of around a dozen men led by an officer would therefore roam the streets of Britain's ports looking for "volunteers" from among the ranks of merchant seamen with maritime experience. They visited pubs, hoping that they might find men too drunk to realize that they were signing up or would trick a man by secretly dropping "the King's shilling" in his drink, and then when he found it at the bottom would claim that he had agreed to serve. It was for this reason that glass drinking vessels became popular: men could see if there was a coin at the bottom. If such methods failed, press gangs might even resort to knocking their targets unconscious and taking them by force, although in such cases the man's friends often resisted, leading to pitched battles in the street. In 1803 on the Isle of Portland off the south coast of England, a crowd of 300 people attempted to block a press gang, resulting in at least three civilian deaths, while sixteen sailors were wounded. Impressment also took place at sea: a naval ship would force a merchant vessel to stop and would press some of the sailors into service. Although it was not legal to impress foreign sailors, it was this practice that contributed to the outbreak of the War of 1812 with the United States, because many Americans at the time had been born in Britain, or at least the British could claim that they had been. The legality of impressment was murky, and civil authorities often supported those who claimed it was a violation of their rights. Impressment, however, allowed the British armed services to avoid conscription. To build its massive Grand Armée, France resorted to conscription in 1798. A powerful navy, however, did not require as many men as an army, and so in Britain the press gang sufficed to full its manpower needs. They continued to supply many of the Royal Navy's recruits until the 1830s, when improved terms of service led to a significant increase in the number of volunteers.

The LIBERTY of the SUBJECT.

Figure 4.6 James Gillray's cartoon "The Liberty of the Subject" (1779) at first glance appears to criticize press gangs for infringing the rights of "free-born Englishmen." But a deeper look reveals that Gillray's sympathy for the impressed victim, who is at center right, is minimal. Weak and cringing, he meekly accepts his fate as his wife wields a mop in an effort to free him. The sailors in the press gang, meanwhile, are much stronger figures as they carry out their duty; Gillray might be criticizing the laws that allowed men to be impressed against their will, but he is not criticizing the men of the Royal Navy who had to enforce them. Catalogue of prints and drawings in the British Museum. Division I, political and personal satires, v. 5, no. 5609 Wright, T. Works of James Gillray, the caricaturist with the history of his life and times, p. 29.

Reproduced courtesy of the Beinecke Rare Book and Manuscript Library, Yale University.

Naval life was hard, but we should not exaggerate the harshness of the discipline, which has been depicted in numerous novels and films. Some captains were martinets, but most were not, and as a result they were able to inspire a sense of comradeship and patriotism. Sailors at least got regular meals and basic medical care, things many lower-class Britons at the time would not have enjoyed. But this relative security came with costs: wages had not been increased for a century, shore leave was minimal and pensions were meager. In 1797, sailors in the fleet anchored at Spithead, off the key naval base of Portsmouth on the south coast of England, mutinied, and the unrest soon spread to the ships anchored at the Nore, at the mouth of the Thames. The mutiny lasted for several months and resulted in the hanging of thirty-six men and the flogging or transportation to penal colonies of hundreds more.

A way had to be found to pay for this enlarged army and navy in a country that was already one of the most heavily taxed in Europe. The 1790s saw steady increases in "Assessed Taxes," which were essentially sales taxes levied on certain goods. This did not generate sufficient revenue, however, and so in 1799 Pitt introduced the first income tax in British history, levied at a rate of 10 percent on annual incomes above £60. It realized £6 million in its first year. The system was improved in 1803, establishing a model that is still used today. Customs duties were also increased by 25 percent over the course of the war. Finally, Pitt relied heavily on loans: in 1796, a "loyalty loan" of £18 million was raised from Britain's wealthiest citizens in only four days, suggesting the degree of elite support for the war.

In 1802, Britain and France, exhausted by a decade of fighting, entered into peace negotiations. The resulting Treaty of Amiens called for the establishment of republics in the territories conquered by France in the Netherlands, Italy and Switzerland, but almost immediately the French began treating them as client states. In August 1802, Napoleon was appointed First Consul for Life (he would elevate himself to Emperor two years later), with the clear ambition of expanding France's territorial reach within Europe and beyond. The British thus reopened the war in April of 1803. (From this point onwards, the conflict is known as the Napoleonic Wars.) Pitt formed a new coalition with Austria, Russia and (later) Prussia, but Napoleon now intended to beat the British at their own game: he assembled a massive fleet to seize control of the Channel, leaving the British helpless to prevent an invasion. Once again, it was Nelson to the rescue: he annihilated the French and Spanish at the *Battle of Trafalgar* in October 1805, eliminating the threat of invasion once and for all. The French and Spanish fleets lost 3200 men, and twenty-two of their thirty-three vessels were captured. The 458 British dead, meanwhile, included Nelson himself, which ensured his permanent enshrinement in the pantheon of the greatest British heroes.

Nelson had staved off disaster, but avoiding defeat was not the same thing as achieving victory. In 1805 and 1806, Britain's Austrian, Russian and Prussian allies lost battle after battle. Austria and Prussia dropped out of the war, while Russia switched to the French side in 1807. The British and French now attempted to defeat one another through economic strangulation. Using the "Continental System," Napoleon closed European ports to all ships coming from Britain. In response, the British issued the Orders in Council, which required that all French and neutral ships be subject to customs duties and be searched for contraband. Both nations suffered from shortages of food and other vital imports as a result of the blockades, as did other, neutral countries. Particularly angry was the United States, and the tensions between the two nations ultimately led to the *War of 1812*, which will be discussed later in the chapter.

Britain's primary attention, however, was directed towards the Iberian Peninsula, where much of the fighting had occurred since 1807. In the Peninsular War, as it became known, the British commander Sir Arthur Wellesley fought a dogged campaign that slowly pushed the French back. By 1813, the British had pressed into southern France. Wellesley's success earned him rapid elevation through the peerage, culminating in his designation as the Duke of Wellington in 1814. In the east, meanwhile, an impatient Napoleon had launched a disastrous invasion of Russia that cost him virtually his entire army of 500,000 men. This proved a decisive turning point: even Napoleon's talent as a commander could not overcome such massive losses, and the French suffered a series of defeats in central Europe. The final blow came at the "Battle of the Nations," or Battle of Leipzig, in October 1813, in which 70,000 French soldiers were killed, wounded or taken prisoner. With his once-invincible army now outnumbered four to one, Napoleon was forced to abdicate in April 1814; the subsequent Treaty of Paris restored France to its borders of 1792. The French monarchy was restored under Louis XVIII, brother of the executed King Louis XVI. But in February 1815, Napoleon escaped from exile on the Mediterranean island of Elba. France's military leaders rallied to his side, allowing him to raise an army of 300,000 men. Facing him, however, were British, Austrian, Prussian, Hanoverian, Dutch and Russian forces totaling more than 550,000. Needing to defeat his opponents before they could unite, Napoleon hurled his forces forward in an attempt to split Wellington's combined British, Dutch and Hanoverian force from its Prussian allies. The battle took place on the 18th of June at *Waterloo*, a Belgian town eight miles south of Brussels. After a hard-fought struggle, the arrival of the Prussians late in the day sealed Napoleon's fate. He abdicated for a second time four days later and was exiled once again, this time to the distant island of Saint Helena in the South Atlantic, where he died in 1821.

The settlement that ended the war was called the *Congress of Vienna*, because it was negotiated in the Austrian capital. Its guiding principle was a "concert of Europe," a loose agreement among European states in which they agreed to maintain a balance of power, maintained through a system of alliances, in order to prevent another large-scale war. Their cooperation would also prevent the spread of the radical ideas of the French Revolution. The European powers agreed to meet frequently in future "congresses," to be held approximately every two years, to discuss important issues and to head off major crises before they began. Even though Britain was now the dominant power in Europe, its diplomats believed that maintaining the balance of power would best protect their country's interests. They also believed that, as much as possible, Europe should be restored to its prewar state. This meant that France, with its restored monarchy, was to be treated generously, because it was essential to the maintenance of the balance of power. In 1818, France was even permitted to join the "Quadruple Alliance" of Britain, Russia, Prussia and Austria that had defeated Napoleon only three years earlier, which now became the "Quintuple Alliance."

British Foreign Secretary Lord Castlereagh was one of the main architects of the Congress of Vienna. For pragmatic reasons, he supported its political conservatism and the sacrifice of liberty at the altar of peace and stability. But in Britain, the strong belief in constitutional government and individual rights sat uneasily with the Congress's defense of absolute monarchy. Most British people had no desire to see the growth of democratic radicalism, but nor did they wish to promote autocracy. Britain thus came increasingly into conflict with autocratic regimes in Austria, Prussia and Russia, who had formed the Holy Alliance to defend hereditary monarchy. Tensions arose over revolts in Spain, Portugal and the Italian states of Piedmont and Naples; the Holy Alliance wished to suppress them, while Britain maintained a noninterventionist stance.

The Revolutionary and Napoleonic Wars had been truly global conflicts that were fought all over the world. This meant that they had global consequences. Britain acquired a number of new colonies: the Ionian Islands, Malta, Heligoland, Trinidad, Tobago, St. Lucia, Guyana, Ceylon, Mauritius, the Cape Colony, and Sierra Leone, as well as trading posts in the Gambia in West Africa. It had now developed and garrisoned a network of some of the world's best harbors, including Gibraltar, Sydney, Cape Town, Halifax in Nova Scotia, and Kingston in Jamaica, along with a string of naval bases stretching from the Mediterranean west to the Caribbean and east to the Indian Ocean. The British had been forced to develop new trade routes and commercial partners in order to circumvent the French blockade, leading to the emergence of new markets in the Mediterranean, the Caribbean, South America and Asia. The war thus had a major impact on both the British Empire and the global expansion of British trade in the nineteenth century. As the historian John Darwin has written, "Vast new worlds were now ready to be explored, exploited, colonized or converted."

The War of 1812

The American Revolution had not settled all the issues between Britain and the new United States. The powerful British Empire and the fledgling republic were not yet economic or military rivals, but the duel between their competing political systems – Britain's constitutional monarchy and limited democracy versus America's republican experiment – continued. This ideological debate took place in real rather than abstract terms along the border that the

United States shared with the British colony of Canada. In 1800, few people on either side would have predicted that the border would still be in essentially the same place today. The British colonial administration believed that another war in North America was inevitable, while the Americans believed that it was their geographical destiny to annex Canada.

 See document "America Contemplates War with Britain in 1812" at www.routledge. com/cw/barczewski.

These ideological differences, however, concealed the shared heritage of the two populations. Almost 40,000 loyalists had fled to Canada during and immediately after the Revolution, and between 1792 and 1812 another 30,000 Americans followed, lured by the cheap land that was offered by the British authorities. (This was at a time when British Canada's total population was less than 100,000.) The American population of 7.5 million, meanwhile, contained thousands of recent immigrants from the British Isles. Many of these newcomers, however, were Irish people, who brought with them a strong sense of political grievance against British efforts to curb growing nationalism in Ireland in the final decades of the eighteenth century.

When war broke out between Britain and the United States in 1812, therefore, it was less an international conflict and more, as the historian Alan Taylor describes, a "civil war between kindred peoples, recently and incompletely divided by the revolution." There were a number of issues that led to war. Most significantly, there was the impressment of American sailors by the British navy. Desperate for naval manpower to fight the French, the British insisted that anyone who had been born a British citizen remained one, even if they had become a naturalized citizen of the United States. They also insisted that they had a right to intercept and search the ships of other countries in order to retrieve these "citizens." There was some basis for their concerns, for as many as 20,000 British seamen had joined the American navy and merchant marine, seeking both better pay and a safe haven from the war. It is estimated that close to half the sailors on board American naval ships in the first decade of the nineteenth century were British- or Irish-born. By 1807, the British had impressed up to 10,000 sailors who claimed to be American citizens, over the vehement protests of the government of the United States.

Two other factors also led to war in 1812. First, the Americans feared that the British were forming alliances with the indigenous peoples who lived along the border with Canada, in preparation for encroaching south into territory that they believed belonged to them. These indigenous peoples had their own reasons for seeking British support: they wanted the British to help them push the Americans back to the Ohio River, thereby restoring the territory they had controlled prior to the American Revolution. Second, the Orders in Council required all neutral ships bound for Europe to stop in Britain and pay customs duties there. The French retaliated by declaring that they would seize any vessel that stopped in Britain, leaving the Americans with no means to trade with Europe. Hoping to damage the British economy, the American government passed an Embargo Act that closed American ports to foreign trade and prohibited American vessels from sailing to other countries. The British, however, quickly found new sources of food and other goods in Latin America; it was instead the American economy that was damaged, as thousands of sailors and other workers who depended on maritime trade were left unemployed. Farmers, too, suffered without access to export markets.

After economic pressure failed to resolve the issues, the American government decided that war was the only option. Many people believed that the American population advantage would lead to an easy victory and to the annexation of Canada. They did not, however, take into account that Britain had been fighting a major war for two decades, and it now possessed military forces that were far larger and stronger than they had been during the American Revolution. The American army numbered 7000 at the beginning of the war, while the British could put 15,000 troops in the field by combining the British Army units that were stationed in Canada with the colony's own forces. Added to this total were the 10,000 indigenous peoples whom the British counted as allies. The Americans hoped to offset this advantage by recruiting regular troops and calling up militia, but the numbers never met expectations. Moreover, these inexperienced soldiers were prone to panic in battle, a tendency that the British exploited by using screaming, war-painted indigenous peoples as the first wave of attackers. In reality, the indigenous peoples were not the bloodthirsty savages of the American imagination, but rather skilled military tacticians who fought for rational objectives. The Americans, however, feared both their prowess in combat and their customs of war, in particular bodily mutilations such as scalping.

The first two years of the war were a disaster for the Americans, as they lost battle after battle. Only the fact that the British were determined to wage a defensive campaign in which they remained behind the Canadian border prevented the fledgling republic from being threatened. By 1814, the conquest of Canada was a distant dream, as Napoleon had been defeated in Europe and the British now had thousands of reinforcements available to send across the Atlantic. At the same time, however, the American army had gained in training and experience, and they were now able to match the British on the battlefield. The British recognized that to continue fighting would be extremely costly. Both sides thus agreed to open peace negotiations, which began in June 1814 at Ghent in Belgium. The Americans were now willing simply to end the war and leave the border with Canada where it was. The British, however, wanted more: the creation of a "buffer zone" along the border that included eastern Maine and a broad swath of land stretching from the Great Lakes south to the Ohio River that was to be recognized as belonging to the indigenous peoples.

Figure 4.7 An American broadside by William Charles that criticizes the British use of indigenous Americans in the War of 1812. On the left, an Indian hands a British officer a scalp dripping with blood. A sign reading "Reward for Sixteen Scalps" hangs from the Indian's musket, while his knife and tomahawk are emblazoned with the initials "GR," a reference to King George III. The officer tells him, "Bring me the Scalps and the King our master will reward you." On the right, another Indian scalps a fallen American soldier while the corpse of another scalped victim lies nearby.

Reproduced courtesy of the Library of Congress.

When they learned of the British demands, the Americans were furious. The British responded by launching an attack on Washington in which the White House and Capitol were burned. In the wake of Napoleon's escape from Elba, however, they were also worried about the resumption of the war in Europe. They thus relinquished most of their demands and agreed that the Canadian border would remain in its prewar position. The Treaty of Ghent was signed on the 24th of December 1814; two weeks later, the British and American armies, which had not yet received the news of peace, clashed at New Orleans. The result was a stunning, if meaningless, victory for the United States: the British suffered almost 1600 casualties, in contrast to a mere seventy-one American losses.

In Britain, the end of the war was greeted with disappointment, as it was felt that the peace terms had been overgenerous. For their part, the Americans, bolstered by their late victory at New Orleans, turned what had largely been a dismal military performance into a triumph. For both nations, the war had achieved little, at a cost of 18,000 lives. But if there was no real winner, the indigenous peoples were clearly the losers. Their position in Michigan and the Ohio Valley was fatally undermined when the British abandoned their alliance with them in order to secure peace. The Americans were now free to push west into their territory. "The ultimate legacy of the war," Taylor writes, "was that the empire and the republic would share the continent along a more clearly defined border more generous to the Americans and more confining to the British – but most ominous to the Indians."

Reform and Repression

Back in Britain, the French Revolution and the ensuing war generated a fierce internal debate. The sides were outlined early. In 1790, the Anglo-Irish Whig politician *Edmund Burke published his Reflections on the Revolution in France*, which defended the value of tradition and predicted a dire end to the French Revolution. Burke argued that that the political system should evolve gradually, rather than being suddenly altered by violent upheaval. Burke's ideas were challenged by Thomas Paine, who had gone to the American colonies in 1774 to support the revolution but had returned to Britain in 1787. In 1791, *Paine published The Rights of Man*, in which he argued that a republic was the best form of government, as all men possessed equal natural rights. He called for universal male suffrage and the abolition of the monarchy, the House of Lords and the aristocracy.

How did Burke and Paine come to such different conclusions about the French Revolution? They agreed that "independence" – defined by freedom from undue influence – was crucial to good government. But they disagreed over the best means to achieve that objective. Burke saw hereditary institutions as providing independence, because they were neither susceptible to political pressures nor the power of public opinion. Paine, however, saw the monarchy and aristocracy as corrupted by self-interest and factionalism and saw the route to good government in the natural rights of the people. Burke and Paine also differed in their views of British history. Burke saw the Glorious Revolution as having established that Britain could achieve change gradually and without bloodshed and as having created a perfect constitutional settlement that required no additional improvement. Paine, in contrast, saw it as having confirmed the right of the people to resist oppression and demand change. He also believed that the past should not constrain people's actions in the present. "Every age and generation must be as free to act for itself, in all cases, as the ages and generations which preceded it," he wrote. "The vanity and presumption of governing beyond the grave, is the most ridiculous and insolent of all tyrannies."

Like their male counterparts, British women were divided in their opinions of the French Revolution. Mary Wollstonecraft grew up watching her two brothers receive her parents' affection and attention, while she was given little formal education and criticized for being too clever. She resented that only a handful of occupations – teacher, governess, seamstress – were open to middle-class women and opted to become a writer instead. In the *Vindication of the Rights of Men* (1791), she fiercely defended the French Revolution. She followed it *a year later with A Vindication of the Rights of Women*, which advocated equal rights for women. In it, she painted an unflattering picture of women as frivolous, weak and irrational, but argued that this was not how they naturally were, but how an unequal society made them. She made her case so forcefully and logically that *A Vindication of the Rights of Women* became a bestseller that was read by many influential people who would have disdained other radical writers.

In sharp contrast was Hannah More. More was a schoolmaster's daughter who grew up in a household in which her cleverness was encouraged. Like Wollstonecraft, she focused in her writings on the place of women, but she was strongly critical of arguments in favor of equality. More argued that differences between the sexes were natural, and that women should not seek to excel at the same things as men. She believed that women should focus on morality rather than intellect, a view encouraged by her evangelical religious beliefs. She was appalled by the French Revolution's atheism, and in response began publishing her "Cheap Repository Tracts," which were aimed at a lower-class audience and which contained simple morals that were intended to promote loyalism and piety. Like Wollstonecraft, More was a successful and popular author, showing that there was room for female as well as male voices from all political perspectives in this period.

Most Britons found Paine's and Wollstonecraft's ideas too radical. Even so, enthusiasm for political change continued, promulgated by the "corresponding societies" that were established by groups of skilled workers in London and other cities in the early 1790s. They supported Paine's call for universal male suffrage and felt that by joining their voices together, they could better formulate strategies to put pressure on the government. They sought change only through peaceful and constitutional means, but in the climate of the French Revolution they were viewed with suspicion. The government responded by building a network of spies and informants, and by passing *an act in 1794 that suspended habeas corpus*, or the right not to be imprisoned without trial. The leaders of the London Corresponding Society, the largest such group, were arrested and charged with treason. They were acquitted by a London jury that was unconvinced that their plan to hold a convention in order to demand universal male suffrage was tantamount to sedition. Afterwards, the London Corresponding Society's membership expanded significantly, boosted by high food prices and rising unemployment as the war cut off continental markets for British goods.

In July 1795, protestors smashed the windows of the prime minister's residence at 10 Downing Street, and three months later a crowd of 200,000 people filled the streets of London to hurl abuse at Pitt and the King as they rode to the opening of Parliament. Pitt's response was to crack down further. The Treason Act made it high treason to "imagine, invent, devise, or intend death or destruction" of the King, while the Seditious Meetings Act limited the size of public meetings to fifty people. These repressive measures were effective in forcing much radical activity underground, but they did not meet with universal approval. Led by Charles James Fox, the Whigs denounced both the conduct of the war and Pitt's repressive measures on the home front. In 1797, Fox led the Whigs in a symbolic "secession" that removed them as a viable alternative to the Tories for the better part of the next decade. Some people saw his actions as dangerous and possibly treasonous, but others saw them as a legitimate defense of British liberties.

In 1800, the domestic situation reached a crisis point. A series of poor harvests led to severe food shortages and high prices. There were riots all over the country, requiring the deployment of local militias. Pitt was so alarmed that he brought several thousand regular troops home from the continent. Rumors flew of secret societies that were stockpiling weapons in preparation for armed insurrection. Better harvests in 1801 and 1802 alleviated the discontentment, but while it had lasted it had shown how Britain was balanced on a knife-edge. The political situation was further destabilized in 1801 when Pitt quarreled with the King over his plan to repeal the Test Acts, which prohibited non-Anglicans from holding public office, and he resigned after seventeen years as prime minister. The Tories remained in power under Henry Addington, but most of their talent had resigned with Pitt, thereby severely weakening the government. There were soon loud calls for Addington's replacement and active behind-the-scenes maneuvering to bring this about. The obvious alternative was Pitt, who returned as prime minister in 1804, but he was a largely spent force and was already suffering from the illness – peptic ulcers, probably exacerbated by alcoholism – that would kill him a year later, in January 1806.

Pitt's disappearance from the political scene left a huge void. The Tories remained in power, but they were divided between their liberal and conservative wings. In 1812, Lord Liverpool, a compromise choice, became prime minister following the assassination of his predecessor Spencer Perceval. (Perceval remains the only British prime minister to be assassinated.) It was a challenging time: the final years of the war saw severe economic distress, exacerbated by the inflation caused by increased military expenditure and by broader changes in the economy. The end of the war in 1815 brought even greater economic disruption, as hundreds of thousands of men were released from the armed services just as wartime demand was diminishing. For the first time, the economic problems hit the agricultural sector, which had prospered during the war due to the decrease in food imports caused by the French blockade. In an effort to bolster agriculture, in 1815 the government passed the Corn Law, which prohibited the import of wheat when prices fell below a certain level. (In British usage, "corn" means "grain.") This was popular with the landed elite and with farmers, but not with most middle- and working-class Britons, who were forced to pay higher prices for the food as a result.

As they sought ways to improve their living conditions, the working classes increasingly defined the attainment of the right to vote as an essential step that would allow them to put pressure on politicians so that more basic "knife-and-fork" issues could be addressed. They began to organize to achieve this goal, forming clubs and societies and even conducting military-style drills to ensure that they could hold large-scale meetings and marches without having them descend into chaos. But although most of their leaders tried to ensure that their activities were controlled and orderly, occasional episodes awakened fears of revolution, such as when the Prince Regent's coach was shot at in 1817. The government resorted once again to repression, suspending *habeas corpus* and reimposing other anti-sedition measures from the 1790s.

In 1818, a poor harvest sparked a fresh round of agitation. In August of the following year, a huge meeting was organized in Manchester at a site called St. Peter's Fields. A crowd of 50,000 people gathered to hear the radical orator Henry Hunt. The local authorities were determined to prevent him from speaking, and the local militia was ordered to place him under arrest. But when the inexperienced volunteers were quickly swallowed up by the angry crowd, the magistrates were forced to send in regular army troops to extricate them. With their sabers drawn, the soldiers forced their way through the crowd, inflicting injuries and inciting panic. The situation quickly degenerated into a stampede in which eleven people were killed and hundreds more injured. When the government praised the conduct of the magistrates, not only radicals but also a considerable portion of the general public was

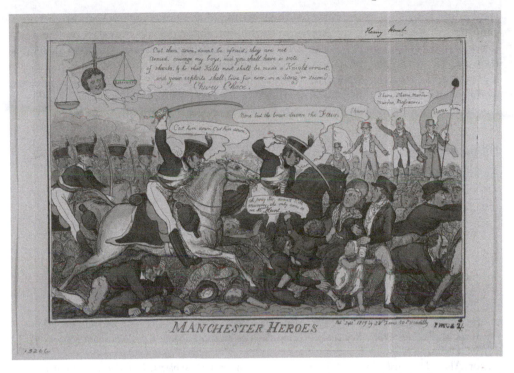

Figure 4.8 Sarcastically titled "Manchester Heroes," this cartoon by George Cruikshank was produced
soon after the "Peterloo Massacre." Reflecting the reaction against the authorities' actions,
it shows a local magistrate at the top left, with his scales of justice very unbalanced, order-
ing the soldiers to "cut down" the protestors, who are mostly women and children, with
their swords.

Reproduced courtesy of the Library of Congress.

outraged. The event became known as the "*Peterloo Massacre*," a satiric reference to the Battle of Waterloo. Undeterred by the criticism, the government clamped down further. A series
of laws known as the "*Six Acts*" imposed tighter censorship on the press, further restricted
public meetings, and limited the right to bear arms. In the short term, these measures were
effective, but they were seen as excessively repressive even by many moderates. Ultimately,
they damaged the Tories by labelling them as the party of reaction, and rejuvenated the
Whigs by allowing them to claim the ground of reform.

Conclusion

Between 1760 and 1820, divergent forces pulled Britain both towards and away from greater
unity. There was great pride in Parliament as a bulwark against tyranny and absolutism, but
much debate about whether the franchise should be extended and borough constituencies
redistributed. The elimination of Jacobitism as a serious threat meant that Scotland could
now be fully incorporated into the United Kingdom, and Scots enthusiastically participated
in government, military and imperial service in the second half of the eighteenth century.
Ireland, however, proved a more complicated case, due largely to the religious differences
between the majority of the population and both the Anglo-Irish elite and the remainder of

the United Kingdom. In the colonies, the meaning of the rights of "freeborn Englishmen" came under pressure during the American Revolution and in debates over slavery. The Revolutionary and Napoleonic Wars with France, meanwhile, proved the strongest unifier, as they directly threatened the nation's survival, requiring a massive mobilization of manpower and resources that touched virtually every Briton. But even they engendered fierce debate, as there were many Britons who sympathized at least in part with the ideals of the French Revolution, or at least wanted some extension of democracy in Britain.

Bibliography

Andress, David, *The Savage Storm: Britain on the Brink in the Age of Napoleon* (2012)

Cash, Arthur H., *John Wilkes: The Scandalous Father of Civil Liberty* (2007)

Colley, Linda, *Britons: Forging the Nation 1707–1837* (1992)

Connolly, Sean, *Divided Kingdom: Ireland 1630–1800* (2008)

Darwin, John, *The Empire Project: The Rise and Fall of the British World System, 1830–1970* (2009)

Elliot, Marianne, *Partners in Revolution: The United Irishmen and France* (1982)

Guldi, Jo, *Roads to Power: Britain Invents the Infrastructure State* (2012)

Herman, Arthur, *How the Scots Invented the Modern World* (2002)

Johnson, Kenneth R., *Unusual Suspects: Pitt's Reign of Alarm and the Lost Generation of the 1790s* (2013)

Knight, Roger, *Britain against Napoleon: The Organization of Victory 1793–1815* (2013)

Lavery, Brian, *Nelson's Navy: The Ships, Men, and Organization 1793–1815*, revised edn (2013)

Overton, Mark, *Agricultural Revolution in England: The Transformation of the Agrarian Economy 1500–1850* (1996)

Taylor, Alan, *The Civil War of 1812: American Citizens, British Subjects, Irish Rebels and Indian Allies* (2011)

Taylor, Alan, *American Revolutions: A Continental History of the United States, 1750–1804* (2017)

Yates, Nigel, *Eighteenth-Century Britain: Religion and Politics 1714–1815* (2007)

5 The Early Victorian Era
Global Power and Its Challenges

Topics covered

- The Industrial Revolution and its consequences
- The Reform Act of 1832
- Chartism
- Repeal of the Corn Laws
- Scotland and Wales under the Union
- The Irish potato famine
- Self-government in the settlement colonies
- Imperial expansion and administration

Timeline

1822	George IV visits Scotland
1829	Catholic Emancipation
1832	First Reform Act
1834	New Poor Law
1837	Queen Victoria's accession
1838	People's Charter
1839	First Opium War begins
1839	Durham Report
1840	Treaty of Waitangi
1842	Retreat from Kabul
1844	Friedrich Engels, *The Condition of the Working Classes in England*
1845	Irish potato famine begins
1845	First Anglo-Sikh War begins
1846	Corn Law repealed
1847	"Treachery of the Blue Books"
1868	Last convicts sent to Australia

DOI: 10.4324/9781003284758-5

Introduction

The next three chapters will trace the Victorian age, which in a formal sense encompassed Queen Victoria's reign from 1837 to 1901 but is often extended back to 1830 or even earlier. Today, views of the Victorians are often influenced by political predilections. People who lean left often see them as sexist, racist and such fervent believers in an unfettered free market that they failed to acknowledge or ameliorate the damage that was done to ordinary Britons, who were forced in consequence to live in overcrowded cities, breathe polluted air and drink poisoned water. People who lean right, meanwhile, tend to see them as highly moral, devoutly religious and so hardworking and inventive that they led Britain to its greatest heights of global power.

Both views are in some measure accurate and in some measure inaccurate. The Victorians were complex, and no attempt to cram them into a neat ideological box will do them justice. To deal with this complexity, historians generally break the Victorian age into three periods: early, mid- and late. The early Victorian period, which this chapter covers, began in the 1830s and lasted until around 1850. By 1830, Britain was the world's leading economic, military and imperial power, but it was still adjusting to its new status. Much of its economic emergence and burgeoning global power is attributed to a shift from agriculture to manufacturing that is conventionally summarized by the term "Industrial Revolution," though as we will see historians now question just how revolutionary it was. The expansion of the British Empire into parts of Africa, Asia and the Middle East created new forms of wealth for Britons and global engagements while challenging the precarious relationship between imperialism and liberal democracy. In politics, the urban middle classes, who were the prime drivers and beneficiaries of industrialization, pressed for the right to vote. A degree of reform was achieved in 1832, expanding the electorate and correcting some of the worst anomalies of the existing system. At the same time, however, the limited extension of the franchise demonstrated the continuing power of the traditional elite; Britain was still a long way from democracy.

The unity of the nation was another source of tension and debate. Though the Act of Union with Ireland in 1800 had brought all four nations of the British Isles together as a single entity for the first time, it was far from a union of equals. The first census in British history, conducted in 1801, showed that while England contained over half of the United Kingdom's population and Ireland a third, only 10 percent of its inhabitants lived in Scotland and only 3 percent in Wales. England also remained the dominant part of the United Kingdom in terms of political and economic power. This was reflected by the fact that over the course of her sixty-four-year reign, Queen Victoria visited Ireland only four times and spent only seven nights in Wales. These disparities engendered much discontentment in the non-English parts of the United Kingdom. Wales and Scotland had clearly retained distinct cultural and economic identities, but it was in Ireland that the differences were most apparent. As the century progressed, many Irish people came to believe that a dramatic alteration to – or even the end of – Ireland's place in the United Kingdom was necessary.

The Victorian world was not limited to the British Isles. Historian John MacKenzie writes, "scarcely a single development . . . was not powerfully influenced by the global context in which the Victorians operated." The Napoleonic Wars had increased the amount of territory under Britain's control, but there were many new questions regarding this expanded empire. In the settlement colonies of Canada, Australia and New Zealand, Britain confronted growing demands for self-government. Nascent nationalist movements emerged in nonsettler colonies, most notably in India. Elsewhere in the Empire, new rivals emerged, in particular

Russia, which increasingly threatened British dominance in India as it sought to expand its own imperial reach into Central Asia. The first half of the nineteenth century thus saw Britain ascend to new heights of power within Europe and around the world, but this also brought new challenges and threats.

The Industrial Revolution

Any discussion of the changing world of nineteenth-century Britain has to begin with the Industrial Revolution. The conventional definition of the term references the shift from an agriculturally dominated economy to manufacturing and factory-based production. Beginning around 1760, industrialization was a global phenomenon, affecting Europe, the United States and Japan in particular, but it began in Britain. Beyond these basic parameters, however, historians continue to debate the Industrial Revolution's meaning and impact, and even the very use of that term to describe the changes in the domestic and imperial British and global economy from the late eighteenth century onwards.

By the early nineteenth century, British people were aware that their economy and society had changed, and was changing, significantly. Indeed, many people felt that the pace of change was unprecedented, in terms of both technological innovation and its consequences, such as urbanization and changes in patterns of work. Two industries have attracted the most attention: iron and cotton. In the century after 1750, the iron industry increased its output by 250 times, thereby providing the materials that would support the paralleling dramatic expansions of manufacturing and transportation. Initially, iron production focused on cast iron, but by the mid-nineteenth century its potential uses were outstripping its capabilities, as a number of dramatic bridge collapses demonstrated. People had long known that steel, an alloy made of iron, carbon and other metals, was stronger, but it was expensive to manufacture. In the 1850s, Henry Bessemer's invention of a more efficient process for smelting steel made possible a variety of new applications.

The cotton industry, meanwhile, had already expanded in the first half of the eighteenth century, thanks to the popularity of colorful calico fabrics that were initially imported from India but soon came to be manufactured domestically. After 1760, mechanization revolutionized the industry. The first was James Kay's flying shuttle in 1733, although it was not widely used until several decades later. It allowed wider cotton cloth to be woven, but most significantly it allowed for the mechanization of looms; the operator now only had to monitor the machine rather than operate it by hand. The acceleration of the weaving phase of textile manufacture, however, created a bottleneck in the other phase: spinning cotton fiber into yarn. This was addressed from the 1760s onwards by a series of inventions. First, James Hargreave's spinning jenny allowed a single machine to operate multiple spindles of thread. In the 1770s, Richard Arkwright's carding and water frames further sped up the conversion of raw cotton to yarn. In the 1780s, Samuel Crompton's spinning mule spun cotton into yarn on over a thousand spindles at a time; it was so efficient that it remained in wide use until 1900. The increased production of yarn led to further improvements in the efficiency of the weaving process, most notably Edward Cartwright's power loom, patented in 1785. The final piece of the puzzle was the invention of a power source that could drive these bigger machines. In 1709, Thomas Newcomen had patented his steam-driven "atmospheric engine," but it was not efficient for factory use. In the 1770s, the Scottish engineer James Watt developed an improved steam engine by adding a separate condenser; Watt also converted the engine to rotational movement, allowing it to be used in textile factories. Together, these inventions dramatically sped up the manufacture of cotton products. By

1830, half of Britain's exports were cotton textiles thanks to new inventions and a steady supply of raw cotton from India and, increasingly, the American South.

All of these new technologies, along with raw materials extracted from the Empire and expanding global trade, changed the pace and rhythm of life. Prior to the 1770s, textile manufacturing was a "cottage industry" that was based in the home. Women and children carded the cotton fibers to prepare them for spinning, then the women spun them into yarn on spinning wheels, and finally the men wove the yarn into cloth on handlooms. The cloth was then sold to a distributor, who paid according to the amount produced, or by the "piece," rather than for the time spent producing it. The large new machines to supply the increased demand for cheap British cotton textiles, however, were housed in factories. By the 1840s, there were over 3000 textile factories in Britain. Workers in these factories were not paid according to the number of pieces they produced, but rather they worked a set shift – up to sixteen hours a day – for a set wage per hour. Whereas a day's work previously spanned from sunrise to sunset, gas light now allowed work to go on after dark; factories often ran all night, using multiple shifts of workers. Instead of performing a variety of tasks that were required to produce a finished product, workers were now responsible for only one part of the process, which required little skill and was extremely monotonous.

Figure 5.1 Women and children carding cotton in a factory in Darton in South Yorkshire. Barfoot, James Richard, 1794–1863.

Reproduced courtesy of the Wellcome Collection.

Many contemporary observers saw these changes as negative. In 1839, the philosopher Thomas Carlyle first called attention to the "Condition of England," by which he meant the detrimental consequences of industrialization for workers. Four years later, Carlyle published his essay "Past and Present," in which he argued that most British people had been better off in the Middle Ages, before paternalism and social cohesion had been swept aside by the profit motive. In 1844, *Friedrich Engels described the terrible conditions* he saw in Manchester and Salford in his *The Condition of the Working Classes in England*. Depictions of the horrors of industrialization were a staple of contemporary literature as well as nonfiction. Charles Dickens set his novel *Hard Times* (1854) in the fictional city of Coketown, where factory workers were reduced to dehumanized "hands."

 See document "Dickens's Coketown" at www.routledge.com/cw/barczewski.

In her novel *North and South* (1855), Elizabeth Gaskell wrote of another fictional town, Darkshire, in which "the air had a faint taste and smell of smoke" and which was filled with "long, straight, hopeless streets of regularly-built houses, all small and of brick." Such depictions showed that many people now had to work long, set hours under strict supervision, performing tedious, repetitive and often dangerous tasks. Women and children, who were paid less to carry out the same unskilled tasks as adult male workers, were particularly exploited. The need for labor to staff factories that produced ever-larger amounts of cheap textiles put pressure on domestic and community life. Workers lived close to their place of work, which meant that people now had to reside in overcrowded, unsanitary housing near noisy, polluting factories that belched toxins into the air they breathed and water they drank.

These problems were not acquiesced to without protest. The years after 1810 saw attempts to destroy machines in the North and Midlands of England, as unemployed workers blamed mechanization for their difficulties. The perpetrators were called "Luddites" because they were supposedly led by a mysterious (and fictional) General Ludd. In 1830, agricultural laborers in southeast England rioted over the introduction of new threshing machines that threatened their livelihoods. They were led by another fictional commander, Captain Swing. Historians see these expressions of popular sentiment, however, less as revolutionary insurrections and more as part of the process of adjustment to economic and technological change. Workers were not demanding that machines be eliminated, only that they be treated fairly in adapting to their introduction.

Some early Victorian employers attempted to address these problems. In the years after 1815, Robert Owen attempted to create an ideal community for workers, including schools, medical facilities and housing, surrounding his cotton factories in New Lanark near Glasgow. Although the cooperative socialism promoted by Owen did not produce lasting results, his efforts did encourage the growth of the trade union movement. Fledgling unions existed by the end of the eighteenth century, as skilled artisans had begun to organize in order to negotiate with employers, but the Combination Act of 1799 prohibited formal unionization. In 1824, however, the act was repealed and replaced the following year with a second Combination Act that allowed unions, albeit within strict limits.

Women workers largely were excluded from early unions due to the belief that their presence in the workforce depressed wages for male workers. Instead, reformers argued that women and children needed protective legislation passed by Parliament rather than union representation to ensure that they could work in safe conditions. This created the false belief that male and female workers had different interests and made gender a central factor in unionization efforts. Women, like children, were considered to be in need of paternalist laws to protect them, rather than equal treatment. This had the consequence of limiting their participation in the labor market. The 1844 Factory Act, which governed work in textile factories, limited children between the ages of eight and thirteen to six-and-a-half hours of work per day, while women were barred from night work and could not work longer than twelve hours per day. In 1842, the Mines Act prohibited the employment of women and female children below ground, and in 1847 another Factory Act legislated a ten-hour workday for women and children only. Though these laws were in many ways beneficial, they contributed to the emergence of gendered notions of work that held that men should work longer hours in order to support their families. This led to even larger disparities in rates of pay for men and women than already existed, as women's labor was devalued as supplementary to that of men.

Male workers in textile factories, meanwhile, joined together in an attempt to improve their working conditions. These early unions soon expanded into organizations of all workers regardless of trade, with the Grand National Consolidated Trades Union, founded in 1833, as the most prominent example. The following year, a group of farm laborers in Tolpuddle in Dorset attempted to form a union after their wages were repeatedly reduced. Alarmed by their activities and under pressure from landowners, the local magistrates ordered six of the group's leaders to be arrested under an obscure law of 1797 that prohibited the taking of secret oaths. They were subsequently found guilty and sentenced to the maximum seven years' transportation to Australia. The harsh punishment of the "Tolpuddle Martyrs" led to protests all over the country, as tens of thousands of workers marched in their support. Two years later, they were granted a full pardon by the Whig government.

How do we view the early stages of industrialization in Britain two centuries later? Unfortunately, we have little detailed statistical evidence that allows us to assess change over time with any certainty. What we do know is that there was sufficient economic growth to allow Britain to feed a population that had tripled in size from 5 to 15 million. (Ireland, as we will see, was a different story.) But such a long-term focus elides periods such as the years after the Napoleonic Wars and the 1840s, in which high food prices and depressed real wages produced serious distress. The Industrial Revolution certainly did not eliminate the problem of poverty; in fact, it was possibly exacerbated by increasing inequalities in the distribution of wealth. At the end of the day, then, the impact of industrialization varied enormously in different places and across different demographic groups.

Certainly, it had different effects on different parts of the United Kingdom. In England, the northwestern county of Lancashire became the center of cotton production, because it offered easy access to fast-flowing waterways for water-powered mills and was near significant deposits of coal once the steam engine came into widespread use. There was already a cottage cotton industry in the region, which meant that a base of skilled workers was readily available. The proximity of the port of Liverpool, into which raw cotton could be imported and from which finished textiles could be exported, was also a factor.

Wales, meanwhile, became a major producer of iron and copper. The city of Swansea was a center of copper smelting, using ore that came first from mines in Cornwall and then, when those deposits were depleted, from South America. It was coal, however, that became Wales's most important industrial product. Coal was much in demand by the Royal Navy for its new steamships and by British industry as a power source. By 1850, Britain was using 70 million tons a year, more than double the demand of only two decades earlier. Deep mine shafts were sunk in the Rhondda Valley in South Wales, which lay atop Britain's largest coalfield. As a result, the population of the two counties, Glamorgan and Monmouth, where the coal was located increased by 400 percent between 1841 and 1911. Welsh industry was often dangerous and unhealthy. In the iron- and coal-producing center of Merthyr Tydfil, life expectancy was less than eighteen years, whereas in the rest of Britain it was close to fifty. Workers did not accept these conditions without protest. In 1831, an armed insurrection took place in Merthyr Tydfil in which more than two dozen demonstrators were killed.

Scotland also played a leading role in Britain's rise to industrial prominence. Similarly to Lancashire, southwest Scotland offered access both to energy sources (first water and later coal) and to global markets by sea. In the early decades of the nineteenth century, Glasgow competed with Manchester for the title of "Cottonopolis." Scotland was also a leading producer of iron, with a thriving industry based in Lanarkshire, the county surrounding Glasgow. Scottish coal production grew steadily over the course of the nineteenth century, and by 1900 Scotland was supplying 27 percent of Britain's coal. Elsewhere, Scottish industry built on the global trade links that had been forged in the eighteenth century. Dundee in northeast Scotland, already established in linen production, became a center of the jute industry. Jute, a natural fiber that was used to make burlap bags, rugs and other textiles, was imported by the East India Company from India. Finished products made from jute and cotton were then sold back to India and other parts of the Empire, in a trade loop that recalled the mercantilist system of the eighteenth century. In India and other colonies, this resulted in the devastation of regional manufacturing and the disruption of local markets, which were flooded with goods made in Britain from colonial raw materials.

The effects of the Industrial Revolution in Ireland were uneven at best. In the 1770s, textile factories appeared in Dublin and Cork, but by 1800 Irish industry was finding it difficult to compete with England. The situation was exacerbated after 1824, when import duties protecting Irish industries were eliminated. With the United Kingdom now a free trade zone, the textile industry in the south of Ireland collapsed. In the northern province of Ulster, however, the story was different. Ulster was a traditional center of linen production, which had suffered during the early years of the Industrial Revolution because the fibers of the flax plant, from which linen is produced, were too fine to be spun by machines. In the mid-1820s, however, the development of a process known as wet spinning allowed linen yarn to be produced in factories. The center of linen production was the city of Belfast, which was described as "Ireland's Manchester." By 1851, Belfast's population was close to 100,000, almost five times what it had been at the beginning of the century. Different patterns of economic development thus helped to divide the Catholic-dominated south and Protestant-dominated north of Ireland even further in the nineteenth century.

The effects of industrialization varied not just by nation and region, however, but also on a local and even individual level. In general, people who were able to adapt to change reaped the largest benefits. Some occupations, however, were rendered obsolete by mechanization, such as the handloom weavers who were displaced by technological innovations in the cotton industry. Prior to 1800, handloom weavers were some of the best-paid skilled laborers in Britain. As late as 1810, there were almost 250,000 of them. But as the number of power looms multiplied, their wages plummeted. "On every hand," wrote Thomas Carlyle in his essay "Signs of the Times" (1829), "the living artisan is driven from his workshop to make room for the speedier, inanimate one." By 1860, only 7000 handloom weavers remained in Britain, most of them Irish immigrants who lacked other employment options.

The degree of scholarly attention afforded to groups such as the handloom weavers has led to a view of the Industrial Revolution as a social disaster that destroyed an older, secure rural world and replaced it with a squalid, impoverished one that was centered on dirty, grim factory towns. Some historians, however, argue that this view was applicable to only a few, largely anomalous sectors of society, such as coal mining. As late as 1850, only 12 percent of the British workforce was employed in factories. Many of the showcase "industries" of Victorian Britain, meanwhile, such as the manufacture of steel cutlery in Sheffield, continued to be organized in small, nonmechanized workshops. Moreover, capital and labor had been slowly migrating away from agriculture since the mid-sixteenth century, meaning that the transition to other economic sectors such as manufacturing had begun long before 1760. As a result, the Industrial "Revolution" now appears to have been more of an "evolution."

But even if historians now debate the scope and pace of change, they concede that change began in Britain earlier than it did elsewhere. Some historians trace this to long-term "incentive" factors such as the growth of religious tolerance, political stability and property rights from the late seventeenth century onwards. Still others look at intellectual developments, arguing that the Enlightenment gave rise to the dominance of science and reason, leading in turn to technological innovations and economic progress. In Britain, as was discussed in the previous chapter, the Enlightenment had what the historian Joel Mokyr calls a "more practical" character. Finally, some historians assert that Britain had high wages and low energy costs – the latter largely thanks to an abundance of coal – relative to other western countries, which tended to have low wages and high energy costs. This meant that there were powerful incentives to create machines that took the place of high-cost human labor and operated on low-cost coal.

Reform

More than industrialization dramatically altered the early Victorian world, though historians continue to debate whether the reforms that occurred in 1832 were merely business as usual or something more revolutionary. After decades of pressure to repair what many people saw as a corrupt and outdated electoral system, the Tories' unwillingness to countenance any measure of parliamentary reform led to a major constitutional crisis. This crisis began with the repeal of the Test and Corporation Acts in 1828, which permitted Protestant Dissenters to hold public office without practicing "occasional conformity" (i.e., occasionally taking the Anglican communion). The ban against Catholics remained, however. In Ireland, where close to three-quarters of the population was Catholic, the achievement of "Catholic Emancipation" therefore remained a major political issue.

In the early 1820s, the Dublin lawyer Daniel O'Connell initiated a campaign for full political rights for Catholics. O'Connell's Catholic Association garnered massive public support. In 1828, he forced Parliament to confront the issue by exploiting a loophole in the law: whereas Catholics could not sit in Parliament, there was no law against a Catholic standing (i.e., running) for a seat. O'Connell therefore decided to stand for County Clare in western Ireland and won by a large majority. The House of Commons refused to seat him, and so he ran, and won, again. Fearful of a rebellion in Ireland, the Tory government granted *Catholic Emancipation* the following year.

Though the repeal of the Test Acts and the passage of Catholic Emancipation were not directly related to the broader issue of parliamentary reform, they marked a significant breach in the previously stalwart defenses against any political change. Now that they had been achieved, parliamentary reform was the next great political question. In 1830, only 516,000 men out of a total British and Irish population of 21 million could vote, as the franchise was still tied to both gender and the ownership of a substantial amount of property. At the same time, hundreds of MPs continued to represent rotten or pocket boroughs that were controlled by the landed elite, and new industrial cities like Manchester continued to be represented only as part of the counties in which they were located. Pressure was building to change these things, from both the middle classes, who felt that their substantial contribution to the nation's economy warranted enfranchisement, and the working classes, who believed that their living and working conditions would not improve until they gained a direct means of influencing their political representatives.

The 1820s saw a number of reform riots in Britain's largest cities. In 1830, a revolution in France that deposed King Charles X reawakened fears similar to those of the 1790s that the radical contagion would spread to Britain. An economic depression that had begun in 1827 further ratcheted up the pressure for change. Also in 1830, the steadfastly conservative King George IV died, bringing to the throne his slightly less intractable brother William IV. The possibility of reform was now widely discussed throughout the political nation, and there was widespread expectation that the Tories would introduce a modest measure, thereby once again restoring confidence in the British political system's ability to adapt to changing times. But the prime minister, the Waterloo hero the Duke of Wellington, was still smarting over hardline conservative accusations that he had surrendered too easily over Catholic Emancipation, and he dug in his heels. In November 1830, he told the House of Lords, "the legislature and the system of representation possessed the full and entire confidence of the country" and pledged to resist all measures of reform.

This was an untenable position, and two weeks later Wellington was forced to resign. The king sent for the Whigs, who had pledged in the 1820s to introduce reform. When the new prime minister Lord Grey did so in March 1831, many people were stunned by its scope. Fifty-six of the smallest boroughs were to be eliminated altogether, and thirty more would lose one of their two seats. As there were a total of 203 borough constituencies, this meant that over a third of all borough seats were to be redistributed. An outraged House of Lords threatened to block the bill's passage, but Grey convinced the King that if something were not done a revolution was inevitable, and thus the King agreed to create sufficient sympathetic peers to ensure the bill's passage. Faced with the dilution of their ranks, the lords gave in and passed the bill in 1832.

The *Reform Act* of 1832, officially titled the Representation of the People Act, marked the first step toward making British elections more representative, fair and democratic. For this reason, it is often called the "Great Reform Act." It standardized the borough franchise for male householders who owned property worth £10 annually or had a long-term lease in which they paid that sum annually in rent. (This latter provision was significant, as it marked the first time in which a man did not have to *own* property to have the right to vote.) The franchise in the county constituencies, meanwhile, continued to be based on the "forty shilling freehold." The electorate grew as a result from 350,000 to 650,000 in England and Wales, from 5000 to 60,000 in Scotland and from 49,000 to 90,000 in Ireland. Twenty-two large towns and cities were given two representatives each and another twenty-one were given one each; important industrial centers like Manchester gained their own parliamentary representation as boroughs for the first time. There was also a minor degree of reduction in England's dominance of the political system, as England lost seventeen seats, while Scotland gained eight, Ireland five and Wales four.

The right to vote, however, remained linked to wealth and gender, and four-fifths of MPs continued to come from landed backgrounds. If one in six adult males could now vote, five in six could not. Only 7 percent of the population as a whole possessed the franchise, as women were still excluded. (The Reform Act had in fact formally *disenfranchised* women for the first time by declaring that the right to vote belonged to men only.) The proportion of voters was not the same in all parts of the British Isles: whereas one in five men in England and Wales could vote, only one in eight in Scotland had the right and a mere one in twenty in Ireland.

And if the franchise varied by nation, it also continued to vary by class. The reforms of 1832 granted a higher percentage of middle-class men the right to vote, but it did nothing for the working classes. In a view supported by a number of later historians, some people at the time felt that the middle classes had been "bought off," in other words that they had used the threat of revolution from below to obtain the right to vote for themselves, and then abandoned their working-class allies in the struggle for reform when they no longer needed them.

Working-class people did not give up the fight for the vote, however. Beginning in the late 1830s, the Chartist Movement demanded six further reforms: universal male suffrage, annual parliamentary elections, the secret ballot, equal electoral districts, the end of the property qualification to sit in Parliament and salaries for MPs.

 See document "The People's Charter" at www.routledge.com/cw/barczewski.

Chartism built upon older traditions of radical, working-class activism, as well as resentment at the limitations of the Great Reform Act. It had its origins in a number of different initiatives. In 1836, a group known as the London Working Men's Association was formed; hundreds of imitators from all over the country followed. A year later, the Irish radical Feargus O'Connor founded a weekly newspaper in Leeds called the *Northern Star*, which soon became the most widely circulated provincial paper in Britain. Emerging as the closest thing that Chartism had to a national leader, O'Connor helped to ally working-class radicalism in the North of England with existing reform movements such as the Birmingham Political Union (established in 1829), which had long called for universal male suffrage. While women participated in Chartism, their role was limited by male leaders, who also excluded them from the demand for universal suffrage.

In 1838, the leaders of the growing movement published a document listing their six demands. It was called the *"People's Charter,"* and so its supporters became known as "Chartists." Their primary strategy was to pressure Parliament to adopt the Charter, and in 1839 they delivered a petition with over 1.2 million signatures to Westminster. Supported by only the most radical MPs, the Charter was voted down 235 to 46. This dismal failure gave rise to a debate among the Chartists as to whether they should adopt more militant tactics. In Wales, where Chartism enjoyed strong support, there was a distinctive strand of "physical force" Chartism, as many Welsh workers favored direct action over further petitions. This led to the Newport Rising in November 1839, in which thousands of Welsh people armed with guns, pikes and knives marched towards the town of Newport to protest Parliament's rejection of the People's Charter. Soldiers opened fire, and over twenty Chartists were killed.

Most Chartists, however, continued to advocate peaceful and constitutional tactics, or "moral force," and in 1842 they presented a second petition to Parliament, this one with over 3 million signatures. The petition was again rejected, and in response a series of strikes occurred in the industrial districts of northern England, where Chartist support was strong. In spite of their lack of immediate success, Chartism continued to serve as a voice of working-class dissent through the 1840s. Historians have suggested that one reason for its continued power was that it drew on a language of popular radicalism that dated back to the late eighteenth century, which linked the economic problems of British workers to their exclusion from political power. The Chartists were also adept at deploying a symbolic and nonverbal vocabulary that appealed to nonliterate people. O'Connor would appear before crowds dressed not as the middle-class gentleman he was but in a suit made of fustian, a thick, cheap cotton cloth that was used for working-class people's clothes.

The climax of the Chartist movement came in 1848, when a new petition campaign coincided with the democratic revolutions taking place on the European continent. The campaign collected 5.7 million signatures, almost double the previous total. The movement's leadership planned a mass meeting in London that was to be followed by a march to deliver the petition to Parliament. Fearing revolution, the government banned the march and took elaborate security precautions, including the placement of cannons to guard Buckingham Palace. (Queen Victoria was sent to the Isle of Wight for safety.) The eighty-year-old Duke of Wellington came out of retirement to take command of the thousands of troops and tens of thousands of civilians who were sworn in as special constables.

The Chartist leadership obeyed the ban on the march and instead delivered the petition to Parliament in three hansom cabs. Three days later, they were informed that less than 2 million of the signatures were genuine; among those allegedly signing the petition included the "Duke of Wellington," "No Cheese" and "Pugnose." Written by opponents of the movement, the earliest accounts of the final Chartist petition depicted it as a fiasco. More recent historians, however, have taken a more sympathetic view. They argue that, while some signatures were forgeries, names such as "Queen Victoria" were in some cases aliases adopted by workers

Figure 5.2 A newspaper photograph, still a novelty at the time, of the "Great Chartist Meeting" on Kennington Common in April 1848. Intended to mark the triumph of Chartism with the delivery of a "monster petition" to the House of Commons by 200,000 marchers, the meeting proved a failure when only around 20,000 people attended. When their march was blocked by police, the Chartist leaders were forced to deliver the petition by taxi, a humiliation from which the movement never recovered.

Reproduced courtesy of Pictorial Press Ltd/Alamy Stock Photo.

who wished to conceal their support of Chartism from their employers. In addition, they note that the leaders canceled the march to Parliament because they realized that serious bloodshed was likely. Chartism had real revolutionary potential in 1848, as was evidenced by the forceful government response. Afterwards, Chartism continued as a collection of local-ized movements, and Chartist ideals continued to influence radical working-class political movements. Except for annual parliamentary elections, all of their demands were eventually realized, though not until well into the twentieth century. Chartism also helped to inspire the women's suffrage movement. In 1851, a group of Sheffield Chartist women formed the Women's Rights Association to campaign for women's suffrage. Although it failed to gain broad-based support, it was a first step towards the more successful suffragist groups that would appear at the end of the nineteenth century.

The problem of social and economic inequality also mobilized the middle classes during this period. Calls for an end to protectionist practices that kept the cost of food high were motivated by an economic downturn in the late 1830s. Reformers campaigned to repeal the Corn Law of 1815, which restricted imports of grain unless domestic prices rose to a certain level. (In British usage, "corn" means "grain.") This policy benefited large landown-ers and farmers over urban middle- and working-class consumers. Established in 1839, the Anti-Corn Law League sought to repeal the Corn Law. They argued that the law negatively impacted Britain's industries by raising grain prices – and therefore wages – and that it dam-aged overseas markets for British industrial goods by encouraging other nations to industrial-ize rather than produce grain for export. The aristocracy, meanwhile, were the staunchest defenders of the Corn Law, as much of their income derived from the agricultural produce of their estates.

The Anti-Corn Law League expanded from its origins in the industrial north of England to become a national organization, with significant support throughout England, Scotland and Wales. While the Chartist leadership was initially hostile to the League, believing that repeal of the Corn Law would allow manufacturers to decrease wages, many industrial workers later came to support it because they thought it would lower food prices. Led by the free-trade advocates Richard Cobden and John Bright, the League adopted tactics that had previously been employed by abolitionists and by the Catholic Association, including the use of pamphlets, petitions, public meetings and speeches. They also attempted to enfranchise additional voters by purchasing property and subdividing it into lots of sufficient value to meet the "forty shilling freehold" qualification in county constituencies. These lots would then be sold to voters who expressed support for repeal. The League dedicated £500,000 to this purpose, with an original target of enfranchising a million new voters. In the end, how-ever, it opted to target only a handful of selected seats, resulting in the addition of a mere 12,000 voters to the electoral rolls. Even so, the strategy paid dividends: Whig candidates, who generally supported free trade and the end of the protectionism that was embodied by the Corn Laws, won three times as many of those seats in 1847 as they had in 1841.

By that point, however, the issue had been decided, and not by the Whigs, who were not in power at the relevant time. The Tories, who had come to be known in the 1830s as the Conservatives and who had won the election of 1841, continued to be closely tied to the landowning interest. ("Tories" continued to be used as a slang term for the party.) They thus initially resisted repeal, on the grounds that protectionism helped agriculture and provided income to the Treasury, thereby benefiting the nation. Over time, however, prime minister Sir Robert Peel came to see the Corn Law as an archaic, protectionist measure that was det-rimental to the British economy. In 1845, the disastrous failure of the potato crop in Ireland and the ensuing famine convinced him that it was time to act; it seemed ludicrous to him to be artificially inflating the price of food and limiting imports at a time when millions of Irish people were starving. The famine was not the cause of Peel's decision, but it did compel him to act more quickly than he might have done otherwise. Using Whig support, Peel *repealed the Corn Law* in 1846, but his decision split his party, as a large portion of Tory MPs were still closely tied to agricultural interests. Less than a third of the Conservatives supported repeal. Afterwards, Peel's Conservative opponents painted him as having made Britain dependent on foreign food, and he was forced to resign only four days after the passage of repeal. He never held political office again prior to his death in 1850.

The repeal of the Corn Law had a lasting impact on Victorian politics, in three ways. First, the success of the Anti-Corn Law League demonstrated that a well-organized, well-funded middle-class pressure group could compel political change. It thus, in tandem with the Reform Act of 1832, confirmed that the middle classes had gained a significant amount of political power by the mid-nineteenth century. Second, it divided the Conservative Party, which influenced the political landscape for decades to come. The Conservatives who had supported the prime minister came to be known as "Peelites." Long after repeal, they continued to function as a loosely defined group in Parliament, at times allying with the Whigs and at times with the Conservatives. While they were committed to traditional Tory policies such as support for the monarchy and the Church of England, they also embraced the Whig causes of free trade and administrative reform. Third, repeal represented the emergence of a new spirit of free trade. In the late 1840s, the system of colonial preference, in which higher duties were imposed on goods from outside the Empire, was ended, and the Navigation Acts, which prohibited foreign vessels from trading with Britain and its colonies, were repealed. It is important, however, not to overstate the consequences of the repeal of the Corn Law. It was far from being a decisive blow to aristocratic influence. Peel had acted at least in part because he was trying to preserve that influence: he feared that if he did not undertake repeal, the Anti-Corn Law League would continue its scheme of creating additional "forty shilling freeholds" in the county constituencies, thereby further undermining the power of landowners. Nor did repeal represent a comprehensive triumph of free trade. Afterwards, many Conservatives supported free trade half-heartedly if at all, and Britain remained a more protectionist nation than France.

Political and economic reform were complemented by a series of social reforms that changed how the state intervened in people's lives. Throughout the early Victorian period, the ideal role for the state was understood by most people in terms of *laissez-faire* (a French phrase meaning roughly "let it be"), a philosophy in which markets were left to regulate themselves with little or no government intervention, in the belief that this would produce the greatest efficiency and wealth through competition and the promotion of self-reliance over dependence. In 1859, the Scottish reformer Samuel Smiles wrote in his popular book *Self-Help*, "Whatever is done for men or classes, to a certain extent takes away the stimulus and necessity of doing for themselves; and where men are subjected to over-guidance and over-government, the inevitable tendency is to render them comparatively helpless." This view has had a long legacy in British politics, particularly among Conservative politicians. In the 1980s, Prime Minister Margaret Thatcher called for a return to "Victorian values," by which she meant that the welfare state had expanded too far and that a revival of *laissez-faire* ideals was in order.

But was *laissez-faire* really the dominant ideology in the mid-nineteenth century? It is true that the government had reduced its size considerably from the era of the Napoleonic Wars, when military demands had led to an expanded capacity for taxation and administration. Government spending, which had peaked at 23 percent of gross national product (GNP) in

1810, declined to a mere 9 percent by 1900. These *laissez-faire* ideals were supported by the philosophy of "liberalism," which dominated political and economic thought. The "classical liberalism" of the Victorian era meant something very different from how we think of the term today. Victorian liberals considered the main struggle of mankind to be one between the liberty of the individual and the authority of the state, with the former as the priority. As philosopher John Stuart Mill wrote in his *On Liberty* (1859), "The only purpose for which power can be rightfully exercised over any member of a civilized community against his will, is to prevent harm to others." At the same time, the state began to pass new legislation to regulate the economy, gender relations and even sexual practices. This has led to the characterization of the Victorian state as "lumpy." This means simply that the role of the state in regulating social, economic and cultural life happened unevenly in the face of a liberal ideology that favored limited government.

The Victorians, however, rarely lived fully up to the gospel of *laissez-faire* in practice. The degree of government intervention in the economy and society might look small relative to today, but it was much larger than it had been in the eighteenth century. The economic displacement and wealth disparities caused by industrialization were so apparent that investigation and action were determined to be unavoidable. Typically, once a problem manifested itself, it was examined by a government commission that collected statistical data and firsthand testimony. The reports of these commissions helped to create the impetus for government intervention to mitigate the worst horrors of unregulated industrial capitalism. Beginning with the passage of the Factory Act, which restricted the employment of children in textile factories in 1833, a series of legislative initiatives attempted to improve the health and welfare of the lower orders of society.

Even so, there is considerable truth to the view of Victorian Britain as a land of *laissez-faire*. Government intervention was reserved only for situations in which living and working conditions were truly abominable; otherwise, it was perceived as a threat to the economy. Moreover, the enforcement of most parliamentary legislation was left up to local authorities, who rarely possessed the resources to ensure that their conditions were fully met. Truly national initiatives, meanwhile, remained rare: Germany introduced a health insurance scheme for its lowest-income workers in 1883, whereas their British counterparts had to wait until 1911.

Their belief in individual liberty led liberals like Mill to espouse freedom of religion, freedom of speech, freedom of the press and other civil rights. Liberalism also had significant economic aspects, as it held that individual liberty and private property were inextricably linked, with each necessary for the other. Liberals believed that people had to be free to sell their labor, to enter into contracts, to run their businesses, and to save and invest their earnings as they saw fit, with minimal interference from the government. In Britain, liberalism created a state that in many ways gave free reign to private enterprise. But at the same time, classical liberals in the nineteenth century were not the same as libertarians today. Most believed in some degree of state intervention in the form of health, safety, financial and other regulations. They also believed in social equality, and that society should work to better the lot of the poor, not abandon them to their fate. Efforts to combat the problem of poverty, however, were not always seen as benevolent by those whom they affected. In 1834, a new *Poor Law* replaced the system of "outdoor relief" that had existed since the reign of Elizabeth I with workhouses that provided food and shelter, but in very unpleasant conditions. This was because many people had come to believe that poverty was caused by laziness. The workhouses were intended to teach the value of hard work and responsibility through menial and often pointless tasks such as breaking stones. Though entrance was voluntary, workhouses acquired a reputation for the harsh treatment of their inmates. Before public pressure encouraged the easing of restrictive rules in 1842, inmates took all their meals in silence and could not leave or receive visitors except under very special circumstances. Parents had no right to see their children even if they were living in the same workhouse, and husbands and wives were kept strictly separate. A new poor law system based on the English model was introduced in Ireland in 1838 and in Scotland in 1845, though in the latter nation greater discretion was left to local parishes, making the law less restrictive than its English counterpart.

Other social reforms also had an impact on the working classes. We have already heard about the Factory Act of 1833, which prohibited the employment of children under nine in textile factories, while workers under eighteen were limited to twelve hours per day. By modern standards, this seems a minor limitation, but at the time it marked a major change in compelling employers to take at least minimal responsibility for their workers. A push to limit all adults to ten hours of work per day, however, met with resistance, and when the "Ten Hour Act" was passed in 1847, as we have seen, it limited the hours of only women and children. The state also began regulating individual liberty in private life. Homosexuality was a capital offence and the 1828 Offences against the Person Act made prosecutions of sodomy easier to prove in court. The last execution for sodomy was in 1835, though the death penalty remained in place until 1861, when it was replaced by a prison sentence of ten years to life. Same-sex female relationships were not subjected to the same degree of cultural and legal scrutiny. Abortion and access to contraception were also regulated. Though birth control was not illegal, the distribution of information about contraception was deemed "obscene" under a law passed in 1824. The first anti-abortion laws were passed in 1803 in an effort to make attempts to end pregnancy a crime. In 1837, while still illegal, the death penalty for aiding in the abortion of a fetus was removed, but women who sought an abortion could still face a maximum sentence of life in prison.

The first Public Health Act was passed in 1848 to compel the cleaning up of cities through regulating the safety of the water supply, sewers and drains though the creation of a Board of Health. Vaccines for smallpox became compulsory in 1853, which sparked the beginnings of the first anti-vaccine movement. Britain relied mostly on quarantine to control the spread of contagious disease in this period, however. The 1825 Quarantine Act created an apparatus to isolate passengers for a period of several weeks on board ships coming primarily from the Americas and West Indies in order to stop the spread of bubonic plague and yellow fever.

Taken in sum, state regulations began to change the relationship of the individual to the state. They were a response to demands from reformers and a changing economic, social and political landscape and, overall, helped preserve the status quo. The political reforms of the second quarter of the nineteenth century, beginning with the Great Reform Act of 1832, decreased the pressure for more radical alterations to Britain's political and social landscape. As a result, Britain avoided any serious threat of revolution, and the landed elite retained its control over wealth, status and power for another half-century. They were now, however, in an uneasy alliance with the middle classes, who would continue to press for changes in recognition of their growing influence as the drivers of the rapidly growing industrial economy. The working classes, meanwhile, would not be content indefinitely with their lack of full political rights.

Scotland and Wales Under the Union

Early Victorian Britain was marked by disparities among its nations as well as between its genders. On the one hand, there was little interest in Scotland or Wales in political independence. One illustration of this is the surge of Victorian interest in the life of William Wallace, a leader of the resistance to the English King Edward I's attempt to conquer Scotland in the late thirteenth century. Wallace was the subject of poetry, ballads and biographies, and numerous places and landmarks were named after him in Scotland. In 1869, the National Wallace Monument was erected, overlooking the site of his greatest victory at Stirling Bridge. For the Victorian Scots, however, Wallace was not an icon of independence, as he was depicted in the 1995 film *Braveheart*. Rather, his victories against the English invaders were seen as paving the way for a Union of equal partners.

At the same time, however, Scotland continued to encompass considerable linguistic and cultural diversity, as close to 20 percent of the population, concentrated in the Highlands, spoke Gaelic. In Wales, meanwhile, language was even more important as a marker of identity. The Welsh had long been subjected to a process of Anglicization that had attempted to compel the population to adopt the English language and English customs. By the eighteenth century, however, Welsh people had begun to make sustained efforts to preserve their language and culture. During the final decades of the eighteenth century, the rise of Romanticism, which praised the nobility and uncorrupted state of "primitive" peoples, further encouraged the preservation of the Welsh language. Also important was Wales's experience of rapid industrialization, which prevented substantial outmigration. Instead of leaving the country, as was the case in Ireland and the Scottish Highlands, many migrants from rural Wales moved to the South Wales coalfields and other industrial areas. These places thus contained high concentrations of Welsh speakers; in the late nineteenth century, the industrial county of Glamorgan had over 300,000 Welsh speakers, the largest number in the country. In 1901, half of the population of Wales spoke Welsh, whereas the proportion of people in Ireland who could speak Irish had fallen to 15 percent and the percentage of Scots who could speak Gaelic to under 5 percent.

Language was the cause of one of the greatest instances of Anglo-Welsh tensions in the nineteenth century. In 1847, a major controversy erupted over a parliamentary report on Welsh education. The 1200-page report, known as a "Blue Book" because of the color of its cover, not only criticized the deficiencies of Welsh education, but also blamed them on the laziness, dishonesty and immorality of the Welsh people, who were accused of clinging to a backward language and culture. The controversy, which garnered tremendous attention in Wales, came to be known as the "*Treachery of the Blue Books*," a reference to a fifth-century event in which Saxon warriors from England massacred several hundred of their Welsh counterparts at a banquet. In response, nationalists decided to create a celebration of Welsh culture by reviving a medieval festival of poetry and music called an *eisteddfod* (meaning "session"). The first national *eisteddfod* was held at Denbigh in 1860.

In Scotland, too, a romantic vision of the past was embraced, as the Highlands came to occupy a special place in the national imagination. The end of Jacobitism as a political force after 1745 made it possible for Scots, and other Britons, to embrace the region's romantic appeal, and the ban on expressions of Highland culture such as wearing kilts and playing the bagpipes was lifted in 1782. In the early nineteenth century, Sir Walter Scott, whose work focused on the people and scenery of the Highlands, became the best-selling author of the era. Not only Scottish people promoted this romanticized view of their history, however, for British monarchs also played a key role. In 1822, *King George IV made the first visit to Scotland* by a British monarch in over 150 years. Scott, who made the arrangements for the visit, ensured that the Highlands were treated as representing Scottish identity. The ceremonial events showcased the Highland clans, each arrayed in their own distinctive tartan, the first time that particular tartans had been assigned to certain clans. In less than a century, the kilt had thus been transformed from a symbol of the rebelliousness of the Highlands into the Scottish national costume. The King himself even donned a kilt that had been specially made to accommodate his ample girth. In 1848, Queen Victoria purchased the estate of Balmoral in northeastern Scotland as a summer residence and decided that she liked it so much that she spent six weeks there each summer. While in the Highlands, the male members of the royal family regularly dressed in kilts, and the Queen danced to Scottish reels and proclaimed herself to be a Jacobite at heart.

The romantic "Cult of the Highlands," however, could not entirely conceal the dramatic social and economic changes that were taking place in the region. This process originated in the last quarter of the eighteenth century, when what became known as the "Highland Clearances" began. The Clearances resulted from attempts by Highland chieftains and other large landowners to make agriculture more efficient and profitable. This required the displacement of thousands of tenant farmers, which was sometimes carried out by eviction and sometimes by indirect methods such as the raising of rents beyond the ability of the tenants to pay. All over the Highlands, people were replaced by sheep, as Scotland came to supply 40 percent of Britain's wool by 1825. The traditional Highland settlement known as the *baile* ("township"), a collective farm housing and supporting around a hundred people, many of whom were kin, all but disappeared. Small farmers now subsisted on tiny plots of land known as "crofts," forcing them to take on other employment in order to support their families.

Historians continue to debate the morality of the Highland Clearances. Some argue that they were a part of the economic and agricultural changes that were taking place all across Europe, in which societies were becoming more urban and industrial and agriculture was becoming more large-scale and efficient. Others, however, condemn it as a form of "ethnic cleansing." Both approaches oversimplify the issues. The first ignores the specifics of the history and culture of the Scottish Highlands, while the second ignores the fact that it was for the most part Scottish clan chieftains who were responsible for the Clearances, not English landlords. Some factors, meanwhile, were beyond anyone's control: bad weather made for a series of poor harvests in the late eighteenth and early nineteenth centuries, at the same time as the population of the Highlands was increasing. Nor were ordinary Highlanders always simply victims of the Clearances, as they often abandoned their traditional ways of life voluntarily, attracted by the promise of a better future elsewhere.

Whatever their morality, the Clearances forever changed the Scottish Highlands, which became one of the most sparsely populated regions of Europe. In 1831, the population peaked at 200,000, or 8.5 percent of the total population of Scotland. By 1931, it had fallen to 127,000, or 2.6 percent of the Scottish population. By comparison, the populations of the Netherlands and Belgium, which are roughly the same size as the Highlands, were around 8 million each in 1930. Even the sheep eventually disappeared: by the late nineteenth century, it was cheaper to import wool and lamb from Australia and New Zealand. Highland land was then mostly converted to sporting estates that were visited by the British upper classes to shoot grouse and deer. Meanwhile, the Highlanders' way of life, which had remained largely unchanged for a thousand years or more, was all but wiped out. The Highlanders did not passively accede to these devastating changes. In the early 1880s, a series of poor harvests left many crofters destitute. This led to the "Crofter's War," the greatest crisis in the Highlands since the Jacobite Rebellion of 1745, in which tenants refused to pay their rents and formed a Highland Land League. Their efforts resulted in legislation that gave crofters rights of fair rent and secure tenure, as well as the establishment of a Crofter's Commission to adjust rents when necessary. This did little, however, to stop the decline in the population of the Highlands. It is ironic that, at the same time as the Highlands were being celebrated in romantic style for their distinctive identity, that identity was being destroyed in reality.

Figures 5.3 and 5.4   Figure 5.3 is John Frederick Lewis's painting *Highland Hospitality* from 1832. The painting offers a highly romanticized view of Highland life in the mid-nineteenth century. Figure 5.4 shows the reality of Highland life at the time. It depicts the remains of a shieling, or cottage, that was abandoned during the Highland Clearances in the nineteenth century. The house was located near the town of Annat in Wester Ross, one of the most rugged and remote parts of the Highlands. Efforts were made to resettle the population in coastal fishing villages, but the scheme failed when the herring deserted the local waters, forcing many people to emigrate.

Figure 5.3 reproduced courtesy of the Yale Center for British Art, Paul Mellon Collection; Figure 5.4 reproduced courtesy of Graham Lewis.

Ireland Under the Union: Repeal and Famine

While the Welsh and the Scots expressed their nationalism primarily in cultural terms, in Ireland events unfolded in a way that created greater pressure for political independence from the United Kingdom. While Catholic Emancipation had gained an important political right for Irish Catholics in 1829, it did not address Ireland's social and economic problems. The Irish population doubled from 4 million in 1760 to 8 million in 1841, making it the most densely populated country in western Europe. At the same time, Ireland, in contrast to a rapidly urbanizing and industrializing Britain, remained overwhelmingly rural and agricultural; as late as 1870, only 15 percent of the Irish population lived in towns with more than 5000 inhabitants.

As we have seen, agricultural innovation in Britain in the last quarter of the eighteenth century had led to the creation of larger, more efficient farms. In Ireland, however, farms remained small, and there was little incentive to innovate, as farmers aspired only to feed their families, not to make large profits. Plots of land were divided and subdivided across succeeding generations, forcing many people to exist on small, marginal plots of land or without land at all as agricultural laborers. Many Irish landlords, meanwhile, were substantially indebted by the early nineteenth century and thus lacked the capital to consolidate their holdings. The west of Ireland in particular remained a land of subsistence agriculture that increasingly relied upon the potato, a cheap and easy-to-grow source of nutrition that could be produced efficiently on small plots. By the 1840s, almost 40 percent of the Irish population was dependent on the potato.

If Ireland's economy and society looked increasingly distinct from other parts of the United Kingdom, so did its system of governance. Although Ireland was represented in the Parliament in London, many historians have argued that its status under the Union is best understood as colonial or quasi-colonial. Over the course of the century, British administrators, regardless of their political outlook, tended to view the Irish as a subject "native" people rather than as equal partners in the Union, and Ireland was governed in ways that resembled the colonial world more than the rest of the United Kingdom. Unlike either Scotland or Wales, the Irish government had a separate executive, which was headed by a lord lieutenant as the Crown's top representative. Ireland's government became more centralized at an earlier date and intervened in Irish society to a greater degree than in Britain. While at times this benefitted Irish people, notably through the establishment of a comprehensive national educational system, officials were also more willing to apply coercive measures such as the suspension of *habeas corpus* in order to quash dissent. In the late nineteenth century, 25,000 soldiers were stationed in Ireland, far more than in any British colony except India. While the police in Britain did not carry firearms, the Irish Constabulary was an armed, centralized, paramilitary force that was responsible not only for combating crime, but also for suppressing agrarian protest and monitoring political activity. In 1867 the force was given the title of "Royal" for its role in defeating an uprising by Irish republican revolutionaries known as the Fenians.

Ireland under the Union also served as a "laboratory for empire," and a number of Ireland's government institutions were exported to British colonies. The office of viceroy of India (established 1858) was based on the Irish lord lieutenancy. Similarly, the Order of the Star of India (1861), bestowed upon loyal Indian aristocrats, was modelled upon the Order of St. Patrick, which lord lieutenants awarded to members of the Anglo-Irish elite from the late eighteenth century onward. Irish land reform acts, which increasingly recognized the traditional rights of tenants, helped inspire colonial legislation such as the Bengal Tenancy Act of

1885, which sought to extend similar protection to Indian peasants. The Irish Constabulary was regarded as the premier police force of the Empire and a model for many colonial forces. In the words of David Cannadine, Ireland's government provided a "proconsular prototype" for colonies across the British Empire.

While some Irish people sought to take advantage of opportunities offered by the connection with imperial Britain, many were unhappy with Ireland's subordinate place in the Union. Following Catholic Emancipation, Daniel O'Connell and his supporters in Parliament worked towards the repeal of the Act of Union and the return of an independent Parliament to Dublin. O'Connell's Repeal Association held mass meetings, dubbed "monster meetings" by the press, which drew crowds numbering in the hundreds of thousands. Yet there was a crucial difference between the campaign for Catholic Emancipation and the repeal movement. In the 1820s, O'Connell had been able to draw upon the support of roughly half of the members in the House of Commons and a substantial minority in the House of Lords, who sympathized with his claim of discrimination against Catholics. In the repeal campaign, however, he had virtually no support from Parliament, as few MPs wished to see the Union broken up. O'Connell was unwilling to risk bloodshed by using more aggressive tactics in the face of government bans on large meetings, and gradually his repeal movement lost momentum.

O'Connell died in 1847 with his goal of an Irish Parliament in Dublin unfulfilled, but the failure of repeal did not mark the end of the debate over Ireland's place in the Union. For by that point, Ireland was experiencing a catastrophic *famine*. The root cause was a blight called *Phytophthora infestans*, which turned potatoes putrid and rotten while they were still in the ground. Borne by spores on the wind, the blight was easily spread, and it soon affected crops throughout Ireland. Between 1845 and 1851, more than 1 million Irish people died of hunger and disease; another million emigrated to avoid starvation. An English Quaker named William Bennett, who visited western Ireland at the height of the famine in 1847, was horrified by the condition of the Irish peasantry. "The scenes of human misery and degradation we witnessed," he wrote, "will haunt my imagination, with the vividness and power of some horrid and tyrannous delusion."

While the famine began as a natural disaster, that only partly explains why so many people suffered within a nation that was at the time the richest and most powerful on earth. The blight struck elsewhere during the mid-nineteenth century, but nowhere was so much of the population dependent on the potato as in Ireland. Ineffective government relief policies also had a major impact. The British government treated the famine as a local rather than a national issue, leaving authorities in Ireland to deal with it as best they could. A final factor was the attitude of Britain's political leadership. Many government officials, such as the undersecretary of the treasury Sir Charles Trevelyan, the man responsible for famine relief, embraced what historians have called a "moralist" stance. Educated Britons believed that the famine was rooted not only in the weaknesses of the Irish agrarian system but in the moral deficiencies of Irish people. Cultural stereotypes, similar to those employed against colonized peoples elsewhere in the Empire, portrayed the Irish "national character" as defective. Irish peasants, contemporary Britons argued, were violent, lazy, stubbornly devoted to primitive and inefficient economic practices and far too dependent on British government assistance.

Describing the famine as an opportunity for "regeneration," Charles Trevelyan and other senior British officials and politicians believed that Ireland's problems could only be corrected through drastic reform. This meant that early relief measures, such as soup kitchens, quickly gave way to works projects that were intended to transform the Irish peasantry into wage laborers. In 1847, a new Irish Poor Law further shifted financial responsibility onto

Irish taxpayers, on the principle that "Irish property should pay for Irish poverty." This led many Irish landlords, who were responsible for paying for poor relief taxes on their tenants' smallholdings, to evict their tenants. This was not always because they were heartless, as many of them were facing financial ruin themselves. In the harsh conditions of the work-house, meanwhile, families were separated, and infectious diseases that were exacerbated by the famine, such as typhus, were rife.

 See document "An English View of the Irish Famine" at www.routledge.com/cw/ barczewski.

The potato blight struck elsewhere in the United Kingdom during the 1840s, most notably in the Scottish Highlands, which, like western Ireland, was a region of poverty and marginal agriculture. There, too, the government's response was limited. Yet Scotland, unlike Ireland, avoided catastrophe. Why? In part, this was because the affected population was much smaller and its diet more varied than that of the potato-dependent Irish. In addition, relief efforts in Scotland were better coordinated, under the auspices of an organization called the Central Board of Management for Highland Relief. Scottish landlords, who were wealthier than their counterparts in Ireland, also assisted their tenants to a much greater degree. Per-haps most importantly, Scotland, unlike Ireland, was urbanizing and industrializing rapidly, more rapidly in fact that any other European nation. A range of jobs was thus available to those who were willing to migrate from the Highlands to Lowland Scotland.

But while the Scottish Highlands avoided mass starvation, the region shared a common fate with Ireland: mass emigration. As we have already seen, in the mid-nineteenth century, a third of the population of the Highlands moved elsewhere. In Ireland, 1.5 million people had already left the country in the thirty years prior to the famine, but after 1845 it became a true "emigration society," in which migration was built into the fabric of rural life.

Immigrants and Refugees 2

Irish Immigration to Britain During and After the Famine

The number of Irish immigrants to Britain was relatively small prior to the potato famine in the 1840s and 1850s. But as the famine's effects intensified, a growing num-ber of Irish people sought employment in England or relief through the English Poor Law system. The port city of Liverpool was the point of arrival for the majority of Irish immigrants. Some went there deliberately to seek employment in the industrial cities of the northwest. Others, however, intended to go on to America or Australia but lacked the funds for the voyage, and so remained in Britain. According to the census of 1851, the number of Irish-born people in Lancashire had doubled to 191,000, com-prising 10 percent of the county's population. Nearly a quarter of Liverpool's popula-tion, meanwhile, was Irish-born. The first wave of Irish immigrants was comprised largely of families, but from the 1860s onwards they tended to be young single men and women who worked as manual laborers and domestic servants. Lacking skills and family support networks, they were extremely vulnerable to economic downturns, and they were forced to live in overcrowded housing in which they were susceptible to outbreaks of epidemic disease; typhus became known as "Irish fever" because so many Irish people suffered from it. Irish immigrants also went to Scotland, where the percentage of the population that was Irish-born increased from 4.8 percent in 1841 to 7.2 percent ten years later. Almost a third of these new arrivals settled in Glasgow, where men found employment on the docks and in coal mines, and women in textile factories. Wales, too, saw an influx of Irish immigrants: nearly 30,000 Irish-born people were registered there in 1861, more than triple the previous number, with many finding employment in the coal mines of South Wales. Because Irish immigrants often lived in poverty and squalid conditions, they were perceived as dirty and lazy and were associated with crime, disorder, drunkenness and violence. But despite the fact that they faced serious discrimination and prejudice, many survived and even flourished in their new home. Later waves of Irish immigration in the twentieth century meant that the Irish remained the largest ethnic group in Britain until the 1970s.

Most of the million Irish people who emigrated during the famine went to the United States and Canada. Bitterness at the British response helped fuel Irish republicanism across the Atlantic, which was later re-exported to Ireland. Immigrants sent funds back to relatives in Ireland and contributed money to the nationalist cause. In 1858, the Irish Republican Brotherhood, a militant republican organization, was founded; an American counterpart, the Fenian Brotherhood, followed the next year. The membership of the Fenians quickly swelled to tens of thousands, but the organization was riddled with government informers, and their actions invariably ended in ignominious defeat. In 1867, a Fenian attempt to invade Canada and an attempted rebellion in Ireland both failed. Despite their lack of success, however, the Fenians re-energized Irish nationalism, and the Anglo-Irish and British political elites recognized that they represented a new force that could not long be ignored.

Self-Rule in the Settlement Colonies

The British Empire experienced significant political change in the early Victorian era. The white settler colonies, including Canada, Australia, New Zealand and South Africa, were not generally viewed as sources of large profits but rather as extensions of the "British world." They each sought increased self-government in the first half of the nineteenth century. The British government was for the most part eager to support these moves towards independence, as they were confident that strong economic ties would survive while the costs of imperial administration declined. They also saw the settler colonies as outlets for surplus population. Emigration from Britain more than doubled in the first half of the nineteenth century, easily outpacing immigration into the country during the same period. These emigrants remained tied to Britain through kinship and a belief that they belonged to a larger British world, but they also sought to establish their own distinctive national identities.

Australia underwent a rapid transformation from penal to settlement colony; the *last convicts arrived* in 1868, but the numbers had been dwindling for decades prior to that date. The Scotsman Lachlan Macquarie, who served as governor from 1810 to 1821, built roads and public buildings, instituted a police force and expanded the wool trade. Sydney became a substantial settlement of 10,000 inhabitants, with cottages, shops, churches and schools, much like an English provincial town. By 1850, the white population had reached 400,000. As the colony's ambitions expanded, so did its desire for increased independence. Australia was organized into six separate colonies for administrative purposes: the mainland territories of New South Wales, Queensland, Western Australia and Victoria, along with the geographically noncontiguous islands of New Zealand and Tasmania. All but sparsely populated Western Australia were granted "responsible government" in the 1850s, in which they acquired autonomy over local matters while the British government retained authority over defense, foreign policy and international trade. The attitudes of nineteenth-century Australians towards the mother country were complex: many people saw themselves as British and attempted to recreate British social and cultural institutions, but others became fiercely nationalist as they sought to create their own distinctive Australian identity.

Canada followed a similar path. "British North America," its official title, was a drain on British finances, costing £2.4 million annually in the 1830s. Its vast territory contained less than a million inhabitants, who produced exports that were of minimal value and purchased few imports from the mother country. To make matters worse, there were constant tensions between Anglo- (Upper) and French (Lower) Canadians, which made the colony extremely difficult to govern. Despite having been part of British North America since 1763, the 450,000 French Canadians remained isolated by their language and Catholic religion. In 1837, the Montreal-born lawyer Louis-Joseph Papineau launched a rebellion in an effort to achieve French-Canadian independence. It was quickly suppressed, but it was clear that French Canadians would continue to be a thorn in the British side.

British "loyalists" who also wanted increased self-rule were emboldened by the French revolt, and Upper Canada attempted its own rebellion in 1837. It, too, was soon quelled, but the British government recognized that Canada was becoming a problem. In 1838, Lord Durham, the former ambassador to Russia, was dispatched to find a solution. The result was the *Durham Report* of 1839, which as the historian Piers Brendon has written, "became a handbook of white colonial development under the Union Jack." Durham comprehended that white settlers were generally proud to be part of the world's most powerful empire and that they appreciated the economic and other advantages that this brought, but they also resented having little say in their own government. They saw rebellion as a genuinely loyal and patriotic act that was intended to restore true British principles of liberty and parliamentary democracy. Durham argued that the key to retaining the settlers' loyalty was to bind them together more closely. Upper and Lower Canada should be merged so as to diminish French separatism, while increased immigration from Britain would also help to make Canada more "British." The construction of a railway network, meanwhile, would link Canada's huge geographical expanse more closely together. But at the same time, the Canadians had to be trusted with greater political autonomy; otherwise, they would continue to chafe against British rule. Given greater control over their internal affairs, they would in fact become more loyal, as their participation in the British Empire would be seen as voluntary rather than coerced. It took another two decades, but in 1867 the British North America Act established Canada (which at the time consisted of Ontario and Quebec as well as the provinces of New Brunswick and Nova Scotia) as a largely self-governing dominion within the British Empire.

South Africa presented a more complex case. The Cape Colony, the territory surrounding the Cape of Good Hope, had been seized by the British from the Dutch in 1795 in order to keep this vital strategic location from falling into French hands. It was formally annexed as a British colony in 1806. The British began encouraging emigration to South Africa in the 1820s, but this led to conflicts with the Dutch settlers, known as the Boers, from the Dutch word for "farmer." In the 1830s, the Boers became increasingly dissatisfied with the imposition of the English language and a British legal system, and a group of 12,000 – known as the *Voortrekkers* – migrated across the Orange River into the territory of Natal in what became known as the "Great Trek." The British annexed Natal in 1843, but they were willing to allow the Boers to remain there so long as they caused no trouble. They even granted them limited autonomy over the two territories of the Orange Free State and the Transvaal. The British-dominated Cape Colony, meanwhile, was given its own elected assembly in 1853.

Though self-rule was achieved in the settler colonies with minimal European bloodshed, it was far from nonviolent. The policy of white minority rule ensured that conflicts with indigenous populations over land and sovereignty continued. Between 300,000 and a million aborigines lived in Australia at the time the British arrived in the late eighteenth century. By the 1880s, disease, loss of land and violence had reduced their population to 80,000. The legal system was firmly on the side of the whites, who were rarely punished for massacring aborigines. By the 1870s, virtually all of the agriculturally viable land in Australia had been appropriated by whites, with the few remaining aborigines pushed to marginal areas or forced to seek employment as menial laborers in the white settlements.

In New Zealand, the British made a gesture towards obtaining the consent of the indigenous Maori. In 1840, 500 Maori leaders signed the *Treaty of Waitangi*. The signatories, however, had very different ideas of the contents of the treaty. The British thought that they had gained indigenous acquiescence to their sovereignty over New Zealand. The Maori believed that they were gaining protection from settler incursion and access to British goods, while still maintaining control over their own affairs. The surge in the settler population from 3000 to 100,000 between 1840 and 1860 made it clear what the British had intended when they drew up the treaty. In 1846, the Colonial Office in London declared that it could not uphold the protection of Maori land rights that the Treaty of Waitangi had guaranteed. By this point, some Maori had already taken up arms to resist further British incursion. The conflict escalated into open warfare in the 1860s; Maori forces fought against 18,000 British troops sent to quell the uprising. Afterwards, vast amounts of land were confiscated by the British. This proved devastating to the survival of the Maori, and by 1870 their population had declined to 37,000.

In South Africa, the British used military force to push the Xhosa and Zulu peoples away from ever-expanding settler territory. After a long series of bloody and brutal conflicts, both were decisively defeated in 1879. In Canada, the indigenous peoples, comprised of hundreds of different groups that are now collectively known as the "First Nations," were subjected to a policy of forced assimilation that sought to eradicate them as a separate culture. Children were removed from their families and sent to residential schools, usually operated by Christian religious denominations, where they were forbidden from speaking their own languages and practicing their own religions. Up to two-thirds of these children died due to poor sanitation, overcrowded accommodations and inadequate medical care.

Imperial Expansion

Beyond the settlement colonies, some historians have argued that in the first half of the nineteenth century there was little interest in imperial expansion, and that any expansion that occurred was a piecemeal, unplanned and accidental process rather than a coordinated, deliberate effort. It was true in this era that there was no concerted, government-backed drive to increase the size of the Empire; nor was there much sustained public interest in Britain's overseas colonies. But even so, an export-driven economy that constantly sought new markets and the re-emergence of European rivalries as the concert of Europe lost influence frequently led to bellicose action, often couched in terms of a "defense" of Britain's strategic and economic interests. In an age in which British enthusiasm for formal colonization was supposedly minimal, the Empire expanded an average of 100,000 square miles each year.

The majority of this expansion occurred in Australia and India but also included the territories that had been acquired during the Napoleonic Wars. In 1821, three of the latter acquisitions, the Gambia, the Gold Coast and Sierra Leone, were united as British West Africa. The Mediterranean possessions of Malta and the Ionian Islands, meanwhile, marked the early stirrings of interference with the Ottoman Empire, which over the next century would lead to major British intervention in North Africa and Asia. Though Java and the Spice Islands were given back to the Netherlands in 1815 in order to bolster Dutch power against the French, Southeast Asian markets had now been opened to British trade, and colonization soon followed. The British established sovereignty over Singapore in 1824; two years later it was incorporated into the colony known as the Straits Settlements, in combination with Dinding, Malacca and Penang. Aden, a port strategically located at the entrance to the Red Sea in what is today Yemen, was seized in 1839, and the Falkland Islands off the coast of Argentina became a British colony in 1840.

In South Asia, major territorial expansion was achieved through warfare. This goes against the conventional perception of Britain as a non-militaristic, or even anti-militaristic, state. In reality, however, as Bruce Collins has written, "The British impact on the wider world and the extension of empire cannot be understood without grasping the extent and frequency of the British use of military and naval force." On India's northeastern border, the Anglo-Burmese War of 1824 to 1826 gave Britain control of the province of Assam and eliminated Burma as a threat to British dominance in the region. In 1852, a second war led to the annexation of Lower Burma. In India, the northwestern province of Sind was conquered in 1843, followed by two *wars against the Sikhs* between 1845 and 1849 that resulted in British control of the Punjab in north India. In the next decade, the provinces of Berar and Awadh were annexed in 1853 and 1856 respectively. The British also fought an unsuccessful war in Afghanistan between 1839 and 1842 in an effort to prevent Russian incursion into India. Only one person survived from the invasion force of 4500 troops and 12,000 camp followers as it *retreated from Kabul* in January 1842. It would take another war in the late 1870s for Britain to secure control of Afghanistan.

Conquest in Africa moved slowly during this period, but it provided the foundation for more rapid expansion during the last third of the nineteenth century. A war against the Ashanti people from 1824 to 1831, for example, served as a basis for the imposition of British power in West Africa. This vast and still expanding empire required a large number of people to oversee its administration and defense. The distance from London often meant that local authorities exercised a great deal of power over their subjects. Governing so much newly acquired territory led to the rise of a new breed of colonial bureaucrats, who were part of the civil service and received special training for colonial duty. The British population, however, could never supply enough manpower to rule such a vast empire directly. Britain was therefore forced to rule its colonies by a variety of means and methods. In India, the East India Company held sway until 1858, but there remained 560 princely states in which British officials known as "residents" advised the local maharajahs. As this example illustrates, governing the Empire was not an exclusively British matter, for it also relied on the cooperation of colonial subjects. To ensure this, the British used a combination of brute force, assertions of cultural superiority and local cooperation. Although the upper ranks of the East India Company's civil service were reserved for Europeans, British authorities came increasingly to rely on Indians to collect taxes and perform day-to-day administrative functions, particularly in rural areas. The British also depended on them for information that would help control their imperial subjects and subvert potential security threats.

The Presence of Empire 4

The Irish in the Empire

We have already seen how Scotland served as the "arsenal of empire" in the era of British expansion that began with the Seven Years' War. In the first half of the nineteenth century, the Irish assumed a similar role. Previously, both the British Army and the East India Company had shunned Irish Catholic manpower, fearing that the loyalties of Irish troops were suspect. By 1800, however, Irish recruits were eagerly sought to secure and garrison Britain's expanding empire. They were prized because, thanks to their potato-based diet, they were healthier and on average 1 to 2 inches taller than their British counterparts. Catholic Emancipation in 1829 enabled Irish Catholics to hold commissions as officers, although their numbers were always fewer than their Protestant countrymen. Despite its hardships, military service in Britain's expanding empire offered an escape from grinding poverty for young Irishmen, many of whom were Gaelic speakers from the west of Ireland. By the 1840s, close to half of the British Army and the East India Company's European soldiers were Irish. Also in the mid-nineteenth century, large numbers of middle-class Irishmen entered imperial service. Irish doctors made up more than a quarter of the new Indian Medical Service, established in 1855, and in 1857, the year of the Indian Rebellion, Irishmen made up almost 40 percent of new recruits to the Indian Civil Service. These imperial servants were influenced by Ireland's distinctive, quasi-colonial status within the United Kingdom. Many Irish doctors had lived among and treated victims of famine and malnutrition in Ireland and tended to be sensitive to similar suffering among India's population, while Irish administrators helped to implement land reform legislation that gave greater security to tenants.

Britain's authority over its "informal empire," which included parts of the Mediterranean, the Ottoman Empire, South America and China, was even less clear. The Chinese permitted British merchants to use only one port, Canton (now Guangzhou), and accepted only one commodity, silver, in exchange for goods such as silks, porcelain and tea. The British government grew increasingly concerned that the China trade was draining the Treasury of its silver reserves, and so the British "hongs," or merchants who were authorized to operate in Canton, turned to another medium of exchange, opium, which was cheaply produced in India. The Chinese government had banned the import of opium in 1796, but many customs officials accepted bribes in return for turning a blind eye. By the 1830s, up to 90 percent of young Chinese males in coastal areas were regular opium smokers, and there were as many as 12 million addicts. Business productivity plummeted, public services all but ceased to function, and the standard of living dropped. In 1839, a frustrated Chinese government ordered Canton to be closed to all foreign merchants. The Royal Navy intervened and secured an easy victory against the Chinese fleet in the *First Opium War*. In 1842, the British forced the Chinese to accede to a treaty that gave them control of much of the coast. A second treaty the following year ceded the island of Hong Kong to Britain and opened four additional "treaty ports" besides Canton (Amoy, Foochow, Shanghai and Ningbo) to foreign merchants. The Chinese government continued to resist the terms of the treaties, however, and a second Opium War erupted in 1856. This time, the British launched a land offensive from Hong Kong that resulted in the looting and destruction of the emperor's Summer Palace in Peking (now Beijing). The Chinese were forced to open four more treaty ports (Hankou, Niuzhuang, Danshui and Nanjing) to foreign merchants and to allow Christian missionaries to proselytize freely. They were also compelled to permit the emigration of indentured Chinese laborers to North America, where they played a major role in the building of the transcontinental railway network.

Conclusion

The early Victorian era saw Britain reach a new height of global economic and imperial power. This was driven by industrialization, which occurred first in Britain, and by the expansion of the Empire that began with the acquisition of territory in the wake of the Napoleonic Wars and continued throughout the first half of the nineteenth century. The resilience and stability of the political system, meanwhile, was demonstrated by the passage of reform in 1832; the electorate was expanded and anomalies eliminated, but the system of limited democracy in which the male elite dominated remained largely intact. In fact, it had been strengthened by the addition of middle-class support, gained through the expansion of the franchise in 1832 and confirmed by the repeal of the Corn Law in 1846.

At the same time, however, the 1830s and 1840s were difficult decades, as the developments detailed earlier all engendered serious debate. This was an age, as the noted British historian Asa Briggs once wrote, in which people were "ranged against each other . . . often in bitterness." In the early part of the period, the struggle over parliamentary reform divided the political universe, and in the end the debate over the repeal of the Corn Laws did the same. Chartism, meanwhile, raised even more difficult questions about Britain's political future, questions that would continue to resonate in the future, even if it was to be decades before they were directly addressed. Regarding the economy, it was now clear that industrialization had changed the country's physical and social landscape, and not always for the better. While the standard of living for some people had improved, others found their lives disrupted and displaced by the upheavals and alterations it engendered. For the first time, the word "class" became a common way to categorize contemporary society. In Scotland and Wales, political nationalism diminished, but the defense of their distinctive cultural identities intensified. Ireland, meanwhile, experienced a catastrophic famine that was exacerbated by British attitudes and government policies.

The expanded empire saw a variety of challenges: growing demands for self-rule from the settlement colonies; a need for an ever-larger military, naval and administrative presence that could defend existing and conquer new territory; and tensions with those parts of the world that were not content to be "informally" dominated by the British. A time of political change and economic and imperial expansion, the early Victorian years showed that dynamism could coexist with underlying stability and that Britain could absorb change while preserving the political and social order. They also showed that its growing economic and global power brought new responsibilities and challenges at home and abroad.

Bibliography

Allen, Robert C., *The British Industrial Revolution in Global Perspective* (2009)
Chase, Malcolm, *Chartism: A New History* (2007)
Clark, Anna, *The Struggle for the Breeches* (1997)

Collins, Bruce, *War and Empire: The Expansion of Britain 1790–1830* (2010)

Donnelly, Jr, James S., *The Great Irish Potato Famine* (2001)

Durbach, Nadja, *Bodily Matters: The Anti-Vaccination Movement in England* (2005)

Gaunt, Richard A., *Sir Robert Peel: The Life and Legacy* (2010)

Jones, Gareth Stedman, *The Languages of Class: Studies in English Working-Class History 1832–1982* (1984)

Mandler, Peter, *Liberty and Authority in Victorian Britain* (2006)

McMahon, Cian, *The Coffin Ship: Life and Death at Sear During the Great Irish Famine* (2021)

Mokyr, Joel, *The Enlightened Economy: An Economic History of Britain 1700–1850* (2012)

Price, Richard, *Making Empire: Colonial Encounters and the Creation of Imperial Rule in Nineteenth-Century Africa* (2008)

Richards, Eric, *The Highland Clearances* (2013)

Roberts, Gwyneth Tyson, *The Language of the Blue Books: The Perfect Instrument of Empire* (1998)

Satia, Priya, *Empire of Guns: The Violent Making of the Industrial Revolution* (2018)

Schonhardt-Bailey, Cheryl, *From the Corn Laws to Free Trade: Interests, Ideas, and Institutions in Historical Perspective* (2006)

6 The Mid-Victorians and Their World

Topics covered

- Improvements in the speed of transportation and communication
- Great Exhibition of 1851
- Population growth and urbanization
- Emergence of system of free, secular, public education
- Religion and Darwin's impact
- Legal changes in women's status and the doctrine of "separate spheres"
- Crimean War
- American Civil War
- Indian Rebellion of 1857
- Rivalry between Disraeli and Gladstone
- Reform Act of 1867

Timeline

1848	Cholera epidemic in London; first Public Health Act
1850	Don Pacifico affair
1851	Great Exhibition
1851	Henry Mayhew's *London Labour and the London Poor*
1854	Britain enters Crimean War
1857	Indian Rebellion
1858	"Great Stink" in London
1859	Charles Darwin's *On the Origin of Species*
1861	Outbreak of American Civil War
1861	Death of Prince Albert
1865	Eyre Crisis
1867	Second Reform Act
1869	First women's college founded at Cambridge
1870	Forster Act
1870	Married Women's Property Act

DOI: 10.4324/9781003284758-6

Introduction

After 1850, Britain moved into what historians refer to as the "mid-Victorian period," which lasted until around 1870. These years are traditionally associated with an economic "boom," in which the difficulties and uneven effects of early industrialization largely dissipated and Britain's impressive manufacturing productivity at long last translated into prosperity for the working classes whose labor had made it possible. In 1851, real wages were 28 percent higher than they had been in 1761. Even if recent research shows that the economic gains were uneven and continued to be interrupted by slumps, there is no doubt that the two decades after 1850 were more socially harmonious and less politically divisive than the two that had come before. The dominant political figure of the age, Lord Palmerston, declared in a speech to the House of Commons in 1850:

> We have shown the example of a nation in which every class of society accepts with cheerfulness that lot which Providence has assigned to it, while at the same time each individual of each class is constantly trying to raise himself in the social scale not by injustice and wrong, not by violence and illegality, but by persevering good conduct and by the steady and energetic exertion of the moral and intellectual faculties with which the Creator has endowed him.

By 1870, the combination of reforms that expanded the electorate, married women's rights and free public education for boys and girls moved British society at least slightly towards greater equality. Although armed conflict was frequent in Britain's colonies, there were no major European wars, contributing to a sense of peace and prosperity at home. This stability allowed the mid-Victorians to develop confidence and a faith in progress that became, in hindsight, characteristics of the age.

   The period was not without its anxieties, however, many of which related to Britain's global position. By the end of the mid-Victorian years, other nations were catching up to the lead in industrial productivity that Britain had enjoyed for the previous three-quarters of a century. Of particular significance was the unification of Germany in 1871, which marked the arrival of a larger and more populous European rival; it would not be long before its economic, military and imperial competition with Britain heated up. Russia, meanwhile, continued to threaten the northwestern frontier of India, and its increasingly active engagement in the Ottoman lands of eastern Europe and the Near and Middle East led to the most serious conflict of the era, the *Crimean War* of 1854–6, which worryingly demonstrated that the quality of Britain's military forces had declined significantly since the Napoleonic era. Equally anxiety inducing was the Indian Rebellion of 1857, the first major uprising against British colonial authority since the American Revolution.

A Smaller World

In the 1850s, the new sense of economic and social stability led to a broader focus on Britain's place in the world. Britons were more conscious of that place because technological innovations and improvements in transportation were creating what the historian Peter Hugill describes as "the most remarkable time-space compression in human history." Within Britain, the most vivid symbol of change was the railway. The first steam-powered passenger railway line connected Stockton and Darlington in 1825. By 1830, trains between Manchester and Liverpool traveled at 30 miles per hour, two to three times the rate of a stagecoach.

The work of the engineer Isambard Kingdom Brunel (1806–59) embodied the shrinking Victorian world. Brunel is probably best known for the design and construction of the Great Western Railway, a 118-mile-long route between Bristol and London that provided the foundation for a national railway network. He also helped to design railways in Australia and India. By 1900, 19,000 miles of track carried over a billion passengers annually, traveling at speeds upwards of 70 miles an hour. The speed of travel and communication increased not only within Britain, however, but also between Britain and the rest of the world. In 1800, crossing the Atlantic by sail had taken forty days or more; by 1900, it took a steamship only five. When Queen Victoria came to the throne in 1837, a letter from London to San Francisco took nine months to reach its destination; by the time of her death in 1901, the telegraph could deliver a message between the two cities in minutes. "The world is growing so small that every patch of territory begins to be looked upon as a stray farm is by a county magnate," commented the *Times* in 1874.

That "smaller" world was clearly having a significant, and for the most part beneficial, impact on Britain. In the mid-1860s, Britain's share of world trade peaked at an impressive 25 percent, and its share of global manufacturing exports at around 40 percent. A third of the world's shipping flew the Union Jack; when the Suez Canal opened in 1869, four-fifths of the ships that passed through it were British. This global commercial dominance was on full display at the *Great Exhibition* of 1851, a precursor of twentieth-century world's fairs. The Exhibition celebrated Britain as the "workshop of the world" and the center of a vast empire. Housed in a building called the Crystal Palace because it was constructed of enormous glass panels supported by an iron framework, it was greeted with tremendous enthusiasm when it opened in London's Hyde Park on the 1st of May. Inside the glass walls was a vast collection of 100,000 inventions and objects from around the world. The numerous displays from the Empire highlighted Britain's rapidly expanding global power, while the products of British industry were presented as a boon for the consumer. Social tensions, meanwhile, were muted. Cheaper admission days were provided so that the working class could see how their labor had helped to build this prosperous new economy. The organizers bragged about their good behavior, claiming that in other European cities, many of which had been convulsed by revolution in 1848, it would have been dangerous to bring so many people together in one place.

The Great Exhibition was by all measures a smashing success. Over 6 million visitors – one in five Britons – traveled to London to see it. The celebratory and self-congratulatory tone of the Exhibition, however, masked a variety of conflicts and tensions in Victorian society. Though in the end the crowds who came to London were peaceful, the fears that they would be intent on riot and revolution were real, and 400 policemen were stationed near the Crystal Palace in consequence. The triumph of manufacturing and mass consumer society that the Exhibition represented was not seen by everyone as a wholly positive development, as many people feared that industrial modernity and urbanization were undermining the traditional, secure, rural world in which they saw Britain's greatness as being rooted. Perhaps the biggest tension that was embodied by the Great Exhibition was the conflict between nationalism and internationalism. On the one hand, the Exhibition displayed the superiority of Britain's political system, economy, society and culture by showing how they had combined to create the most prosperous, productive, harmonious and stable nation in the world. But on the other, it celebrated the material progress of the entire world by bringing together inventions from every country and promoting peace, the exchange of ideas and a global spirit of cooperation. The liberal reformer Richard Cobden declared that the Exhibition would "break down the barriers that have separated the people of different nations."

Figure 6.1 The transept of the Crystal Palace during the Great Exhibition, showing three tiers of exhibits on the sides with larger objects in the center. The image gives a sense of the Exhibition's scale. Mayall, J. E. (John Jabez Edwin), 1813–1901.

Reproduced courtesy of the Wellcome Collection.

In truth, the Great Exhibition represented a view of the world that was both global and Anglocentric, because it was geographically expansive but centered on the idea of British dominance. We often think of nationalism and imperialism as distinct and conflicting concepts, but for the mid-Victorians they were mutually reinforcing. The Victorians embraced the idea of the Pax Britannica, which held that the British Empire would help to keep the world peaceful. At the Great Exhibition, fifty-six British colonies, all except Gambia and Gibraltar, featured displays. Britons did not see these displays as reflecting the colonies' own artistic and manufacturing achievements, but rather as extensions of the mother country that bound them all together. The superiority of the British system would not have been in doubt to most Victorians, who believed that they had the right and obligation to rule over non-European peoples.

 See document "A Visit to the Great Exhibition of 1851" at www.routledge.com_cw_barczewski.

The Great Exhibition was an important event not only because of its overwhelming popularity, but because it embodied in physical form Britain's conception of the world in the nineteenth century. This conception was increasingly global, in that it encompassed a wide variety of peoples and places, many of them far distant from Britain. But at the same time, it was increasingly informed by the assumption that British economic philosophies and political systems were superior. In the second half of the nineteenth century, this was very much how Britons saw the world.

In reality, the age of Pax Britannica did not live up to its ideals regarding the pursuit of peace. Almost 200 small-scale wars and two larger-scale ones in the Crimea and South Africa helped to quadruple the size of the Empire during Queen Victoria's reign from 1837 to 1901. This is not surprising given that political leaders from both of the main parties supported imperial expansion, albeit in different ways and for different reasons. While Conservatives embraced territorial expansion more overtly and aggressively, Liberals took a more providential view, believing that the British Empire had, in the words of W. E. Gladstone, a "mighty mission" to defend "the cause of public right, and of rational freedom." This tension between ideals and reality was noted by contemporary observers. The writer Rudyard Kipling sardonically referred to Britain's many "savage wars of peace" in his poem "The White Man's Burden" (1899).

Urbanization

At the time of the first British census in 1801, the population of England, Scotland and Wales was 10.5 million, while that of Ireland, which was not included in the census, was between 4 and 5 million. By 1901, the population had increased to 41.5 million. If France's population had grown at the same rate as Britain's in the nineteenth century, today it would have a population of around 150 million, instead of its current 66 million. Equally as significant as the rapid rate of Britain's population growth were changes in where people lived. In general, there was movement away from rural, agricultural areas such as the southwest of England, the Scottish Highlands and North Wales, and towards London, the southeast of England, and industrial regions such as the North of England and South Wales. In the census of 1851, for the first time the majority of the population was classified as "urban," meaning that they lived in towns with more than 2500 inhabitants. (We probably would not call a town of 2500 "urban" today, but over a third of the population lived in towns larger than 20,000, which by the standards of the time was a big place.) By 1901, 77 percent of Britain's population lived in urban areas. By comparison, only one in five French and German people lived in cities in the mid-nineteenth century, and it was not until 1921 that the majority of Americans were classified as "urban."

Over the course of Queen Victoria's sixty-four-year reign, the number of cities in England and Wales with a population greater than 100,000 increased from six to twenty-three. London, the largest city in the world, had less than a million inhabitants in 1800 and almost 7 million by century's end. The industrial cities of the North of England and central Scotland also saw phenomenal rates of growth. Manchester's population increased from 40,000 in 1770 to 600,000 in 1900, while Bradford in Yorkshire grew from 6000 in 1801 to nearly 300,000 by 1911. In Scotland, Glasgow's population almost quadrupled from 200,000 in 1830 to 760,000 by 1900.

This rapid growth transformed Victorian cities into unhealthy places. Careful planning had ensured the elegance and orderliness of **Georgian** towns such as Bath or the New Town of Edinburgh, but their Victorian successors were filthy, polluted and overcrowded. In the 1850s, half the families in Newcastle-upon-Tyne in northeastern England lived in single rooms, the vast majority of which lacked indoor plumbing. In the summer of 1858, London was affected by the "*Great Stink*," which resulted from raw sewage being carried into the Thames. The stench was so bad that people refused to cross the river by boat, and the curtains of the House of Commons had to be soaked in bleach so that Parliament could carry out its business. These unsanitary conditions had predictable consequences for people's health. In 1851, a child born in Liverpool had a life expectancy of only twenty-six, while one born in rural Devon could expect to live to fifty-seven. The municipal corporations that governed cities invested little in urban infrastructure such as sewers and drainage, and water-borne diseases such as cholera and typhoid killed thousands. Even the royal family was not safe: Queen Victoria's husband *Prince Albert* died of typhoid in 1861.

A number of contemporary observers attempted to draw attention to the problems. Edwin Chadwick's *Report on the Sanitary Conditions of the Labouring Population* (1842) detailed the horrific state of urban housing. At the end of the decade, the journalist and reformer Henry Mayhew published a series of articles in the *Morning Chronicle* that described the horrors of life in London's slums. In 1851, the articles were *collected and published* in a single volume entitled *London Labour and the London Poor*. Mayhew's revelations shocked many people. "Do you devour those marvellous revelations of the inferno of misery, of wretchedness, that is smouldering under our feet?" wrote Mayhew's fellow journalist Douglas Jerrold to a friend in 1850. The French artist Gustave Doré presented a similarly grim view of the capital's poverty in the collection of 180 engravings that were published in *London: A Pilgrimage*, with text by the journalist Blanchard Jerrold, in 1872.

Eventually, the appalling conditions of Victorian cities created pressure for change. In 1848, a *cholera epidemic* killed 21,000 people, leading to the passage of the Public Health Act, which placed the control of the water supply, sewerage and drainage under a General Board of Health. Two Smoke Nuisance Abatement Acts in 1853 and 1856 attempted to curb pollution, and the Sanitary Act of 1866 gave local authorities the power to carry out sanitary inspections, demolish slums and remove other impediments to public health. Two further Public Health Acts in 1872 and 1875 gave local governments additional powers to improve sanitation. These efforts met with considerable success, and by the end of the nineteenth century urban life expectancies equalled their rural counterparts. Cities had become not only healthier places to live by the end of the mid-Victorian period, but also culturally richer ones. Birmingham led the way; there, the mayor Joseph Chamberlain, who was elected in 1873, embraced an urban activism that was so fervent it came to be called a "civic gospel." Other cities followed suit and built schools, parks, art galleries and other public amenities.

The long struggle to improve Victorian cities shows the continuing dominance of *laissez-faire* economic philosophies, in which government intervention was kept to a minimum. But the eventual emergence of a new vision of civic government shows that by the 1870s the notion of the common good was increasingly being used as a justification for expanded public oversight. On a national level, the government was now more willing to authorize actions to improve people's lives, though it did not generally require them or provide a means of enforcement. In the 1860s and 1870s, a series of reforms led to increased industrial regulation, while anti-poverty efforts continued to intensify. In 1864, for example, safety regulations previously limited to mines and textile mills were extended to other "dangerous industries," including match making and pottery making. To be sure, there was no dramatic shift towards a collectivist view of society, but by the end of the mid-Victorian era a new sense had arisen that the state should provide greater security against the ups and downs of modern life.

Education and Religion

This new sensibility could be seen in the far-reaching changes that occurred in public education in this period. For the first three-quarters of the nineteenth century, education for the working classes was limited. In 1870, however, the *Forster Act* made elementary education for boys and girls both compulsory and free. The development of compulsory public education affected the four nations of the British Isles differently. In England, the establishment of locally elected school boards in the 1880s increased community control over schooling and reduced the influence of the Church of England on children's education. Though there were still over 11,000 Anglican-run schools in Britain at this time, the founding of these boards marked a key step towards the creation of a national, secular system of schools.

Because it had maintained a separate system of education, Scotland was not affected by the Forster Act, but like England it moved away from a church-dominated system towards free, state-sponsored schools. The Education Act of 1872 made education compulsory for all Scottish children between the ages of five and thirteen. In Wales, the Forster Act did apply, and initially it enhanced efforts to eradicate the Welsh language. If a child spoke Welsh in school, the teacher would hand him or her a stick or marker, known as a "Welsh Not." It was then passed to the next child who did so, until the end of the lesson, when the child left holding the Not was punished. It was not until the passage of the Local Government Act in 1888, which restored autonomy to local governments, that instruction in Welsh once again became the norm in the parts of the country where it was widely spoken. In Ireland, religious divisions complicated efforts to improve public education. In an effort to overcome the Protestant–Catholic divide, multidenominational "National Schools" were established in 1831. Within a few decades, however, most of them had come to be dominated by a single faith. In any event, education was neither free nor compulsory in Ireland until 1892, so only a small percentage of the population completed even a primary level.

Throughout the United Kingdom, higher education remained the province of elite males, who attended a handful of prestigious universities. In England, Oxford and Cambridge continued to dominate. The two institutions did, however, broaden their admissions policies somewhat. Subscription to the Thirty-Nine Articles, the core tenets of the Anglican faith, was eliminated as a requirement for matriculation and graduation at Oxford in 1854 and at Cambridge in 1856. Founded in 1869, *Girton College* at Cambridge became the first women's college, though women could not earn degrees on an equal basis as men until 1920 at Oxford and 1948 at Cambridge. Things changed faster at newer institutions. The University of London, which had been founded in 1826 as the first English institution to admit students without any kind of religious requirement, allowed women to receive degrees on equal terms with men from 1878 onwards. University education was still in large measure oriented towards the production of "gentlemen," however. It was not until the first decade of the twentieth century that the **"redbrick universities,"** based predominantly in the North of England, began providing technical and industrial education to middle-class men. In Scotland, the four "ancient universities" of Edinburgh, Glasgow, St. Andrews and Aberdeen were gradually brought under a single system of governance, beginning with the passage of the Universities (Scotland) Act in 1858. Wales, meanwhile, did not get its own university until the creation of the University of Wales, with three colleges in Aberystwyth, Bangor and Cardiff, in 1893.

In Ireland, higher education mirrored society in being divided along religious lines. The most prestigious institution, Trinity College in Dublin, continued to be closely linked to the Protestant Ascendancy. Catholics had been permitted to enter and take degrees since 1793, though few did so as the Catholic Church prohibited its members from attending. (This "episcopal ban" lasted until 1970.) Three secular universities, Queen's College Belfast, Queen's College Cork and Queen's College Galway, were created in 1845, but they aroused controversy, as many people felt that the government of the United Kingdom should not be spending so much money on higher education at a time when the famine was devastating the Irish population. It was not until 1854 that the first Catholic university, the Catholic University of Ireland in Dublin, was established. It was later restructured as University College Dublin.

The slow but steady increase in educational opportunities at all levels contributed to important cultural changes. Rapidly rising literacy rates – Britain would achieve close to full adult literacy by 1900 – meant that a world of print replaced an iconographical one that conveyed information through symbols and pictures. In 1843, the novelist William Makepeace Thackeray observed, "there are a thousand men [who] read and think today for one who read on this same day of April 1743." In 1855, the stamp duty on newspapers was repealed; issues now cost only a halfpenny or penny, making them affordable to the working classes. Over the subsequent decades, what historians call the "new journalism" focused on exciting, at times sensationalist, stories that attracted a broad readership. The local papers that had proliferated over the previous century were soon supplanted by national ones, which achieved circulations of over a million copies daily. The same trends towards greater literacy and reduced taxes enhanced the sales of periodicals, which were enjoyed predominantly by the middle classes. The popularity of novelists such as Charles Dickens, Arthur Conan Doyle and George Eliot derived from the appearance of their work in serial installments in periodicals. These authors were now able to rely on sales rather than patronage; upon his death in 1870, Dickens left a fortune of £93,000, a vast sum for the time.

The mid-Victorians read more than novels, however. Nonfiction, too, was very popular, as people sought to understand the changed and changing world in which they lived. Tales of exploration were often bestsellers: Dickens sold an impressive 35,000 copies of *Bleak House* in 1853, but four years later the African explorer David Livingstone sold twice as many of his *Missionary Travels and Explorations*. *Charles Darwin's On the Origin of Species* (1859), meanwhile, quickly sold out its first two editions. Darwin presented a model of a natural world that was based on the principle of evolution, which explained why some species survived and others did not. He contended that all living things derived from a common ancestor due to a process of "natural selection," in which the differences that enhanced the adaptive qualities of particular species of plants and animals over time became dominant traits, because the individuals who possessed them tended to survive and reproduce in greater numbers. Darwin's ideas had a major impact not only on science, but also on social thought, thanks to the work of the philosopher and biologist Herbert Spencer. Spencer's notion of the "survival of the fittest" understood progress as reliant on evolutionary processes. This made science a reliable predictor of social outcomes that the state could advance or interrupt through policy changes. Through Spencer's work, "social Darwinism" was assimilated by policy makers and social critics, who considered evolutionary thinking to be a roadmap to social progress.

Darwin's theories, which challenged the centrality of God's role in the making of the natural world, made people more skeptical and willing to question biblical truth and traditional Christian morality. In consequence, many historians argue that the mid-Victorian period saw a steady decline in the importance of organized religion in Britain and that a more secular worldview gradually came to supersede traditional religious beliefs. Darwin, however, was not single-handedly responsible for this change. In 1851, eight years before his work appeared, a religious census that measured the number of church attendees on a particular Sunday revealed that only slightly over half of the British population was going to church regularly.

Some people blamed the established church for failing to maintain its hold over a rapidly changing population. The Church of England had already seen one attempt at revitalization. In the 1830s, the Oxford Movement had attempted to bring Anglicanism closer to its Catholic roots. The emphasis on ritual and tradition led its critics to charge that the movement was seeking a reconciliation between Anglicanism and Catholicism, while the movement's leaders claimed that their goal was to stress the importance of continuity and tradition to the Anglican Church. But in 1841 in the ninetieth and final publication of the series *Tracts for the Times*, the Oxford Movement's most prominent leader, John Henry Newman, argued that Roman Catholic and Anglican doctrine were compatible. Four years later, Newman converted to Catholicism; he later became a cardinal. For most British people, this was too far to travel along the road to Rome, and the Oxford Movement's ability to bring about changes in the Church of England dissipated.

A sense that religion was declining as a force in society remained, however, and the 1850s witnessed a rise of evangelicalism among Anglicans and Nonconformists alike, who shared a belief in a strict adherence to the Bible and moral codes of conduct that included sobriety and sexual continence. Evangelicalism was popular among industrialists, who saw it as both spiritually appealing and conducive to the discipline that factory work required. Their influence helped to spread evangelicalism among their employees. The spiritual zeal of more adventurous evangelicals found an outlet in missionary movements, which sent representatives to the British Empire as well as to other parts of the world, including China and the Ottoman Empire. At home, a domestic mission movement looked to aid the poor by combining religion with philanthropy. In 1865, the Methodist preacher William Booth and his wife Catherine founded the Salvation Army to serve London's impoverished East End. By 1886, the Salvation Army was operating 1749 "mission churches" throughout Britain.

Despite fears that its influence was waning, religion remained a powerful presence in the mid-Victorian world. Many people were able to accommodate the new scientific theories within their religious views. Some intellectuals, like Benjamin Jowett, attempted to demonstrate that Christianity and science were not mutually antagonistic by pressing for nonliteral interpretations of the Bible. Others, like Philip Gosse, argued that the fossil record on which Darwin had based his theory of evolution was, like everything else, a creation of God, rather than a true indication of the course of natural history. Still others, like the future prime minister Arthur Balfour, asserted that religion and science were two separate but equal spheres of intellectual authority.

The diversity of these ideas shows that the Victorian religious universe was becoming less unified and that religion was becoming an individual rather than a communal matter. This privatization of religion was given added impetus by the severing of some of the links between church and state that had long been a part of religious practice in Britain. In the mid-Victorian period, state churches lost their exclusive privileges to record births, deaths and marriages and to provide education and poor relief. In 1869, the (Anglican) Church of Ireland was **disestablished**, though it would it take until the 1920s for the Anglican Church in Wales and the (Presbyterian) Church of Scotland to follow. Despite these structural changes, however, religion continued to influence social privilege and political life, as non-Anglicans, though increasingly tolerated, remained in many ways, outsiders.

Women and Separate Spheres

The unequal treatment of women was embedded in the Victorian legal system. The legal principle of coverture, which held that upon marriage the woman's legal identity was subsumed by that of her husband, still prevailed. There were, however, some calls for change. In 1837, Caroline Norton published her *Observations on the Natural Claim of a Mother to the Custody of Her Children* in order to protest her estranged husband's refusal to allow her to see her sons after his unsuccessful attempt to divorce her. Her plea was successful: in 1839, the

Custody of Children Act gave separated or divorced mothers who could prove their good character access to their children. Beginning in 1855, a series of Matrimonial Reform Acts granted some autonomy to married women.

 See document "A Woman's Voice" at www.routledge.com_cw_barczewski.

It was not until the end of the nineteenth century, however, that a series of Married Women's Property Acts gave married women the same property rights as unmarried women, effectively ending coverture. An *act of 1870* gave married women control of their own wages and allowed them to retain ownership of any landed property and cash up to £200 that they inherited. This marked a key step in redefining the ideal of marriage as a union between two equal partners rather than between a superior husband and a subordinate wife. Two additional acts in 1882 and 1893 further increased married women's property rights. Divorce laws, however, continued to enforce inequality. In 1857, the Matrimonial Causes Act made divorce easier to obtain, but it also established a higher standard for women than for men. Men could divorce based on a single instance of adultery, but women had to prove ongoing unfaithfulness, along with additional causes, usually physical abuse or incest.

Women also continued to be denied full political rights. In 1867, the liberal philosopher John Stuart Mill, at the time MP for Westminster, introduced a measure supporting the right to vote for all householders regardless of sex, but it garnered only seventy-three votes. Two years later, Mill published his essay "The Subjection of Women," which made a strong case for female suffrage. "Marriage is the only actual bondage known to [English] law," Mill wrote. "There remain no legal slaves except the mistress of every household." Women, too, increasingly demanded the right to vote. In 1870, Lydia Becker founded the *Women's Suffrage Journal* to advocate for the franchise.

Though it would be 1918 before women over thirty who met the property qualification obtained the parliamentary franchise, they did see some improvement in their political status in the nineteenth century. One of the most influential female voices of the era was Harriet Martineau, who argued for changing customs and practices that stood in the way of women's financial independence. Her case against gender inequality was built on the argument that bad laws and restricted opportunities prevented women from fully participating in Victorian life. Her work inspired organizations such as the Langham Place Circle, which supported the educational and professional aspirations of middle-class women. By the late 1860s, these voices in favor of increased rights for women were having an impact. The Municipal Franchise Act (1869) allowed female ratepayers (i.e., taxpayers) to vote in local elections, and the following year the Forster Act gave them the right to sit on local school boards.

The unequal legal and political treatment of women upheld the idea of "separate spheres," in which men occupied the public sphere – politics and work – and women the private – the home. In his essay "Of Queen's Gardens" (1864), the cultural critic John Ruskin wrote that men should "pursue rough work in [the] open world," while for the "true wife" the "home is always round her." Women were supposed to embrace a "cult of domesticity," in which the home became a retreat from the outside world. In 1890, the magazine *The Christian Miscellany and Family Visitor* described the ideal woman: "She is the architect of home, and it depends on her skill, her foresight, her soft arranging touches whether it shall be the 'lodestar to all hearts,' or whether it shall be a house from which husband and children are glad to escape either to the street, the theater, or the tavern."

The emergence of these views was encouraged by new patterns of work. Previously, middle-class, professional men had worked out of rooms in their houses, while shopkeepers lived in rooms above their street-level retail premises. By the mid-nineteenth century, however, work and domestic spaces were increasingly differentiated, as the people who could afford it moved out of dirty, crowded, polluted cities to new, leafy suburbs, from which they commuted to their jobs. Improvements in transportation made it possible to live a significant distance from one's place of employment for the first time. The hero of F. G. Trafford's novel *City and Suburb* (1861) observed of London, "the mass of business people I see take a journey for the sole purpose of going to sleep; they eat and drink, and walk, and read in the city, and then they get into a close ill-ventilated omnibus, and drive five or six miles to bed." Among the best-off members of the working classes, meanwhile, the ability of a woman to stay home and tend to the children and household while being supported by a male breadwinner was increasingly seen as an indication of respectability.

Work outside of the home remained a reality for many women despite the emerging ideal of the male breadwinner. But this labor was not valued in the same way as it was for men, and the unionization of women workers came more slowly than it did for male workers. The Women's Trade Union League was not founded until 1874. Women, however, found other ways to form organizations that supported remunerative employment for women, in part inspired by John Stuart Mill's writing on political economy from the late 1840s. Founded in 1859, the Society for Promoting the Employment of Women (SPEW) provided financial backing and institutional support for women-run employment training programs. This cooperative investment plan was made possible by the Limited Liability Act of 1855 and the Joint Stock Companies Act of 1856, which permitted individuals to incorporate and invest in business ventures while being more protected from avaricious creditors. SPEW's leaders Barbara Leigh Smith Bodichon and Bessie Rayner Parkes promoted working- and middle-class women's employment, particularly in the printing trades and publishing.

Thus, the separation of men's and women's "spheres" was never complete. A third of all women worked in paid employment in the nineteenth century, as their earnings were necessary to support themselves and, if married, their families. Smaller family sizes, meanwhile, gave middle-class women increased time to devote to activities outside the home. In 1820, a married woman could expect to bear seven children; by 1900, that number had declined to three. At the same time, the average age at which a woman had her last child fell from forty-one to thirty-four. This allowed women to undertake a variety of philanthropic activities, such as visiting the poor and infirm and gathering and distributing clothes and food. Women were also actively involved in their churches, as Sunday school teachers or, in some Dissenting sects, as lay preachers. Despite their inability to vote, women joined and led political pressure groups, most prominently the campaign to abolish slavery in America and the temperance movement.

As the nineteenth century wore on, the sharp distinction between the "public" and "private" spheres eroded further. Many men became more immersed in the domestic world, as they devoted greater attention to their familial responsibilities as husbands and fathers. Whereas previously respectable women had not appeared on city streets without a chaperone, by the 1870s they were shopping and carrying out other tasks alone, at least in the daytime. Finally, it should be noted that a separation of the male and female "spheres" was often actively supported by women, rather than something that was imposed on them by men. Some women saw it as a way to define spaces in which they could exercise power and independence, rather than be subordinate to men. "Separate spheres" was thus more complex than a clear-cut division between men's and women's roles in society and the family. While many middle-class women and women of the lower gentry found solace, privilege and comfort in private life and embraced domesticity, others believed that women's exclusion from public life stood in the way of political and social equality between the sexes. The campaign for women's suffrage was for middle-class women in particular part of a larger quest for equal treatment before the law. Women's participation in politics as full citizens was increasingly coming to be seen as the key to their social and economic equality.

Foreign Policy

In the middle decades of the nineteenth century, the direction of Britain's interactions with the external world fell primarily to the Whig politician Henry John Temple, 3rd Viscount Palmerston, who served as foreign secretary, home secretary, and prime minister between 1830 and 1865. A stereotypically diligent Victorian, Palmerston had a special desk designed so that he could work standing up, in order to prevent himself from falling asleep when he labored late into the night. He was also a staunch patriot who saw the British Parliament as a perfect political institution and as a model for other nations. A Frenchman once attempted to compliment the British by saying to Palmerston, "If I were not a Frenchman, I should wish to be an Englishman." Palmerston replied, "If I were not an Englishman, I should wish to be an Englishman." His foreign policy sought to use Britain's "moral weight" to defend and promote political movements in Europe against autocracy, endearing him to a public that embraced liberty as a British ideal.

Palmerston believed in the importance of the armed forces, particularly the Royal Navy, as a means of asserting Britain's point of view. In 1850, he dispatched a naval fleet to secure compensation for *Don Pacifico*, a Portuguese Jew who was a British subject because he had been born in the colony of Gibraltar. In 1847, Pacifico was living in Athens, Greece, when his house was attacked and looted by an anti-Semitic mob. He appealed to the Greek government for compensation, but when none was forthcoming, he asked the British government to intervene. Palmerston sent a Royal Naval squadron to blockade Piraeus, the port used by Athens; after eight weeks the Greeks yielded and paid Pacifico the requested compensation. The House of Lords criticized Palmerston's decision as an excessive use of force, but the Commons supported him after he delivered a patriotic speech in which he declared, "as the Roman, in days of old, held himself free from indignity, when he could say *Civis Romanus sum*; so also a British subject, in whatever land he may be, shall feel confident that the watchful eye and the strong arm of England will protect him against injustice and wrong." The claim was tantamount to a declaration of "might is right," but it was wildly popular with the British public.

Experience of Warfare 4

Palmerston's Follies

During the Napoleonic Wars between 1805 and 1812, 101 defensive towers were constructed to guard Britain's south and east coasts. The work continued even after the British naval victory in the Battle of Trafalgar removed the threat of a French invasion. These were known as "Martello towers" because they were inspired by the tower at Mortella (Myrtle) Point in Corsica, which had withstood an attack by two British warships in 1794 and had to be taken by land. After Napoleon was defeated in 1815, however, the need for coastal defenses diminished, and many of the towers fell into disrepair. But after the July Revolution of 1830 that brought Louis Philippe I to power, the tone of Anglo-French relations changed, and so the towers were repaired. Relations deteriorated further after Louis Philippe was deposed in 1848, transforming France to a republic that saw Louis-Napoleon Bonaparte, Napoleon's nephew, elected as its first president. Louis Napoleon would overturn the republic in 1852 and proclaim himself Emperor Napoleon III; he began espousing a more aggressive foreign policy in which he hinted at the conquest of newly independent Belgium. In response, the prime minister Lord Palmerston, who believed that a French invasion of Britain was likely, ordered the construction of a new set of coastal defenses. This construction initially focused on protecting the main naval dockyard at Portsmouth, but was expanded to the other naval dockyards at Plymouth, Milford Haven, Cork, Dover and the Thames estuary after a report was issued by the Royal Commission on the Defence of the United Kingdom in 1860. They became known as "Palmerston's Follies" because the first fortifications at Portsmouth had most of their guns facing inwards to protect against an attack from land, and so many people believed that they had been built facing the wrong way. The French threat receded after France was defeated in the Franco-Prussian War of 1870, but many of Britain's nineteenth-century coastal fortifications were rearmed during the First and Second World Wars. They were finally taken permanently out of service in 1956, when the need for coastal defense was deemed obsolete. None of the forts was ever used for its intended purpose of defending Britain from invasion.

Figure 6.2 No Man's Land Fort in the Solent off Portsmouth on the south coast of England. One of "Palmerston's Follies," it was begun in 1865 and completed in 1880, long after the threat of a French invasion had receded.

Reproduced courtesy of Shutterstock/balipadma.

Palmerston saw such saber rattling as a means of preventing war; despite his bellicose rhetoric, he believed that wars were expensive and therefore undesirable. They were not, however, always avoidable. In 1853, the outbreak of the Crimean War, so named because it was fought on the Crimean Peninsula in the Black Sea, marked the death knell of the concert of Europe. Fought over the expansion of Russian imperial interests in the East, the war drew Britain and France into the conflict as allies of the Ottoman Empire in 1854. British forces were woefully unprepared, as inadequate supplies and deficient medical services indicated the sorry state of a military administration that had not managed a large-scale conflict since the Napoleonic era. As one soldier put it in a letter home, "We are certainly the worst clad, worst fed, worst housed Army that ever was." The war was responsible for the emergence of two female heroes, Florence Nightingale and Mary Seacole. Both women went to Crimea to assist with the war effort and became known for their efforts on behalf of soldiers. Nightingale, immortalized as the "Lady with the Lamp," helped modernize nursing and legitimate nursing as a respectable profession for women. Seacole, a Caribbean-born healer, aided and provided housing for soldiers at her British Hotel in Crimea.

Figure 6.3 Philip Hermogenes Calderon's painting *Lord, Thy Will Be Done* (1855). In it, a young woman sits holding an infant, while a picture of her absent husband, who has gone to fight in the Crimean War, hangs above the mantel. The room's simple décor suggests that she is from the lower ranks of society. The painting uses the war to illustrate the Victorian idea of "separate spheres," in which men played public roles and worked outside the home, while women remained confined to the private, domestic realm. The image's ambivalent depiction of the husband's absence, however, suggests that the notion that the Victorians were both blindly patriotic and firmly committed to separate spheres requires questioning.

Reproduced courtesy of the Yale Center for British Art, Paul Mellon Fund.

The Crimean War became infamous for mismanagement and tactical errors on both sides. The failures shone a light on the outmoded army traditions and practices. In the mid-nineteenth century, the officer ranks of the British Army were dominated by men from elite backgrounds who had attended **public schools**, rather than the military academy at Sandhurst, and who had purchased their commissions and promotions rather than acquiring them by merit. They thus had little in the way of formal military training; only two of the six generals who commanded divisions in the Crimea had any experience of battlefield command. For the British, the most notorious example was the disastrous charge of the Light Cavalry Brigade, which took place on the 25th of October 1854 during the Battle of Balaclava. During the charge, the Light Brigade attacked a battery of Russian artillery that was deployed at the end of a mile-long valley. The valley was flanked on both sides by guns that fired down on them from above. The action, which was in defiance of every basic principle of warfare, was due to the erroneous interpretation of an ambiguous order given by Lord Raglan, commander of all British forces, to Lord Lucan, commander of the British cavalry. Of the approximately 670 men who participated in the Charge, almost 300 were killed, wounded or taken prisoner. The debacle was immortalized in Alfred Tennyson's poem "The Charge of the Light Brigade," which was written immediately after Tennyson read the first accounts of the charge in the British press and published only six weeks after the event. The rapidity with which Tennyson was able to produce his poem showed how much the speed of global communications had increased by the 1850s, as the Reuters telegraph agency delivered information from the front within days.

Britain and its French and Ottoman allies ultimately prevailed in the Crimea, but the attention that had been drawn to Britain's poor military preparedness led to important changes. A royal commission was established in 1858 to examine the reasons for the failures, though it would be over a decade before any significant change was achieved. Beginning in 1868 and spearheaded by the secretary of war Edward Cardwell, reforms eliminated the harshest forms of corporal punishment, permitted shorter terms of enlistment and abolished the purchase of officers' commissions. The necessity of these reforms was an indication that Britain was growing increasingly nervous about its international position. Concerns focused not only on the continuing Russian threat to India, but also on a new rival: Prussia (and after 1871 the unified German confederation), which threatened to upset the balance of power that Britain had striven to maintain in Europe since the end of the Napoleonic Wars. The speed of Germany's victory over France in the Franco-Prussian War (1870–1) set off serious alarms at Westminster.

The Crimean War also had major geopolitical consequences that still echo today. European interference in the region that is today known as the "Middle East", a term that for Britain designated the regions location in relation to its empire in India, increased as a result of what Victorians referred to as the "Eastern Question." As the Ottoman Empire weakened, Palmerston saw an opportunity to extend British influence in the region through a system of alliances that would increase Britain's informal power over its affairs. Siding with the Ottoman Empire during the Crimean War and playing a key role in negotiating the peace settlement did just that. The Eastern Question, however, was far from settled, and it remained an important issue for the remainder of the nineteenth century. "The eternal Eastern Question is before us again," declared the foreign secretary Lord Derby in 1876, in reference to Britain's proposed purchase of the Suez Canal. By the 1870s, Conservatives like Derby argued for a greater investment of British capital in the Ottoman lands, while Liberals (the new name for the Whigs, as will be discussed later) worried that propping up a weakening Ottoman Empire would result in greater misery for the Christian minorities living within its borders.

The contest over the "sick man of Europe" thus became a more important part of the Victorian political world as the nineteenth century wore on.

Britain and the American Civil War

When *war broke out* between America's northern and southern states in 1861, Britons were divided as to which side to support. The 4 million bales of cotton that were imported annually from the South fueled a textile industry that was responsible for 40 percent of Britain's total exports. At a dinner in Charleston in 1861, the *Times* correspondent William Howard Russell, who had become famous for his dispatches from the Crimean War, was told by a confident southerner, "Why, sir, we have only to shut off your supply of cotton for a few weeks, and we can create a revolution in Great Britain." Most British people, however, opposed slavery, and thus their moral sympathies, if not their economic interest, lay with the North.

These two factors alone made Britain's position extremely complex, but there were a number of other complicating issues. Though today we think of Britain and the United States as close allies, in the mid-nineteenth century relations between the two countries were tense. This was partly due to hard feelings that lingered from the American Revolution and the War of 1812, but also to the United States' desire to see Britain displaced entirely from the North American continent. In particular, the Americans coveted the Oregon Territory, which had been claimed by Britain since George Vancouver's explorations in the 1790s. Tensions over Oregon had peaked in the mid-1840s, when war between Britain and the United States seemed imminent, but diplomacy prevailed, and a treaty establishing the boundary at the 49th parallel was signed by both nations in 1846.

In popular rather than diplomatic terms, British attitudes towards the northern and southern states were complex. Antislavery sentiment was widespread. Harriet Beecher Stowe's novel *Uncle Tom's Cabin*, published in 1852, sold a million copies in Britain, three times as many as in America, and its success led to demands for the British government to exert greater pressure on the United States to end slavery. Other Britons, however, thought that southern independence was inevitable or that the South had a right to self-determination. "The South fight for independence; what do the North fight for," asked the home secretary, Sir George Cornewall Lewis, "except to gratify passion or pride?" Many Britons believed that slavery would soon be abolished in the South even if it won the war, a view that southern agents in Britain were only too happy to encourage, even if it had little basis in reality. Some upper-class Britons, meanwhile, felt that southerners retained more of their British heritage and had not been "contaminated" by the influx of immigrants from other European countries as had occurred in the North. At a banquet in Sheffield in August 1862, the Liberal MP John Roebuck asserted, "the North will never be our friends. Of the South you can make friends. They are Englishmen, and not the scum and refuse of Europe." These elite Britons saw the South as an agrarian paradise that was untouched by the twin scourges of industrialization and social equality.

Throughout the war, the British government maintained a stance of strict neutrality and prohibited the sale of arms to either side, which was a greater blow to the Confederate government than to its Union counterpart as the industrialized North could more easily manufacture its own munitions than the agrarian South. The South was desperate for formal recognition as a sovereign country, which would be an enormous psychological victory. But it never came. Even a desperate offer as the war neared an end to abolish slavery in return for recognition failed to bring about any alteration in Britain's stance. Britain's maintenance of neutrality, however, was complicated by the economic pressure imposed by the collapse of the cotton trade. Mill owners in Lancashire were forced to lay off tens of thousands of workers and reduce the hours of hundreds of thousands more. Relations between the American and British governments thus remained tense. In November 1861, two Confederate diplomats, James Mason and John Slidell, who were traveling on the R.M.S. *Trent*, a British merchant vessel, were seized and imprisoned by the American Navy. The incident nearly led to war, but at the last moment the American government backed down and released the two men.

 See document "The Trent Affair" at www.routledge.com_cw_barczewski.

Had the North been willing from the beginning to state clearly that the war was being fought to abolish slavery, British attitudes might have been different. Although he was the most pro-Confederate member of the British cabinet at the time, the future Liberal prime minister William Gladstone declared, "if we could say that this was a contest of slavery and freedom, there is . . . hardly a man in all England, who would for a moment hesitate upon the side he would take." The American president Abraham Lincoln, however, was fearful that a strong declaration of abolitionist intent would alienate the neutral border states and drive them into the southern camp. It was not until September 1862 that he issued the Emancipation Proclamation, which declared that all southern enslaved people would be "forever free" once the nation was reunified. Though British politicians suspected that the proclamation was a desperate gesture by a president who feared that he was losing the war, it was enough to check any serious talk of recognizing the Confederacy. Tensions between the British and American governments remained high, however, as despite its purported neutrality the former allowed private contractors to build ships for the Confederate navy, so long as they were not fitted out as warships until after they left British ports. It was not until 1863 that Britain began threatening to detain vessels that were clearly being built for military purposes.

In the end, both the Union and Confederate sides felt resentment towards the British. The Confederate government was angry because Britain had failed to recognize it and because the British had conceded the legality of the Union blockade of southern ports. The Union government was frustrated because Britain had not viewed the conflict as one between a legitimate government and a rebellious internal faction. In addition, the toleration of the construction of Confederate ships by British companies in the early years of the war led to the capture of dozens of ships bound for northern ports. Claims for compensation from these raids dragged on for years after the war, focusing in particular on the damage done by the C.S.S. *Alabama*, a Liverpool-built sloop that had captured sixty-five Union merchant ships. These claims were finally resolved in 1871, when a tribunal in Geneva decided that Britain owed the United States $15.5 million.

For its part, the British government was frustrated by the Union leadership's failure to understand that its commitment to neutrality had been maintained despite considerable pressure to recognize the South, and that its refusal to bend on this score had prevented other European countries, France in particular, from doing so. They were equally frustrated, however, with the Confederacy's repeated attempts to drag Britain into the war on their side, and with their efforts to stir up anti-northern feeling in Canada in order to provoke a war between Britain and the United States. They were frustrated with both sides for their "crimping," or forced conscription, of thousands of British citizens into the two armies, despite numerous diplomatic protests. It was slavery, however, that ultimately proved the key issue. As the historian Amanda Foreman writes, southerners continually "confused sympathy for southern suffering . . . with acceptance of southern slavery."

Challenges to British Imperial Authority

The mid-Victorian period saw little formal colonization of new territory. Wars waged during this period were largely fought to consolidate British rule in and around territories already under its influence. Beyond these areas, Britain is sometimes said to have created an "informal empire," where it exercised outsized economic dominance over less industrialized countries. The commitment to free trade was maintained only when it was thought to be economically advantageous; in other cases, such as in India, commercial transactions continued to be highly regulated in quasi-mercantilist fashion. "Informal empire" in the regions outside of direct British control has come to be seen as such a slippery concept that some scholars dispute whether it has any meaning at all. One part of the world that has occasioned particular debate over the existence of "informal empire" is South America. In particular, Britain's relations with Argentina are often held up as a prime example of "informal empire" in the mid-nineteenth century. Some historians, however, argue that the British government exercised little influence over Argentine politics in this period and that the two countries enjoyed a relatively equitable economic relationship.

What is not in dispute is that the mid-Victorian period saw the British metropolis linked more closely to the Empire through major innovations in transportation and communications. As steam gradually replaced sail, ships were able to reach distant parts of the world much faster. By 1900, it took only three weeks to sail from London to Bombay, down from the six months it had taken a century earlier. India was linked to Britain by telegraph in 1866, making communication between the British government in London and colonial administrators in Calcutta a matter of minutes rather than the ten weeks it had taken previously.

But if empire and metropolis were being bound more closely together by new technologies and economic relationships, other forces were pushing them apart. In 1857, the outbreak of *rebellion in India* represented the strongest challenge to British rule in the subcontinent to date. It began as a mutiny by the Indian troops, or "sepoys," serving in the East India Company's forces in India. In the mid-nineteenth century, approximately 300,000 of the Company's 350,000 troops were Indian, though the officer ranks remained overwhelmingly British. Over the previous seventy-five years, the Company had attempted to increase the quality of its soldiers by recruiting sepoys from among higher-caste Hindus. This required the Company's army to adapt to their religious practices, however, and so the sepoys were promised that they would not have to serve overseas (defined as any place to which they could not march), which was considered polluting. Hindu and Muslim sepoys were given separate dining facilities and other religious accommodations as well. This avoided tensions in the short term, but it set up a situation in which the sepoys were extremely sensitive to any infringement of their religious rights.

Earlier in the nineteenth century, several incidents had caused unrest among the sepoys and among the Indian population as a whole. The British had attempted to abolish *sati*, a religious ritual in which newly widowed Hindu women burned themselves to death. They also had attempted to replace education in indigenous languages with western-style education in English. Lord Dalhousie, governor-general of India from 1848 to 1856, was determined to modernize India along western lines, which included the expansion of the railways, the institution of a postal service and the establishment of English-language schools. At the same time, he expanded the British footprint in India by further limiting the power of the Indian princes who still ruled in parts of the subcontinent. Making it illegal for princes who lacked heirs to adopt sons eased Britain's annexation of territories that now had no recognized hereditary ruler. Conflicts over property taxation further exacerbated the situation, as British notions of private property did not mesh with traditional Indian land-use practices.

There were also mounting religious tensions. The growing number of missionaries in India aroused suspicion that the British were planning mass conversions of Hindus and Muslims. As the East India Company's territory continued to expand, it was forced to dispatch troops to distant places like Burma, thereby violating the promise not to send sepoys overseas. This requirement was at first imposed only on new recruits, but veterans feared that it would soon be extended to them. The sepoys also resented the slowness with which they obtained commissions, promotions and raises, due to the overwhelming dominance of the British among the officer ranks.

These were longstanding grievances, however. Why did the sepoys mutiny in 1857? That year, a new Enfield rifle was introduced into the army. It had a tighter barrel, and so the paper cartridges used to load it were pre-greased with tallow. As part of the loading process, the sepoys were required to bite off the end of the cartridges in order to release the gunpowder they contained. Rumors spread that the cartridges were greased with pig or cow fat. The minority of soldiers who were Muslim were forbidden by their faith from eating pork, while the Hindu majority was forbidden from eating beef. The British attempted to remedy the situation by issuing ungreased cartridges that the sepoys could then lubricate with whatever they preferred, but it was too late. Many sepoys now believed that the British were attempting to destroy their caste status, and along with it their religion.

The rebellion began in May of 1857 at Meerut in the Northwest Provinces, where 2400 sepoys and 2000 British soldiers were stationed. A British officer ordered ninety of his men to perform firing drills, which required them to use the controversial cartridges. When all but five refused, the other eighty-five were court-martialed, and many were sentenced to ten years' hard labor. The condemned men were humiliated by being publicly stripped of their uniforms and marched off to prison in shackles. The next day, the sepoys mutinied, released the eighty-five prisoners and set the cantonment (military base) on fire; around fifty British soldiers and civilians were killed in the ensuing violence. Gathering support as they marched south, they captured the city of Delhi, about forty miles away, and declared the restoration of the Mughal emperor Bahadur Shah II. As the news spread, the mutiny led to additional uprisings against British authority in northern and central India that involved both sepoys and civilians.

For this reason, historians still debate whether the events of 1857 are more accurately termed a mutiny or a rebellion. In reality, it was most likely what the historian Thomas Metcalf has described as "something more than a sepoy mutiny, but something less than a national revolt." The rebels soon controlled a swath of northern India that was 400 miles long and 200 miles wide, running from Meerut to Benares.

The Presence of Empire 5

The Cawnpore Massacre

No single episode better demonstrates the brutality of the Indian Rebellion of 1857 than the events at Cawnpore (now Kanpur) in the Northwest Provinces. In early June, the British cantonment at Cawnpore was besieged by 12,000 to 15,000 rebel sepoys. The cantonment was inhabited by around 300 British soldiers and 300 women and children, and 300 Indian merchants and servants. The unfinished barracks in which the British took refuge contained little food and only a single well, the location of which was exposed to enemy fire. Poor sanitation meant that dysentery, cholera and other diseases were soon rampant. When the desperate garrison surrendered after three weeks, they were promised safe passage to the nearby city of Allahabad, which was under British control. As they made their way to the boats that would carry them along the Ganges River, however, the surrounding sepoys opened fire – whether deliberately or accidentally is still disputed – and most of the men were killed. Between 125 and 200 women and children survived; they, along with a handful of men, were taken prisoner. But as British forces neared Cawnpore two weeks later, they were massacred with cleavers, knives and axes.

When British forces retook the city, they were horrified by the remnants of the carnage. The houses of local civilians were looted and burned, and any rebel prisoner who could not prove that he had not been involved in the massacre was summarily executed. Before they were hanged, some were forced to lick the dried blood from the walls and floor of the compound where the massacre had occurred. "Remember Cawnpore!" became a battle cry that inspired British soldiers for the remainder of the campaign. The British press overflowed for weeks with outrage, as the response to the rebellion came to be seen as a crusade against Indian treachery that sought to restore the honor of the helpless victims, women in particular. The British built a memorial garden over the well in which the bodies of the massacred women and children had been dumped; the Indian citizens of Cawnpore, who were blamed for not resisting the rebels, were forced to contribute £30,000 towards its construction, even though it was off-limits to them. In 1948, a year after India achieved its independence, the memorial was destroyed by the departing British, who feared its defacement by Indian nationalists.

Figure 6.4 From 1865, Samuel Bourne's photograph of the memorial garden at Cawnpore attempted to minimize the violence and divisiveness of the Indian Rebellion by depicting Indians enjoying the now-peaceful setting, even though in actuality they were banned from visiting the site.

Reproduced courtesy of the Samuel Bourne, Getty Museum.

The British response was confused and slow, as commanders were unsure whether their troops could be trusted. The mutineers remained confined to one of the East India Company's three armies, that of Bengal, while the armies of Bombay and Madras remained largely unaffected. Even in the Bengal Army, however, many sepoys remained loyal. Sikh soldiers from the Punjab, for example, feared a restoration of the Mughals, under whom they had been viciously persecuted. Gurkha troops from Nepal also fought for the British. The fighting was often brutal, but by the end of 1857, the British had gained the upper hand. Delhi was recaptured in September, and by the following spring British authority had been restored. Reprisals were swift and harsh, and showed the extent to which the rebellion had shaken British conceptions of their rule in India, and in particular their belief in the willing acquiescence of Indians to it. Some captured rebels were hanged, but others were strapped to the front of cannons that were then fired, a form of punishment adapted from the Mughals. Back in Britain, any hint of moderation met with sharp criticism in the metropolitan press.

Figure 6.5 Felice Beato's photograph of the badly damaged Sikander Bagh, a building in the city of Lucknow that was occupied by thousands of sepoys who had mutinied during the Indian Rebellion of 1857. Taken in early 1858, it shows what were supposedly the bones of the sepoys scattered over the ground in front of the Sikander Bagh, although in reality they had been dug up for the purpose of making the scene more dramatic.

Reproduced courtesy of the Felice Beato, Getty Museum.

Lord Palmerston's government swiftly instituted reforms in order to avoid a political crisis. The number of British soldiers in India was doubled, while the Government of India Act (1858) transferred all authority from the East India Company to the British Crown, thereby ending two-and-a-half centuries of private oversight of the British Empire in India. It also provided for the regular parliamentary review of Indian affairs and the appointment of a viceroy to replace the governor-general. The British were determined to establish that they and not the Mughals were India's legitimate rulers.

The events of 1857 changed the way Britons understood the importance of India. A vast, expanding empire that would eventually cover one-third of the globe after World War I required new institutions and people to fill roles in its administration and the military. In addition, missionaries began to find new opportunities in an empire where religious Dissenters and Anglicans alike could go to find new converts. The Government of India Act necessitated the rise of a new breed of colonial bureaucrat. These men were part of the civil service and trained for a career as mostly mid-level administrators in the colonies. The distance from London often meant that they exercised a great deal of formal and informal power over their subjects. Governing the Empire also relied on the cooperation of its subjects. Although very few educated Indians made it to the upper ranks of the colonial administration, the British came increasingly to rely on this group to administer taxes and handle day-to-day business in Indian towns and villages. These local administrators played a crucial role in imperial governance as the British came to rely on them for information and knowledge in order to control local populations and subvert potential security threats. A similar administrative system that co-opted the power of tribal elites grew up in nonsettler colonies in Africa.

Missionaries remained a presence in the British Empire with an estimated 10,000 serving overseas by end of the nineteenth century. Hundreds of missionary publications appeared during this period, including the Church Missionary Society's flagship publication *The Gleaner*, which from 1841 onwards chronicled the activities of Anglican missionaries around the globe and familiarized readers with far-off regions of the Empire. Missionaries set up new churches and educational institutions that were often critical of traditional religious and cultural practices. One missionary claimed, "Civilization is to the Christian religion what the body is to the soul." Women comprised two-thirds of all missionaries by the turn of the century. As teachers and doctors working through missionary institutions, they instructed indigenous women about western practices in ways that sometimes led to tensions with local leaders because they interfered with indigenous systems of belief and women's traditional roles in society.

India was not the only place where British imperial authority was questioned. The abolition of slavery in 1834 had not significantly improved the lives of the Afro-Caribbean population, as land and wealth remained overwhelmingly concentrated in the hands of the white minority. Jamaica was a case in point: in 1864, fewer than 2000 black Jamaicans could vote, out of a total population of 436,000. A two-year-long drought that led to poor harvests generated rumors that the white plantation owners were contemplating the reimposition of slavery. In 1865, a rebellion was led by 300 impoverished former enslaved people at Morant Bay. The colony's governor, *Edward Eyre*, declared martial law; 437 people were hanged and over 700 flogged, many more than who had actually participated in the rebellion. When the news reached Britain, Eyre's actions became the topic of tremendous controversy. Some commentators defended him, using familiar racist tropes. The philosopher Thomas Carlyle described Eyre as a "brave, gentle, chivalrous and clear man" who was needed to discipline the "idle black gentleman, with his rum bottle in his hand." The popular novelist Charles Dickens also praised Eyre. John Stuart Mill and Charles Darwin, on the other hand, were extremely critical. The British government for the most part supported the latter camp: Eyre was recalled and the autonomy of the white planters was significantly reduced by bringing Jamaica under direct rule as a crown colony, paralleling the British response to the Indian Rebellion.

The Great Rivalry: Disraeli and Gladstone

After fifteen years of relative calm, the temperature of British politics heated up after 1865. By the late 1850s, the old Whig Party had become an uneasy coalition of its traditional aristocratic wing, based in the House of Lords, and a more radical faction, based in the House of Commons. Comprised predominantly of MPs from the new manufacturing towns, the latter group favored social and political reform, free trade and the avoidance of foreign entanglements, as well as more traditional Whig policies such as the reduction of the power of the monarchy and the Church of England. In the 1840s, this increasingly inchoate alliance had added another group: the Peelites who had defected from the Conservatives over the repeal of the Corn Laws. Despite their differences, the three groups found sufficient common ground to serve as a foundation for a new party, which united around the broad principles of limited government expenditure and intervention and lukewarm support for imperialism, principles that they did not always uphold in practice. The formal foundation of the Liberal Party is usually dated to a meeting that took place in London on the 6th of June 1859, when 274 Whig, Radical and Peelite MPs agreed to cooperate to defeat the Conservative government.

In the 1860s, the power of the old Whig aristocratic wing diminished rapidly. Through the early part of the decade, the party had been headed by two aristocrats, Lord Palmerston and Lord John Russell, but the death of the former in 1865 and the retirement of the latter in 1868 marked a transition to a new kind of leader. Their successor, William Gladstone, increasingly directed his appeal and policies to the middle and working classes. Though Gladstone was wealthy and had been educated at the elite institutions of Eton and Christ Church, Oxford, his background was in trade. His father Sir John Gladstone was a Scottish-born, Liverpool-based merchant who traded in a variety of global commodities. He was thus in the Victorian world very much "new money," with little connection to the landed elite. Commercial origins do not entirely explain the trajectory of Gladstone's political career, however. He began in the 1830s on the far right of the Tory Party and migrated steadily leftward until his retirement in 1894 at the age of eighty-four, by which point he had served as chancellor of the Exchequer and as prime minister four times each. This long journey was made possible by his political acumen, which included brilliant oratorical skills and a keen mind when it came to budgets, but it was motivated by his religious and moral convictions. Its duration caused him to be labeled the "Grand Old Man," but his increasingly radical brand of Liberalism made him the "People's William."

The first major issue that Gladstone confronted as Liberal leader was political reform. By the 1860s, pressure for a further measure of reform was growing. The middle-class-dominated National Reform Union sought a modest extension of the franchise, while the more radical Reform League pressed for universal male suffrage. When Gladstone's government tried and failed to pass a moderate reform bill, the League escalated its campaign. Their rallies became increasingly boisterous, culminating in a massive meeting of 200,000 people in Hyde Park in July 1866. When the police attempted to prevent the crowd from entering the park by standing guard in front of the locked gates, the reformers charged through the railings. Fears of revolution were rife. The League's leaders, however, recognized that such actions were likely to alienate middle-class supporters, and after the "Hyde Park Railings Affair" their meetings became more peaceful and orderly.

Gladstone's Liberal government had fallen in 1866 when the right wing of the party voted with the Conservatives against the reform bill. In this environment, it hardly seemed likely that the Conservatives, who had opposed the Liberals' extremely limited measure of reform, would pass a more radical reform act of their own, but that is precisely what happened. The Tory chancellor of the Exchequer, Benjamin Disraeli – who led the party in the House of Commons because the new prime minister, the Earl of Derby, sat in the House of Lords – came to a very different conclusion about the current political situation than his Conservative colleagues. Disraeli's rise to the top of what he called the "greasy pole" of Victorian politics was the most remarkable such ascension of the century. Born in London into a family of Jewish merchants who had emigrated from Italy only a half-century earlier, Disraeli was far more of an outsider than Gladstone. He converted to Christianity as an adolescent, but he did not attend university and quickly abandoned a mainstream career as a lawyer. Instead, he opted to pursue a unique double track: in the 1820s, he began publishing a series of successful novels, and in the 1830s, he began trying to get elected to Parliament, failing four times before finally gaining a seat in 1837. After a disastrous maiden speech, in which his flamboyant oratorical style made him a laughingstock, he made his name by attacking Sir Robert Peel over his abandonment of the Corn Law.

Disraeli was no landed aristocrat who ardently believed in the necessity of agricultural protectionism; rather, he was seeking vengeance for Peel's failure to appoint him to office when the Tories took power in 1841. It was here that the rivalry with Gladstone began; he had supported Peel and hated Disraeli for destroying his hero. Many political rivalries balance ideological opposition with mutual respect, but Gladstone and Disraeli genuinely loathed each other. The former was serious and high-minded, while the latter was theatrical and witty. Their rivalry can be readily seen in the debates over reform in 1867. Disraeli recognized that reform was inevitable and that if the Conservatives did not pass it, the Liberals would, thereby getting the credit from the newly enfranchised voters. Moreover, he believed that the working classes were not radical, as most Conservatives feared, but instead were naturally conservative and would over time improve the party's electoral prospects. He also recognized that for most of the nineteenth century, the Conservatives had focused on opposing change rather than developing an agenda of their own. This caused them to be thought of by many people as the "stupid party," in other words as a party that was focused on defending the interests of the landed elite and that had not adapted to modern, industrial society. In consequence, the Whigs and their successors the Liberals had been in power for all but thirteen of the fifty-five years between 1830 and 1885.

Disraeli thus saw the situation as an opportunity for the Conservatives to discard the label of the "stupid party" and to gain popular support among the urban middle and working classes. He believed that the newly enfranchised voters would be grateful to the Conservatives. Expecting the Conservatives to balk, the Liberals tried to thwart Disraeli's strategy by adding a series of increasingly radical amendments to the bill, but Disraeli foiled this plan by simply accepting them. As a result, the *Reform Act of 1867* was far more expansive than anyone had expected: it increased the electorate from 1 million to 2 million, or around a third of the adult male population in England, Wales and Scotland. (In Ireland, only one in six men could vote.) The granting of the franchise to all householders (i.e., local taxpayers) in the boroughs gave some of the best-off members of the working class the right to vote, and the electorate was now a quarter working class. Many politicians were alarmed by its extent, and the phrase "leap in the dark" was used to describe the bill. In some ways, it marked the beginning of mass politics in Britain, with candidates now required to campaign for votes in a way that we would recognize today.

Any whiff of radicalism in 1867, however, was due to Disraeli's political machinations, not a conscious movement towards democracy. Only fifty-two seats were redistributed, correcting a few lingering anomalies from 1832, but parliamentary representation remained tilted in favor of rural areas. Even after 1867, 106 of 263 borough MPs represented towns with fewer than 20,000 inhabitants. Most significantly, the right to vote in Britain remained firmly linked to property and not to any conception of it being a natural right. The Second Reform Act thus did not bring about the fundamental changes in the British political system that many people had feared, or hoped for.

It did, however, achieve Disraeli's goal of altering the Conservative Party's fortunes in the decades to come. His prediction that many working-class voters were natural Tories was proven correct. After replacing Derby as party leader in 1868, Disraeli led the Conservatives to victory in 1874, using a new electoral strategy of associating conservatism with patriotism. He recognized that invoking voters' allegiance to the nation presented a more potent appeal than rational appeals to their specific interests. To ensure that nationalism and conservatism became closely linked, he focused on two key institutions: the monarchy and the Empire. Fiercely loyal to the monarchy as an institution and to Queen Victoria personally, he understood that a monarchy whose political power had largely dissipated still had a key role to play as a symbol of national unity. This could in turn be coupled with increasing popular support for empire. Disraeli had a romantic view of the Empire as a place of quasi-medieval hierarchy and pageantry, but he also saw it pragmatically as a vital source of British power in the world. In 1863, he referred to the Empire as "the national estate . . . which gives to the energies and abilities of Englishmen an inexhaustible theater." In 1876, he made Queen Victoria the Empress of India, a symbolic gesture that simultaneously linked the two main props of his new brand of conservatism.

Disraeli's turn towards empire mirrored that of British politics in the 1860s and 1870s. Both Liberals and Conservatives agreed that the main goal of foreign policy in this period was to maintain a balance of power in Europe while protecting Britain's imperial interests, but they pursued different strategies for achieving these goals. By the late 1870s, Disraeli's government was taking an arm's length approach to foreign policy that opted for informal influence over foreign affairs rather than direct intervention. Gladstone's Liberals, on the other hand, continued to embrace a more activist stance. One of the key issues was the ever-present Eastern Question, in which Europeans vied for control over a weakening Ottoman Empire. Britain gradually came to take the lead in policing Ottoman internal affairs while attempting to defend its own political and economic interests. The contest over the "sick man of Europe," as the Ottoman Empire had come to be called, complicated attempts to enforce the balance of power that had guided British foreign policy since the end of the Napoleonic Wars.

In dealing with the Eastern Question, the Conservatives put Britain and the Empire first. Gladstone and the Liberals, in contrast, believed that Britain had a responsibility to support freedom abroad, even if it was sometimes contrary to British interests. The differences between them were on display in the late 1870s, when rising nationalism in the Balkans dragged Russia and the Ottoman Empire into conflict once again. In 1876, the slaughter of as many as 100,000 Bulgarian civilians by the Ottoman forces led Gladstone to launch a national campaign against the "Bulgarian Atrocities" in which he called for British intervention. Disraeli, whose Conservatives were in power at the time, discounted the reports of the massacre and refused to send troops. "Our duty at this critical moment," he said, "is to maintain the empire of England."

Disraeli's government played a key role in negotiating the Treaty of Berlin that ended the Russo-Turkish War in 1878. Gladstone and his supporters, however, worried that the treaty did not guarantee civil liberties for Ottoman religious minorities. During the election campaign of 1880, Gladstone promised to help defend British interests by supporting the ambitions of oppressed minorities through diplomatic pressure. The Liberals swept to a landslide victory, showing popular support for a humanitarian diplomacy that defended minority rights.

But although it is tempting, and in some ways accurate, to see the Bulgarian crisis as pitting Disraeli's hardheaded pragmatism against Gladstone's idealistic moral fervor, there were other forces at work as well. Gladstone took up the Bulgarian cause not only because he opposed the actions of the Turks, but also because he saw it as a way to whip up popular opinion against the Conservatives at home, a strategy that proved extremely successful. The mixture of moral and political motives that Gladstone displayed in his response to the Bulgarian Atrocities was typical of his foreign and imperial policy. He was quite capable of abandoning his idealism in the face of the complexities of international geopolitics and Britain's role as the ruler of the largest empire in the history of the world. Long a believer in the right of national self-determination, he was initially sympathetic when a revolt broke out in opposition to increasing European influence in Egypt in 1879. As the revolt grew in scale, however, he altered his view, and by 1882 he had come to see it as a dangerous and destabilizing force. That summer, he ordered the bombing of Alexandria, which was followed by a military invasion that secured British domination of Egypt for the next half-century. Gladstone defended the takeover of Egypt as necessary for upholding the balance of power in Europe, for if Britain had not stepped in, he believed some other European power, most likely France, certainly would have.

Conclusion

The mid-Victorian era was a time of shifting priorities and values, and some long-held norms that governed gender and class relations began to change. The 1867 Reform Act marked another step in the expansion of democracy, thereby further eroding upper-class dominance of British politics. Parliament also passed legislation that allowed women to retain their property after they married, while increased opportunities for women's education challenged the idea of separate spheres. Although religion remained a very powerful force in many people's lives, the secularization of education and Darwin's ideas about evolution reduced its power.

These political and social changes took place in a domestic context that was increasingly shaped by issues beyond Britain's shores. The debates over the Bulgarian Atrocities and the situation in Egypt reflect that, although Disraeli and Gladstone differed on many points, they both were forced to operate as politicians in a world that was dominated by foreign and imperial concerns. The historian John Darwin refers to "the pervasive effects of Britain's external connections on its institutions and outlook" in this era. Few actions by contemporary politicians failed in some way to account for imperial concerns. Debates over the establishment of the Church of England, for example, frequently referred to the Empire, as the Liberals argued that its application to the colonies would unite non-Anglican colonial subjects against British rule. The pervasive commitment to free trade, meanwhile, often functioned as a means of disguising the extent of Britain's formal conquest and economic domination of its colonies. In these ways, mid-Victorian Britons existed very much in a global and imperial world.

Bibliography

Aldous, Richard, *The Lion and the Unicorn: Gladstone vs. Disraeli* (2007)

Auerbach, Jeffrey A., *The Great Exhibition of 1851: A Nation on Display* (1999)

Bender, Jill C., *The 1857 Indian Uprising and the British Empire* (2016)

Buchanan, Angus, *Brunel: The Life and Times of Isambard Kingdom Brunel* (2002)

Colin, Jonathan, *Evolution and the Victorians: Science, Culture, and Politics in Darwin's Britain* (2014)

Foreman, Amanda, *A World on Fire: Britain's Crucial Role in the American Civil War* (2011)

Gleadle, Kathryn, *British Women in the Nineteenth Century* (2001)

Gough, Barry, *Pax Britannica: Ruling the Waves and Keeping the Peace in the Century before Armageddon* (2014)

Hadley, Elaine, *Living Liberalism: Practical Citizenship in Mid-Victorian Britain* (2010)

Hall, Catherine, Keith McClelland, and Jane Rendall, *Defining the Victorian Nation: Class, Race, Gender, and the British Reform Act of 1867* (2000)

Hoppen, K. Theodore, *The Mid-Victorian Generation 1846–1886* (2006)

Hunt, Tristram, *Building Jerusalem: The Rise and Fall of the Victorian City* (2006)

Jenkins, Roy, *Gladstone: A Biography* (2002)

Kriegal, Lara, *The Crimean War and its Afterlife* (2022)

Wagner, Kim A., *The Skull of Alum Bheg: The Life and Death of a Rebel of 1857* (2017)

Wolmar, Christian, *Fire and Steam: How the Railways Transformed Britain* (2009)

7 Britain and Empire, 1870–1910

Topics covered

- Monarchy and the Empire
- Scramble for Africa
- Britain in Egypt and the Sudan
- Strategies of colonial rule
- Impact of empire on the British metropolis
- British and colonial critiques of the Empire
- Boer War
- Rising nationalism in India

Timeline

1869	Suez Canal opens
1877	Victoria becomes Empress of India
1879	Anglo-Zulu War
1882	British occupation of Egypt begins
1885	Indian National Congress founded
1889	British South Africa Company established
1892	Dadabhai Naoroji elected to Parliament
1893–4	First Matabele War
1897	Diamond Jubilee
1899–1902	Boer War
1905	Partition of Bengal and beginning of *Swadeshi* movement

Introduction

We have already seen how empire formed a prominent part of Britain's economy, culture and society in the eighteenth and first half of the nineteenth centuries. In the eighteenth century imperial commodities such as tea became everyday items, while the returning wealth of the Indian nabobs sparked concerns about their impact on the political and social elite of Britain. By 1800, Britain ruled a global empire, composed of peoples of many races, ethnicities and religions. In the early and mid-Victorian era, the British Empire continued to expand,

DOI: 10.4324/9781003284758-7

aided by new technologies such as the steamship and the telegraph. These not only helped the British to suppress a major rebellion in India in the mid-nineteenth century, but also helped ensure that it and other imperial events seized the attention of the British public. Thus, neither imperial expansion nor the influence of empire on British culture was new in the last decades of the nineteenth century.

These things, however, became so prominent in this era that we have decided to treat the late Victorian empire in a separate chapter, which will explore the strengths and the vulnerabilities of the British Empire during the period from the 1870s to the First World War. In the final two decades of the nineteenth century, the scale and pace of imperial expansion increased. Back home in Britain, meanwhile, the Empire was on more prominent public display in London, which was both an imperial and a national capital, and it came to occupy an increasingly large place in the consciousness of many Britons. An increasing number of peoples from Britain's colonial empire traveled to Britain and experienced the culture and society of the metropolis firsthand. Some offered pioneering critiques of imperial rule. While Britons gloried in their imperial achievements, there was also a growing sense that the Empire was threatened from without by the rising power of other nations and from within by the resistance of indigenous peoples and the beginnings of modern nationalist movements that sought a share in colonial governance. As modes of ruling the Empire shifted to deal with this latter threat, racial hierarchy and the privileged status of the white colonial elite became even more apparent.

The Diamond Jubilee and the Monarchy

In 1897, Queen Victoria celebrated her *Diamond Jubilee*, commemorating her sixtieth year on the throne. The Jubilee was an imperial celebration of an imperial monarch, culminating in a splendid six-mile procession through the heart of London. All eleven prime ministers of the self-governing colonies of white settlement were in attendance, along with numerous Indian princes. Over 45,000 soldiers – making it the largest military display ever held in Britain – from around the Empire marched, including troops from India, the Caribbean, Africa, Canada and Australia. The *Daily Mail* wrote, "up they came, more and more, new types, new realms at every couple of yards, an anthropological museum – a living gazetteer of the British Empire." The focal point was Queen Victoria herself, who rode in an open carriage driven by eight cream-colored horses. American writer Mark Twain was in attendance and observed, "in her the public saw the British Empire itself. She was a symbol, an allegory of England's grandeur and the might of the British name."

Twain's comment illustrates how the role of the monarchy had shifted over the course of the nineteenth century. Despite the erosion of royal power since 1688, at the beginning of Victoria's reign the monarchy still wielded considerable influence over the affairs of state. Her two predecessors, George IV and William IV, had actively intervened in a variety of political issues; the latter, in a reign of only seven years, had dismissed ministries on three occasions and dissolved Parliament twice. The young Victoria, meanwhile, had sparked the "Bedchamber Crisis" in 1839, when Lord Melbourne's Whig government fell and she refused to accede to the new prime minister Robert Peel's request that she dismiss those women among her ladies in waiting who were the wives or relatives of Whig politicians. (The fact that Peel even felt it necessary to make such a request shows that he feared political interference from a monarch who was influenced by the views of his opposition.) Victoria's husband, Prince Albert, contributed to her efforts to influence politics by attempting to redefine the monarchy as an impartial and independent executive that could govern for the entire nation without being biased by partisan perspectives.

Figure 7.1 & 7.2 Queen Victoria's Diamond Jubilee was celebrated not only in Britain, but also throughout the British Empire. Figure 7.1 shows a 60-foot-high clock tower in Penang, now in Malaysia but then the capital of the British colony called the Straits Settlements; Figure 7.2 shows a fountain in Victoria, the capital of the Seychelles. Both were built in honor of the Diamond Jubilee.

Figure 7.1 reproduced courtesy of CEphoto, Uwe Aranas; Figure 7.2 reproduced courtesy of Marco Verch.

By the end of Victoria's reign, however, things were very different. The growth of the electorate after the political reforms of the nineteenth century and the emergence of modern party politics both diminished royal power. Albert's death from typhoid fever in 1861 removed a tremendous source of energy and creativity from the royal household and plunged the Queen into a state of deep mourning. For the next decade, Victoria rarely appeared in public, leading to calls from a small but vocal minority for the monarchy to be abolished and for Britain to become a republic. But rather than disappearing, the monarchy evolved. Some of these changes began even before Albert's death. Victoria's status as a woman made it possible to recast the monarchy as a symbol of domesticity. With her nine children and harmonious marriage, she embodied the contemporary feminine ideal. Victoria embraced this role; despite her status as the titular head of the world's largest empire and most powerful nation, she did not believe in female power. In 1870, Victoria wrote of "women's rights" as a "mad, wicked folly": "It is a subject which makes the Queen so furious that she cannot contain herself. God created men and women different – then let them remain each in their own position." Her favorite painters, Edward Landseer and Franz Winterhalter, ensured that the public saw images of the royal family that portrayed her as a wife and mother first and a ruling monarch second.

In the 1870s, Victoria's symbolic role took on another dimension. The Conservative leader Benjamin Disraeli, with whom Victoria enjoyed a warm relationship, was able to use his wit and charm to coax the Queen into resuming a more visible role. In this role, Victoria was recast in a new light: as the head and unifying symbol of the British Empire. In 1876,

Disraeli's government passed the Royal Style and Titles Act, *which made Victoria the Empress of India*. Over the final decades of her reign, the Queen's image appeared on stamps and medals throughout the Empire; statues of her were erected in dozens of colonial capitals; and her portrait was displayed in public buildings and private homes all over the world. A wide range of natural and man-made geographical features were named after her, ranging from islands and mountains to parks and entire cities.

For her part, Victoria was keenly interested in her imperial possessions. She protested vehemently when the government agreed to cede Heligoland to Germany in return for recognition of Britain's claim to Zanzibar and for other territorial concessions in East Africa. She never traveled beyond Europe, but she surrounded herself with gifts and objects from her colonial realms. At the time of the Golden Jubilee in 1887, which celebrated her fiftieth year on the throne, two indigenous peoples were selected to become her servants; one, Abdul Karim, to whom Victoria gave the title "Munshi" (Urdu for "teacher"), became so beloved by the Queen that it made her other attendants jealous. In the 1890s, she took an active interest in the design of an Indian-style "Durbar Wing" at Osborne House, her home on the Isle of Wight where she spent much of her time after Albert's death.

Historians have traditionally interpreted the increasing association between the monarchy and the British Empire in the late nineteenth century as a further indication of the diminishment of the institution's real political powers and of its growing role as a symbol of national unity. But there was more to the Queen's new imperial role than mere symbolism. The historian Miles Taylor writes that Disraeli sought to make her Empress of India not merely to flatter her, but to underline Britain's global power to its rivals, Russia and Germany in particular. The monarchy thus played a part both in the increasing centrality of empire to British culture in the late Victorian era and in Britain's efforts to maintain its global position.

At the same time as it displayed the monarchy's emerging role as a symbol of imperial unity and of Britain's global power, however, the Diamond Jubilee raised questions about the future of the British Empire. Although a staunch advocate of empire, the poet laureate Rudyard Kipling struck a cautionary note in his poem "Recessional," in which he warned that all empires ultimately decline and fall:

> Far-called, our navies melt away;
> On dune and headland sinks the fire:
> Lo, all our pomp of yesterday
> Is one with Nineveh and Tyre!
> Judge of the Nations, spare us yet,
> Lest we forget – lest we forget!

Kipling's fears about the future were not entirely unfounded: in spite of the display of imperial military might at the Jubilee, Britain's status as a world power had by 1897 clearly declined since its mid-Victorian apex. Other European nations, notably the newly unified Germany and the United States, were not only challenging but surpassing Britain's industrial output and had established their own overseas empires. The American victory in the Spanish–American War and its acquisition of Guam, the Philippines and Puerto Rico confirmed its emergence as another rising global power. Beginning in the 1880s, Germany acquired territory in east, west and southwest Africa, as well as in New Guinea and Samoa in the South Pacific.

The Jubilee also engendered debates about the future of the Empire within the United Kingdom and beyond its shores. In Dublin, nationalists advocating Home Rule attended the Jubilee celebrations with black flags and a coffin labeled "British Empire," which they flung into the River Liffey. In India, the Jubilee took place amidst a terrible famine. Policies implemented by colonial officials placed strict limitations on the ways in which relief could be administered, contributing to the deaths of a million Indian men, women and children from disease and starvation. In 1897, two Hindu men in the western city of Pune assassinated a British official as he was returning from a Jubilee celebration. These stirrings of discontentment would continue to grow throughout the Empire. Within two years, Britain would be embroiled in a war in South Africa that would lead many people to question the fitness of the British as an imperial race, and in the following decade, Indian nationalism would assume new and more radical forms, challenging imperial rule with protests, boycotts and acts of violence.

Imperial Conquest and Expansion

The conquest and annexation of territory was a continual process across the nineteenth century, but after 1870 the pace of imperial expansion accelerated. In part this was due to the technological changes that were noted in the previous chapter, which revolutionized communications and transportation. Steamboats, which were able to travel up rivers, made the exploration of the African continent possible and greatly contributed to knowledge of the terrain, natural wealth and resources of Africa. In 1830, it took about two years for a person in Britain to receive a reply from a letter to India. By 1850, steam-powered mail boats had cut that time to two or three months, and by the 1870s, with the invention of the telegraph, a telegram from London to India arrived in a matter of hours, and a reply could be received on the same day.

Technology did not just speed up travel and communications, however. It also made possible the rapid conquest of territory. Steam-powered ships could quickly move British and colonial troops to where they were required. New weapons such as breech-loading rifles, repeating rifles and machine guns provided accuracy and rapid fire. In many imperial locales prior to the middle of the nineteenth century, the British had faced roughly equivalent armaments, and conquest was a process measured in decades. After 1870, however, the arms advantage shifted decisively towards Britain. This advantage enabled the rapid conquest of millions of square miles and millions of people. One of the most striking examples of this was the Battle of Omdurman in 1898, in which 25,000 British and Egyptian troops faced more than 50,000 Sudanese soldiers. Over 10,000 Sudanese were killed and another 13,000 wounded, while the Anglo-Egyptian forces lost only fifty men.

The Experience of Warfare 4

The Battle of Omdurman and the New Weapons of the Late Nineteenth Century

On the 2nd of September 1898, British and Egyptian forces faced the army of the independent Islamic state in the Sudan, which had been established after the British gained control of Egypt in 1882. Despite being outnumbered two-to-one, the combined British and Egyptian force easily prevailed. Of the 52,000 men in the Sudanese army, 12,000 were killed, 13,000 wounded and 5,000 taken prisoner. The British and Egyptian army, meanwhile, had only fifty men killed and 380 wounded. What had made such a lopsided victory possible, and turned a battle into a slaughter? The British and Egyptian side possessed fifty pieces of artillery and forty Maxim machine guns capable of firing 600 rounds per minute, as well as a few twelve-barreled Nordenfelt organ guns, which could fire 1,000 rounds a minute. Their troops were armed with Lee Metford or Lee Enfield rifles, which had a range of 2,800 yards and which an experienced soldier could fire ten times a minute. The Sudanese soldiers were, according to the young Winston Churchill who was working as a war correspondent at the time, armed with swords and spears. This was an exaggeration: they did possess some captured rifles and a few captured artillery pieces and machine guns, but they were poorly maintained and short on ammunition. Their biggest deficiency, however, was tactical awareness. The Sudanese commander, the Khalifa, ordered a series of frontal charges, but they were mowed down by artillery fire before they got within fifty yards of the British trenches. One eyewitness described it as "not a battle but an execution." The Battle of Omdurman provides one explanation for how the British were able to conquer so much territory in the final decades of the nineteenth century: superior weaponry. Previously, the armaments of the British and those who resisted imperial conquest in Asia and Africa had been roughly similar, but now the gap in lethality was enormous. The British, however, did not learn the lesson that battles like Omdurman taught. In the First World War, generals would order frontal charges against an entrenched enemy armed with machine guns and heavy artillery, with predictably bloody results.

BATTLE OF OMDURMAN. FRIDAY. SEPTEMBER 2. 1898.

Figure 7.3 This contemporary chromolithograph shows the Battle of Omdurman, making clear its lopsided nature as massed ranks of red-coated British troops fire into the Sudanese ranks, many of whom already lie dead or wounded. Sutherland, A., active, 1898.
Reproduced courtesy of the Wellcome Collection.

Yet while these technological innovations brought many advantages, they were not the exclusive province of the British, and they also made possible the imperial expansion of other European nations such as France and Germany as well as the United States. While in 1860 Britain produced half of the world's iron and coal and owned a third of the world's merchant shipping, by the following decade Britain's industrial and commercial dominance was no longer secure. The economies of the nations who had industrialized later grew faster than Britain's, and they were able to achieve pre-eminence in new industries such as chemical dyes. Empire thus became even more important to the maintenance of Britain's global position, and the massive acquisition of territory that took place in the final decades of the nineteenth century, called by historians the "New Imperialism," was intended to preserve Britain's position as a world power. This was illustrated by a statement by the English cultural critic John Ruskin, who in 1870 declared, "This is what England must either do, or perish. She must found colonies as fast and as far as she is able."

Between 1870 and 1900, Britain acquired as colonies or protectorates over 750,000 square miles of territory, with a population of 20 million people, in Asia and the South Pacific, and about 4.4 million square miles of territory, with a population of 60 million people, in Africa. As these figures suggest, the primary theater of this drive for expansion was what became known as the "Scramble for Africa." Prior to the 1880s, Britain's formal control of African territory was limited to parts of West Africa and the Cape Colony at the continent's southern tip. Close to 80 percent of the continent remained under the control of indigenous rulers in 1880, but over the following three decades, the situation changed dramatically. By the beginning of the First World War in 1914, only the states of Ethiopia and Liberia retained their independence from European rule.

British expansion in specific regions was often sparked by concerns that other European powers would establish a dominant position there. In West Africa, an increasing Dutch, French and German presence caused British traders to fear that they would lose access to both goods and markets further inland. The response was the annexation of large areas of territory in present-day Ghana, Nigeria and Sierra Leone. In southern Africa, British expansion was fueled by a goal of containing both Germany, which had established territorial claims in modern-day Namibia, and the Afrikaners or Boers, the descendants of seventeenth- and eighteenth-century Dutch settlers, in the Transvaal region. These rivalries extended into Asia as well. In 1884, the British partitioned the island of New Guinea with Germany, while in the following year, fears of a French extension of their territory in Indo-China lay behind the conquest of Upper Burma.

Simply cataloguing the possessions acquired by the British does not explain the process of imperial expansion, however. In fact, it can give a false impression of the ease and inevitability of the growth of the British Empire in this era. This was the view expressed by one influential contemporary, the historian Sir John Seeley, who wrote in *The Expansion of England* (1881) that Britain had "conquered and peopled half of the world in a fit of absence of mind." In reality, imperial expansion was undertaken for a variety of concrete and often tightly interwoven motivations: political, strategic and economic.

The expansion of British economic and political power in Egypt, culminating in its conquest, illustrates the multiplicity of motives in the process of late nineteenth-century imperialism. Egypt was nominally part of the Ottoman Empire, but by the mid-nineteenth century it was a quasi-independent nation under the rule of an official called the khedive. Britain had already intervened in Egyptian affairs several times in previous decades, principally because Egypt occupied a strategic position between India and the Mediterranean. Egypt's importance was further enhanced by the construction of the *Suez Canal*, completed with French engineering and financial assistance in 1869. The canal's immense value quickly became evident, particularly to the British, who were responsible for 80 percent of the traffic that passed through it. When the financial problems of Ismail Pasha, Egypt's spendthrift khedive, forced him to sell his shares in the Canal Company in 1875, prime minister Benjamin Disraeli arranged for the British government to purchase them. In the years that followed, the khedive's financial position continued to deteriorate, and the Egyptian government came to be dominated by his French and British creditors. In 1879, Britain and France prevailed upon the Ottoman sultan to replace him with his son Tewfik Pasha.

Increasing Egyptian opposition to European control of their country's affairs led in 1882 to a nationalist revolt, led by an army officer, Colonel Ahmed Urabi. (His name was often spelled "Arabi" by the British.) The following year, after riots in the port city of Alexandria caused the deaths of fifty Europeans, Britain intervened militarily, first by bombarding Alexandria from naval ships and then by dispatching 40,000 troops. In September 1882, British forces defeated Urabi at the battle of Tel-el-Kebir.

 See document "Colonel Urabi's Revolt in Egypt" at www.routledge.com_cw_ barczewski.

While the Liberal prime minister William Gladstone supported Egyptian liberation from the Ottoman Empire, he also ordered the bombing of Alexandria and the British occupation of Egypt. In the ensuing decades, though Egypt never formally became a British colony, it was run as one, with a consul-general who directed the khedive's ministers and a colonial administration that was second in size only to India's. By 1906, there were over 600 British officials in Egypt. At the outbreak of the First World War in 1914, when the Ottoman sultan allied with Germany, the khedive was deposed and a British protectorate established. Egypt was restored to independence in 1922, but British influence over Egyptian affairs remained powerful until the 1940s.

The long saga of Britain's involvement in Egypt shows the complexities of the motivations that underlay imperial expansion in the late nineteenth century. First, there was the obvious strategic value of Egypt and the Suez Canal in particular. Second, there was competition with France, who might assume a dominant role if the British relinquished theirs. Third, there were financial considerations: British banks had supplied massive loans to the khedive, and they demanded that their government ensure that he did not default. In addition, many British investors, including Gladstone himself, owned stock in the Suez Canal Company, and in consequence they did not wish to see the canal seized by Egyptian nationalists.

Ruling an Empire

The colonies of Britain's late-nineteenth-century empire were extremely diverse, and so were the British methods of ruling them. The Indian Civil Service, with strong representation from public schools and **Oxbridge**, was the most prestigious of the colonial services. Most colonies, however, did not develop such elaborate administrations, for fundamental to empire was profit, and profit required that colonies be administered cheaply. As a result, the late nineteenth century witnessed a revival of conquest and administration that was carried out by chartered companies like the former East India Company. These companies were responsible for much of the British colonization of Africa. From 1888 onwards, the Imperial British East Africa Company administered Kenya and Uganda. In 1889, the British government gave the *British South Africa Company* (BSAC) the right to administer a huge area of southern Africa and to conquer further territory. The BSAC, like other chartered companies, offered British governments the prospect of economic development at minimal cost, as well as an influx of white settlers who would establish Britain's "effective occupation," and therefore validate their legal claim.

The prime mover behind the BSAC was Cecil Rhodes. Born in England in 1853, Rhodes traveled to South Africa at the age of seventeen in an effort to improve his poor health. He began buying up diamond mines in the vicinity of Kimberly, which he consolidated under the De Beers Mining Company. By the late 1880s, he had a virtual monopoly on the diamond trade. He gradually extended the territory under his control north to the Zambezi River, where he created two new colonies called Northern Rhodesia (now Zambia) and Southern Rhodesia (now Zimbabwe). Rhodes had a strong, but deeply racist, imperial vision that espoused the unity not only of the British Empire, but also of everywhere that was inhabited by the "Anglo-Saxon race," including the United States. It was to foster unity with America, which he felt would one day rejoin the Empire, that he created the Rhodes Scholarships to Oxford University.

 See document "Cecil Rhodes's Imperial Vision" at www.routledge.com_cw_barczewski.

While some Britons considered Rhodes to be a demagogue and an unprincipled adventurer, his ideas reflected important currents in late-nineteenth-century thinking about empire. His vision shows that, while profit was a vital motive, also critical to the imperial ideology of the late nineteenth century was the idea of a "civilizing mission." In addition to the profits and benefits that the colonizers derived from empire, they were supposed to be bringing progress, education and moral enlightenment to their colonial subjects. By the turn of the twentieth century, there were 10,000 British missionaries around the world. Modernization was another important element of imperial ideology, and science and statistics were widely deployed in the colonial empire. For many colonial servants and social scientists, knowledge of colonial societies and their cultures and customs translated directly into an ability to rule the diverse peoples of the Empire effectively. The 1881 Indian census epitomized this quest for knowledge of the Empire's peoples, as it incorporated not only statistical information, but also extensive data about India's religions, customs and economy. The railways and other infrastructure improvements that were constructed in Africa, India and elsewhere in Asia were another facet of the modernizing aspect of colonialism. The economic benefits of these projects, however, largely accrued to the British. By 1910, for example, India had the fourth-largest railway system in the world, but the substantial profits from its construction went largely to private investors in Britain, who were offered guaranteed returns of up to 5 percent annually on their investment. Indians provided the unskilled labor, but the skilled engineers came from Britain. To be sure, railways benefited the people of India. Among the middle classes and elite, the ability to travel around the country helped to build a sense of India as nation. Yet the location of railway lines was determined in large part by the need to move troops quickly in order to suppress attempts at rebellion.

The railways led not to industrialization in India, but to a further dependence on British goods, as they facilitated the export of raw materials, including cotton, jute and later tea, and the import of British finished goods to India. As more Indian farmland was devoted to crops for export such as wheat and cotton, food reserves of rural communities decreased and food insecurity increased. Farmers who turned to producing cotton during the American Civil War saw prices plummet as American cotton returned to British markets after 1865.

Figure 7.4 An ostrich next to a railway carriage in South Africa in 1905. In partnership with the engineer Sir Charles Metcalfe, Cecil Rhodes dreamed of building what he termed an "African Trunk Line" that would stretch the entire length of Africa from north to south. Rhodes saw this "Cape to Cairo" railway, as it was quickly nicknamed, as the precursor to the creation of a continuous chain of British colonies extending from Egypt to South Africa. The latter actually occurred following Britain's acquisition of the former German colony of Tanganyika (now Tanzania) after the First World War. But although sections of the route from Cape to Cairo were completed, the entire project was not, as the difficulties of climate and topography, international rivalries and economic factors intervened. British Association for the Advancement of Science.

Reproduced courtesy of the Wellcome Collection.

The worldwide agricultural depression that began in the 1870s further depressed grain prices and pushed many farmers into debt.

As India's rural economy was being transformed by colonial rule, drought conditions caused by the failure of seasonal monsoon rains caused widespread crop failure. The 1866 famine in Orissa killed over a million people, around one-third of the population. When Queen Victoria was proclaimed Empress of India in an elaborate ceremony in Delhi on the first day of 1877, large numbers of her Indian subjects were dying following another monsoon and crop failure. Between four to five million perished in the Madras famine between 1876 and 1878; millions more died in a famine that stretched from 1899 until 1902. Photographs by missionaries documented the starvation and suffering of famine victims, whose emaciated bodies reached the stage of extreme malnourishment known as skeletonization.

While climatic conditions were at the root of crop failures in late nineteenth-century India, they were not the primary cause of famine. As in Ireland, economic change and famine policies led to widespread human suffering. Famine morality rates in India were in fact even higher than during the Irish potato famine. Indian grain prices skyrocketed as crops failed, and the Government of India held rigidly to the *laissez-faire* economic doctrine that government intervention in the market was unnecessary and harmful to the economy. Wheat exports continued in the midst of famine; over 300,000 tons of Indian wheat were exported to Europe during 1877–8 alone. Famine outbreaks were, as in Ireland, typically dismissed as the product of peasant laziness or improvidence, not the structural changes that colonial rule had brought to India's economy or the inadequacies of government relief measures. While the new railways played an important role in transporting supplies for famine relief, aid to famine victims – as in mid-nineteenth-century Ireland – was often limited by restrictions that prevented many sick and starving individuals from obtaining adequate assistance. Until the end of the century, adult Indians receiving famine relief were expected to labor on railroad and canal construction. A "distance test" was applied that prohibited able-bodied adults and older children from receiving famine relief within ten miles of their home. These works projects in many instances proved fatal to sick and malnourished indigenous peoples who worked on them.

"Modernization" thus involved the transformation of colonial economies for the benefit of Britain. It also meant the promotion of the English language. Many members of the Indian middle classes actively sought English language skills and English education, which offered opportunities for careers in colonial administration. By the early twentieth century, half a million Indians were studying English in universities, and many young men (and sometimes women) sought higher education in Britain. Yet the British, while recognizing that an English-educated colonial elite was crucial to the maintenance of their empire, also tended to be suspicious of indigenous peoples' growing desire for a share in colonial rule. Queen Victoria's Proclamation of 1858, issued in the wake of the Indian Rebellion, had promised Indians government employment in accordance with their "education, ability, and integrity." But although thousands of Indians filled the lower ranks of the army, police, and colonial bureaucracy, in 1880 only sixteen could be found among the 900 members of the elite Indian Civil Service.

In both India and Africa, British administrators tended to cultivate the "traditional" elites of colonial society rather than the western-educated middle classes. Frederick Lugard, high commissioner for northern Nigeria at the turn of the twentieth century, pioneered a widely emulated system of "indirect rule" in which African chieftains were recruited to keep the colonial state running. In the **Raj**, the British favored the Indian maharajahs who ruled the princely states under British control. These Indian princes featured prominently in splendid ceremonies known as durbars (a term adapted from a Mughal court ritual), which celebrated events such as the coronations of British monarchs.

The late-nineteenth-century British Empire was complex, and its ideals were often contradictory. One contradiction was to have major consequences in the twentieth century. The "civilizing mission" of colonialism was meant to prepare the colonized for the responsibilities of self-government. In 1839, the historian and East India Company servant Thomas Babington Macaulay, who argued for a system of English education for the Indian elite, had predicted that when such a day came "it will be the proudest day in English history." Yet while "responsible self-government" had been progressively granted to the white settlement colonies, similar concessions were denied to the non-white parts of the Empire. By 1885, the first moderate Indian nationalist organization, the *Indian National Congress*, had convened; its goal was to petition not for independence, but for a greater Indian role in colonial government. But whereas early nationalist organizations were moderate, even deferential, by the twentieth century they were calling more assertively for self-rule.

The Empire at Home

By the turn of the twentieth century, for many Britons the idea of a Britain without its global empire was unthinkable. Accordingly, the Empire played a prominent role in British popular culture. The historians Catherine Hall and Sonya O. Rose have observed that for "the majority of Britons . . . their everyday lives were infused with an imperial presence." Not only did British consumers encounter a wide range of imperial goods, but also advertisements in this era prominently featured the Empire. In 1902, Bovril, a popular brand of beef extract, used the colonies of the Empire to spell out its product's name, one of several imperial-themed advertisements that the company produced.

Imperial themes featured prominently in popular entertainment as well. A prominent example was music hall, which combined song, comedy, acrobatics and dancing. During the age of the "New Imperialism," music hall was at the height of its popularity, as theaters expanded from the city centers into the suburbs, where they attracted an audience from the upper ranks of the working class as well as the lower middle class. The audiences and performers were predominantly male, and many performances espoused a masculine, militarist form of patriotism. It was from music hall that the term "**jingoism**" – meaning enthusiastic, bellicose patriotism – emerged. The term originated in a song written in 1877, when Russia threatened the Ottoman capital of Constantinople, which Britain viewed as a threat to the Mediterranean and the Suez Canal.

 See document "Jingoism" at www.routledge.com_cw_barczewski.

The patriotic and imperial content of music halls was obvious and prominent. How empire was woven into the fabric of British life in more subtle ways is demonstrated by the zoo in Regent's Park, one of London's most popular recreational sites. Many of the animals came from British colonies in Africa and Asia. Some were donated by explorers or by colonial peoples. The zoo's famous elephant, Jingo, had been brought home by the Prince of Wales from his tour of India in the mid-1870s, while exotic birds such as ostriches and emus were the gifts of British Army regiments who had served in Africa. Guidebooks depicted the "taming" of the animals as an illustration of Britain's natural right to rule a great empire. A 1905 guidebook called *My Book of the Zoo*, for example, spoke of the "terrible destruction" that tigers wrought on the people of India, and how British hunting of tigers helped to alleviate their woes: "To shoot a tiger not only gives pleasure to the sportsman but also confers a great benefit upon the natives of that country."

Empire also featured prominently in the education of British children, not only to justify expansion, but also as part of an effort to use nationalism and imperialism to promote a cohesive society in the face of contemporary fears of class conflict and socialism. Both children and adults became enthusiastic consumers of popular adventure stories featuring imperial themes. These included novels by Henry Rider Haggard, who had served in the administration of the British colony of Natal in southern Africa. Haggard crafted stories of masculine adventure and exploration in exotic and fantastic African locales. Rudyard Kipling's stories and poems depicted the lives of the British in India and praised the British and Irish soldiers whose exploits had won and maintained the Empire. G.A. Henty produced over seventy popular adventure novels, many of which featured imperial themes. A genre of magazine known as the "boys' story paper" achieved an even greater readership, with a combined circulation of over a million. Though aimed primarily at an upper-middle-class audience, they were read widely by boys from other classes. In the late Victorian era, these boys' magazines contained numerous stories featuring gentlemanly heroes – dutiful, athletic and able to deal with seemingly any situation – who traveled the globe to explore and conquer new territories for Britain.

Britons also encountered the Empire via the numerous people from the colonies who traveled to the metropolis. These included not only colonial subjects, but also British-born men and women who had served the Empire for long periods of time in Asia, Africa and the Caribbean. Returnees from India were a particularly prominent group who brought their tastes, experiences and political views home to Britain; at the same time, they had to adjust to a life in Britain that was different in many ways to that in colonial India. The experience of these **British-Indians** demonstrates the prominence of race within the British Empire, as one of the greatest adjustments they had to make was that in Britain their racial status as whites no longer automatically branded them as a member of the elite. Most had to make do with far fewer servants than they had enjoyed in India and with a less opulent lifestyle; instead of being driven about in a private carriage, they rode the omnibus (and later the **Underground**) in London, which many found to be a novel experience. These British-Indians also influenced the tastes of British society, as they brought back their fondness for foods such as curry. They tended to settle in communities close to other British-Indians and close to shops where they could purchase Indian goods. So many returnees (along with Indian visitors and migrants) settled in the London neighborhood of Bayswater that the district was nicknamed "Asia Minor."

The Presence of Empire 6

Curry

In 2001, Foreign Secretary Robin Cook proclaimed an Indian curry, chicken tikka masala, to be the British "national dish." Cook was correct to recognize curry's hybridity as an invention of British India. With a name derived from a British adaptation of a Portuguese word, the term "curry" referred to Indian food prepared to appeal to the palate of Europeans. Returning British-Indians brought their taste for curries

Figure 7.5 Opened in 1926, Veeraswamy is London's oldest Indian restaurant.
Reproduced courtesy of stephenrwalli.

home, and recipes began to appear in British cookbooks in the mid-eighteenth century. In the early nineteenth century, Dean Mahomed's Hindustanee Coffee House in London, Britain's first Indian restaurant, catered to the British taste for curry. Most curries, however, were cooked at home by the servants of the middle classes. Later, visitors to imperial exhibitions in which the culture and society of India were showcased, such as the Empire of India Exhibitions in 1895 and 1896 and the British Empire Exhibition in 1924, could sample curries in their cafés and restaurants. The oldest Indian restaurant in London, Veeraswamy's, was established in 1926, with interior décor deliberately designed to conjure up the atmosphere of the Raj.

Retired colonial servants were not the only white peoples of the British Empire to establish a presence in Britain at this time, however. By the turn of the twentieth century, more than 10,000 Australians and New Zealanders had made the long voyage back to the "Mother Country." They were attracted to London as the first city of the British Empire and as a place where there were cultural, educational and professional opportunities not available in the colonies. In spite of their status as white men and women from a British Dominion, however, they were in many ways outsiders, viewed as different from and subordinate to native Britons.

Estimating the exact number of black and Asian Britons in this era is difficult, since census records rarely specified a person's race or ethnicity. By the late nineteenth century, however, the sight of Indians and other colonial peoples on the streets of London was far from uncommon. While people from India traveled all over the British Isles, they were particularly drawn to London, the center of imperial power that to colonial subjects also represented the heart of British civilization. According to one estimate, by 1900 there were approximately a thousand Indians in London, a city with a population at the time of 7 million. There were also a significant number of temporary visitors. In this era, many Indian aristocrats traveled to the metropolis, where they were often presented at court to Queen Victoria. Indians from the opposite end of the social spectrum traveled to Britain as servants or lascars, or seamen. In spite of efforts to repatriate maritime workers, desertion rates from ships were high, and many lascars stayed in London. The missionary Joseph Salter, who was attached to the Stranger's Home, complained that the Indian presence had turned the capital into "an Asiatic jungle of courts and alleys."

We should not assume, however, that all migrants from the Caribbean or India were either from the highest or lowest levels of society. Many were middle-class people who came to pursue educational opportunities not available at home. This included enrolment at the elite English universities of Oxford and Cambridge, which were opened to non-Anglican religions in the 1870s. Some elite and middle-class men and women from the colonies took up permanent residence in the United Kingdom after completing their education. One prominent example was John Alcindor, who became one of the first black West Indians to practice medicine in Britain. Alcindor worked in several London hospitals and established his own medical practice in 1917. Indians in London established societies to discuss and debate imperial policy and make appeals to the British government. One of the most influential was the East India Association (1866), whose members included students, politicians and retired British colonial administrators. Other colonial migrants pursued political careers. Unlike colonial legislatures, the British Parliament did not have a formal color bar, and in 1885 the Calcutta lawyer Lalmohan Ghosh became the first-ever

Indian to stand (unsuccessfully) for election. Seven years later, the Liberal *Dadabhai Naoroji* and the Conservative Mancherjee Bhownagree, both of Indian origin, were elected to the House of Commons. While Bhownagree was a supporter of British rule who opposed the idea of Home Rule for India, Naoroji was a pioneering critic of colonialism. He made alliances with British suffragists, socialists and labor activists and Irish nationalists, championing causes such as Irish Home Rule, an eight-hour workday and women's voting rights as well as a greater Indian role in colonial government and administration. According to historian Dinyar Patel, Naoroji "placed India within the ranks of leading progressive causes in Late Victorian Britain."

Naoroji's life in Britain highlights the important role colonized peoples played in formulating critiques of imperialism. For western-educated Indians like Naoroji, their country's devastating late-nineteenth-century famines underscored both the damage that colonial rule had done to India's economy and the need for Indian political representation. The 1866 Orissa famine led Naoroji to begin decades of detailed investigation into Indian poverty. He carried out much of this research in Britain, where he had arrived in 1855 to establish offices for the Bombay Indian merchant firm of Cama and Cama in Liverpool and London. While Indians had long contended that British rule had impoverished India, Naoroji's detailed statistical research established a direct link between imperial rule and impoverishment. He demonstrated that as much as a quarter of tax revenues collected in India were not reinvested in the country, but rather used to enrich the British treasury and balance Britain's international trade deficit. In contrast to rosy official statistics, his research documented the profound and widespread poverty of India. Subsequent generations of nationalists were to expand on Naoroji's pioneering "drain theory."

Naoroji presented his research to British audiences and over time helped to convince many educated Britons, including colonial administrators, of India's impoverishment. Other colonial subjects made direct appeals to the British public and government as well. In 1895, three rulers from Bechuanaland Protectorate in south-central Africa traveled to Britain in an effort to prevent Cecil Rhodes from incorporating their kingdoms into the British South African Company's territories. Led by King Khama III of the BagammaNgwato people and assisted by the London Missionary Society, they embarked on what David Olusoga calls "one of the best organized and most effective public relations operations in British history." Thousands of Britons attended their meetings and talks across England and Scotland, and the three monarchs – Khama, Sebele and Bathoen – became national celebrities. Everywhere they went in Britain, colonial subjects, on the basis of their skin color, were subject to intense scrutiny, whether they wore western clothes or traditional Indian or African attire. Presenting themselves as beneficiaries of the British imperial "civilizing mission," the three rulers attracted considerable public sympathy and met with Colonial Secretary Joseph Chamberlain as well as Queen Victoria. Khama and his associates were ultimately able to convince the government to allow Bechuanaland to remain a British protectorate, rather than being incorporated into Cecil Rhodes's territories. Bechuanaland retained this status until 1960, when it became the independent nation of Botswana.

As the visit of King Khama demonstrates, attitudes towards colonial peoples who came to Britain were complex. Social class could mitigate negative racial attitudes, although in an era in which biologically informed definitions of racial difference were the norm, romantic relationships between even "respectable" Africans or Asians and British women were considered scandalous. London's "Bobbies" actively policed racial boundaries, often intervening on the streets to prevent potential romances between Indian men and English women. John Alcindor's marriage to a white Englishwoman led to her being disowned by her family, while

KHAMA, CHIEF OF BAMANGWATO

Figure 7.6 King Khama III of the BagammaNgwato people of Bechuanaland (now Botswana), whose visit to Britain in 1895 created a sensation.

Reproduced courtesy of the British Library.

the public outcry over the engagement of Peter Lobengula, a London stage performer who claimed to be an African prince, to an Englishwoman illustrates the limits of racial tolerance in the Victorian era.

Although some colonial subjects, such as the young Mohandas Gandhi (whose life in Britain is discussed later), were intimidated by the imperial metropolis, many confidently returned the scrutiny of Britons' curious gazes and hostile stares. Indians who visited, worked and studied in Britain wrote guidebooks offering advice to their compatriots on topics such as touring London, arranging accommodations and meeting other people from India. Their recommendations included riding the omnibus for a panoramic view of the city, settling in "Asia Minor" and maintaining cordial relations with English landladies and

an air of superiority toward servants. Indians in Britain wrote admiringly of the achievements of British civilization (although many found Paris more beautiful than London) but
also critiqued both British urban poverty and colonial policies. One Indian visitor to the
1886 Imperial Exhibition in London bitterly contrasted the British fascination with Indian
commodities while "half of India goes half-naked for want of means to purchase the necessary clothing."

Race 4

Prince Peter Lobengula

In May of 1899, a show called "Savage South Africa" premiered at the Empress Theatre
in London. This imperial spectacle featured 200 black African "warriors" and white
South Africans who re-enacted events from the British conquest of southern Africa,
including the 1896 rebellion of the Ndebele people. The show was a tremendous
success, drawing crowds of thousands of Londoners for its twice-daily performances.
While "Savage South Africa" was designed to highlight the heroism of British men,
who were shown in one scene singing "God Save the Queen" as they were cut down
by African "savages," audiences also responded positively to what they saw as the martial prowess of the Africans. One white performer, to a round of applause, ad-libbed
the line, "a brave man is a brave man, whatever the color of his skin." One of the
show's stars was a man who claimed to be the son of the Ndebele king who had led
the uprising. "Prince Lobengula" became a celebrity in London, and there were stories
that he shared a bottle of champagne with the Prince of Wales when he attended the
show. But Britons' attitudes to Lobengula abruptly shifted when it was reported in the
press that he was to marry a respectable young Englishwoman named Kitty Jewell.
There was a public outcry, and newspapers criticized "the inexpressibly disgusting
. . . mating of a white girl with a dusky savage." The couple did marry, but Kitty later
ran away from her husband. Lobengula rejoined "Savage South Africa" for a tour of
English provincial cities and settled in the northern industrial city of Salford after
the tour ended. He worked as a coal miner, and later had five children with an Irish
woman. Shortly before the First World War, Lobengula came to British media attention once again when he attempted to gain a pension, attracting sympathetic coverage as "the Prince in Poverty." Lobengula's career on the London stage demonstrates
not only the appeal of imperial spectacles to late Victorian audiences, but also how
Britons could valorize non-white subject peoples of the Empire while still upholding
a sense of racial hierarchy and white racial superiority.

Challenges to Empire

The early twentieth century was a time of both internal and external tensions for Britain. The
British Empire was by far the largest in the world, three times the size of its French equivalent and ten times that of Germany. Even so, Britain's grip on its empire seemed increasingly
vulnerable. Internally, there were an increasing number of critics of empire. Some people
believed that, rather than bringing progress and modernization, British rule was draining

India of its wealth and impoverishing its people. The journalist William Digby helped to call public attention to widespread famine in southern India in the late 1870s. As a result, more than £800,000 was raised in famine relief. Other commentators offered alternative visions of colonial administration, particularly in Africa. Mary Kingsley, the daughter of a London physician, spent close to two years traveling in West Africa in the 1890s and became a prominent lecturer and writer on the subject. While Kingsley regarded African peoples as inferior, she argued against the imposition of European-based models of civilization on them. Her pioneering anthropological research and her arguments that the development of African indigenous culture should be encouraged provided the intellectual framework for what became known as the policy of "Indirect Rule," in which the British sought to rule through African intermediaries. Some Liberal and socialist politicians and social thinkers expressed similar skepticism about the ability of the British to export civilization to colonized societies. The socialist and future Labour Party prime minister Ramsay MacDonald argued in 1898, "there are other civilizations besides that of the West." The economist and social theorist J. A. Hobson, who was one of MacDonald's colleagues in the association of Liberal and socialist thinkers known as the Rainbow Circle, also rejected the premise that western civilization was the best model for colonized societies. He contended that empire had negative consequences for both colonizer and colonized. After serving as a correspondent for the left-wing *Manchester Guardian* during the Boer War, Hobson argued in his influential *Imperialism: A Study* (1902) that the engine of imperial expansion was financial, as wealthy capitalists sought outlets to invest their wealth. "An ambitious statesman, a frontier soldier, an overzealous missionary, a pushing trader, may suggest or even initiate a step of imperial expansion," Hobson wrote, "but the final determination rests with the financial power." Hobson argued that a better distribution of wealth within Britain would provide stronger internal markets for manufactured goods and eliminate the need for imperial conquest in search of new markets and areas of investment.

The Edwardian era saw more sustained discussions of the abuses of empire. In the general election of 1906, Liberal and Labour politicians called attention to the use of Chinese indentured labor in the gold mines of the Transvaal. The harsh treatment of these Chinese laborers, they argued, constituted not only barbaric and uncivilized treatment, it also deprived British workers of the opportunity for employment. In the same years, the widespread abuses of African laborers in the Congo Free State, a private colony of the Belgian King Leopold II, drew sustained criticism. The Congo Reform Association, formed in 1904 by the French-born journalist E. D. Morel, and Roger Casement, an Anglo-Irish consular official and later an Irish revolutionary, was effective at keeping the issue in the public spotlight. The lobbying of the Congo Reform Association helped to persuade the Belgian Parliament to take control of the colony in 1909 and to enact reforms.

Externally, the greatest imperial crisis of the decade was the South African War (1899–1902), or as it was more commonly called, the *Boer War*. The conflict took its name from Britain's opponents, the Boers or Afrikaners, descendants of seventeenth- and eighteenth-century Dutch settlers in southern Africa against whom the British had already fought a war two decades earlier. The Anglo-Boer conflict was prompted by both strategic and economic interests. From the 1840s onwards, the Boers controlled two independent republics, the Transvaal and the Orange Free State. In the ensuing decades, the republics had seen the arrival of a significant number of *uitlanders*, or British immigrants, but they were not given full political rights. The two republics were considered to be of little economic value until the discovery of diamonds (1867) and gold (1886) in the region. The British also feared the potential for an alliance between the Transvaal and Germany, which would threaten the sea routes to India. As a result, they used the issue of the lack of political rights for the *uitlanders* to provoke a war.

When the war began in 1899, it appeared to be a huge mismatch, in which the might of the British Empire was pitted against 60,000 Boer farmers. British military commanders expected a quick and easy victory. It did not work out that way, however, as British forces become involved in a brutal guerilla war. Pretoria, the Boer capital, fell in June of 1900, but the Boers took to the surrounding remote and rugged country. After a prolonged and costly struggle, the British were only able to defeat the Boers by using scorched-earth tactics. Troops removed over 100,000 civilians from rural areas to deprive Boer guerillas of support and moved them into prison settlements known as "concentration camps." (This was the first time this phrase was used.) Some 28,000 Boer prisoners, most of them women and children, died of malnutrition and disease due to poor sanitation. The war ultimately cost the lives of 22,000 British soldiers.

Religion and Difference 5

Anti-Semitism During the Anglo-Boer War

It is frequently argued that Britain has been less historically anti-Semitic than other European countries. Even so, Britain has a long history of anti-Semitism dating back to the Middle Ages, after the first significant migration of Jews there following the Norman Conquest. There were massacres of Jews in York in 1189 and during the Barons' Wars in the 1260s. In 1290, they were expelled from England and not permitted to return legally until 1656, although a small number of Spanish and Portuguese *conversos* (Jewish converts to Christianity) practiced Judaism secretly. By the 1730s, there were around 6000 Jews in England. In the eighteenth and nineteenth centuries, Jews were relatively tolerated, and Jews who fled to Britain from pogroms in Russia and Eastern Europe generally found a safe refuge. Between 1882 and 1919, Britain's Jewish population quintupled to 250,000. Full Jewish emancipation came in 1858 when the requirement to swear a Christian oath to hold public office was removed, allowing Jews to sit in Parliament for the first time. Lionel de Rothschild became the first openly Jewish MP that same year; the House of Commons has never been without a Jewish member ever since. In 1874, Benjamin Disraeli became the first (and still only) prime minister to be born Jewish, although he had converted at a young age to the Church of England and was a practicing Anglican. When the Second Anglo-Boer War broke out in 1899, however, some Britons blamed Jewish bankers and mining magnates, whom they saw as trying to protect their financial interests. These accusations came in particular from the left wing of British politics, as trade union leaders and the recently founded Independent Labour Party (the forerunner of today's Labour Party) accused "Jewish capitalists" of promoting an "imperialist" war. These opinions contributed to an increase in anti-Semitism in Britain in the early twentieth century, as some working-class communities began to see Jews as scapegoats for their economic difficulties. In the struggling coal-mining town of Tredegar in South Wales, many local shops and small businesses were owned by Jews. On the night of August 11, 1911, out-of-work miners attacked a Jewish shop, which led to a full-scale riot. The anti-Semitic violence soon spread to other South Welsh towns; after a week of unrest, Home Secretary Winston Churchill was forced to dispatch troops to restore order. Responding to public pressure, beginning in 1905, the British government enacted a series of restrictions on immigration that targeted Jews. Even so, Jews served their country proudly in the Anglo-Boer and First World Wars. Around 2800 fought in the former conflict, 125 of whom were killed. The 41,000 who later served in the First World War, meanwhile, represented one of the highest per capita rates of participation of any ethnic group. Among them were two of Britain's most noted war poets, Isaac Rosenberg and Siegfried Sassoon. Sassoon survived, but Rosenberg became one of 2425 Jews who lost their lives.

In 1910, the Boer republics and Cape Colony entered into the Union of South Africa. But while the British were ultimately victorious, the South African War demonstrated the weakness rather than the strength of the Empire. Within Britain, the long and costly war sparked fears of national decline and degeneracy, particularly when it became public that thousands of British Army recruits had been rejected for service due to their poor health and physical condition. Britain also experienced increasing pressures in India. There, radical nationalism increasingly appealed to a younger generation of nationalists. Instead of the moderate tactics of petitioning and appealing to British public opinion hitherto employed by the Indian National Congress, they employed more militant strategies such as public demonstrations and boycotts. In an effort to blunt the impact of Indian nationalism, Lord Curzon, viceroy of India from 1899 to 1905, *partitioned the province of Bengal* in order to divide its Hindu and Muslim populations. This led to the campaign known as the *Swadeshi* ("own country") movement. When petitioning failed, the Swadeshi protestors adopted more confrontational tactics: a boycott of British imported goods and an attempt to replace them with indigenous Indian products. Middle-class Swadeshi protestors made bonfires of piles of British textiles and forced people to purchase Indian-made cloth. The Swadeshi protests were nonviolent, but some Indian revolutionaries adopted more radical tactics, carrying out assassinations of British officials and indigenous peoples who served the colonial state. In 1909, the revolutionaries brought their campaign to Britain, when an Indian student in London shot and killed Sir William Curzon Wylie, political aide-de-camp to the secretary of state for India. Two years later, during the first and only visit to colonial India by a reigning monarch, King George V announced both the revocation of the partition of Bengal and the movement of India's capital from Calcutta, a center of Indian nationalism, to the former Mughal capital of Delhi. Neither strategy put an end to the violence. In 1912, Indian revolutionaries threw a bomb that wounded the viceroy, Lord Hardinge, as he made a ceremonial entrance into Delhi on an elephant. While neither the Swadeshi movement nor more revolutionary tactics succeeded in achieving Indian independence in the short term, they posed an increasing challenge to the British Raj, as more nationalists began to embrace the goal of "Home Rule" for India.

Conclusion

The early life of Mohandas Gandhi, who later became the most important leader of the movement for Indian independence, reveals much about the British Empire in the late nineteenth and early twentieth centuries. He was born in 1869 in Gujurat in western India, where his father was an official of the Kathiawar Agency, one of the "princely states" in which a member of the nobility exercised sovereignty on a local level but recognized the authority of the British Presidency in Bombay. Gandhi would thus have been aware of the workings of the British Raj from an early age. As his family wished for him to follow his father into princely service, he was sent to London to be educated as a lawyer. On the voyage, he

Figure 7.7 Mohandas Gandhi in 1906.
Reproduced courtesy of Dinodia Photos/Alamy Stock Photo.

cowered in his cabin because he came from a vegetarian sect of Hinduism and was afraid to ask if the food contained meat. Arriving in London in 1888, he enrolled in the **Inner Temple** to study law. In his autobiography, Gandhi recalled not only the intense loneliness of his early days in London and his difficulty at maintaining a vegetarian diet, but also his extensive efforts to make himself into a Victorian gentleman. "I wasted ten pounds on an evening suit made in Bond Street, the center of fashionable life in London," Gandhi later wrote, and "directed my attention to other details that were supposed to go towards the making of an English gentleman. I was told it was necessary for me to take lessons in dancing, French and elocution." Gandhi's experience illustrates how colonial subjects developed identities that were not simply "colonial" or "metropolitan," but hybrid.

Gandhi, however, soon rejected this embrace of Englishness and adopted a more austere and ascetic lifestyle. But he did not entirely reject the west: he studied the Bible, finding much to admire in the New Testament in particular, and made a number of non-Indian friends. After three years in London, Gandhi briefly returned to India in 1891, but he quickly found a position with an Indian trading firm that did business in South Africa. A few days after he arrived, he was ordered off a train because a white passenger refused to share a carriage with an Indian, even though he had a first-class ticket. This became the most important moment of Gandhi's life. At this time, there was a significant number of Indians in South Africa, some of them middle-class merchants and others working-class indentured laborers. They were subject to various forms of discrimination, ranging from restrictions on where they could live to a denial of the right to vote. Gandhi had only been supposed to stay in South Africa for a year, but ended up remaining for over two decades to fight for equal rights for the Indian population. His argument was premised on Indians' status as citizens of the British Empire, as expressed in Queen Victoria's proclamation of 1858 in the wake of the Indian Rebellion, which had declared that all her subjects of "whatever race or creed, be freely and impartially admitted to office in our service." To demonstrate his own loyalty to the Empire, he served as a stretcher bearer in the Boer War. Gandhi's appeals to imperial solidarity and equality fell on deaf ears, however, as the colonial authorities in London were unwilling to intervene in South Africa. He came to believe that a different strategy – peaceful, coordinated resistance – was the only means of achieving change.

In 1915, he returned to India. His efforts in South Africa had achieved little for the Indian population, but they had transformed Gandhi. He had gradually abandoned his western clothing in favor of a simple loincloth and shawl made of *khadi*, or homespun fabric. This symbolized his opposition to modernity, which he associated with exploitation, oppression and state-sponsored violence. His vision for an independent India was rural and traditional, and he would work for the remainder of his life to achieve this, as we will see in a future chapter. Gandhi's journey for the first forty-five years of his life thus incorporated the British Empire in a variety of ways. His familial origins lay in service to a princely state of the Raj. After traveling to London as a young law student, he attempted to convert himself into an English gentleman, in similar fashion to other middle-class Indians of the time. But a western education and exposure to western ideas often instilled not permanent loyalty to the Empire, but a desire for independence and equality. For Gandhi, these ideals were confirmed in South Africa, where he encountered virulent racial discrimination for the first time. He initially appealed to the Empire to recognize the loyalty and equality of its subjects, but when this failed he came to believe that independence and a rejection of the modernity that colonialism had brought was the best path forward. His journey had been long and complex, but throughout it had been shaped by his experiences as a subject of the British Empire.

Bibliography

Belich, James, *Replenishing the Earth: The Settler Movement and the Rise of Angloworld* (2009)

Bell, Duncan, *The Idea of Greater Britain: Empire and the Future of World Order, 18607–1900* (2008)

Buettner, Elizabeth, *Empire Families: Britons and Late Imperial India* (2004)

Burton, Antoinette, *At the Heart of the Empire: Indians and the Colonial Encounter in Late-Victorian Britain* (1998)

Collingham, Lizzie, *Curry: A Tale of Cooks and Conquerors* (2006)

Darwin, John, *The Empire Project: The Rise and Fall of the British World System, 1830–1970* (2009)

Davis, Mike, *Late Victorian Holocausts: El Niño Famines and the Making of the Third World* (2001)

Hall, Catherine and Sonya O. Rose, eds., *At Home with the Empire: Metropolitan Culture and the Imperial World* (2006)

Headrick, Daniel, *Tools of Empire: Technology and European Imperialism in the Nineteenth Century* (1981)

Kennedy, Dane, *Britain and Empire 1880–1945* (2002)

MacKenzie, John M., ed., *Imperialism and Popular Culture* (1986)

Metcalf, Thomas R., *Ideologies of the Raj* (1994)

Olusoga, David, *Black and British: A Forgotten History* (2016)

Patel, Dinyar, *Naoroji: Pioneer of Indian Nationalism* (2020)

Rotberg, Robert I., *The Founder: Cecil Rhodes and the Pursuit of Power* (1990)

Schneer, Jonathan, *London 1900: The Imperial Metropolis* (1999)

Woollacott, Angela, *To Try Her Fortune in London: Australian Women, Colonialism, and Modernity* (2001)

8 Late Victorian and Edwardian Britain
Social and Political Change

Topics covered

- Home Rule for Ireland
- Conservative dominance 1886–1906
- Aristocratic decline
- Changing role of women in workforce and society
- Complexity of attitudes towards sexuality and homosexuality
- Immigration
- Joseph Chamberlain and tariff reform
- Liberal resurgence after 1906
- "People's Budget" of 1909 and diminishment of power of House of Lords
- Women's suffrage movement
- Founding of the Labour Party
- Campaign for "national efficiency"
- Anglo-German naval rivalry

Timeline

1881	Land Law (Ireland) Act
1883	*The Bitter Cry of Outcast London* published
1884	Third Reform Act
1885	Criminal Law Amendment Act
1886	First Home Rule Bill
1886	Repeal of Contagious Diseases Act
1889	Naval Defence Act
1893	Second Home Rule Bill
1893	Independent Labour Party founded
1895	Jameson Raid and Kruger Telegram
1897	National Union of Women's Suffrage Societies founded
1900	"Khaki Election"
1901	Taff Vale decision
1903	Joseph Chamberlain launches campaign for tariff reform
1903	Women's Social and Political Union founded

DOI: 10.4324/9781003284758-8

1906	Liberal landslide
1905	Sinn Féin founded
1908	*Scouting for Boys* published
1909	"People's Budget"
1911	Parliament Act
1912	Third Home Rule Bill

Introduction

In 1886, Alfred Tennyson, Britain's poet laureate, published a poem entitled "Locksley Hall Sixty Years After." A sequel to his poem "Locksley Hall" (1835), in which Tennyson had expressed hopes for a utopian future, the later poem makes it clear that those hopes had not been achieved. Instead, it expresses pessimism and disillusionment:

> Truth for truth, and good for good! The Good, the True, the Pure, the Just; Take the charm "For ever" from them, and they crumble into dust. Gone the cry of "Forward, Forward," lost within a growing gloom; Lost, or only heard in silence from the silence of a tomb.

Literary scholars often point to "Locksley Hall Sixty Years After" as an encapsulation of the late Victorian and Edwardian eras, which were characterized by economic and social difficulties and growing anxiety about Britain's international and imperial position. The end of the nineteenth century brought fears that Britain's period of economic, military and imperial dominance was also coming to an end.

Not all of the changes were negative, as the relative stasis of the mid-Victorian years gave way to a renewed social dynamism that pushed Britain towards what we would think of as modernity, as measured by increased democracy and equality. At the time, however, it was not clear where change might lead. "All is doubt, hesitation, and shivering expectancy," declared the Liberal politician John Morley in 1874. At home, a restless population demanded increased voting rights for both working-class men and women, while more workers joined trade unions to press for higher wages and improved working conditions. The surge in labor activity would eventually lead to the creation of the Labour Party, which by the 1920s had supplanted the Liberals as the primary opposition to the Conservatives. At long last, the dominance of the landed interest was giving way to democracy, a change that was accelerated by the increasing difficulties of the upper classes as their incomes were reduced due to declining agricultural profits.

In Ireland, nationalists pressed harder for self-rule, with the majority of them supporting devolved government, or "Home Rule," but others a complete break with the Union. Further afield, serious rivals to Britain's global economic dominance emerged for the first time in a century, with Germany and the United States leading the way. This changed situation led to a divisive debate over whether to abandon Britain's longstanding commitment to free trade. Germany emerged as a military rival as well, as its efforts to build a navy as powerful as Britain's led to a major arms race between the two nations. With hindsight, it was clear that the long period of peace in Europe was coming to an end, though few people in 1900 or even 1910 would have predicted that the most devastating war in human history was just over the horizon.

Disuniting the Kingdom: The Home Rule Debate

In the last quarter of the nineteenth century, Ireland loomed large in British politics. Although land was the most immediate issue, the questions it engendered soon expanded to encompass broader demands for increased Irish independence. Beginning in the 1870s, a worldwide agricultural depression meant that many Irish tenant farmers were unable to pay their rents, prompting landlords to respond with evictions. An organization called the Irish National Land League called for tenants to protest by refusing to pay their rents and offered them financial and legal assistance. In what became known as the "Land War," the Land League urged its members in the late 1870s to socially ostracize landlords, their agents and those tenants who cooperated with them. Their actions contributed the term "boycott" to the English language after Captain Charles Boycott, an agent on Lord Erne's estate in County Mayo, was shunned when he and Erne refused to lower rents.

Though they were both born in 1846, the two main leaders of the Land League could hardly have been more different. Michael Davitt, a Catholic and former Fenian, had personally experienced eviction and its consequences. Born in County Mayo at the height of the potato famine, Davitt was four years old when his family was evicted for nonpayment of rent. The family immigrated to Lancashire, where Davitt went to work in a cotton mill at the age of nine. Two years later in 1857, he lost his right arm in an accident after being ordered to monitor a machine normally supervised by an older boy. Davitt never forgot the experiences of his youth, and he grew up strongly committed to Irish independence and the end of the existing system of landownership in Ireland.

The Land League's other leader was Charles Stewart Parnell, a Protestant from a landowning family in County Wicklow. In stark contrast to Davitt, Parnell grew up among the Anglo-Irish elite: he spoke with an upper-class English accent and enjoyed the gentlemanly sports of hunting and cricket. While a student at Cambridge, however, Parnell was outraged by the execution of the "Manchester martyrs," three Fenians who were hanged in 1867 for killing a policeman during an attempt to rescue several of their compatriots from an English prison. By the 1870s, he had become committed to Home Rule for Ireland. Home Rulers sought to fundamentally alter the framework of the United Kingdom by restoring a Parliament in Dublin that would manage Irish domestic affairs. By 1874, fifty-nine of the 103 Irish members of Parliament endorsed Home Rule. Parnell joined them the following year, when he was elected MP for County Meath.

For the next fifteen years, Ireland was a dominant issue in British politics. At a time when the political world was closely divided between the Conservatives and the Liberals, the Irish Home Rulers held the balance in Parliament. They used this to their advantage by negotiating with both sides, though the Liberals were always a better bet, as the Tories had been recast as the party of the Union and the Empire under Disraeli's leadership in the 1870s. The Liberal leader, William Gladstone therefore became the focus of the Home Rulers' hopes. Initially, his policy was to simultaneously coerce and conciliate Irish nationalists. The government responded to the Land War with restrictive legislation, leading to Parnell's imprisonment for six months. Gladstone also, however, secured the passage of the 1881 *Land Law (Ireland) Act*, which granted three principal demands of Irish tenants, known as the "3 F's": fair rent, fixity of tenure and freedom of sale. Over the next three decades, additional land acts established schemes for the purchase of land by Irish tenants. By 1920, over 300,000 tenants had purchased 11.5 million acres of land, out of a total of 20 million acres in all of Ireland. A social revolution in Irish landownership had taken place.

As the Land War began to achieve important victories, the campaign for increased political independence for Ireland gained momentum. "We are determined to take the power of governing Ireland out of the hands of the English Parliament and people, and transfer it to the hands of our own people," Parnell declared in 1880.

 See document "The Case for Home Rule" at www.routledge.com_cw_barczewski.

In the mid-1880s, Gladstone committed himself to Home Rule. He saw increased independence for Ireland as consistent with his belief in national self-determination, and he recognized that Ireland – and thus the United Kingdom – would never be stable without it. He also hoped that it would unite the Liberal Party around a common cause and that it would strengthen the union of England, Scotland and Wales. "The concession of local self-government," he stated, "is not the way to sap or impair, but the way to strengthen and consolidate unity." In order to justify a devolved government for Ireland within the Union, Gladstone looked to the Empire as a model. He argued that Ireland's new position would be similar to that of a self-governing colony such as Canada or Australia, which would benefit both Britain and Ireland. "The connection between this country and her colonies is not a selfish and sordid connection . . .," he declared, "It is at once a connection of interest, of honor, feeling, and duty."

Gladstone, however, failed to convince enough members of his own party that Home Rule was good for either the Union or the Empire. Instead, many Liberal MPs saw it as a major step towards the disintegration of both. They felt that allowing Home Rule for Ireland would open up the entire constitutional structure of the United Kingdom to debate. They also did not understand why, at a time when Britain was seeking to expand the Empire in Africa and elsewhere, they would let territory so close to home move towards independence. Further complicating the situation were the views of most Irish Protestants, especially in the northern province of Ulster, where most of them lived. For Ulster Protestants, the flourishing shipbuilding and other industries in Belfast were proof that the Union had delivered on its promises of economic prosperity. British Conservatives stoked fears that their wealth and religious freedoms would be eradicated by a Catholic-dominated Home Rule parliament. In 1886, Lord Randolph Churchill, a leading Conservative politician and father of the future prime minister Winston Churchill, urged resistance to Home Rule in Belfast with a ringing call to arms: "Ulster will fight, and Ulster will be right!" Ulster Unionism would continue to function as a serious obstacle to increased Irish independence for decades to come.

Alongside such strident rhetoric, Gladstone's exhortation to Liberal MPs to think "not for the moment, but for the years that are to come" seemed hopelessly idealistic. When the *Home Rule Bill* came to a vote in the House of Commons in 1886, it was defeated 341 to 311; only 229 of the 333 Liberal MPs voted for it. Ninety-four "Liberal Unionists," led by the radical reformer Joseph Chamberlain, voted against the bill. Initially, the Liberal Unionists did not see their stance as marking a permanent split in the Liberal Party, but over the next quarter-century they gradually moved closer to the Conservatives before formally merging with them in 1912. Most Liberal Unionists came from the aristocratic "Whig" wing of the Liberals; many of them were themselves Irish landowners and thus stood to lose significant wealth if Home Rule became a reality. Home Rule thus spelled the death knell of traditional Whiggism; from the 1880s onwards, the landed interest was overwhelmingly Tory.

Gladstone took his case to the country, but lost the ensuing election. The split in the Liberal Party opened the way for Conservative domination of British politics for the next two decades. In 1892, however, the Liberals briefly returned to power in a minority government. At the age of eighty-two, Gladstone was the oldest prime minister in British history. Recognizing that this would be his last chance, he immediately began drafting a *second Home Rule Bill*. Hoping to quell fears that the Union was being dismantled, this time the bill called for Irish MPs to continue to sit in the Parliament of the United Kingdom. His strategy was partly successful: the bill managed to pass the House of Commons, but it was overwhelmingly defeated in the House of Lords. Gladstone wanted to call an election as he had done in 1886, but he was persuaded not to by his cabinet and instead let the bill drop. Gladstone's success in steering the second Home Rule Bill through the House of Commons serves as a reminder, as his biographer H.C.G. Matthew writes, that "imperial Britain was not inevitably unionist," and that the constitutional arrangements of the United Kingdom remained a source of debate and dissension. But in the end, the desire to preserve the Union as it was won out.

Conservative Politics in the Late Nineteenth Century

Thanks to the Liberal split, British politics in the final decades of the nineteenth century was dominated by the Conservatives. This did not mean, however, that the status quo was unquestioningly maintained. Instead, the Conservatives were forced to adapt to a changing world, both at home and beyond Britain's shores. A key factor in bringing about this change was the Representation of the People Act, or "*Third Reform Act*," of 1884, which further extended the franchise. The act granted the right to vote to male householders (heads of households) who had been in residence for at least a year. This increased the number of eligible voters from 2.6 million to 5.6 million; two out of every three adult males in England and Wales, three out of five in Scotland and one out of two in Ireland could now vote. For the first time, the franchise encompassed a significant number of working-class men. The Third Reform Act also redistributed 150 seats according to population. These changes generally benefited urban places: London, for example, increased its representation in Parliament from twenty-two MPs to sixty-two. For the first time, the number of urban and suburban voters exceeded rural ones. Joseph Chamberlain declared, "the center of power has shifted, and the old order is giving place to the new." This was an exaggeration: millions of men, and all women, still lacked the franchise. But Chamberlain was right to point out that a significant change had occurred and that the age of mass politics, which had been born in 1867, was now reaching maturity.

The Third Reform Act was coupled with two other pieces of legislation: the Corrupt and Illegal Practices Act (1883), which limited the amount of money that could be spent on a single election, and the Redistribution Act (1885), which evened out the size of parliamentary constituencies and ensured that urban areas were represented equally with rural ones. All of these acts helped to diminish the political influence of the traditional elite. In this context, it is tempting to see the Conservative governments of the late nineteenth century as archaic anomalies. Their dominant political figure, the 3rd Marquess of Salisbury, who served as prime minister three times between 1885 and 1902, was an aristocrat from one of the most distinguished families in Britain; his ancestor Lord Burghley had been Elizabeth I's chief minister in the late sixteenth century. He grew up in Hatfield House, an impressive mansion surrounded by vast acreage in Hertfordshire, and attended Eton, Britain's most exclusive public school, before going on to Christ Church, Oxford, the preferred college of the elite. In 1853, at the age of only twenty-three, he was elected to the House of Commons as MP for Stamford in Lincolnshire, a pocket borough that was controlled by his relative the Marquess of Exeter. He then ascended effortlessly up the political ladder, serving as secretary of state for India and foreign secretary before becoming the leader of the Conservatives upon Disraeli's death in 1881.

Today, Salisbury is often remembered for his reactionary statements, such as his comment in 1887, "whatever happens will be for the worse, and therefore it is in our interest that as little should happen as possible." In the changing political landscape of the late nineteenth century, he seemed a throwback to an earlier age. There is some truth to this view: Salisbury was the last of his kind, as no other British prime minister has been a member of the House of Lords since his resignation for reasons of ill health in 1902. He sincerely believed that rule by the upper classes was in the best interest of the British nation and its people and that democracy was dangerous. But at the same time, Salisbury was an astute politician who was well aware that the political universe was shifting beneath his feet. Born two years before the First Reform Act was passed, he first became prime minister in the same year as the passage of the Third. His goal was to find a way for conservatism to adapt to this new world, not to lead a doomed crusade to try to prevent it from coming into being. As the Conservatives went on to govern Britain for more of the twentieth century than any other political party, he was in many ways successful.

As prime minister, Salisbury presided over the high imperial age of the final decades of the nineteenth century. He disliked jingoism as a manifestation of the popular politics that he loathed, but he also, like Disraeli before him, recognized its value in increasing votes for his party by linking it to the Empire. Moreover, he saw that the bombast that surrounded empire in late-nineteenth-century Britain concealed the increasingly precarious nature of Britain's global dominance, as the competition from other countries grew for trade and colonies. Salisbury might best be described as a "skeptical imperialist." He believed in empire as an enhancement to British power and prestige and admired the way in which a hierarchical, authoritarian world existed in the colonies in a way that it no longer did in Britain. But he did not believe in acquiring colonies merely to add to the amount of territory that Britain ruled, and he acknowledged that an overly aggressive approach to empire would inevitably make enemies and involve Britain in unwelcome foreign entanglements and expensive wars.

Salisbury also understood that the British Empire was fragile, depending as it did on colonial administrations and military forces that were massively outnumbered by indigenous populations. He did not share the messianic sense of a mission to spread British values or the Christian religion throughout the world of many of his contemporaries. He did, however, share their sense of superiority, seeing the world as organized into a hierarchy of peoples with the British at the top, though his worldview was determined more by class than race. He believed that overt racism would ultimately undermine Britain's authority over its colonies and was critical of its worst expressions, such as the mistreatment of the indigenous Maori by the white settlers of New Zealand. In this attitude, he was a true aristocratic paternalist who saw it as his duty to protect those who were beneath him on the social ladder. But at the same time as he wanted to prevent empire from doing moral evil, he was not much interested in using it as a force for moral good: the suppression of the slave trade in Africa, which excited the passions of many late Victorians, was of minimal interest to him.

At the end of the day, Salisbury's view of empire was pragmatic: if it was good for Britain, then it should be pursued, if not, the world should be left to its own devices. Why, then, did he preside over such a significant expansion of the British Empire in the 1880s and 1890s? It was not because of its economic worth: the territory added in that period contributed only 2.5 percent of Britain's total trade, and the total value of trade with the Empire dropped from £90 million to £81 million between 1883 and 1892. It was instead because Salisbury recognized that the competition for colonies was an inherent component of contemporary international politics, and as a result that competition needed to be managed by the British in an orderly fashion, so as to prevent it from provoking a European or, worse, global war. He also believed that Britain would rule its colonies more benevolently than other countries and that it would use them to spread free trade in ways that would benefit Britain's industrialized economy, not to create trade barriers and protectionist markets.

Much of the international world in which Salisbury's career took place was not of his, or even Britain's, making. His preference was for a continuation of the policy of "splendid isolation" – in which Britain held aloof from European entanglements – that the Conservatives had pursued under Disraeli. But he faced a variety of threats to the cornerstones of that policy: a secure empire, a strong navy and diplomatic leverage. Russian incursion on the northwest frontier of India and the interest of other European powers in acquiring colonies in Africa forced him to devote considerable attention to the Empire, and Germany's naval construction program forced him to concentrate on Britain's own fleet. In the mid-1890s, the massacre of 200,000 Ottoman Armenian subjects once again drew Britain into the internal affairs of the Ottoman Empire and brought the Eastern Question to the forefront of foreign policy concerns. By this time, the Eastern Question had grown to encompass both securing British trading interests in the East and the acceptance of moral responsibility for oppressed civilians living under despotic regimes.

In this sense, the global dominance that Britain had enjoyed was beginning to diminish, as it increasingly reacted to rather than determined international developments. Salisbury maneuvered adeptly in these changing circumstances, but there was no doubt that Britain's place in the world was changing too. A burgeoning humanitarian movement took root in this period that was focused on the rise of the "new slaveries." Largely focused on Africa, the source of many raw materials used in products consumed in Europe, British reformers protested against the practices of other empires. In the mid-1890s, forced labor in the Belgian Congo, which was privately owned by Belgium's King Leopold II, captured the attention of antislavery advocates who published exposes of atrocities on its rubber plantations in the press. British manufacturers were guilty of abetting similar practices, however. The exposure of slave-like labor conditions on the plantations in Portuguese West Africa that supplied the cocoa used in Cadbury's chocolate created a scandal, though it did little to end exploitative labor practices in Africa.

Immigration was another complex issue in a globalizing world. Britain had relatively open borders in comparison to continental Europe during much of the nineteenth century. Revisions to the Aliens Act of 1793, however, show how the question of immigration challenged British ideas about the right of an individual to seek refuge in the case of persecution. The lapse of the act in 1826 meant that all foreigners now had a right to enter Britain. This remained the case until the passage of a new Aliens Act in 1905 that distinguished between migrants seeking refuge from persecution and what we might today call economic migrants, with the primary goal of limiting Jewish immigration from Eastern Europe. In the early twentieth century, passport controls came into force that further restricted immigration.

Social Change

Salisbury and the Conservatives also presided over significant social developments. Traditional forms of spiritual life were challenged by new ideas about religion. In the late nineteenth century, spiritualism emerged as a movement largely among middle-class women, who began to explore alternative forms of spirituality that included communicating with the dead through séances. A small but culturally prominent minority of Victorians came to view Asian religions such as Buddhism and Hinduism as sources of spiritual insight. The Theosophical Society, founded in the United States in 1875 by the Russian émigré Madame Blavatsky, sought to achieve a state of universal brotherhood that transcended divisions of race, class and religion. The British Theosophist Annie Besant advocated Indian self-determination after her arrival in India in 1893. Besant went on to found the Indian Home Rule League during the First World War and in 1917 became the first female president of the Indian National Congress.

Other changes related to increased leisure time. Legislation limiting work hours led to the emergence of the six-day work week, with a half-day on Saturday. This meant that there was now a clear distinction between work and leisure, which in turn led to the emergence of new forms of mass entertainment. Local cricket and football (soccer) clubs were increasingly popular, with the former appealing primarily to the middle class and the latter to the working class. The most prominent teams in English football today – Manchester United (1878), Arsenal (1886), Liverpool (1892) and Chelsea (1908) – all date from this period. Inexpensive transportation and affordable tickets made it possible for millions of Britons to spend their days off watching their favorite team compete. Music halls continued to attract large audiences, but they faced new competition from cinema, which first appeared in the 1890s, though it did not become true mass entertainment until after the First World War. Drinking remained a popular pastime, and the pub remained a focus of social life, particularly for the working classes. Some observers estimated that working-class families spent as much as a third of their incomes on alcohol.

A broader range of people were now able to travel. The extension of the railways into more rural parts of the country made it possible for large numbers of Britons to take trips to the countryside and the seaside for the first time. Daytrippers visited the gardens and parks of the great landed estates, which became increasingly popular as tourist destinations after 1850, or wilder landscapes such as the Peak District in north central England, which was readily accessible by train from the large urban centers of Lancashire. The seaside also lured workers from Lancashire's cotton mills, as Blackpool became the first truly working-class seaside resort. Collectively, these new forms of entertainment added up to the emergence of the first modern mass culture, as the working class began to form its own distinct identity by embracing new leisure activities and experiences.

This rosy picture of late Victorian and Edwardian life as filled with fun and entertainment, however, could not entirely conceal a number of serious social issues. Though conditions had improved in Victorian cities, urban poverty remained a significant problem. In 1883, a Congregationalist minister from Scotland named Andrew Mearns published a twenty-page pamphlet entitled *The Bitter Cry of Outcast London*, in which he revealed the extent of poverty and squalor in London's East End. Mearns's work caught the attention of a wide range of people, including the prominent journalist W.T. Stead, who two years later published in the popular periodical the *Pall Mall Gazette* a series of articles entitled "The Maiden Tribute of Modern Babylon" that focused in lurid – and exaggerated – form on child prostitution in London. Less sensationalist and more scientific, but no less revelatory, was the philanthropist Charles Booth's seventeen-volume *Life and Labour of the London Poor*, which appeared between 1892 and 1903.

Urban poverty was not only a problem in London: inspired by Booth's work, Seebohm Rowntree spent two years investigating poverty in the northern English city of York. In 1901, Rowntree published the results as *Poverty: A Study of Town Life*, in which he showed that over a quarter of York's population was living in destitution. He argued that poverty was not caused by the indolence and drunkenness of the lower classes, as many people assumed, but rather by low wages. The observations of these authors helped to spark the settlement movement, in which high-minded young reformers moved into impoverished urban areas in order to provide social aid and education to the local population. The first settlement house, Toynbee Hall, was established in the East End of London in 1884.

Urban poverty was, unfortunately, nothing new. Serious financial problems for the British upper class, however, were. For the first three-quarters of the nineteenth century, Britain remained a society that was dominated by the landed elite. As late as the 1870s, 7000 upper-class families owned over two-thirds of the land in Britain. In Scotland, this concentration of acreage was even greater, with a mere 1700 families in possession of 92 percent of the country's land. Up to this point, the ownership of land still meant the possession of wealth, as it offered the most reliable means of generating a substantial income. After 1880, however, the world of the landed elite changed rapidly. As the prices for British agricultural products were undercut by competition from abroad, their incomes fell. The westward expansion of the United States opened up vast new lands for agricultural development, while other countries such as Russia and Argentina also brought large amounts of land into agricultural production. British grain imports increased from 1.7 million tons in 1870 to 3.9 million in 1900; in consequence, prices fell by half. The advent of refrigerated steamships, meanwhile, meant that it was now possible to import even highly perishable commodities such as beef.

Farmers who were earning less from their crops could not pay as much in rents, which fell by a quarter between the 1870s and 1890s. Land values also collapsed, which meant that the longstanding practice of borrowing against the value of an estate was no longer a valid strategy for getting through a difficult period. Many landowners had no choice but to sell off acreage in order to improve their cash flow, but this raised far less money than it would have previously due to the reduced prices for land. It also represented a short-term gain at long-term expense, because a reduced estate meant less income from rents. For Britain, this situation led to even more reliance on imported food. Between 1886 and 1903, over 5 million acres of farmland went out of cultivation, and by 1910, less than 10 percent of the population was employed in agriculture. At the same time, the landed elite faced an increasing tax burden. In 1894, the government introduced the death duty, or inheritance tax. It started at a rate of 8 percent on estates worth over £1,000,000, but it was repeatedly increased over the subsequent decades. The income tax and taxes on land were also increased in the first decade of the twentieth century. These increases were not arbitrary, but were imposed with the deliberate goal of redistributing wealth from its concentration in elite hands.

For the upper classes, the double blow of declining agricultural rents and increased taxes was severe. They were forced to sell not only land but also works of art, antiques and other possessions that had been in their families for centuries. In some cases, they were forced to sell their entire estates: between 1910 and 1922, Britain saw the largest transfer of land since the dissolution of Catholic monasteries during the English Reformation in the 1530s. There were not enough buyers for all of these properties, and in England, one in six country houses fell victim to the wrecking ball. Once the richest people in the world, by 1900 the British aristocracy saw their wealth outstripped by that of American plutocrats such as the Vanderbilts, Mellons, Carnegies and Rockefellers. Their political position declined alongside their fortunes. After 1885, the landed interest no longer dominated the House of Commons, and after 1905 the upper classes no longer comprised a majority of the cabinet.

The landed elite were not the only people who felt the impact of social and economic change after 1880. Women's lives, too, altered significantly as employment opportunities increased, though not all classes benefited evenly. At the lowest end of the social scale, the changes were least apparent. Domestic service continued to employ a third of women between the ages of fifteen and twenty-one, while other working-class women sought jobs in factories or as seamstresses and dressmakers. In 1906, female industrial workers earned less than half of the wages of their male counterparts. Many of them, moreover, were employed in dangerous industries that their male counterparts shunned. The trade union movement did not initially represent women workers, but eventually they were able to organize in ways that helped to improve working conditions. In London in 1888, the Match Girl Strike protested the use of cheap phosphorus in matches that caused a high percentage of workers to develop bone cancer. The women and girls who worked in the industry succeeded in forcing management to improve working conditions and shorten work hours.

For women from the upper end of the working classes and the middle classes, improved educational opportunities created new possibilities for respectable employment. The number of clerical jobs increased, as office work and the civil service expanded and employers sought to hire women for lower wages than they paid men. According to British census returns, the employment of female clerks increased from zero in 1871 to 17,859 two decades later. The invention of the typewriter, telegraph and telephone also created a demand for female workers, who were considered both to have greater dexterity in operating the machines than men and to be more adaptable to sedentary work. In cities and towns, Britain's burgeoning number of retail establishments required a growing number of "shop girls" to work behind the counters. By the early twentieth century, the majority of department-store employees were women. Other growth in female employment came in the fields of teaching and nursing, both of which expanded significantly in the late nineteenth century with the growth in state-sponsored education and the beginnings of a national health system. All of these jobs were considered to be superior to domestic service and factory work and came with higher rates of pay and greater respectability. For the first time, a woman who wished to preserve her status could find work as something other than a governess.

Although women continued to earn less than their male counterparts, their presence in new places in the workforce marked a departure from traditional divisions of labor. The Anglo-American novelist Henry James popularized the term "New Woman," which described his well-educated and independent heroines such as Isabel Archer in *Portrait of a Lady* (1881). Some people embraced the New Woman as an indication of social progress towards greater equality, casting her as a modern, independent symbol of progress. Others, however, saw her as threatening to overturn traditional gender roles. The press was full of satirical cartoons of trouser-clad women riding bicycles and smoking cigarettes, while late Victorian novels also featured a number of negative exemplars. The character of Sue Bridehead in Thomas Hardy's *Jude the Obscure* (1895) is a case in point. On the one hand, Hardy depicts her as spirited and intelligent and presents her unhappiness in her marriage to her dull husband in a sympathetic light. But her initial attractiveness is soon outweighed by her self-centeredness, shallowness and unreliability. She suffers a terrible punishment – the deaths of all three of her children and a resulting mental breakdown – for her decision to abandon her marital vows. The more conservative elements of late Victorian society doubtless approved. Victorian feminists eventually appropriated the idea of the New Woman as a symbol of liberation.

The New Woman was only one part of a wider story of changing social mores regarding sex and gender. For most of the nineteenth century, there were vast differences in conceptions of male and female sexuality. Men were considered to possess strong sexual urges and to be naturally polygamous. Though they were supposed to curb these impulses in order to support the "cult of domesticity," they enjoyed considerable license to resort to mistresses, prostitutes or pornography in order to achieve sexual satisfaction, so long as they preserved a façade of respectability. Women, on the other hand, were thought to have only occasional feelings of sexual desire and to be naturally monogamous. In *The Functions and Disorders of the Reproductive*

Organs (1857), William Acton declared, "the majority of women (happily for them) are not very much troubled by sexual feelings of any kind." Women suffered far greater consequences if they sought sex beyond the confines of marriage or engaged in unconventional sexual behavior.

The legal treatment of prostitutes demonstrated this double standard. Once tolerated as a fact of life, in the 1850s prostitution became the focus of a near-hysterical morality movement. In sermons and newspaper editorials, they were increasingly depicted as depraved, disease-carrying harlots who threatened to undermine contemporary society. This campaign led to the passage of three Contagious Disease Acts that allowed police to subject women suspected of prostitution to forced medical examinations and to detain them if evidence of venereal disease was found. Similar acts were passed to govern prostitution in the British Empire. The feminist Josephine Butler argued that the civil rights of these women were being infringed upon and that it was male lust that was to blame. Her speeches shocked many people, who were not accustomed to hearing a woman speak so frankly and publicly about sexual matters. Her success in securing the *repeal of the Contagious Diseases Acts* in 1886, however, shows that sexual attitudes were becoming less restrictive and that women's roles in the public sphere were changing.

Equal complexity existed in Victorian attitudes to homosexuality. For much of the nineteenth century, the penalty for sodomy was death. It is often assumed that the harshness of this sentence limited the number of prosecutions in cases involving acts between consenting adults, but in reality nearly 9000 cases were brought between 1806 and 1861, resulting in 404 death sentences and fifty-six executions, the last of which took place in 1835. In 1861, the penalty was changed to a maximum of life imprisonment.

The difficulty of proving that sodomy had actually occurred, however, led to a new legal strategy to curb homosexuality in the late nineteenth century. In 1885, the *Criminal Law Amendment Act* imposed a maximum two-year sentence for what was referred to as "gross indecency." (Sodomy remained a separate crime.) The author of the relevant section of the law was Henry Labouchere, a Liberal MP, and thus it became known as the "Labouchere Amendment." Along with a number of other contemporary politicians and journalists, Labouchere believed that there was an epidemic of homosexuality in Britain. As he had hoped, his amendment led to a rash of prosecutions, since the phrase "gross indecency" was sufficiently broad to cover even the slightest hint of homosexual conduct. Many other men, meanwhile, fell victim to blackmailers, as they sought to avoid public trials that would ruin their reputations and careers. The most famous case was that of the author Oscar Wilde, who in 1895 sued the Marquess of Queensberry for calling him a sodomite. The evidence that emerged during the trial led to Wilde's own prosecution for gross indecency and a two-year prison sentence. Wilde left prison bankrupt and with his reputation in tatters, and he was forced to spend the remainder of his life in exile in France.

Sexuality and Gender 3

The Trial of Oscar Wilde

The author of hit plays like *The Importance of Being Earnest* (1895), Dublin-born Oscar Wilde was one of the most successful authors of the late nineteenth century and was as well known for his witty remarks as he was for his writing. He was also gay, at a time when homosexuality remained illegal in Britain. In 1891, he began an affair with Lord Alfred Douglas, the son of the Marquess of Queensberry. Wilde was married to a woman and was discreet about his sexuality, but Douglas was as "out" as it was possible to be in late Victorian Britain. His father loathed his son's lifestyle, and he waged a campaign of harassment against Wilde in an effort to force him to end the affair. Queensberry brought a prizefighter to Wilde's house and threatened to beat him up, and he planned to disrupt the premiere of *The Importance of Being Earnest* by leaping on to the stage and revealing his sexuality. (Wilde prevented this by having the theater surrounded by police.) The last straw came when he visited Wilde's favorite London club, the Albemarle, and left a card reading, "For Oscar Wilde, posing as a somdomite [*sic*]," which was essentially a public accusation of homosexuality. Against the advice of his friends, Wilde sued Queensberry for libel. He lost the case when Queensberry's lawyer threatened to call as witnesses several men whom Wilde had paid for sex. Wilde withdrew the libel charge and was forced to pay Queensberry's legal expenses. Worse was to come: he was arrested and charged with "gross indecency." The jury in the first trial failed to reach a verdict, but he was retried, found guilty and sentenced to the maximum penalty of two years' hard labor. His reputation was ruined, and, after two years spent walking for hours on a treadmill and picking oakum (i.e., untwisting strands of rope), so was his health. His wife changed the names of his two sons in order to protect them from the scandal; Wilde never saw them again. After his release, Wilde moved to France to escape from prying eyes. He was virtually penniless and alternated between staying with friends and in cheap hotels. When he was recognized on the street, he was often abused. He wrote very little in his final years, apart from *The Ballad of Reading Gaol* (1897), a poem about the brutality of the Victorian penal system. Wilde died in 1900, aged only forty-six. Today, Wilde's trial stands as a symbol of the wrongful legal persecution of gay men in Britain prior to legalization of homosexuality in 1967. In 2017, he, along with 50,000 other men from the past, was pardoned for acts that were no longer crimes.

Even with these legal restrictions, however, the final decades of the nineteenth century saw the emergence of small but growing gay subcultures in Britain. In 1889, the Cleveland Street Scandal revealed the existence of a male brothel in London that was frequented by an elite clientele. In 1891, Wilde's friend George Cecil Ives founded a secret organization called the Order of Chaeronea, which promoted homosexuality as a normal lifestyle and fought discrimination against gay men and women. Lesbianism, meanwhile, was never illegal, and a number of prominent middle-class female couples were viewed with at least limited toleration. The appearance of the word "homosexuality" in English for the first time in 1892 indicated that views of same-sex love as a disease were giving way to views that it was a psychological state. There was still much prejudice against gay men and women, but this was a small but important step towards the greater acceptance that would come in the twentieth century.

Conservative Dominance and Tariff Reform After 1900

At the beginning of the twentieth century, the Liberal Party's return to power seemed unlikely. The one Liberal administration from 1892 to 1895 was a minority government that only survived with the support of Irish nationalists. The Conservatives won a huge parliamentary majority in 1895, which was followed by another convincing victory in the "Khaki Election" held during the South African War in 1900. (The election was named after the uniforms worn by British soldiers in that conflict.) The Tories' dominance of British politics was more fragile than these electoral results indicated, however, as party unity had become increasingly precarious by the early twentieth century.

The most divisive issue was *tariff reform*, which was the brainchild of the colonial secretary Joseph Chamberlain. The first British industrialist to hold high political office, Chamberlain was a radical who believed in the power of government to enact social and economic reform. While he was mayor of Birmingham in the 1870s, the city's government assumed control of local utilities. His variety of municipal reform, known as "gas and water socialism," was influential throughout the industrialized world. Chamberlain combined his zeal for social and economic reform with an ardent imperialism. One of the most prominent Liberals who had split with Gladstone over the issue of Irish Home Rule, he favored granting greater powers of local government to Ireland but argued that Home Rule would cause the "dismemberment of the British Empire." As colonial secretary, Chamberlain sought to bring the diverse colonies of the British Empire into a closer political union.

 See document "A Vision of Imperial Unity" at www.routledge.com_cw_barczewski.

The campaign for tariff reform linked Chamberlain's dual concerns of domestic reform and imperial unity. He called for Britain to impose a tariff (or duty) on imported agricultural products, which would be reduced for colonies that lowered duties on British exports such as manufactured goods. This system, known as "Imperial Preference," was thus designed to benefit both British industry and agricultural production in colonies such as Canada. It represented an attempt to transform Britain's ramshackle collection of overseas colonies, dominions, protectorates and other territories into a coherent economic entity that would allow Britain to overcome competition from bigger and potentially more powerful rivals such as Germany, Russia and the United States. In May 1903, Chamberlain launched the campaign with a speech in his home city of Birmingham in which he called for the British Empire to "stand together, one free nation, if necessary, against all the world." Failure to accept tariff reform, Chamberlain warned, meant Britain must "accept our fate as one of the dying empires of the world."

That September, Chamberlain resigned as colonial secretary in order to campaign full time for tariff reform. While he believed passionately that his policy would secure industrial jobs for British workers and strengthen the unity of the Empire, the issue provoked considerable controversy across the political spectrum. Tariff reform attracted strong criticism from Liberals who were devoted to the ideal of free trade. It also, however, divided the Conservative Party, as many Tory politicians felt that it would harm British agricultural interests. Prime Minister Arthur Balfour, Lord Salisbury's nephew and successor, attempted to pursue a middle course, endorsing tariff reform in principle while refusing to commit to its specifics.

In 1906, the Liberals, who had campaigned aggressively for free trade, won a landslide victory, ensuring that Chamberlain's vision never became a reality. The fact that tariff reform had become a matter of serious debate, however, showed that Britain's economic position had altered. The commitment to free trade had derived from Britain's dominance: in a world in which everyone traded on equal terms, the nation that was able to produce the most goods and sell them at the lowest prices would prevail. For the first three-quarters of the nineteenth century, that had been Britain, but after 1880 its advantage in both manufacturing output

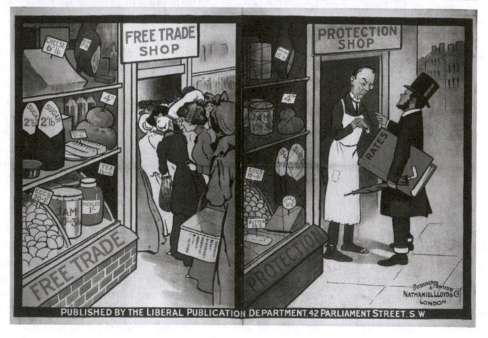

Figures 8.1 and 8.2 Two posters from the early twentieth century arguing for and against tariff reform. Figure 8.1 shows a farmer sitting dejectedly on his hops and eggs, unable to sell them because of the arrival of cheaper agricultural imports on the "Foreign Produce Express." He believes that tariff reform is the only way to make his small farm profitable. Figure 8.2 is a Liberal Party poster in which the "Free Trade" shop on the left is full of goods and customers, while the "Protection" shop on the right, with a caricature version of Chamberlain as its proprietor, has no customers, cobwebs covering its goods and a tax collector at the door.

Both figures reproduced courtesy of the London School of Economics Library.

and price competitiveness decreased significantly. In 1886, the United States began to out-pace Britain in steel exports; seven years later, Germany, too, caught up. Britain's relative position slipped even further in the ensuing decades. It was responsible for 83 percent of the world's coal exports in 1900, but only for 50 percent by 1913. At the outbreak of the First World War in 1914, Britain produced only half as much steel as Germany and a fourth as much as the United States. Britain's long head start in the race to industrialize had thus been erased. That head start had in fact become a disadvantage, as Britain's industrial infrastructure was now aging and often obsolete. Though Britain could lay claim to the pneumatic tire and the steam turbine engine, most of the great innovations and inventions of the late nineteenth century – such as the telephone, electric light and the automobile – happened elsewhere.

Liberal Landslide, the Origins of the Labour Party and Constitutional Crisis

At the end of 1905, after the Conservatives lost a series of **by-elections**, Balfour resigned as prime minister, despite the fact that he still had a comfortable majority in the House of Commons. Historians still debate the reasons for his drastic action. He may have been eager for retirement at a time when the confidence of his party in his leadership was diminishing, or he may have been gambling that the Liberals would be unable to form a lasting government. If the latter was the case, he was quickly proven wrong. In the ensuing general election, which took place in January 1906, the Liberals focused their campaign on the issues of free trade, cheaper food prices and a higher standard of living. With populist slogans such as "Hands Off the People's Food," they painted the Conservatives as defending the interests of big business against the consumer. The Liberals won in a *landslide*, increasing their number of MPs from 184 to 400, while Conservative and Unionist MPs declined from 402 to 157.

The Liberal resurgence was further aided by an alliance with a new political party that represented the interests of workers: the Labour Party. The Labour Party emerged from the growing strength of the British trade union movement. After the failure of Chartism in the late 1840s, trade unionism had revived as an alternative means of improving workers' lives. These "new model" unions were less radical than their early Victorian predecessors, preferring negotiation and arbitration over strikes and more militant forms of action. In keeping with contemporary middle-class values, they emphasized aspiration, self-help and the attainment of respectability by their members. Even so, the pace of labor organization continued to increase. In the 1860s, Trades Councils, which brought together the leaders of individual unions, were established in most large cities. In 1868, a Trades Union Council (TUC) for England and Wales was formed in order to provide a unified voice on political issues affecting workers. A Scottish Trades Union Congress was formed in 1896 to support Scottish workers in a similar fashion. The British government acknowledged the growing importance of unions in 1871, when Parliament passed the Trade Union Act, which recognized unions as legal entities, meaning that they were now protected by law. By 1900, there were over 1300 trade unions in Britain, with over 2 million members.

While women workers increasingly became involved in the agitation for better working conditions and shorter hours, the trade union movement continued to exist almost exclusively for male workers. Some women workers, however, found creative new ways through cooperative societies to protect their interests and create employment opportunities. In the printing trade, this meant founding enterprises run by women. From the 1850s, male workers and labor organizations blocked women's entry into the printing trades, which prompted the rise of a small number of women-owned printing organizations in England, Scotland and Ireland. The Women's Cooperative Printing Society, formed by the trade union organizer Emma Paterson in 1876, gave women workers a share in the profits while challenging culturally determined understandings of the relationship between gender and work.

At the same time, the expansion of the electorate through the reform bills encouraged male workers to explore strategies to increase their political power. In the 1880s, labor representatives had begun standing as candidates for Liberal constituencies. Referred to as "Lib-Lab" candidates, twelve were elected to Parliament in 1885. Many labor leaders, however, felt that workers needed their own political party, and in 1893 the *Independent Labour Party* (ILP) was founded. It was a socialist party whose primary objective was "to secure the collective ownership of the means of production, distribution and exchange." It was, however, more conservative than many comparable parties on the European continent, which were more committed to a full-blown socialist agenda. Initially, the ILP achieved little electoral success: in the election of 1895, its twenty-eight candidates won only 44,325 votes. Its leader, the Scotsman James Keir Hardie, decided that a new strategy was needed for the party to win more votes. In 1900, the ILP combined with the TUC and with two other socialist groups, the Social Democratic Federation and the Fabian Society, to form the Labour Representation Committee (LRC), with the goal of obtaining more parliamentary representation for workers. The following year, Labour's quest for increased political representation was boosted by the *Taff Vale case*, in which the courts awarded substantial damages to a Welsh railway operator that had filed a claim against the railway workers' union for lost profits due to a strike. The verdict threatened to break the power of the unions by holding them liable for damages suffered during trade disputes. It drove many workers to political action, and between 1900 and 1906 the number of Labour MPs increased from two to twenty-nine.

Recognizing the growing political power of the trade unions, the Liberal Party agreed to form a "progressive alliance" with the LRC. In 1906, the Liberals did not contest forty seats in industrial areas in order to give Labour candidates a better chance of winning. The progressive alliance also helped to motivate a series of far-reaching social reforms that were enacted after the Liberals' landslide victory. The widespread support for these sweeping changes suggests that a shift had taken place in the way people understood the role of government from the Victorian belief in *laissez-faire*. The most significant changes occurred after Henry Campbell-Bannerman resigned as prime minister in 1908 for health reasons. His successor, Herbert Henry Asquith, appointed two young reformers to high office: David Lloyd George, who became chancellor of the Exchequer, and Winston Churchill, who replaced Lloyd George as president of the Board of Trade.

Raised in relatively humble circumstances in North Wales, Lloyd George was a native Welsh speaker and a fiery debater. As a young MP, he led unsuccessful campaigns for the **disestablishment** of the Church of England in Wales and for Welsh Home Rule. Although Lloyd George's political focus had shifted to the national stage by the twentieth century, Wales continued to deeply inform his political views. He became a staunch advocate for trade unions, labor issues and working people more generally. In stark contrast to Lloyd George's humble origins, Winston Churchill was the grandson of the Duke of Marlborough. His father, the prominent Tory politician Lord Randolph Churchill, was the Duke's third son, however, and Winston thus inherited little wealth. This forced him to seek paid employment. After serving as an army officer, with a sideline as a war correspondent, in India, the Sudan and South Africa, he entered Parliament in 1900 as a Conservative MP. He broke with Balfour's government over tariff reform, and in 1904, he "crossed the floor" to join the

Liberals. His decision was motivated by political ambition as well as principle, as Churchill believed that his chances for high office would be greater with the Liberals. He was soon proven correct: four years later, he became president of the Board of Trade at the age of only thirty-three.

In the years prior to the First World War, Lloyd George and Churchill championed a series of social reforms. The Old Age Pensions Act of 1908 guaranteed five shillings per week for people over the age of seventy who earned less than £31 10s. per year. Churchill implemented the creation of Labor Exchanges, where employees could seek work and employers could advertise job vacancies. In 1911, the National Insurance Act promised workers between the ages of sixteen and seventy security against sickness and unemployment through a plan jointly funded by the state, the employer and the employee. Other social legislation included an eight-hour workday for miners and the prohibition of the imprisonment of children under the age of fourteen. These reforms demonstrated that the *laissez-faire* liberalism of the nineteenth century was giving way to a more interventionist vision of the role of the state in people's lives. Historians label this changed attitude the "New Liberalism."

The issue of how to fund these new reforms led to one of the most important political battles of the era. In 1909, Lloyd George introduced what became known as the *"People's Budget."* This included a number of new taxes, most of which were aimed at wealthy landowners, including an increase in the death duty, new taxes on land, higher income taxes and a "super tax" on incomes greater than £5000 per year. The objective of the "People's Budget" was not simply to balance the budget or even to pay for the new social welfare programs. Rather, the goal was to establish the use of taxes, in the words of Lloyd George's biographer Roy Hattersley, as "the engine for social policy, the sinews of the war against poverty."

Although the budget passed the House of Commons, it was handily defeated in the Tory-dominated House of Lords. This was far from a routine occurrence, for while the lords were allowed to amend bills dealing with finances, their outright rejection of a budget bill went against precedent. Lloyd George scornfully referred to the lords as "five hundred men . . . chosen accidentally from the unemployed," and asked whether they should be allowed to "override the judgment – the deliberate judgment – of millions of people who are engaged in the industry which makes the wealth of the country?" The Liberals called a general election in January 1910 that was fought on the issue of the "People's Budget." While the Liberals' large parliamentary majority declined, they clung to a slender margin of two seats.

When the People's Budget was reintroduced in 1910, the lords, acknowledging that they had overreached, passed it. The Liberals were not content to stop there, however, and they used their victory as an opportunity to eliminate the lords' power once and for all. In 1910, they introduced the Parliament Bill, which prevented the lords from blocking budgetary legislation and imposed a limit of two years on its veto power over all other measures passed by the Commons. Crucially, the Liberals were able to secure the support of the new monarch, George V, who became king when Edward VII died in May 1910. (It was Edward who gave his name to the first decade of the twentieth century.) Recalling the passage of the Great Reform Act in 1832, the new king promised to create enough peers to ensure the passage of the Parliament Bill if another general election confirmed support for the Liberal Party.

A second general election held in December 1910 produced almost identical results to its predecessor. The lords now faced two unappealing alternatives: either they could vote to diminish permanently their own power or be flooded with newly created peers, who would be Liberal in their politics and who would pass the bill anyway. "The question," stated Lord Selbourne, "is shall we perish in the dark, slain by our own hand, or in the light, killed by our enemies." While most of the lords chose not to attend the debate on the bill, it passed by a vote of 131 to 114 in 1911. The lords' power to alter or block legislation passed by the House of Commons had been massively reduced.

An Edwardian Crisis?

In 1935, a young English historian named George Dangerfield published a book with the provocative title of *The Strange Death of Liberal England*. Dangerfield argued that in the years following the passage of the Parliament Act, Britain faced a series of crises. If the outbreak of the First World War had not intervened, he asserted, the parliamentary system would have collapsed. Few historians today would accept Dangerfield's contention, but the idea of an "Edwardian crisis" has been enduring. It was certainly the case that the United Kingdom faced considerable unrest in the years leading up to the Great War in three areas: the campaign for women's suffrage, widespread labor strikes and the threat of civil war in Ireland.

In the decades before 1900, calls for women to be given the right to vote had slowly gained momentum. The first individuals and groups who promoted women's suffrage were called "suffragists"; they believed in using only peaceful, constitutional methods to achieve their objective. Because most Victorian suffragists were middle class, they did not call for all women to be granted the vote, but rather for women to be granted the vote on the same terms as men, which meant that it would still be tied to the ownership of property. It was only later that their goal was expanded to universal suffrage, or the right to vote for all adult men and women. In 1897, various suffragist groups joined together to form the *National Union of Women's Suffrage Societies* (NUWSS). Some suffragists, however, were dissatisfied with the slow pace of change. In 1903, mother and daughter Emmeline and Christabel Pankhurst founded the *Women's Social and Political Union* (WSPU), which took a more militant approach; the WSPU's motto was "deeds not words." The WSPU's supporters were dubbed the "suffragettes" by the *Daily Mail* newspaper, a term that was intended to belittle them, but which they embraced as distinguishing them from the suffragists. In contrast to the NUWSS, some suffragettes were working-class women or socialists. Drawing on longstanding traditions of British radicalism, they used civil disobedience, predominantly in the form of demonstrations, as their main tactic, leading to the arrest of a number of their members.

Both the suffragists and the suffragettes hoped that the election of a Liberal government in 1906 would aid their cause. Many Liberals were sympathetic, seeing women's suffrage as an extension of their longstanding commitment to increased democracy. The prime minister Herbert Henry Asquith, however, was adamantly opposed to women's suffrage, as was David Lloyd George, who believed that female votes would benefit the Conservatives. Two bills were brought forward in 1907 and 1909, followed by a series of "Conciliation Bills" in 1910, 1911 and 1912 that would have given the right to vote to around a million women who owned a significant amount of property. All failed. The failure of the first Conciliation Bill in 1910 led to "Black Friday," in which around 300 members of the WSPU protested outside of the House of Commons. The police aggressively intervened, and many women suffered serious injuries; one later died.

In response, the tactics of the WSPU became more radical. Suffragettes set fire to mailboxes and empty buildings, smashed windows and committed other acts of vandalism, such as the slashing of Diego Velázquez's seventeenth-century painting the *Rokeby Venus* in the National Gallery. In the most dramatic gesture, Emily Wilding Davison was killed at the 1913 Derby when she stepped in front of a horse belonging to King George V. When imprisoned for these acts, many suffragettes resorted to hunger strikes. Attempts to force-feed them, which was a brutal process requiring the women to be physically restrained,

Figure 8.3 A suffragette being arrested in London around 1910.
Reproduced courtesy of the Library of Congress.

aroused strong public criticism. In response, in 1913 the government passed the Prisoners (Temporary Discharge for Ill Health), or "Cat and Mouse Act," which allowed prisoners to be released and then rearrested after they had recovered their strength. But this, too, was unpopular: the Labour MP George Lansbury railed in the House of Commons that Asquith would "go down in history as the man who tortured innocent women."

 See document "Votes for Women" at www.routledge.com_cw_barczewski.

Historians continue to debate which strategy, that of the suffragists or the suffragettes, was more effective in finally gaining women over thirty the right to vote in 1918. Some argue that the suffragettes have been given too much attention, and that it was in fact the suffragists who were more responsible for the movement's eventual success. It is true that the WSPU never totaled more than 2000 members, while by 1914 the NUWSS boasted over 50,000. The activities of the WSPU may have in fact delayed women in gaining the right to vote, by making politicians reluctant to appear as if they were giving in to their destruction of private property and other illegal activities. Other scholars, however, argue that the suffragettes' militancy was crucial in keeping the cause of women's suffrage at the forefront of politics, at a time when many Liberal politicians would have preferred to ignore it. In truth, the activities of both the NUWSS and the WSPU put the issue of women's suffrage on the national agenda. While the suffragettes challenged modes of accepted "feminine" behavior in a more dramatic fashion, more mainstream suffragists made inroads in persuading British politicians that the enfranchisement of women would not destroy family life and traditional gender roles.

Another challenge was posed by the labor movement in the years preceding the First World War. Between 1910 and 1914, union membership increased from 2.5 million to 4.1 million. Although unemployment was generally low in this period, workers believed that their working conditions were deteriorating. Many industries introduced new techniques of scientific management that sought to break down jobs into smaller component parts, a practice that decreased workers' control over their labor. Prices also generally rose faster than wages between 1900 and 1914. Labor militancy was also spurred by a legal decision in 1909 by the House of Lords, known as the "Osbourne judgment," which ruled that trade union funds could not be used as donations to political parties. (In 1913, the Osbourne judgment was reversed by the Trade Union Act.) In addition, a more radical trade union leadership emerged in the years prior to the war. As a result, strikes became a common feature of industrial disputes. In 1912, the year of the greatest industrial unrest, 41 million working days were lost to strikes. The foreign secretary, Edward Grey, expressed the fear that it was "the beginning of a revolution." This proved an exaggeration, but there was no doubt that British workers were becoming increasingly militant. While some strikes, such as the coal miners' strike in Wales in 1910, ended in failure, in other cases workers gained concessions from employers.

While the militancy of the suffragettes and the labor unions did not lead to civil war, Irish Home Rule almost did. After the failure of the second Home Rule Bill in 1893, increased self-government for Ireland appeared to be a dead issue. The dependence of the Liberal Party on Irish nationalist support after the 1910 elections, however, put it back on the political agenda. In April 1912, Asquith introduced a *third Home Rule Bill*. With the House of Lords now only able to delay legislation for two years, passage seemed assured. Neither Irish nationalists nor the Liberals, however, fully anticipated the depth of hostility to the idea of Home Rule among Ulster Protestants. On the 28th of September 1912, almost half a million Unionists expressed their opposition by signing the "Solemn League and Covenant," which declared Home Rule to be "disastrous to the material well-being of Ulster as well as the whole of Ireland." Unionists maintained that they were loyal subjects of the King, but that they would use "all means which may be found necessary" to defeat any attempt to make Ireland more independent. This militant stance was encouraged by British Conservatives, who saw Home Rule not only as dissolving the Union and threatening the Empire, but also as a political issue that they could use against the Liberals. The Conservative leader Andrew Bonar Law stated, "I can imagine no length of resistance to which Ulster can go in which I should not be prepared to support them." The "length of resistance" that Unionists were willing to go to was demonstrated by the formation of the Ulster Volunteer Force, essentially their own army.

At the same time, Irish nationalism had become more radical after the failure of the second Home Rule Bill. The Irish Republican Brotherhood enjoyed a revival, bolstered by a new Irish–American republican secret society known as Clan na Gael. The IRB attracted a new generation of republican recruits who were influenced by the cultural nationalism of organizations such as the Gaelic League, which promoted the Irish language and its literature, and the Gaelic Athletic Association, which promoted the playing of traditional Irish sports such as hurling and Gaelic football. In 1905, a new political organization called *Sinn Féin* (Gaelic for "We Ourselves") was founded in Dublin. Sinn Féin regarded the Union as illegitimate and called upon Irish MPs to withdraw from the Parliament in London and establish a separate Irish legislature.

While nonviolent, Sinn Féin represented a new, more militant form of Irish nationalism. It was thus not surprising that Irish nationalists responded to the formation of the

Figure 8.4 Ulster Volunteers march through the center of Belfast around 1915.
Reproduced courtesy of the Library of Congress.

Ulster Volunteer Force by organizing their own quasi-military organization, the Irish Volunteers, which quickly grew to over 150,000 men. Both sides imported weapons in gunrunning operations, though the Unionists, tacitly encouraged by British Conservatives, did so far more successfully. The government worried that the British Army in Ireland would not act against Unionists to implement Home Rule. There were good reasons for these concerns. In 1914, fifty-seven of the seventy army officers stationed at the Curragh Camp in Ireland publicly stated that they would refuse to obey if ordered to act against the Ulster Unionists. The next day, the third and final reading of the Home Rule Bill was passed by the House of Commons. Home Rule was set to take effect in September 1914, but to many observers, a civil war seemed likely to break out before that date; the *Times* referred to the situation as "the greatest crisis in the history of the British race." Before Home Rule could become a reality, however, a far greater crisis – the First World War – intervened.

National Efficiency

Internationally, the Edwardian period was marked by increasing anxieties about Britain's empire, military capacity and place in the world. These concerns were sparked in part by the Boer War, which lasted far longer and produced far more casualties than expected. This unsatisfactory performance gave rise not only to debates about the conduct of the war, but also to a more general concern for what came to be known as "national efficiency," a phrase that derived from the socialist economist Sidney Webb's *A Policy of National Efficiency* (1901). At the core of national efficiency was the idea that Britain had to ensure the physical well-being and education of its people in order to maintain its position as a world power. During the first year of the Boer War in 1899, close to a third of army recruits had been rejected as physically unfit, for problems ranging from their small stature to deficiencies such as heart disease, weak lungs and bad teeth. As one Liberal MP observed in 1905, "Empire cannot be built on rickety and flat-chested citizens." One response to these concerns was a series of legislative acts that were intended to improve the health of infants and children. In 1906, local authorities were allowed (though not required) to provide free school meals for poor children, and by 1914 over 150,000 children were being fed. In the following year, mandatory medical inspections were introduced in schools. The Children's and Young Persons Act of 1908 introduced a number of provisions related to child welfare, including the banning of alcohol and tobacco sales to minors and the ability to prosecute parents for the abuse or neglect of their children. These concerns about the health of Britain's youth had an impact on gender roles. There was a renewed emphasis on the role of married women as mothers, as good motherhood came to be seen as essential to a healthy British "race." Reformers and philanthropists attempted to improve what were seen as the deficiencies of working-class mothers, although these efforts tended to overlook the entrenched problem of poverty that substantially impacted the health of their children.

"National efficiency" was often entwined with patriotic appeals, as patriotic leagues and societies flourished in Edwardian Britain. The largest and most influential of these groups was the National Service League (NSL), which argued for compulsory military service for British men. Initially a small organization, the membership and profile of the NSL expanded rapidly after 1905, when Frederick Lord Roberts, former commander-in-chief of the British Army and one of the most famous men of the era, became its president. Under Roberts, the League's membership approached 100,000. The NSL's arguments went beyond jingoistic appeals to patriotism, for they also focused on social reform. Compulsory service, the League argued, would "counteract the physical and moral degeneracy attendant upon industrial life in crowded cities" through compulsory physical exercise and outdoor activities.

Similar concerns about counteracting the "degeneration" of the British race also permeated one of the most popular youth organizations established during the Edwardian age: the Boy Scouts. Founded by Robert Baden-Powell, a hero of the Boer War, scouting attempted to address fears of racial decline through an emphasis on physical culture and healthy outdoor activity. In his *Scouting for Boys* (1908), Baden-Powell argued that the Roman Empire fell because its young men abandoned "soldiering and manliness"; he warned that the British Empire could face a similar fate. By 1909, over 100,000 British boys, mostly from the middle and lower middle classes, had become Scouts.

The Anglo-German Rivalry

Edwardian anxieties about the "degeneration" of the British race focused in particular on the growing Anglo-German rivalry. Many Britons admired Germany's achievements in culture, industry, science and technology, while advocates of compulsory military service looked enviously at Germany's national system of conscription. Social reformers, meanwhile, sought to emulate German social insurance schemes. At the same time as Germany served as a model for reform, however, it also was perceived as an increasingly dangerous threat to Britain's position as a great power.

One place in which the new German threat was felt most keenly was in the British Empire. The leaders of the newly unified Germany felt that it was essential to acquire a colonial empire, and they had focused in particular upon southern Africa, which they saw as a market for the products of German industry. They were particularly interested in the Boer republic of the Transvaal, which was inhabited by "Teutonic" Dutch settlers, as a future home for German immigrants. This was to lead to a major diplomatic incident. In 1895, the British launched a clumsy attempt to topple the Boer government of the Transvaal. Cecil Rhodes, the gold and diamond mining magnate who had ascended to become prime minister of the Cape Colony in 1890, was keenly interested in the gold deposits of the Transvaal. With Rhodes's active support, in 1895 a British settler named Leander Starr Jameson and a small group of mercenaries launched a raid on the Boer republic's capital of Johannesburg. The British colonial secretary Joseph Chamberlain had approved Rhodes's plan in principle, but he disapproved of the timing and attempted to prevent the raid. Rhodes and Jameson went ahead anyway: they hoped that the raid would inspire the *uitlanders*, or British settlers, to launch an uprising; the British could then claim that in order to restore order they had to seize control of the Transvaal. Jameson and his mercenaries, however, were captured by Boer forces well before they reached Johannesburg. Once the knowledge of Rhodes's collusion became public, he was forced to resign as prime minister in 1896 and his mining consortium was compelled to pay £1 million to the Transvaal's government in compensation. Jameson spent fifteen months in a British prison. Upon learning that the *Jameson Raid* had been thwarted, the German government lent its support to the Boers. A telegram from Kaiser Wilhelm II to the Transvaal's president, Paul Kruger, congratulated the Boer leader for preserving "the independence of his country against external attack." The "*Kruger Telegram*" provoked outrage in Britain, as the press launched a barrage of anti-Boer jingoism. The Germans were forced to back down, as they lacked the means to project their power in the region, but the incident had continuing ramifications for years to come.

The tensions between Britain and Germany over the Jameson Raid and the Kruger telegram provide a good example of how colonial rivalries strained relations among the European powers in the late nineteenth and early twentieth centuries. Germany was not Britain's only colonial rival in this period. Russia's activities on the northwest frontier of India continued to be a source of concern, and in East Africa an increasingly ambitious France was interested in dislodging the British from the Sudan, and possibly Egypt as well. In 1898, the French dispatched a small force to seize Fashoda on the White Nile, in what is now South Sudan. In response, the British sent a flotilla of gunboats, and both nations began preparing for war. The commanding officers on the spot remained calm, however, and eventually a diplomatic solution was negotiated in which the French agreed to withdraw and to leave the Sudan to the British.

Fashoda did not lead to war between Britain and France. Nor did it prevent the two countries from forming an alliance only six years later. We thus should be careful in assuming that colonial rivalries were a major contributing factor to the outbreak of the First World War in 1914. But in the specific case of Britain and Germany, they did undoubtedly add to the burgeoning tensions between them. After the Jameson Raid, the desire of Kaiser Wilhelm II to build a powerful navy that could compete with the British became an obsession. Initially, plans called for nineteen battleships, but in 1900 the number was doubled and in 1909 the target was increased further to forty-nine.

The British felt that they had to respond. In 1889, Parliament passed the *Naval Defence Act*, which required the Royal Navy to maintain a "two-power standard." This meant that it had to possess more battleships than the next two biggest navies (at the time those of France and Russia) combined. This led to an additional £21,500,000 in naval expenditure over the next five years, which funded the construction of ten new battleships, eighteen torpedo gunboats and thirty-eight cruisers. But if the purpose of the Naval Defence Act was to serve as a deterrent to Britain's rivals, it failed, as it spurred them to undertake major expansions of their own fleets. The United States began construction of a navy second only to Britain's, while Germany's naval program posed an even greater threat.

This burgeoning Anglo-German imperial and naval rivalry became increasingly costly after 1906, when the new dreadnought-class battleships, with their heavier caliber guns and steam-turbine engines, first came into service. Each dreadnought cost £2 million, twice the expense of a conventional battleship. While Britain continued to spend less on its all-volunteer army than any other European power, its naval spending outpaced all rivals. Naval budgets increased by over 60 percent between 1907 and 1914; by the latter date, Britain's naval expenditure was double that of Germany's. In total, per capita defense spending in Britain was the highest in Europe during these years. The Anglo-German naval rivalry did not automatically lead the two countries into war; as Christopher Clark observes, "British policy-makers were less obsessed with, and less alarmed by, German naval building than is often supposed." Even so, it was an indication of the mounting international tensions that were soon to lead to the outbreak of the first major European war in a century.

Conclusion

The death of Queen Victoria in 1901 caused many Britons to feel that an era had come to an end. As she watched the Queen's coffin pass by, novelist Elinor Glyn felt that she was "witnessing the funeral procession of England's greatness and glory." This has become the conventional view of the late Victorian era: that it was an era of disillusionment, as Britain's confidence faded and its anxieties increased in the face of a relative decline of its global economic and imperial position. At home, the Irish question threatened to disunite the kingdom, while urban poverty engendered fears that the British population was in a state of fatal physical decline. The Edwardian era was even more unsettled. Militant trade unionism and the suffragettes challenged the ability of the political system to accommodate gradual change, while Home Rule brought Ireland to the brink of civil war. At the same time, the external pressures on the Empire and the economy grew more intense.

Before identifying the signs of Britain's twentieth-century decline so early, however, it must be remembered that in the decade after 1900 Britain still ruled the largest empire in the history of the world, which contained a quarter of the earth's population. It still possessed the world's most powerful navy, and it still accounted for a fourth of all global trade. Moreover, change was not always for the worse. Britain was a significantly more democratic society at the end of the nineteenth century than it had been at the beginning: a significant portion of the working class had obtained the right to vote, and both universal male and women's suffrage were now serious topics of discussion. At the beginning of the Victorian era, "democracy" had been for many Britons a negative term with implications of mob rule and continental-style chaos and violence. By the end of the Edwardian years, people viewed its gradual extension without revolution as a uniquely British achievement.

Bibliography

Bell, Duncan, *The Idea of Greater Britain: Empire and the Future of World Order, 1860–1900* (2007)

Boyce, D. George and Alan O'Day, eds., *Gladstone and Ireland: Politics, Region, and Nationality in the Victorian Age* (2010)

Cook, Matt, *London and the Culture of Homosexuality, 1880–1914* (2008)

Grant, Kevin, *A Civilised Savagery: Britain and the New Slaveries in Africa* (2005)

Hattersley, Roy, *David Lloyd George: The Great Outsider* (2012)

Holton, Sandra Stanley, *Feminism and Democracy: Women's Suffrage and Reform Politics in Britain, 1900–1918* (2003)

Jackson, Alvin, *Home Rule: An Irish History 1800–2000* (2004)

Koven, Seth, *Slumming: Sexual and Social Politics in Victorian London* (2006)

Levine, Philippa, *Victorian Feminism 1850–1900* (2005)

Pugh, Martin, *Speak for Britain!: A New History of the Labour Party* (2011)

Shaw, Caroline, *Britannia's Embrace* (2015)

9   The First World War

Topics covered

- British entry into the First World War
- Popular support for the war
- Military course of the war
- Domestic response of the government to the war
- Manpower crisis and the implementation of conscription
- The British Empire in the war
- Easter Rising in Ireland
- Social changes caused by the conflict and the rise of state intervention
- Costs and consequences of the war

Timeline

July 1914	Diplomatic crisis in Europe
August 1914	Britain declares war on Germany and Austria–Hungary
September 1914	Indian troops arrive on the Western Front
April 1915	First landings on Gallipoli Peninsula
May 1915	Formation of coalition government
January 1916	Conscription introduced
April 1916	Easter Rising in Dublin
July 1916	Battle of Somme begins
December 1916	Lloyd George becomes prime minister of new coalition government
April 1917	United States declares war on Germany
July 1917	Third Battle of Ypres (Passchendaele) begins
December 1917	Russia makes peace with Germany
February 1918	Representation of the People Act
March 1918	German offensive on the Western Front
November 1918	Armistice

DOI: 10.4324/9781003284758-9

Introduction

The First World War (often referred to in Britain as the "Great War") was a shock to the British. Fought largely in an effort to preserve the status quo in terms of both Britain's international position and the domestic political and social order, the war instead significantly altered both. Yet it did not represent a total rupture with the past: Britain was not convulsed by revolution as were some other European countries that fought in the war. Britain's political system and social structure were forced to bend and adapt, but they did not break.

Britain's Entry Into the War

Immediately after the Archduke Franz Ferdinand was assassinated by a Serbian nationalist in Sarajevo in June 1914, it was not clear that the dispute between Austria–Hungary and Serbia would escalate into a major war. Across Europe, many hoped that this would be yet another of the conflicts that had plagued the Balkan region since 1908, none of which had activated the two great European alliances that had been in place since the 1890s. On the one hand, there was the Triple Alliance of Germany, Austria–Hungary and Italy; on the other, there was the Dual Alliance of France and Russia. British politicians, meanwhile, proudly referred to their country's lack of European entanglements. Yet Britain's apparent isolation was deceptive, for throughout the nineteenth century, the British had worked to maintain a balance of power in Europe. Moreover, a subtle reorientation of British foreign policy had occurred during the decade leading up to 1914. In the late nineteenth century, Germany had been viewed as a potential ally by Britain, but its aggressive diplomacy and pursuit of colonies engendered suspicion. Meanwhile, colonial disputes between the British and French and the British and Russians were partially papered over by two agreements, or *ententes*, in 1904 and 1907. These were not formal alliances, but the *ententes* did signal that Britain would not automatically remain neutral in a European war. Although Britain and France were historical enemies, the alliance between them was not totally unprecedented. They had fought, for example, on the same side in the Crimean War against the Russians in the 1850s. Prior to 1900 they continued to be bitter rivals over empire in Africa and elsewhere, but Germany's increasingly aggressive foreign and imperial stance, combined with its decision to build a navy of equivalent strength to Britain's, forced Britain's leaders to rethink their traditional conception of the European balance of power. Germany, rather than France or Russia, now seemed the greatest threat to that balance.

Initially, hopes that the archduke's assassination would not lead to war seemed likely to be realized, as the immediate reaction from the Austro-Hungarian government was muted. But over the next month, *diplomacy failed to halt the momentum towards war*. After Austria–Hungary declared war on Serbia on the 28th of July, Germany, Russia and France quickly entered the conflict as well. In Britain, the foreign minister Sir Edward Grey tried to convince his cabinet colleagues that Britain had both a moral obligation and a strategic imperative to join the war on the side of France. The moral case Grey set out was based on the military and naval discussions that the British had been conducting with the French since 1911, which had been kept secret from most of the cabinet. He argued that Britain had an obligation to meet the expectations that these discussions had generated.

Grey's most powerful argument, however, was strategic: Britain would be vulnerable if it remained neutral. A victorious Germany would dominate Europe, severely threatening Britain's security. Since 1815, Britain's pursuit of a balance of power was predicated on the principle that no one state should achieve dominance over the continent. Germany was poised to do just that. Fighting Germany now, alongside France and Russia, was preferable to facing a strengthened Germany alone in the future. His arguments proved persuasive, and Britain issued an ultimatum to Germany not to violate the neutrality of Belgium, which had been guaranteed by Britain in a treaty of 1839. Germany's military strategy, however, called for a rapid advance through Belgium, with the ultimate goal of defeating France quickly, before Russia could bring the full might of its forces to bear on the Eastern Front. German armies moved into Belgium on the 3rd of August 1914. *Britain declared war the next day.*

Enthusiasm for War?

The day before the declaration of war, as many as 10,000 people gathered outside Buckingham Palace in London to express support for the government's ultimatum to Germany.

 See document "A Burst of Patriotism" at www.routledge.com_cw_barczewski.

Once war was actually declared, there were further demonstrations of enthusiasm and a rush of volunteers to enlist in the army. With hindsight, after the horrors of the war became apparent, some politicians claimed that "war fever" had tied their hands in the summer of 1914 and that they had no choice but to declare war. These facts have led many scholars to argue that war was welcomed by the British public. There are strong reasons to doubt these views, however. There is no evidence that the Liberal government paid much attention to public opinion in making its decision to go to war, but even if they had, it would have offered little guidance, as the British public was divided. In the days before the declaration, there were as many demonstrations *against* British involvement as there were pro-war rallies, with anti-war sentiment particularly strong amongst socialist organizations and trade unions. Some newspapers, including the *Times*, promoted British involvement, but much of the liberal press was vehemently opposed to intervention. Two cabinet ministers, John Morley and John Burns, resigned from their posts in protest, as did the leader of the Labour Party, Ramsay MacDonald.

After the declaration of war, however, opposition rapidly drained away. As the previously staunchly anti-war *Daily News* noted the day after war was declared: "Being in, we must win." Neither the British population nor most of its leaders understood the enormity of the challenge. It was still assumed by most people that Britain could rely on the Royal Navy and the regular army to conduct the war. The government implicitly encouraged this perception by proclaiming that, while the war was prosecuted, for the rest of the country it would be "business as usual."

Other government actions, however, suggested otherwise. Britain's most famous soldier, Lord Kitchener, was appointed minister for war, normally a position held by a civilian. The public put tremendous faith in the man who had led Britain to victory against the Boers, but Kitchener had few illusions about the challenge Britain now faced. Virtually alone among allied military leaders, he recognized that war in the new industrial age would be long, bloody and brutal, and that it would require a massive expansion of the nation's armed forces. He knew that the British army was miniscule, only about 225,000 men. Only 150,000 of these, known as the British Expeditionary Force (BEF), could be quickly deployed overseas. The BEF consisted of a mere six divisions, compared to the seventy divisions each that could be mobilized by France and Germany.

Cooperation with the French was now essential, but it was not immediately or easily achieved. British and French military commanders had differing views of where and how their forces should be deployed. The French wanted British forces to be placed under their command, but the British made it clear that was not an option. The language barrier did not help: the French commanders did not speak English and their British counterparts did not speak French. On the 21st and 23rd of August, the French, in danger of being enveloped by the German advance, first did not advance along with the British and then withdrew without informing them, thereby endangering the British flank. The British commander Sir John French threatened to withdraw the BEF altogether, but fortunately cooler heads in London prevailed and prevented him from doing so. Even after the German advance was halted at the Marne, there continued to be tensions, as French commanders were frustrated with the failure of the British to take on anything approaching an equal share of the military burden. In early 1915, the French had seven times more troops on the Western Front than the British, and they held a line that was fourteen times longer. British commanders knew that in order to preserve the alliance with the French, and ultimately to win the war, in the future they would have to take on a much larger share of the fighting.

Figure 9.1 A poster from October 1914 encouraging men to volunteer for the "New Army" which the war secretary Lord Kitchener, who believed it was going to be a long war, was attempting to recruit.

Reproduced courtesy of Shutterstock/Everett Collection.

Towards this end, Kitchener called on the government to create a new army of volunteers. Some 100,000 men enlisted in the first three weeks of August. This was the beginning of what would come to be known as the "New Army," but it would be months before these untrained men were ready to go overseas. In the meantime, the BEF was rushed into position on the left flank of the French armies that had been deployed along the Belgian border. In the third week of August, the full force of the German offensive hit the BEF at the small industrial town of Mons, forcing the severely mauled British troops to fall back to the Marne River, only 30 miles northeast of Paris. There, the German advance was finally halted. The Battle of the Marne resulted in 500,000 casualties, divided roughly evenly between the French and Germans. Only 13,000 of these casualties were British, demonstrating the small size of the BEF relative to other European armies in the early stages of the war.

Germany's failure to defeat the French quickly meant that the war now became a two-front conflict. On the Western Front, where British forces would be engaged for the next four years, the combatant armies dug lines of trenches along a 460 mile frontline, stretching from the North Sea to France's border with Switzerland. The British defended only about 85 miles of that front. Their sector, however, was at the northeastern end of the line, which meant that it lay in flat, soggy Flanders, some of the front's worst terrain for fighting. There, even a small hill was "high ground." To defend this front, the British dug 6000 miles of trenches.

The Experience of Warfare 5

The Myth of the Christmas 1914 Football Match in No-Man's Land

A well-known story about the first Christmas of the First World War in 1914 is that troops on both sides called an impromptu truce in which they exchanged gifts, took photographs and even played games of football (i.e., soccer) against each other. But how much of this actually happened? It is true that as the war intensified there were occasional informal truces in quiet sectors of the front line so that both sides could repair their trenches and retrieve their dead from no-man's land. And certainly there were such truces in some places at Christmas 1914, in which British and German soldiers exchanged greetings and possibly gifts. They also took advantage of the lull to bury their dead. But in other parts of the line the fighting continued, and commanders on both sides prohibited such events in the future for fear they would decrease the men's fighting spirit. And what about the football matches? Historians dispute whether they took place at all. A soldier from the Queen's Own Rifles recalled British troops kicking a ball around, but he made no mention of them playing against the Germans. The other accounts of such matches, meanwhile, were all second-hand. An image that is frequently claimed to show one of these Christmas-truce football games in fact shows British soldiers playing soccer in 1915 in the Greek city of Salonika. No photos of an actual match on the Western Front at Christmas 1914 survive. So why has the myth of the Christmas 1914 football matches survived? In part because we want to believe in it as an indication of our common humanity in a brutal and bloody war. In addition, as the historian Dan Snow has pointed out, football is traditionally a working-class sport, and so the matches support the British view of a war in which ordinary soldiers were innocent victims of callous generals. Whatever the reason, the myth of the Christmas football matches lives on.

Figure 9.2 The "Football Remembers" memorial at the National Memorial Arboretum in Staffordshire. Unveiled in 2014 by Prince William, it commemorates the football match that was supposedly played between British and German soldiers during the Christmas truce in 1914, although there is no clear evidence that such a match actually occurred.

Reproduced courtesy of DeFacto.

As the war settled into a stalemate, the most important task of the British army was to expand as rapidly as possible. In the first weeks, boyish idealism inspired many new recruits, but they were not motivated by patriotism alone. For many potential volunteers, especially the married, working-class men who comprised the bulk of the male population, national pride was balanced by other concerns, especially the uncertain financial future facing their families if they enlisted. Thus most of the initial recruits were young, single, middle-class men. By September, however, recruitment patterns began to alter. In the first two weeks of the month, 310,000 men volunteered, with a higher percentage of them married and from the working class. These men enlisted for two reasons. First, the BEF appeared on the edge of catastrophic defeat, as the German army advanced rapidly through France. Second, they faced the prospect of unemployment, for as businesses saw demand for their peacetime products and services plunge, 10 percent of the workforce was laid off. The resulting rush of volunteers was so great that it overwhelmed the recruiting system. Kitchener had to raise the minimum height of recruits to 5'6" to give recruiting offices a respite. Some 1.9 million men volunteered for Kitchener's New Army over the next twenty months. This was the second largest nonconscripted force in military history; only the British Indian Army in the Second World War was larger. But it was still not enough: the unceasing demands of the army led to the conscription of another 2.5 million men into the armed services between mid-1916 and late 1918.

The Military Course of the War

As there was no way for the British and French to outflank the Germans on the Western Front, they had to choose between either direct attacks or moves against Germany's allies in other parts of Europe and the Middle East. In pursuit of the latter strategy, Britain sent troops to Italy and the Balkans and launched the Dardanelles campaign against the Otto- man Empire, but these efforts devolved into stalemates as well. Even where the British were successful, as in Africa against Germany's colonies there, the result did nothing to dislodge the Germans from their positions in France and Belgium.

The fighting on the Western Front was akin to medieval siege warfare with twentieth- century weapons. The defender held a clear advantage, with the attackers forced to try to break through using frontal assaults against artillery and machine guns. Between battles, the troops in the front lines spent their time in the trenches, since anything above ground in daylight was an easy target for machine gunners or snipers. The strip of land between the opposing trenches, which was anywhere from a 100 yards to a mile across, was called "no-man's land." British troops were rotated through the front-line and supporting trenches, spending about two weeks a month in dangerous positions. There, they were exposed to the elements in muddy fields that had been churned up by constant shelling, surrounded by the decaying flesh of unburied corpses and pestered by rats and lice.

The British army learned slowly which trench warfare tactics worked and which did not. Later, it was often claimed that men's lives were recklessly and needlessly thrown away by generals who were slow to adapt. Certainly, generals on both sides of the conflict did not shrink from engagements in which they knew there would be terrible casualties, and many made costly mistakes. But this was not because they were callous or because with more imagi- nation they could have succeeded without such appalling loss of life. Rather, they faced a conflict whose size and technology were entirely beyond their experience and in which the breaking of the stalemate was inevitably going to be bloody. "For years," writes Nick Lloyd, "these men have been characterized as 'donkeys' or 'butchers': unfeeling military aristocrats fighting the wrong kind of war, unable to adapt or change to the new realities unfolding on the battlefield. The truth was a much messier picture of trial and error, success and failure, with each promising development followed by an equally effective counter-measure."

The generals quickly grew to understand that no attack could hope to succeed without a preliminary artillery bombardment, but the downside of this was that it gave away the element of surprise. Artillery killed more men than any other weapon in the war, but it was not usually used in a very sophisticated manner. Only in the last twenty months of the conflict did the British utilize tactics that made the best use of it. As much of the terrain on the Western Front was boggy and interspersed with canals and rivers, artillery bombardments churned it into a sea of mud. At the battle of *Passchendaele* in the fall of 1917, significant numbers of British and dominion troops literally drowned in the mud while trying to attack across waterlogged fields. Even in drier conditions, troops could not move fast enough to take advantage of breaches in the German defenses that the artillery managed to open. And until the last year of the war, artillery was neither mobile nor accurate enough to keep up with the infantry when they were successful in advancing into a breach in the enemy line. Because artillery fire often destroyed communication links, generals had to make crucial decisions without adequate information. Most of the time, the generals became mere spectators to the battles that they launched, unable to provide direction fast enough to influence the result.

British commanders looked to any strategy or technology, old or new, that promised to break the stalemate, even if they did not always at first understand its limitations or full potential. Medieval siege warfare methods were adapted, for instance, in the digging of deep tunnels under the German trenches. In a new twist to this old method of "sapping," huge piles of explosives were set off at the end of the tunnels. These "mines" proved effective at opening gaps in the German defenses, but they took months to prepare and then sometimes failed to explode on cue. New technologies proved equally difficult to use. Poison gas, first used by the Germans in 1915 and thereafter by the allied armies, depended on the prevailing winds and sometimes caused more casualties for the side deploying it than for the enemy. Tanks, which were introduced by the British in 1916, were slow, liable to mechanical breakdown, susceptible to getting bogged down in mud and to catching fire, and easily put out of action by artillery. Although they had improved by the last phase of the conflict, far too few tanks were produced to make a decisive difference in the war. Submarines, observation balloons, airship bombers, fighter and bomber airplanes, flame-throwers, railway-mounted artillery guns – all these new weapons were introduced during the war, but none of them proved to be the "miracle weapon" that could win it.

In the summer of 1916, the British launched the first major offensive using their New Army. Planned for months, the battle was in part a response to demands from the French, who called for the British to relieve pressure on their beleaguered forces at Verdun, where the Germans had launched an attack that was intended not to achieve a decisive breakthrough but to inflict maximum casualties. This goal had been achieved: since it began in February 1916, the Battle of Verdun had produced 70,000 casualties a month, divided roughly evenly between the French and Germans. As pressure on the French mounted, the British commander-in-chief, General Douglas Haig, fended off their pleas for a large-scale offensive. But by the summer of 1916, he at last felt that his New Army was ready. His forces now contained fifty-eight divisions, making it by far the biggest and best-equipped army in British history.

In his battle plan, which was so meticulously detailed that it extended to fifty-seven pages, Haig envisioned a decisive breakthrough. His plan called for an advance on a fourteen-mile front along the Somme River. The attack was to include eleven divisions, with 66,000 men in the first wave, thereby ensuring that the British would significantly outnumber the Germans. He did not fully trust his men, however, as they had been trained in haste and were not battle-tested. Two-thirds of the soldiers deployed at the Somme were from the New Army, and no battalion had more than a quarter of its men who were from the old BEF. Six of the eleven divisions had never seen battle at all. Haig therefore chose to rely on the strength of his artillery. The breakthrough would be achieved by pounding the Germans with an around-the-clock bombardment for a full week before the infantry assault. In this bombardment, the British would launch over 1.7 million shells, more than they had fired at the Germans in the entire war up to this point. Haig believed that so few Germans would survive such a massive barrage that the infantry assault would meet with little opposition. He left the precise tactics, however, to his subordinate officers, some of whom ordered their troops to rush across no-man's land, while others told them to seek whatever cover they could find on the way, and still others to march across shoulder-to-shoulder behind a moving barrage of artillery fire. Many of the men carried 66 pounds of equipment in anticipation of a long stay in the German trenches. In the end, the tactics chosen mattered little, for although some enemy trenches were taken, many of the British troops did not even make it out of their own trenches and into no-man's land.

This was because, although it was psychologically devastating, the bombardment killed relatively few Germans, who took refuge in deep dugouts that were impenetrable to all but a direct hit from the largest shells. The inexperience of the artillery gunners of the New Armies was also a factor, as was the high percentage – as much as a third – of dud shells. Finally, in their effort to ensure that the barbed wire that protected the German trenches was cut, most of the British shells were shrapnel, which did not penetrate the ground. (Nor, as it turned out, did they significantly damage the wire.) So the Germans waited, frightened, stunned and deafened by the constant explosions, but alive and awaiting the assault that they knew would inevitably follow the barrage. Haig may have had six months to prepare his battle plan, but the Germans had had two years to prepare their defenses, which along the Somme extended 12 miles deep. The front line alone was 4000 yards thick, an impenetrable tangle of barbed wire and trenches, interspersed by frequent redoubts, or strongpoints, and fortifications on every bit of high ground. A thousand machine guns were in position, which meant that there was one approximately every 75 feet. Requiring little skill and even less precise aim, these machine guns could fire so many bullets that as far as a mile away advancing troops could not hope to move forward without being hit. In fact, a significant number of British troops were picked off by artillery and machine gun fire behind their own front lines as they moved forward to join the attack.

All of these factors added up to disaster. The first day of the *Battle of the Somme* – the 1st of July 1916 – produced the worst one-day losses the British army has ever seen. Nearly 20,000 British troops were killed and another 40,000 were wounded, most within the first hour of the attack. The official log of the battle required 212 pages to record the names of all the dead. The Royal Newfoundland Regiment began the day with over 800 men; only sixty-eight were able to answer the roll call the following morning. Haig, however, was not deterred by the appalling casualty rate, and the battle continued for another five months. The British suffered 82,000 additional casualties in July and August. In September, they pushed the Germans back a few miles by using tanks and more sophisticated artillery tactics, but even this minor advance was halted the following month. In November, when the winter weather began to set in, Haig reluctantly called off the offensive. The British forces were still more than six miles from Bapaume, a French town that had been their objective on the first day of the battle.

 See document "The Battle of the Somme" at www.routledge.com_cw_barczewski.

In the Battle of the Somme, 600,000 British and French soldiers were killed or wounded, as compared to 450,000 German casualties. The following year, the British suffered nearly as many losses at the *Battle of Passchendaele* (also referred to as 3rd Ypres), with equally limited results. As a result of these heavy casualties, the British public and some politicians began

Figure 9.3 Soldiers from New Zealand in action on the Somme in September 1916.
Reproduced courtesy of Archives New Zealand.

seriously to question the strategy of their military leaders. After Passchendaele, *David Lloyd George, who had become prime minister* in 1916, complained, "Haig does not care how many men he loses. He just squanders the lives of these boys." Today, a century later, battles such as the Somme and Passchendaele remain controversial. For decades after the war, the view that brave men had been needlessly sent to their deaths by callous and incompetent generals prevailed. In recent years, however, some historians have argued that these battles were necessary to grind down the strength of the German army and to transform the New Army into a battle-tested and formidable fighting force.

Though it is the trench warfare of the Western Front for which the First World War is remembered today, not all of the fighting took place on land. At sea, the battleships of the Royal Navy proved vulnerable to submarines and mines; the brand-new dreadnought HMS *Audacious* sank after hitting a mine off the Irish coast in October 1914. In consequence, the bulk of the British fleet spent most of the war at its base at Scapa Flow in the Orkney Islands of Scotland, waiting for signs that the German navy had put to sea, which it did on a major scale only once, in June 1916. The two navies clashed at the Battle of Jutland, but although the British fleet suffered greater casualties, the German battleships retreated to their bases for the duration of the war. British naval forces also helped to enforce a maritime blockade of Germany and its allies, hoping to starve them of resources. The Germans countered this blockade with unrestricted submarine warfare, which threatened Britain's food supply, but was ultimately foiled by convoy tactics and the immense material resources of the United States.

The German submarine campaign helped bring the United States into the war. The American president, Woodrow Wilson, had attempted to keep the United States out of the conflict, though he did agree to make substantial loans to Britain and France. American public opinion initially supported a policy of neutrality, but it was stirred by (frequently embellished) stories of German atrocities. In 1915, anti-German sentiment was further inflamed by the sinking of the passenger vessel R.M.S. *Lusitania* by a German U-boat off the Irish coast, at a cost of 1200 lives, 128 of them American. When Germany agreed to suspend submarine attacks on passenger ships, Wilson was able to keep the United States out of the war for two more years. But in 1917, when the Germans resumed unrestricted submarine warfare and also attempted to form an alliance with Mexico, his hand was finally forced, and the *American Senate voted to enter the conflict* in April 1917.

The entry of the Americans into the war eventually tipped the balance in favor of the Allies, but initially their contribution was minor. By June 1917, only 14,000 American soldiers had arrived in France, and it appeared as if the arrival of more substantial numbers might come too late. In the wake of the Bolshevik Revolution, *Russia signed an armistice with Germany* in December. With their eastern flank now secured, the Germans were able to concentrate their resources on the Western Front. In March 1918, they *launched an offensive* that pushed the Allies back towards Paris and threatened to drive a wedge between the British and French armies. The Germans, however, ran into the same problems of exploiting their breakthrough that had dogged allied attacks over the previous two years. After suffering enormous casualties and with their remaining troops exhausted, the German advance ground to a halt in the summer of 1918. By then, 10,000 American troops were arriving on the Western Front each day, and by May 1918, over a million were stationed in France. A counter-attack, led by experienced British, Canadian and Australian units and supported by new American ones, pushed the Germans back past their old front lines. Even this advance required bloody frontal assaults: the British casualty rates in 1918 were the worst of the war. But for the first time on the Western Front, the defenders of a major assault suffered significantly greater casualties than did the attackers. By September, the formidable Hindenburg Line, the last line of the German defenses, had been breached, and the German High Command called for an end to the war before Germany itself was invaded. An *armistice* was signed on the 11th of November 1918. Sixteen million soldiers and civilians had lost their lives in the war, 720,000 of them British, with another 250,000 from the Empire.

Government, Politics and the War Effort

In the initial stages of the war, Prime Minister Herbert Henry Asquith's Liberal government managed the war and the home front by focusing on political unity. The appointment of Lord Kitchener as secretary of state for war put the government above partisan criticism, and a decision to eliminate parliamentary **by-elections** for the duration of the war reduced political infighting amongst the parties. Policy was left in the hands of the cabinet, supported by a newly created Council of War, consisting of the heads of the army and navy and a select group of ministers. Increasingly, the Council became the main decision-making body.

The government quickly passed a series of emergency measures known as the Defence of the Realm Acts (DORA), which contained sweeping powers to rule by decree (i.e., without the consent of Parliament), censor the press, suppress dangerous "agitators" and repatriate or intern "enemy aliens" (i.e., German people living in Britain). The property of German nationals was also confiscated. The war generated much popular anti-German sentiment, leading British people with German or Austrian ancestry to change their surnames. This included the royal family, whose family name was altered from "Saxe-Coburg-Gotha" (which had come from Queen Victoria's German husband Prince Albert) to "Windsor" in 1917. Perceived German atrocities, such as the sinking of the *Lusitania*, led to mobs attacking the shops and houses of people in Britain of "enemy" ancestry, including non-German Jews and naturalized British citizens. By 1916, the government had interned over 40,000 enemy aliens in special camps, though very few of these people represented a real threat. Paranoid fears of spies led to the investigation of hundreds of suspects, with only about two dozen ever determined to be real enemy agents.

The lack of British military success on the battlefield, however, led to problems for Asquith and his ministers. Military commanders attempted to justify their failures by claiming that they were being starved of necessary munitions. In 1915 the conservative press made much of a "shells scandal," in which the government was blamed for a shortage of artillery shells on the front lines. As public confidence in the government decreased, it seemed likely that the Liberals would lose the next general election, scheduled for that December. In May, Asquith offered to form a *coalition* with members of the Labour and Conservative parties in which he would remain prime minister. The Conservative leader Andrew Bonar Law agreed to join, and a general election was postponed until the conclusion of the war. Seeing it as a violation of their political principles, some Liberal MPs were outraged by the decision to include the other parties in the government. Most, however, supported the coalition, including David Lloyd George, the fiery Welsh radical who emerged as the leader of the "we must win at all cost" group within Parliament. Lloyd George was successful in using the shells scandal to reduce Kitchener's administrative responsibilities and to establish a new Ministry of Munitions, which he headed himself. This was a key political development, as munitions production had emerged as vital to the successful prosecution of the war.

As the conflict became mired in stalemate by the end of 1914, the BEF had exhausted all of Britain's prewar stock of weapons and ammunition. Industry now had to produce arms and ammunition for two armies: the BEF fighting in France, which needed artillery and vast amounts of shells, and Kitchener's New Armies in training, which needed everything, especially rifles and uniforms. Lloyd George attacked the problem by concentrating on three aims: increasing the output of ammunition through the building of new government-run factories; stimulating the growth of private production by offering guaranteed government contracts; and investing in scientific and technological research. He effectively created an entirely new industrial landscape wherein supply rather than costs ruled, as firms were guaranteed that the munitions they produced would be bought by the government. Over 250 new "national" munitions factories under direct government control were established. These were supplemented by some 20,000 "controlled" establishments, or private firms with guaranteed munitions contracts.

This system allowed munitions production to increase rapidly. The output of medium-size artillery guns increased by 380 percent in the first year, while the production of heavy guns increased by 1200 percent. By 1917, munitions were the primary product of Britain's industrial economy. Such rapid expansion led to some problems: about a quarter of the big guns produced after 1915 were flawed, and, as we have seen, a third of the 1.7 million shells fired in the barrage that preceded the Battle of the Somme in 1916 were duds. Both the quantity and quality of production, however, improved over the course of the war. The Ministry of Munitions also expedited the development of new military technologies like the tank and the airplane, but it was simpler developments that proved more vital. A good example was the steel combat helmet. British troops went to war in 1914 in cloth hats. Within a year, it became obvious that the alarming number of head wounds suffered by soldiers in the trenches could be reduced by issuing steel helmets. By the end of the war, 7 million helmets had been delivered to the army.

An even greater challenge than munitions was the recruitment of troops to fill the ranks of Kitchener's New Army. The effort was spearheaded by an all-party Parliamentary Recruiting Committee (PRC). The PRC surveyed households to identify potential recruits, held rallies at music halls and sporting events, and produced propaganda films. It initially appealed primarily to patriotism, but later exploited tales of German atrocities and encouraged women to pressure their husbands and sons to enlist. The PRC's propaganda output was prodigious: it issued 54 million posters and 5.8 million leaflets, organized 12,000 public meetings and sponsored 20,000 speeches. To encourage married men to enlist, separation allowances were offered to their wives by the government. Another recruiting strategy was the formation of "Pals Battalions." Men were more likely to want to serve in units alongside their neighbors, friends and colleagues. Numerous units were thus created that exploited the bonds of locality or occupation. Battalions were created for artists, stockbrokers and bicycle enthusiasts, as well as for specific counties, towns and urban neighborhoods. The Pals Battalions proved a very effective recruiting tool, but when one of these units suffered badly in battle, the effect upon the community was devastating. During the Somme offensive, some villages and urban neighborhoods lost almost all their enlisted men in a single engagement.

The Experience of Warfare 6

War Posters

In January 1915, a Londoner observed, "Posters appealing to recruits are to be seen on every hoarding, in most shop windows, in omnibuses, tramcars, and commercial vans. The great base of Nelson's pillar (in Trafalgar Square) is covered with them." Early recruiting posters tended to be blown-up versions of handbills, often simply providing the technical terms of enlistment and usually printed in only one or two colors. They contained no visual images and relied on simple slogans such as "Your Country Needs You." Soon, however, the posters began to feature striking graphic images and to become more sophisticated and psychologically manipulative. Some made reference to Germany's violation of Belgian neutrality and other purported war crimes, while others appealed to young men's camaraderie, masculinity and desire for adventure and were not above using shame as a motivation. Perhaps the most famous example was the poster that asked "Daddy, What Did You Do in the Great War?" It depicted a middle-aged man sitting comfortably in an armchair after the war, while his son played with toy soldiers on the floor and his daughter sat on his knee, reading an account of the war as she innocently asked the damning question. The bullying tone of these posters engendered criticism, and by the end of 1915 their effectiveness in the recruitment effort was being questioned. Propaganda posters continued to be issued, but the implementation of conscription in 1916 led to a shift in their primary purpose away from recruitment and towards home-front issues such as service in munitions factories, the restriction of food consumption and the buying of war bonds.

"ANIBYNIAETH
SYDD YN GALW
AM EI
DEWRAF DYN"

Figures 9.4 and 9.5   Two recruiting posters from the First World War that show the diversity of populations at whom recruiting efforts were aimed. Dated 1916, the one on the left is in Welsh; it shows British artillerymen loading a howitzer above words that translate to "independence demands the bravest men." The one on the right appealed to the loyalty of men from Britain's Caribbean colonies as it sought to recruit men for the British West Indies Regiment.

Reproduced courtesy of the Library of Congress.

Civilian groups and individuals also encouraged men to enlist. Most notoriously, some women handed out white feathers, symbolizing cowardice, to men not in uniform. These women saw themselves as pioneers who were defying gender stereotypes and demonstrating their patriotism. The practice sometimes backfired, however, as some of the men who were given a feather were soldiers on leave or men who had been wounded at the front, and they

YOUNG MEN
OF THE BAHAMAS

The British Empire is engaged in a Life and Death Struggle. Never in the History of England, never since the Misty Distant Past of 2,000 years ago, has our beloved Country been engaged in such a conflict as she is engaged in to-day.

To bring to nothing this mighty attack by an unscrupulous and well prepared foe, HIS MOST GRACIOUS MAJESTY KING GEORGE has called on the men of his Empire, MEN OF EVERY CLASS, CREED AND COLOUR, to

COME FORWARD TO FIGHT

that the Empire may be saved and the foe may be well beaten.

This call is to YOU, young man; not your neighbour, not your brother, not your cousin, but just YOU. SEVERAL HUNDREDS OF YOUR MATES HAVE COME UP, HAVE BEEN MEDICALLY EXAMINED AND HAVE BEEN PASSED AS "FIT."

What is the matter with YOU?

Put yourself right with your King; put yourself right with your fellowmen; put yourself right with yourself and your conscience.

ENLIST TO-DAY

THE GLEANER CO. LTD. PRINTERS, KINGSTON JAMAICA.

did not take kindly to having their courage questioned. In order to avoid such social shaming, men who worked in essential war industries (and who were therefore not allowed to enlist) were given badges to wear in public.

Recruiting efforts were largely successful: 2.4 million men voluntarily enlisted, but the army always required more, and calls for conscription grew ever louder. Conservatives argued that the war required individual liberty to be subordinated to the needs of the nation as a whole, but the Liberals who dominated the coalition argued that joining up must remain a matter of conscience. Ultimately, the demand rendered these political arguments moot. After all alternatives had been exhausted, Asquith reluctantly introduced the Military

Service Act in January 1916. Passed by the coalition with predominantly Conservative support, it imposed *conscription* on all single men between the ages of eighteen and forty-one.
Ireland was excluded, however, because it was argued that the introduction of conscription
there would lead to rebellion against British rule.

The act contained a clause permitting exemption from military service on grounds of
special hardship, essential war work or conscientious objection. Local military tribunals
adjudicated exemption claims. Staffed by magistrates, military representatives and prominent local people, these tribunals had to make difficult decisions. In the first six months of
1916 alone, some 750,000 exemptions were submitted for consideration. Those opposed to
conscription accused the tribunals of being biased and perfunctory, but others complained
that they were too liberal in granting exemptions. Between March 1916 and March 1917,
nearly 780,000 men gained exemptions, while 370,000 were denied. The vast majority of
the exemptions were on the grounds of essential war work or special hardship, such as being
the sole provider for a large family or taking care of an infirm relative.

The number of exemptions based on moral or religious conscience was small. Over the
course of the war 16,500 men registered as conscientious objectors, and about 80 percent
of them received some form of exemption. Some men refused to fight but agreed to carry
out alternative civilian duties or to serve as medical personal. But 1298 men, known as
"absolutists," refused to apply for an exemption or undertake service of any kind. They
were imprisoned for their stance, and a few died in custody as a result of ill treatment.
Without an exemption they were technically conscripts, so their stance placed them under
the jurisdiction of military law. If they were sent to France, their refusal to fight was considered desertion, an act punishable by death. Thirty-four absolutists were sentenced to
death, although all these sentences were commuted to ten years' hard labor. Though the
courage of these men came to be celebrated after the war, during the conflict "conchies"
were widely reviled.

The army's demand for manpower created shortages in other crucial areas. Some 120,000
highly skilled workers had enlisted by 1915, threatening munitions production, and Lloyd
George had to plead with the army for their return. In 1916, the Ministry of Munitions
kept 1.4 million men from military service, while teenagers, elderly men, and women were
used in many sectors of the economy. In 1917, a new Ministry of National Service assumed
responsibility for both army and labor recruitment. Most nonessential industries were closed
by the government and their workers redistributed to military service, munitions or food
production. Despite these efforts, throughout 1917 and 1918 there remained a shortage
of both war workers and soldiers. In the spring of 1918, the Ministry raised the upper age
limit of military recruits to fifty and, more controversially, extended conscription to Ireland,
though to decrease opposition it came with a promise of the quick implementation of Home
Rule after the war. (In any event, it was never implemented in the face of strong opposition
from Irish nationalists.)

The issue of conscription fatally undermined support for Asquith from the Liberal Party.
In November 1916, Lloyd George and Bonar Law confronted him with a plan to impose
executive control over the ministries and the military. The ensuing crisis brought down the
coalition and prompted Asquith's resignation from the premiership. A new coalition was
formed, with Lloyd George as prime minister and a cabinet dominated by Tory appointees.
This fractured the Liberal Party, as very few of its most prominent members joined. Some
middle-class Liberals found common ground with working-class radicals, the first step in the
political realignment that would see Labour supplant the Liberals after the war. Although
Lloyd George created a five-man executive war cabinet, control of the military conduct of

the war continued to elude him. He failed to muster the political will to remove Haig, the general whom he most blamed for the high casualty rate on the Western Front. Following the success of the German offensive in March 1918, however, he did manage to secure the cooperation of the British and French armies under the leadership of the French General Ferdinand Foch, thereby significantly reducing Haig's role.

The Home Front

The war had a profound impact on British people's lives. Since Britain imported most of its food in 1914, securing food supplies from abroad and boosting domestic food production were key strategic imperatives. Food prices rose sharply in the fall of 1914, due in part to hoarding, yet the government was at first reluctant to interfere with agricultural production or to regulate food prices. A strong global harvest in 1915 temporarily relieved fears of a food crisis, but a year later the situation was dire. Domestic crop yields fell below prewar levels, and mounting shipping losses to German U-boats further reduced the supply of food. Prices rose sharply: by the end of 1916 food expenditure was taking two-thirds of working-class families' wages. In 1917, the shortages were even more serious, with women in some towns forming lines at food shops as early as 5 a.m. Some male munitions workers stopped working in order to assist their wives in queuing for food.

These shortages tended to magnify existing social inequalities, as the wealthy did not suffer the same privations as the working population. In November 1917, the socialist news-paper the *Daily Herald* was outraged at the revelation that, while some working families in the East End of London survived solely on a diet of bread, potatoes, tea and cabbage leaves, patrons of the Ritz Hotel were being served six-course meals that included salmon, meats and cheeses, and elaborate desserts. It was widely known that many shop owners kept key items like sugar from their regular customers and sold them at high prices to their wealthier patrons. Such practices generated widespread anger, and in a few cases shops known to be withholding food supplies were raided. Government intervention in the production and sale of food steadily increased, and by 1917 many staple foods were being rationed.

Even before the war, there had been a significant shortage of housing. Overcrowding (defined as more than two people per room) was the norm for the poorest 10 percent of the population; in Glasgow, over half of the city's population was jammed into tiny flats in multifamily dwellings called "tenements." The war intensified this crisis. As a result of a decrease in the construction of new housing stock, the migration of workers to new places of employment for war work, and the demands of the army to house trainees, the number of families who shared a dwelling doubled. Thousands of people lived by the "box and cot" routine, in which night-shift workers occupied beds by day before turning them over to day-shift workers at night. In some places, ten people shared a single room. Housing shortages led to rising rents. In Glasgow and London, rents rose by as much as 25 percent in the first year of the war. Such rapid increases caused anger amongst tenants, some of whom went on rent strikes. At the end of 1915, the government froze rents at prewar levels, but this only exacerbated the shortage of housing, as builders were not interested in projects that had no hope of turning a profit. Local governments were forced to build a large number of new homes themselves, a trend that continued after the war.

War also imposed new challenges on workers. The demand for munitions led to the most persistent source of workplace friction: the diminishment of the prewar privileges of skilled workers. The speed of munitions production was increased by breaking down tasks that had previously been performed by a skilled worker into multiple parts, to each of which an unskilled worker was assigned. These practices, known as "dilution" and "substitution," were opposed by skilled workers, who had trained in lengthy apprenticeships and who had fought for decades to keep their privileges (and wages) from being eroded by employers. They were particularly concerned that the use of female workers in traditionally male trades would depress wage rates, since women were paid less than men. Differences in wages between skilled, semi-skilled and unskilled workers indeed diminished in many industries. Skilled laborers, however, were given a variety of incentives and bonuses that kept their earnings ahead of those of unskilled workers. For the most part, they grudgingly accepted the new situation after extracting promises from employers and the government that dilution and substitution would end after the war.

Workplace rights were further curtailed in 1915 by the passage of the Munitions War Act, which outlawed strikes, prohibited employers from poaching workers from other establishments at higher rates of pay, and prevented workers from changing jobs. Within two weeks of its passage, the toothlessness of the law was exposed by south Welsh coal miners, who struck over a pay dispute. The strikes were illegal, but the government could not imprison 200,000 men who worked in a vital industry, so the miners' demands were met without penalty. Workplace unrest continued throughout the war, due to high rents and food prices; the constant demands of the military for more men; and the huge profits being made by factory owners. Three million workdays were lost to strikes in 1915, 2.5 million in 1916 and 5.5 million in 1917. This was a much lower rate of strikes, however, than before the war: in 1912, 41 million workdays had been lost to labor action.

Women became a much larger proportion of the workforce during the war, but this was mainly because there were fewer male workers rather than because of a huge influx of women into the workplace. Prior to the war, between 5 and 6 million women, most of them unskilled industrial workers or domestic servants, worked outside the home. This number grew by between 1.2 and 1.4 million during the war, an increase of about 20 percent. Most women's paid work during the war was in "traditional" areas – textile manufacturing, clerical positions, nursing, retail and social work – rather than war industries. Some women, however, found work in new fields such as commerce, banking, government, finance and transport. Around 900,000 women – the famous "munitionettes" – did work in munitions factories, comprising about 12 percent of the total female workforce during the war.

Since industrial wage rates nearly doubled over the course of the war, some conservative critics complained that the working class was "benefiting" from the conflict. In reality, in the first two years of the war earnings lagged behind price increases. It was only in the last eighteen months of the war that the gap between wage rates and prices narrowed, due to government intervention in the form of increased wages and food rationing. Wartime work was arduous, as at the outset of the war the government suspended many regulations in the drive to increase munitions production. The standard forty-eight-hour week was extended to fifty-three hours, plus mandatory overtime. At the Woolwich Arsenal in London, six twelve-hour shifts per week were the norm. Gradually, however, excessive hours were cut back, as it was discovered that munitions workers were becoming exhausted. By 1918, the average working day for women had been reduced to eight hours in most factories, and Sunday once again became a day off.

To keep up the pace of production, machine operators routinely disregarded safety procedures. In bomb factories, explosions caused by unstable chemical compounds occurred with terrible frequency. In January 1917, an explosion at the Mond munitions factory in East London killed sixty-nine men and women, injured over a thousand and damaged hundreds of houses in the surrounding neighborhood. Poisoning from chemicals was more insidious,

Figure 9.6 Male and female workers in a warehouse at the National Shell Filling Factory in Chilwell, Nottinghamshire, around 1917. During the war, this factory filled 19 million shells with high explosives, or half the total number of shells fired by British forces. Women were employed there from the time it opened in 1915; the chemicals in the explosives often turned their skin yellow, earning them the nickname the "Chilwell Canaries." In July 1918, pressure to increase production led to a massive explosion that destroyed a large portion of the factory. A total of 134 workers were killed and another 250 injured. Only thirty-two of the dead could be identified; the rest were buried in a mass grave in a local churchyard.

Reproduced courtesy of IWM Collections.

but just as lethal. Female workers who were exposed to TNT on a daily basis found that their skin turned bright yellow, earning them the nickname "canaries." Around 400 women died from TNT poisoning, and thousands of others became seriously ill. Initially, the government responded by censoring news of the problem, but later weekly medical checks, mechanized shell-filling and the use of respirators and protective clothing were instituted.

Ultimately, the dangers of war work pushed the government to enact welfare policies to improve workplace conditions and practices for female workers in particular. This led to the provision of meals, rest breaks and improved washing and toilet facilities, as well as the establishment of recreational and educational activities and child-care facilities in factories. The welfare supervisors were almost always middle-class women. Combining the roles of social worker and moral guardian, they dealt with complaints, carried out rudimentary medical and dental examinations and enforced discipline. By the end of the war, about a thousand welfare supervisors had been appointed, one for every 300 female employees. They were loved and loathed in equal measure by the working-class women who worked under their watchful eye.

The Empire in the Great War

When Britain declared war in August 1914, it brought millions of people in the colonies into the war as well. Though we think of the First World War primarily as having been fought on the Western Front, significant action also occurred in Africa and the Middle East, with more minor campaigns taking place in Central Asia and East Asia. Troops from Australia and New Zealand led assaults on Germany's territories in the South Pacific, while South African forces attacked Germany's possessions in South West and East Africa. Other soldiers from the Empire saw action farther from home: Indian troops fought in China and the Middle East; in the latter theater, they were joined by volunteers from the West Indies. Imperial troops, however, did not only fight in imperial locales. Large numbers also fought on the Western Front and elsewhere. Over 140,000 Indian soldiers served on the Western Front; 8500 died, out of the total of 75,000 Indian war dead. Perhaps the best-remembered contribution by imperial forces, however, is that of troops from Australia and New Zealand in the *failed invasion of the Gallipoli Peninsula* in Turkey in 1915. Over 10,000 of these "Anzacs" died; in both Australia and New Zealand today, Anzac Day (25th of April) remains the most important annual commemoration of national military history. Over 1600 Indian soldiers were also killed at Gallipoli, which represented more than half the total number who fought in the campaign, a staggering casualty rate.

Overall, the contribution of the British Empire to the First World War was massive. One and a half million men from India fought for the British, along with 1.3 million from the dominions (Australia, New Zealand, Canada, South Africa and Newfoundland) and 16,000 from the West Indies. New Zealand lost 5 percent of its total male population between the ages of fifteen and forty-nine. Why were Britain's colonies willing to make such an immense sacrifice in a war that had started so far away? Some historians have answered this question by suggesting mercenary motives, particularly in the case of India. Indian soldiers were paid eleven rupees a month, a substantial sum for men who often came from the poorest castes. But many colonial recruits, both white and non-white, felt genuine loyalty to the Empire. This was reinforced by colonial elites, who for the most part enthusiastically supported the war effort by raising funds and recruiting large numbers of troops. The war engendered a true sense of imperial solidarity and common identity.

At the same time, however, the war exacerbated differences between Britain and its colonies. At the beginning of the war, the use of non-white troops on the Western Front was controversial. In August 1914, the *Times* began publishing a "History of the War" in weekly installments. One of the early issues observed, "the instinct which made us such sticklers for propriety in all our dealings made us more reluctant than other nations would feel to employ colored troops against a white enemy." As casualties mounted, however, such scruples (or prejudices) quickly diminished. By the end of September 1914, *two corps of Indian troops had been sent to France.* They were later joined by soldiers from the West Indies, though they served as pioneers (construction workers) rather than in combat. But even if in some ways the war led to a diminishment of racial prejudices within the British military establishment, others lingered. Even if official policy evolved to treat troops more equitably, non-white soldiers frequently encountered discrimination and racism within the armed forces. The British continued to sort colonial peoples into "martial" and "non-martial races," with the former the subject of more intense recruiting efforts than the former. Among South Asian recruits, for example, men from Nepal and the Punjab were considered to be more "warrior-like" – and also more obeisant to the authority of white officers – than men from other parts of India. During the war, men from the Punjab provided 54 percent of the Indian Army.

Figures 9.7 and 9.8 Imperial troops on the Western Front. At the top, Sikh soldiers from India. On the bottom, Mohawk troops fighting in the Canadian Army.

Both images reproduced courtesy of Shutterstock/Everett Collection.

For colonial peoples, the experience of war was complex. After Turkey joined the war on the German side in October 1914, Muslim soldiers from India faced a decision as to whether to prioritize their religious identities or their loyalty to the British Empire. Most chose the latter, but a few deserted, and on at least three occasions Muslim troops mutinied because they did not want to fight against the Turks, since they were fellow Muslims and the Ottoman emperor was regarded as the *caliph*, or successor to Mohammad. Exposure to western lifestyles and values also elicited a variety of responses. Some men were astonished by the wealth of European cities, but others saw them as decadent and overly focused on material display. Some admired the educational attainments and intellectual abilities of European women, but others saw them as immoral and lacking in modesty. In the colonies themselves, the war had far-reaching consequences. In many colonies, in particular in India, Egypt and the Middle East, the war increased desires for independence. Even as colonial peoples fought alongside the British, they saw their loyalty as a means to demonstrate their worthiness of greater autonomy in the future. Many of them went to war consciously expecting that that their service would strengthen the case for independence in the years to come. Some Irish nationalists, as we will now see, harbored similar hopes.

The Easter Rising

As they focused on the war effort, British politicians paid little attention to Ireland. In Ireland, however, the impact of the war was dramatic. Prior to 1914, the issue of Home Rule had seemed likely to cause a civil war between Irish nationalists and Ulster Unionists. Once the war began, however, the implementation of the Home Rule legislation that had been passed by the House of Commons was deferred. John Redmond, the leader of the Irish Parliamentary Party, and the Unionist leader Edward Carson both pledged their support for the war effort. Their objectives were similar: they hoped that by proving their loyalty to the British Empire, they would achieve their political goals. Members of the Ulster Volunteer Force formed the nucleus of the 36th (Ulster) Division of the British Army, which suffered heavy casualties on the first day of the Battle of the Somme. Redmond, meanwhile, called upon Irishmen to serve "wherever the firing line extends." Many heeded his call: in total, over 200,000 Irishmen, both Unionists and nationalists, served in the war, over 30,000 of whom were killed.

On the whole, the war effort enjoyed popular support in Ireland, and high prices for agricultural products benefited Irish farmers. As the war dragged on, however, and the goal of Home Rule seemed no closer to reality, many nationalists became disillusioned with Redmond and the Irish Party. Some 12,000 members of the Irish Volunteers, the prewar army formed to fight for Home Rule, rejected Redmond's call to enlist in the British Army and continued to organize and drill in Ireland. The leadership of the revolutionary Irish Republican Brotherhood (IRB), who believed the nineteenth-century nationalist leader Daniel O'Connell's dictum that "England's difficulty was Ireland's opportunity," began planning an insurrection in order to establish an independent Irish republic. Enlisting the aid of the Germans, these revolutionaries attempted to import arms via U-boat in support of a rebellion planned for Easter Sunday, 1916. When the shipment was intercepted off the southwest coast of Ireland in April, the leaders of the Irish Volunteers attempted to call off the rising, but the leadership of the IRB decided to go ahead. The rebellion took place on the Easter Monday **bank holiday**, 24th of April, and it thus became known as the *"Easter Rising."* It took place primarily in Dublin, where around 1500 rebels, including 100 women, occupied key buildings around the city. On Easter Monday, the leader of the revolt, Patrick Pearse, read a

"Proclamation of the Irish Republic" outside of the General Post Office in central Dublin, which became the headquarters of the rising.

 See document "The Proclamation of the Irish Republic" at www.routledge. com_cw_barczewski.

Although the rebels were poorly equipped, they managed to hold out for a week against British military forces. Around 450 people were killed, including over 100 British soldiers and more than 200 civilians, while British artillery fire reduced much of central Dublin to

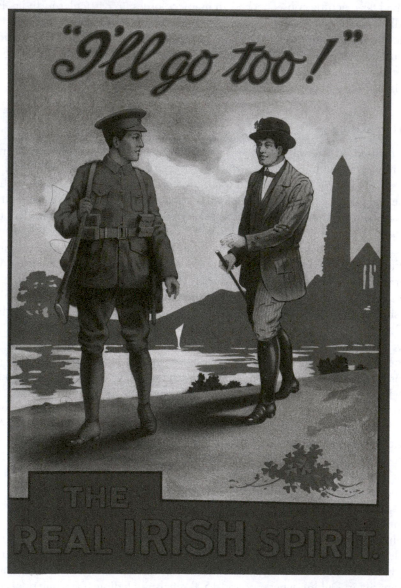

Figure 9.9 A recruiting poster targeting Irishmen.
Reproduced courtesy of the Library of Congress.

ruins. Many Irish people initially reacted with anger at the rebels for causing such death and destruction for such a hopeless cause. The British government's response to the rising, however, dramatically altered Irish public opinion. In the midst of the Great War, with the major offensive at the Somme approaching, no leniency was given to the rebel leadership. Military trials sentenced ninety rebels to death; fifteen were executed between the 3rd and 12th of May, including Pearse and the other six signatories of the Proclamation of the Irish Republic. The condemned included the socialist republican James Connolly, who had been badly wounded in the fighting and had to be strapped to a chair in order to face the firing squad because he could not stand up. Another 3500 people, most of whom had little or nothing to do with the rising, were arrested and detained. The harsh British response swung Irish opinion firmly behind the rebels. In June 1916, General Sir John Maxwell, commander-in-chief in Ireland and the man who had ordered the executions, noted that army recruiting in Ireland had "practically ceased."

Although the radical nationalist party Sinn Féin had nothing to do with the Easter Rising, afterwards it became the political arm of the Irish rebels and a renewed force in Irish politics. In 1917 and 1918, several members of the party were elected to Parliament in by-elections, including Eamon de Valera, the senior surviving member of the Easter Rising's leadership. (Recognizing the effect that the executions were having on Irish opinion, the British government had called a halt to them before de Valera's turn had come.) The newly elected Sinn Féin MPs refused to take their seats in Parliament; instead, they acted as if the Irish republic was already in existence and rejected the authority of the United Kingdom. By the end of the war, Home Rule was no longer an acceptable political solution to the majority of Irish nationalists, and armed conflict between Britain and Ireland erupted soon afterwards.

The Costs and Consequences of the War

The alteration of the political situation in Ireland was only one of many ways in which the First World War had a dramatic impact on the United Kingdom. Although Britain did not suffer as many casualties in the First World War as did France, Germany or Russia, the figures were still shocking: over 720,000 British soldiers had been killed, which when combined with the losses from the dominions, was rounded up to a "million Empire dead." A further 1.6 million were wounded, with many permanently maimed or crippled. Tens of thousands more suffered serious psychological trauma, known at the time as "shell shock." In total, one in eight servicemen died, and one in four was wounded. The losses were greatest amongst the young; the age with the highest percentage of war losses was twenty. Though the subsequent claim of a "lost generation" was exaggerated, the deaths of so many young men produced profound grief. During the war, public mourning had been restrained by the need to keep up morale. The period that followed, however, saw a vast number of memorials and commemorative ceremonies in honor of the war dead.

The Experience of Warfare 7

The First World War in British Memory

The First World War looms large in British popular memory in part because of the way in which it was commemorated. War memorials focused on sanctifying the sacrifice of those who had been killed and on offering consolation to their bereaved

Figures 9.10, 9.11, and 9.12 After 1918, war memorials dotted the landscapes of Britain, Ireland and the Empire, as well as marking the places where British and colonial solders had fought and died. The memorial in Figure 9.10 is typical of examples in rural English towns. Located in Wiltstone in Hertfordshire, it takes the form of a Celtic cross and lists the names of the nine men from the village who died. In Figure 9.11, a memorial to the soldiers from New Zealand who fought at Chunuk Bair during the Gallipoli campaign in 1915 is unveiled in 1925. Figure 9.12 shows the unveiling ceremony for the Chattri Memorial outside Brighton on the south coast of England. It commemorated the service of the 1.5 million Indian soldiers who fought for the British. Thousands of wounded Indian troops were brought to hospitals in Brighton for treatment and recuperation. The Brighton Royal Pavilion, formerly a royal palace built by King George IV, was converted to a military hospital, ostensibly because its Indian-style architecture would make the Indians feel at home. The memorial was placed on the site of the ghat, or funeral pyre, that was used to cremate the remains of fifty-three Hindu soldiers who died in Brighton, in accordance with their religious practices. Paid for by the India Office and the Brighton Corporation, the memorial was unveiled by the Prince of Wales, the future King Edward VIII, in 1921.

Figure 9.10 reproduced courtesy of Chris Reynolds/Wilstone War Memorial; Figure 9.11 reproduced courtesy of Archives New Zealand; Figure 9.12 reproduced courtesy of Royal Pavilion and Museums, Brighton and Hove.

THE "LAST POST". 1664.

H.R.H. THE PRINCE OF WALES UNVEILING THE INDIAN CHATTRI ON THE DOWNS PATCHAM · FEB. 1. 1921.

loved ones. New, nondenominational, nonhierarchical forms of remembrance were intended to commemorate all those who had died. Designed by Sir Edwin Lutyens, the Cenotaph in London took the form of a stone plinth with an "empty tomb" at its top. An "unknown soldier" was exhumed from the fields of Flanders and buried in a special tomb in Westminster Abbey. Across Britain on every Armistice Day (11th of November), two minutes of silence, in which everything stopped in honor of the fallen, was observed at 11 a.m. Tens of thousands of war memorials were built in British cities, towns and villages, almost all of them listing the local dead. As the bodies of the dead were not repatriated but were interred in special cemeteries near where they were killed, thousands of people made pilgrimages to the graves of their loved ones in France and Belgium.

All of these commemorative activities meant that the war cast a shadow over postwar society long after it had ended. A myth developed in Britain of a younger generation that had been sacrificed in a futile war by the old. This view was largely created by middle-class writers who had been in the conflict and who came to view their service and sacrifice differently when British society did not seem to change for the better after the war. The high quality of their writing, which resonated with later generations due to their emphasis on the horror and futility of war, made them worthy of attention, but they were not as representative of the trench experience as they were presumed to be. Much of the disillusionment associated with Great War literature was in fact a product of the postwar era. Robert Graves, whose book *Good-Bye to All That* (1929) was both a commercial and critical success, was far more bitter about his war experience when he wrote it ten years after the armistice than he was in his personal correspondence at the time.

The war also had serious economic consequences for Britain. Total British expenditure on the conflict exceeded £9.1 billion. To meet this enormous cost, government spending as a percentage of gross national product rose from 13.5 percent in 1914 to 59.3 percent in 1918. This level of expenditure required substantial increases in taxation and massive borrowing. The standard rate of income tax rose from 5.8 percent to 30 percent in 1918, while the "super tax" on annual income over £3,000 was raised to 4 percent, and another 15 percent was levied on income over £11,000. The majority of government tax revenue, however, came from a tax on "excessive profits," which climbed to 80 percent by the end of the war, and from increased duties on commodities such as tobacco, alcohol, tea, cocoa and coffee. The government raised some £2.7 billion over the course of the war, but this was only 29 percent of total expenditure. The remainder was met by borrowing, both from the British public and from overseas allies. The largest creditor for the British was the United States. Britain's foreign debts in 1919 were £840 million to the United States, £113 million to its European allies and £92 million to Canada. By 1919, the national debt had ballooned to £6.1 billion.

The war also had a profound impact on British politics. The war tore the Liberal Party apart, giving Labour a chance to challenge it for votes on the left of the political spectrum. The real winner, however, was the Conservative Party, which dominated British politics for the next two decades. The war was also the catalyst for the largest single expansion of the electorate in British history: in 1918, men over twenty-one and most women over thirty were enfranchised by the *Representation of the People Act*. The electorate nearly tripled, from 7.7 million in 1912 to 21.4 million in 1918. A significant shift in the basis of citizenship underlay this increase: for men it was their service during the war, rather than the ownership of property, that now became the basis of their right to vote. Women's service in support of the war, meanwhile, helped to secure their right to vote over the objections of the die-hard opponents. But for women, property rights remained tied to the vote, as the 1918 Act stipulated that voting women had to be at least thirty and either the owner or the wife of the owner of property. This meant that most of the women who had worked in the munitions factories were not enfranchised. They would have to wait another decade for the right to vote.

Despite the immense importance of women's contribution to the war effort and the challenging of gender norms that was evident in female wartime work and the achievement of female suffrage, at the end of the war there was a concerted effort to re-establish the prewar gender order. Women were encouraged to leave the workplace in order to make way for male veterans. Many willingly did so, but others who had enjoyed the financial independence and workplace camaraderie of the war years resisted being pushed back into traditional female occupations. Thus, while the existing gender order was not overturned by the war, prewar trends towards greater freedom for women were significantly advanced.

Conclusion

Even before the First World War ended, questions were raised about whether the massive offensives launched by the British in 1916 and 1917 were worth the staggering casualties that they generated. Certainly, they gained little in the way of territory. One line of thinking, which began during the interwar years and developed into near-orthodoxy after the Second World War, was that the British had fielded fine armies filled with brave soldiers, but they had been led by a bunch of incompetent, reckless and callous generals, who sat safely miles behind the front line and who lacked the imagination to order anything but murderous frontal assaults. This notion of "lions led by donkeys" also contained a class dimension, as it was argued that the British high command was dominated by aristocrats and gentry who were both socially distant from and contemptuous of the middle- and working-class men they sent to their deaths.

In reality, however, it was the scale of the armies, the new technologies that were employed and the geography of the battlefield that made the First World War so shockingly bloody, rather than the decisions of the generals. Victory required massive casualties, whatever tactics were employed. Indeed, the rate of casualties on the Eastern Front in Russia and during times when there was significant mobility on the Western Front, such as March to November 1918, was considerably higher than in the period of stalemate. The casualty rates on the Western Front were comparable to those of the American Civil War fifty years earlier, and later in the great land battles of the Second World War. The only antidote to the slaughter was to not fight at all.

The First World War had complex consequences for the people of Britain, Ireland and the Empire. While voluntary recruiting and the army's regimental system initially emphasized local identities, the experience of mass casualties and the introduction of conscription in 1916 enhanced a sense of Britishness. Men from all parts of the British Isles fought in the same units and suffered from the same horrific conditions, and the sense of shared sacrifice cemented bonds of unity. Civilians in England, Scotland and Wales experienced a weakening of national loyalties in the face of a shared British identity. Tens of thousands of male English workers were employed in Scottish factories, and vice versa, while thousands of women moved from their homes to munitions factories that were dispersed around the British Isles. While moving did not entirely undermine local identities, the shared experience of the workplace did tend to deepen social connections, and for many people class differences became more significant than national or regional ones. Moreover, the service of almost 3 million soldiers from Britain's colonies and dominions fostered a sense of imperial camaraderie. In other ways, however, the war weakened rather than strengthened ties to the British Empire. This was most immediately apparent in Ireland, where by 1918 a far larger number of people were convinced that full independence from the United Kingdom was the right path for the country's future. Also in the interwar years, nationalists in other British colonies would begin to think along the same lines.

Bibliography

Bourne, Stephen, *Black Poppies: Britain's Black Community and the Great War* (2019)

Dewey, Peter, *War and Progress: Britain, 1914–1945* (1997)

Fanning, Ronan, *Fatal Path: British Government and Irish Revolution 1910–1922* (2013)

Gregory, Adrian, *The Last Great War: British Society and the First World War* (2008)

Gullace, Nicoletta, *"The Blood of Our Sons"*: Men, Women, and the Renegotiation of British Citizenship During the Great War (2002)

Holmes, Richard, *Tommy: The British Soldier on the Western Front 1914–1918* (2004)

Lloyd, Nick, *The Western Front* (2021)

Philpott, William, *Bloody Victory: The Sacrifice on the Somme* (2009)

Robb, George, *British Culture and the First World War* (2002)

Simmonds, A. G. V., *Britain and World War One* (2012)

Townshend, Charles, *Easter 1916: The Irish Rebellion* (2005)

Watson, Janet S. K., *Fighting Different Wars: Experience, Memory and the First World War in Britain* (2004)

10 The Interwar Years

Topics covered

- Britain's role in the new international order
- Rise of nationalism in the British Empire
- Irish independence
- Changed political landscape after the First World War
- Economic depression, structural unemployment, racial tensions and labor unrest
- Interwar Scotland and Wales
- British society and culture in the "Jazz Age"
- Appeasement in the 1930s

Timeline

1918	First postwar general election
1919	Paris Peace Conference
1922	Irish Free State established
1924	First Labour government
1926	General Strike
1929	Wall Street crash; beginning of the Great Depression
1931	"National Government" formed under Ramsay MacDonald
1931	Statute of Westminster
1935	Government of India Act
1936	Abdication crisis
1938	Munich Pact
1939	Britain declares war on Germany

Introduction

The First World War did not completely shatter British society, as was the case for a number of other European combatants. Even so, the British economy was fundamentally disrupted, social relations were thrown into a state of flux, and the political landscape was permanently reshaped. Historians have tended to characterize the period between the end of the First World War in 1918 and the start of the Second in 1939 as "lost decades" that were

DOI: 10.4324/9781003284758-10

dominated by unemployment, economic decline, intensifying ideological conflict and growing international tensions. There is much truth in this depiction: Britain's economy was fundamentally altered by the war, and Britain's leaders often proved unable to cope with the crises that ensued. Instead, they tried the solutions of the past, which did little to solve the country's economic problems, particularly after a global depression began after 1929. To be sure, the difficulties varied by region, age group and social level. Some economic sectors performed well, and the standard of living improved for many people. But in general, this was a troubled and unsettled period in which few people felt secure.

Internationally, Britain struggled to maintain its prewar international position. The British Empire emerged from the aftermath of the war larger in geographical extent than it had ever been, but with new challenges in the form of increased responsibilities and nationalist demands for independence. These pressures would build to a breaking point first in Ireland, where armed conflict erupted in 1919, leading to its partition and the granting of self-governing dominion status to the majority of the island. European affairs were also a source of continuing anxiety, culminating in the desperate search for a peaceful solution to the rise of extremist regimes on the continent in the 1930s, a quest that ultimately failed.

The New Postwar Order

Immediately following the armistice, Prime Minister David Lloyd George called a *general election*, the first since 1910, which was held in December of 1918. Campaigning as "the man who won the war," he swept back into power with a majority of over 200 seats, as he continued to enjoy coalition support from Conservatives as well as from his own Liberal Party. Working with the Conservative leader Andrew Bonar Law, he identified candidates who agreed to support him and got them to cosign a letter of endorsement, known as a "coupon." As a result, the 1918 contest became known as the "coupon election." But although Lloyd George remained prime minister and the coalition remained in power, the political landscape had changed significantly. The Conservatives won the most votes, but only around a third of the total number cast, while the Liberals won a quarter, split evenly between those who supported Lloyd George's coalition and those who did not. The Labour Party, meanwhile, received 21 percent of the vote. Though this gained Labour only fifty-seven seats in Parliament, it was still a significant increase over their forty-two in 1910.

For the government, the first task after the election was to tackle the building of a new Europe at the *Paris Peace Conference*, which opened in January of 1919. Lloyd George and the British delegation were forced to mediate between the idealism of the American president, Woodrow Wilson, who aimed to build a new world order based on the principles of national self-determination, collective security, liberal democracy and free trade, and the pragmatism of the French president, Georges Clemenceau, who aimed to protect France from a German juggernaut that had invaded his country twice in the previous half-century. Britain's role was rendered all the more difficult by the shattered and unstable state of Europe, the influenza pandemic of 1919 (which killed more Europeans than the war), and revolutionary uprisings across the continent that were inspired by the Bolsheviks in Russia. At the conference, Lloyd George attempted to take a moderate position, viewing Wilson's idealism as impractical and Clemenceau's hard line as certain to create future conflict. He recognized that it was in Britain's economic interest to have a strong rather than devastated Germany. A significant portion of Britain's prewar trade had been with Germany, and thus the quick recovery of German markets was necessary for the revival of Britain's economic health.

It was a reflection of America's burgeoning power and Europe's exhaustion that Wilson's vision prevailed in the Treaty of Versailles, which was signed in June of 1919. The principle of national self-determination was applied to a variety of European situations, as liberal democracy was actively promoted and Wilson's notion of collective security was enshrined in the League of Nations, a precursor to the United Nations whose primary role was to maintain global peace. The French, however, won a victory in imposing disarmament and massive reparations payments on Germany. Lloyd George returned from Paris reasonably satisfied with the results of the conference, though some members of the British delegation, in particular the economist John Maynard Keynes, believed that Germany had been treated too harshly.

 See document "A British View of the Treaty of Versailles" at www.routledge. com_cw_barczewski.

The Postwar "Crisis of Empire"

The peace settlement altered the contours of the British Empire. During the negotiations, Lloyd George had focused on preserving the Empire and had attempted to dampen Wilson's calls for self-determination, recognizing that they could be interpreted as encouraging anticolonial nationalism. He was largely successful in at least the former goal, and Britain emerged with the Empire not only intact but enlarged, thanks to the addition of territories held as "mandates," or quasi-colonial possessions that were officially administered on behalf of the League of Nations. These included Mesopotamia (modern-day Iraq) and Palestine (comprising modern-day Israel, Jordan, the West Bank and the Gaza Strip), both formerly part of the now-dismantled Ottoman Empire, as well as the former German colony of Tanganyika (now Tanzania) in southeastern Africa. The foreign secretary, Lord Curzon, proudly proclaimed, "the British flag has never flown over a more powerful and united empire."

 See document "The British Empire Exhibition" at www.routledge.com_cw_barczewski.

But this expanded size concealed growing internal problems, as the Empire faced a new series of challenges from nationalist movements seeking independence from colonial rule. These challenges were sufficiently formidable that some historians refer to Britain as facing a "crisis of empire" in the years immediately following the war. In part, as Lloyd George had feared, the difficulties were inspired by Woodrow Wilson's rhetoric of national self-determination during the Paris Peace Conference of 1919. Wilson's call for "a free, open-minded, and absolutely impartial adjustment of all colonial claims" inspired many colonial nationalist leaders to demand self-government. These nationalists displayed a keen awareness of the activities of their counterparts elsewhere in the British Empire, helping to spread the "crisis" throughout the British world. In February 1920, the Irish republican leader Eamon de Valera, whose own country was well on its way to achieving independence, addressed Indian nationalists in New York City. Stating "our cause is a common cause," he stressed the need for solidarity among anticolonial activists in Ireland, India, Egypt and the Middle East. Statements such as these sparked British fears of anticolonial collaboration among nationalists, Communists, Pan-Islamists and labor organizers.

The postwar "crisis of empire" began within the United Kingdom. The Easter Rising of 1916 initiated a major shift in Irish politics in which the goal of nationalists became full independence rather than a more limited form of autonomy such as Home Rule. In the spring of 1918, large-scale protests took place when the government attempted to impose conscription in Ireland. Though it was never implemented, conscription increased support for Irish separation from the Union. In December 1918, the *first general election* held after the end of the war confirmed the dominance of the republican Sinn Féin party, as only seven members of the pro–Home Rule Irish Party maintained their seats, while seventy-five Sinn Féin MPs were elected. In an historic moment, Countess Constance Markiewicz (her title came from her marriage to a Polish aristocrat) became the first woman elected to the British Parliament. Like the rest of the Sinn Féin MPs, however, she refused to take her seat.

Instead, the Sinn Féin MPs convened their own Parliament in Dublin, or Dáil Éireann, which met for the first time in January 1919. At the same time, Irish republicans resumed the armed struggle for independence. By 1920, the republican forces, which became known as the Irish Republican Army (IRA), had succeeded through assassination and intimidation in demoralizing the Royal Irish Constabulary (RIC). In consequence, demobilized British Army veterans were recruited to fill the ranks of the depleted RIC. They became known as the "Black and Tans," because their uniforms combined the khaki trousers of the British Army with the dark green jackets of the RIC. Even more notorious in the eyes of many Irish civilians were the Auxiliaries, or "Auxies," 2000 (mostly) former British Army officers who were recruited to form a special paramilitary unit within the RIC. The Black and Tans and Auxiliaries engaged in a brutal struggle against the IRA that was marked by indiscriminate violence on both sides.

Figure 10.1 An Auxiliary on the streets of Dublin in 1921.
Reproduced courtesy of the National Library of Ireland.

As the fighting intensified in the spring of 1920, Parliament passed a fourth (and final) Home Rule Bill. Called the Government of Ireland Act, it established two Parliaments for Ireland, one in Belfast and one in Dublin. While Unionists in Ulster accepted an offer that kept the province within the United Kingdom, the offer of a Dublin Parliament – a goal long sought by earlier generations of Irish nationalists – was rejected by Sinn Féin. The republican insurgency continued until July 1921, when a truce was declared. By this point, the British had serious doubts as to whether the IRA's campaign could be defeated. Moreover, Britain's actions in Ireland were meeting with increasing criticism abroad. Over the next several months, negotiations produced the Anglo-Irish Treaty, which granted twenty-six counties of Ireland dominion status as the *Irish Free State*, while six counties of Ulster, in which Protestant Unionists formed a majority, remained part of the United Kingdom as the new state of Northern Ireland.

When King George V opened the new Northern Irish Parliament in 1921, he appealed to "all Irishmen to . . . forgive and forget and to join in making for the land which they love a new era of peace, contentment and goodwill." Ireland, however, would continue to be marked by conflict for much of the twentieth century. Northern Ireland was dominated by Protestant Unionists, while the 40 percent of the population that was Catholic was subjected to discrimination in employment and housing. Electoral districts were drawn in order to ensure that Unionists maintained control of local government. The new Irish Free State was also divided, as the Anglo-Irish Treaty became a source of violent conflict. Many republicans objected to the fact that the Free State remained part of the British Empire and that an oath of allegiance to the King was required for members of the Dáil. By the end of June 1922, pro- and anti-Treaty forces were engaged in a brutal civil war. With assistance from the British government, the Free State's forces prevailed, but political divisions over the Treaty continued to dominate Irish politics for decades afterwards. Even today, two of the most important political parties in Ireland, Fianna Fáil and Fine Gael, are descended from the conflict over the treaty in the early 1920s.

Colonized peoples not only embraced Woodrow Wilson's rhetoric of national self-determination but also closely observed the events that led to the foundation of the Irish Free State. Irish news was widely reported in the British and French colonial press, and nationalists in colonies such as India and Algeria wrote detailed histories of the Irish independence movement. Ireland's violent decolonization, partition and short but bitter civil war provided cautionary tales for nationalists. Nonetheless, many anticolonial activists were further inspired by the ideology and achievements of Irish republicanism.

The Jamaican-born Pan-Africanist Marcus Garvey deeply admired Eamon de Valera and studied how Irish activists had generated publicity for the republican cause in New York City in planning his own campaign there in support of an independent African republic. Other colonized peoples scrutinized the Irish Republican Army's guerilla campaign for lessons about fighting colonial security forces. IRA commander Dan Breen's memoir, *My Fight for Irish Freedom* (1924), was translated into multiple Indian languages. The Government of India banned all editions of Breen's book, fearing its influence as a "text book for the revolutionaries of India." These fears were not unfounded; in April 1930, a small group of Indian insurgents staged an uprising in the eastern port of Chittagong that was inspired by the Easter Rising.

Colonial subjects also sought to build alliances across the British Empire and within Europe and North America during the interwar era, constantly seeking to avoid the scrutiny of police and intelligence forces. An important vehicle for anticolonial collaboration in the interwar period was the League Against Imperialism (LAI), established in 1927 at a congress on anti-imperialism in Brussels. While the League was founded under the auspices of the Communist International or Comintern, which sought to export the Soviet Union's Bolshevik rebellion to the colonial world, for most of its ten-year existence the League reflected diverse political viewpoints. Communists, liberals and nationalists were all part of its membership, which came from Europe, America and both the colonial and semi-colonial world.

The founding of the LAI was an important moment for independence movements across the world, and its internationalist outlook significantly influenced prominent nationalists such as future Indian prime minister Jawaharlal Nehru. With its focus on exposing the evils of imperialism as a global system, the League enabled anticolonial activists to learn about conditions in other colonies and build relationships with their counterparts elsewhere. The London branch of the LAI organized protests against events such as the Meerut Conspiracy Case, in which more than two dozen left-wing British and Indian trade unionists and labor organizers were put on trial for conspiring against the Raj, and the 1935 Italian invasion of Abyssinia. The LAI also provided a space for prominent anticolonial intellectuals and activists such as the Pan-Africanists George Padmore and C. L. R. James of Trinidad to meet with other Europeans, Americans, Africans and Asians who opposed colonial rule.

The British dealt with these challenges in a variety of ways. In the so-called white dominions (Australia, Canada, Newfoundland, New Zealand, South Africa and the Irish Free State), demands for greater autonomy were generally met, as a series of imperial conferences led to the passage of the *Statute of Westminster* in 1931. This law acknowledged the self-government of the dominions, though the British monarch continued to function as the official head of state. From this point onwards, no act of Parliament could become law in the dominions without their consent.

The story was different, however, elsewhere in the Empire. In India, the London-educated lawyer Mohandas Gandhi emerged as a skilled organizer of mass civil disobedience campaigns. One-and-a-half million Indians had served in the armed forces of the British Empire during the First World War, and nationalists had the expectation of substantial reforms, including the granting of dominion status to India, following the end of the war. While legislation known as the Montagu-Chelmsford Reforms gave Indians some increased independence, it fell far short of expectations, and control of India's government remained firmly in British hands. Adding to the grievances of Indian nationalists, the detention without trial and the use of special tribunals to try suspected terrorists was extended into the postwar period.

In response, Gandhi launched the first of his civil disobedience campaigns, which was called the *satyagraha*, a Hindi word coined by Gandhi that roughly translates to "insistence on truth." His supporters organized a series of public demonstrations and general strikes in Indian cities to protest the Rowlatt Act. In some places, the demonstrations led to confrontations with police, and martial law was declared. The worst violence occurred in the city of Amritsar in the Punjab, where on the 13th of April 1919 thousands of Indians gathered in an enclosed square. Indian soldiers under the command of the British General Reginald Dyer opened fire on the unarmed and peaceful crowd, killing close to 400 people and wounding over a thousand. In Britain, Dyer's conduct sparked a debate about the administration of India. The Labour Party denounced his "cruel and barbarous actions," but he also had many defenders who believed that his actions had saved British rule in India. Dyer's supporters collected over £25,000 for his legal defense, but he was never put on trial, though he was relieved of his command. Dyer's actions demonstrate how violence came to play a prominent role in the final decades of British colonial rule in the twentieth century.

As Dyer's conduct was being debated in the summer of 1920, Gandhi, now working in concert with the Indian National Congress, organized a new civil disobedience campaign, the Non-Cooperation Movement. The new campaign called for *swaraj*, or independence, for India within a year. The visit of the Prince of Wales, the future King Edward VIII, in 1921 was boycotted by many Indians, and his tours of many cities took place along deserted streets. By the end of the year, Gandhi and thousands of other protestors had been arrested and imprisoned. Nationalist frustration with their lack of immediate success led to escalating violence, culminating in an attack on a police station in the village of Chauri Chaura in which twenty-two policemen were killed. From his prison cell, Gandhi decided to bring Non-Cooperation to an end in February 1922. He remained in prison for two more years.

In 1929, the Congress's new president, Jawaharlal Nehru, committed it to the goal of *purna swaraj*, or complete independence for India. In March 1930, Gandhi began a new civil disobedience campaign with a 240-mile march from his base at the Sabarmati Ashram near Amedabad in Gujarat to India's west coast. Known as the salt *satyagraha*, or "Salt March," the trek protested the government's monopoly on salt production and the tax it imposed on salt. In the ensuing months, millions of people broke the law by making their own salt or by buying it illegally. More than 100,000 Indian men and women were arrested, including Gandhi himself. The campaign quickly expanded into a more general boycott of British goods. The government's efforts to bring the situation under control by declaring the Congress to be illegal had little effect. Gandhi's commitment to nonviolence garnered sympathy for his cause around the world, putting increasing pressure on the British.

The issue was temporarily settled by the Gandhi–Irwin Pact of 1931, in which Gandhi agreed to end the civil disobedience campaign and the British agreed to allow the Congress, with Gandhi as its representative, to join a conference that was taking place in London on India's constitutional arrangements. Though the pact fell far short of Gandhi's goals, it was greeted with hostility by British conservatives. The future prime minister Winston Churchill was appalled by "the nauseating and humiliating spectacle of this one-time Inner Temple lawyer, now seditious **fakir**, striding half-naked up the steps of the Viceroy's palace, there to negotiate and parley on equal terms with the representative of the King Emperor." Much of what was discussed at the conference subsequently went into the *Government of India Act* (1935), which granted greater autonomy to the provinces of British India and increased Indian representation in local government. The act was intended as a conservative measure that would ensure the retention of British control over India. It also, however, further increased the power of the Indian National Congress, which dominated the elections held in 1937.

During the interwar years, Britain also confronted nationalist protests in Egypt, which, after decades of being under quasi-colonial control, had formally become a British protectorate in 1914 in order to prevent it from joining the Ottoman Empire in its alliance with Germany. By the end of the war, nationalists were eager to regain Egypt's independence, and they responded eagerly to Wilson's rhetoric of national self-determination. They hoped to send representatives to the Paris Peace Conference to plead their case, but their leader Saad Zaghlul Pasha, founder of the nationalist Wafd Party, was denied permission to attend. In March 1919, he and three colleagues were arrested and deported to Malta. Their arrest sparked weeks of rioting and attacks on colonial authorities in Cairo, leading to the declaration of martial law. Repression was only a temporary expedient, however, as Britain was forced to recognize the growing force of Egyptian nationalism. Zaghlul Pasha was released from detention and allowed to attend the Peace Conference, though he achieved little, since

Wilson had already recognized the legality of the British protectorate. But the British could not withstand the force of growing nationalist sentiment indefinitely, and in 1922, Egypt was granted nominal independence. Britain, however, continued to dominate Egyptian politics for the next three decades. It also retained control of the Suez Canal, and a large number of British troops continued to be stationed in the country.

In addition to nationalist resistance in India and Egypt, Britain faced revolt in Mesopotamia, one of the new additions to the Empire. In 1916, the secret Sykes–Picot Agreement had created British and French spheres of influence in the Ottoman lands of the Middle East, and after the war Britain gained control of Mesopotamia and Palestine, which were ruled as mandates on behalf of the League of Nations. Mesopotamia was strategically important, both as a rich source of petroleum at a time when the Royal Navy was converting from coal- to oil-powered ships and as part of a British sphere of influence stretching from Egypt to India. For many Arabs, however, the new mandate merely traded one set of imperial rulers (the Ottomans) for another (the British), and by June 1920, the British faced a revolt in Mesopotamia. To suppress it, the Royal Air Force pioneered the use of a tactic known as "air policing," or the aerial bombardment of rebels. This resulted in substantial civilian casualties, and as many as 10,000 Arabs (and 500 British and Indian soldiers) died in the three-month-long revolt. While the use of air power was initially appealing to both politicians and members of the British public as a seemingly low-cost way of supporting empire, it ultimately cost over £40 million and provoked intense hostility among the Arabs. Unwilling to continue paying such a high price, the British opted to restructure their governance of Mesopotamia from direct to indirect rule. In 1921, they established the quasi-independent Kingdom of Iraq and installed King Faisal ibn Husayn as monarch. He had worked closely with the British during the First World War and was thought to be friendly to British interests, though he soon became an active promoter of Arab nationalism. Iraq gained full independence in 1932, but, like Egypt, it remained part of a British sphere of influence. Britain retained the use of Iraqi airfields until 1958, when a revolution toppled the monarchy and established a republic.

The British also faced a revolt in the mandate territory of Palestine. In an effort to enlist the support of the local Jewish population during the First World War, the British government had issued the Balfour Declaration of November 1917, which had pledged to support "the establishment in Palestine of a national home for the Jewish people." At the same time, the British gave assurances to Palestinian Arabs that their land rights would be upheld. In the 1930s, the rise of fascism in Europe and the reluctance of Britain and the United States to accept Jewish refugees dramatically increased Jewish emigration to Palestine. In 1936, this led to a revolt by Palestinian Arabs, who felt their right to the land was being threatened. By 1939, the revolt had been crushed, but at a cost of over 3000 Palestinian lives.

The British Empire thus faced a number of challenges in the years after the Great War. It also, however, withstood, at least temporarily, these challenges, in some instances through political concessions and in others through violent coercion. More broadly, the Empire continued to play a prominent role in Britain's status as a great power. Between 1910 and 1914, 25 percent of Britain's import trade and 36 percent of its export trade was with its colonies, but by the late 1930s, those percentages had risen to 40 percent of imports and almost 50 percent of exports. Increasingly, British corporations not only purchased raw materials from the Empire, but also were involved in their production. The Dunlop Rubber Company, for example, began purchasing rubber plantations in Malaya prior to the Great War, and by 1926 it was the largest landowner in the British Empire. British people were very much conscious of the continuing importance of the Empire. In *The Road to Wigan Pier* (1937), George Orwell emphasized how empire played an important role both in the British economy and

Figures 10.2 and 10.3   As anticolonial nationalism grew in the interwar period, British efforts to suppress it became increasingly violent. Figure 10.2 shows bullet marks in the walls of the buildings surrounding the square Jallianwala Bagh in Amritsar, where nearly 400 unarmed Indians were killed by soldiers from the Indian Army acting on the orders of the British General Reginald Dyer in April 1919. Figure 10.3 shows British soldiers on patrol near the Jaffa Gate in Jerusalem during the Arab Revolt in 1938.

Figure 10.2 reproduced courtesy of Shankar S.; Figure 10.3 reproduced courtesy of the Library of Congress.

in people's sense of national prestige. "Apart from any other consideration, the high standard of life we enjoy in England," he wrote, "depends on our keeping a tight hold on the Empire, particularly the tropical portions of it such as India and Africa." If the Empire were to vanish, Orwell argued, England would be reduced "to a cold and unimportant little island where we should all have to work very hard and live mainly on herrings and potatoes."

Despite the previously described challenges, during the interwar years Orwell's fears seemed unlikely to come true. The British government certainly assumed that the Empire had a long future ahead of it. A new naval base at Singapore, considered to be impregnable, was completed in 1938 at a cost of £60 million. The prominent architect Edwin Lutyens designed a magnificent new capital for India at New Delhi, which was intended to rival former imperial capitals such as Rome and Constantinople. In London, the importance of empire was displayed at the 1924 British Empire Exhibition, which featured exhibits from fifty-eight different colonies; only Gambia and Gibraltar did not take part. A tremendous popular success, the Exhibition was attended by 27 million Britons.

The popularity of the Empire was also demonstrated in a number of hit films of the era, such as the British productions *Sanders of the River* (1935), *King Solomon's Mines* (1937) and *The Four Feathers* (1939) and the Hollywood film *Gunga Din* (1939), which drew large audiences on both sides of the Atlantic. Cinema presented the British Empire as an exotic venue for masculine adventure in similar fashion to the boys' stories of the late nineteenth century. Heroic Britons, loyal colonial subjects and benevolent depictions of British rule all featured prominently in these imperial films.

In other ways, as well, the Empire continued to be a part of the lives of Britons in the interwar period. It offered career opportunities not only for the elite, but also for middle- and working-class Britons. In the years immediately after the First World War, hundreds of thousands of emigrants left Britain, a large number of whom sought new lives in the Empire. The British government offered free passage to the dominions for ex-servicemen who were unable to find work in the troubled postwar economy. Between 1919 and 1921, 17,000 of them went to Australia and another 13,000 to New Zealand. In 1922, the Empire Settlement Act provided assistance to families wishing to immigrate to the dominions of Australia, New Zealand, Canada and South Africa. Aided by such encouragement, over 130,000 Britons settled in Canada. But while independence remained a distant prospect for the vast majority of Britain's colonies into the 1930s, the political and economic impact of the Second World War would bring about dramatic changes in the years following 1945.

Party Politics in the 1920s and 1930s

Since the late nineteenth century, the platform of the Conservative Party had been based upon the defense of the Union and the Empire, and thus the granting of self-government to the Irish Free State and the concessions that Lloyd George made to Indian nationalists were anathema to many Tories. This led the Conservatives to withdraw their support for the coalition in 1922. They successfully fought the election later that year on their own, and they dominated the remainder of the interwar period. Following Bonar Law's resignation due to throat cancer in 1923, Stanley Baldwin became prime minister. From a middle-class background, Baldwin astutely cultivated the image of an ordinary Briton in order to appeal to those who yearned for an imagined "simpler" time that had existed before the war. Baldwin was particularly skillful at using the press and the new medium of radio, and he was in consequence personally very popular. He served as prime minister on three occasions, from May 1923 to January 1924, from December 1924 to June 1929, and from June 1935 to May

1937. Winston Churchill called him "the most formidable politician I ever encountered," though he was later sharply critical of Baldwin's failure to pursue rearmament more vigorously in the 1930s.

The Liberals, meanwhile, were still divided over the polarizing figure of Lloyd George, and many of their working-class supporters had switched to the Labour Party. By the late 1920s, they were condemned to third-party status in a political system designed for two, while Labour emerged as the main party of opposition. Under the leadership of the Scotsman Ramsay MacDonald, *Labour formed its first government* in 1924, though it was a minority one that lasted for only ten months. Though Labour's 1918 party manifesto declared its allegiance to socialism, in a practical sense this meant little more than a call for the state to nationalize a few key industries. Most of Labour's leaders were pragmatically minded and interested in "bread and butter" issues rather than ideology. Even so, Labour was forced to expend much energy in defending itself from Conservative accusations that they were radical Bolsheviks.

Labour formed another minority government in 1929, when it received over 37 percent of the vote and gained 287 seats in Parliament, the first time that it had surpassed the other two parties. MacDonald became prime minister for the second time. They had been handed a poisoned chalice, however. The *Great Depression* had begun, and by the end of 1930, 2.5 million Britons were unemployed. In 1931, the cabinet split over the issue of whether to reduce public spending, including unemployment benefits, in response to the mounting crisis. MacDonald broke with his own party and agreed to form a "*National Government*" in coalition with the Conservatives and the Liberals; coalition governments would remain in power until 1945. Many Labour leaders were furious at MacDonald's decision, and he and his supporters were expelled from the party as a result. Fears that the National Government would be Conservative-dominated were soon proved to be well founded, as it contained few non-Tory ministers of any influence. After MacDonald's resignation due to ill health in 1935, Baldwin replaced him as prime minister; two years later, Baldwin retired and was succeeded by his fellow Conservative Neville Chamberlain.

As was the case elsewhere in Europe, the 1930s in Britain saw the growth of extremist parties on both the left and the right of the political spectrum. Many intellectuals, especially at British universities, were sympathetic to the left wing of the Labour Party or to the Communist Party. Certainly, the left's critique of capitalist democracy in Britain was compelling, given the ongoing depression and the rise of fascism on the European continent. To be sure, the Communist Party of Great Britain (CPGB) remained a fringe party with only a few thousand members and rarely more than one MP. But thousands of young British men joined the International Brigades to fight for democracy and socialism in the Spanish Civil War, and a number of prominent artists and intellectuals embraced socialist or communist ideas. The Left Book Club, which began in 1936, aimed to make books by authors of left-wing views accessible to a wide audience. The Club brought together supporters of the Labour Party and the Communist Party, as well as trade unions and socialist pressure groups. Its subscriber base had grown to nearly 60,000 by 1939, with a readership of its periodicals and books estimated at 250,000.

On the right, the British Union of Fascists (BUF) was led by Sir Oswald Mosley. A baronet and veteran of the Western Front in the Great War, Mosley had been elected as a Conservative MP at the age of only twenty-one in 1922. After falling out with the Conservatives over the use of the Black and Tans to suppress the rebellion in Ireland, he first became an independent and then joined the Labour Party in 1924. He was at this point a committed socialist, with close ties to a group called the Fabians, who believed in non-revolutionary change and social justice. In the late 1920s, some people saw the handsome and charismatic Mosley as a future Labour leader, but when the party won the election of 1929, he was given only the minor post of chancellor of the Duchy of Lancaster. He was also assigned the task of reducing unemployment, but his radical proposals for high tariffs, the nationalization of industry, and a public works program to create jobs were rejected by the cabinet. Disillusioned, he left Labour in 1930 and founded the New Party, which initially advocated the granting of wide-ranging government powers to solve Britain's economic problems, but gradually became more authoritarian and aligned with the fascist movements that were emerging in Germany, Italy and Spain.

Immigrants and Refugees 3

Jewish Refugees in the 1930s

After Adolf Hitler and the Nazi party came to power in Germany in 1933, German Jews began to be targeted by anti-Semitic laws and by popular hostility; the intent was to make life so difficult that Jews would choose to leave the country. By 1938, about 150,000 German Jews, or a quarter of the total number, had already emigrated. Many others were convinced to leave by the events of the 9th of November 1938, the "Night of the Broken Glass," when Jewish businesses across Germany were vandalized. Despite widespread awareness of what was happening in Germany, however, most other countries were reluctant to take in large numbers of Jewish refugees. In 1938, President Franklin Roosevelt called for an international conference to address the issue. The conference met in the French town of Evian; the delegates expressed sympathy for the plight of the refugees but refused to accept significant numbers. British officials argued that an influx of Jewish refugees into Britain would lead to an increase in anti-Semitism and would put additional pressure on an already strained jobs market. Britain did accept around 70,000 Jewish refugees by the outbreak of the Second World War, including around 8000 children as part of the much-publicized "Kindertransport" program. This gave rise to a myth that Britain had been generous in its attitude towards Jewish refugees. In reality, however, British policy was determined by British interests and not concern for Germany's Jews. Refugees were admitted only after Britain's Jewish community agreed to take on all responsibility and expense for their support, so that they would not require any public funds. In 1939, the British also restricted Jewish immigration into their colony of Palestine, in order to quell growing Arab unrest there. Sadly, however, the British record looks fairly good in comparison to that of its North American allies. Canada admitted only 5000 Jewish refugees between 1933 and 1945, and the United States, with a population almost three times the size of Britain's, only 33,000.

In 1932, the New Party was transformed into the BUF. It attracted considerable attention via a number of highly visible marches. At the "Battle of Cable Street" in 1936, a march of 3000 BUF supporters through the East End of London was met by between 50,000 and 100,000 anti-fascists. Though the BUF marchers dispersed, the police clashed with the anti-fascists; 175 people were injured and 150 arrested. In response, the government passed the Public Order Act of 1936, which forbade the wearing of political uniforms such as the BUF's black shirts. The BUF was more notorious than politically relevant, however. It never attracted more than a few thousand serious supporters, and it was electorally insignificant, though some politicians on the right of the Conservative Party sympathized with its views. After the mid-1930s, when reports of Nazi atrocities towards Jews began to reach Britain, its support melted away. The authorities continued to keep a watchful eye on it, however, and Mosley and some 700 party members were imprisoned at the outbreak of the Second World War.

A Struggling Economy and Racial Tensions

Britain faced serious economic challenges throughout the interwar period. After 1918, the demobilization of the army led to unrest and rioting. Demobilization was carried out on the principle of "first in, first out," meaning that those who had served longest were the first to be discharged. This was fair but bad for the economy, as those called up last tended to be the most skilled and therefore the most needed by industry as it attempted to regain its prewar footing. It quickly became apparent that neither the economy nor employment opportunities were the same as before the war. Britain had lost its position of global dominance of finance and trade to the United States. Its key industries, such as textile manufacturing, coal mining, shipbuilding and steel production, faced declining demand and increasing global competition. Overseas markets that had long been dominated by British products were now being served by the new industrial powers of the United States and Japan. Britain's colonies and dominions, meanwhile, had developed industries and trade networks of their own, making them far less dependent on British manufactured goods.

The weaknesses of Britain's interwar economy brought racial tensions to the forefront of British society. The year 1919 witnessed some of the worst race riots in the history of twentieth-century Britain. Violence took place in port cities around England, Wales and Scotland, including London, Cardiff, Glasgow, Hull and Liverpool. Africans, Afro-Caribbeans, Chinese, Indians and Arabs were all targeted. Many were seamen who had served in the merchant marine or British armed forces during the Great War. While large numbers of these men, like their white counterparts, found themselves unemployed after the war, others moved into factory jobs previously occupied by white working-class men. Despite their wartime service, these black and Asian men found that they were not welcome in post–Great War Britain.

Competition for jobs in the postwar economy was only one cause of the 1919 riots, however. A Jamaican man arrested for allegedly assaulting a Liverpool policeman in April 1919 declared in court that he was "as good as any white man. My blood is just the same: it isn't black and I've done my bit . . . for King and country." While black men believed that their wartime service had proved their equality with white Britons, working-class men in cities such as Liverpool widely resented what they saw as their "aggressive attitude" and their romances with and marriages to white British women. In Liverpool, where some of the worst riots took place, retaliation against attacks on the black community quickly led to an escalation of violence. Hundreds of black men and their families were forced to seek refuge in police and fire stations. Charles Wootten, a young man from Bermuda, was chased by a stone-throwing crowd into the River Mersey, where he drowned.

In response to the 1919 riots, the Colonial Office advertised incentives for men who wished to voluntarily repatriate: £5 was offered for resettlement expenses for "British coloureds" plus £2 to clear any debts in Britain. While the government in this instance resisted calls for forced deportation and upheld the principle of the free movement of British subjects, greater restrictions were imposed on black and Asian seamen in the interwar period. The Coloured Alien Seamen Order (1925) required "coloured" sailors who could not prove their status as British subjects to register as aliens. In practice, seamen found it difficult to prove their nationality since they were not required to carry passports, although an appeal process was instituted.

Race 5

Lascars and the Coloured Seaman's Act (1925)

As Britain's overseas trade expanded dramatically after 1700, a large number of sailors were needed for the merchant fleet. The pressure to find more qualified men was particularly acute in times of war, when white seamen were drafted for service in the Royal Navy. During the Napoleonic Wars in the late eighteenth and early nineteenth centuries, non-white sailors from South and Southeast Asia and Africa took their places on many merchant ships; they became known in Britain as "lascars," a term which originally came from the Arabic "Al-Ashkar," meaning "sailor from East India" but came to be used as shorthand for any non-white, non-European sailor serving on a British vessel. At the peak of Britain's imperial and overseas trade in the late nineteenth century, lascars often formed the majority of the crew on many merchant vessels; captains preferred them because they were paid lower wages and were used to working in hot climates, and many were Muslims who did not drink alcohol. When they were not serving on ships, many lascars settled in London and other port cities such as Cardiff, Hull, Liverpool and South Shields, where they lived in slum conditions in lodging houses. Some opted to leave behind the harsh life of a merchant seaman and find permanent employment on shore, but many employers refused to hire non-white men, and so they too lived in extreme poverty. They were often reduced to begging and therefore were frequently in trouble with the police; their neighborhoods, such as "Tiger Bay" in Cardiff and "Little Arabia" in South Shields, were depicted in the media as places of crime and danger. In 1925, the Coloured Seaman's Act required all non-white sailors who could not prove their British citizenship to register as aliens, which made it easier to deport them. The historian Laura Tabili describes the act as "the first instance of state-sanctioned race discrimination inside Britain to come to widespread notice." It was enforced aggressively, leading to the deportation of many men who were in fact British subjects. Despite these obstacles, however, many lascars managed to remain in Britain and build lives for themselves, as they married British women and set up successful cafés, shops and laundries. They were responsible for some of Britain's first multicultural communities.

To be sure, race riots and discrimination were not the sole experience of Black and Asian Britons during the interwar era. Historians have recently shown that South Asian migrants intermarried, raised families and became established parts of local communities in a number of British cities. Many were former lascars, who had developed valuable industrial and entrepreneurial skills on board ships. Indian traders selling a variety of products featured prominently in working-class communities. The "Indian toffee man," a street vendor who sold candy and sweets, was a fondly remembered figure among British men and women who grew up in working-class neighborhoods between the world wars. Indian traders, café owners and industrial workers in turn offered loans and assistance to new arrivals, further strengthening migration networks from colonial India.

As interwar British society changed, Britain needed to radically transform its economy and move into new industrial arenas, but this did not happen. Instead, the government attempted to continue as before the war. A rapid decrease in the level of government involvement in the economy was accompanied by drastic cuts in public spending. Initially, it seemed that this course of action would have positive results, as industry's transition to peacetime production and the need to replace machinery led to a "restocking boom" from 1919 to 1920. Pent-up demand for consumer goods not available during the war also contributed to the surge. The gains proved short-lived, however. In 1921, overseas trade began to contract, while domestic markets were saturated with unsold goods and many businesses were buried under a mountain of debt. The underlying structural weaknesses of the British economy now became apparent. The slump continued throughout the 1920s, exacerbated by the global depression. Britain's heavy manufacturing industries suffered the most. The productivity of coal mining, cotton textiles and shipbuilding all declined; by the end of the 1930s, these three industries were producing only 79, 37, and 31 percent respectively of what they had in 1913. The government made these problems worse due to its reluctance to abandon traditional fiscal policies. Throughout the 1920s, regardless of which party was in power, the belief remained strong that the free market was self-regulating and would right itself without government interference.

The government did act, however, to maintain the value of **sterling** against other currencies. In 1925, the chancellor of the Exchequer Winston Churchill was prevailed upon by London's financiers to return Britain to the gold standard at the prewar exchange rate of $4.86 to the pound. While helpful to the financial sector, this move caused British manufacturing exports to become overpriced by 10 percent at a single stroke, thereby making them even less competitive on world markets. The depression forced Britain to go off the gold standard once again in 1931, but by that time the damage to the manufacturing economy had been done. The worsening economic situation of the early 1930s also led to the abandonment of free trade. In 1932, a system of imperial preference was initiated in which Britain and the Empire traded on more advantageous terms than were granted to other countries. Such protectionist measures were a common response by countries around the world to the depression, but they had little positive impact on the British economy.

The situation was not all bad, however. Postwar economic difficulties forced some businesses to increase their efficiency through mergers. Several giant conglomerates, including Imperial Chemical Industries and Unilever, were created in the 1920s, while iron and steel manufacturers formed a cartel in 1932. From one of the most fragmented industrial economies in 1914, by 1939 Britain had become one of the most concentrated. The hundred largest British companies in 1939 were responsible for over a quarter of Britain's industrial output. New industries joined the old in this remade interwar economy. Automobiles were produced in large numbers for the first time; Britain was second only to the United States in the number of motor vehicles produced. The new industries were aided by a new capacity for the generation of electrical power. In the 1920s, the government instituted the world's first national electrical transmission grid, which linked virtually the entire country to a network of efficient generating stations. Cheap electricity led to a consumer boom in products such as radios, stoves, vacuum cleaners, washing machines and irons.

One of the distinctive characteristics of these new industries was their location, which was generally in the Midlands and southeast of England, where they enjoyed ready access to

London, by far the biggest consumer market in the nation. But in the country's traditional industrial regions, such as the North of England, South Wales and the vicinity of Glasgow in Scotland, the story was very different. In these areas, structural unemployment, in which the supply of labor outstripped the demand, became the norm. The national unemployment rate peaked at 22.5 percent in 1932, but was much higher than that in some industries. That year, 35 percent of coal miners, 36 percent of pottery makers, 43 percent of cotton operatives and 62 percent of shipbuilding workers were jobless. In Tyneside, the area surrounding the city of Newcastle-on-Tyne in northeastern England, the depression caused a complete collapse in the demand for new ships. Among the worst affected places was Jarrow, which had an unemployment rate of 80 percent in 1932. The distress led to the Jarrow Hunger March, in which unemployed workers marched 300 miles to London to gain sympathy for their plight.

Large loans of American capital helped to sustain European economies in the 1920s, but the *crash of the stock market* in late 1929 brought this aid to a sudden halt. As the American economy went into shock, the market for European imports contracted sharply. Making matters worse, in 1930 the United States Congress imposed new tariff barriers. Foreign governments needed to sell the Americans exported goods in order to pay back the loans, but the high tariffs made this much more difficult. As the crisis mounted, the government enacted a number of policies, including the provision of loans to shipyards and the imposition of tariffs on imported manufactured goods, in an effort to stimulate growth and reduce unemployment in the most severely distressed areas. These policies, however, were not carried out on a sufficiently large scale to make a significant impact on the high rates of unemployment. It was not until the mass production of armaments began in 1938 that the economy began to improve significantly.

The persistence of structural unemployment during the interwar years was one of the most difficult problems faced by successive governments. After the war, Lloyd George's unemployment insurance scheme of 1911 was extended to cover more than 12 million workers, but many people were still excluded from the system, and benefits were denied to those who were deemed to not be "vigorously looking for work," even when there was no suitable work to be found. Moreover, the expanded benefits were payable only for a short period. Anyone who was unemployed for longer than fifteen weeks had to rely on the meager welfare relief provided by local governments. To make matters worse, benefits were paid out according to the amount of contributions rather than according to need. Hundreds of thousands of workers who had been too poorly paid to make insurance contributions were thus left out of the scheme. With the mass unemployment of the 1930s, contributions to the insurance fund dried up quickly, creating a long-term funding crisis that could only be managed by massive government borrowing. In 1931, unemployment relief was made subject to a means test, which meant that anyone applying for unemployment compensation had to endure an inspection by a local government official to make sure that they had no hidden earnings or savings, or physical assets they could sell. Investigations of working-class households by middle-class inspectors were humiliating experiences that were much resented.

Many workers looked to trade unions to push back against employers and a government that seemed indifferent to their plight. But although many Conservative politicians and business leaders feared their power, the unions never managed to unite fully in the interwar period and were a far less potent force than their opponents claimed. This was dramatically demonstrated by the failure of the *General Strike* of 1926. The strike began in the coal-mining

Figure 10.4 Because public transportation did not function during the General Strike of 1926, some people had to cycle to work.

Reproduced courtesy of Shutterstock/Everett Collection.

industry, which was unprofitable even before it was hit hard by the postwar economic slump. By the early 1920s, it was languishing from the collapse of foreign demand, resulting in high unemployment and decreased wages. In 1925, the miners convinced the Trades Union Congress (TUC), which represented all trade unions, that the decline in the miners' wage rates would soon be paralleled in other industries if no action were taken. The TUC threatened to call a general strike of the members of all of its affiliated unions in support of the miners. In response, the government summoned a commission to study the problem and delayed any further cuts to workers' wages. The commission's report, however, acknowledged that the mining industry was badly in need of reform and that further wage reductions were inevitable. The mine owners used the report to increase miners' hours and to justify another round of wage cuts; the million miners who refused to accept the new conditions were locked out of work.

This action spurred the TUC to call for a general strike that encompassed over 1.5 million workers in the heavy industry and transport sectors. The strike began on the 3rd of May 1926 and lasted for nine days, shutting down much of Britain's economy. It was perceived by the government as a direct challenge to its authority; thousands of special constables were drafted to bolster the ranks of the police, while soldiers were used to guard food convoys and run essential services. Faced with the stiff resolve of the government, the TUC called off the strike on the 12th of May. The miners were not permitted to return to work until the end of the year, when they were forced to accede to the terms offered by the owners before the strike. The government subsequently passed legislation that made general strikes illegal. While the depression lasted, the trade unions were thus unable to significantly improve the lot of their members.

Wales, Scotland and Ireland

The industrial areas of Wales, in particular the coal-mining areas in the south of the country, were particularly affected by Britain's interwar economic malaise. More than other British coal-producing regions, Wales depended on the export trade. A variety of factors, including increased coal production in other countries, the high cost of Welsh coal due to the sterling exchange rate and the switch to oil as a source of fuel, meant that Welsh collieries faced tremendous difficulties after the end of the immediate postwar boom. By January 1922, miners' wages were less than half what they had been a year earlier, a portent of even worse problems to come. From 1921 to 1939, 241 Welsh collieries closed, and as a result, unemployment rates in Wales were the highest in Britain between the world wars. In 1935, unemployment in Merthyr Tydfil reached 51 percent.

These economic problems pushed Welsh politics to the left. Beginning with the 1922 election, the Labour Party eclipsed the Liberals as the dominant party in Wales, while Conservative support eroded sharply. In the 1929 election, only one Tory MP was elected in Wales. Labour enjoyed particularly strong support in the coal-mining areas of the south. In 1931, when the Labour Party was reduced to only fifty-two seats in the House of Commons, sixteen of their MPs came from South Wales. In keeping with their left-wing politics, the Welsh coalfields were a center of trade union militancy. The South Wales Miners' Federation, known as "the Fed," was the largest union in Britain, and its members voted for radical policies more readily than their English and Scottish counterparts did. While Welsh miners successfully struck for higher wages in 1920, in the following year a lockout over the return of coal mines to private ownership lasted for three months and led to a drastic reduction in miners' wages. The Fed's membership dropped by more than half, though it remained a force in Welsh Labour politics.

Many of the major political figures of interwar Wales came from coal-mining backgrounds. These included the Labour MPs James Griffiths, former president of the Fed, and Aneurin Bevan, the son of a coal miner from the southeast Welsh town of Tredegar, where two-thirds of the adult male population worked in the local mines. Politicians like Griffiths and Bevan were deeply influenced not only by trade unionism, but also by the deeply communitarian ethos of the Welsh coal-mining regions. They both went on to play important roles in the establishment of the welfare state in the post–Second World War Labour government.

The economic downturn in Wales significantly affected the status of the Welsh language. In 1891, more than half the population spoke Welsh. By 1931, the proportion had declined to 36 percent. Prior to the First World War, the decline of the Welsh-speaking population was due largely to inward migration from western England, Scotland and Ireland. During the interwar years, however, Wales experienced significant outmigration, as many young Welsh people in search of employment left both the rural areas of north and western Wales and the industrial regions of South Wales. Altogether, almost 400,000 people migrated from Wales between 1925 and 1939, and the Welsh population did not again reach its level of 1925 until the 1970s.

In an effort to preserve Wales's distinctive identity, in 1925 a new political party called Plaid Cymru, or the National Party of Wales, was established with the goal of preserving the

Welsh language. In 1932, the party pledged itself to Home Rule for Wales as well. In 1936, three members of the party set fire to a Royal Air Force (RAF) bombing school at Peny-berth in northwest Wales, which they saw as a symbol of English oppression of the Welsh. The action did not change Plaid Cymru's electoral fortunes at the time, as it remained a small and elite organization that made few inroads into the industrial regions that were the Labour heartland. Later, however, it came to be seen as an important symbolic moment in the campaign for Welsh cultural independence.

In Scotland, the issue of self-government remained a minority concern in the interwar period, but nationalist and cultural movements emerged that in the longer term would have an important impact on the Scots' sense of identity and their relationship to the United Kingdom. For many Scots, Scotland's prominent role in the British Empire continued to be a powerful argument against altering the Union. "Why should we want to be a daughter state," the prominent novelist John Buchan asked in 1932, "when we are a mother state?" On the left, meanwhile, support for increased independence diminished. Given the weak state of Britain's economy in the interwar period, the idea of self-government for Scotland made little economic sense to many Scottish Labour MPs and trade unionists. In 1931, the Scottish Trades Union Congress abandoned its commitment to Scottish Home Rule. Its leadership believed that in the midst of the depression, the best way to improve the conditions of Scottish workers was through closer collaboration with their English counterparts through the formation of all-British unions, not political separation.

The indifference of the Labour Party and the trade unions to Home Rule, however, gave rise to a new Scottish nationalist organization. In 1934, the National Party of Scotland and the Scottish Party merged to form the Scottish National Party (SNP), whose goal was "self-government for Scotland on a basis which will enable Scotland as a partner in the British Empire with the same status as England to develop its national life to the fullest advantage." The initial political impact of the SNP was minimal, in part because it was divided between those members who wanted to focus on outright Scottish independence and those who, believing that independence could most effectively be achieved in stages, wished to focus on measures such as **devolution**. In its first general election in 1935, the SNP lost all eight seats that it contested.

While nationalists pursued the goal of Scottish self-government, a number of interwar writers sought to assert a distinctive Scottish identity within the United Kingdom. John Buchan opposed the breakup of the Union, but he argued, "every Scotsman should be a Scottish nationalist." His interwar novels increasingly reflected on Scotland's past and future. Buchan was one of a number of authors associated with the Scottish literary renaissance, a movement that sought to develop a distinctive Scottish voice. The movement's leading figure was Christopher Murray Grieve, who wrote as Hugh MacDiarmid. MacDiarmid sought both to reverse the Anglicization of Scottish culture and to overturn the romanticized vision of the Scottish past that had been put forward by an earlier generation of authors such as Sir Walter Scott. Writing in Scots rather than English, he and the other writers of the Scottish literary renaissance sought to foster a new cultural identity that reflected the economic and social realities of modern Scotland as well as its history and tradition.

As we have seen, only in Ireland did a movement towards political independence from the United Kingdom gain sufficient momentum to succeed. In the 1930s, the Irish government became increasingly focused on the assertion of a separate Irish identity from Britain. Shortly after Fianna Fáil's victory in the election of 1932, the Irish president Eamon de Valera utilized one of the most emotive issues in Anglo-Irish history – land – to challenge

British authority. De Valera announced that Ireland would make no further payments to the British government on what were known as the Land Annuities, the payment for purchases of land by Irish tenant farmers under various land acts while Ireland had still been part of the Union. This refusal led to what was called the "Economic War" between Britain and Ireland. Britain retaliated by placing high import duties on Irish agricultural products, while Ireland in turn placed high duties on British industrial products. Both economies suffered, but Ireland's was hit harder, as it was overwhelmingly dependent on trade with Britain.

The dispute was ultimately resolved when under the Anglo-Irish Trade Agreement of 1938 the Irish government agreed to make a one-time payment of £10 million for the outstanding Land Annuities. In return, the British prime minister Neville Chamberlain agreed to give up control of three "Treaty Ports," naval bases that Britain had retained control of under the terms of the Anglo-Irish Treaty. By this point, Ireland, though still officially a dominion of the British Empire, was a republic in all but name. In 1936, the Irish government passed the External Relations Act, which sought to remove all references to the King from the Free State's constitution. The following year, the Dáil approved a new constitution, largely authored by de Valera, which changed the name of the country from the Irish Free State to Éire and claimed sovereignty over the "whole island of Ireland," including Northern Ireland. Éire's separation from the British Empire was to become even more apparent during the Second World War.

Social and Cultural Change

If British society was unsettled by economic difficulties, however, the interwar years also saw a desire for stability that was occasioned by the dislocations caused by the war. For women, the death of more than 720,000 men in the war is often seen as the defining factor of the era, as they purportedly struggled to find husbands. In reality, marriage was a vital institution in this period, as people sought the security that long-term, legally sanctioned relationships could provide. A greater percentage of British men and women married in the 1930s than had done so in the decade before 1914, and they tended to marry at a younger age.

Increased social stability was also reflected in a decline in crime, as both petty offenses such as drunkenness and more serious acts such as murder decreased in frequency. The prison population in England and Wales fell to 11,000 in 1930, down from 21,000 twenty years earlier.

It is one of the paradoxes of the interwar period that, despite the economic dislocations of the era, for those who *were* employed the standard of living improved. People in the upper echelons of the working and middle classes enjoyed higher incomes, lower prices, more leisure time and access to a wide range of new consumer goods. The average length of the working week declined from fifty-five hours to forty-five. Britons filled the extra time with a variety of leisure activities. For young people, dancing was popular; by 1925, there were over 11,000 nightclubs in London. Cinema also attracted large audiences, and by 1939, 23 million people were attending films each week.

Sexuality and Gender 4

Radclyffe Hall's *The Well of Loneliness*

In 1928, Radclyffe Hall published her semi-autobiographical novel *The Well of Loneliness*, about a lesbian relationship. Hall, who was known to her family and friends as "John" and who wore traditionally masculine clothes, lived openly as a lesbian.

The novel was possibly based on her relationship with Mabel Batten, an older married woman whom she had met while traveling in Germany. The heroine Stephen Gordon, like Hall herself, believed that she was a sexual "invert," a concept invented by the sexologist Havelock Ellis in which a person's gender role differed from their biological sex. Hall deliberately wrote the novel to, as she put it, "speak on behalf of a misunderstood and misjudged minority." In contrast to those between men, sexual acts between women were not illegal in Britain at the time. There were concerns, however, that lesbianism was on the rise, as there was a shortage of men in Britain after 750,000 lost their lives in the First World War. The novel was therefore controversial, due to fears that it might encourage women to seek out same-sex relationships, and many commentators called for it to be banned. The publisher, Jonathan Cape, sent a copy to the home secretary, Sir William Joynson-Hicks, in the hope that he might deem the novel acceptable, but Joynson-Hicks instead labeled it "gravely detrimental to the public interest." Cape halted its publication in Britain, but he leased the rights to an English-language publisher in France who began shipping copies to England for sale. In response, Joynson-Hicks seized the shipments and summoned Cape to court to show why they should not be destroyed. Cape called as witnesses some of the leading authors of the day to defend the book; some demurred as they did not wish to be embroiled in the controversy, but Virginia Woolf and E. M. Forster, among others, did turn up. Despite this support, the judge found the novel to be obscene and ordered it to be withdrawn from shops and all copies to be pulped. *The Well of Loneliness* would not be published again in Britain until 1949. Even at the time, however, most reviews were positive, as critics praised Hall's book for bringing attention to an overlooked group in society. For decades afterwards, it remained the most well-known novel featuring a lesbian relationship at its center, and many people relied on it as a guide to their own experience when few other such texts were available.

When people opted to stay home, they enjoyed significant improvements in the quality of Britain's housing stock. One of the promises made by Lloyd George in the 1918 election was that his government would build "homes fit for heroes to live in." This promise was not entirely fulfilled, but local governments did clear some of the worst urban slums and build over 2 million new homes that were rented to tenants as **council housing**. Private builders added another 2 million houses, which raised the proportion of housing that was owner-occupied from 10 percent in 1914 to 35 percent in 1938. This benefited the working classes as well as the middle classes, as low interest rates and an abundant supply kept prices and mortgage payments affordable.

Social services also improved in the interwar years. The school-leaving age was raised from twelve to fourteen, and merit scholarships were created in order to help talented young men (and a few women) from the working class go to secondary schools and, on a limited basis, universities. Even so, in 1938 only 2 percent of nineteen-year-olds attended a post-secondary institution. There were also efforts to improve public health. A new Ministry of Health was created in 1919, more nurses were hired, modern hospitals were established in impoverished areas and a national health insurance scheme was made available for those with low incomes. Additional health insurance was provided by businesses for their employees, though this tended to benefit the middle rather than working class. These efforts were in some ways successful: the mortality rate for children declined steadily during the interwar years. In 1929, the nineteenth-century Poor Law, which had forced the most destitute members of society into the workhouse, was scrapped and responsibility for welfare assistance placed in the hands of local authorities. This reduced the stigma attached to poor relief, but it did not significantly reduce the poverty that still dogged a significant portion of the population.

These enhanced social services were paid for out of increased tax revenues. Income tax rates had increased sharply during the war and remained high afterwards. Prior to the war, the wealthiest people in Britain had paid income tax at the rate of 8 percent; immediately afterwards the rate was 42.5 percent, and in 1938 they were still paying 39 percent. The progressive nature of the tax system, in which the wealthiest members of society paid a higher rate of taxation, meant that for the first time in British history the working classes collected more in social benefits from the state than they paid in taxes. But although this helped to reduce income disparities, Britain remained a highly unequal society.

If in some ways Britain's economic problems exacerbated the distinctions between different parts of the country, cultural changes had the opposite effect, as more and more people heard, read and saw the same things. The popular press remained the main form of mass communication, with a large number of newspapers competing for readers. In the late 1930s, about two-thirds of adults read a newspaper daily, and some papers, like the *Daily Express* and *Daily Herald*, sold upwards of 2 million copies a day. The growing popularity of radio also helped to promote cultural homogeneity. By the end of the 1930s, nearly 75 percent of the population had access to radio. The medium was dominated by the British Broadcasting Corporation (BBC), which was founded in 1926. Although it was a public institution that enjoyed a monopoly of the airwaves, the BBC was largely free from government intrusion. Its early years were dominated by the views of its first director-general, John Reith, a man of Victorian sensibilities who wanted the medium to be instructional and morally uplifting, rather than merely entertaining. He, along with many other members of the British cultural elite, was concerned about the "Americanization" of British culture, which he felt would lead to celebrity-driven programming of dubious artistic and moral value. He countered this with a mixture of classical music, news, intellectual discussions, drama and live broadcasts of special events and religious services. But in recognition of popular tastes, "light" programming such as dance music and sports was also offered. Reith's insistence that all BBC broadcasters had to have a nonregional, upper-class accent meant that radio also helped to smooth over differences between the various parts of Britain. The term "middlebrow," which was coined in the 1920s by critics of its programming, encapsulates the BBC's appeal, which fell somewhere between the commercial culture of the masses and the high culture preferred by intellectual elites.

Foreign Policy and Appeasement

After the Paris Peace Conference, Britain's international position declined, from one of relative strength in the 1920s to one of weakness in the 1930s. The early 1920s were dominated by the problem of ensuring that the terms of the Treaty of Versailles were fulfilled by a bitter and recalcitrant Germany, as well as by the repayment of war debts. Germany's refusal to pay the required reparations led Britain and France to occupy the Ruhr, Germany's industrial heartland, in 1923, which only served to exacerbate German economic problems and promote hyperinflation. The following year, the crisis led to the creation of the Dawes Plan, which attempted to resolve the issue through the provision of substantial American loans to Germany. This economic settlement was bolstered by the Locarno Treaty in 1925, which bound all parties to accept the territorial changes made by the Treaty of Versailles in western Europe. The "spirit of Locarno," a belief that Germany was finally accepting its place within the new Europe, engendered a sense of optimism about the future of international relations. For most of the 1920s, British policy makers continued to display good will towards Germany and to make efforts to restrain lingering French vindictiveness.

The Dawes Plan, however, linked Germany's reparation payments to Britain to loans from American banks. After the stock market crash in 1929, when these banks called in their German loans, no further reparations payments were forthcoming. As Europe followed America into depression, the optimism of the Locarno era was replaced by growing anxiety about Britain's worldwide commitments and the dwindling resources of its treasury. The British had already relinquished their global mastery of the seas with the Washington Naval Agreement of 1922, which pegged the size of the world's major naval fleet to one another in a set ratio, with Britain and the United States sharing the pre-eminent position. The biggest concern of the era, however, was the rise of air power. Fears pervaded British culture of the ability of aerial bombardment to wreak havoc amongst the civilian population, and civilian air-raid precautions were first discussed in 1935.

Although they recognized that Britain's status as an island was no longer sufficient to protect it from invasion, the nation's political and military leaders were slow to prepare for a future war. To be sure, Britain's military, naval and aerial power in this period was not as poor as some historians claim. Britain retained one of the two largest navies and one of the most modern air forces in the world; the RAF replaced all of its planes three times over as designs and capabilities improved. Moreover, Britain's annual defense spending was greater than it had been in the last years of peace prior to 1914. The latter figure, however, reflected more the expense of modern weaponry than a high level of military preparedness. Throughout the 1920s, military planning and spending was premised on the "ten-year rule," which assumed that Britain would not need to fight a major war for at least another decade. First initiated in 1919, this policy became a rolling deadline, with the result that spending on major rearmament was continually delayed. In hindsight, this decision was criticized, but prior to the 1930s, there seemed to be no pressing need to put Britain on a war footing. In 1932, the ten-year rule was rescinded and an enhanced, although still modest, amount of rearmament was undertaken. It was not until the late 1930s, however, that the rearmament program kicked into high gear. The acceleration of rearmament was a response to the growing international dangers that Britain now faced, which policy makers believed overrode economic constraints.

It is within this context that the pursuit of the policy of appeasement must be understood. Appeasement refers to efforts to reduce international tensions through the granting of concessions to aggrieved states. It was not a new means of conducting diplomacy; arguably, the British had long been using it. But in previous instances, Britain had the military muscle to back up the threats and ultimatums that accompanied the concessions. In the 1930s, however, the British no longer possessed that military might. Moreover, the British Empire was facing a barrage of threats, ranging from the growing imperial ambitions of Japan in Asia and the Pacific to the bellicose rhetoric of the fascist regime in Italy, which was aiming at the domination of the Mediterranean. The appointment of Adolf Hitler as chancellor of Germany in 1933 compounded these concerns, as he openly displayed his contempt for the Treaty of Versailles. Although these three potentially dangerous states were not yet allied with one another, British military planners knew that they could not effectively counter aggressive moves made by all of them at once.

The League of Nations proved to be ineffective in dealing with these mounting international tensions. When Japan invaded Manchuria in 1931 and Italy attacked Abyssinia in 1935, the economic sanctions imposed by the League failed to halt the aggression. After the Spanish Civil War erupted in 1936, the British and French refused to intervene, while the Germans and Italians assisted the fascist Spanish Nationalist rebels. That same year, the British government proved reluctant to stand up to the Germans over the remilitarization of the Rhineland, on Germany's western border, which had been demilitarized by the Treaty of Versailles. In direct defiance of the treaty, Hitler sent troops into the Rhineland in March of 1936. A weak French government looked to the British for leadership, but Britain refused to act, as there was little domestic appetite for a war over what most people saw as a minor issue in which the nation's interests were not at stake. The Rhineland was after all German territory; as Lord Lothian stated, the Germans were "only going into their own backyard."

Germany was thus not restrained in 1936. Nor, two years later, did Britain put up significant resistance to the *Anschluss*, or unification of Germany and Austria, which had also been prohibited by the Treaty of Versailles. That same year, when Germany began demanding to annex the Sudetenland, the German-speaking region of Czechoslovakia, Prime Minister Neville Chamberlain met with Hitler three times in September in an effort to defuse the situation. This time, war was seen as a strong possibility; the British began building air-raid shelters and mobilizing their armed forces. Chamberlain's effort to reach a compromise was thus undertaken in a climate of intense domestic anxiety. In the agreement that ensued, known as the *Munich Pact*, Czechoslovakia was compelled to surrender the Sudetenland, thereby satisfying German demands and (temporarily) averting war. This marked the apex of appeasement. Chamberlain believed that he had negotiated the end of German expansionism, and upon his return home he was greeted by ecstatic crowds. The prime minister made an impromptu speech, during which he waved a document given to him by Hitler that proclaimed Anglo-German friendship and declared that he had secured "peace in our time."

 See document "Appeasement" at www.routledge.com_cw_barczewski.

Chamberlain, however, was less optimistic about the future than his off-the-cuff remarks suggested. He had not been duped by Hitler at Munich, nor did he act in a cowardly manner, as was later claimed by his opponents. He understood that the Nazi regime was brutal and aggressive, but he believed that Hitler's demands were not infinite and that a reasonable agreement could be reached. Few people in Britain wanted war or accepted that it was inevitable. In addition, Chamberlain was convinced that British military power was inadequate. Even if it had declared war, Britain had no means of enforcing a demand to halt the annexation of the Sudetenland. The policy of appeasement thus emerged from, and was in many ways necessitated by, Britain's perceived position of weakness, and the concessions were based on the assumption that Hitler would abide by his word.

There were other reasons, as well, for appeasement. The British saw some of Germany's grievances as legitimate, stemming as they did from the overly punitive Treaty of Versailles. Pacifism was pronounced in Britain in the 1930s, as revulsion against the horrors of the Great War remained strong. In 1933, the prestigious Oxford Union debating society voted by 257 votes to 153 that "this house will in no circumstances fight for King and Country." The results shocked many people, but they reflected the degree of anti-war sentiment that had developed in Britain, particularly among the elite. Britain was distracted from European affairs by imperial concerns, in particular growing anticolonial nationalism in India and the Middle East, as well as by Italian and Japanese expansionism in Africa and Asia. Imperial unity was also tenuous, as both Canada and South Africa declared that they would not go to war over the Sudetenland. British diplomats constantly misread the German domestic political situation and believed that there was a "peace party" that would rein in Hitler if his aggression began to seriously threaten war. In reality, Hitler faced no significant opposition from within Germany. Britain's two most important allies, France and the United States, could not be counted on, as the former was intent on maintaining a defensive posture behind the **Maginot Line** and the latter had retreated into isolationism.

Finally, many British political leaders believed that Stalin's communist Russia was a greater threat than Hitler's fascist Germany. In 1937, the deputy prime minister Lord Halifax visited Germany and congratulated Hitler "on crushing communism in Germany and standing as a bulwark against Russia." Other Britons admired Hitler for having rebuilt Germany into a powerful nation once again, while on the far right of the Conservative Party, there was even some sympathy with Nazi ideology, as fascism appeared to offer a way to reimpose the authority of the elite over an increasingly democratic society. In 2005, documents were released by the Foreign Office that included telegrams from Lord Rothermere, the publisher of the popular newspaper the *Daily Mail*, which praised Hitler's work in "regenerating" Germany as "great and superhuman." In the summer of 1939, only two months before the outbreak of the Second World War, Rothermere wrote to the German foreign minister Joachim von Ribbentrop, "Our two great Nordic countries should pursue resolutely a policy of appeasement for, whatever anyone may say, our two great countries should be the leaders of the world."

Conclusion

Assessed as practical policy that was intended to prevent war, appeasement must be judged a failure. In March of 1939, Hitler ordered the invasion of the rest of Czechoslovakia. This time, the British response was swift: a guarantee of security was publicly issued to Poland, which was rightly seen as Germany's next target. The British were no more able to assist the Poles than they had been the Czechs, but the guarantee was an indication that they would not allow German aggression to go unchecked indefinitely. When Germany invaded Poland in September 1939, Britain (and France) immediately *declared war*, and for the second time in twenty-five years, the British population prepared to resist a German military onslaught by dispatching an expeditionary force to France.

Bibliography

Faber, David, *Munich, 1938: Appeasement and World War II* (2009)
Fanning, Ronan, *Fatal Path: British Government and Irish Revolution 1919–1922* (2013)
Gardiner, Juliet, *The Thirties: An Intimate History of Britain* (2011)
Hattersley, Roy, *Borrowed Time: The Story of Britain between the Wars* (2009)
Leeson, D. M., *The Black and Tans: British Police and Auxiliaries in the Irish War of Independence* (2011)
Macmillan, Margaret, *Paris 1919: Six Months That Changed the World* (2003)

Manela, Erez, *The Wilsonian Moment: Self-Determination and the International Origins of Anticolonial Nationalism* (2009)

McKibbin, Ross, *Classes and Cultures: England 1918–1951* (2000)

Moulton, Mo, *Ireland and the Irish in Interwar England* (2014)

Overy, Richard, *The Morbid Age: Britain and the Crisis of Civilization, 1919–1939* (2010)

Pugh, Martin, *We Danced All Night: A Social History of Britain between the Wars* (2009)

Taylor, D. J., *Bright Young People: The Rise and Fall of a Generation 1918–1940* (2008)

11 The Second World War

Topics covered

- Outbreak of war in 1939
- Churchill's emergence as a war leader
- Battle of Britain
- The Blitz and aerial bombing
- American aid and entry into the war
- Economic, social and political impact of the war
- War in Wales, Scotland, Northern Ireland and Éire
- Effect of the war on the British Empire
- Allied victory

Timeline

September 1939	Britain declares war on Germany
May 1940	Churchill replaces Chamberlain as prime minister; German invasion of France, Belgium and the Netherlands; Dunkirk evacuation
June 1940	France surrenders
July–September 1940	Battle of Britain
September 1940–May 1941	The Blitz
June 1941	Germany invades Soviet Union
August 1941	Atlantic Charter
December 1941	Japanese bomb Pearl Harbor; United States enters the war
February 1942	Japanese capture Singapore
November 1942	British victory at El Alamein
February 1943	Soviet victory in the siege of Stalingrad
September 1943	Allied invasion of Italy
June 1944	Allied invasion of France
May 1945	Germany surrenders
July 1945	Labour victory in general election
September 1945	Japan surrenders

DOI: 10.4324/9781003284758-11

Introduction

Although the First World War set in motion long-term processes that fundamentally changed Britain's economy and society, few people understood this in the immediate aftermath, as they tried to return Britain to its prewar status. This would not happen after the Second World War. A much greater degree of government intervention in the economy and society was necessary between 1939 and 1945 for Britain to emerge victorious from this larger and longer conflict. The changes wrought by the Second World War were both immediate and lasting, and there was a widely shared recognition that there could be no return to the prewar status quo.

The British people shared the trials and tribulations of the war far more equally than had been the case between 1914 and 1918. This contributed to the emergence of a consensus that the government had a major role to play in regulating the economy and in providing social security. In political terms, this consensus translated into a belief that the Labour Party could and should be entrusted with governing and with enacting widespread social reform. The population's experience of being targeted by German bombing and the massive civilian effort required to keep Britain fighting ensured that this was a "People's War," and those same civilians demanded that it be followed by a "People's Peace."

1940–1: Britain Alone

Britons were not surprised that Germany invaded Poland in September 1939. Nor were they opposed to the *declaration of war* against Germany that swiftly followed. No burst of public enthusiasm followed as in 1914, however, for Britons now understood what modern warfare meant. They felt that Prime Minister Neville Chamberlain had done everything possible to appease Germany, and in consequence that war was now unavoidable. For his part, Chamberlain was not eager to enter the conflict. Even after the guarantee of security had been given to Poland in March 1939, he had hoped that peace might be preserved through diplomatic efforts.

When diplomacy failed, the British Expeditionary Force (BEF) took up its position alongside the Belgians and the French, who had manned the Maginot Line, a system of fortifications that was intended to protect them from a German invasion. The situation was in some ways worse than in 1914, as the Russians had signed a nonaggression pact with Hitler in August, which meant that Germany would not have to face a two-front war. Nor could the British do much to defend Poland, which was quickly overrun by the Germans from the west and the Russians from the east. After that, however, the pace of military action slowed. From the conquest of Poland in early October 1939 until April 1940, a period of over six months, there was little fighting in Europe, which led contemporaries to dub this phase of the conflict the "Phoney War."

The respite offered the British a chance to assess whether Chamberlain was the right man to lead the war effort. The question as to who, if anyone, should replace him was complex. In the late 1930s, Winston Churchill had emerged as the leading spokesman against appeasement. He had also recently been appointed **First Lord of the Admiralty**, but he had spent most of the previous decade in the political wilderness, seemingly at the end of a long career that had been punctuated by a series of controversial moments. These included his decision to invade the Gallipoli Peninsula in Turkey while previously serving as First Lord of the Admiralty during the First World War; his decision to return Britain to the gold standard while serving as chancellor of the Exchequer in 1925; and his staunch opposition to increased independence for India in the 1930s. Most of his fellow Conservatives distrusted Churchill, and they expected that the recklessness, exuberance and pugnaciousness that had characterized his career up to this point would resurface once again.

This very nearly occurred, for in April 1940 Churchill supported a British invasion of Norway in order to prevent the Germans from securing supplies of iron ore from neighboring Sweden. The invasion turned into a debacle that led to a heated debate in the House of Commons, but it was Chamberlain rather than Churchill who was attacked by MPs from his own party, as they were frustrated by his lackluster leadership. In the ensuing vote, the government retained its majority, but nearly 120 Conservative MPs failed to support it. Faced with this visible draining away of his support, Chamberlain resigned two days later, on the 10th of May 1940.

But even with Chamberlain's demise, Churchill was far from his obvious successor. Many people saw the Earl of Halifax, who was foreign secretary at the time, as the leading candidate, since he enjoyed the support of the majority of Conservatives, the Labour Party and King George VI. Halifax had been a proponent of appeasement prior to the Munich Pact, but thereafter, recognizing that the concessions had gone too far, he had advocated a policy of vigorous rearmament. At this critical moment, however, he realized that Churchill's energy and determination made him a better choice, and he did not press his case. There were also concerns that Halifax would find it difficult to lead the country from the House of Lords, in which no prime minister had sat since Lord Salisbury's resignation in 1902. Chamberlain, Halifax and Churchill agreed that it was *Churchill who would be recommended to the King*. The widespread lack of faith in his character and leadership abilities was demonstrated when the House of Lords greeted the news with stony silence.

The relentless energy and combativeness that had long been decried by his enemies, however, made Churchill an ideal leader at this time of national crisis. He immediately assembled a coalition government that brought the most capable Labour and Liberal leaders into the cabinet. The Labour leader Clement Attlee was made deputy prime minister; Herbert Morrison, another Labour politician, became home secretary; and Ernest Bevin, secretary of the Trade Union Council, became minister for labour and national service. But Churchill reserved the most important wartime position, minister of defence, for himself. He was determined that, unlike in the First World War, there would be no conflict between military and civilian authorities.

Churchill needed all of these men's skills and abilities, for as he was taking office *Germany invaded Belgium, the Netherlands and France*. The speed of the German advance made it apparent that there would be no repeat of the stalemate on the Western Front that had developed in the First World War. Dubbed "blitzkrieg" (lightning war), the German offensive used air power and fast-moving tanks to punch holes in the Allied lines at strategic weak points. The BEF was pushed back towards the French coast, where it was pinned down in a pocket around the port of Dunkirk and surrounded by German forces. Fortunately, however, Herman Göring, the head of the *Luftwaffe*, or German air force, convinced Hitler that the BEF could be forced to surrender by aerial bombardment alone. This proved a mistake, as it gave the British time to organize an *evacuation*.

The "miracle" of Dunkirk, which occurred in the last week of May, was one of three defining events in 1940 that determined the course of the rest of the war for the British. The Royal Navy, with the assistance of thousands of volunteers in a variety of civilian vessels, rescued 240,000 British and 100,000 French troops from the beaches of Dunkirk. This represented the vast majority of Britain's trained army. The story of the courage of both the civilians, who transported around 8 percent of the evacuated troops, and the British (and French) troops who were sacrificed to buy the time necessary for the rescue was genuinely inspirational, and it was turned into a major propaganda victory by Churchill in his speeches to the nation. The rescue significantly bolstered civilian morale, and the contribution of the civilian "little boats" subsequently helped to create the notion of the "People's War," a war in which the British population as a whole, and not only its soldiers, fought, worked, suffered and sacrificed. But it should not be overlooked that Dunkirk was in reality a retreat from a disastrous defeat, not a victory. The British effectively abandoned their allies, allowing the Germans to encircle the Belgian army. They did not tell the French that they were evacuating their forces until three days into the operation. It was only towards the end of the operation that the British agreed to evacuate the French troops who were trapped in Dunkirk as well. The soldiers returned demoralized and lacking their equipment, which had been left on Dunkirk's beaches; it took nearly a year to resupply the army with what it had lost.

France surrendered on the 22nd of June 1940. Paris and the north and west of the country were occupied by the German military, while the rest of the country and its empire were placed under the control of a collaborationist regime based in the town of Vichy and led by Marshal Philippe Pétain, a hero of the First World War. A "Free French" government-in-exile was established in London under the leadership of General Charles de Gaulle.

Now, Britain (with the support of its empire) was the only major state at war with Germany, which meant that it now faced the possibility of invasion. The Home Guard, or militia, had been armed and given minimal training, but it was well understood by Britain's military and political leaders that should the Germans manage to land in numbers, resistance would be futile. Preventing a landing was the job of the Royal Navy and the Royal Air Force (RAF). Even before the fall of France, Churchill had ordered the RAF to bring its aircraft back to British bases. This deprived the French of air power they desperately needed, but it preserved the RAF for the coming German onslaught against Britain. Churchill and Hitler both knew that a successful invasion of Britain required control of the skies over the English Channel. Without such control, an invasion force would be vulnerable to attack from the sea and the air.

The Battle of Britain and the Blitz

During the summer of 1940, the Luftwaffe attempted to achieve the air superiority necessary to launch Germany's invasion of Britain. The operation, codenamed Operation Sea Lion, had a secondary objective of convincing the British that the situation was so hopeless that they must make peace with Germany. Thus began the *Battle of Britain*, the second defining event of 1940. The battle occurred over southern England between July and September. The Luftwaffe targeted the RAF's airfields with bombs, while the RAF sent Hurricane and Spitfire fighters to intercept them. Massive aerial dogfights ensued. In one of his most famous speeches, Churchill declared, "never in the field of human conflict was so much owed by so many to so few." He was referring to the 3000 RAF pilots and crewmen who fought in the battle. They were young men of an average age of only twenty; 544 of them lost their lives.

Much was made at the time and afterwards of the pilots' bravery and skill, but there were additional reasons why the British prevailed. At the beginning of the battle, the Germans had at their disposal about 800 modern fighter aircraft and 1500 modern bombers, along with another 1000 older aircraft. The RAF had about 700 modern fighters with which to resist these attacks. The German's numerical advantage was offset, however, by the fact that in 1940 the British produced new fighter planes twice as fast as the Germans'. Moreover, the battle occurred over British territory, which meant that British planes that were shot down could sometimes be recovered and repaired, and their pilots rescued and returned to action, whereas downed German planes were lost and their pilots, if they survived, were taken as prisoners of war. Because they had to fly a long way to get to Britain, the German fighters could not always protect the bombers all the way to their targets, making them vulnerable to attack. The bombing of small targets like airfields had to be done in daylight, depriving the Luftwaffe of the cover of darkness and making their interception by British fighters more likely.

Figure 11.1 The original version of what has now become the most famous British propaganda poster of the Second World War. It and two other posters ("Freedom Is in Peril Defend It with All Your Might" and "*Your* Courage *Your* Cheerfulness *Your* Resolution Will Bring Us Victory") were printed even before the war began in 1939. The first two were printed and posted widely beginning in August 1939, but the 2.5 million copies of "Keep Calm and Carry On" were held back so that they could be used in the event of a German invasion. It was thus never used, and most of the copies were later pulped as paper shortages mounted. An original copy, one of only fifteen still known to be in existence, was discovered by a bookstore owner in Alnwick, Northumberland, in 2000. When he framed it and posted it in the store, it became a sensation. The design is old enough to be in the public domain, which explains the number of products that have been sold using it in recent years.

Another factor that favored the British was their development of the world's first radar system, with stations dotting the coast. Radar, in which radio waves are used to determine the range, altitude, direction and speed of objects at a distance, allowed the British to "see" impending aerial attacks long before the planes reached their targets. Combined with volunteer aircraft spotters and anti-aircraft batteries, radar allowed the British to direct their aircraft to meet the threat quickly. Moreover, it did not require its pilots to be constantly patrolling the coasts waiting for attacks. The British had fewer pilots than they had planes, so preventing unnecessary fatigue was crucial. Even given these British advantages, however, the Battle of Britain was closely fought. By mid-September 1940, the British had lost 1134 aircraft to the Germans' 1155. But a draw was equivalent to a British victory: the continued resistance of the RAF meant that Operation Sea Lion had to be postponed as winter approached.

This delay caused Hitler to alter his strategy towards a new focus on breaking the morale of Britain's civilian population. When the war began, it was widely recognized that the emergence of air power meant that civilians as well as combatants were potential targets. The American president Franklin Roosevelt had issued a request to all the participants to avoid conducting air raids on nonmilitary targets. The British and French agreed, but only if the other combatant nations agreed to abide by Roosevelt's request as well. The definition of what constituted a military target in an age of aerial warfare, however, was slippery. In May 1940, the British bombed industrial targets in Germany's Ruhr Valley, hoping to disrupt the production of munitions. In August, the Germans bombed airfields on the outskirts of London, as well as the cities of Aberdeen and Bristol and the coalfields of South Wales. At the end of that same month, the British launched their first bombing attack on Berlin. A furious Hitler ordered the Luftwaffe to begin bombing London and other British cities in retaliation.

This change in tactics represented a tacit acknowledgment that the Luftwaffe's primary objective – air superiority over the Channel – had not been achieved. In late September, Operation Sea Lion was postponed indefinitely. The RAF had succeeded in preventing an invasion, and more significantly, the tenaciousness that the British had displayed had convinced many neutral observers, particularly in the United States, that they were not going to be defeated nearly as easily as had been widely assumed after the fall of France. The Americans now began to consider ways of increasing their support for Britain without actually joining the war. For British civilians, however, the new German tactics were terrifying. At night, the Luftwaffe's bombers flew with relative impunity over British cities, as the RAF's fighters could not operate effectively in darkness. German aircraft losses were thus significantly less than they had been during the daylight raids of the summer, and the tonnage of bombs dropped increased. Fortunately for the British, however, the Luftwaffe was not an air force designed for such a sustained bombing offensive, and it never possessed the heavy bombers that the British (and later the Americans) deployed on long-distance raids.

Nonetheless, the "*Blitz*," as the German bombing campaign came to be called, had a major impact on British cities. Over the course of eight months in 1940 and 1941, over 37,000 civilians were killed, nearly 30,000 of them in London, and another 50,000 were seriously injured. Over 800,000 houses were badly damaged or destroyed, leaving millions of people homeless. The list of damaged buildings included the Houses of Parliament and Buckingham Palace. The worst effects of the bombing were felt by people living close to industrial targets, such as the densely populated working-class districts near the docks in the East End of London. The bombings caused large numbers of people to leave major cities every evening in search of safety in the countryside or to take refuge in bomb shelters. Most of the shelters were in the form of either tin backyard dugouts covered in earth (named "Anderson shelters" after Sir John Anderson, who as Lord Privy Seal had been responsible for preparing civilian air-raid defenses prior to the war) or, for those who lacked gardens or cellars, steel cages placed under tables (called "Morrison shelters" after Home Secretary Herbert Morrison). Only a small segment of the population regularly sought refuge in communal shelters or in the **London Underground**, although photographs of hundreds of people sleeping in Tube stations came to be one of the most iconic images of the Blitz.

The Experience of Warfare 8

The Blitz: Myth and Reality

The response of the population to the Blitz fired the British imagination in a way that no other aspect of the Second World War did. To be sure, the bombing of British cities was neither new nor unexpected. During the interwar years, the preparations for defense against aerial attack were derived from the experience of zeppelin raids during the First World War, which led British officials to believe that bombing would be far more devastating than it turned out to be. Government planners feared that the populace would not be able to withstand sustained attack and that bombing would result in domestic chaos and demands for the government to end the war. To meet this threat, an Air Raid Precautions (ARP) Department was established in 1935. It advocated a policy of crowd dispersal, in which people should not gather in large air-raid shelters, in order to avoid the threat of panicked mobs and the devastating impact on morale if such a shelter should suffer a direct hit. There was also concern over the development of a "deep shelter mentality," in which people would choose to remain underground in safety and not perform the day-to-day activities that were necessary for the war effort.

ARP policy in the first year of the war thus advocated that families should take refuge in small shelters in their own homes or backyards. This was the reason for the development of the Anderson backyard shelter and the Morrison indoor shelter. It was also why, during the first days of the Blitz, the authorities in London tried to prevent the use of Underground stations as shelters. They were ultimately compelled, however, to accede to public demands on this issue, especially in hard-hit areas like the crowded East End of London, where there were few alternatives. Even so, a "shelter census" taken in November 1940 found that just 4 percent of Londoners used the Tube stations as shelters, while another 9 percent used other public shelters. The remainder used family shelters, left the city entirely or felt no need to shelter at all. The postwar remembrance of sheltering during the Blitz as a collective experience with people of vastly different social backgrounds sharing the same space was thus not the norm. Even so, the collective experience of being bombed helped cement the idea of a "People's War." It also played a role in increasing people's desire for government intervention in society and the economy. If the war was being brought to civilians as a means of attacking the state, many people felt that this meant that the state had an obligation to protect its citizens. The Blitz thus helped to smooth the way for the establishment of the social welfare policies that were enacted during and after the war.

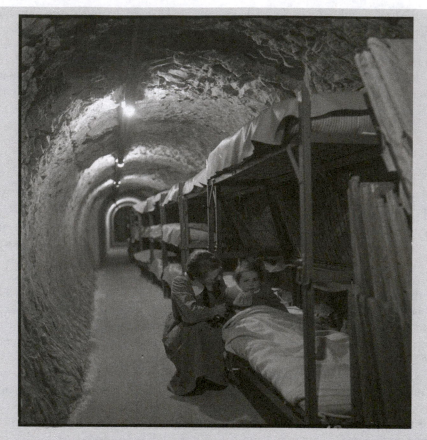

Figure 11.2 A mother tucks her child into bed in a deep shelter in London during the Blitz. Taken by the American photographer Toni Frissell, this photo was used to show Americans how calm and resilient the British people were being in response to German aerial bombardment. In reality, relatively few people used such large public shelters.

Photographer: Frissell, Toni, 1907–1988. Reproduced courtesy of the Library of Congress.

The aerial bombardment of London was the third defining event of 1940. It solidified the idea of the "People's War," not only for Britons themselves, but also for Americans, who learned about the Blitz from radio broadcasts and newspaper stories via the reporting of American journalists in London like Edward R. Murrow, Quentin Reynolds, Helen Kirkpatrick and Ernie Pyle. Although the United States was still neutral, these journalists were both witnesses to and victims of the air raids, and they became partisans for the British cause. Their reports helped to construct an image in America of a suffering British population that was nonetheless resolute in its determination to resist the tyranny and barbarism of the Nazis.

 See document "An American Journalist's View of the Blitz" at www.routledge.com/cw/barczewski.

The government's preparations to deal with the aerial attacks, known as "air-raid precautions" or ARP, were at first sharply criticized for their inadequacy, but political leaders and civil servants worked diligently to improve them. This enormous undertaking involved tens of thousands of civilian volunteers, who each night maintained public order during raids, spotted bombers in the air and directed the emergency services to bomb sites and fires. Some 3.5 million children, pregnant women and mothers with young children were evacuated from large cities and moved to "reception areas" in the country. Those who lacked family or friends with whom they could stay were billeted in the homes of strangers, who were paid an allowance for their upkeep from the government. About 20,000 children, mostly from wealthier families, were evacuated to overseas locations, primarily Canada, but this practice was halted in late 1940 due to the danger to transatlantic shipping posed by U-boats. The experience of the evacuees varied widely; some established lifelong friendships with their hosts, while others were treated with contempt and exploited as free labor. The placement of working-class evacuees with middle-class hosts (and vice versa) brought into sharp focus the persistence of deep social divisions in Britain. While in some cases an understanding ensued, in others the experience reinforced class prejudices.

By May of 1941, the worst of the Blitz was over. Hitler ordered the cessation of sustained bombing, as he needed to conserve Germany's air resources for the upcoming campaign against Russia, which began the following month, marking the end of the nonaggression pact between Germany and the Soviet Union. Britain would suffer sporadic air raids for the remainder of the war, however. In 1944, the Germans began launching an unmanned rocket bomb called the V-1, which was guided by a preset magnetic compass and gyroscope. It was succeeded by the V-2, the first long-range ballistic missile, meaning that it was guided only at the beginning of its flight and then relied on the laws of physics to reach its target. Between June and September 1944, when the last launch sites within range were overrun by Allied forces, about 9000 V-1s were launched at British targets, though almost half of them were destroyed before they hit the ground. The V-2, which had a longer range and traveled at a much faster speed, was far more difficult to intercept, and 2750 civilians in London lost their lives to this terrifying new weapon. But after the British supplied false intelligence to the Germans that the bombs were missing the center of London, the Germans recalibrated them to land further south, where most of them fell harmlessly in thinly populated areas. In March 1945, the V-2 launch sites were also overrun, ending German bombing raids on civilian targets in Britain once and for all.

Bombing left deep physical scars on Britain. By the end of the war, 60,000 British civilians had been killed and another 250,000 injured. Two of every seven houses had been destroyed or severely damaged. Britons' sense of moral authority – of being the victims of bombing – made it possible for the public to countenance, and even relish, visiting the same fate on the enemy. Britain conducted its own strategic bombing offensive against German cities, a campaign that intensified with the arrival of the American Air Force in Britain in 1942. But although British people saw the bombing of Germany as justified retaliation for the Blitz, as we have seen, the British had begun targeting industrial sites in Germany's Ruhr region as early as May 1940, months before the Blitz began. In July, Churchill declared that there was "one thing" that would bring Hitler "down": "An absolutely devastating, exterminating attack by very heavy bombers from this country upon the Nazi homeland."

Britain's aerial offensive against Germany was one of the most prolonged and extensive endeavors in the nation's military history. Immense resources were diverted from other aspects of the war, and entire industries were given over to the design and production of

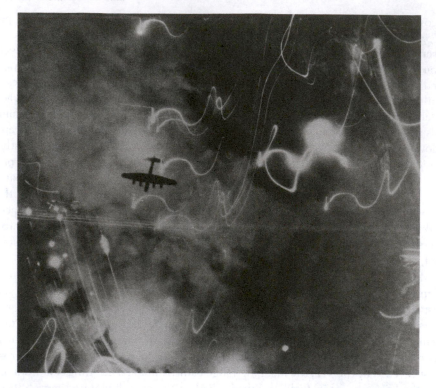

Figure 11.3 In a photo taken during an attack on the shipyards in Hamburg, Germany, in January 1943, a British Lancaster bomber is silhouetted against trails of light emitted by incendiary bombs dropped by other planes.

Reproduced courtesy of Shutterstock/Everett Collection.

heavy bomber aircraft, radio navigation aids, ground-mapping radar and huge amounts of ordnance. Some 1.4 million workers – about 42 percent of the total workforce that was engaged in military production – were assigned to the Ministry of Aircraft, with a further 400,000 producing support equipment and ordnance. In total, the effort consumed approximately a third of Britain's total wartime expenditures and accounted for a large portion of the foreign debt owed at the end of the war.

The military effectiveness of the British bombing offensive continues to be debated, as does its morality. German morale was not shattered, even though the scale of the bombing was much greater than what Britain suffered. Instead of weakening the grip of the Nazis on the German population, bombing might have strengthened it. The historian Richard Overy writes, "The effect of the bombing was not, in the end, as the Allies hoped, to drive a wedge between people and regime, but the opposite, to increase dependence on the state and the party." Nor did bombing significantly dent German wartime production, which peaked in 1944, three years after the campaign started. On the other side of the ledger, however, Germany did have to divert significant resources to its air defenses and to protecting its industry. The moral debate about bombing, meanwhile, focused on the issue of deliberately targeting civilians. Over 350,000 Germans were killed, which represented more than half the total number of European civilians who died from bombing in the war.

Turning the Tide

Even before the beginning of the Blitz, it was apparent to the government that Britain could not long continue the war effort without substantial material help from other nations, in particular the United States. Much British wartime propaganda, and much of Churchill's own efforts, were thus devoted to gaining American assistance and, ultimately, to bringing the United States into the war. Though hamstrung by the strength of isolationist sentiment, President Roosevelt not only sympathized with Britain's plight, but also recognized that American security would be threatened if Britain were to fall to the Germans. Roosevelt did as much as he could: he allowed the British to buy American armaments and gave them fifty aging destroyers to assist in convoy protection, in return for which the United States was permitted to build naval bases in British colonies in the western hemisphere. By the beginning of 1941, however, the British treasury was empty. The situation was so dire that iron railings were removed from houses and parks so that they could be melted down for armaments. A plan was even contemplated to confiscate all wedding rings in the country and melt them down for gold. The latter measure never had to be implemented, however, because in March Roosevelt announced the Lend-Lease Program, whereby America would sell, lend or lease Britain the supplies and armaments it needed, with repayment not required until after the war. Having little choice, the Churchill government mortgaged Britain's economic future to the United States. Lend-Lease supplied a quarter of British munitions in 1943 and 1944.

In June 1941, *Germany invaded the Soviet Union*, and British and Soviet diplomats began moving towards an alliance. In July, Britain and the Soviet Union signed a pact in which they agreed to lend assistance to each other and to refuse to make a separate peace with Germany. In August, British and Soviet forces launched a joint invasion of Iran to prevent the Germans from seizing the country's oil supplies. The following month, representatives from the United States participated in a conference in Moscow in which a plan for supplying weapons and vital resources to the Soviet Union was formulated. The United States was not yet formally in the war, but that changed in December 1941, after the *Japanese bombed Pearl Harbor*. Britain immediately declared war on Japan, and Germany declared war on the United States four days later. The war aims of the new allies were outlined in the *Atlantic Charter*, which had been signed by Britain and the United States in August. In crafting an idealistic vision for the postwar world, both countries agreed that they would not seek territorial gains and not make territorial adjustments without the consent of the affected peoples. They also declared that all people had a right to political self-determination, and that they would promote global economic cooperation and improvements in social welfare.

 See document "An Anglo-American Vision for the Postwar World" at www. routledge.com/cw/barczewski.

Even with the American entry into the war, however, in early 1942 victory was still a distant prospect. The Soviet Union appeared to be on the verge of defeat; the British strategic bombing offensive had yet to seriously dent the German war effort; and neither Britain nor the United States had the military means to invade continental Europe. Late 1941 and early 1942, in fact, marked the nadir of the war for the British, as a number of key imperial possessions in the East, including Singapore, Hong Kong, Borneo and Malaya, fell to the Japanese. The *loss of Singapore* was particularly devastating: over 100,000 troops surrendered, and two of Britain's newest battleships, the *Prince of Wales* and the *Repulse*, were sunk by Japanese air attacks. At the same time, British successes in North Africa against the Italians were reversed when German troops were brought in to bolster Axis forces. Most worryingly, German U-boats were sinking more allied shipping in the Atlantic than could be replaced.

In 1943, however, the Allies began gaining ground on a number of fronts. American aircraft carrier operations in the Pacific led to the liberation of some of the Japanese-occupied islands, and the British also began to make progress against the Japanese in Burma. In January 1943, the Soviets inflicted a major defeat on the Germans at *Stalingrad*, ending Hitler's long-cherished dream of conquering Russia. After the brilliant defense of *El Alamein* in western Egypt in November 1942, the British and Americans pushed the Italians and Germans out of North Africa. The first allied foothold on the continent since 1940 was regained in July 1943 with the invasion of Sicily, followed by an *invasion of the Italian mainland* two months later.

By this point, however, differences had emerged among the Allies regarding the strategic direction of the war. Churchill, who believed Italy to be the "soft underbelly" of the Axis, endorsed the campaign there. Popular support for the war was waning among Italians, leading to the deposition and imprisonment of the fascist dictator Benito Mussolini in July. But this strategy enraged the Soviet leader Joseph Stalin, as Russia was still suffering more than 4000 casualties a day. Stalin wanted an attack on Germany itself to commence as soon as possible, via an invasion of northern France. The British and Americans argued they were not yet ready to tackle the "Atlantic Wall" defenses that had been erected by the Germans on the French and Belgian coastline, nor did they yet have the required air superiority over the English Channel. The attack on France was thus postponed until the summer of 1944. Meanwhile, after its initial success the invasion of Italy bogged down when the defense of the country was taken over by German troops. The Allies struggled up the Italian boot in a slow and brutal campaign that was very different from Churchill's prediction of an easy victory. Italy was not defeated until the spring of 1945, shortly before *Germany itself surrendered*.

The Home Front

By 1943, the idea of the "People's War" had become entrenched in the British imagination. But although the difficulties of the conflict brought out the best in many British people, everyone did not suffer them equally. Crime diminished but did not disappear, and even some houses that were bombed in the Blitz were looted. Some people exploited evacuees or refused to take them in at all. Expressions of overt class antagonisms surfaced: at the beginning of the Blitz, some residents of the East End of London expressed resentment that they were being hit more heavily than the wealthier neighborhoods to the west, where people also had access to better shelters.

But if national unity was more precarious than postwar mythology suggested, the war effort still required a tremendous commitment from the British people. A massive effort was made to improve domestic food production and people's eating habits, with victory the ever-present goal. For example, one campaign claimed that carrots helped to improve eyesight and therefore aided in the spotting of enemy aircraft. A "Dig for Victory" drive asked homeowners to turn their backyards into vegetable gardens. The rationing of food and consumer goods was introduced, based on a combined coupon and points system that allowed consumers some choice of what they could acquire on a weekly basis. But while the principle that rationing was the only means of ensuring fairness for all was broadly endorsed, few people were above complaining about how it worked in practice. The growth of the black market in rationed goods meant that by 1944 the government employed over 900 inspectors to ensure compliance with rationing regulations. These inspectors had the power to impose draconian punishments in order to retain public confidence in the "fair shares" principle that underpinned the rationing system.

Figure 11.4 King George VI and Queen Mary visit a Ministry of Agriculture Harvest Camp in 1944. These camps were established so that Britons could volunteer to spend their holidays performing agricultural labor in order to increase food production. Images like these, in which the royal family and ordinary Britons shared their wartime experiences, helped to solidify the notion of a "People's War."

Reproduced courtesy of the *Daily Herald* Archive at the National Media Museum.

The Experience of Warfare 9

Rationing

Before the start of the war, the British government planned to implement the rationing of food and other essential consumer items such as clothing and gasoline. The program went into effect in January 1940. Important lessons had been learned from the First World War, and care was taken to ensure that the rationing scheme provided both an adequate intake of calories (set at 3000 per adult per day) and some consumer choice. Unlike the rationing of food in other countries, the British system left cereals and vegetables unrationed and kept bread prices stable through a subsidization scheme. In fact, only about half of the average person's caloric intake was regulated by rationing. The rationed items, which were acquired via coupons found in government-issued ration books, included meat, butter, cheese, sugar, jam, tea and coffee. They were distributed in set amounts depending on the age of the consumer, who was put in one of three categories: adults, children aged six to seventeen, and children under six. Other rationed items could be purchased via a points system, which allowed consumers to spend a weekly allowance as they wished on scarce foods like biscuits or canned fish.

It was quickly determined, however, that the 3000-calorie target, while fine for a person in a desk job, was insufficient for workers in heavy industry. The government therefore encouraged, and sometimes enforced, the establishment of industrial canteens in factories and large workshops that provided workers with at least one unrationed meal per day. Government-run "British Restaurants" were also set up near smaller workshops and businesses to allow working people to eat decent food at reasonable prices and without having to use their precious ration coupons. By 1944, there were over 2000 British Restaurants and 18,500 industrial canteens, feeding 12 million people per day. As in the First World War, private restaurants continued to operate, but they were typically the preserve of the wealthy and their menus became more limited.

Rationing was popular, particularly with women, who tended to do the bulk of the family shopping, because it managed scarcities well and meant that price alone did not determine what food could be acquired. The system was complex and required careful planning by its users, but it was justified by the idea of "fair shares for all." This did not, however, prevent grumbling about shortages or resentment of those who could afford more. It also failed to stop people from resorting to the black market for particularly desirable items, although those who profited – known colloquially as "spivs" – were publicly derided. But in general the rationing system served the British population well. For most people, their caloric intake remained close to what it had been before the war, and for those in the lowest income groups, it actually increased. Rationing lasted in Britain until 1954, as the country continued to face shortages. By the early 1950s, however, the public's tolerance of rationing was wearing thin, and the call for consumer choice and a return to the free market was one of the key issues in the elections of those years.

As the war was considered to be a just one by the vast majority of the population, there were fewer controversies regarding the power of the government to compel its citizens to fight and work than there had been during the First World War. Conscription had been enacted even before the war began, and there were far fewer applications from conscientious objectors this time around. The economic difficulties of the previous two decades were quickly overcome by wartime demand. By early 1941 there was a huge shortage of labor, with an additional 2 million workers needed to sustain the war effort. Workers were imported from Britain's dominions and colonies, and, as in the First World War, women were encouraged – and even conscripted – to join the workforce. By 1943, 46 percent of all women between the ages of fourteen and fifty-nine were in paid employment, and about 500,000 women were serving in auxiliary roles in the armed services or in ARP positions. Women even helped to operate anti-aircraft guns, though prevailing gender norms prevented them from being allowed to actually fire them. Concerns that the war might "de-sex" women led to some magazines to promote a "beauty is duty" campaign, with tips on how women could remain feminine in appearance while wearing a uniform or the "utility clothing" that was the product of wartime shortages.

Figure 11.5 Women working at the General Engineering Company's munitions factory in Scarborough, Ontario. As in Britain, tens of thousands of Canadian women volunteered to perform jobs formerly held by men. Though they were paid less than their male counterparts, many enjoyed their independence and pursued new employment opportunities even after the war ended. Others, however, were happy to return to their prewar domestic lives.

Reproduced courtesy of the Archives of Ontario.

Sexuality and Gender 5

Gay Men in World War II

Male homosexuality was not only illegal in Britain during the Second World War, but for servicemen it was a court-martial offense, meaning they could be thrown out of the armed services if they were caught. Gay men were believed to be cowards, and if straight men were forced to serve alongside them it was seen as bad for morale. But many gay men fought in the war, with their comrades often fully aware of their sexual orientation. When they fought just as bravely as their straight counterparts, it helped to overturn stereotypes that all gay men were effeminate and cowardly. Indeed, two of Britain's most prominent war heroes were gay. Ian "Widge" Gleed was an RAF flying ace who was credited with shooting down thirteen German aircraft.

Although he was offered a desk job in 1942, he arranged to be posted to the North African campaign, and was shot down and killed in Tunisia on the 16th of April 1943. Before his death, Gleed had authored a memoir of his flying exploits, but the publisher was concerned that his claim to be a "confirmed bachelor" would arouse suspicion about his sexuality. Gleed therefore invented a fictional girlfriend named Pam. More famous than Gleed today is Alan Turing. Turing was a promising young mathematician at the University of Cambridge when at the beginning of the war he was approached by the Government Code and Cypher School (GC&CS) to serve as a codebreaker. He was sent to the GC&CS secret facility at Bletchley Park, a requisitioned country house in Buckinghamshire, to try to break the codes generated by Germans' supposedly unbreakable Enigma machine. Turing built "the Bombe," an electro-mechanical machine that was a precursor to our present-day computers. His success in deciphering the Enigma codes meant that Allied ship convoys in the Atlantic could be diverted away from German U-boats, thereby saving not only the vital supplies they carried but also thousands of lives. In 1946, Turing was awarded the Order of the British Empire for his wartime service. But in 1952, he was arrested for committing an act of "gross indecency" with another man. After pleading guilty, instead of going to prison, he agreed to receive estrogen injections that would chemically castrate him. Two years later, his housekeeper found him dead in his bed; he had committed suicide by eating an apple laced with cyanide. He was forty-one years

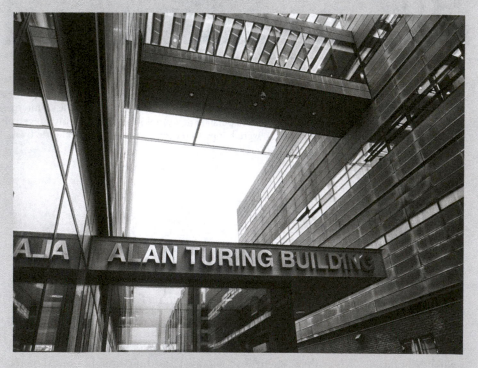

Figure 11.6 The Alan Turing Building, which houses the School of Mathematics at the University of Manchester, opened in 2007. It reflects Turing's transformation from outcast to national hero.

Reproduced courtesy of www.vitastudent.com.

old. The documents revealing the full extent of his wartime achievements were not declassified until the 1970s. Finally, Turing could be celebrated as a war hero. Since then, his reputation has only grown. In 2009, he received an official apology from Prime Minister Gordon Brown, and four years later he was granted a pardon under the Royal Prerogative of Mercy. He appeared on a Royal Mail postage stamp in 2012, and he was portrayed by Benedict Cumberbatch in the 2014 film *The Imitation Game*. When in 2019 new £50 notes went into circulation, Turing replaced the inventors of the steam engine, James Watt and Matthew Boulton, on it. Also in 2019, he was named the greatest person of the twentieth century by BBC viewers, beating out Muhammed Ali and Nelson Mandela.

The requirements of the war meant that cost-effectiveness was sacrificed in favor of the volume and speed of production. There was a race to develop new technologies and weapons that might prove decisive. Important innovations – radar, jet propulsion, antibiotics and atomic energy – were all pioneered by British scientists in the late 1930s and early 1940s. Many of them, however, had to be turned over to the Americans to realize their full potential, as the British lacked the means to fully develop them during the war. Huge amounts of munitions and fuel had to be imported to maintain the war effort, which is why limiting the effectiveness of U-boat attacks in the Atlantic was so crucial. The Atlantic convoys also transported hundreds of thousands of servicemen to Britain from the Empire and later some 3 million American soldiers who arrived in preparation for the invasion of the European continent.

This American "occupation" of Britain generated its own problems. The complaint that American GIs were "oversexed, overpaid, and over here" was a joke, but it revealed the fears of many British men that their glamorous and wealthy American allies would "steal" their women. There was some basis to these concerns: the GIs were better paid than British servicemen and had more access to cigarettes, nylon stockings and other scarce goods. Their novelty and outgoing personalities also made them attractive to British women. By the end of the war, 70,000 British women had married American GIs, and 9000 babies were born out of wedlock from liaisons between British women and American servicemen.

Ultimately, however, the presence of so many Americans as part of the Allied war effort cemented rather than undermined the "special relationship" between the two nations, which would become a linchpin of the postwar order. Long before the end of the war, British people were envisioning their hopes for the postwar world. The author J.B. Priestley's "Postscripts" broadcasts on the BBC celebrated the British people and their achievements during the conflict and looked forward to a more egalitarian society afterwards. Almost a third of the population listened to Priestley's weekly broadcasts in 1940, much to the discomfiture of many Conservatives, including Churchill, who disapproved of what they saw as their radical political content. Despite their popularity, the BBC canceled Priestley's broadcasts the following year. But no amount of censorship could disguise the fact that the British population would not be satisfied with vague promises for a better world after the war. Instead, politicians had to demonstrate that the government was committed to providing a more equitable future for all. Real policies were thus enacted, with more promised after the war. In 1941, the **means test** for welfare provision was eliminated, and allowances were paid to families whose breadwinner(s) had joined the armed services. Free milk was provided to pregnant women and young children above the quotas of the rationing system. Ernest Bevin, the minister for labour, raised the minimum wage and allowed workers to bargain collectively for better wages. As a result, average wage rates rose by 80 percent over the course of the war. The Education Act of 1944 created a tripartite system of secondary education that was divided into **grammar schools** for the top quarter of students (as measured by an examination taken at the age of eleven or twelve), secondary technical schools that emphasized mechanical, scientific and engineering skills, and secondary modern schools for everyone else. The Family Allowances Act of 1945 gave women a payment for each child in their family beyond their first-born. These measures, promoted largely by the ranks of the younger, more progressive wing of the Conservative Party, indicated that a degree of consensus over the nature of the postwar world was emerging.

The most important social welfare initiative that occurred during the war, however, was the Beveridge Report, which appeared in 1942. The report was the work of Sir William Beveridge, who had earned a knighthood for his work at the Ministries of Munitions and Food during the First World War and had spent most of the interwar years as director of the London School of Economics. In 1939, Beveridge was appointed by Ernest Bevin to head a committee investigating the reorganization of social services after the war. Going far beyond what the government expected, Beveridge aimed to eliminate what he called the "five giant evils": want, squalor, idleness, ignorance and disease. His recommendations called for the various piecemeal social programs that had been instituted since 1911 to be brought together and made part of a comprehensive welfare system that would be available to all British citizens. Thus, unemployment benefits would for the first time cover the entire population; workplace compensation for injury and illness was to be reformed and increased; and complicated old-age pensions were to be converted into a single, simple plan. In addition, a new National Health Service to which everyone would have access regardless of income would be created. Lastly, Beveridge argued for government policies that would ensure full employment, which would reduce the benefits that had to be paid out and keep contributions high.

The enthusiasm with which the report was received made it seem a far more radical set of proposals than it was. The Conservative government reinforced perceptions of the plan's radicalism with their reluctance to fully endorse it. In reality, Beveridge's proposals drew on, and in some respects stepped back from, policies that already existed or had long been under consideration. The benefits proposed were not more generous than those already offered; what was new was their rationalization and their universality. Every citizen was now entitled to them, rather than their being applied only to those in demonstrated need. Ultimately, the recommendations in the report, only slightly modified, became the basis of the British welfare state after 1945.

Ireland, Scotland and Wales in the Second World War

The wartime experience of Scotland, Wales and Northern Ireland in some ways paralleled that of England, but in others it was distinctive, as people fought for their individual nations as well as for Britain. Wartime patriotism, the rhetoric of the "People's War" and common experiences such as air raids and rationing helped to foster a sense of British identity. All over Britain, as the historian Martin Johnes has observed, the war "brought together people from different regional, class, and linguistic backgrounds in a way that really had no precedent." Even in the most remote parts of the United Kingdom, people were aware of what was happening in the war, and they found ways to contribute to the war effort by donating money to build planes and ships, collecting scrap metal and waste paper, knitting hats and gloves for the troops and growing food.

The war also, however, revealed people's ignorance about each other. A Welsh woman who joined the Women's Royal Naval Service commented, "I don't think I'd ever heard of a Scouse person or a Geordie until I joined up. Then, suddenly, all these different accents [are] all around you. A lot of people didn't know my accent. I'd be asked what part of Scotland I came from. Or Ireland – was I north or south?" Cultural institutions such as the BBC helped to unify the United Kingdom, but they could also emphasize divisions. Welsh listeners chafed at BBC commentators' descriptions of the conflict as "England's war," which occurred frequently despite admonitions from the Ministry of Information that broadcasters should not say "England" when they meant "Britain." In any case, in rural Wales, many households did not have access to a radio, and 40,000 people spoke only Welsh. The twenty minutes a day of BBC programming in Welsh did little to overcome their isolation.

The war presented new opportunities for both cultural exchange and cultural conflict between Welsh and English people. As it was unlikely to be targeted by German bombs, most of rural Wales was designated a "reception area" for children who were evacuated from London and the industrial north of England. Tens of thousands of children were housed in Welsh villages, often in places where English was not widely spoken. For some, the adjustment was challenging. Rural Wales was quiet and pious, and many children loathed being made to go to chapel three times on Sunday. Their host families could be very poor, and the experience of being in a household that spoke Welsh as its first language could be bewildering. The language barrier meant that English children were often educated separately from the local population. One evacuee recalled, "we didn't mix much with the locals, it was them and us." Welsh people, meanwhile, feared that evacuees from England's slums would bring disease and moral degradation to their towns; a child's first experience in a Welsh home was often being dipped in disinfectant. Nationalists were concerned that the influx of English children would swamp their culture. Saunders Lewis, a former leader of Plaid Cymru, referred to the evacuation as "one of the most horrible threats to the continuation and to the life of the Welsh nation that has ever been suggested in history."

Figure 11.7 Children evacuated from London to Wales learn Welsh in school.
Reproduced courtesy of piemags/Alamy Stock Photo.

In many cases, however, the experience of evacuation led to enhanced mutual understanding. Many English children learned to speak at least some Welsh, and they often enjoyed less crowded and healthier living conditions than they had experienced at home. Some evacuees even continued to live with their adoptive families after the war, while those who returned home often had fond memories of Wales. For Welsh people living in industrial areas that had been hard-hit by the depression, war brought welcome employment opportunities. Unemployment in the industrial town of Merthyr Tydfil in South Wales had reached 62 percent before the war, but quickly dropped as production geared up. When 25,000 Welsh coal miners enlisted between 1938 and 1941, a labor surplus suddenly became a labor shortage. To combat the shortage, mining was made a "reserved occupation," which meant that miners could not be conscripted. This failed to alleviate the problem, however, and so in 1943 a scheme was introduced in which one in ten eighteen-year-olds were sent into the mines rather than the armed forces. Though trade union leaders were committed to the war effort, miners often expressed discontentment over their working conditions, and in 1944 100,000 struck for better wages.

But if the war brought new employment opportunities, it also brought terror. While no other part of the United Kingdom experienced the sustained bombing of the London Blitz, the urban areas of Wales also suffered attacks. Cardiff in South Wales was first bombed in June 1940; by the end of the war, more than 30,000 houses in the city had been destroyed and 355 civilians had been killed. On three successive nights in February, the Luftwaffe dropped more than 30,000 bombs on the city of Swansea, destroying more than half of the city center and killing 227 people. In total, almost a thousand Welsh civilians died as a result of bombing attacks during the Second World War.

In general, Welsh people responded to the call to arms with equal patriotism to their English counterparts, though many saw themselves as fighting for Wales as well as for Britain. The strong tradition of evangelical Nonconformism in Wales, however, made pacifism more prevalent there than it was elsewhere in the United Kingdom. Some Welsh nationalists, meanwhile, did not want to fight in a British cause. The nationalist party Plaid Cymru declared its opposition to the war, and some of its more extreme members hoped for a German victory. In consequence, its activities during the war were monitored by the British Secret Service. The British government tried, however, not to inflame Welsh nationalism and thereby undermine Welsh support for the war. A few Welshmen were allowed to claim the status of conscientious objectors due to their nationalist convictions, though some of them were imprisoned.

Scotland, as well, experienced the war in distinctive ways. Britain relied heavily on Glasgow's Clydeside industries to build ships and munitions. This made the city into a target; in March 1941, two nights of bombing attacks, later termed the "Clydebank Blitz," killed 538 civilians and left almost 50,000 people homeless. As in England, however, morale generally held. "The cool, unwavering courage of the people is evident," observed the *Glasgow Herald*, "and when the full story of their heroism in the face of the Luftwaffe is told, they will take their place alongside the citizens of London and Coventry." Other Scottish cities, including Edinburgh, Aberdeen and Dundee, were also bombed, and by the end of the war, 2250 Scottish civilians had died in bombing raids. The intensity of the bombing required the evacuation of thousands of Scottish children from urban areas. Though a few were sent overseas, most remained within Scotland and were sent to homes in the Highlands or other rural areas. Some English children, as well, were evacuated to rural Scotland.

Scotland's geographic position in the far north of Britain caused it to experience the war in unique ways. Its relative isolation made it an attractive location for both airfields and prisoner-of-war camps, as well as for secret training facilities that were used to prepare commandos for raids on the coast of continental Europe. Some of the most remote areas of the Highlands were requisitioned for military purposes, and entire villages were evacuated in order to preserve secrecy. British intelligence services combined with the Norwegian government-in-exile to form a clandestine organization based in the Shetland Islands that delivered aid to the Norwegian resistance. Called the "Shetland Bus," the group used small vessels disguised as fishing boats to ferry nearly 200 agents and 400 tons of weapons and supplies to Norway. As it had done in the First World War, the Royal Navy used Scapa Flow in the Orkney Islands as its main naval base, primarily because it was out of the range of most German aircraft. "Blockships" were sunk to prevent U-boats from entering the harbor, and cable nets were strung across its entrances. These defenses proved inadequate, however, and on the 14th of October 1939, U-47 sank the battleship H.M.S. *Royal Oak* as it lay at anchor. A total of 833 British servicemen were killed.

During the war, Scotland was not defended by Scottish or even British troops but by Poles. Scotland had been left bereft of troops after the 51st Highland Division had surrendered during the fighting in France, and so the Poles were deployed as a deterrent against a German invasion of Britain via Norway. The Poles had no barracks and were forced to spend their first winter living in tents and Nissen huts. The remnants of the Polish Navy, meanwhile, were based at Greenock on the west coast, where they served as escorts for Atlantic convoys and later assisted with troop landings on the continent. After the war, some Polish ex-servicemen chose to remain in Scotland. They found, however, that the same people who had welcomed them during the war now wanted them to leave. Led by the trade unions, a "Poles Go Home" campaign claimed that Polish immigrants threatened to take jobs away from Scottish workers. This was effective in keeping the Poles out of industrial employment, but many did find jobs in agriculture, teaching and other fields. Some married Scottish women and even changed their surnames in order to better assimilate to their new home.

In Scotland, as in Wales, some nationalists opposed participation in the war. The Scottish National Party (SNP) leader Douglas Young argued that the terms of the Act of Union of 1707 prohibited conscription from being introduced in Scotland. When he refused to register for conscription or as a conscientious objector, he was imprisoned for twelve months. The homes of several other SNP leaders were searched by the police due to their links with the Scottish Neutrality League, a pacifist organization that was suspected of German sympathies. One, Arthur Donaldson, was arrested and imprisoned for six weeks, until petitions to the secretary of state for Scotland compelled his release. Donaldson's activities during the war remain controversial. Documents that were released by MI5 in 2001 claimed that he was actively working to set up a Vichy-style collaborationist regime in Scotland, as he saw it as a means of achieving a break with England. The SNP's present-day leaders, however, adamantly deny that Donaldson had any such plans and attribute the reports to the wartime paranoia of British intelligence.

In other ways, however, war, as it had done since the eighteenth century, brought Scotland more closely into the Union. The secretary of state for Scotland, Tom Johnston, convinced Churchill to allow him to form a Council of State comprised of his predecessors as Scottish secretary. This both increased administrative efficiency and convinced the Scottish public that their national interests were being attended to. Johnston was able to institute a far-reaching hydroelectric power scheme in the Highlands, to bring important wartime industries to Scotland and to enact a wide range of educational and social welfare legislation. On a personal level, he sympathized with the cause of Home Rule for Scotland, but his efforts at the Scottish Office were crucial in outlining a significant role for the British state in postwar Scotland's economy and society.

Northern Ireland, too, played an important part in the war. Over 100,000 British troops were stationed there in 1940, and between 1942 and 1944 120,000 American soldiers arrived in preparation for the D-Day landings. As in Wales and Scotland, the war stimulated industry in Northern Ireland. In the first half of 1939, over £6 million in government contracts were received for military supplies and equipment. The Harland and Wolff shipyard in Belfast produced tonnage exclusively for the Royal Navy during the war. Between 1939 and 1945, over 700 warships were built in Belfast, and 1000 more were repaired. As was the case for other industrial areas, this productivity attracted the attention of the Luftwaffe. In March and April of 1941, Northern Ireland suffered two devastating series of air raids. On the 15th of April, 1100 people in Belfast were killed, the highest single-night death toll suffered by any city in the United Kingdom outside of London. The damage was exacerbated by the fact that the authorities had not expected the Germans to bomb Northern Ireland, and so there were few anti-aircraft defenses in place.

The sense of shared danger from German bombing and a rise in living standards helped, temporarily at least, to submerge differences between nationalist Catholics and Unionist Protestants, though Northern Ireland was the only part of the United Kingdom where conscription was never introduced, for fear of alienating nationalists. Political divisions did not entirely disappear, however, as the war effort was complicated by the partition of the island of Ireland. After the fall of France in June 1940, German U-boats could be based on the southwestern coast of France, thereby extending their range to the west and south. This meant that Britain's Atlantic convoys had to be rerouted from their normal routes around the south

Figure 11.8 An "Éire" sign on Capel Island in County Cork on the south coast of Ireland. Eighty-three such signs were built near coastal Lookout Posts in order to signal to combatant aircraft that they were over neutral Ireland.

Reproduced courtesy of Shutterstock/D. Ribeiro.

coast of Ireland and instead sent around the north coast of Ireland through the North Channel that separates northeastern Ireland from southern Scotland. A base was needed for these convoys that lay as far west as possible, and Londonderry in Northern Ireland was the best option. The River Foyle and Lough Foyle that led out to sea from Londonderry, however, lay along the border with Éire (today the Republic of Ireland), which, as we will see later, was neutral. The British feared that using the waterway without permission from the Éire government would inflame the opinions of Irish nationalists not only in Éire and Northern Ireland, but also in America. Historical research by British legal experts, however, determined that the border between Éire and Northern Ireland lay on the north side of the waterways. The British therefore decided that they were not violating Éire's sovereignty by using them, and as Éire never objected to their actions, they continued to do so for the remainder of the war.

While Northern Ireland was an important part of the British war effort, the rest of Ireland's experience of war was very different. Though it was officially still part of the British Empire, Éire remained neutral in the war. In 1938, the British had returned the three ports (Berehaven, Queenstown and Lough Swilly) that they had retained after the creation of the Irish Free State in 1921, and the Irish government denied access to them after the outbreak of the war. In the summer of 1940, when a German invasion of Britain seemed likely, Churchill offered to relinquish British claims to Northern Ireland in return for Irish participation in the war. This offer was rejected by the Irish government, in large part because it seemed to expose Éire to attack by Nazi Germany at a time when British victory in the war seemed unlikely. In practice, however, Irish neutrality leaned towards the Allies. British pilots forced to parachute to safety in Ireland were discreetly returned to Britain, whereas German pilots were interned for the duration of the war. The Irish authorities arrested suspected German agents and shared intelligence with the British. When the dissident Irish Republican Army attempted to collaborate with Nazi Germany, hundreds of its members were detained by the Éire government. Close to 50,000 Irish men and women voluntarily enlisted in the British Army during the war, and thousands more immigrated to Britain to work in war industries.

The Empire at War

In the summer of 1940, the American journalist Ben Robertson described Britain as "the island fortress that was guarded by the Empire." Robertson's observation reflected the fact that Britain relied heavily on the support of its colonies. Australia's declaration of war on Germany immediately followed Britain's, and almost a million Australians fought for the Allies in the European and Pacific theaters. About 27,000 Australians were killed, another 23,000 were wounded and 29,000 were taken prisoner, mostly by the Japanese. A third of the latter group died, many from malnutrition and disease while working as forced labor on the Burma Railway. Canada, too, quickly followed Britain into war. Over a million Canadians fought for the Allies, and by war's end Canada possessed the world's fourth-largest air force and third-largest naval fleet. Some 42,000 Canadians lost their lives in the conflict.

But if the war in some ways brought Britain and the dominions closer together by enlisting them in a common cause, its long-term effects pushed them farther apart. The British did little to protect Australia when it was threatened by a Japanese invasion and its northern city of Darwin was subjected to bombing raids. As a result, many Australians felt abandoned, as the British focused their attention on the defense of the United Kingdom and the war in Europe. This helped to spur the development of a more independent foreign policy by the Australian government. The war also accelerated the growth of industry in Australia, making it less dependent on British manufactured goods and leaving it with a booming postwar economy. In Canada, meanwhile, the war helped to foster unity between French and Anglo-Canadians. Though French Canadians volunteered in significantly lower numbers than their Anglo-Canadian counterparts did, when conscription was introduced in 1944 there was less opposition to it in Quebec than there had been in the First World War. In a broader sense, Canada, like Australia, emerged from the war with its status as an independent country enhanced.

The Second World War also had a major impact on India. Most Indian nationalists, including Mohandas Gandhi, had supported the British war effort in the First World War. Their response to the Second World War, however, was dramatically different. In 1939, the viceroy of India, Lord Linlithgow, declared India to be at war with Germany without consulting Indian nationalist leaders. Two months later, a number of these leaders resigned from the provincial government posts to which they had been elected in the wake of the Government of India Act of 1935. Their actions compelled Britain to rule India under emergency legislation. The viceroy's action underscored what was to become a key issue for many Indians – as well as for other Asians, Africans and Afro-Caribbeans – during the war. While Britain claimed to be fighting a "People's War" in support of freedom and democracy, these ideals did not seem to apply to the peoples of the British Empire.

The British were not unaware of this issue. In an attempt to enlist support for the war effort, they offered concessions to Indian nationalists. Sir Stafford Cripps, a leading Labour politician, was dispatched to India in April 1942 with an offer of independence following the end of the war. This offer, however, appeared less generous as Britain's military position in Asia deteriorated. In February 1942, the supposedly impregnable garrison at Singapore fell to the Japanese, and over 100,000 British and Commonwealth troops surrendered. The British Empire in Asia no longer looked invincible, and the Congress Party rejected Cripps's offer. Gandhi referred to the promise of postwar independence as "a postdated cheque on a failing bank."

Declaring "we shall either free India or die in the attempt," Gandhi convinced the Indian National Congress to launch the last of his nationwide civil disobedience campaigns, the Quit India movement, which began in August 1942. Gandhi and the other Congress leaders were immediately arrested and imprisoned. Quit India was intended to be a nonviolent campaign, but the arrests left local leaders in charge, and many of them interpreted Gandhi's call to "do or die" as an endorsement of violence. Quit India became the greatest internal threat to British rule in India since the Indian Rebellion of 1857, as nationalists attacked police and government offices and cut telegraph lines. Colonial authorities responded with military force, which included the deployment of more than fifty battalions of British troops. By the end of 1942, more than 60,000 Indian men and women had been arrested.

The detention of the leadership of the Indian National Congress opened political space for what would emerge as one of the most important political movements in postwar India, the Muslim League. Established in 1906, the League had long remained a small organization; in the 1937 election, it garnered less than 5 percent of the Muslim vote. By the late 1930s, however, the League had swelled to 2 million members, and it was pressing for a homeland for India's Muslims. It called this land "Palestein," meaning "the land of the pure," and it encompassed territory in both the northwest and northeast of India, the two regions where Muslims constituted a majority. The Muslim League's leader, Mohammad Ali Jinnah, did not necessarily intend to create an independent Muslim state, but he wanted to ensure that Muslims would be equal players in the negotiations that would determine the shape of post-independence India. British officials responded positively to the League's growing popularity among Indian Muslims. Colonial officials thought of India as an aggregate of many religions, castes and ethnicities that were held together only by the British Raj. Given their difficulties with the Indian National Congress, the British were eager to enlist the support of India's Muslims for the war effort.

In the fall of 1942, a cyclone devastated rice crops in the northeastern province of Bengal, leading to a famine. Wartime decisions made by British and colonial authorities exacerbated the situation: rice imports from Burma were cut off by the Japanese advance in 1942, and rice supplies were removed from coastal regions of Bengal in order to prevent them from falling into the hands of the enemy. The Government of India prioritized the supply of food to urban locations that were seen as more essential to the war effort, which left many people in rural areas to starve. The British government in London, meanwhile, prioritized the supply of food for the home front and the British Army above relief for India. In consequence, as many as 3 million people starved to death in Bengal.

 See document "The Effect of the Second World War on India" at www.routledge. com/cw/barczewski.

In spite of growing nationalism, however, India fulfilled its longstanding role as a source of military manpower for the British Empire. The Indian Army swelled to 2.5 million men, eclipsing the British Army in the First World War as the largest all-volunteer army in history. It suffered over 100,000 casualties, and its soldiers won thirty-one Victoria Crosses. There was, however, a difference from the past use of Indian troops: for the first time, the British government agreed to pay for the use of Indian military forces in the defense of the Empire. Indian troops were evacuated from Dunkirk, where they were praised by their British counterparts for their discipline amidst the chaos. In September 1940, when the Royal Air Force desperately needed pilots due to the losses it had sustained in the Battle of Britain, twenty-four pilots from the Indian Air Force were sent to Britain. The Indian Army went on to play an important role in the North African campaign and carried out important garrison duties in Southeast Asia. After the fall of Singapore, over 60,000 Indian soldiers were taken prisoner by the Japanese. Disillusioned by the collapse of British leadership, a third of them chose to join the Indian National Army (INA), which later fought on the side of the Japanese against British and Indian troops in Burma.

Also in 1940, a group of West Indian pilots was recruited to help cover the losses in the Battle of Britain. By the end of the war, 16,000 men from the Caribbean had fought for the British. They were joined by over a million Africans, both white and black. For non-white soldiers to serve in British forces, however, the color bar stating that only "British subjects of pure European descent" could join had to be temporarily lifted. It was removed permanently in 1948, though some elite regiments such as the Household Cavalry refused to admit black soldiers until the 1960s. In 1961, an Army document declared, "the strength of the British Army has always depended on the reliability of the individual soldier. The reliability of colored soldiers is not certain and therefore too great a dilution of British units would be dangerous." It was not until 1988 that a black soldier was finally allowed to participate in the Changing of the Guard at Buckingham Palace.

Victory

Although both Germany and Japan were clearly on the defensive by the end of 1943, bringing them to the point of surrender required taking the war to their respective homelands. In the Pacific, the Allies slowly and painfully retook the territory that the Japanese had occupied. In April 1945, they reached the Japanese island of Okinawa, only 340 miles from mainland Japan. In Europe, the Italian offensive continued to stall, but the Soviet Red Army steadily pushed German forces out of Russia. In Europe, meanwhile, the British and the Americans were finally ready to launch their invasion of France in the summer of 1944. Operation Overlord, the name given to the invasion of Normandy on the north-western French coast, was a colossal undertaking involving 2 million British, American, Canadian, Free French, and Polish troops. In the run-up to the launch of the amphibious assault on *D-Day*, the 6th of June 1944, the RAF and the American Air Force secured air superiority over northern France, and British and American intelligence agencies executed a clever operation to deceive the Germans about where the landings would occur. Dummy armies, including inflatable tanks and wooden airplanes, were set up around southern England to trick German aerial reconnaissance. The ruse worked, and for several days after the first landings in Normandy, the German high command remained convinced that a second landing was planned further up the French coast. They held back their armor reserves in consequence, allowing the landings to succeed, though they were still difficult and bloody.

Two beaches, codenamed Gold and Sword, were assigned to British forces; two, Utah and Omaha, to the Americans; and one, Juno, to the Canadians. These beachheads provided a foothold for the vast amount of troops and equipment needed to liberate France and ultimately to invade Germany. The logistics of the operation had been meticulously worked out over the course of the previous year. Within days of the landing, two British-built floating harbors were towed across the Channel and moored on the French coast, which enabled allied ships to unload their cargo directly onto the beaches. A pipeline was laid from England to France under the Channel to provide the vast amount of fuel needed for allied vehicles.

Over the course of the next year, British and American troops pushed east, liberating France, Belgium and the Netherlands in succession. On the Eastern Front, the Russians pushed the Germans into Poland and towards Germany's eastern border. By March 1945, the fighting was in Germany itself, and Berlin fell to the Russians in late April. Germany's

Figures 11.9 and 11.10   On the left, Gurkha soldiers from Nepal fight in the British Army in the North African campaign in July 1942. On the right is the British military cemetery at Kandy in Sri Lanka. Of the 203 soldiers who are interred there, 107 are British, thirty-seven are East African, twenty-six are Sri Lankan, twenty-three are Indian and six are Canadian, showing the contribution of Britain's colonies to the war effort.

Figure 11.9 reproduced courtesy of the National Museum of the US Navy; Figure 11.10 reproduced courtesy of Shutterstock/saiko3p.

unconditional surrender soon followed, celebrated by the Allies as VE (Victory in Europe) Day on the 8th of May 1945. The war in the Pacific continued until August, when the United States dropped two atomic bombs on the Japanese cities of Hiroshima and Nagasaki. *Japan sued for peace* on the 15th of August, which became known as VJ (Victory over Japan) Day. The Second World War was over.

Conclusion

For Britain, the consequences of victory were wrenching, long-lasting and ultimately far more transformational than those of the First World War. The 295,000 soldiers who were killed in combat represented only about 40 percent of the total from the First World War, but civilian casualties added another 60,000 dead. Many British cities were devastated by bombing damage, and the government had exhausted all of Britain's capital reserves and borrowed huge sums from the Commonwealth and the Americans. Britain's national debt soared from about £500 million at the start of the war to over £3.5 billion at its end. The war also led to major changes for the British Empire. Lend-Lease assistance had come with pressure from the Americans for decolonization, especially for India. India had supplied 2.5 million troops to aid the British war effort, but much of the subcontinent had become virtually ungovernable by the end of the war. Indian nationalist leaders sensed that Britain's international and economic position had been fundamentally weakened. As we will see in a future chapter, India attained independence only two years after the war's conclusion. Most of the rest of Britain's colonies followed over the next two decades. The speed of postwar **decolonization** reflects that the prestige Britain earned as the only major western state to resist German aggression from the very beginning of the war to its conclusion was not reflected in its international political stature after the war. Churchill assumed that Britain would be one of the "Big Three" global powers, alongside the United States and the Soviet Union. By the end of the war, however, there were only two "superpowers," with Britain reduced to a secondary role in the emerging Cold War between them.

In July 1945, the first British general election in ten years was held. The result was an *outright majority for the Labour Party*, the first in its history. Polling nearly 12 million votes (48 percent of the total number cast), Labour won a massive majority of 145 seats in the House of Commons. While opinion polls throughout the war had indicated a consistent swing towards Labour, many people were surprised by the scale of the Conservatives' defeat. This was not a vote against Churchill as a wartime leader, but a vote for Labour's promise to enact a wide-ranging social welfare program. The voters for Labour wanted to build a new world, not merely return to the same one that had existed before the war.

Bibliography

Allport, Alan, *Britain at Bay: The Epic Story of the Second World War 1938–1941* (2020)

Brooke, Stephen, *Labour's War* (1992)

Calder, Angus, *The Myth of the Blitz* (1991)

Edgerton, David, *Britain's War Machine: Weapons, Resources and Experts in the Second World War* (2012)

Feigel, Laura, *The Love-charm of Bombs: Restless Lives in the Second World War* (2013)

Fisk, Robert, *In Time of War: Ireland, Ulster, and the Price of Neutrality, 1939–1945* (1985)

Gardner, Juliet, *Wartime: Britain, 1939–1945* (2005)

Grayzel, Susan, *At Home and Under Fire: Air Raids and Culture in Britain from the Great War to the Blitz* (2012)

Hastings, Max, *Winston's War: Churchill, 1940–1945* (2010)

Lukacs, John, *Five Days in London: May 1940* (1999)

Mukerjee, Madhusree, *Churchill's Secret War: The British Empire and the Ravaging of India during World War II* (2010)

Nicholson, Virginia, *Millions Like Us: Women's Lives During the Second World War* (2012)

Overy, Richard, *The Battle of Britain: Myth and Reality* (2010)

Overy, Richard, *Blood and Ruins: The Great Imperial War, 1931–1945* (2021)

Ponting, Clive, *1940: Myth and Reality* (1990)

Rose, Sonya, *Which People's War? National Identity and Citizenship in Wartime Britain 1939–1945* (2003)

Royle, Trevor, *A Time of Tyrants: Scotland and the Second World War* (2012)

Todman, Daniel, *Britain's War, Volume I: Into Battle 1937–1941* (2016) and Volume II: *A New World 1942–1947* (2020)

12 "Let Us Face the Future"
The Postwar Era

Topics covered

- Postwar welfare state
- Transition from austerity to a consumer economy
- Cultural transformation of the 1960s
- Consensus politics
- The "Troubles" in Northern Ireland
- Economic difficulties of the 1970s
- Social issues in the 1970s

Timeline

1945	Labour victory in general election
1953	Coronation of Queen Elizabeth II
1954	Food rationing ends
1961	Britain's application to the European Economic Community (EEC) rejected
1969	British troops sent to Northern Ireland
1971	Collapse of Bretton Woods system of currency exchange
1972	First of major mining strikes leads to power cuts
1972	Bloody Sunday in Northern Irish city of Derry
1973	Britain enters EEC
1976	Britain negotiates loan from International Monetary Fund
1978	Referendums on devolution of government in Wales and Scotland fail
1978	"Winter of discontent" begins
1979	Conservative victory in general election

Introduction

The state of Britain in the early 1950s was symbolized by the *coronation of Queen Elizabeth II* on the 2nd of June 1953. Though it included traditional elements such as the anointing of the sovereign with consecrated oil, it was not an archaic ritual but rather a thoroughly modern event that was intended to foster mass support for the monarchy. More than 8000 guests attended the ceremony at Westminster Abbey, but more significantly, 20 million

DOI: 10.4324/9781003284758-12

British people watched it live on television. Another 11 million listened on the radio; in total, these viewers and listeners comprised five out of six people living in Britain at the time. This was not only the first time that a coronation had been shown, but also for many British people, as they gathered in the homes of their neighbors to watch, the first time that they had ever watched television at all. The coronation was broadcast in forty-four different languages, demonstrating that the British monarchy had become a truly global institution.

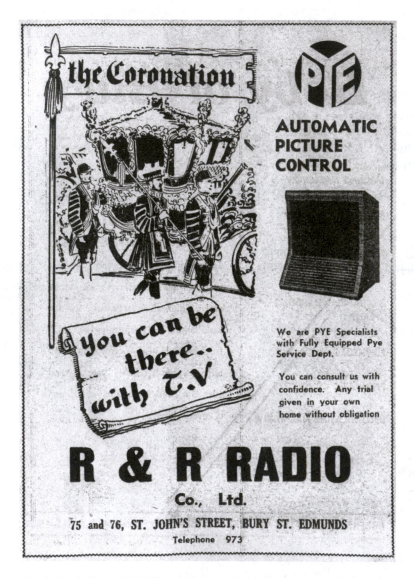

Figure 12.1 On the 2nd of June 1953, Queen Elizabeth II's coronation became the first time that the full ceremony in which a British monarch was crowned was shown in live television. Twenty million people watched, almost double the number who listened on the radio. On a website celebrating its hundredth anniversary in 2022, the BBC declared, "the event that did more than any other to make television a mainstream medium."

Reproduced courtesy of Karen Roe.

The coronation's message about the state of the British nation was complex. On the one hand, it reflected the optimism that many Britons felt in the early 1950s. The young queen declared, "my coronation is not the symbol of a power and a splendor that are gone but a declaration of our hopes for the future." Commentators hailed the dawning of a "new Elizabethan age" that would rival its sixteenth-century predecessor in terms of national glory and achievement. That morning, the news reached Britain that Edmund Hillary and Tenzing Norgay had made the first successful ascent of Mount Everest. The BBC announced, "the ascent of Mount Everest by British climbers is a victory worthy to resound through history." But although the expedition of which they were a part was British-led, neither Hillary nor Tenzing was in fact "British." The former was from New Zealand, while the latter was a Sherpa who had been born in Nepal but had lived in India and considered himself a resident of both nations; he waved the flags of Britain, Nepal and India from Everest's summit.

Alongside the conquest of Everest, the coronation itself also reflected the changes that had come to postwar Britain. David Cannadine writes that the increasingly elaborate royal ceremonies of the second half of the twentieth century were less a "re-opening of the theater of power" and more "the premiere of the cavalcade of impotence." Since *rationing remained in effect*, applications to follow tradition and roast an ox in the new monarch's honor had to be approved by the Ministry of Food. Eighty-two were granted, but only to places that could prove that they had roasted an ox on previous coronations. The coronation also hinted at growing tensions within the United Kingdom. Three years earlier, Scottish nationalists had stolen the Stone of Scone, which was used in ceremonies crowning the monarchs of Scotland from the tenth century until it was seized by King Edward I in 1296, from its place under the Coronation Chair in Westminster Abbey. The stone was recovered four months later and was back in place in time for Elizabeth II's coronation, but the fact that the British authorities declined to prosecute the thieves for fear of further inflaming Scottish nationalist opinion was telling. Finally, the coronation presaged the post-imperial, multicultural Britain that would emerge by the late twentieth century. The dish that was invented to feed the guests at Buckingham Palace after the ceremony, a cold chicken salad in curry mayonnaise, demonstrated the increasing influence of the Empire on British cuisine and culture. Called "Coronation Chicken," it remains popular in Britain today.

The Welfare State and Its Limits

After 1945, the *newly elected Labour government* moved swiftly to enact the bold legislative program laid out in their pre-election manifesto "Let Us Face the Future." This was a huge task, as Britain grappled with crippling foreign debt, growing nationalist resistance around the Empire and an uncertain international situation. With full employment and increased exports of manufactured goods as its primary objectives, Labour set about rebuilding the economy using a mixed approach of nationalizing industries in key areas, while allowing the free market to operate elsewhere. They also set about systematizing and improving health and social welfare provisions along the lines advocated by the Beveridge Report in 1942. Despite the budgetary constraints, much was accomplished in the immediate postwar period. Building on the piecemeal welfare provisions that had been enacted in Britain since the turn of the century, the Labour government under Clement Attlee attempted to establish a welfare safety net for all British citizens.

 See document "A Vision for the Welfare State" at www.routledge.com/cw/barczewski.

Two key elements of the new slate of programs built on existing legislation. Apart from raising the school-leaving age to fifteen, Labour left alone the 1944 Education Act, which had established a system of free, meritocratic secondary schools. It also kept the 1945 Family Allowances Act, which granted a payment of five shillings a week to mothers for each child after the eldest, up to the age of eighteen. Beyond those existing acts, however, Labour extended the interwar policy of subsidizing municipal authorities in the building of government-owned homes (known as "**council housing**") that would be made available for cheaper rents than on the open market. Housing was sorely needed, as the war had destroyed or seriously damaged a significant portion of the nation's stock. In 1945, it was estimated that about 3 million new homes were needed. More than 1.25 million homes were built between 1945 and 1951, but alleviating the shortage of housing would continue to be a major political issue for governments into the 1960s.

Other Labour initiatives, however, were more innovative. In 1946, the government passed the National Insurance Act, which created a single comprehensive social security program and increased the existing unemployment, sickness and old-age benefits to a uniform level. Labour sought to diminish class divisions and reduce the stigma attached to state support by making its welfare provisions available to everyone regardless of their income. This was not fiscally possible, however, and so when the government passed the National Assistance

Figure 12.2 Prefabricated houses, or "prefabs," were a key part of efforts to address Britain's housing shortage after the Second World War. Passed by Winston Churchill's Conservative government, the Housing (Temporary Accommodation) Act of 1944 called for the construction of 300,000 prefabs within ten years of the end of the war, although ultimately only around 150,000 were built. There were a number of designs; these houses in south Birmingham are Phoenix prefabs, which utilized a steel frame clad with aluminum.

Reproduced courtesy of Oosoom.

Program in 1948, which replaced the hated Poor Law of 1834, the aid it provided was means-tested and gender-based. Entitlements were seen through the lens of traditional family norms, with a male breadwinner making contributions to the national insurance scheme through his employment. Thus, the social security scheme actually reinforced female economic dependency, as the right to benefits for married women who did not work outside the home depended on their husbands' contributions. Family allowances similarly reinforced women's traditional roles as unpaid wives and mothers.

The most far-reaching of the welfare programs introduced by Labour was the National Health Service (NHS), which was launched in 1948. For the first time, healthcare was incorporated into a national system, based on need rather than the ability to pay. Large segments of the population who previously had limited or no access to healthcare were brought into the system. (As a concession to the British Medical Association, which represented the doctors who fought the measure tooth and nail, private health care continued for those who wished to pay for it.) The NHS was the crowning achievement of Labour's social policies. It was designed to promote social justice and equality and to provide all Britons with access to an optimal level of healthcare as a right. British health standards improved markedly, and life expectancy at birth rose by five years over the following two decades. General approval of the NHS, however, coexisted with growing anxiety about its costs and efficiency. Excessive bureaucracy, geographical disparities, lengthy wait times and low employee morale developed over time. Moreover, improvements in average standards of health were more pronounced in other European countries in this period. Nor did the NHS fully achieve its goal of reducing social inequality: the major beneficiaries were generally those in the middle-income brackets, rather than the poor.

Although Labour's social programs sought to eliminate poverty and reduce inequality, significant disparities remained a defining feature of postwar Britain. Poverty is a relative measure of deprivation from societal norms, so what was perceived as poverty during the affluent 1960s was very different from its definition in the depressed 1930s. Even so, studies found that in 1960 about 7.5 million people (14.2 percent of the population) were living below the poverty line. This was not due to a lack of government attention. Social security exceeded the defense budget as the most expensive item of government expenditure for the first time in the mid-1960s. Welfare payments continued to grow over the next decade, reaching a staggering 55 percent of all government spending in 1977. Even so, high numbers of people continued to live below the poverty line.

Why? Postwar British governments attempted to use the taxation system to redistribute wealth. Top income earners paid extremely high rates of tax; in 1974, the top rate was increased to 83 percent on income over £20,000. Over time, however, the tax burden came to fall more heavily on lower income brackets. This was particularly true after the implementation of the Value Added Tax (VAT), a 10 percent national sales tax, by the Conservatives in 1973. In addition, inflation reduced the lowest threshold at which income tax became payable. By the mid-1970s, some families had to pay income tax even though their earnings were below the official poverty line. Thus, even in the heyday of the welfare state, the tax system only marginally redistributed income and primarily benefited middle-income earners rather than the poor.

Another form of economic inequality related to gender. By 1980, women made up 40 percent of the workforce, but they earned less pay per hour than men. In 1970, the Equal Pay Act sought to establish equal pay rates for men and women for equivalent work, but industry compliance was voluntary until 1975 and was frequently evaded by various means thereafter. Women's rates of pay did rise steadily after the passage of the act, but in the late

1970s women's wages still averaged only 70 percent of those of men. Women were also shut out of more lucrative occupations. In the 1981 census, three-quarters of working women were employed in just four of sixteen fields: personal services; clerical positions; health, welfare and education; and sales. Amongst the highest-paying professions, meanwhile, women made up only 1 percent of engineers, 3 percent of surgeons, 22 percent of general-practice doctors and 21 percent of lawyers.

Inequalities also persisted in the educational system. A cornerstone of Labour's policies was that education would become more meritocratic and would therefore promote social mobility. In the early 1960s, however, only 11 percent of working-class children made it into grammar schools, the most prestigious state schools, even though they made up almost 70 percent of the population. In the 1960s, the system of determining at age eleven which children were suited to go on to university was largely abandoned, and "comprehensive" secondary schools for all children regardless of their intellectual abilities were established. This new system proved somewhat more effective in overcoming the social barriers to higher education. In the 1930s, only 1.7 percent of all eighteen-year-olds went on to a university; by 1967, that percentage had grown to 6.3 percent. This was still, however, far below the 20 percent who went to college in the United States. Only 3.1 percent of British university students, meanwhile, were from working-class families.

Managing and Reconstructing the Economy

In 1945, Britain was broke. It had lost an estimated £7 billion in capital, investments and resources during the war. Its exports in 1946 were less than a third of prewar levels, and the government had accumulated more than £3 billion in external debts. Much of that debt was created by the American decision to end the Lend-Lease program a month after the war ended. The United States wrote off the wartime balance of $650 million, but British industry was not yet ready to shift to peacetime production, and Britain found itself in desperate need of food and other vital supplies. Lacking the funds to purchase them, the British were forced to take out a $3.75 billion loan from the Americans, with another $1.19 billion coming from Canada. Repayment occurred in fifty installments; the final payment of $83.3 million was not made until 2006.

Another problem for Britain related to the postwar financial system that had been created to rebuild international economies after 1945. At a conference at Bretton Woods in New Hampshire in 1944, delegates from all forty-four Allied nations agreed to peg the value of their currencies to the American dollar. This was intended to create global economic stability, but it led to a situation in which the participating countries could not simply put more money into circulation in the event of a budgetary shortfall, because this would decrease the value of their currency relative to the dollar. A country that was running a budget or trade deficit therefore could simply run out of money. The British faced this threat repeatedly over the next two decades, as their manufactured goods became increasingly uncompetitive in international markets and rising consumer demand resulted in increasing imports. This created a growing "balance of payments deficit," which meant that a much smaller amount of money in payment for British goods was coming into the country than the amount of money to pay for imports that was going out.

The British government thus faced a variety of economic challenges in the postwar era that made the funds necessary for the construction of the new welfare state hard to come by. Its solution was to maintain as close to full employment as possible, thereby ensuring a robust tax base and minimizing the number of people requiring benefit payments. To ensure a steady supply of jobs, a number of ideas were adopted in order to smooth out the boom and bust cycles of the economy. First, food rationing and price and import controls were all retained after the war. This was due partly to the difficulties of paying for foreign imports, but also to Labour's belief that during the period of reconstruction there should be "fair shares" for all. The austerity that resulted was grim: the minimum caloric intake provided by rationing was reduced to 2650 calories from its wartime standard of 3000. In 1947, when Britain suffered the coldest winter in decades, there were severe coal shortages. During the purportedly morale-boosting exercise of hosting the first Olympic Games after the war in London in 1948, there were difficulties in feeding and housing the athletes, which caused the event to be labeled the "austerity games."

The government also used its planning powers to ration key materials such as building supplies so that they could be used for factory reconstruction. Regional economic policies were pursued that aimed to foster industrial employment in depressed areas such as the North of England, South Wales, and Clydeside in Scotland. Another planning tool used by Attlee's government was the nationalization of key industries and economic institutions, including the Bank of England, civil aviation, the nascent telecommunication industry, coal mines, rail and long-distance road transport, the gas and electrical industries, and iron and steel production. Generous compensation, totaling £2.6 billon, was paid to their former owners. By 1951, about 20 percent of economic activity in Britain was owned by the state.

Six years after the end of the war, Britons were weary of seemingly endless austerity, and in the election of 1951, the Conservatives, still led by seventy-seven-year-old Winston Churchill, returned to power with a slim majority. The burden of austerity had fallen disproportionately on women, who usually managed rationing in the family, and a significant number of them voted Conservative due to their promises to begin a return to normal economic conditions. It is a measure of the popularity of the welfare programs that Labour had introduced, however, that the Conservative governments of the 1950s and 1960s made no attempt to scale them back. Postwar Conservative leaders recognized the claims of the "People's War," and they understood that they risked permanent removal from power if they tried to unstitch the new social safety net. Their embrace of this consensus allowed them to remain in power until 1964.

For decades after the war the Conservative and Labour parties agreed on two basic issues. First, they agreed that the welfare state that had been created in the late 1940s was to be maintained. Second, they agreed that full employment and a mixed economy in which there was at least some degree of government intervention would remain the cornerstones of economic policy. Recent historical research, however, has reduced the areas of policy in which there was a real meeting of the minds between the two parties, and emphasized that there were many internal disagreements within them about what course to follow. Consensus should thus not be thought of as agreement between the parties about what programs and policies should be pursued, but rather as a working compromise that was dependent on the social and economic conditions of the time. There was, for example, clear disagreement between the two parties on the universalism of the welfare state. Labour generally wanted to eliminate means-testing so as to preserve cross-class unity, while the Conservatives wanted benefits to be targeted at only those in need. There was also disagreement on economic policy. The pursuance of full employment required the Conservatives to display a less antagonistic attitude towards trade unions than in the past. They also wanted less state ownership than did Labour, and thus for example moved to denationalize the steel industry in 1952. One of the most divisive of all consensus-era social policies was housing. Conservatives viewed the rights of private property as sacrosanct, while Labour saw them as potentially damaging to the economic interests of the working class. In some ways, the only real area of postwar consensus was in foreign policy. The Conservatives and Labour agreed that Britain should support the Commonwealth, move towards decolonization, oppose Soviet communism, retain membership in the North Atlantic Treaty Organization (NATO) and develop its own nuclear capability. Both parties were hostile to British involvement in European unification, which began via the European Defence Community in 1950, and both supported the "special relationship" with the United States.

The Conservatives benefited from a period of economic growth, subsequently dubbed the "age of affluence." Between 1951 and 1973, the British economy grew at an average annual rate of 2.4 percent. This impressive performance was matched by low unemployment figures. While in the interwar years unemployment had averaged over 12 percent, between 1951 and 1973 it was barely 2 percent. To be sure, these figures concealed substantial regional differences, as unemployment rates were lower in southeastern England than in other parts of the United Kingdom. In 1965, for example, when the average rate of unemployment for all of Britain was 1.4 percent, it was 1 percent in the South and Midlands of England, but three times higher in Scotland and six times higher in Northern Ireland.

Low unemployment caused wages to rise, leading to better standards of living. Even taking inflation into account, the average male manufacturing worker saw his real wages double between 1950 and 1973, while the work week declined from 47.5 hours to 44.5 hours. Women's rates of pay, meanwhile, increased in absolute terms, but they fell further behind men relatively. Women working full time in industry earned, on average, 62 percent of a male worker's wages in 1950 and only 59 percent in 1970. For most people, Britain's new affluence was measured by what they could now afford to own. While less than a third of households owned their homes in 1950, by 1973 more than half did. Over the same period, car ownership increased from 4.6 percent of the population to 24.7 percent. The number of households with refrigerators increased from 3.2 percent to 68 percent, washing machines from 7.5 percent to 66.9 percent, and televisions from 2 percent to 90 percent. These new domestic luxuries led to new patterns of living. For many working-class people, the home rather than the community (i.e., the street, neighborhood or pub) became the primary focus of life outside of work.

Although the economy grew in absolute terms, observers worried about Britain's relatively poor economic performance compared to its international competitors. In the 1950s and 1960s, Britain's growth was less than half of West Germany's and less than a third of Japan's. Britain's share of global manufacturing diminished from 25 percent in 1950 to less than 10 percent in 1975. Some economists blamed government economic policies for this poor performance. The **Keynesian** economic thinking that dominated the postwar era was predicated on the notion that high levels of inflation would be accompanied by low levels of unemployment. Consequently, in an effort to keep employment rates high, successive governments sought to stimulate the economy by a combination of state spending and tax reductions aimed at encouraging private investment. Yet, as companies hired more workers, the resulting labor shortage pushed wages up, which was then spent on imported consumer goods, hurting the balance of trade and inflating domestic prices. Once inflation and the trade deficit rose, the government tried to dampen the economy through credit restrictions and tax increases. As inflation cooled and imports declined, unemployment would start to rise again, so the government returned to inflationary spending and tax cuts.

This cycle of government-led inflation and deflation of the economy came to be known as "stop-go." By the late 1960s, the stop-go cycle was blamed for Britain's faltering economy. This conclusion is dubious, however, as other European economies pursued similar policies and experienced similar, if not larger, fluctuations over the same period. Even so, they enjoyed greater overall growth. Britain's long-term economic difficulties were rooted not in stop-go, but in its overreliance on undercapitalized industrial employment and low levels of productivity (i.e., the amount produced per worker). The postwar Labour government had tried to finance economic and social reconstruction through the export of manufactured products, the same source of British industrial expansion in the nineteenth century. By 1955, manufacturing accounted for almost half of all paychecks, the highest level in British history. But these impressive levels of industrial employment were not matched by investments in productivity or innovation, and were only possible because the other industrial economies of Europe had been decimated by the war. Over the next quarter-century, the percentage of people working in industry dropped steadily, as Britain faced increased competition from recovering economies. By 1973, the manufacturing sector employed less than a third of the workforce.

Even with increased competition, Britain might have suffered a lesser degree of industrial decline had its productivity been higher. Two reasons have been suggested for why it was not. First, the level of domestic investment was low, as much of the available capital in the 1950s and 1960s went overseas. This was often because British business tended not to embrace the aggressive new practices found in other economies, especially in America. Britain's early industrial success was here a disadvantage, as a disinclination to tamper with what had worked in the past discouraged innovation. Larger businesses tended to be led by a small clique of university graduates from the upper sectors of society. Coined in the late 1950s, the term "the Establishment" signified the entrenched attitudes of an "old boys" network that dominated government, business and the major civil and cultural institutions. Second, Britain's economy suffered from chronically poor industrial relations, as the unions and management constantly blamed each other for low productivity and growth. Every dispute, no matter how trivial, escalated due to long-simmering class tensions. Managers were frequently socially isolated from their workforce and dismissive of their complaints. The unions, meanwhile, sought to make economic gains for their members in the "go" phases of the cycle and to defend those gains in the "stop" phases. As these demands were made regardless of whether workers' productivity justified the raises, the resulting inflationary wage and price spiral added to the competitive disadvantage of British industry.

A good example of the long-term problems of British industry was automobile manufacturing. Prior to the Second World War, dozens of companies produced cars in Britain, and some continued to be successful into the early 1960s. Rolls-Royce, Jaguar and Aston Martin remained global leaders in luxury vehicles, and in 1959 the British Motor Corporation, a merger of the manufacturers Austin and Morris, produced the iconic Mini Cooper. British automobile production peaked in 1973 at almost 2 million vehicles annually. But over the next several decades, British automotive production declined sharply. By the 1980s, fewer than 900,000 cars were being produced per year. The last British-owned mass-manufacturer, the Rover Group, was sold to BMW in 1994.

For a time, however, these problems were papered over by a boom in consumer spending, which in political terms most benefited the Conservatives. In 1957, Harold Macmillan became prime minister. He seemed to embody a new spirit of British conservatism. Despite his pedigree as the son of a wealthy publisher, his experience as a junior officer during the First World War and as an MP for a northern constituency that had suffered high unemployment during the depression had led him to rebel against Conservative orthodoxy. He concluded that capitalism required regulation and advocated for a mixed economy based on both private enterprise and state intervention in his book *The Middle Way* (1938). He cemented his reputation as an advocate of the new mass consumer as minster of housing in the early 1950s, when he oversaw the building of 300,000 houses annually. Macmillan concentrated on raising living standards by making credit easier to obtain and by stimulating the economy through low taxes. The result was higher real wages and a consumer boom. Home ownership increased; foreign holidays became more popular; and automobile ownership nearly doubled between 1955 and 1960. Famously, in a 1957 speech Macmillan told the nation that it had "never had it so good." The consumer boom, however, fostered inflation and another series of balance of payments crises, which ultimately forced Macmillan to apply the "stop" phase of the stop-go cycle. His "middle way" thus failed to break the cycle of economic uncertainty that plagued Britain after 1945.

Domestic economic problems helped to determine Macmillan's foreign policy. By the mid-1950s, Britain's trade with Europe was on the rise, while that with its colonies and the Commonwealth was declining. After an internal audit revealed the costs of maintaining its remaining colonies, Macmillan steered Britain towards rapid decolonization, as will be discussed in the next chapter. Beyond the Empire, neither the "special relationship" with the United States nor Britain's possession of its own nuclear weapons seemed likely to ensure that the British would have a major influence on world affairs. One remedy was to turn away from a crumbling empire towards the European Economic Community (EEC). Many politicians distrusted the idea of a European supranational organization, as they feared that British sovereignty would be compromised. Some younger political leaders, however, felt that the reluctance of Britain to participate actively in European affairs after 1945 had been a mistake. They carried the day, and in 1961, despite fierce opposition from within his own party, Macmillan *applied for British membership in the EEC*. That application, however, was vetoed by the French president Charles de Gaulle, who worried that Britain's entry would bring with it unwelcome American influence. It was certainly the case that Macmillan was primarily interested in increasing Britain's prestige and in transforming the European alliance into a transatlantic partnership, not in being a good European citizen. But even though the reasons for it were in some ways legitimate, the rejection was another postwar humiliation for Britain.

By the early 1960s, the popularity of the Conservative government was declining. Macmillan resigned in 1963 and was replaced by Alec Douglas-Home, but the change of leadership did not alter the overall political climate, and the following year Labour returned to power for the first time in thirteen years. The new prime minister, Harold Wilson, was immediately confronted by a huge balance of payments deficit. To deal with this problem, he followed deflationary policies to curb domestic demand for imported goods. These policies reduced the deficit, but at the cost of killing economic growth. The only alternative was to devalue the currency – a cheaper pound would make British exports more competitive on the international market – but this was politically unpopular. In order to avoid devaluation, Wilson needed American help, but President Lyndon Johnson's price for bailing out sterling was British support for America's military intervention in Vietnam. Although the left wing of the Labour Party was vehemently opposed to the rapidly escalating war, Wilson's government refused to condemn it, once again demonstrating the subordination of Britain's international position to America's.

Wilson's strategy succeeded in shoring up sterling for the time being, and Labour won another election in 1966 with an increased majority. But this was only a temporary expedient: the balance of payments deficit simply built up again, and America would only continue to bail out sterling if Britain sent ground troops to Vietnam. Wilson knew that such a move would bring down his government, and he was thus finally forced to devalue the currency in 1967. The government hoped that increased sales of exports would stimulate manufacturing and create jobs at home, but the action was vehemently criticized by the Tories and even by many prominent Labour politicians, including the chancellor of the Exchequer, James Callaghan, who resigned in protest. The following year, the government announced the withdrawal of Britain's military presence "east of Aden" (that is, in Asia east of the Persian Gulf). This left the United States as the sole western power in the region and clearly demonstrated that Britain's days as a global power had come to an end.

Cultural Change

As postwar austerity gave way to increased consumer spending, it also allowed for major transformations in the lifestyles of ordinary people, as they enjoyed higher incomes, more leisure time and greater access to a wider variety of goods. Young people in particular had more leisure time and more money to spend, and their extra income was spent on products that helped to distinguish them from the rest of society. Discontented with the drabness and tedium of postwar Britain, some young people chose to participate in subcultures that challenged social conventions. These subcultures included the Rockers, who embraced American popular culture by listening to rock and roll music, wearing leather jackets and motorcycle boots and styling their hair in elaborate pompadours. Another youth group was the Mods, short for "Modernists," who rode Vespa scooters, wore expensive Italian suits and featured hairstyles that imitated the French movie stars of the era. Musically, the Mods favored rhythm and blues, soul, beat music and **ska**, a genre brought to Britain by Caribbean immigrants. The rivalry between Mods and Rockers went beyond fashion and musical taste. In the early 1960s, they clashed violently on the beaches of several seaside resorts in the south of England. The British public was sufficiently alarmed for the sociologist Stanley Cohen to coin the term "moral panic" in his examination of the sensationalist media coverage of the conflicts. Cohen argued that such fights between young men were nothing new, but the shrill tone of the press turned the Mods and Rockers into symbols of delinquency and deviance.

The Mods reflected a change in the tastes of British youth, who were moving away from an obsession with American music and fashion. A key factor in this change was the British Invasion, which saw British bands come to dominate popular music around the world. The British Invasion began in 1962 when the Beatles, four working-class lads from Liverpool, had their first hit with "Love Me Do." By 1964, they were a global cultural phenomenon, and they were soon joined by other British bands, including the Rolling Stones, the Who and the Kinks. In the first week of May 1965, nine of the top ten singles on the American charts were by British acts.

Demonstrating that Britain had finally recovered from the war, the British Invasion, along with increasing economic prosperity, gave rise to a new cultural confidence that quickly spread beyond music. Both the Mods and the British Invasion were closely identified with "Swinging London," a term that was first used in a *Time* magazine cover story in 1966 but was inspired by a comment made by Diana Vreeland, the editor of *Vogue* magazine, who observed, "London is the most swinging city in the world at the moment." Shopping districts such as Carnaby Street in the West End and the King's Road in Chelsea were filled with British youth flaunting new styles. In 1962, the mini-skirt was introduced by the designer Mary Quant. Over the next several years, as hemlines got progressively shorter, it became a symbol of young women's liberation from staid conventions.

Figure 12.3 Carnaby Street, the epicenter of "Swinging London," in 1968.
Reproduced courtesy of H. Grobe.

Britain's newfound cultural vibrancy extended beyond London. Literature was given a new energy by the "Angry Young Men" movement, a label that was derived from John Osborne's play *Look Back in Anger* (1956). Osborne and other authors such as Kingsley Amis, John Braine, Alan Sillitoe and Shelagh Delaney (not all of the Angry Young Men were male) attacked what they saw as Britain's complacency and stifling social mores. The supposedly malign influence of the Establishment also engendered a boom in political satire in the early 1960s. Founded in 1961, the satirical magazine *Private Eye* skewered the social and political elite, and the following year the hit television series *That Was the Week That Was* depicted the nation's leaders as comically hapless and out of touch.

British cinema, too, benefited from a closer focus on social issues. In the late 1950s, there was a move away from adventure and war films towards more realistic and relevant subjects. Films such as *Room at the Top* (1959), *Saturday Night and Sunday Morning* (1960) and *The Loneliness of the Long Distance Runner* (1962) were gritty dramas based on fiction by the Angry Young Men. The male protagonists, usually from the working class, chafed against the social hierarchy while they drank, swore and engaged in promiscuous behavior. These films became known as "kitchen sink dramas" because of their settings in cramped working-class homes and grimy, smoke-filled pubs, often located in locales in the North of England that had suffered badly from postwar industrial decline. Not all British films focused on social criticism, however. Some of the most popular films of the era were entries in the slapstick *Carry On* series, thirty examples of which appeared from 1958 onwards. Beginning with *Dr. No* in 1962, Ian Fleming's popular James Bond novels were turned into the most successful film franchise of all time. In the novels, Bond was a serious Cold War warrior, but in the movies he was transformed into a playboy who fit perfectly with the increasing materialism and sexual permissiveness of the era.

Television, too, flourished. By the end of the 1960s, Britons watched more than twenty hours a week per person, more than any other European country. The British Broadcasting Corporation (BBC) lost its monopoly when the commercially run ITV was founded in 1955; within five years, the new network boasted the ten most-watched British programs. This revived fears of excessive American influence over British culture, and in 1962 a new public channel, BBC 2, was launched. It was devoted to "serious" topics, and ITV was also required to provide space for educational programming on its schedule. Ironically, this left BBC 1 able to experiment with more popular programming. Two influential examples were the gentle satire of *Dad's Army* (1968–77), which followed the misadventures of a fictional Home Guard unit during the Second World War, and *Till Death Do Us Part* (1966–75), which satirized contemporary "Little Englander" xenophobia via the cockney anti-hero Alf Garnett.

By the end of the 1960s, many people felt that traditional values were retreating in the face of social liberation; whether they welcomed or feared this depended on their age and perspective. The laws relating to obscenity in print had been relaxed as a result of the 1960 trial over *Lady Chatterley's Lover*, the novel by D.H. Lawrence that had been banned in Britain since its publication in 1928. The censorship of the theater was eliminated in 1968, just in time for nude hippies to appear on the London stage in the musical *Hair*. But it was the year 1967 that was arguably the highpoint of government-led sexual reform in the second half of the twentieth century. In that year abortion was made available to women, if not on demand, at least on a more secure legal footing for those who were less than twenty-eight weeks pregnant. The Labour government also empowered the National Health Service for the first time to provide contraceptive advice to all women regardless of their marital status through the National Health Service (Family Planning) Act.

Sexuality and Gender 6

The Wolfenden Report

Published in 1957, the Wolfenden Report marked an important step in decriminalizing male homosexuality in Britain. The earliest legal restrictions on sexual acts between men were imposed by the Buggery Act of 1533, and such acts remained punishable by death until 1861. The last executions for homosexuality occurred in 1835. After the Second World War, the British government intensified its prosecutions of gay men; in 1952 alone, there were 670 prosecutions for sodomy and 1686 for gross indecency. This surge in prosecutions, however, led to increased public scrutiny of the laws prohibiting homosexual acts and ultimately to a determination that it was time to re-examine them to see whether they were effective. A committee chaired by Sir John Wolfenden was established for this purpose in 1954. Why had the government suddenly proved willing to re-examine the laws? There were two main reasons. First, there were concerns that homosexual members of the military and civil service might be blackmailed by the Russians, who would threaten them with revealing their sexuality and thus subject them not only to embarrassment but also potentially to criminal prosecution. These concerns became particularly acute after the "Cambridge Five," a ring of spies that passed information to the Soviet Union from the 1930s to the 1950s, was discovered. Two of the five spies were gay, and there was speculation that they had been coerced into giving state secrets to the Soviets. Second, several high-profile men were caught committing homosexual acts in the 1950s. They included the actor John Gielgud and the 3rd Baron Montagu of Beaulieu, who was arrested for gross indecency on two occasions and spent a year in prison in consequence. Montagu's case aroused considerable sympathy from the British public, and it played a significant role in pushing the government to set up the Wolfenden Committee. The committee conducted dozens of interviews over a period of three years; while it was sitting Wolfenden found out that his son was gay. The report concluded, "homosexual behaviour between consenting adults in private should no longer be considered a criminal offence." The government, however, initially rejected the report's findings; it had expected the committee to recommend that the laws regarding homosexuality should be tightened, not repealed altogether. It took another decade before male homosexuality was decriminalized in Britain in 1967.

Private homosexual acts between consenting adults were decriminalized, although the age of consent for homosexuals was set at twenty-one, as opposed to sixteen for heterosexuals. Moreover, this last legislation did not apply in Scotland and Northern Ireland, where the strength of evangelical Protestantism ensured continued political opposition. In 1969, divorce was made available on the grounds of the breakdown of a marriage; a cause such as adultery or cruelty was no longer required. These changes to the legal frameworks around sexuality and marriage became the hallmarks of the claim, welcomed in some quarters and criticized in others, that Britain had become a "permissive society." Traditional morals did not immediately or entirely disappear, however. Publicly discussing sex was still viewed as shocking by most Britons, and the contraceptive pill, available in Britain from the mid-1960s onwards, was not widely used for another decade.

The Troubles in Northern Ireland

Born from the strife of the struggle for Irish independence in the early 1920s, Northern Ireland saw its Protestant and Catholic populations coexist uneasily, but relatively peacefully, for the next half-century. The Protestant majority, which comprised two-thirds of the population, tended to identify themselves as British, while the Catholic minority perceived themselves as Irish. Aided by the drawing of electoral boundaries that favored Unionist candidates, Protestants dominated local government. Catholics were also discriminated against in other ways: council housing was allotted disproportionately to Protestants, and Protestant areas received more government investment. Catholics were frequently harassed by the police, and they were rarely appointed to civil-service jobs. These tensions were exacerbated in the 1960s, when the Northern Irish economy, which was dependent on heavy industries such as shipbuilding, declined precipitously alongside the rest of the United Kingdom's industrial base.

In 1966, there were two important fiftieth anniversaries: that of the Easter Rising, which was a touchstone for Catholics, and that of the Battle of the Somme, which served the same purpose for Protestants. This caused tensions to boil over, and by the late spring of that year disorder was rampant. This was the beginning of over two decades of sectarian violence and bloodshed that would become known as "the Troubles." There were attempts, however, to enact change nonviolently. In 1967, Catholics founded the Northern Ireland Civil Rights Association (NICRA), which agitated peacefully for full citizenship rights for their community using techniques imported from the American civil-rights movement. But in the city of Derry in 1968, a protest march was violently dispersed by the Protestant-dominated Royal Ulster Constabulary (RUC). The resulting outcry forced the British government to intervene, and over the next year a number of reforms would be suggested. These efforts culminated in the "Downing Street Declaration," a communiqué issued jointly by the British and Northern Irish governments that called for an end to discrimination.

Though in an effort to satisfy Protestants the declaration had confirmed that Northern Ireland would remain part of the United Kingdom, it led to a backlash from hardline Unionists that was spearheaded by the fundamentalist Presbyterian preacher Ian Paisley. By now, there were paramilitary groups acting lawlessly and violently on both sides of the sectarian divide. The Irish Republican Army (IRA), which had largely become dormant by the early 1960s, had thus far remained quiescent, but in 1969 a more militant "Provisional" IRA broke off from the mainstream group. Unionists, meanwhile, formed the Ulster Volunteer Force (UVF), which carried out its own program of violence and reprisal. With the violence escalating rapidly, in 1969 the *British government sent in the Army.* The troops were initially welcomed by Catholics, who saw them as protectors, but they rapidly came to be seen as enforcers of the unsatisfactory status quo. This was confirmed in 1972, when in what came to be known as *"Bloody Sunday,"* British soldiers killed fourteen protestors in Londonderry (known as "Derry" to its Catholic population) who were peacefully marching for increased civil rights for Catholics. A British government inquiry, the results of which were published in 2010, confirmed that the protestors were unarmed and that the British troops had "lost control" of the situation, in several cases fatally shooting people who were fleeing or who were trying to help those who had been wounded.

 See document "The British Government Apologizes for Bloody Sunday" at www.routledge.com/cw/barczewski.

After Bloody Sunday, the British Army was regarded with hostility by Ulster's Catholics, and they were targeted by IRA bombs. The IRA's bombing campaign also crossed the Irish Sea to London and other major British cities. In 1974, twenty-six people were killed and more than 200 injured in pub bombings in the English cities of Guildford and Birmingham. Also in the wake of Bloody Sunday, the British government escalated their intervention into Northern Ireland by introducing "direct rule" from London and by dissolving the Northern Irish Parliament, known as "Stormont" because it met in Stormont Castle outside Belfast. After a failed attempt to establish a new assembly and an executive council in which power was shared between Protestants and Catholics, direct rule lasted for the next twenty-five years. In the short term, increased British intervention did little to stem the violence, and 496 people were killed in 1972, the highest total for any year during the Troubles. The next decade would see a variety of peace initiatives, none of which succeeded. The seemingly unsolvable Northern Irish problem would remain at the center of British politics for another quarter-century.

Figure 12.4 A "peace line" or "peace wall" in Belfast separating Catholic and Protestant neighbor-hoods. The first peace lines were built in 1969 at the start of the Troubles; today, there are forty-eight in Belfast and other Northern Irish cities, stretching for a total of over 20 miles. In recent years, as the peace process has taken hold, there have been discussions about removing them, but a survey in 2012 revealed that 69 percent of people in Belfast believed that they were still necessary.

Reproduced courtesy of Sonse.

Britain in the 1970s

In 1977, the punk-rock band the Sex Pistols released a single called "God Save the Queen," a deliberately provocative reference to the national anthem. The timing of the song's release was clearly intended to cause outrage. This was the year of the Silver Jubilee, the twenty-fifth anniversary of Queen Elizabeth II's accession to the throne, which was marked by celebrations across the country. "God Save the Queen" was banned from the radio by the government, but this did not prevent it from reaching the top of the charts, where it was listed as a black rectangle rather than by name. Media pundits seized upon the song's success as a sign of the state of Britain in the 1970s.

Today, the 1970s are remembered as a decade of crisis. A combination of high inflation, low levels of productivity and rising unemployment led to the coining of a new term: "stagflation." Public spending far outstripped revenue, and in 1976 the Labour government was humiliated by having to *negotiate a $3.9 billion loan*, the largest in its history, from the International Monetary Fund. Because the terms of the loan imposed restrictions on spending, Labour was forced to abandon one of its core principles: the commitment to full employment. Without government stimulus, unemployment doubled between 1975 and 1977. Spending on welfare programs was decreased, as were public sector wages, which in the context of the double-digit inflation amounted to a significant cut in real earnings for many people.

At the beginning of the decade, however, there had been some basis for economic optimism. After returning to power in 1970, the Conservatives inherited a healthy budget surplus. Long committed to joining the EEC, Prime Minister Edward Heath was successful in *securing British admission* on its third application in 1973, primarily because France now viewed Britain as a potential counterweight to an increasingly dominant West Germany.

 See document "Britain Contemplates Entry into the European Common Market" at www.routledge.com/cw/barczewski.

In 1971, the currency was modernized through decimalization. Previously the pound had consisted of twenty shillings, with twelve pence in each shilling; now, there were a hundred pence in a pound. But Conservative policies proved unable to alter the structural problems that had plagued the British economy throughout the postwar era. In an effort to address rising unemployment, the budget of 1972 adopted a policy of "reflation," or an increase in the money supply. This stimulus did heat up the economy, but it also generated a familiar problem: inflation, which the government proved unable to control through efforts to limit increases in prices and incomes. In 1975, inflation reached the unprecedented level of 25 percent.

The government's attempts to curb wage increases brought it into conflict with the trade unions, which fought back using strikes. In 1972, 23 million working days were lost to strikes, more than any year since the General Strike of 1926. The National Union of Miners (NUM) was particularly militant. It developed a system of coordinated "flying pickets" in which strikers set up roadblocks outside coal distribution centers, thereby severely disrupting the movement of coal to where it was needed. As Britain was still heavily dependent upon coal for electrical generation, a national crisis ensued. The government was forced to declare a state of emergency and to impose a *three-day work week* in order to conserve coal. In February 1974, Heath went to the polls in an effort to gain public support to tackle industrial militancy. This proved a miscalculation. There was widespread sympathy for the unions, as almost two-thirds of British men and a third of women belonged to one. Labour won the most seats, though not a sufficient number to secure an outright majority. Eight months later, a second election confirmed the result, as Labour increased its total to 319 seats, enough for a slim four-seat majority.

One of the first tasks of new Labour government was dealing with unrest within the party itself, notably about Britain's entry into the EEC. Many within the Labour Party distrusted the EEC and feared it would stymie domestic social initiatives. Prime Minister Harold Wilson thus arranged for a national referendum on the issue of EEC membership held in 1975. The result confirmed the public's acceptance of membership by a two-to-one margin, which quelled Labour opposition to the EEC if not backbencher criticism. The referendum was perhaps more significant as a precedent. Although more limited referenda had been previously held in local communities, this was the first use of a national referendum in British history, and it sat in awkward tension with parliamentary sovereignty as it had evolved since 1688. That principle held that whatever satisfied a majority in both of the Houses of Parliament became law and could be changed or rescinded by a subsequent parliament. Consequently, referenda within a parliamentary system could only ever be advisory and not automatically binding, nor could referenda forever settle an issue. But the very act of sending an important question to be voted on directly by the people brought with it justifiable expectations that the democratic will of the people would be followed. This tension between the representative democracy embodied by Parliament and the direct democracy of referenda would increase over the subsequent decades as a number of difficult national political questions were also put to referendums.

One such question was the place of Scotland and Wales within the United Kingdom. In the second election of 1974, the Scottish National Party (SNP) increased its share of the vote in Scotland to 30 percent. The growing support for the SNP north of the border was indicative of how Britain's economic problems led to a powerful surge in nationalist sentiment in the 1970s. For most of the twentieth century, Scottish and Welsh identities had been expressed predominantly in cultural terms, while political nationalism made little headway. After 1945, the popularity of the welfare state provisions, improved regional planning and rising affluence further diminished demands from Scotland and Wales for greater autonomy. But by the 1960s, industrial decline in both countries was spurring nationalist sentiment, boosting the popularity of the SNP and the Welsh nationalist party Plaid Cymru. In Scotland, the economic growth rate was only half that of the rest of Britain. By the late 1960s, some Scottish nationalists were calling for independence, a goal now thought realistic because of the discovery of oil off the North Sea coast. Nationalism was further fueled when the revenues from the oil fields were treated as British by the Westminster government rather than as Scottish.

The rise of nationalist parties in both Wales and Scotland in the 1960s and 1970s led to demands for Home Rule, or complete control over domestic affairs. In response, the Labour government proposed a policy of limited devolution, in which elected assemblies would be granted to both nations. Harold Wilson resorted again to referendums, this time to gauge the depth of public demands for devolution. Not only would the pro-devolution side have to win the vote with an outright majority, but also at least 40 percent of the total Scottish and Welsh electorate regardless of the percentage who participated in the referendum would have to vote in favor of devolution before it would go into effect. When the referendums were held in 1978, they *both failed to get the requisite support*. In Wales, the English-speaking population, who were worried that a Welsh assembly would be dominated by nationalists, voted overwhelmingly against devolution or did not vote at all. Only 12 percent of eligible voters supported the measure. In Scotland, there was anger that Wilson's bill did not give the country control over the North Sea oil, and although a majority of those who voted supported devolution, only 33 percent of the total electorate voted yes. As a result, devolution was shelved for the next two decades.

Devolution was far from the only issue that caused conflict within the Labour Party. The rank-and-file of the party had moved to the left of its leaders and was pushing for unilateral nuclear disarmament, the abolition of the House of Lords and more nationalization of industry. Amongst the Conservatives as well, internal revolt was brewing. Many people on the party's right were dissatisfied with Heath's reflationary policies and Keynesian-style economic intervention, as well as with his electoral failure in 1974. They demanded a leadership contest, which was surprisingly won by Margaret Thatcher, the first woman to lead a major British political party. From the party's right wing, Thatcher argued for an end to a mixed economy and the welfare state.

For now, however, it was the Labour government that had to contend with Britain's economic difficulties, in particular union demands for wage hikes, as inflation continued to cut into real earnings. Over the *"winter of discontent"* in 1978–9, a number of unions went on strike, paralyzing public services. As uncollected garbage piled up on the streets of Britain's cities, Labour's chance of re-election diminished. To be sure, strikes were hardly unique to Britain, and the industrial relations record of the United States in the 1970s was worse. In 1978 and 1979, more days were lost to sickness and accidents in Britain than to strikes, and 98 percent of private companies experienced no work disruptions at all. Even so, the perception that the government was powerless to control either the unions or the economy led the Conservatives to a *narrow electoral victory* in 1979. Recession, rising unemployment and runaway inflation were seen by a significant portion of the electorate as a failure of the Keynesian consensus that had existed since 1945. The Conservatives took full advantage of the discontent, and after 1979 they would attempt to chart a new direction for British politics and society.

While the persistent sense of crisis about the economy dominated political discussions, socially and culturally, the 1970s saw as much change as the 1960s. In particular, second-wave feminist activists called for easier access to abortion and birth control, as earlier concerns about women's rights in relation to suffrage, motherhood and the family were supplanted by calls for full equality. They sought to defend the gains of the late 1960s and engage in consciousness-raising campaigns around continuing discrimination facing women and those whose sexuality was perceived outside of traditional norms.

There were good reasons for keeping up the pressure for reform: over the course of the 1970s and 1980s, abortion rights came under sustained attack from Conservatives using private members' bills. The first effort came less than two years after the 1967 Abortion Act was passed, and there were subsequent attempts to restrict abortion that were debated in Parliament in 1975, 1977, 1979 and 1989. Parliamentary defenders of these rights tended to be found within the Labour Party, although Labour was divided on the issue. But pushed by activists within and beyond its ranks, Labour governments in the 1970s attempted to address gender inequalities in the workplace through the Equal Pay Act of 1970 and the Sex Discrimination Act of 1975, with only limited success.

A gay rights movement also developed in the early 1970s, with the short-lived Gay Liberation Front being perhaps the most famous activist group. In addition to addressing the social stigma towards gays and lesbians that was prevalent in British society, the main priorities of the gay liberation movement were the equalization of the age of consent, removing sanctions against gays and lesbians in the military and bringing Scotland and Ireland into line with the English law of 1967. There were some successes. Scotland legalized homosexual acts in 1980, and decriminalization in Northern Ireland occurred in 1982 after a European Court of Human Rights case on the issue. But for most of the 1980s, despite slowly growing acceptance of homosexuality in society, gay activists found themselves fighting a rear-guard action to defend their community's rights against a Conservative government that demonized them and against the misperception among many Britons that AIDS was a "gay plague." The women's and gay rights movements of the 1970s reflected the beginning of a broader change in British society, not fully realized until the twenty-first century, in which individual identities rather than traditional class, sexual and gender norms came to be prioritized by a wide swath of society.

British culture evolved in significant ways in the 1970s. In music, British artists continued to have an outsize influence on global trends. Rock musicians acquired both more respectability and greater notoriety in the 1970s, as excessive drug use and the destruction of hotel rooms regularly featured in the news, while some high-profile musicians, like the Rolling Stones, moved to other countries in order to avoid the high rates of taxation of the super-rich in Britain. But there was substantial musical innovation too. The end of the 1960s had seen the musical experimentation of psychedelia, which morphed into "progressive rock." Over the next decade, some of the most influential bands in this genre, such as Pink Floyd, Yes and Genesis, stressed innovative musicianship and elaborate live performances. The perceived self-indulgence of "prog rock" would help lead to the backlash that produced punk at the end of the decade.

At the same time, Led Zeppelin became the most famous rock band of the decade, pushing blues-inspired music toward a more intense and harder-edged sound that was dubbed "heavy metal." The music of the bands who embraced that label, who included Black Sabbath and Judas Priest, tended to be apolitical, focusing on themes that appealed to their mostly young male audiences such as love, sex and fantasy. Glam rock, however, was more directly tied to the changing mores around gender and sexuality. The key figures here were David Bowie and Marc Bolan of the band T-Rex, who presented stage personas that emphasized androgyny and ambiguous sexuality.

Conclusion

The three decades that followed the end of the Second World War comprised a complex period for Britain, with significant social and cultural change taking place against a background of growing economic problems. Though the establishment of the welfare state provided a solid social safety net and postwar austerity gave way to increased affluence for many people, this was in general a period of economic pain. The rapid decline of British industry was the main factor in a sharp decrease in the country's global competitiveness, and the former "workshop of the world" found itself with a massive balance of payments deficit. These problems gave rise to tensions over the meaning of Britishness, as Scottish and Welsh nationalists voiced louder demands for independence. The 1970s would be remembered as a difficult decade that was characterized by failed attempts to curb rising inflation and unemployment and by labor militancy that frequently paralyzed the country. At the same time, major social advances were achieved through both government legislation and direct activism. Culturally, Britain continued to have an outsized influence on the world, while by the end of this era individual identities were increasingly coming to be defined in new ways. Britain's continuing decline as a global power, however, would be further demonstrated by the rapid disintegration of the British Empire between the late 1940s and the mid-1960s. In less than two decades, as we will see in the next chapter, an empire that had taken over 300 years to be built was almost completely dismantled.

Bibliography

Beckett, Andy, *When the Lights Went Out: What Really Happened to Britain in the Seventies* (2010)
Bew, John, *Citizen Clem: A Biography of Attlee* (2016)
Black, Lawrence, *Redefining British Politics: Culture, Consumerism and Participation 1954–70* (2010)
Black, Lawrence and Hugh Pemberton, *An Affluent Society: Britain's "Golden Age" Revisited* (2004)
Brooke, Stephen, *Sexual Politics* (2011)
Donnelly, Mark, *Sixties Britain* (2005)
Dutton, David, *British Politics Since 1945: The Rise, Fall and Rebirth of Consensus* (1997)
Edgerton, David, *The Rise and Fall of the British Nation: A Twentieth-Century History* (2019)
Fielding, Stephen, *Labour: Decline and Renewal* (1995)
Fielding, Stephen, Peter Thompson, Nick Tiratsoo, *England Arise! The Labour Party and Popular Politics in the 1940s* (1995)
Marwick, Arthur, *British Society since 1945* (2003)
Morgan, Kenneth, *Britain since 1945: The People's Peace* (2001)
Turner, Alwyn W., *Crisis? What Crisis? Britain in the 1970s* (2008)
Turner, Alwyn W., *Glam Rock: Dandies in the Underworld* (2013)
Weight, Richard, *Mod: A Very British Style* (2013)

13 The Postwar Empire

Topics covered

- Independence and partition in South Asia
- Reconstruction of the postwar Commonwealth
- Nationalism and counterinsurgency
- Suez crisis and the increased pace of decolonization after 1960
- "New Commonwealth" immigration to the United Kingdom

Timeline

1947	Independence of India and Pakistan
1948	Independence of Burma and Ceylon
1948	Republic of Ireland declared
1948	*Empire Windrush* arrives in England
1952	Emergency in Kenya begins
1956	Suez crisis
1957	Independence of Ghana (the Gold Coast)
1961	South Africa leaves the Commonwealth
1962	Commonwealth Immigrants Act
1963	Kenyan independence
1968	Enoch Powell's "Rivers of Blood" speech

Introduction

The Second World War had a dramatically different impact on the British Empire than on the United Kingdom. While the war in many ways unified Britain, it contributed to the dissolution of the Empire. Humiliating defeats at Japanese hands undermined the prestige and authority of colonial rule in Asia. The military situation grew so dire that it compelled the British to do something that would have been unthinkable prior to the war: offer independence to India. And even though Britain ultimately was on the victorious side, the postwar era would see rapid decolonization that not only transformed the British Empire, but also impacted society and culture in Britain itself. In the two decades following the war, the population under British rule decreased from 700 million people to only 5 million, while men and women from the Empire increasingly came to settle in Britain.

DOI: 10.4324/9781003284758-13

This chapter will examine the causes, patterns and impact of postwar decolonization. It occurred in three broad phases: the achievement of independence by India and other Asian colonies in the late 1940s; the independence of African and West Indian colonies in the 1950s and 1960s; and the achievement of independence by other British colonies and possessions after the 1960s. But although decolonization occurred quickly, the British did not surrender their empire passively. Instead, they sought to reconstruct it as a source of power and prestige in a postwar world that was dominated by the two superpowers of the United States and the Soviet Union. This process was marked by the high ideals of the British Commonwealth of Nations, but also by the brutal violence on the part of colonial authorities who sought to maintain British control; the idea of a peaceful and orderly British withdrawal from empire is largely a myth. Lastly, this chapter will explore important aspects of empire's impact on life in Britain, which continues to this day.

Independence and Partition in South Asia

The British Empire had always depended on the cooperation of colonized peoples. Following the upheavals of the Second World War, however, the loyalty of the Indian population could no longer be taken for granted. The rise of nationalist sentiment was illustrated when three soldiers from the Indian National Army, which had fought on the Japanese side against the British, were tried for treason in Delhi in the fall of 1945. The men attracted a huge amount of popular support, and many prominent politicians joined their defense team. While the three were found guilty and sentenced to life imprisonment, the public outcry was so great that they were simply expelled from the army and released. In February 1946, a mutiny in the Indian Navy spread to seventy-eight ships and encompassed 20,000 sailors, a further sign that the loyalty of the armed forces, the foundation of British rule in India, was rapidly decreasing.

In the spring of 1946, in what was called the Cabinet Mission, a delegation of Labour Party ministers traveled to India to negotiate the colony's independence. Their complex solution preserved Indian unity through a transfer of power to a single successor state, while its federated system of three tiers of provinces attempted to satisfy the Muslim League's demand for a Muslim "nation" within India. Muhammed Ali Jinnah and the Muslim League approved the proposal, but the Congress Party, now led by Jawaharlal Nehru, refused to accept it. The Congress leaders were concerned that the central government would be too weak and that they would be unable to implement their ambitious plans for an independent India, which included a state-controlled economy and massive industrial development. In response to Congress's rejection of the Cabinet Mission Plan, Jinnah and the Muslim League announced a "Direct Action Day" for the 16th of August 1946. Intended as a day of demonstrations in favor of a Muslim homeland called Pakistan among Indian Muslims, it instead highlighted the escalating tensions between Hindus and Muslims and hinted at the violence that would accompany the transfer of power. In what became known as the "Great Calcutta Killing," over 8000 Hindus and Muslims died and thousands more were injured in four days of rioting and sectarian violence. Thousands also died in violence elsewhere in India.

By the end of 1946, the British Raj had only a tenuous grasp on power in the subcontinent. Towards the end of the war Congress's leaders, including Nehru and Mohandas Gandhi, had been released from prison, and elections were held for provincial legislations in 1945 and 1946. The Congress gained control of local governments in eight of India's eleven provinces, but the elections also confirmed that the Muslim League was now a political force, as it won 75 percent of the Muslim vote. "Pakistan" was still a vague concept, but the idea of a Muslim homeland was gaining in appeal for Indian Muslims, who feared the domination of the predominantly Hindu Congress Party in post-independence India.

As the British moved towards the granting of independence, the provincial governments were charged with electing representatives to a national Constituent Assembly. Showing its dominance of Indian politics, Congress won 70 percent of the seats. The viceroy's Executive Council functioned as the executive branch in this new government, with Nehru, the Council's vice-president serving as prime minister rather than the viceroy. Believing that a policy of cooperation better suited their interests, Congress leaders did not call for a renewed uprising against the British, but even so sectarian violence continued to increase. The viceroy, Lord Wavell, advised the government in London that he could not envision the British continuing to rule India for much longer, unless the government was willing to commit substantial British military forces to secure the Raj.

 See document "The Impact of Indian Independence on the British Commonwealth" at www.routledge.com/cw/barczewski.

In early 1947 Prime Minister Clement Attlee decided to replace Wavell with the man who would be the final viceroy of British India: Lord Louis Mountbatten. Mountbatten was an unusual choice for a Labour government as their chief representative in the most important part of the British Empire. A great-grandson of Queen Victoria, he had close connections to the royal family; the future King Edward VIII had been best man at his wedding. However, his wife Edwina had left-wing views, and Mountbatten himself held pragmatic beliefs about empire. He arrived in India in February 1947 with instructions to transfer power by mid-1948. Within two weeks, he decided that the deadline needed to be moved forward to August 1947.

By March, though Attlee was still publicly advocating a goal of "a unitary government for British India" within the British Commonwealth, he had come privately to endorse a rapid British departure, even if it meant the transfer of power to a divided state. This shift to a definite and a quick deadline for independence dealt a huge blow to Jinnah's strategy, which depended on the British being in power to negotiate a settlement for Indian Muslims. A further round of negotiations between the British, the Congress and the Muslim League resulted in an agreement to transfer power to a divided subcontinent. The provinces of the Punjab in the northwest and Bengal in the northeast would be divided, and *two new states, India and Pakistan*, would come into existence. Both nations would become self-governing dominions within the British Empire.

At midnight on the 15th of August 1947, Nehru, as the first prime minister of an independent India, spoke to the Indian Parliament in Delhi, famously telling them, "at the stroke of the midnight hour, when the world sleeps, India will awake to life and freedom." Yet independence and partition were also marked by the largest migration in human history, as around 15 million people crossed the newly drawn borders between India and Pakistan. Brutal violence ensued, and hundreds of thousands of people died in sectarian massacres, mostly in the Punjab. Virtually no violence was directed against the departing British; rather, Hindus and Sikhs murdered Muslims trying to reach Pakistan, and Muslims did the same to Hindus and Sikhs leaving Pakistan for India. Attlee maintained that the British had long contemplated the independence of India and had carefully planned for how the transfer of power would occur. Yet the process as it actually occurred was clearly the product of multiple, more immediate forces, including British policies, the demands of Indian politicians, high-level diplomatic maneuverings and the brutal forces of violence that were unleashed at the grassroots level by ordinary people thrust into a situation in which the very fabric of their lives was rapidly changing.

The Commonwealth

Given what occurred in India, it might appear that the Labour Party's priority was to dissolve the Empire as rapidly as possible. The Labour Party's 1945 election manifesto, "Let Us Face the Future," included only one sentence on the Empire, and Atlee and other Labour leaders were sympathetic to anticolonial nationalism. Nor was India the only colony from which Labour opted to retreat in the late 1940s. In 1948, the British abruptly withdrew from Palestine, which they had held as a mandate territory since the end of the First World War. In the face of a campaign of terrorism by members of the Jewish population of Palestine, who wanted a Jewish state, as well as a United Nations resolution that called for the creation of two states, one Jewish and one Palestinian, the British decided simply to depart. As in India, conflict ensued, as a war between a coalition of Arab states and Palestine's Jewish population was won by the latter, leading to the establishment of the state of Israel.

Events in India and Palestine notwithstanding, however, the Labour government did not set out to deliberately dismantle the Empire. To be sure, Labour's primary focus was on the construction of the welfare state, but their concept of "welfare" applied not only at home, but also to Britain's colonial subjects. Rather than abandoning it altogether, the Labour Party desired to make the Empire, in the words of the historian John Darwin, "more dynamic, efficient and productive . . . a perfect combination of profit and virtue." Moreover, the continuing possession of a large empire would help to bolster Britain's claim to be a world power in an era in which the United States and the Soviet Union had emerged as the two global superpowers. Thus, while the Labour government recognized that Indian independence was inevitable, it did not seek to sever connections with the "white dominions" or with Britain's colonies in Africa and the West Indies.

Indeed, the tropical empire was seen as an important part of the postwar British economy, as exports such as cocoa, coffee, rubber and tin could help to balance Britain's trade deficit. In return, the British would bring modernization and economic development to the colonies. This vision was in some ways fulfilled: some colonies, such as tin- and rubber-rich Malaya, produced lucrative exports. Other examples of imperial economic development, however, were far less successful, such as an attempt in 1947 to produce groundnuts (peanuts) in the East African colony of Tanganyika (modern Tanzania), which resulted in a loss of £36.5 million by the time the program was ended four years later. These efforts at economic development also disrupted British relationships with traditional elites in the colonies, who often objected to the new policies, and gave an impetus to nationalists, who wished not for development but for independence.

In addition to economic development in the tropical empire, an important goal of both the Labour and Conservative governments of the 1950s was to foster the growth and allegiance of the British Commonwealth. At the Imperial Conference of 1926, former prime minister Arthur Balfour had outlined a vision of Britain and its dominions as "autonomous communities within the British Empire, equal in status, in no way subordinate to another in any aspect of their domestic or external affairs, though united by common allegiance to the Crown." This organization was to be called the "British Commonwealth of Nations." The principle of member "communities" of equal status within the Empire was enshrined in law in the Statute of Westminster of 1931, in which Parliament renounced its right to legislate for the dominions.

A key role for the Commonwealth was to support Britain in maintaining its status as the third postwar global power alongside the United States and the Soviet Union. It also helped to maintain the links of the dominions and their peoples to Britain. The inhabitants of Australia, Canada and New Zealand continued to identify strongly with Britain and to think of themselves as "British" nations in the 1950s. A significant portion of the exports of these countries, meanwhile, continued to flow to Britain. The original vision for the Commonwealth encompassed only the white colonies of settlement, but after the Second World War, the British expanded it to include newly independent Asian and African nations. Both India and Pakistan joined the Commonwealth upon their independence in 1947, as did *Ceylon* (Sri Lanka) when it gained its independence the following year.

Not all former British possessions were convinced to join, however. None of Britain's colonies in the Middle East opted to do so, and *Burma* (modern Myanmar), which became independent in 1948, also declined, as relations with Britain had been bitter since the Japanese occupation of most of the country in the Second World War. Éire, which had a far older and more difficult relationship with Britain, also refused. The External Relations Act (1936) had greatly reduced the monarch's role in Ireland's governance, and in the following year Éire's government introduced a new constitution establishing Irish sovereignty over its own affairs. Although Ireland continued to maintain a relationship with the British monarchy for specific purposes such as diplomatic appointments, by the end of the Second World War, Ireland's connection to the Commonwealth was, in the words of historian Deirdre McMahon, "almost invisible." In 1949 the southern twenty-six counties of the island formally became the *Republic of Ireland* and departed the Commonwealth.

Ireland nonetheless continued to provide a precedent for British colonies during decolonization. Indian political leaders closely watched Ireland's gradual separation from the Commonwealth and sent a delegation to Dublin at the end of 1947 to meet with the Irish government about Éire's future constitutional relationship with Britain. When India became a republic in 1950, the British government faced the question of whether a republic could join the Commonwealth, as the British monarch remained its titular head. The solution that the British government essentially offered was for India to follow Ireland's External Relations Act, a pragmatic decision that permitted a Commonwealth headed by a monarch to include nations that had renounced monarchy. India merely accepted King George VI as "the symbol of the free association of its independent member nations and as such the head of the Commonwealth." Another new republic, however, was not permitted to remain in the Commonwealth. When South Africa became a republic in 1961, its continued membership drew fierce criticism from Commonwealth nations in Africa and Asia who objected to its system of discrimination against its black population, known as **apartheid**. Worried that it would face the embarrassment of being expelled, the South African government withdrew its application and *left the Commonwealth*.

Apart from controlling its membership, however, the Commonwealth soon proved to have little real power. In 1965, Southern Rhodesia, where a white minority ruled under a constitution that denied basic rights to the country's black population, declared independence in defiance of British wishes. Unwilling to use military force against a white settler population, the British resorted to economic sanctions, but the Rhodesian regime was able to rely on trade with South Africa. Britain appeared weak, and many Commonwealth nations strongly criticized the Labour prime minister Harold Wilson for betraying the organization's ideals. By the late 1960s, the European Economic Community seemed to offer greater promise than the Commonwealth did for bolstering Britain's economy and world standing.

The "Dirty Wars of Empire"

Violence marked the final decades of the British Empire. The "readiness" of colonies for independence was always determined more by issues of political expediency than by any other criteria. But where British economic and strategic interests were at stake or the white settler population was substantial, both reform and brute force were used to maintain imperial rule for as long as possible. The British carried out ten major **counterinsurgency** campaigns in the period from 1945 to 1967, beginning with Palestine in the late 1940s and ending with Britain's withdrawal from Aden in present-day Yemen in 1967.

One of the earliest counterinsurgency campaigns took place in Malaya. The reimposition of British rule following the wartime Japanese occupation was meant not only to impose a progressive imperialism that would improve the health and welfare of the population, but also to secure British access to valuable commodities such as rubber and tin, which were vital in balancing Britain's trade deficit with the United States. A planned "Union of Malaysia" was shifted to a looser "Federation" to placate Malay nationalists, but this sparked a guerilla revolt in 1948 by communist insurgents among the minority Chinese population. One of the main architects of British counterinsurgency policy in Malaya, General Sir Gerald Templer, came to be closely identified with the policy of winning the "hearts and minds" of rebels. Templer fully utilized methods of propaganda such as radio, cinema and the distribution of millions of leaflets, including 100,000 coronation portraits of Elizabeth II, in an effort to win Malayan support. At the same time, however, the British launched a coercive campaign against the communist insurgents. Templer gave the resettlement areas that were intended to deprive rebels of support from the local population the euphemistic name "New Villages." This more attractive nomenclature, however, could not conceal the fact that almost half of the 2 million Chinese residents of Malaya were forcibly relocated in the 1950s.

Violence was even more pronounced in the East African colony of Kenya. Here, a small minority of 21,000 white settlers monopolized the colony's economic wealth, particularly the fertile agricultural land of the "White Highlands." The settlers' leader, Lord Delamere, owned over 150,000 acres. A strict color bar operated, and schools, cinemas, churches and public lavatories in the capital of Nairobi were segregated. During the interwar period, the White Highlanders tried to replicate the lifestyles of the English upper classes, though they hunted jackals rather than foxes. Its members enjoyed a well-deserved reputation for decadence and excess; at one of Lord Delamere's parties, the 250 guests consumed 600 bottles of champagne. British settlers preferred to be "verandah farmers" who relied on African labor, predominantly the Kikuyu people, many of whom had been dispossessed of their land by white settlers. They were attracted by their right as "squatters" to work land for themselves in return for their service to white farmers.

Nearly 100,000 black Kenyans fought for the British Empire in the Second World War, though they were commanded by white officers and not permitted to rise above the rank of warrant officer. They returned home to find that preferential treatment was being given to a new wave of white settlers: former British servicemen who were granted land, loans and other economic incentives. This situation led to calls for "land and freedom" that by the early 1950s had generated a movement known as Mau Mau, which drew on both the impoverished rural Kikuyu and the urban poor for support. A secret society, Mau Mau advocated violence and terror to oust the British from Kenya. White settlers were appalled by its rituals, which involved animal blood and entrails, and labeled it an "evil" and "bestial" phenomenon. Mau Mau killed around a hundred white settlers, but a far greater number of casualties was inflicted by the colonial state. In 1952, the government declared a *state of emergency*, which was not

Figures 13.1 and 13.2 In the decades after the Second World War, anticolonial unrest led the British to undertake a number of counterinsurgency operations. Figure 13.1 shows British troops deploying during the Malayan emergency in 1959. Figure 13.2 shows British and African soldiers on patrol near Nyeri during the Mau Mau uprising in Kenya in the early 1950s. As many as 35,000 people died in the ensuing violence.

Figure 13.1 reproduced courtesy of Trinity Mirror/Mirrorpix/Alamy Stock Photo. Figure 13.2 reproduced courtesy of INTERFOTO/Alamy Stock Photo.

lifted until 1960. A network of detention camps, which were established ostensibly to "civilize" the members of Mau Mau, became zones of abuse and torture.

At least 160,000 Kikuyu were detained without trial, and as many as 20,000 Mau Mau insurgents and suspected insurgents were killed. In addition, almost 70 percent of the Kikuyu and other Kenyan supporters of Mau Mau were forced to move to 800 newly established villages, a resettlement program that was far more extensive than those carried out by other colonial empires at the time, including the French in Algeria and the Portuguese in Mozambique. The British experience in postwar Malaya and Kenya, along with the violence that accompanied the partition of India, demonstrates that British decolonization was by no means a nonviolent process.

The Presence of Empire 7

Archives and Empire

In establishing their global empire, British colonial officials created vast archives of government records in both the colonies and London. These predominantly reflect the viewpoints and concerns of colonial officials, but if read carefully and critically, they can be used to illuminate the experiences of colonial subjects as well. The documents relating to the Mau Mau uprising in Kenya in the late 1950s and early 1960s are a prime example. British colonial officials in Kenya were believed to have destroyed the documents relating to the detention camps in which suspected members of Mau Mau were incarcerated. In April 2011, however, four elderly Kenyans, three men and one woman, were given a hearing in the High Court in London. All four had been prisoners in the British detention system in Kenya in the 1950s. The prosecution claimed that they had been the victims of torture and abuse at the hands of colonial authorities and that their suffering (including the castration of two of the men) had been part of a systematic response by the colonial state to the Mau Mau insurgency rather than isolated instances of brutality. The High Court ruled that the British government was answerable to the charges. In the legal maneuverings that preceded the hearing, it was discovered that more than 1500 files from Kenya that were believed to be lost still existed at a top-secret government facility called Hanslope Park. The documents, which revealed the far-reaching extent of counterinsurgency efforts, lent further credence to the four Kenyans' accounts of the brutality they had suffered. The documents' storage in a secure location was originally intended to hide material that might prove embarrassing to colonial governments or incriminating to colonial policemen and soldiers. Over time, however, the staff lost track of them. As the historian David M. Anderson commented, they represented a "colonial conspiracy" followed by a "bureaucratic bungle" which led to the files being concealed for decades. In addition to the Kenya documents, more than 8800 additional files from thirty-six other British colonies were discovered at Hanslope Park. While these "migrated archives" focused largely on routine matters of colonial administration, their discovery nonetheless has raised new questions about the final decades of the British Empire and the incomplete nature of the surviving archival record of decolonization.

Although many details of what happened in Kenya have come to light only very recently, the British campaign against Mau Mau did attract public attention and criticism at the time. The Labour MPs Barbara Castle and Fenner Brockway raised the issue repeatedly in Parliament, while missionaries sent reports of the brutalities committed by colonial forces back to London. New organizations such as Brockway's Movement for Colonial Freedom and the Kenya Committee, which was formed by a group of Kenyan expatriates in London, sought to bring to light the injustices of colonial rule, and letters from detainees were published in the British press. During a parliamentary debate in July 1959 on the deaths of ten detainees, the young MP Enoch Powell, who had recently broken with the Conservative Party, argued, "We cannot say, 'We will have African standards in Africa, Asian standards in Asia and perhaps British standards here at home' . . . We cannot, we dare not, in Africa of all places, fall below our own highest standards in the acceptance of responsibility." Harold Macmillan's Conservative government, however, defended the colonial regime by asserting that the savagery of the Mau Mau insurgency necessitated a forceful response and that the allegations of atrocities were exaggerated. In spite of the attention that human rights abuses in Kenya received in Britain, the plea for an official inquiry into the system of detention camps fell on deaf ears.

The Suez Crisis and the "Wind of Change"

While force could be effective in maintaining colonial control for a time, Britain's ability to project imperial power in the postwar era diminished. Between 1951 and 1955, defense spending fell from 14 to 8 percent of GDP, and even the lower figure continued to strain government finances. An event in 1956 underscored this growing weakness. After invading Egypt in the 1880s, Britain had dominated the country for the next three-quarters of a century. Egypt had formally achieved independence in 1922, but the British had continued to exercise significant influence over its affairs. In 1952, however, the Arab nationalist Gamal Abdel Nasser unseated the pro-British monarch King Farouk in a coup. Nasser intensified pressure for the British to withdraw their troops from the Suez Canal Zone. Since its construction in 1869, the Suez Canal had been owned by the private Suez Canal Company and was legally defined as a neutral zone that was overseen by the British military. The canal was still an important route for British shipping, and in the postwar era it was more strategically important than ever as a base for projecting British power in the Middle East. In 1951, there were 81,000 British troops stationed in the canal zone, making it the largest military base in the world. The Egyptians had long been unhappy with the presence of so many foreign soldiers in their country, and the British government had already agreed to withdraw them in a treaty of 1936.

Events, however, outpaced diplomacy. Nasser wanted to build a massive dam at Aswan on the Nile River in order to control flooding and generate hydroelectric power. The British and the Americans initially agreed to lend financial support to the project, but withdrew it when they became suspicious that Nasser was becoming more closely allied with the Soviet Union. In retaliation and to raise the funds required to build the dam, Nasser nationalized, or assumed government control of, the Suez Canal. The British government's lawyers found that the move was legal, so long as shareholders were compensated and so long as the canal remained open to international shipping. The British prime minister Anthony Eden, however, felt that acceding to the move was akin to appeasement, and he colluded with Israel to invade Egypt. This allowed the British and French to occupy the canal zone under the auspices of protecting the important international waterway. The military operation was swiftly accomplished, but the United Nations called for its own peacekeeping forces to occupy the canal zone instead of the British and French. The operation was also condemned by the Commonwealth. When US president Dwight Eisenhower learned of the invasion, he asked Eden, "Anthony, are you out of your mind?" Under pressure from the Americans, British forces withdrew after a week. The debacle seriously undermined Britain's international prestige and stimulated nationalist movements throughout the Empire.

The shock of their isolation during the *Suez crisis* brought home to the British their diminished standing in the world. Rather than securing a strategic asset for the British Empire, the failed invasion caused an economic crisis in which the value of the pound dropped sharply and had to be shored up with support from both the United States and the International Monetary Fund. Although public opinion polls suggested that the majority of the British public supported the military intervention, Suez marked the end of Eden's political career, as he resigned in January 1957.

For many Britons, the impact of Suez was equivalent to that of the fall of Singapore in 1942, as it demonstrated that the power and prestige of the Empire had been sharply reduced. It is too simplistic, however, to say that Suez led directly to decolonization. While the Sudan received its independence in 1956 and the Gold Coast became the first sub-Saharan African nation to achieve independence (as *Ghana*) a year later, plans for a transfer of power in both places were underway prior to the Suez crisis. But the crisis did help to accelerate the pace of decolonization. The changing landscape of the British Empire was illustrated in a speech made by Eden's successor as prime minister, Harold Macmillan, in South Africa in February 1960. Macmillan spoke of the "wind of change" that was blowing across Africa. Although his main purpose was to criticize the system of apartheid in South Africa, he referenced the strength of African nationalism.

"Whether we like it or not," Macmillan observed, "this growth of national consciousness is a political fact. We must all accept it as a fact, and our national policies must take account of it."

 See document "Change Comes to the British Empire" at www.routledge.com/cw/barczewski.

Over the next decade, more than two dozen colonies became independent nations. Nigeria and the Mediterranean island of Cyprus gained independence in 1960; they were soon followed by the African nations of Sierra Leone (1961), Tanganyika (1961), Uganda (1962) and *Kenya* (1963), along with Jamaica (1962) and Trinidad and Tobago (1962) in the Caribbean and Singapore (1963) in Southeast Asia. The dismantling of the Empire was virtually complete when the Labour prime minister Harold Wilson announced in January 1968 that within three years Britain would withdraw from all its territories in East and Southeast Asia (Hong Kong excepted) and the Persian Gulf region.

British decisions to grant independence to nations were based on a variety of factors. Nationalism played an important role, and anticolonial campaigners employed nonviolent as well as violent methods of protest. In the southeast African colony of Nyasaland, the African National Congress used strikes and demonstrations to protest a 1953 federation with the white settler-dominated colonies of Northern and Southern Rhodesia. After a police shooting killed more than fifty protestors and thousands were detained or imprisoned during a state of emergency declared in 1959, the Congress made appeals to the international press and the United Nations. At the UN, representatives of Ghana used the findings of a British commission of inquiry to condemn Nyasaland's "police state." Caroline Elkins concludes, "the combined impact of Kenya, Cyprus," where insurgents began an armed independence campaign in 1955, "and Nyasaland was *the* tipping point for widespread colonial retreat."

Decolonization was, however, far from a simple capitulation to resistance, protests and calls for independence from colonial peoples. Decisions to decolonize were also impacted by the actions of imperial rivals. In 1959, the French president Charles de Gaulle, although he was still fighting a bloody war against nationalists in Algeria, offered to grant independence to any French colony that requested it. A year later, Belgium abruptly decided to leave its vast central African colony of the Congo. In 1961 Macmillan's colonial secretary, Iain MacLeod, told the cabinet, "pressure from the United Nations, now that Belgium and France are dropping out as colonial powers, will increasingly concentrate on us." The Cold War was also a constant reference in government debates about decolonization. British politicians feared that if decolonization were too rapid, it would create a power vacuum in Africa and Asia into which Soviet power and influence would flow. Accordingly, much attention was devoted to attempting to determine the political affiliation of anticolonial activists, many of whom combined nationalist and Marxist beliefs. In the late 1940s and early 1950s, the Colonial Office feared that nationalist leader Kwame Nkrumah would turn an independent Ghana into a Soviet satellite. The British intelligence agency MI5, however, was able to assure the government that while Nkrumah held strong Marxist beliefs, he was no puppet of the USSR and "would turn a deaf ear to any encouragement to adopt revolutionary tactics." MI5 and other British intelligence agencies played an important role in advising the Colonial Office throughout the era of decolonization and also helped to secure British interests in newly independent nations. MI5 officers known as SLOs (security liaison officers) provided an important secret channel of communication between the United Kingdom and former colonies.

In the same era, British military intervention was also used to oust nationalists who were believed to be under Soviet influence from positions of influence. In the South American colony of British Guiana, a combination of Cold War fears, American pressure and economic calculations caused the British to depose the democratically elected chief minister Cheddi Jagan in 1953. Both the United States and Britain feared that he would establish a Soviet puppet state that would control the colony's valuable bauxite mining industry. In 1961, when Jagan appeared once again to be in a position to lead British Guiana into independence, Britain authorized the United States to use covert warfare in order to subvert his influence. CIA-sponsored strikes and demonstrations led to the deaths of 200 Guyanese. When British Guiana gained independence in 1966, it was not Jagan, but the American-backed candidate, Forbes Burnham, who became its first prime minister.

Empire Windrush and "New Commonwealth" Immigration

For most of the twentieth century, emigration outwards from Britain far outpaced inward migration. This remained the case in the postwar period: from 1946 to 1954, 1.3 million people emigrated from Britain, mostly to settle in the "white dominions" of Canada, Australia and New Zealand, further strengthening the Commonwealth bonds among them. Beginning in the late 1940s, however, an increasing number of immigrants from the Caribbean, South Asia and Africa began to settle in Britain. In 1948, the Labour government passed the Nationality Act, which defined everyone residing in the British Empire and the Commonwealth as a British subject, giving them the right to settle in the United Kingdom. In the late 1940s, a mass influx of immigrants was not seen negatively; at the time, the government was scouring displaced persons' camps in Europe for potential immigrants, even from Britain's former enemies, due to the severe labor shortage. Irish immigration was also encouraged,

Immigrants and Refugees 4

Postwar Migration to Australia

During the depression in the 1930s, the Australian birth rate fell sharply, and there was little net immigration. Population growth remained sluggish after the Second World War. To address this problem, the Australian government adopted a policy of "Populate or Perish," a key part of which was to persuade people to move to Australia. Between 1945 and 1965, two million immigrants arrived in the country, which resulted in Australia's population almost doubling from 7.5 to 13 million between 1945 and 1975. The largest number of these arrivals, about a third of the total, arrived from the United Kingdom, where the Australian government advertised heavily. Faced with a labor shortage of their own, British politicians tried to discourage people from leaving, but the Assisted Passage Migration Scheme, in which the Australian government subsidized the cost of the voyage, proved very popular. By 1947, more than 400,000 Britons had registered their intention to move to Australia; they became known as "Ten-Pound Poms" because adult immigrants were charged only a £10 processing fee for their passage, the equivalent of around £500 today. ("Pom" was Australian slang for a British person.) The government's emphasis on attracting immigrants from Britain, however, was a legacy of the prewar "White Australia" policy that had tried to bar non-white immigrants from Asia and the Pacific Islands. Although the official bans on non-white immigration were gradually dismantled from 1949 onwards, many Australian politicians saw the efforts to attract European and specifically British immigrants as a way to keep the country majority white.

Figure 13.3 The Elder Park Migrant Hostel in Adelaide, Australia, which was converted from World War II–era military housing to provide migrants to Australia from Britain with temporary accommodation. It could house up to 180 people at a time in rooms ranging from cubicles to large dormitories; dining and bathrooms were communal. Most new arrivals spent only a few nights there before moving on to other accommodations.

Reproduced courtesy of the History Trust of South Australia.

and even though after 1948 Ireland was no longer a member of the Commonwealth, Irish citizens were given special rights of entry into Britain.

One of the unforeseen results of the 1948 Act, however, was a relatively small but steady number of non-white immigrants from the Empire, in particular the Caribbean, South Asia and East Africa. Although persons of color had resided in Britain for centuries, these populations had been small and concentrated in London and other port cities. The beginning of mass non-white migration to Britain is often claimed to have begun in June 1948, when 492 men from Jamaica and other British colonies in the Caribbean *arrived on board a ship called the Empire Windrush* at Tilbury Docks at the mouth of the Thames.

The arrival of the *Windrush* was sufficiently novel to make headlines, but there was little public apprehension of the prospect of large-scale West Indian migration. After being housed briefly in an air-raid shelter, all of the passengers found employment. Although Labour politicians and Colonial Office officials privately expressed misgivings about the prospect of further black settlement in Britain, at the time no proposals were made to limit immigration. The Labour government, with its goals of creating a more just and equitable society at home and of reorienting the Commonwealth to include African and Asian nations, was reluctant to restrict the flow of people into Britain. But despite the postwar labor shortage, no further efforts were made to recruit black or Asian labor.

 See document "Colonial Immigrants in the United Kingdom" at www.routledge. com/cw/barczewski.

Over the course of the 1950s, West Indian immigrants were joined by people from South Asia. These included both workers who came in response to the need for factory labor and Indian sailors, or *lascars*. Many of the latter, along with Cypriot and Chinese immigrants, went on to operate cafés in working-class areas such as London's East End. These cafés served Indian dishes adapted for British tastes alongside the staples of the working-class diet, such as fish and chips. West Indian immigrants, meanwhile, brought new styles of music to Britain. One of the passengers on the *Empire Windrush* was the Trinidadian calypso star Lord Kitchener. Kitchener had composed a new song on the *Windrush* in anticipation of his arrival called "London Is the Place for Me," which he sang for newsreel crews on the docks at Tilbury. He remained in Britain until 1962, achieving chart success with a number of calypso songs that were popular both with the West Indian immigrant community and with white Britons. By the early 1960s, the rhythmic and syncopated Jamaican music known as ska, a forerunner of reggae, became popular among young black Britons in urban dance halls. Following the appearance in 1964 by the Jamaican ska star Prince Buster on the pop music television show *Ready, Steady, Go* and the international hit "My Boy Lollipop" by young Jamaican singer Millie Small that same year, ska gained an audience among white British youth as well.

But while the introduction of South Asian food and West Indian music to Britain was seen by some commentators as enlivening a drab postwar Britain, the reality for most immigrants was long hours of toil, a marginal place in British society and racial prejudice. E.R. Braithwaite, a Cambridge-educated veteran of the Royal Air Force from British Guiana, was denied housing and employment based on his race – which was not illegal in Britain in the late 1940s – and was only able to find a job teaching in a school in London's working-class East End. As a member of the colonial elite and a veteran of the Second World War, Braithwaite had firmly believed in what he described as "the ideal of the British way of life." After his arrival in Britain, however, he bitterly observed, "I was British, but evidently not a Briton."

As the presence of immigrants from the British Empire continued to grow, there were growing calls for restrictions on immigration. These calls accelerated after there were disturbances in the London neighborhood of Notting Hill in 1958. There had already been episodes of violence against blacks and Asians in the late 1940s, but the disturbances in the next decade were on a far wider scale. Notting Hill was already an economically depressed area when West Indian immigrants began to settle there in the late 1940s, and both black and white residents lived in dilapidated Victorian housing. But while poverty and deprivation were factors in the riots, the presence of right-wing organizations such as the Union Movement, the successor to the prewar British Union of Fascists, exacerbated racial tensions. Attacks on black residents of Notting Hill began on Sunday, the 24th of August, and lasted for the next ten days. Crowds of thousands of whites attacked West Indians with knives, razors and iron bars. The rioters were not all local, as white youths from suburban London had come to join in the attacks. Over a hundred people were arrested.

Race 6

Notting Hill Riots

After World War II, a small but increasing number of non-white settlers from Britain's colonies in the West Indies migrated to London and other British cities in search of employment. By the early 1960s, London's West Indian immigrant population was over 100,000, with many of them concentrated in a part of west London called Notting Hill. Tensions grew as local white residents became increasingly concerned that these new arrivals were putting pressure on housing and jobs. Right-wing political organizations began attempting to stoke these fears, while white working-class "Teddy Boys" began expressing increasingly open hostility to black Londoners. On the 20th of August 1958, several black businesses were vandalized; four days later, nine black men were attacked in west London, leaving three seriously injured. On the 30th of August, the violence escalated dramatically, as 400 white youths, armed with knives, iron bars, milk bottles and petrol bombs, chased the black residents of Notting Hill through the streets. In response, young black men armed themselves and began fighting back. The riots continued for a week, leading to the arrest of 140 people, most of them white. In the aftermath, the government sought to frame what had occurred as the result of hooliganism on both sides, which led to a debate about continuing black immigration to Britain and contributed to white demands for tighter immigration policies. In reality, the Notting Hill riots were the product of white racism. They did have, however, a positive legacy in the form of the Notting Hill Carnival, a celebration of West Indian culture in London that began in 1966 and is now one of the world's largest street festivals. In 2006, the carnival was voted onto a list of 100 "icons of Englishness" compiled by the BBC.

The Notting Hill riots provoked much public commentary. The anonymous narrator of Colin MacInnes's novel *Absolute Beginners* (1959) despairs of how a nation that established a global empire cannot seem to accommodate a small percentage of immigrants: "In the history books, they tell us the English race has spread itself all over the dam [*sic*] world . . . No one invited us, and we didn't ask anyone's permission, I suppose. Yet when a few hundred thousand come and settle among our fifty millions we just can't take it." The Notting Hill riots provided an impetus for the West Indian community to organize. Most famously, they led to the establishment of an annual carnival in the neighborhood that remains extremely popular among Londoners, black and white, today. Among white Britons, however, the riots focused attention on "black criminality" rather than white racism. One proposed solution was the deportation of West Indians. The power of the British government to deport men and women who had been resident less than five years for both crimes and behavior deemed socially disruptive was enshrined in the 1962 *Commonwealth Immigrants Act*. Throughout the 1950s, both Labour and Conservative governments had opposed restrictions on immigration, as they feared their negative impact on the Commonwealth. The 1962 Act, however, limited entry to students, members of the armed forces and immigrants with employment vouchers that guaranteed jobs or who could otherwise prove that they possessed the means to support themselves. The use of deportation and immigration controls thus became normalized as a strategy for dealing with immigration to Britain.

The 1962 Act received widespread popular support. In the short term, however, it actually increased immigration. In the eighteen months prior to its passage, as many black and Asian immigrants came to Britain as in the previous five years combined, as they attempted to gain entry before the restrictions came into effect. In 1965, the Labour government further restricted immigration by limiting the number of employment vouchers for skilled workers. Tensions over immigration continued, however. In 1968, Asians in now-independent Kenya, the majority of whom were of Indian descent, had to make a choice regarding their citizenship in response to the government's "Africanization" policy, which barred noncitizens from positions in the government and the economy. In order to claim Kenyan citizenship, however, they had to renounce the United Kingdom citizenship that had been granted to them by the 1948 Nationality Act. The policy was deliberately intended to exclude Asians from positions of influence in government and business, as the government knew that few would be willing to surrender their British citizenship. Faced with such blatant discrimination, 23,000 Kenyan Asians migrated to Britain. Many British people feared that more of Kenya's 200,000 Asians would seek entry to the United Kingdom. In response, the Labour government passed a new Commonwealth Immigrants Act in 1968, which further restricted the right of immigration to only those people with a "qualifying connection" to the United Kingdom, meaning that they had to have been born there or to have at least one parent or grandparent who had been born there.

The fears of white Britons regarding black and Asian immigration were highlighted once again later that same year, when the Conservative MP Enoch Powell made one of the most infamous speeches in British history. Powell declared, as he watched the number of immigrants increase, "I am filled with foreboding; like the Roman, I seem to see 'the River Tiber foaming with much blood.'" This latter phrase, a reference to Virgil's classical Roman epic the *Aeneid*, caused Powell's oration to be labeled the *"Rivers of Blood" speech*, although Powell never actually uttered that phrase. He was abandoned by the Conservative Party for his comments, which were seen by many people as racist, and he became a political pariah. He also, however, received over 100,000 private letters of support.

Race 7

Enoch Powell's "Rivers of Blood" Speech

In the 1960s, the debate over non-white immigration continued. Many white Britons welcomed immigrants from Africa, Asia and the West Indies and acknowledged their contribution to the labor force; the National Health Service, for example, recruited heavily from the Jamaica and Barbados to supply its workers. Others, however, felt threatened by the newcomers and demanded the numbers be reduced. The government struggled to deal with these competing views: a series of acts from 1962 onwards restricted non-white immigration, but the Race Relations Act of 1965 made it illegal to deny housing or employment on the basis of race, color or ethnicity. On the 20th of April 1968, Conservative Member of Parliament Enoch Powell gave a speech to the West Midlands Area Conservative Political Council in the city of Birmingham. Powell described the opposition of many of his constituents to further non-white immigration and claimed that if it continued, violence would inevitably ensue. Powell's address became known as the "Rivers of Blood" speech because in it he quoted from the ancient Roman poet Virgil's *The Aeneid*: "As I look ahead, I am filled with foreboding; like the

Roman, I seem to see 'the River Tiber foaming with much blood.'" The response was swift: Conservative party leader Edward Heath condemned the speech for its "racialist" tone and removed Powell from his position as shadow secretary of state for defence. He remained a political pariah for the remainder of his career. But Powell received hundreds of thousands of letters in support of his views, and a poll conducted shortly afterwards suggested that almost three-quarters of the British population agreed with at least some of what he had said. The Conservatives went on to win the general election in 1970, a victory that is often attributed in part to widespread support for Powell's views.

Figures 13.4 and 13.5 In Figure 13.4, students from Bristol University demonstrate against Enoch Powell three weeks after his "Rivers of Blood" speech in 1968. In Figure 13.5, people in Powell's constituency of Wolverhampton South West march to show their support.

Figure 13.4 reproduced courtesy of Tony Byers/Alamy Stock Photo; Figure 13.5 reproduced courtesy of Black Country Images/Alamy Stock Photo.

Social scientists and historians continue to debate the depth of racial prejudice in postwar Britain. The conventional view, which was enunciated by commentators at the time and which has been echoed by many historians since, was that Britain's "race problem" began with the arrival of significant numbers of non-white immigrants. Their presence was tolerated by most people in a British society that was broadly liberal about race, but a minority of the population was hostile. Least tolerant were working-class people, who competed with the new immigrants for housing and work. The attitude of the social and political elite towards non-white immigration, meanwhile, was more liberal than that of the population as a whole. Beginning in the late 1950s, the government tried to restrict immigration informally in an effort to reduce tensions, but this proved impossible, and so formal restrictions were introduced through legislation. In this view, racial tensions were inevitable and had to be managed by the government through immigration controls and other methods. Governments were thus simply reacting to events and to illiberal attitudes within British society.

Some scholars, however, have challenged this view. They argue that the government was a major contributor to intolerant attitudes. It was not, in other words, popular racism but political and bureaucratic views of who "belonged" in Britain that drove the restrictive policies of the 1960s. Race was the crucial variable: white Europeans were welcomed and helped to assimilate, while peoples of color from the Empire, who often not only spoke English but also had British-style educations, were not. The truth is complex. In contemporary opinion surveys, the vast majority of British people denied that they were racially prejudiced, but many favored immigration restrictions. A survey in the mid-1960s revealed that four out of five Britons agreed with the statement, "too many immigrants had been let into the country." Public expressions of overt racism diminished, but there were clear exceptions, such as the Notting Hill riots. The transition to the multiracial society that Britain is today was not an easy one.

Immigrants and Refugees 5

The Expulsion of Asians From Uganda (1972)

In the late nineteenth century, the British began encouraging people to migrate from their colonies in South Asia to their newly acquired territory in East Africa, in order to help build railways and other infrastructure. In the decades around 1900, 30,000 people from India arrived in Uganda in order to help build railways there. In their wake came middle-class workers such as clerks, merchants and professionals, who soon came to form an important layer of society. As the cotton, tea, coffee and sugar trade with Britain boomed, these South Asians served as intermediaries between Africans and their colonial rulers. This led, however, to tensions between Africans and Asians, as Ugandan Africans saw Asians as profiting at their expense. In the mid-twentieth century, Ugandan political leaders increasingly began to blame Asians for the economic struggles of Africans and to pursue policies of "Africanization" that targeted Asian businesses. Aware of these tensions, the British government allowed the approximately 85,000 Ugandan Asians to retain their British passports after Uganda gained its independence in 1962. In 1972, the dictator Idi Amin ordered the expulsion from Uganda of all people of Asian origin who did not hold Ugandan citizenship. In the intervening period since Ugandan independence, however, Britain had tightened its immigration laws, and most Asian British passport holders were no longer permitted to live and work in the United Kingdom. Only after intense international pressure was brought to bear did the Conservative prime minister Edward Heath permit around 28,000 Ugandan Asians to enter the country. At a time when the British economy was performing badly and unemployment was rising, they met with staunch opposition from right-wing anti-immigrant political groups such as the National Front, although many white British people and already-established South Asian communities welcomed the newcomers with open arms and helped them to assimilate. Today, the Ugandan Asians are generally seen as an immigration success story in Britain, even if their initial arrival was controversial.

Conclusion

For the first time since the American Revolution, the British Empire significantly contracted in size in the decades after the Second World War. Decolonization was a multifaceted process. It was not simply a matter of colonial nationalists winning independence; nor was it a benevolent process of Britain granting the gift of independence to colonial peoples who requested it. When British and colonial governments perceived that their strategic interests were threatened by anticolonial campaigns, the response could be brutal. It is no surprise that during the recent wars in Iraq and Afghanistan, the British experience of counterinsurgency has been scrutinized for insights into how to fight irregular opponents.

Repression and violence were not the entire story of the postwar British Empire, however. Both Labour and Conservative governments made considerable efforts to come to terms with the new forces of African and Asian nationalism that were reshaping both the colonial world and the postwar world of the Cold War. The economic development of the Commonwealth and its opening to non-white nations seemed, at least for a time, to be a way for Britain to maintain its own status as a major power in a world divided between the superpowers of the United States and the Soviet Union.

A prominent theme throughout the history of the British Empire is how its history was intertwined with that of Britain itself. Empire was never something that happened purely overseas, but rather it impacted the economic, political, cultural and social life of Britons at home. This was more evident than ever in the postwar era, when the immigration of Asian, African and Afro-Caribbean peoples to Britain reached new levels and raised new political and social issues. From the legacy of empire in film to the revelations of new archival records of the processes of decolonization, the British Empire continues to impact Britain today.

Bibliography

Anderson, David, *Histories of the Hanged: The Dirty War in Kenya and the End of Empire* (2005)
Bailkin, Jordanna, *The Afterlife of Empire* (2012)
Boyce, D. George, *Decolonisation and the British Empire, 1775–1997* (1999)
Brendon, Piers, *The Decline and Fall of the British Empire, 1781–1997* (2008)
Buettner, Elizabeth, *Europe after Empire: Decolonization, Society and Culture* (2016)
Darwin, John, *The Empire Project: The Rise and Fall of the British World-System, 1830–1970* (2009)
Elkins, Caroline, *Imperial Reckoning: The Untold Story of Britain's Gulag in Kenya* (2005)

Elkins, Caroline, *Legacy of Violence: A History of the British Empire* (2022)

French, David, *The British Way in Counter-Insurgency 1945–1967* (2011)

French, Patrick, *Liberty or Death: India's Journey to Independence and Division* (1997)

Gopal, Priyamvada, *Insurgent Empire: Anticolonial Resistance and British Dissent* (2019)

McMahon, Deirdre, "Ireland, the Empire and the Commonwealth," in Kevin Kenny, ed., *Ireland and the British Empire* (2004)

O'Malley, Kate, *Ireland, India and Empire: Indo-Irish Radical Connections, 1919–1964* (2008)

Phillips, Trevor and Mike Phillips, *Windrush: The Irresistible Rise of Multi-Racial Britain* (2009)

Santhnam, Sanghera, *Empireland: How Imperialism Has Shaped Modern Britain* (2021)

Thompson, Andrew, *The Empire Strikes Back? The Impact of Imperialism on Britain from the Mid-Nineteenth Century* (2005)

Toye, Richard, *Churchill's Empire: The World that Made Him and the World that He Made* (2010)

Ward, Stuart, ed., *British Culture and the End of Empire* (2001)

Watson, Calder, *Empire of Secrets: British Intelligence, The Cold War and the Twilight of Intelligence* (2013)

14 1979–1997
Thatcherism and Its Discontents

Topics covered

- Margaret Thatcher as prime minister
- The Labour Party in the 1980s
- Hunger strikes in Northern Ireland
- The Falklands War
- The miners' strike
- The city of London and the creation of new wealth
- Popular culture
- Thatcher's resignation
- The Conservative government after Thatcher

Timeline

1979	Margaret Thatcher becomes prime minister
1981	Brixton riots
1981	Social Democratic Party founded
1981	Death of Irish republican hunger-striker Bobby Sands
1981	Marriage of Prince Charles and Lady Diana Spencer
1982	Falklands War
1983	Second Conservative victory under Thatcher
1984	Brighton hotel bombing
1984	Miners' strike begins
1987	Thatcher becomes first twentieth-century prime minister to win three general elections
1990	John Major replaces Margaret Thatcher as prime minister
1991	Maastricht Treaty
1992	Conservatives win re-election

Introduction

An examination of British politics, and in many ways of British history, in the 1980s largely comes down to an assessment of the impact of a single person: *Margaret Thatcher, who served as prime minister* from 1979 to 1990. That assessment, in turn, depends very much on the

DOI: 10.4324/9781003284758-14

assessor's political attitudes. Any attempt to present Thatcher even-handedly cannot help but be filled with sentences beginning with "her supporters argued," followed by others beginning with "her opponents, on the other hand, asserted that." There is, in other words, no way to achieve a consensus view of Thatcher; she was the most polarizing figure in recent British history. Much of the controversy that still surrounds her relates to her efforts to alter two pillars of British policy that had stood for decades. Since the First World War, the theories of John Maynard Keynes, based on a mixed economy in which the government should at times intervene in order to improve the efficiency of the private sector, had generally been accepted by all political parties. And since 1945, the welfare state, in which the government maintained programs to secure the health, employment, education and basic social security of the population, had been a sacrosanct area of policy that both Labour and Conservative governments had endorsed. Thatcher challenged both of these presumptions.

A Polarizing Figure

In 1979, the electorate voted for the Tories out of desperation for a dramatic change that could lift the nation out of its economic doldrums. By the late 1970s, British per capita income was only 46 percent of West Germany's and 41 percent of France's. People thus had good reason for wanting something different, and that was what Thatcher promised. In the early 1970s, she and other prominent Conservative politicians had begun to favor a radical approach to the economy that departed from accepted Keynesian principles. Known as monetarism, this policy was inspired by the ideas of the American economist Milton Friedman, who argued that a government's sole responsibilities in managing the economy were to limit inflation and maintain the value of the currency by controlling the amount of money in circulation. This theory had obvious appeal in a country that had been plagued by high rates of inflation since the early 1970s.

Initially, the results of monetarism were negative. Inflation reached 22 percent in 1980, and gross domestic product fell by 5.5 percent. Manufacturing output tumbled as the high value of the pound made British industry noncompetitive on the international market. Interest rates soared to 17 percent, and unemployment rose faster than it had since 1930, reaching 3.6 million in 1982. The government's approval rating fell to 18 percent and Thatcher's to 25 percent, both the lowest ever recorded. The explanation for what happened next – Thatcher became the longest-serving prime minister since Lord Liverpool in the early nineteenth century – depends very much on one's political perspective. Thatcher's supporters argue that she remained resolute against calls to deviate from the course she had set. As the public, the press and even some members of her own cabinet demanded that she return to the normal presuppositions that had governed British economic policy for decades, she stood firm. At the Conservative party conference in the fall of 1980, she famously declared, "To those waiting with bated breath for that favorite media catchphrase, the U-turn, I have only one thing to say. You turn if you want to. The lady's not for turning." Her fans argue that her resolution paid off. By 1983, inflation had fallen to 5.4 percent, the lowest rate since 1970, while productivity was increasing.

Thatcher's critics, on the other hand, argue that the economy was bound to improve eventually and would have done so faster had a different approach been taken. They claim that Thatcher made a bad situation worse by sticking dogmatically to a failed theory, and in the process she permanently destroyed Britain's industrial base and created high unemployment. Between 1979 and 1989, unemployment averaged 9.1 percent, compared with 3.4 percent for the period from 1973 to 1979. Thatcher's critics also point to economic statistics indicating rising inequality, leading to the creation of a permanent underclass. This was most visible in urban areas due to the growing number of homeless people, but it could also be seen in rising rates of welfare dependency, child poverty and crime. Particularly hard-hit was the industrial north of England, where unemployment was 60 percent higher than it was in the south.

Not only the regional divisions within England but also those between England and the rest of the United Kingdom were exacerbated during these years. As it was reliant on mining and other forms of heavy industry, the Welsh economy struggled. Scotland, meanwhile, remained committed to a more collectivist way of life that was in sharp opposition to Thatcher's individualist vision. The number of people employed in the public sector continued to be significantly higher in Scotland than it was in England, and more Scots continued to belong to trade unions and to live in council housing. These differences began to create a new electoral map, which in many respects still exists in Britain today. The election of 1987 saw a decisive shift towards the Labour Party in Scotland, Wales and the North of England. The industrial hubs of Manchester, Liverpool and Newcastle did not return a single Tory MP, and the Tories lost eleven of their twenty-one seats in Scotland and six of their fourteen in Wales. The Conservatives, meanwhile, won 227 of the 260 seats in the south of England and the Midlands.

The divisions created by what came to be known as "Thatcherism" were apparent in other ways as well. Prompted by tensions between the police and black communities and exacerbated by the economic struggles of minorities under Thatcher, the early 1980s saw a spate of riots in Britain's cities. The most explosive riots occurred in 1981 in the south London neighborhood of *Brixton*, where the majority of the population was Afro-Caribbean, but that summer saw upheavals in many other cities. The cause of the riots was a subject of debate. Thatcher saw them as the consequence of a "permissive society," while Labour blamed unemployment and racism. Certainly, unemployment was significantly higher among black Britons, while the sputtering economy had increased racism among whites, who felt that black immigrants were taking their jobs. Some people, such as the members of the neofascist group the National Front, advocated an end to all immigration and forcible deportation for the minorities who were already in the country. Most Britons were unwilling to go that far, but many feared that the country was losing its national identity as the numbers of black and Asian immigrants grew. Thatcher was not entirely unsympathetic to these latter views, saying in 1979 that Britain was being "swamped by people with a different culture." In 1981 and 1984, her government passed two Nationality Acts, which strictly limited the right of immigration from the Commonwealth and clearly targeted Asian, African and Caribbean immigrants.

In response to the charge that her policies were increasing inequality, Thatcher asserted that the free market would ultimately lift all, or at least most, boats. She proclaimed the virtue of individualism over egalitarianism, with the welfare state seen as a minimal safety net rather than a mechanism to promote greater socioeconomic equality. "There is no such thing as society," she famously said in 1987. "There are individual men and women, and there are families. And no government can do anything except through people, and people must look to themselves." For her model of an ideal society, Thatcher looked to Britain's past. In 1983, a television interviewer suggested that she was trying to restore "Victorian values," an idea that she enthusiastically embraced although he had meant it as an insult. She wrote in her memoirs that the Victorians "distinguished between the 'deserving' and the 'undeserving' poor" in a manner that did not "reinforce the dependency culture," but rather restored "their self-discipline and their self-esteem."

Sexuality and Gender 7

Margaret Thatcher and Gender

Margaret Thatcher, the first woman to hold the top political office in a major western democracy, was often seen as someone who attempted to deny her gender and even took lessons to lower the pitch of her voice. The impact of gender on Thatcher's career was, however, undeniable. After she became prime minister, some of her male colleagues had trouble accepting her authority; her employment secretary Jim Prior admitted, for example, that he found it "difficult to stomach" working for a woman. But her gender also worked for her. It gained her a seat in the cabinet earlier than she might otherwise have obtained one. Labour prime minister Harold Wilson had included a woman, Barbara Castle, in his cabinet in 1964, and when the Tories returned to power six years later Edward Heath wanted to be seen as equally progressive and so appointed Thatcher as minister of education. After she became Conservative leader, she deliberately cultivated an image of what Campbell terms "an ordinary housewife, old-fashioned, home-loving, and non-feminist, thus allaying both male fears and female disapproval." She often had herself photographed while performing mundane household tasks such as cooking and taking out the garbage. She was well aware that men of her generation felt a need to treat her with chivalry,

Figure 14.1 Margaret Thatcher in the kitchen of the flat on the top floor of 10 Downing Street in 1989. She often had herself photographed in such domestic contexts in order to calm fears that a female prime minister might challenge traditional gender roles.

Reproduced courtesy of Peter Jordan/Alamy Stock Photo.

and she used this to her advantage, bludgeoning her opponents into submission while they struggled with how to simultaneously disagree with and remain gallant towards a woman. The Labour leader Neil Kinnock wrestled with the issue of how to challenge her in the House of Commons without seeming, as he put it, "vile." Kinnock felt that there were "punches" that he "could not throw" against a woman, because the public would see it as "disrespectful." At the end of the day, the fact that Thatcher's foes, and sometimes her friends, frequently referred to her as "that woman" or "that bloody woman" was no accident. Over the course of her political career, her gender defined her in many ways, despite her insistence that it did not.

Because of statements like this, there is a debate about whether Thatcher was a true conservative or was instead someone who wanted to return to the *laissez-faire* liberalism of the nineteenth century. Many people within her own party, whom Thatcher denigrated as the "wets," believed that conservatism by definition encompassed a paternalist view of society in which the better off were supposed to take care of those at the bottom. They also believed that conservatism should be defined by a pragmatic and commonsense approach to problems, not be bound by ideology and moral conviction. Thatcher countered by arguing that the Conservative Party had since the Second World War abandoned its true principles and followed Labour down the path of government intervention to address economic and social problems. They had thus abetted the transformation of Britain into a socialist nation. She argued that the Conservatives had to rediscover their fundamental identity as the party of free markets and minimal government.

In keeping with this vision, she reduced the government's role in the economy through the **privatization** of a variety of state-owned industries, including British Petroleum, British Rail, British Telecom, British Airways, British Steel and the automobile manufacturers Jaguar, Rolls-Royce and Rover. In all, Thatcher sold off forty companies that employed a total of 600,000 workers. In addition, her economic policies called for a shift from direct forms of taxation such as the income tax to indirect forms such as the value-added tax (VAT, or what Americans would think of as a national sales tax, which was raised from 8 to 17.5 percent). Broadly, she supported the dismantling of restraints upon the operations of the free market and a sharp decrease in public spending. Little of this was truly new, but what defined Thatcherism was less its content than the force with which it was enacted. It was not, as one historian writes, a "coherent body of thought or ideology," but rather "a series of non-negotiable precepts."

Divided Opposition

In spite of the polarizing nature of Thatcher's economic policies, her opponents were unable to mount a serious challenge, largely because they lacked unity. After James Callaghan's resignation in 1979, the Labour Party selected as its leader Michael Foot, who was decent and sincere but devoid of the telegenic appeal necessary for political success in a modern media age. He was also hamstrung by a badly divided party. Some Labourites interpreted their defeat in the 1979 election to their failure to endorse stronger left-wing policies. They drove the creation of the 1983 party manifesto, which called for unilateral nuclear disarmament; greater trade union power; greater spending on the National Health Service; increased pensions for the elderly; the renationalization of many of the industries that Thatcher had recently sold off; withdrawal from the European Economic Community in order to protect British industry; and the elimination of the House of Lords. One Labour MP derisively called it "the longest suicide note in history." He had a point, as the party did not return to power for fourteen more years. The electorate had shifted, and the traditional working-class voters, employed in industrial jobs, who had been Labour's core constituency no longer existed as a large and homogeneous group. By the 1980s, people employed in manual labor comprised only half of all British workers, while middle-class, service-sector jobs – whose holders were more likely to vote Tory – were growing. Some members of the Labour Party recognized this change. In 1981, a group of Labour leaders broke ranks because they felt that the party had moved too far to the left. They *formed the Social Democratic Party* (SDP). Their primary appeal was to the people who were disgusted with both the extremes of Thatcherite conservatism and the leftward tilt of the Labour Party. But this meant that they lacked a clear identity, and they were never able to translate their early promise into substantial electoral gains.

Even so, their impact on the political world was substantial, as they split the vote on the left. They also led to the creation of a third party in British politics, the Liberal Democrats. In 1981, the SDP formed an alliance with the Liberal Party, which had survived, barely, since its precipitous decline in the first half of the twentieth century by clinging to a handful of seats in Scotland and Wales. Seven years later, the SDP and the Liberals merged as the Liberal Democrats, or "Lib Dems." Significantly, the Liberal Democrats have been the most consistently pro-European national party within Britain. In their first general election in 1992, they won 17.8 percent of the vote and twenty seats in Parliament. In recent years they have regularly received over 20 percent of the vote, but the Liberal Democrats are hampered by the **"first past the post"** voting system in parliamentary elections, which prevents them from gaining seats in proportion to their electoral success. In 2010, however, they played a crucial role in the formation of a coalition government, as we will see in the next chapter.

Two Victories, and a Bomb

In the early hours of the 12th of October 1984, the Grand Hotel in Brighton, where the Conservative Party was holding its annual conference, was rocked by the explosion of a bomb planted by the Irish Republican Army (IRA). Four people were killed and dozens injured. The most audacious act of political violence that the IRA would ever carry out on British soil, the bombing reflected the degree of animosity that had arisen between Thatcher and Irish republicans. She had inherited a difficult situation in Northern Ireland. Though the violence associated with the Troubles had diminished from its peak in the early 1970s, bombings and murders on both Northern Irish and British soil remained a constant threat. *The Brighton bombing* was not the first time that the violence had touched Thatcher directly: her mentor Airey Neave had been killed by a car bomb planted by the Irish National Liberation Army, a republican paramilitary group, in 1979.

Beyond her personal feelings, Thatcher also opposed Irish republicanism on principle. She was a resolute Unionist and repeatedly declared her intention for Northern Ireland to remain part of the United Kingdom. The sense that as long as Thatcher was prime minister a negotiated settlement was unlikely led to an upsurge in republican violence after 1979. That year, Lord Mountbatten, a military hero of the Second World War, the last viceroy of British India, and a member of the royal family, was blown up while on vacation in the west of Ireland. In 1980, Irish republican inmates in Northern Irish prisons launched a hunger-strike campaign in protest of the denial of their status as political prisoners by the British government. Initially, thirty-seven prisoners in the Maze prison near Belfast vowed to starve themselves to death. This was called off, but in the spring of the following year a prisoner named *Bobby Sands* began another fast. Thatcher refused to budge: she felt that the prisoners were being treated humanely and that granting them the status of political prisoners was submitting to terrorist blackmail. (Recently released documents show that privately the British government worried that "international confidence in British policy" was eroding, and that the cabinet discussed the possibility of "compulsory" – i.e., intravenous – feeding.) In April 1981, Sands stood for election to the British Parliament in a by-election and won; four weeks later, he *died of starvation*. That summer, seven more prisoners starved themselves to death before the IRA called for an end to the hunger strikes. Whichever side was right in a moral sense, it was a tremendous propaganda victory for Irish republicanism, as world opinion was overwhelmingly sympathetic to the hunger strikers. Large sums of money flowed to the IRA from Americans of Irish descent, and Bobby Sands's face continues to adorn republican posters to this day. Thatcher vehemently denied this view and argued that the real martyrs were the victims of republican violence. But the hunger strikes and their aftermath – including a spate of bombings in London that killed sixteen people and injured dozens more – pushed Thatcher towards a political solution to the Northern Irish problem, and negotiations were opened in late 1983.

 See document "The Hunger Strikes in Northern Ireland" at www.routledge.com/cw/ barczewski.

Talks were still ongoing when the IRA bomb exploded in Brighton a year later. Thatcher's secretary had come to her hotel room get her to sign a letter before she went to bed; otherwise, she might have been in the bathroom, where the bomb's effects were more devastating. Though she recognized almost immediately that she had been the target of an assassination attempt, she gave a calm interview to the BBC that night and then gave her speech to the party conference as scheduled the next day, only acknowledging the previous night's horrific events when she pronounced, "all attempts to destroy democracy by terrorism will fail." It was, even her detractors had to acknowledge, an impressive demonstration of her mettle.

The Brighton bombing occurred between the two most important victories of Thatcher's political career. The first, in the *Falklands War*, was for her an unqualified triumph, at least in a political sense. A British dependency since 1833, the Falkland Islands lay 8000 miles from Britain but only 300 miles off the coast of Argentina. The issue of sovereignty over the islands, which in Argentina are called the Malvinas, had long been more important to the Argentines than to the British. In 1982, they were targeted for invasion by Argentina's military dictatorship, led by General Leopoldo Galtieri, in an effort to distract the population from the country's severe economic problems. Though the vast majority of the islands' 1800 inhabitants wished to remain British, the Argentines assumed that the distance from the United Kingdom, along with the Falklands' complete lack of strategic value, would ensure a minimal response from the British government and would score a major propaganda victory for their tottering regime.

But although prior to 1982 few British people had even heard of the Falklands, when the Argentines invaded, the islands suddenly became the linchpin of British prestige. Initially, most people expected yet another humiliation as the long history of the British Empire drew to its painful close. Thatcher, however, saw it as a moment in which to awaken the ghosts of British greatness. Backed by the public, she hastily assembled a naval task force and dispatched it to the Falklands. To be sure, some people were disturbed by the bellicose and chauvinistic attitudes that the war awakened, particularly when Thatcher's order to sink the cruiser *General Belgrano* resulted in the loss of 323 Argentine lives. This order proved a source of great controversy later, as the Argentine government claimed that the *Belgrano* was outside the British-imposed Total Exclusion Zone and was steaming away from the Falklands when it was sunk. (Recently revealed British intelligence reports, which assert that the *Belgrano* was intending to attack any British vessel within range, suggest otherwise.) But at the time no one worried about ensuring the attack was justified. The prevailing attitude was captured by the headline in the *Sun* newspaper, which proclaimed "Gotcha!," a repetition of the outburst by the paper's editor Wendy Henry after she heard the news.

Four thousand British troops landed on the Falklands on the 21st of May. Over the next three weeks, they fought their way to the capital, Port Stanley. The young Argentine conscripts stood little chance against the well-equipped and well-trained British forces. The Argentines surrendered on the 14th of June; in London, crowds gathered outside 10 Downing Street and sang "Rule Britannia." In the three weeks of the conflict, 255 British soldiers and 649 Argentines lost their lives. The conflict cost £3 billion; as Thatcher's biographer John Campbell writes, "it would have been cheaper to give every islander £1 million to settle elsewhere." But the cost was not the point. Thatcher had been convinced from the beginning that this was a crucial moment in British history, and she had transformed it into one by sheer force of will. It had been her war from start to finish; no other event was as significant in defining her as a political leader. The polls were clear: the Tories now had a solid lead, and Thatcher's personal approval rating rose above 50 percent for the first time.

 See document "The Conflict in the Falklands and a New Vision for Britain" at www. routledge.com/cw/barczewski.

The conflict in the Falklands demonstrated that, despite the fact that very little of it remained, the British Empire continued to play a prominent role in British politics in the 1980s. Some people believed that Thatcher was interested in reviving the days of Britain's imperial supremacy. She was far too pragmatic, however, to harbor such romantic dreams: she admired the Empire and saw it as having had a beneficial impact upon the world, but she also thought of it as a thing of the past. In Rhodesia in 1981, she negotiated a settlement that ended the supremacy of the white population and created the independent nation of Zimbabwe. She explored the possibility of keeping Hong Kong under British administration beyond its scheduled reversion to Chinese sovereignty in 1997, but she did not press the issue when Beijing balked.

The victory in the Falklands had major political consequences, as the *Tories swept to a large majority in the 1983 election*. Michael Foot resigned as Labour leader and was replaced by the Welshman Neil Kinnock. Kinnock came from the party's left, but he recognized the need to move Labour towards the center of the political spectrum. At the party conference in 1985, he emphatically denounced those members who clung to "rigid dogmas" that were "outdated, misplaced and irrelevant to the real needs" of the British people. Over the next decade, Labour became a center-left party instead of a far-left one. It abandoned its traditional goals of state ownership of industry and unilateral nuclear disarmament and called for a decrease of the maximum rate of income taxation to 50 percent. (The Tories had cut it from 83 to 60 percent soon after taking power and would further reduce it to 40 percent in 1988.) The party also began to distance itself from the trade unions by renouncing its support of the closed shop, in which all workers in a particular place of business had to belong to the union, a stunning refutation of what had been a sacred component of party doctrine only a few years before. These major changes in Labour's policies demonstrated the extent of Thatcher's impact on the British political world, which had shifted significantly to the right. Thatcherism, which had so recently seemed novel and unusual, now seemed entrenched and inevitable. She would go on in 1987 to become the *first prime minister of the twentieth century to win three consecutive general elections.*

The conflict in the Falklands had displayed Thatcher's signature qualities – unwavering resoluteness, commitment to principle, a willingness to take bold action and a ruthless streak – in a setting in which they appeared as assets. These character traits were again visible, though more controversially, in her next confrontation, which took place in a domestic rather than foreign context. Immediately upon becoming Tory leader, Thatcher made her hostility to labor unions clear. She saw their constant demands for increases in pay and benefits as driving up inflation and interfering with the operations of the free market. She also recognized the political consequences that their unbridled power could have. Industrial disputes had brought down both Edward Heath's Conservative government in 1974 and James Callaghan's Labour government in 1979. The next time around, she was determined to secure a different outcome. After passing a series of legislative acts intended to curtail union power, in early 1984 the government brought the conflict with the unions into the open when it announced its intention to close twenty coal mines in South Yorkshire, which would put 20,000 miners out of work.

Coal was already a dying industry: in the face of declining stocks and increased international competition, the number of British coal miners had fallen from 1.1 million in 1900 to 240,000 in 1983. (Today, there are less than 3000.) Arthur Scargill, the leader of the National Union of Mineworkers (NUM), was as divisive a figure as Thatcher, inspiring fierce loyalty and intense loathing in equal measure. Despite the fact that by the early 1980s three-quarters of British pits were unprofitable and only a £1 billion annual subsidy from the government was keeping the industry alive, the NUM had proven that it was still powerful by forcing substantial concessions from the government in every recent clash. There was no reason to think that this time would be any different. But the government had stockpiled large amounts of coal, and the miners made the mistake of *striking* in the spring, when demand was lower. Their chances of victory were further diminished when a significant number of the miners who worked in the unaffected pits refused to strike. In spite of these obstacles, the miners refused to give up: the strike dragged on and on, with the strikers reduced to desperate poverty. But as the government stood firm and the prospect of victory evaporated, the miners slowly drifted back to work. In March 1985, eleven months after it had begun, the NUM voted to end the strike.

It was a crushing defeat, the worst in the history of the British labor movement. It would never fully recover. Union membership fell from 13.5 million in 1980 to less than 10 million by the time Thatcher left office a decade later; today it stands at around 7 million. The *miners' strike* remains one of the most divisive events in postwar British history. The majority of British people disliked Scargill and disapproved of the frequent strikes of the 1970s. Many of them believed that the breaking of the strike was a victory for democracy over the tyranny of the unions. But they also saw the miners as standing up for a way of life that had long kept the nation's houses warm, against cold economic reality and a colder government. Even many conservatives recognized that miners were hard-working men who toiled in dangerous jobs, and they were discomfited by Thatcher's brutal tactics in putting down the strike. When in July 1984, three months into the strike, Thatcher referred to the miners as "the enemy within," in direct comparison to the Argentine "enemy without" that she had defeated in the Falklands, many people were uncomfortable with her language. They also disliked her aggressive use of the police, which threatened to turn the affected parts of Britain into quasi-military states. In contrast to the conflict in the Falklands, Thatcher's victory over the miners did not increase her popularity. The same character traits – resolution, ruthlessness, an absolute conviction that she was right – were once again on display, and though she won in the end, not everyone, even among her supporters, liked what they saw this time around.

New Wealth and Popular Culture

Far from the coalfields of South Yorkshire, people in other parts of Britain were living very different lives. As in the United States, the deregulation of financial markets in the mid-1980s created a bevy of new stock-trading millionaires. In Britain, the so-called Big Bang of 1986, in which the government eliminated many of the regulations that had governed the markets for centuries, transformed the city of London from an old boys' club into a place in which aggressive, upwardly mobile young men could make large fortunes. Nor were the financial markets the only source of higher incomes. The privatization of many of Britain's largest industries sent executive salaries soaring upwards, and wealth-flaunting "yuppies" in a variety of professions became the increasingly denigrated symbols of the decade's vulgarity and excess. (This did not stop them from being much envied and emulated.) The greed associated with the relentless pursuit of cash was satirized in literary works such as Caryl Churchill's play *Serious Money* (1987), a more humorous version of Oliver Stone's film *Wall Street*, which was released in the United States the same year. Gordon Gekko's iconic phrase "greed is good" resonated in Britain as well. There, it was embodied by "Loadsamoney," a character created by the comedian Harry Enfield, who had been inspired by seeing fans of the London-based Tottenham Hotspur football club waving £10 notes at fans from northern cities where unemployment rates were high.

Rising incomes led to a boom in consumer spending; like their American counterparts, Britons in the 1980s enthusiastically embraced shopping malls and chain superstores. The spending spree was given added impetus by the ready availability of credit. By 1989 British consumers owed £304 billion, much of which was in the form of mortgage loans. The rush to acquire property was particularly pronounced in London, where prices increased by an average of 20 percent annually in the mid-1980s. But also as in America, the fragility of an economy that was now based on finance and consumer spending was demonstrated on "Black Monday" – the 19th of October 1987 – when stock markets around the world plummeted. In London, the Stock Exchange lost £50.6 billion, 24 percent of its value and its biggest ever one-day drop. The British economy ended the 1980s as it had begun them: in recession.

On the surface, the glossy, synthesizer-dominated sound of the "New Wave" music that dominated the charts in the 1980s seemed to perfectly embody the wealth-driven spirit of the decade. Bands such as Duran Duran, Wham!, and the Police emphasized the catchiness of their melodies and the good looks of their members far more than they did commentary on the state of British society. The aggressive striving of these bands for chart success, and the wealth that accompanied it, seemed to be in tune with the new age of entrepreneurship and materialism unleashed by Thatcher. Boy George, the lead singer of the band Culture Club, observed "a new pop superficiality. Suddenly it was OK to be rich, famous and feel no shame. Some saw it as the natural consequence of Thatcherism."

But at the same time, many 1980s bands embedded sharper political messages within their slick sounds. The synthpop band Heaven 17's first single was titled "(We Don't Need This) Fascist Groove Thang," and even Wham! sang about unemployment in "Wham Rap." Other bands tackled contemporary politics head-on. The 1981 single "Stand Down Margaret" by the Beat (known as the English Beat in America) featured the line "our lives seem petty in your cold grey hands" alongside the chorus's repeated calls for Thatcher's resignation. The multiracial ska band the Specials sang about the race riots of the early 1980s in "Ghost Town." Elvis Costello recorded "Shipbuilding," a thoughtful critique of the Falklands War, while Gang of Four used their spiky, minimalist sound to criticize what they termed "capitalist democracy" in songs like "Damaged Goods," "Cheeseburger," "Paralysed" and "Capital (It Fails Us Now)." These impulses diminished as the decade wore on and Thatcherism became more entrenched and accepted, but they did not disappear completely. The Pet Shop Boys satirized the materialism of Thatcher's Britain in songs like "Opportunities (Let's Make Lots of Money)" (1985) and "Shopping" (1987).

Older bands, too, offered a critical perspective on the 1980s. The punk band Clash released their album *London Calling* in December 1979; the timing made it simultaneously the culmination of punk's achievements and a call to arms in Thatcher's Britain. The album featured songs like "Clampdown," a strident demand for British youth to resist the forces of oppression; "The Guns of Brixton," which captured the mood of discontentment and fore-shadowed the race riots that occurred two years later; and the title track, with its apocalyptic vision of the capital's future. The Jam opted for a more cerebral approach in songs such as "The Eton Rifles," about class conflict, and "That's Entertainment," an unromanticized depiction of working-class life, both from the 1980 album *Sound Affects*.

Pop music also challenged the status quo in another arena: gay rights. In the 1980s, being openly gay or lesbian was still not yet tolerated in mainstream British culture. In 1988, a survey revealed that 74 percent of the population felt that homosexual relationships were wrong, up 12 percent from five years earlier. The chart success of pop bands like Frankie Goes to Hollywood and Bronski Beat, members of whom were openly gay and who sang about gay issues, helped to undermine such prejudice. The latter band's hit "Smalltown Boy" (1984) told the story of a young man forced to leave his hometown because he was caught flirting with a man at a local swimming pool.

The most obvious challenge to anti-gay stereotypes, however, came from Boy George, whose band Culture Club recorded a string of hits, beginning with "Do You Really Want to Hurt Me?" in 1982. Though there was considerable discussion of George's androgyny and sexuality in the media on both sides of the Atlantic, he was for the most part accepted by a broad, multigenerational audience. George, however, did not openly declare that he was gay until the publication of his autobiography in 1995. "I wanted people to know I was gay," he wrote later. "It went against every corpuscle of my body to deny it. [But] those around me, management, record company, were worried about sales potential." Other performers, meanwhile, continued to keep their sexual identity a secret. George Michael, the lead singer of Wham!, remained closeted until 2007.

Sexuality and Gender 8

Section 28

The Local Government Act of 1988 was an otherwise innocuous piece of legislation about rules for putting contracts out for bid. The Conservative MP Dame Jill Knight, however, inserted an amendment into it – "Section 28" – which declared that local governments could not "intentionally promote homosexuality" or teach "the accept-ability of homosexuality as a pretended family relationship." Prime Minister Margaret

Thatcher held similar views. She often proclaimed that she wished to see a return to "Victorian values," by which she meant traditional morality. About Section 28, Thatcher said, "children who need to be taught to respect traditional moral values are being taught that they have an inalienable right to be gay. All of those children are being cheated of a sound start in life." These conservative views represented one side of a debate over the place of same-sex relationships in British society in the 1980s. At the time, people were less accepting of such relationships than they are today, and in fact anti-gay sentiment was increasing. A poll in 1983 found that 50 percent of those surveyed thought same-sex relationships were "always wrong." Four years later, that percentage had risen to 67 percent, as the AIDS pandemic led to increased homophobia. A more direct factor that led to Section 28 was a Danish children's book called *Jenny Lives With Eric and Martin* by Susanne Bösche, which was intended to show children that having two gay parents was normal. After the book was published in English in 1983, the Inner London Educational Authority acquired a copy for its libraries. When the right-wing press discovered the book in 1986, the tabloids were full of headlines such as "Save the Children from Sad, Sordid Sex Lessons." Not everyone agreed with these views, however. There were protests around the country, as not only gay Britons but also many people on the political left expressed opposition. In a radio debate about the bill, the actor Ian McKellen revealed that he was gay; the following year he co-founded the gay rights group Stonewall. The constant pressure for its repeal eventually succeeded: Section 28 was revoked in 2000 in Scotland and 2003 in England and Wales. (It had never applied in Northern Ireland.) In 2009, the Conservative party leader David Cameron apologized for his party's passage of the law. Today, Section 28 is often seen as having galvanized the gay rights movement in Britain. But even if it ultimately had a positive legacy, at the time it caused many gay children and young people to suffer, as teachers and local government authorities were afraid to confront homophobic bullying or even to say that it was acceptable to be gay, for fear of running afoul of the law.

Another prominent strain of alternative voices in British popular music came from the North of England. In the 1980s, a number of northern cities produced successful bands, including Leeds (the aforementioned Gang of Four), Sheffield (the Human League and Cabaret Voltaire) and Liverpool (Echo and the Bunnymen), but it was Manchester that became the region's most sonically creative city. The Fall addressed the city's post-industrial grime and decay in songs like "Industrial Estate" and "Fiery Jack," while Joy Division's epic, spare sound provided a perfect soundtrack for northern despair. After recording their biggest hit, "Love Will Tear Us Apart," the band's lead singer Ian Curtis hanged himself in May 1980. But much like the North itself, Joy Division became a symbol of resilience. The remaining members of the band morphed into New Order and enjoyed far greater chart success than they had in their previous incarnation. Manchester, meanwhile, continued throughout the 1980s to produce bands that were popular, critically lauded and politically engaged. The lead singer of the Smiths, Morrissey, was outspoken regarding his antipathy for Thatcher. After the IRA bomb exploded in Brighton, he publicly expressed his regret that it had not killed her. In his song "Margaret on the Guillotine," released on his solo album *Viva Hate* in 1988, he asked, "When will you die?" over and over again.

A final aspect of British popular culture in the 1980s that bears examination is the strong presence of the British Empire, despite is massively shrunken size. The videos for songs such as Duran Duran's "Hungry Like the Wolf" (1982) and Spandau Ballet's "Gold" (1983) were set in unidentified exotic locales that provided appealing backdrops for the handsome band members to romp around in safari dress. Imperial nostalgia, however, was most prevalent in a spate of films about British India. The independence and partition of India in 1947 had occasioned surprisingly little public reaction in Britain, and for decades afterwards the place of the Raj in popular culture seemed to be marked by historical amnesia. During the 1980s, however, a number of films and television programs about British India appeared: the historian Antoinette Burton observes that there was "an inexhaustible market for the exotic allure of British imperialism." These included Richard Attenborough's Academy Award–winning film biography *Gandhi* (1982); the film adaptation of E.M. Forster's novel *A Passage to India* (1984); and the television mini-series *The Far Pavilions* (1984) and *The Jewel in the Crown* (1984). The latter, a fourteen-part adaptation of Paul Scott's *Raj Quartet* novels, averaged an impressive 8 million viewers per episode. These productions did not always depict colonial rule in glowing terms. *A Passage to India* emphasized the racism of the British community in India during the interwar years, and one of the main characters in *The Jewel in the Crown*, the British police officer Ronald Merrick, takes a sadistic delight in beating the Indians in his custody. But they also presented more positive views of the Empire and emphasized the glamor, romance and exoticism of their settings. The pomp and ceremony of the Raj, including dinners with Indian princes, rides on elephants and journeys by steam train through tropical landscapes, were on prominent display. At the same time, the depiction of the Raj and its demise focused almost exclusively on the British community rather than on the millions of Indian men, women and children who were affected.

The Presence of Empire 8

Film and Empire

By the early twentieth century, going to the cinema was an established form of recreation throughout the Empire, as audiences enjoyed Hollywood and British films in locales ranging from the Caribbean to Australia. Colonial authorities viewed these films as more than mere entertainment, however, as they closely monitored their content to ensure that it did not undermine the objectives of imperial governance. On the one hand, they sought to harness the new technology of film for propaganda and educational purposes; on the other, censorship was utilized to prevent the production or screening of films seen as likely to damage colonial authority. Cinema also contributed to the impact of the Empire on Britain. By the 1930s, Britain boasted over 5000 movie theaters, and a large segment of the British population went to the cinema each week. The same decade saw the emergence of what the film historian Jeffrey Richards has called the "cinema of empire." A series of popular feature films such as *Gunga Din* (1939) and *The Four Feathers* (1939) conveyed stories of imperial adventure. These films emphasized the masculine heroics of British soldiers and adventurers and painted flattering portraits of colonial rule. In the postwar era, however, the depiction of empire, like the British Empire itself changed. Films such as *Lawrence of Arabia* (1962), *Zulu* (1964) and *The Man Who Would Be King* (1975) continued the tradition of the imperial epic but offered a more critical view of empire. The enduring strength of the imperial epic continued to be felt into the 1980s, particularly in Richard Attenborough's Academy Award–winning biopic *Gandhi*. While the film depicted its subject reverently, it also seemed to absolve the British of any responsibility for the violence that accompanied the end of colonial rule.

Why were these nostalgic depictions of Britain's imperial past so popular in the 1980s? The patriotic climate after the British victory in the Falklands War, itself a legacy of the British Empire, helped give these productions a warm reception. Thatcher's bellicose stance on foreign affairs convinced many people that the days of empire had returned, at least in spirit. But at the same time, the process of decolonization was largely over by the 1980s, and the Empire, including its racism and brutality, could be viewed as something that was safely in the past. Lastly, depictions of the Raj, with their period costumes and romantic settings, became part of the burgeoning "heritage industry" in contemporary Britain. *The Jewel in the Crown* chronicled the demise of the Raj much like the wildly popular mini-series *Brideshead Revisited* (1981) depicted the decline of the aristocracy.

Some Britons, however, felt that the legacy of empire should not be treated so romantically. The Labour MP Diane Abbott declared in 1989,

> It is a common fallacy among Americans to believe Europeans are nicer than Americans and more liberal than Americans. Far from Britain being a nicer and more liberal society, the British invented racism. They built an empire on which racism was the organizing principle. I believe Britain is one of the most fundamentally racist nations on earth.

By that point, an increasing number of voices, often writing from **postcolonial** perspectives, were addressing the legacy of empire in Britain more critically. In literature, notable authors included the novelists Salman Rushdie, Penelope Lively and Timothy Mo and the poet-musician Linton Kwesi Johnson. Perhaps most influential was the filmmaker (and later novelist) Hanif Kureishi, the London-born son of an English mother and Pakistani father, whose films *My Beautiful Laundrette* (1985) and *Sammy and Rosie Get Laid* (1987) presented complex views of people of South Asian heritage in Britain. Kureishi's work played a key role in helping to overturn stereotypes and in opening the way for the explosion of postcolonial and multicultural literature that would make British culture so dynamic in the following decade.

Downfall

In the late 1980s, Thatcher's invincibility crumbled. That her will was no longer sufficient to get her way was demonstrated in 1989, when she attempted to replace traditional local rates of taxation, based on property values, with a fixed-rate charge per household, based on the number of people living there. She labeled the new tax a "community charge," but it was quickly termed a more derogatory "**poll tax**." Opposition surged when it was revealed that more than 90 percent of the population would be paying more than they had under the old system. In March 1990, a demonstration against the poll tax in Trafalgar Square drew 200,000 protestors. It led to some of the worst riots in London's history, in which 450 people were injured. When the tax went into effect the following month, some areas reported that half their residents refused to pay. Thatcher had with one miscalculation succeeded in alienating many of the middle-class voters that she relied upon for her electoral success. Polls showed that Labour was now running more than twenty points ahead of the Conservatives.

Thatcher's power was of a sufficient magnitude, however, that it would take more than one crisis to fatally undermine it. The second issue that led to Thatcher's downfall was European unification. The Conservatives had traditionally favored engagement with Europe, but in the 1980s the **Euroskeptic** wing of the party grew in strength. Thatcher herself followed this line, moving from half-hearted enthusiasm for Europe in the 1970s to hostility. Thatcher, who enjoyed a close relationship with the American president Ronald Reagan, believed the "special relationship" with the United States was more important than Britain's links to Europe.

As an enthusiast for free trade, she supported the creation of a single market, but not a single currency, and she was adamantly opposed to the move towards federalism that began to develop in the mid-1980s. "We have not successfully rolled back the frontiers of the state in Britain, only to see them re-imposed at a European level with a European superstate exercising a new dominance from Brussels," Thatcher said in 1988. She enjoyed playing the role of the defender of Britain's sovereignty, so much so that at times she seemed to be fighting the Second World War all over again, treating the continental nations as either enemies or inferior allies. The fall of the Berlin Wall only exacerbated this attitude, as she feared the enhanced power of a reunified Germany, which would surely be, and indeed became, the dominant state in a federated Europe. In 1989, she told one of her foreign policy advisors, "we've been through the war and know perfectly well what the Germans are like and . . . how national character basically doesn't change."

 See document "Thatcher's Vision for the European Union" at www.routledge.com/cw/barczewski.

Thatcher's rhetoric ensured that Britain was identified as unified Europe's most reluctant member. It was during her time in office that European politicians began to refer to the "Bloody British Question," as they despaired of finding a way to keep Britain in the union without having to endure constant protests from Thatcher that its national sovereignty was being threatened. Her stance not only alienated political leaders on the continent, it also created massive dissension within her own party. Her increasing stridency caused a breach with her chancellor of the Exchequer, Nigel Lawson, and her foreign secretary, Geoffrey Howe, who both felt that it was imperative for Britain to remain a part of a unified Europe. In the summer of 1989, they threatened to resign if she did not give way. She backed down temporarily, but subsequently removed Howe from his post, demoting him to speaker of the House of Commons. She was now committed to a firm anti-Europe stance, and she reveled in her isolation, both within Europe and within her own cabinet, without realizing how dangerous it had become to her political future.

In 1989, Thatcher spoke of going "on and on" as prime minister. Her ministers, however, were weary of her autocratic and combative style. The public, too, had seen enough: in the spring of 1990 her approval rating stood at 25 percent, back in the depths where it had been in her first years as prime minister. Conservative politicians were deeply worried about their prospects if they went into the next election with Thatcher as leader. Still, few predicted her imminent demise. It was Europe that served as the catalyst. As the continent moved towards a single currency, the British government's economic team proposed a less radical alternative called a "hard ecu," which would be used primarily by multinational businesses and tourists. But Thatcher scuttled her ministers' efforts to take even this moderate position. In consequence, Howe resigned as speaker of the House. Over the next few days, Tory MPs called increasingly loudly for a leadership contest. Expecting to win easily, she called one for the 20th of November, two weeks hence. Thatcher's main challenger for the leadership was Michael Heseltine, former secretary of state for defence, who was from the left wing of the party.

A few days later, Howe went before the Commons and excoriated Thatcher for her "nightmare image" of a Europe "teeming with ill-intentioned people" who sought to undermine democracy and British sovereignty. He concluded with an open challenge to her leadership, saying, "perhaps the time has come for others to consider their own response to the tragic conflict of loyalties with which I have myself wrestled for so long." The effect was devastating: it was not so much what was said but who had said it, for Howe had long been one of Thatcher's most loyal supporters. Thatcher won the subsequent leadership vote by 204 to 152, but she was four votes short of the 15 percent margin required to prevent a second ballot. Most of her cabinet ministers told her they would not support her the next time around, which meant that if she continued to battle, Heseltine would become prime minister. If she stepped aside now, she could ensure that her successor would continue her legacy. Four days later, *Margaret Thatcher waved goodbye from the steps of 10 Downing Street for the last time*, and *John Major, whom she favored as her successor, became prime minister*. The suddenness with which British politics can change is very different from the lengthy electoral process in America. But even in a nation accustomed to quick changes in the political landscape, Thatcher's disappearance from the scene was stunningly abrupt.

The Conservatives in Government After Thatcher

Under Prime Minister *John Major* the Conservatives went from being well behind in the polls to being well ahead almost overnight. Major was selected because of what he was not: not Thatcher, certainly, but also not Michael Heseltine, the option on the party's left, who was simply too liberal and too flashy a personality for many Tory traditionalists. The son of a mother who was a circus performer, Major was from the humblest origins of any British prime minister. He had grown up in a house with a shared lavatory and had dropped out of school at sixteen. Once in office, his consensual style provided a much-needed level of comfort, in stark contrast to Thatcher's confrontational and divisive approach. He would never, however, manage to get out from under the towering shadow of his predecessor. Famously depicted by the satirical television puppet show *Spitting Image* in black and white while everyone else was in color, Major was doomed to spend his premiership healing the wounds created by his predecessor rather than being able to define his own agenda.

Some of those wounds were still bleeding. Major's gentler style could not bridge the bitter Conservative division over Europe. The issue nearly came to a head over the *Maastricht Treaty* of 1991, which brought the European Union (EU) into being as a true political, social and economic union for the first time. The Labour and Liberal Democratic parties supported the treaty, while the "Euroskeptic" wing of the Tories adamantly opposed it. Major ultimately negotiated a precarious compromise in which Britain signed the treaty but opted out of the currency union and the "social chapter," which covered issues relating to workers' rights and trade unions. To add to his difficulties, the British economy remained in recession, and when he called for an election in 1992, many people expected a Labour victory.

Instead, the *Conservatives emerged the winners*, for reasons that are still debated. Some blamed Labour's "shadow budget," which had called for the top rate of income tax to be raised from 40 to 50 percent. Others attributed the victory to the popular press: on election day, the conservative *Sun* newspaper ran a headline asking "the last person to leave Britain" to "turn out the lights" if Labour won. Still others blamed the triumphalism of the Labour Party, which had come to expect an easy victory. Afterwards, statistical analysis cited a "shy Tory factor," in which people did not want to admit they were voting for the Conservatives due to peer pressure within both traditionally Labour-voting working-class constituencies and liberal-leaning middle-class ones. Whatever the reason, when the votes were counted, the Conservatives had a majority of forty-five in the House of Commons. Having lost its fourth straight election, Labour was forced yet again to regroup, and this time it was clear that the party had to undergo a thorough house cleaning. Neil Kinnock resigned as leader and was replaced by John Smith, an affable Scotsman who continued to move the party towards the center. His most important achievement was to eliminate the trade union block vote at Labour Party conferences and replace it with the principle of "one member one vote," which seriously diminished union power.

At the same time, however, the victorious Tories faced serious political difficulties, with the crisis once again occurring over Europe. In 1979, Britain had refused to join the European Exchange Rate Mechanism (ERM), which was intended to stabilize European currencies in preparation for the transition to the euro. But in 1990, the pro-Europe left wing of the Conservative Party gained sufficient clout to compel Britain's entry into the ERM. The pound was pegged to the German deutsche mark, but parity between the two currencies was always going to be tricky to maintain, because at the time Britain's rate of inflation was three times higher than Germany's. The situation was exacerbated when the economic pressures imposed by German reunification required Germany to raise interest rates, forcing Britain to follow suit. This put enormous pressure on credit and housing markets. As the value of sterling plummeted, Major had to authorize the spending of billions of pounds in a desperate attempt to prop it up. It did not work: when foreign currency traders continued their massive sell-off of sterling, the government was forced to announce a humiliating withdrawal from the ERM. The Conservatives dropped more than ten points in the polls overnight. After threatening for years to destroy the Tories, Europe had finally come close to doing so.

Domestically, although he personally evinced a less doctrinaire approach to governing than his predecessor, the John Major years were characterized by many of the same policy initiatives that had been pursued by Thatcher's governments. Despite mass protests, the remaining coal mines and British Rail were both privatized, the former leading to pit closures and redundancy packages for those that lost their jobs, the latter to competing private sector franchises that run the routes and a publicly subsidized company that maintains the infrastructure. Under Major, law and order issues rose to the fore. The home secretary, Michael Howard, introduced numerous reforms to the criminal justice system, including ending the "right to silence" of an accused person (meaning that refusal to answer police questions could itself be inferred as evidence in a trial), increasing prison sentences and cracking down on squatting, fox hunt sabotage and the increasingly popular but illegal warehouse parties known as raves. In education policy, Major's government introduced standardized testing and an independent school inspectorate that made public its results in school ranking tables, with the aim of giving parents more information and choice about where their children were educated. These reforms were resisted by teachers' unions, and critics pointed out that only those financially better off were really able to exercise the choice of where to send their children. The post-secondary system was also revamped, with the division between the so-called polytechnic colleges and universities ended and most polytechnics becoming full-fledged universities. By the end of Major's term in office, university attendance in Britain was the largest in its history. Approximately one-third of those who finished secondary school now went onto university, a figure approaching North American attendance numbers.

Throughout his term in office, Major faced criticism from within his own party, mostly from the right, who wanted the government to press on with the Thatcher agenda more aggressively and who were increasingly hostile to further European integration. Tired of the incessant snipping at him from his own backbench MPs, Major abruptly resigned as head of the Conservative Party in June 1995 and called for a leadership contest, while remaining prime minister until the leadership issue was resolved. Major won the contest with over two-thirds of the vote, which he hoped would end the divisions and internal criticism of him from within the Party once and for all. It did not. Moreover, thereafter the party and his government became embroiled in a series of financial and sexual scandals at the very same time Major was calling for a return to "traditional" moral and family values. Major later recounted that practically every weekend he would be warned by an advisor of the next embarrassing news story about to break. Disgust among the Tory ranks, defections to other parties and by-election losses meant that by the end of 1996, the Tories had lost their majority in the Commons. A perception of "sleaze" hung over Major's government and the Conservatives generally as they prepared for the next election in 1997. By this time, after eighteen years in power, with widespread public perception of the Tories as hypocritical and corrupt and facing a rejuvenated Labour Party with a charismatic new leader, few political pundits thought Major had a chance to win the election. The pundits proved correct.

Conclusion

Whatever one's opinion of what the 1980s and early 1990s had wrought, there was no doubt as to who had played the starring role. Alone among twentieth-century prime ministers, Margaret Thatcher has come to have her name linked to a particular set of policies; not even Winston Churchill managed that. To be sure, the extent of Conservative dominance in the 1980s must be kept in perspective. Though Thatcher's parliamentary majorities were substantial, the highest percentage of the popular vote that the Conservatives ever received under her leadership was 43.9 in 1979. In 1983, it fell to 42.4 and in 1987 to 42.2. After the Conservative loss in the election of 1997, they would remain out of power for thirteen years, their longest stretch since 1906. All of this serves as a reminder that much of Thatcher's electoral success was the product of divisions in her opposition rather than her personal popularity or that of her policies.

Nonetheless, Thatcher's impact on twentieth-century Britain was substantial. She fundamentally changed the nature of the Tory Party, making it less elitist and more middle-class, with fewer public school and Oxbridge-educated MPs and more from the professional and business worlds. This new breed of Tory MPs still tended to be wealthy, but their money was now self-made rather than inherited. Thatcher changed the Labour Party as well. During the 1980s, Labour abandoned any pretense, rhetorical or real, of socialism and embraced the economics of the free market. Thatcher thus succeeded in moving the entire spectrum of British politics to the right.

Beyond the realm of partisan politics, Thatcher's impact on Britain was twofold. First, she was widely perceived to have arrested the long, slow, painful national decline that had been occurring since the end of the Second World War. "We have ceased to be a nation in retreat," she declared after the Falklands War. Decline can be measured in economic statistics, but it is also an issue of cultural perception. Even many of Thatcher's enemies concede that she did much to change the perception of terminal decline. Second, Thatcher was the architect, for better or worse, of fundamental changes in the British economy. Taken as a whole, Britain's economic record during the Thatcher years was mixed. The financial, retail and other service sectors did well, while the country's industrial capacity declined by 15 percent. Between 1979 and 1990 British productivity rose by 11 percent, but over the same period America's productivity grew by 65 percent and Germany's by 25 percent. Britain's rates of economic growth during the 1980s barely exceeded those of the much-maligned 1970s, and they lagged seriously behind that of countries like Germany, Japan and the United States. At a micro- rather than macroeconomic level, overall prosperity increased, with the average real incomes of British families rising by 37 percent from 1979 to 1992. But these gains were disproportionately felt at the top: the incomes of the wealthiest tenth of British society grew by 61 percent, while those of the bottom tenth fell by 18 percent. Over the same period, the number of Britons living below the poverty line rose from 5 million to 14 million.

For these reasons, Thatcher continued to inspire visceral hatred long after she had disappeared from the political stage. At the time of her death in 2013, she had not been prime minister for almost a quarter-century and had been absent from the public eye for several years due to the fact that she was suffering from dementia. Even so, some Britons held parties to celebrate, and a re-release of the song "Ding Dong! The Witch Is Dead" from *The Wizard of Oz* peaked at number two on the British charts after a Facebook campaign. The vitriol of the response demonstrates the extent of Thatcher's impact upon Britain. During her premiership, many of the norms that had underpinned government actions were significantly altered; no subsequent government has attempted to return things to the way they were before her arrival at 10 Downing Street. As the *Guardian* declared in its obituary, "Thatcher broke the pattern of postwar politics and changed its nature."

Figures 14.2 and 14.3 Two images from the day of Margaret Thatcher's funeral on the 17th of April 2013 showing how she continued to polarize opinion over two decades after her resignation as prime minister. Taken at 5 a.m., Figure 14.2 depicts people camped out in London overnight in order to ensure that they got a good view of the procession. On the barrier fencing hangs the flag of the Falkland Islands, a reminder of the patriotism the British victory had bestirred in 1982. Figure 14.3 shows that some spectators had a different opinion of Mrs. Thatcher.

Figure 14.2 reproduced courtesy of John Pannell; Figure 14.3 reproduced courtesy of Sebastian Remme/Alamy Stock Photo.

Bibliography

Augar, Philip, *The Death of Gentlemanly Capitalism* (2000)

Beresford, David, *Ten Men Dead: The Story of the 1981 Irish Hunger Strike* (1987)

Campbell, John, *The Iron Lady: Margaret Thatcher, from Grocer's Daughter to Prime Minister* (2009)

Evans, Eric J., *Thatcher and Thatcherism*, 2nd edn (2004)

McSmith, Andy, *No Such Thing as Society: A History of Britain in the 1980s* (2010)

Middlebrook, Martin, *The Falklands War* (1985)

Reynolds, Simon, *Rip It Up and Start Again: Postpunk, 1978–1984* (2006)

Stewart, Graham, *Bang!: A History of Britain in the 1980s* (2014)

Turner, Alwyn, *Rejoice! Rejoice!: Britain in the 1980s* (2010)

Vinen, Richard, *Thatcher's Britain: The Politics and Social Upheaval of the Thatcher Era* (2009)

Young, Hugo, *One of Us: A Biography of Margaret Thatcher* (1989)

15 New Labour to Brexit

Topics covered

- Tony Blair and the rise of New Labour
- New Labour's achievements and the role of "spin"
- Good Friday Agreement in Northern Ireland
- Blair and the Iraq War
- 7/7 bombings in London and the debate over multiculturalism
- Return of Conservative government in 2010
- Referendum on Scottish independence
- The Brexit referendum

Timeline

1994	Tony Blair becomes Labour leader
1997	Labour wins general election; Blair becomes prime minister
1998	Scottish Parliament and National Assembly for Wales created
1998	"Good Friday" Agreement signed
2001	Labour wins re-election
2003	Iraq War begins
2005	Labour wins third term
2005	Terrorist attacks on London public transportation system
2007	Blair resigns; Gordon Brown becomes prime minister
2010	First coalition government since 1945; David Cameron becomes prime minister
2014	Scotland votes to stay in the United Kingdom
2016	Britain votes to leave the European Union

Introduction

Following the upheavals of Thatcher's governments, both major political parties underwent significant evolutions. In the 1990s, Labour remade itself into "New Labour," which took the party to its greatest-ever heights of success, with three general election victories in a row between 1997 and 2005. But by the end of the party's period in power in 2010, the questions as to whether it had "sold its soul" in order to win elections were growing ever

DOI: 10.4324/9781003284758-15

louder. Internal convulsions within the ranks of the party would eventually lead to the rise of a new leader, Jeremy Corbyn, in 2015, who in some ways represented a return to the views of the pre–New Labour left. Popular with party members and with youth generally, Corbyn was disliked and distrusted by most of his fellow Labour MPs. Seemingly turning his back on the New Labour approach that had been so successful, he would lead the Party in two elections with mixed results. The retreat of the Conservatives from the "Thatcher Revolution," meanwhile, allowed them to achieve victory in 2010, albeit in coalition with the Liberal Democratic Party. For half a decade David Cameron's less combative, more inclusive version of conservatism seemed likely to endure, but Tory divisions between their own left and right wings over Europe, social policy and immigration would in 2016 destroy his premiership and plunge Britain into the most convulsing political crisis since the 1930s.

These political changes took place in the context of, and in many ways have been driven by, a changing British society. Britain had become a far more diverse place than it was even a few decades earlier, thanks largely to the arrival of a significant number of immigrants from Asia, Africa and the Caribbean, and also from migrants from the European Union. The extent of the changes they have brought can be exaggerated: the demographics of many parts of rural Britain today remain largely unchanged. But the revelation in the 2011 census that "white Britons" were now a minority of London's population was undeniable evidence that the diversity of many urban areas had increased markedly.

At the same time, the diversity of the United Kingdom was demonstrated in other ways. In the late 1990s, Scotland and Wales were granted their own devolved legislative assemblies, which had authority over most domestic affairs, while international matters and energy policy remained under the jurisdiction of the Westminster Parliament. In Northern Ireland, the negotiation of the Good Friday Agreement in 1998 held out the promise of a lasting peace; there, too, a new assembly led to a more autonomous state in which Catholic nationalists and Protestant Unionists shared power, albeit sometimes uneasily. This new devolved system of governance meant that the constitutional arrangements of the United Kingdom became more complex than ever. While MPs representing Scotland, Wales and Northern Ireland continued to sit in the Westminster Parliament and to vote on English affairs, MPs representing England did not have the same privilege in the devolved assemblies. Though this system in some ways acknowledged and redressed the longstanding imbalance of power among England and the other parts of the United Kingdom, it was also politically anomalous and eventually led to a rise in English political nationalism. Devolution also did not prevent the surge in popularity of the Scottish National Party, which successfully demanded a referendum on Scottish independence in 2014. The result of that vote did not reach the threshold needed to begin negotiations on Scotland leaving the United Kingdom, but it was sufficiently close for the issue to remain alive for the foreseeable future.

Britain's growing social, cultural and political diversity also engendered debate. From the early 2000s onwards a backlash developed against it in some areas, fueled by anger over immigration, by growing regional inequality and by a perceived lack of accountability for the devastating effects of the global economic crisis of 2008. Amongst Labour supporters a divide developed between young, cosmopolitan, largely middle-class urbanites who supported progressive cultural policies such as women's and LGBT rights (and embraced cultural diversity and European integration), and the party's more socially conservative traditional working-class supporters in the older industrial towns of the Midlands and North of England. This backlash was also evident in the rise of the populist United Kingdom Independence Party (UKIP), which seriously challenged the Conservatives for votes on the right of the political spectrum but also siphoned off support from Labour. When Cameron decided to call a referendum in 2016 on Britain's continued membership in the European Union, he intended it to silence his own Euroskeptic backbenchers and quell the anxieties of Tory MPs about how much UKIP was cutting into their voter base. The result, however, was a surprise victory for those who wanted Britain to leave the EU.

Tony Blair and the Rise of New Labour

For much of the 1980s, it appeared as if the Labour Party was doomed to irrelevance. Even as Thatcher's personal vice-grip on the political world weakened, Labour was unable to present a viable challenge, as it continued to be riven by divisions between traditionalists and modernizers. Labour's attempt to rebuild after the calamity of the 1992 election was thrown into crisis when Labour Party leader John Smith died suddenly of a heart attack in May 1994. The resulting election for the leadership was the most soul-searching that the party had ever faced. The battle between the traditionalists and the modernizers was now fully out in the open: no patchwork compromise was possible this time around. The contest was between the traditionalist John Prescott, a burly Welsh former trade union activist (albeit one with a degree from Oxford) and the modernizer *Tony Blair*, who was young (forty-one), charismatic and the possessor of a megawatt smile. By this point, the party recognized that it needed a leader who could appeal to middle-class voters, particularly in England, where Labour support had been steadily eroding. Blair was easily elected leader, besting Prescott with 57 percent of the vote to 24 percent.

Blair was a keen observer of American politics, and he took much of his inspiration for remaking the Labour Party from what was happening there in the early 1990s. By 1992, the American Democratic Party, like Labour, had lost three consecutive elections and had spent twelve years out of power (as compared to Labour's thirteen). As he watched the centrist Bill Clinton lead the Democrats to an emphatic victory over an incumbent president in 1992, Blair saw a model for Labour to follow. Elections, he came to believe, were not about attracting the greatest number of true believers but about winning the middle ground of moderate swing voters. In his first act as leader, Blair declared his intention to rewrite Clause IV of the Labour constitution, which called for the nationalization of the economy. Though the language had long been seen as archaic and the change was purely symbolic, it was viewed by many observers as the moment in which the "old" Labour Party was transformed into the "new."

Blair was an astoundingly gifted politician, with a rare ability to understand and appeal to voters' emotions and to capture the national mood in a speech or even a phrase. If the Falklands War marked the apex of Margaret Thatcher's premiership in terms of her ability to judge and respond to the national mood, then for Tony Blair that moment came with the death of Princess Diana in a car accident in Paris in 1997. Unlike many Labour politicians, Blair was a committed supporter of the monarchy. He enjoyed his weekly meetings with the Queen and always spoke of the royal family with respect. But he was not always adept at dealing with the royals directly. When Bill Clinton visited Britain in 1998, Blair's team forgot to arrange a meeting with the Queen, irritating Buckingham Palace. On the day of his first **Queen's Speech** as prime minister, Blair walked to the Houses of Parliament from Downing Street, upstaging the Queen's arrival as he shook hands with people along the way.

The relationship became even more fraught in the wake of Diana's death. On the night of the 30th of August 1997, Blair was at Myrobella, his house in his **constituency** in Sedgefield in County Durham, when the phone rang at 2 a.m. Blair was informed that there had been a serious accident in Paris in which Diana's lover Dodi Fayed had been killed and the Princess seriously injured. An hour-and-an-half later, Blair learned that Diana was dead. Blair was genuinely devastated, but he also recognized immediately that the news, as he told his press secretary Alastair Campbell, was "going to produce real public grief on a scale that is hard to imagine." As he sipped a cup of tea alone in the early morning hours, he determined that he would need to make a statement, a decision that was confirmed when he heard that the royal family would not be offering any praise for the Princess, only an acknowledgment of the shock of her sudden death. The next day, a visibly emotional Blair stood outside his local church and described Diana in glowing terms. He concluded with words, written by Campbell, that would be repeated many times over in the days ahead: "She was the People's Princess and that is how she will stay, how she will remain in our hearts and our memories forever."

After the initial shock receded, Blair saw his role as trying to mitigate the damage to the royal family that was being caused by their apparent hostility towards Diana. Blair feared that the intense emotional response of the British public was going to go "horribly wrong" if the monarchy was not seen to be treating Diana's death appropriately. He played a key role in convincing the royal family to give Diana a public rather than a private funeral. He convinced the Queen to return to London from Balmoral, her estate in the Scottish Highlands; to fly the royal standard at half-mast over Buckingham Palace; and to make a statement expressing her grief. Blair thus played a vital role in saving the monarchy from the serious damage it might have suffered had the royal family not ameliorated its stance. He had acted out of a genuine commitment to and respect for the monarchy, but the events of that extraordinary week forever altered the relationship between the Labour government and the Queen. Some members of the royal household resented the perception that the Queen had only acted at Blair's urging. Others felt that the politicians had tried to exploit the situation for their gain. Blair did not pay much mind to these criticisms. In this period, his approval rating soared to a stratospheric 93 percent, the highest ever recorded for a prime minister.

Blair's detractors derided him as a mere actor who lacked true convictions, and he was never trusted by the left of the party. But Blair won three elections and served four years longer than any other Labour prime minister in British history. None of this occurred by accident. He had one goal when he became leader: win elections. This was accomplished in 1997 by stressing that the party had abandoned its commitments to large-scale state intervention, "tax-and-spend" economic policies and a welfare state that emphasized social security over individual responsibility. Such positions clearly resonated with the British public that had absorbed almost two decades of Thatcherite Conservatism. A massive swing to Labour gave the party a majority of 179 seats in the House of Commons, the biggest it had ever had. Garnering only 31 percent of the vote, the Conservatives lost a staggering 178 seats, including substantial numbers in traditionally solid-Tory **Middle England**. It was their worst electoral performance since 1832. There was not a single Conservative MP left in Scotland and Wales and only a handful in the urban areas of England. "Nothing will ever equal that defeat," recalled the former Tory minister Anne Widdecombe. "It was shattering." Labour would go on to win the next two elections, in 2001 and 2005; it was the greatest run of electoral success the party had ever enjoyed.

In keeping with New Labour's youthful image, the 1990s saw a resurgence of British culture that the media called "Cool Britannia." Cool Britannia was most closely associated with popular music, and specifically with the emergence of Britpop, which sought to revive the simple, catchy pop songs of the British Invasion of the 1960s. Britpop bands like Blur and Oasis focused on British themes in their lyrics and featured British imagery, especially the Union Jack, in their music videos. Most critics regard Blur's albums *Modern Life Is Rubbish*

(1993) and *Parklife* (1994) and Oasis's *Definitely Maybe* (1994) and *What's the Story Morning Glory?* (1995) as the apex of Britpop. Both bands were invited to 10 Downing Street, as Tony Blair sought to link them to his efforts to create a youthful, vibrant image for his government. A more mainstream exemplar of Cool Britannia was the Spice Girls, best known in America for their 1997 hit "Wannabe." The Spice Girls very much emphasized their Britishness, most famously in the form of band member Geri Halliwell's Union Jack minidress.

Beyond music, Cool Britannia was also associated with art, and specifically with the emergence of the Young British Artists, or YBAs. The YBAs garnered much of their support from the art collector Charles Saatchi, co-founder of the advertising agency Saatchi and Saatchi. Saatchi almost singlehandedly revived the contemporary art market in Britain in the mid-1990s. The most prominent artist associated with the YBAs was Damien Hirst, whose best-known creation was *The Physical Impossibility of Death in the Mind of Someone Living* (1991), which consisted of a 14-foot-long tiger shark suspended in formaldehyde in a glass case. Cool Britannia did not last long. In 1995, Blur and Oasis each released albums (*The Great Escape* and *Be Here Now*) that most critics panned, and though they both continued to enjoy considerable popularity, their days of dominating the British music scene were over. By 2000, politicians and pundits, and even the musicians themselves, were declaring themselves heartily sick of the whole thing.

Figures 15.1 A feature of Britpop was its embrace of patriotic symbols. For the 1997 BRIT Awards, Spice Girl Geri Halliwell (i.e., Ginger Spice) wore a Union Jack dress, made from a tea towel sewn by Halliwell's sister onto a black Gucci minidress. It became a massive fashion success; in a 2010 poll by the *Daily Telegraph*, it was named the most iconic dress of the last fifty years, topping even Princess Diana's wedding dress. This Ginger Spice doll from 1997 confirms the dress's fame.

Reproduced courtesy of author's collection.

New Labour's Achievements and the Role of "Spin"

In some ways, New Labour became a victim of its own success. Almost immediately upon taking office in 1997, the government's main objective became winning the next election, in order to prove that Labour's resurgence was real and not a fluke. New Labour thus expended massive energy on presentation and media relations; the word most commonly associated with the Blair years was "spin." Many observers viewed Blair's two key media advisors, Peter Mandelson and Alastair Campbell, as the behind-the-scenes puppet masters of a government that lacked a clear policy agenda beyond the clever catch phrases and carefully polished image. Campbell in particular was given unprecedented authority, as he became the first press secretary to attend cabinet meetings and was the possessor of special Orders in Council that allowed him to give orders to civil servants.

The concern with political consequences was apparent when it came to dealing with Europe, which continued to be the most divisive issue in British politics. Seeing it as a key part of making Britain a modern, globally oriented nation, Blair referred on numerous occasions to full membership in the European Union, including the single currency, as Britain's "destiny." He wanted Britain not only to join but also to play a leadership role in the European Union, which he recognized would be difficult if Britain did not join the euro. He was aware, however, that the majority of the British public did not favor giving up the pound, and ultimately he was unwilling to take the political consequences of trying to persuade them. Nor was he willing to take on Gordon Brown, his chancellor of the Exchequer, who emphatically opposed Britain's entry on economic grounds. In Brown's view, the fundamental problem was that Britain traditionally maintained higher interest rates than other European nations; lowering the rates would mean either substantial tax increases or cuts in spending, neither of which he was prepared to undertake. Even so, Britain did play a more active role in the EU under Blair than it had under Thatcher.

On the domestic front, New Labour succeeded in lowering unemployment and interest rates and in achieving rates of economic growth that were higher than in most European countries. The government boosted funding for education and the National Health Service (NHS); by 2010, there were 42,000 more doctors and 90,000 more nurses employed by the NHS, and deaths from cancer, heart attacks and strokes had declined. There were also 42,000 more teachers in the classroom, and almost 4000 schools had been built or rebuilt. The National Minimum Wage Act ensured that workers at the bottom of the economic scale were better protected. Other measures granted greater equality to gay people: the age of consent was equalized at sixteen for gay and straight couples, the ban on gays serving in the military was lifted and adoption by gay couples was legalized. New Labour was also responsible for significant constitutional change. The House of Lords was reformed, though Blair backed off his campaign promise to eliminate hereditary privilege altogether and transform it into an elected body. Instead, it continued to contain ninety-two hereditary peers alongside around 700 **life peers**. The most important constitutional reform, however, was the creation of devolved Parliaments for Scotland, Wales and Northern Ireland. The *Scottish Parliament*, which sat at Holyrood and was established following a referendum voted on by the Scottish electorate, was granted powers over education, health, justice, agriculture and the environment – almost everything but energy, foreign policy and national security. The *National Assembly for Wales* (usually referred simply as the "Welsh Assembly") at Cardiff was initially more limited in scope: it could not initiate legislation or fiscal policy until 2006, and it had no direct law-making powers until a referendum of 2011 granted it similar status to its Scottish counterpart.

The Good Friday Agreement

Northern Ireland, as always, presented a more complicated case. Though Blair had also promised to grant it an elected assembly, bringing that body into being required the cooperation of Unionists and Nationalists. Blair was willing to retreat from both Labour's customary support for the nationalist cause and Thatcher's demonization of the republicans, which won him the respect of both sides. The Belfast Agreement of 1998, usually referred to as the *"Good Friday" Agreement* because of the day on which it was signed, was arguably Blair's greatest achievement. The agreement committed the signers to "exclusively democratic and peaceful means of resolving differences on political issues." It stated that Northern Ireland's ultimate fate would be decided by the people of Ireland. This language was of immense significance, as it granted Irish people, north and south, the right to determine their island's fate without interference from Westminster. Both governments, British and Irish, made huge concessions. The British government acknowledged that it was willing to remove itself from Irish political affairs altogether if that was what the people of the island of Ireland wished, while Unionists conceded that they shared Northern Ireland with republicans whose political beliefs were valid and worthy of respect. The Irish government, meanwhile, granted that Irish unity could only be achieved with the consent of a majority in Northern Ireland, an enormous concession in historical terms, as it required the territorial claim to the six Ulster counties to be removed from the Republic of Ireland's constitution.

 See document "A Peace Plan for Northern Ireland" at www.routledge.com/cw/ barczewski.

Since the Good Friday Agreement, a minority of people on both sides of the conflict have found it difficult to adjust to the new world, and occasional acts of violence have continued to occur. The working-class neighborhoods of Belfast are still divided by "peace walls," or concrete-and-steel barriers that prevent Catholics and Protestants from mixing. Elections to the Northern Irish Assembly continued to reflect ongoing polarization, as the staunchly loyalist Democratic Unionist Party and the equally staunchly republican Sinn Féin generally received the most votes. There is no doubt, however, that the violence decreased markedly: deaths in sectarian conflicts declined from a peak of almost 500 in 1972 to only one in 2010. There were still, however, occasional reminders that the peace remains uneasy. In early 2013, a decision by the Belfast City Council to follow the precedent of other cities in the United Kingdom and only fly the Union Jack over City Hall on eighteen officially designated public holidays, rather than every day as had been done up to that point, provoked outrage from many Unionists. In the ensuing protests, which lasted for months, over a hundred police officers and hundreds more civilians were injured. More lay behind the disturbances than the controversy over the flag. The vote not to fly the Union Jack was made possible because Irish nationalists now held a majority on the Belfast City Council, which in turn reflected the fact that the Catholic population of Northern Ireland was growing faster than its Protestant counterpart. In the 2011 census, 48 percent of the population identified themselves as Protestant, a 5 percent decline since 2001, while 45 percent identified themselves as Catholic, a 1 percent increase. Since Northern Ireland's continuing place in the United Kingdom (as well as the prospect of its joining the Republic of Ireland) is pegged to a popular referendum that may occur at some point in the future, this demographic trend alarmed many Unionists. Moreover, the decision in 2016 of a slim majority in the Protestant areas of Northern Ireland to vote in favor of Britain leaving the European Union, while Catholic areas overwhelmingly supported remaining, further underscores the continuing cultural divisions despite the otherwise clear success of the Belfast Agreement.

Blair and the Iraq War

When he learned of the terrorist attack on the United States on September 11, 2001, Tony Blair instantly understood the magnitude of what had occurred. He told those around him after the second plane hit the World Trade Center, "this will change everything." In the months that followed, he made it clear that terrorism, not Islam, was the enemy, but he made it equally clear that he saw the war on terrorism as a moral crusade in which the future of the world was at stake. Blair shared with the American president George W. Bush a deep-rooted Christian faith that in large measure determined their responses to the attack. To be sure, they did not worship in the same denominations: Bush was a Baptist, Blair officially an Anglican who frequently worshipped with his Catholic wife. (He converted to Catholicism soon after leaving Downing Street in 2007.) Bush's faith had evangelical and fundamentalist elements, while Blair was an ecumenical who believed that all major world faiths led to the same God. But they both believed in a world of clear-cut divisions between good and evil, and this shaped their mutual commitment to the war on terrorism.

Figure 15.2 In 2008, protestors march in Manchester to demand an end to the wars in Iraq and Afghanistan. The man on the right carrying the sign is wearing a Tony Blair mask, showing that many British people blamed him for the decision to go to war.

Reproduced courtesy of Pete Birkinshaw.

September 11th led Blair to embrace the role of a world leader; a friend recalled, "he saw it as a moment of destiny." He thought that he could use the tragedy as a springboard to solving a host of international issues, such as the Israeli–Palestinian conflict. This was in many ways admirable, but also pointed to a messianic streak in Blair's character. This streak had previously been on display in the peace process in Northern Ireland and in Kosovo in 1998, when Blair had convinced a reluctant Bill Clinton to agree to send in ground troops if necessary to stop the ethnic cleansing of Bosnian Muslims. To be sure, Blair worked much harder than Bush to reassure moderate Muslim opinion in Britain and throughout the world. He also worked to try to convince Bush that a measured and multilateral response, focused on al-Qaeda and backed up by clear evidence, was the best approach. But Blair's peace-making efforts, and his political credibility in Britain, were in the end undermined by his unwavering support of American military initiatives. Between 2003 and 2011, 46,000 British troops participated in *operations in Iraq*; 179 of them lost their lives.

As the wars in Afghanistan and Iraq dragged on, costing an ever-rising number of British, American and civilian lives and seemingly accomplishing little, most British people came to see them as being promulgated by right-wing hardliners in America and as having little to do with Britain or with fighting al-Qaeda or terrorism. By September 2003, only 38 percent of the British public thought that the war was justified. Blair's most significant political error in his handling of the war was to stake Britain's participation on Saddam Hussein's possession of "weapons of mass destruction," or WMDs. When it turned out that Saddam did not in fact possess WMDs, the issue of how aware the Labour government was of this became the subject of much discussion in the press and ultimately the focus of two parliamentary enquiries. Coming under particular scrutiny was the issue of whether Blair's team had "sexed up" the main intelligence dossier analyzing the data on WMDs. Released in September 2002, the dossier was supposed to provide a clear justification for Britain's participation in the war by definitively establishing that Saddam Hussein had WMDs. The British intelligence agencies, MI5 and MI6, provided the data for the dossier. Initially, they presented their information as sketchy and speculative, but when Downing Street pressed for a more emphatic statement, they attempted to oblige.

 See "The 'Dodgy Dossier' and the Iraq War" at www.routledge.com/cw/barczewski.

The dossier was rewritten multiple times, with major input coming not only from intelligence experts, but also from Labour's press relations staff. One government expert on Iraq and WMDs, Dr. David Kelly, secretly revealed to the BBC in 2003 that the government had exaggerated much of the intelligence contained in the dossier. When his identity was discovered by Downing Street and leaked to the press, Kelly committed suicide. It appeared as if Blair had Kelly's blood on his hands, and he was forced to summon a government enquiry into the matter. The enquiry exonerated Blair, but the public and many members of his own party remained unconvinced about his veracity regarding the dossier, his role in leaking Kelly's name to the media and his responsibility for leading Britain into a war that few people thought was justified. Blair was forced to call for a second inquiry that was more broadly focused on the use of intelligence in the march to war. Its conclusions were much more critical of the prime minister's actions.

The Experience of Warfare 10

Britain and the Iraq War

After the attacks on the United States on September 11, 2001, Prime Minister Tony Blair committed to stand with his American ally. British troops participated in the war to oust al-Qaeda from and overthrow the Taliban regime in Afghanistan, and in 2003, they took part in the invasion of Iraq. Blair had been reluctant to join the latter campaign without parliamentary approval, however, and so British forces were unable to prepare fully for what was termed Operation Telic, from the Greek for "purposeful action." This resulted in delays and shortages in equipping them with the requisite supplies, weapons and vehicles. Moreover, few British soldiers had experience in active combat. The British fought alongside the Americans in the initial "shock and awe" assault that was intended to overwhelm Iraqi defenses; the main British assignment was to secure Basra, Iraq's second-largest city. But once the initial victory was secured, the British, like the Americans, became bogged down in a counterinsurgency operation after attempts to impose a new government and establish political

Figure 15.3 British soldiers from the 3rd Battalion, Parachute Regiment, maintain vehicle checkpoint security for US Marines at landing strip Viper in southeast Iraq in 2003.

Reproduced courtesy of Department of Defense, American Forces Information Service, Defense Visual Information Center.

stability failed. In contrast to the more aggressive American approach, the British used a "softer" strategy in the territory they occupied in southern Iraq, in an effort to win popular support, which largely failed. In 2006, British military commanders decided to focus their efforts on Afghanistan and began a gradual withdrawal from Iraq. The last Operation Telic personnel left the country in May 2009. One hundred forty thousand men and women served in Operation Telic; 179 were killed. In 2009, Blair's successor Gordon Brown launched an inquiry into the decision to go to war that was chaired by Sir John Chilcot. After a seven-year investigation, the Chilcot Inquiry concluded that the intelligence suggesting that Saddam Hussein possessed WMDs should not have been presented as being so certain, that the legal basis for the war had been shaky and that military intervention in Iraq was unnecessary. By that point, the British public agreed: by 2015, only around 25 percent of those polled thought that the decision to go to war was correct.

Blair emerged from the Iraq war as a damaged leader in the eyes of the public, the media and his own party. For many British people, it was a question of national pride, as Britain's independence on the international scene seemed severely compromised. His morale sapped by Iraq, Blair nearly resigned in 2004 to make way for Gordon Brown, once his close friend but now his archrival. As a newly elected MP in the mid-1980s, Blair had shared an office at Westminster with Brown, another of Labour's rising stars. Brown was, as Blair biographer Anthony Seldon puts it, "simply everything Blair wasn't." Blair was all about flash and dash, charisma and charm; Brown was all about diligence, attention to detail and deep thought, about economic policy and budgets in particular. Blair had been a diffident student at Oxford; Brown had a doctorate in history and had already authored three books. But the two men shared one characteristic: they were both fiercely ambitious. For a time, this bound them together, as they channeled their drive into the remaking of the Labour Party, to which they were both deeply committed. Brown claimed, "there's no closer relationship in the world."

But there was room for only one of them at the top at a time, and as the years passed their rivalry tore New Labour apart from within. The two men met several times to try to resolve the issue, including a now-famous dinner in 1994 at a restaurant called Granita in Islington, a neighborhood in north London. There is no record of what exactly was said, but subsequently it emerged that three things had supposedly been agreed upon: first, that Blair would seek the leadership; second, that if Blair became prime minister he would step down after a time in favor of Brown; and third, that Brown would be given charge of the government's economic and social policy.

A decade later, that dinner would tear the Labour Party apart. It was an extraordinary situation. Instead of fighting it out in a leadership contest, which Blair would have easily won, he struck an unprecedented political deal with Brown in which he promised to hand over the premiership to him at some point in the future. This was in many ways supremely generous and a reflection of how much regard Blair truly had for Brown. But it was a colossal mistake. Knowing that he would never have to fight a leadership election, Brown failed to cultivate the relationships with his fellow politicians that would have been necessary had he assumed the leadership by a more conventional path. Moreover, the rivalry between the two men accounts for some of Labour's caution in its first term, as Brown did not want to risk a loss in the next election that would scupper his chances of becoming prime minister in the future. Most importantly, Brown never got over his jealousy of Blair for becoming prime minister first.

By 2001, the two men were barely on speaking terms, even if they still agreed on most political issues. When Blair spoke, Brown could barely hide his contempt. In private meetings with Blair, he would shout, "I want the job now!" Once able to keep their disagreements out of the public eye, the two men now fought openly, hurling expletives at each other while government business stalled. In the summer of 2004, when Blair made up his mind to continue as prime minister through the next election, he did not tell Brown prior to announcing it to the party, because he knew what the response would be. Blair's decision destroyed any remaining shred of their once-close friendship. With hindsight, the Blair–Brown relationship tends to be read as a political marriage gone wrong, in which two men who once were very close became bitter enemies, nearly destroying their party and their government. In many ways, it is a tribute to both of their abilities that, in spite of their growing rancor, they were able to accomplish as much as they did. But their rivalry also prevented New Labour from accomplishing much more.

Blair managed to win a third election in 2005, but New Labour was by then largely a spent force. By the summer of 2006, more than his own party was turning against Blair. In his final term, he was often forced to rely on Tory votes to pass key legislation, such as his effort to reform education by allowing more school choice. Public opinion was further soured by the "cash for coronets" scandal, in which Labour was found to have been granting honors (i.e., peerages or knighthoods) to wealthy donors in exchange for loans that had supported the 2005 electoral campaign. Though similar exchanges had long been taking place in British politics, the blatancy of this current episode led to a criminal investigation in which Blair was interviewed by the police, an embarrassing first for a sitting prime minister. The case was ultimately dropped without any charges being filed, but Blair's once squeaky-clean image now appeared to be mired in sleaze. As the pressure mounted, Blair was pushed from all sides to name the date on which he would vacate the prime minister's office. With Labour polling at its lowest level in two decades, he had no choice but to announce a firm departure date. Blair resigned from office on the *27th of June 2007*, having spent ten years as prime minister.

The 7/7 Bombings and the Debate Over Multiculturalism

On the 6th of July 2005, the government announced that London's bid to host the 2012 Summer Olympics had been successful. Jubilant Londoners poured into the streets to celebrate; Trafalgar Square was filled with a cheering crowd. The next morning, at ten minutes to nine o'clock at the peak of rush hour, *three bombs were detonated* within one minute of each other on the London Underground. An hour later, a fourth bomb destroyed a bus full of commuters. Fifty-two people, plus the four bombers, were killed, and more than 700 were injured. It was the deadliest bombing attack on London since the Second World War. Though much of it was up and running by the next day, parts of the city's transportation network were affected for months afterwards.

Initially, the explosions were attributed to a power surge, but within hours they were determined to be the result of terrorism. The investigation revealed that, although they may have had some contact with al-Qaeda, the bombers had not come to Britain from the outside; as the former commissioner of the Metropolitan Police Lord Stevens declared, they did not "fit the caricature al-Qaeda fanatic from some backward village in Algeria or Afghanistan." Three of the four were the sons of Pakistani immigrants, but they themselves had been born in Britain. The fourth had been born in the former British colony of Jamaica. They were described by the investigators as "cleanskins," meaning they had no known connections to terrorism previously. The bombing was planned in the northern English city of Leeds.

The events of 7/7 gave rise to an intense debate in Britain over their cause and the best means of preventing similar attacks in the future. Fresh questions were raised about Blair's promises that the wars in Afghanistan and Iraq would make Britain a safer place. All he had succeeded in doing, it seemed, was to convince portions of Britain's own Muslim population to join the terrorists, and in making Britain a prime target. Commentators on the left, who had opposed the Iraq War, were particularly drawn to this explanation. The next day, the British Pakistani writer Tariq Ali declared in the *Guardian*, "as long as western politicians wage their wars and their colleagues in the Muslim world watch in silence, young people will be attracted to the groups who carry out random acts of revenge." On the right, commentators called for decreased tolerance towards Islamic fundamentalism.

Religion and Difference 6

Secularism in Britain

Today, Britain is one of the most secular countries in the world. In some recent polls, more than half of British people do not identify with a particular religious faith and either do not believe in a deity or are agnostic. There is a long intellectual tradition of atheism in Britain. The romantic poet Percy Bysshe Shelley published an essay entitled "The Necessity of Atheism" when he was a student at Oxford in 1811, and the atheist periodical *The Oracle of Reason* was founded in 1841. One of its authors, George Holyoake, coined the term "secularism" in 1851 to describe his vision for the separation of religious and civil life. In 1911, John Gott, a trousers salesman from Bradford in Yorkshire, became the last person to be jailed for blasphemy in Britain, although the law against it remained on the books until 1977. In recent decades, secularism has increased markedly. The number of Britons who do not identify as members of a particular faith rose from 7.7 million in the 2001 census to 14.1 million in 2011, and polls suggest that the number has continued to increase significantly since. With a third of their populations professing no religion, Scotland and Wales are the most irreligious parts of the United Kingdom, while in England the percentage is about a quarter. Only Northern Ireland remains strongly religious, with only 7 percent of its population not identifying with a particular faith. Attendance at Church of England services has halved since the 1980s; for every new convert, the church currently loses twelve members. With younger people increasingly identifying as having "no religion," it seems likely that the trend towards secularism will continue.

The government's response was to increase surveillance and intelligence efforts. Additional funding poured into MI5, and at least twenty other terrorist plots were foiled over the next five years. The price for this success was high: Britain became the most watched society in the world, with one CCTV camera for every thirty-two people. Blair grew more authoritarian after 7/7 and expressed frustration when the legal system would not allow suspected terrorists simply to be rounded up and interrogated or deported. Many members of the Labour Party opposed what they saw as the creation of a police state.

More broadly, the 7/7 bombings engendered a discussion of multiculturalism in Britain. The right-wing British National Party distributed leaflets with a picture of the damaged bus that was captioned, "Maybe now it's time to start listening to the BNP." Conservative journalists also pointed to multiculturalism as the cause of the bombings. Writing in the *Daily Mail* a week later, Melanie Phillips asserted that the bombings had resulted from the "disastrous doctrine of multiculturalism," which "refused to teach Muslims . . . the core of British culture and values. Instead, it has promoted a lethally divisive culture of separateness." Other Britons, however, pointed to the cultural vibrancy and richness that multiculturalism had brought to Britain in recent decades.

One point that was not open to debate was that Britain had become a far more diverse society. The 2011 census revealed that in the ten years since the last census, the proportion of white British people living in England and Wales had dropped from 87.5 percent to 80.5 percent. Immigrants had accounted for two-thirds of the increase in the British population by 3.7 million people. Some 7.1 million foreign-born residents were living England and Wales, meaning that around one in seven people had been born elsewhere. (The percentage of the American population that is foreign-born is roughly equivalent; in Germany it is 9 percent.) The changes were most striking in London, which became the first place in Britain where white British people were a minority. Only 45 percent (3.7 million) of the people living in the capital described themselves as "white British," a decrease from 58 percent (4.3 million) ten years earlier. London also had the highest percentage in Britain of people born outside the United Kingdom (37 percent).

Many of those people living in British cities but born outside the United Kingdom were Eastern Europeans who had come to Britain looking for work after the EU was enlarged in 2004. Alone amongst the existing EU countries, the United Kingdom and Ireland placed no restrictions on the migration of these new EU citizens. The Blair government had anticipated that the net influx of Eastern European migrants looking for work would amount to less than 13,000 new residents in Britain per year. In actuality, almost a million had moved to Britain by 2011. This large influx of new EU citizens, many of whom spoke little English, antagonized many within Britain. Surveys suggested that British people were more hostile to immigration than all other Europeans except the Greeks. Since the British economy was doing relatively well prior to 2008, however, these growing immigration anxieties outside London were largely dismissed by the government. Yet this anti-immigration sentiment fueled the electoral gains made by the United Kingdom Independence Party, which wanted to curb immigration and end Britain's membership in the European Union, after 2010. In 2014, UKIP won 27.5 percent of the popular vote in Britain's elections for the European Parliament and sent twenty-four representatives to Brussels, the largest number of any British political party.

Immigrants and Refugees 6

Migrants From Eastern Europe Countries After 2004

In 2004, the European Union saw its largest expansion as ten new countries joined: Cyprus, the Czech Republic, Estonia, Hungary, Latvia, Lithuania, Malta, Poland, Slovakia and Slovenia. Although the free movement of peoples from one country to another is a firm principle of EU membership, most of the older member states enacted policies that placed temporary limits on the numbers of people who could migrate from the new members, with the intention of introducing free movement from them in a phased process. Austria and Germany, for example, only opened their labor markets fully to people from the new members after seven years. The United Kingdom, however, adopted no such limits, as government studies assumed that other EU members would fully open their labor markets and therefore the number of migrants from Eastern European countries would be small, only an estimated 5000 to 13,000 per year. In fact, between 2004 and 2011, 850,000 people moved to the UK from Eastern Europe, comprising around 3 percent of the working-age population. In the past, most Eastern European migrants to the UK had been high skilled and had settled in London, but this new generation were generally low skilled and could not afford to live in the capital. Almost three-quarters of them moved to other, less affluent parts of the UK, which in many cases had little previous experience with migration from Eastern Europe. The largest numbers came from Poland; by 2017, there were over a million Polish people living in the UK. An example of a post-2004 Polish community was in the south Welsh industrial town of Merthyr Tydfil, where many Poles found work in local meat-processing plants. Between 2001 and 2011, Merthyr's population of foreign-born residents rose from 807 to 2641. Some residents welcomed the Poles, whom they saw as hard-working contributors to the local economy, but others worried that they were putting pressure on schools, housing and the National Health Service and that they were decreasing wages and taking jobs away from longtime residents. In the Brexit referendum in 2016, 58.4 percent of Merthyr's residents voted for Britain to leave the EU. This was typical of other places in the UK that had seen an influx of migrants from Eastern Europe after 2004. A study conducted by social scientists at the University of Warwick found that such places saw a significant increase in anti–European Union sentiment after 2004 and an increase in support for anti-Europe political parties such as the United Kingdom Independence Party (UKIP).

If most British people thought that fewer immigrants should be admitted to the country in the future, however, they were more positive about the effects of those who have already entered. A survey in 2013 revealed that 90 percent of Britons thought that their country had become more multicultural, and 70 percent thought that this was a good thing. This was true even among Conservative voters, 71 percent of whom supported multiculturalism. Only 6 percent of Britons, meanwhile, thought that "being white" was an important attribute of being British, though 26 percent thought that "being born here" was and 41 percent that "speaking English" was. Regardless, in 2011, Prime Minister David Cameron gave a controversial speech in which he declared that "state multiculturalism" had failed because it promoted the maintenance of separate identities by people who had recently arrived in Britain. Cameron asserted that Britain needed to develop a stronger national identity in order to prevent the kind of dangerous extremism that could lead people to commit terrorist acts.

 See document "The End of Multiculturalism?" at www.routledge.com/cw/barczewski.

Cameron's speech engendered an intense discussion about not only multiculturalism, but also the nature of British identity. His critics argued that most immigrants assimilated fairly quickly and that the separateness from the mainstream of British society had been exaggerated. A survey in 2007, for example, revealed that 89 percent of Britons of Indian or Pakistani origin felt "fairly or very strongly" that they "belong to Britain," in comparison to 85 percent of white Britons. Cameron's detractors also asserted that there is no such thing as a homogeneous, monocultural "Britishness." During the 2010s this debate over multiculturalism, and the meaning of British identity in the twenty-first century, was far from resolved; indeed, it would underlay the debate over whether Britain should remain part of the European Union in 2016.

The End of New Labour and the Return of the Conservatives

In 2007, Gordon Brown got what he had long wanted: to become leader of the Labour Party. He was the first person to become prime minister without at least an internal leadership contest since Anthony Eden had succeeded Winston Churchill in 1955. But Blair had handed Brown a poisoned chalice. By mid-2007, Labour was ten points behind in the polls and had little chance of winning a fourth consecutive election. Brown faced the problem of having to demonstrate to a dissatisfied electorate why his premiership would bring change. It was a formidable task: reinvigorating the left that Blair had alienated while not alienating the center that he had worked so hard to win over.

Initially, Brown's plodding, less polished communication style seemed a breath of fresh air after the all the slick spin of the Blair years. But within months, worrying signs were emanating from Brown of a tendency to micromanage, to seek scapegoats to blame when problems arose and to be even more concerned with media coverage than Blair had been. Warm, witty and engaging in private, he froze before the cameras, turning into a stiff and unsmiling robot. It was one of the tragic ironies of Brown's premiership that he got the job because people were tired of spin, but once it was gone they soon wanted it back. Within eight weeks of Brown taking office, there was a twenty-point swing to the Tories, from ten points behind to ten points ahead. Brown descended into isolation and introspection, punctuated with bursts of anger; stories of objects being thrown and furniture being kicked trickled into the media. The atmosphere at 10 Downing Street was dark, distrustful and depressed.

That fall, the global economic bubble, based on easy credit and rising housing prices, burst. The first tremors were felt in August, when it became clear that the American market in subprime mortgages, which had been repackaged in complex financial instruments known as credit derivatives and sold all over the world, was in serious trouble. British banks, like everyone else, had invested heavily in these derivatives, and they were suddenly left with billions in toxic assets. When the banks panicked and stopped lending money, credit markets seized up. By the spring of 2008, housing prices were plummeting, taking retail spending and consumer confidence with them. A number of British banks were in deep trouble, and government action was desperately needed to prevent a panic. A particular source of concern was the Royal Bank of Scotland (RBS), which had outstanding loans in an amount greater than the entire British GDP. The only answer was a massive injection of public funds. Brown felt that the money had to be given directly to the banks to recapitalize them, as politically distasteful as that would be given growing taxpayer wrath at the seemingly endless bailouts. He tried to convince the Americans to follow suit, but Secretary of the Treasury Hank Paulson preferred to use $700 billion to create a dumping ground for bad debts, the Troubled Asset Recovery Program (TARP). Nor did Germany and France follow the British strategy. Brown was isolated and nervous, but he knew the political price he would pay for recapitalizing the banks was less painful than what would ensue if the entire British financial system collapsed. A sum of £500 billion was pumped into the banks, making the government the majority owner of RBS and the part owner of two other banks, Halifax and Lloyds TSB. When it worked, other European countries came around to the British solution and began recapitalizing their banks as well. Paulson abandoned TARP and began pumping money directly into American banks. It was Brown's finest moment as prime minister. He no longer had to deal with the myriad complexities of government; all he had to do was focus on the economy, which was his strength.

But Brown's newfound popularity was not to last. As more was revealed about the banks' risky behavior and their executives continued to receive massive salaries and bonuses, questions were raised about the government's failure to impose stronger regulations and punishments. Though Brown tried to blame the crisis on America, it was increasingly clear that British banks had followed virtually identical practices. The massive bailouts and falling tax revenues, meanwhile, sent deficits ballooning, making taxpayers very nervous. Things got worse when it was revealed that MPs were claiming large sums in expenses by exploiting a loophole that allowed them to deduct the costs of the accommodation that was necessary for them to do their jobs. A number had used this loophole to purchase second homes in London or their constituencies, which they had then resold and pocketed the profits. Other expense claims included massage chairs, patio heaters, plasma TVs and Jacuzzis. By June 2009, more than £500,000 had been paid back, but the damage was done. Though both parties were guilty, the Conservatives were quicker off the mark to apologize and to take steps to end the abuses, while Brown struggled to get on top of the crisis. In a scandal that significantly increased the public's distrust in government, the party in power was bound to bear the brunt of the blame.

Brown's authority was fatally damaged. The *Sun* newspaper, which had steadfastly supported New Labour since the mid-1990s, announced that it was switching to the Tories. Polls showed that people did not particularly like the Conservatives but that they had developed even more negative feelings towards Brown. The only thing that kept him in office was the fear on the part of Labour MPs that a second change of leader would seal their fate in the upcoming election, now only four months away. There was no one waiting in the wings who seemed capable of rescuing the party and no point in undertaking what was sure to be a bitter fight within the party if they were only going to lose anyway.

They did lose, though it was in the end much closer than most people anticipated. The Conservatives fought the election under a young, charismatic new leader, *David Cameron*, who represented a more modern incarnation of Toryism that clearly showed the influence of New Labour. Since their landslide defeat in 1997, the Conservatives had been in utter disarray. While New Labour focused on the economy, which was the most important issue to voters, the Conservatives continued to be obsessed with the European Union, which was not. They also devoted considerable attention to immigration, which threatened to brand the party as racist in the eyes of moderates. In the short term the political consequences were disastrous. The party appealed to an ever-narrower spectrum of the electorate, primarily older white voters in the southeast and middle of England. In the mid-1990s, the average age of party members was sixty-three. The 1997, 2001 and 2005 defeats were respectively the worst, second-worst, and third-worst defeats in party history. Between 1834 and 1997, there had only been one Conservative leader, Austen Chamberlain in the early 1920s, who had failed to become prime minister. But between 1997 and 2010, there were three in succession: William Hague, Iain Duncan Smith and Michael Howard.

Cameron was charged with reversing this dire state of affairs. Only thirty-nine, he had been an MP for less than five years and a **shadow cabinet** minister for less than one. But as the son of a wealthy stockbroker whose family tree was dotted with peers, baronets and the occasional royal, he exuded the breezy self-confidence of a man whose place in the elite was secure. Describing himself as a "practical Conservative," he distanced himself from the harsh tone and ideological purity of the Thatcher years. An adept communicator, he delivered many of his speeches without the help of notes or a teleprompter. He recognized that the Tories needed a "Clause IV moment," meaning that they needed to find a way to demonstrate that the party had changed. In the 2010 election, his campaign was built around the concept of the "Big Society." "In this modern, compassionate Conservative party," he proclaimed, "everyone is invited." He promised to increase funding for public services, to address climate change and other environmental issues and to increase the diversity of Conservative MPs. (Of the 198 elected in 2005, there were only seventeen women; of the 181 men, only one was black and one Asian.) Cameron made it clear that greater social and economic equality was now a key goal of Conservative policies. After almost two decades of fealty to Thatcherism, the change was rapid and striking.

Cameron's "New Tories" thus competed for the same center ground as New Labour had done, and they staked a convincing claim to represent the future while Labour seemed exhausted and out of ideas. But in a Britain in which class still very much mattered, a modernizer who had gone to Eton, the most elite public school in the country, was in the eyes of many people an oxymoron. Cameron was distrusted not only on the left but also on the right, where he was seen as betraying traditional Conservative values and policies. Norman Tebbit, formerly a member of Thatcher's cabinet, complained of Cameron's first policy document as leader that "every one of these things could be listed in a Labour manifesto." Support for the Tories remained overwhelmingly concentrated in the south of England, while they continued to struggle in the north. In Scotland and Wales, meanwhile, disenchantment with Labour benefited the nationalist parties, not the Conservatives.

If people loathed Brown, they had not yet embraced Cameron. Though they were clearly gaining in popularity, the Conservatives had a mountain to climb: they needed a massive 117 seats to gain a majority in the House of Commons. A divided electorate that was unenthusiastic about the usual two options put the Liberal Democrats in a strong position. As the only major party to oppose the Iraq War, the Lib Dems had gained in popularity since 2001, and by April 2010 they were polling at around 28 percent. As a result, many polls predicted a **hung parliament**. This would put the Liberal Democrats in the position of negotiating to form a coalition with either Labour or the Conservatives. When their leader, Nick Clegg, performed well in the three American-style debates – a first for a British election – that were held in the weeks before voters went to the polls, their position became even stronger, and they threatened to move into second place behind the Conservatives and ahead of Labour.

Things became even more uncertain when disaster struck Brown and Labour. On the 28th of April 2010, only nine days before the election, Brown was campaigning in Rochdale, a town in the North of England. He encountered a sixty-five-year-old woman named Gillian Duffy, who assailed him about a number of issues, including immigration, and complained about "all these eastern Europeans." Brown answered her politely, telling her that she was "a very good woman" who had "served your community all your life." Mrs. Duffy was pleased and told a reporter that she was planning to vote for Labour. But when Brown got back to his car, he forgot that he was wearing a live microphone on his lapel and complained to his team about his encounter with that "bigoted woman." A few minutes later, one of Brown's staff noticed the microphone. By the time he got to his next engagement, a radio interview, the story had already broken. "We just lost the election," said a member of the Labour team at their campaign headquarters.

On election night, the Tories came in first, but with only 36 percent of the vote, a mere three points higher than in 2007. They had gained ninety-seven seats, their largest increase since 1931, but were still twenty short of a majority. Labour held on to second place with 29 percent, but lost ninety-one seats in their second-worst performance since 1918. The Lib Dems came in a disappointing third with 23 percent, but were still in a strong position because the other parties needed them in order to form a coalition. After five tense days of negotiations, Clegg decided that he did not want to be in the position of propping up a government that nobody wanted, and so he struck a deal with the Conservatives. On the 11th of May 2010, David Cameron became prime minister. If the power of Thatcherism in the 1980s had forced the Labour Party to move to the right, in turn the Conservatives were compelled by the appeal of New Labour in the 1990s to move back to the left. "I am the heir to Blair," Cameron proclaimed at the Tory party conference two months before being elected leader.

The Cameron-Clegg Coalition

In both the 2010 election campaign and his subsequent premiership, Cameron was guided by his belief in the "Big Society" doctrine. This idea, which germinated in the immediate post-Thatcher years amongst Conservatives eager to distance themselves from the Iron Lady's hard-edged stances, sought to integrate the free market with social solidarity at a community level. Intellectually, the concept draws on Edmund Burke's ideas about the role of civil society and from Benjamin Disraeli's promotion of "one-nation" conservatism in the nineteenth century. Practically, it meant an emphasis on devolving power to local communities; encouraging volunteerism within those communities; supporting cooperative and social enterprises; and making government more open and transparent. Cameron proposed a number of initiatives along these lines, but the Liberal Democrats were keen to use their voice in the coalition to push forward progressive social policies around individuals and their rights. Much of the coalition's legislation thus reflected an uneasy compromise between the two approaches.

The coalition did pass a number of socially progressive measures during its tenure, including legalizing same-sex marriage in 2015 and giving women equality to men in the royal succession, making the first-born the heir to the throne regardless of gender. Future heirs to the throne were also permitted to marry Catholics in 2013. Another major reform was the Fixed Term Parliaments Act in 2011, which dictated general elections would be held every five years, and that prime ministers could only call an early election if they lost a confidence vote in the House of Commons or if two-thirds of the Commons voted for an early dissolution.

Sexuality and Gender 9

Same-Sex Marriage in Britain

Same-sex marriages did not become legal in England, Scotland and Wales until 2014 and in Northern Ireland until 2020. But for centuries, same-sex British couples have found ways to unite. In some cases, they may have been aided by sympathetic clergymen. The parish records of Taxal in Cheshire state that Hannah Wright and Anne Gaskill were married on the 4th of September 1707 and Ane Norton and Alice

Pickford on the 3rd of June 1708. Perhaps half of these names actually belonged to men despite being traditionally female, but the information is intriguing, especially because the two weddings were so close together in time. There were also cases in which women disguised themselves as men in order to marry another woman. Arabella Hunt, who played the lute at the Stuart royal courts of the late seventeenth and early eighteenth centuries, applied for her marriage to be annulled in 1680 because her "husband" James Howard was actually a woman, and in 1734 a couple in London was denied a marriage certificate because they were suspected of being two women. By the end of the eighteenth century it was relatively tolerated for two women to live together as close companions. Anne Lister, the focus of the BBC/HBO television series *Gentleman Jack*, exchanged vows and rings with her partner Ann Walker in 1834. Male same-sex relationships were more controversial, but men too found ways to make more permanent unions with their partners. In the eighteenth century, the molly houses mentioned in a previous chapter were often the scene of mock marriage ceremonies; some of these were merely in jest but others seem to have been intended to signify more serious relationship commitments. The Reverend John Church, the chaplain of the "Marrying Room" in the White Swan molly house in 1810, is sometimes described as the first ordained minister to perform same-sex marriages. He was himself gay and later served two years in prison when he was caught in a homosexual act. Another strategy was for a gay man and a lesbian to marry each other in order to provide "cover." Perhaps the best-known example is the marriage of Vita-Sackville West and Harold Nicolson, two members of the literary and artistic Bloomsbury Group in the early twentieth century. Vita continued to have affairs with women, most famously with Virginia Woolf, and Harold with men, but they also seem to have had a genuine affection for one another. Their "marriage of convenience" lasted for forty-nine years, from 1913 until Vita's death in 1962.

The shadow of the 2008 financial crisis was long, however, and the Cameron government's most notable actions between 2010 and 2015 was the enaction of a series of "austerity budgets." In an effort to get the skyrocketing national budget deficit caused by the bank bailout under control, a new Office for Budget Responsibility was created, and the chancellor of the Exchequer, George Osborne, slashed spending and the annual transfers to local municipal and county council governments. Over £100 billion was cut in the first five years. The government claimed that the National Health Service and education were exempted from direct cuts, but other welfare benefits programs were impacted. Over £30 billion had been cut from welfare payments, housing subsidies and other social services by 2019. A number of separate welfare benefits programs were also merged into a single "universal credit" system, although this has yet to be fully implemented.

In the face of massive cuts, local governments were forced to raise taxes to remain solvent, but this merely added to the misery in areas of high poverty. The worst-hit areas were the post-industrial cities and towns of the Midlands and the North of England. After declining steadily between 1998 and 2012, the number of children living in poverty began rising again, from about 3.5 million to over 4.1 million by 2019. The number of children regularly using food banks tripled over the same period. Despite Cameron's attempts to argue that food banks were the "Big Society" in action, the increased need for them prompted much criticism of the government in Parliament and by British churches. Local arts programming was slashed, nearly 800 public libraries were forced to close and over 200,000 local government employees lost their jobs. The wages of nearly five million public sector employees were frozen for two years and then capped so that annual increases averaged less than 1 percent per year after 2013, a rate below that of inflation, which means that in real terms those workers were effectively getting pay cuts year after year. By the time of the next election, in 2015, the government had managed to cut its annual budget deficit in half, but this fell well short of its target of a balanced budget.

Moreover, despite no mention of it in either the Tory or Liberal Democrat election platforms, the National Health Service was subject to its most extensive reorganization since its founding. The stated aim of the reforms was to remove local bureaucracy, increase innovation through competition and give users of the system more choice. Critics noted the main purpose seemed to be to increase the role of the market and private-care providers. Opposition to the new system was voiced by all the major organizations and unions representing health-care providers. Large public demonstrations also took place, to no avail. The Health and Social Care Act was enacted in 2012, and over the next five years as the reforms were put in place it became clearer that they did indeed lead to greater marketization of the NHS and to more top-down reorganization with complex and confusing accountability procedures. The resulting system did not serve local planning needs, overall bureaucracy was not substantially reduced and a stated objective of the changes – increased user choice – did not materialize. By 2019 it was clear the NHS needed another major overhaul: the policy of competitive choice was abandoned, and plans were put in place to create integrated care systems (i.e., partnerships of organizations who plan, buy and provide health-care services) on a regional basis. This represented a compromise between the 2012 reforms and what had existed prior to them.

Cameron and the Tories were notably more hostile to immigration and asylum seekers than the Labour government they succeeded, although this was an issue that created tensions with their Liberal Democratic partners. Cameron promised to bring down net immigration to Britain from 150,000 in 2011 to below 100,000. In 2013, however, net arrivals increased to over 200,000. Illegal immigration also became a hot issue for the Cameron government, with estimates of the number of undocumented British residents ranging between 400,000 and 800,000. From 2012 onwards, a "hostile environment" policy was officially maintained by the government, aimed at pushing illegal residents to voluntarily leave the country by making life difficult for them through such means as making identity checks necessary for use of the NHS and other social services. This was followed in 2014 by legislation that prevented landlords from renting houses to people who could not prove they had legal status to reside in the UK.

While aimed at reducing the number of undocumented immigrants, the hostile environment policy and the 2014 Act also led to hundreds of legal residents being deprived of their homes, jobs, medical care, passports, re-entry to the UK when they temporarily left and, in 83 cases, wrongly deported from the UK entirely. This was because those who had moved to the UK from Commonwealth countries between 1948 and 1971 were legally British citizens but were never given, or asked to provide, documentary evidence of their right to remain. The zeal with which the government pursued its hostile environment policy with a "guilty until proven innocent" approach, which targeted mostly black Britons, generated a major public scandal. The home secretary, Amber Rudd, was forced to resign in 2018, as parliamentary inquiries were launched and the government was pressured into issuing a formal apology.

Immigrants and Refugees 7

The Windrush Generation

People who arrived in the United Kingdom from Caribbean and other Common-wealth countries between 1948 and 1971 have become known as "the *Windrush* Generation." This name comes from the ship *Empire Windrush*, which landed at Til-bury docks east of London on the 22nd of June 1948, carrying 1027 passengers from Jamaica, Barbados, Trinidad and other Caribbean islands. Responding to an ad in a Jamaican newspaper calling for workers to fill a postwar labor shortage, around 700 of them, including many former servicemen who had fought for Britain in the Sec-ond World War, intended to settle and work in Britain. The British Nationality Act (1948) granted British citizenship and the right to work in Britain to all inhabitants of Britain's colonies. Although the arrival of the *Windrush* has often been romanticized as the origins of a multicultural postwar Britain, its passengers met with an ambiva-lent response at the time. The government had not expected such a large number of Caribbean immigrants, and there were no plans in place to house, feed or employ them; they were housed temporarily in the deep underground wartime bomb shelter at Clapham in south London. The Labour government immediately contacted the colo-nial authorities in the Caribbean to tell them to prevent such voyages in the future. Almost immediately tensions arose with Britain's white community: although jobs were relatively plentiful, housing was not, as numerous homes had been destroyed by German bombing during the war. Even so, many other immigrants followed, not only from the Caribbean, but also from other British colonies, before tighter restrictions began to be imposed in the early 1960s. In 1971, immigration policies were changed so that a British passport holder who was born overseas could only immigrate to the United Kingdom if they could obtain a work permit and had a parent or grandpar-ent who was born there. Today, more than 500,000 residents of the United Kingdom arrived from a Commonwealth country prior to 1971, making them part of "the *Win-drush* generation." They were legally permitted to stay by the terms of the 1971 Act, but in many cases had little proof as to when and how they had arrived. In 2010, the British government ordered the destruction of the cards they had filled out when they landed, which for most was the only documentation of their right to British citizen-ship. In the years that followed, many of them faced difficulty in proving their right to access public services such as the National Health Service. As the British government increasingly cracked down on undocumented immigrants under what was called the "hostile environment" policy, some of them were threatened with, and even subjected to, deportation; around eighty-three were wrongfully removed from the country and sent back to the Caribbean, despite the fact that they had been legally living in Brit-ain since at least the early 1970s. After widespread publicity brought attention to their cases, the British government launched an inquiry in 2018, which led to a public apology, the establishment of a compensation scheme and the creation of an annual "*Windrush* Day" on June 22nd to celebrate the contribution of immigrants to British society and culture. But although around 15,000 people were eligible for compensa-tion, only a quarter of them came forward, as many were still afraid of being targeted by the Home Office.

Two Referendums: Independence for Scotland and Brexit

In Scotland, the Scottish National Party had been for decades making slow but steady gains amongst the electorate with its program of demanding that more powers be given to the Scottish Parliament and by promoting socially progressive policies. In the 2007 election, the SNP for the first time became the largest party in the Scottish Parliament at Holyrood, although it fell short of an absolute majority. (The Scottish Parliament uses a form of proportional representation that makes getting an overall majority of seats very difficult.) With support from the Scottish Green Party, the leader of the SNP, Alex Salmond, became first minister of Scotland. Salmond was an economist by training with socialist political leanings; he had served as an SNP MP in the House of Commons from 1987 until 2010. As SNP leader, Salmond moderated his left-wing views and pushed the party to embrace a gradualist approach towards the question of independence. During his first term, Salmond and his deputy Nicola Sturgeon oversaw a government study of the options available for a referendum on Scottish independence in 2009. A draft bill was drawn up for a referendum with the option of further devolution for the Scottish Parliament or full independence for Scotland. But as it was a minority government and no other party in the Scottish Parliament supported the plan, the SNP could not pass its bill.

In the 2011 elections for the Scottish Parliament, the SNP obtained a majority, winning 53 percent of the seats with 45 percent of the vote. Armed with an absolute majority, Salmond and Sturgeon pressed forward with their referendum plan. In 2012, David Cameron agreed to hold a referendum, provided it was "fair, legal and decisive." Confident that most Scots would chose to stay in the United Kingdom, Cameron wanted to settle the independence issue for the foreseeable future. A legal process was worked out and codified in the Edinburgh Agreement of October 2012, in which both governments agreed on the terms of the referendum. The date for the vote was set for the 18th of September 2014, with the question put to the electorate: "Should Scotland be an independent country?" All British, Commonwealth and EU citizens who were legally resident in Scotland were eligible to vote.

The campaigns for and against independence kicked off in the late spring of 2012, with the SNP leading the "Yes Scotland" campaign and all the other major political parties working to solicit a "no" result with their "Better Together" campaign. The "yes" campaign emphasized the benefits to the Scottish people of having complete control over social policy, of negotiating a better deal with regards to North Sea oil and of creating a Scottish political constitution. The "no" campaign emphasized the risk to the Scottish economy; argued Scotland would not automatically be admitted to the EU if it left the United Kingdom; and pointed out that there was no guarantee that Scotland would be able to use the British pound as its currency after independence. Defense issues – the SNP was opposed to both membership in NATO and to the possession of nuclear weapons – and other questions about dividing up government assets and liabilities were also contentious.

For most of the two-year campaigning period it appeared that the "no" side had the advantage. Certainly, there was little doubt in Westminster about the result, and thus minimal attention was paid to the issue. That complacency was shattered in early September 2014 after the second official debate (which Salmond was widely perceived to have won), when public opinion polls indicated that the "yes" side was effectively tied with "no" among decided voters. With the prospect of an independent Scotland now very real, the panicked major political parties in Westminster sprang into action. A series of dire pronouncements about the dangers to the economy followed, with businesses and the big British banks all encouraged to sound the alarm about the consequences of Scotland leaving the union. It was at this moment that the former Labour prime minister Gordon Brown emerged as the unofficial leader of the "no" campaign. He spent the last two frantic weeks of the campaign touring Scotland and shoring up support for the "no" side. Brown also brokered a deal with Cameron's government to issue a declaration just days before the referendum that if the Scots voted against independence extensive new powers would be given to the Scottish Parliament.

Brown's public and private campaigning made a major difference. In particular, his brokered promise of greater autonomy for Scotland if they voted no to independence – "the Vow" as it was called by the newspapers – helped shift support back to the "yes" side. In the end 55.3 percent of voters opted to remain in the United Kingdom. Turnout was very high, with nearly 85 percent of the 4.3 million eligible voters going to the polls. Subsequent studies demonstrated that the opponents to independence were concentrated among women and the young. Those living in poorer regions, meanwhile, were more likely to vote "yes" than those living in affluent areas.

Cameron made good on his promise to grant sweeping new powers to the Scottish Parliament, including over taxation and the NHS in Scotland. But these came with a catch. In a move widely denounced as cynically partisan – the Conservatives had practically no electoral support at all in Scotland – Cameron announced that Scottish MPs at Westminster would no longer be able to vote on issues that solely concerned England. Moreover, similarly sweeping new powers were to be given to the devolved Parliaments of Northern Ireland and Wales and also to the local councils of the largest urban areas like Greater London. While there was an intellectual case for these additional changes, which fit broadly within Cameron's "Big Society" vision, it seemed to the SNP that this was a betrayal of "the Vow." Salmond, who had resigned as leader of the SNP after the referendum, protested that the electorate had been duped by a phony pledge. This would become a major issue in the national election campaign the following year. Given that the Scottish Referendum had raised the possibility of the dissolution of Great Britain, there was much anticipation that the results of the 2015 election would turn on the future of the union. All the national parties addressed what powers they thought should be devolved to the regions and urban areas, as well as the proposed "English votes for English laws" policy. The issue of immigration and the government's hostile environment policy were also front and center in the 2015 campaign, with the Tories proposing that legal migrants to Britain be barred from accessing any government social services for four years after their arrival. The third issue that dominated the 2015 election was the place of Britain in Europe. David Cameron had pledged that, if the Tories obtained a majority, the new government would hold a referendum on Britain's continued membership in the EU. This promise had been made by Cameron in January 2013 largely to silence the Euroskeptics on the Tory backbenches. Cameron himself was pro–European Union, but much of his caucus was not, and moreover many were worried by the continued uptick in support for UKIP.

The promise received relatively little attention at the time because it seemed unlikely that the Conservatives would win a majority. Instead, another coalition with the pro-European Liberal Democrats, who would never agree to such a referendum, was predicted. The results, however, surprised the pollsters. In England, the Conservatives won 60 percent of the seats in Parliament on just 41 percent of the popular vote, and emerged with a majority of fifteen. In Northern Ireland, the Democratic Unionist Party won 44 percent of the seats. Labour did well in Wales, getting 63 percent of the seats, but was virtually wiped out in Scotland. Its support galvanized by anger over what was perceived to be duplicity of the implementation of "the Vow," the SNP won all but three Scottish seats with 50 percent of the popular vote. As a result, the SNP surpassed the Liberal Democrats, who were reduced from fifty-six MPs to only eight, as the third-largest party at Westminster.

With this surprise victory, Cameron felt compelled to follow through on his promise to his backbenchers. Despite gaining further concessions from the EU, Cameron set the 23rd of June 2016 as the date of the promised referendum on Europe. Because the vote was called to deal with a rift within the Conservative Party, Cameron allowed his MPs to choose the side for which they wished to campaign. Cameron, much of the cabinet, a majority of Tory MPs, the remaining Liberal Democrats, the SNP and most of the opposition Labour Party all backed the "Remain" campaign. A handful of high-profile Tory MPs, however, organized the official "Vote Leave" campaign, including Justice Secretary Michael Gove and former mayor of London Boris Johnson. Both men saw the referendum as an opportunity to raise their own profiles and stake a claim to Tory leadership in the future. In his prior career as a journalist Johnson had ridiculed the EU, but it was later revealed that he had been undecided about which side to support prior to Cameron's announcement of the referendum date.

Meanwhile, the leader of UKIP, Nigel Farage, organized a parallel campaign called Leave. EU. Farage was a former stockbroker who had once supported the Tories but had left the party due to his Euroskepticism. He co-founded UKIP in 1993, and from 1999 onwards was repeatedly elected as a member of the European Parliament, where he organized an anti-EU bloc. But UKIP was more than just a single-issue political party: it tapped into general discontentment with the status quo and offered an explicitly anti-elite, populist message. Its electoral base was older, mostly male, working-class, white and generally did not have a post-secondary education. They mixed deep Euroskepticism with concerns about immigration and the ways in which British society and culture were changing. UKIP members viewed the established political parties as dominated by highly educated, socially liberal people who were comfortable in an ethnically and culturally diverse, outward-looking society. Socially very conservative, UKIP members on the other hand were not comfortable with that vision of Britain, and they deeply resented what they viewed as the condescension of experts and policy makers towards their views. On economic issues, UKIP's membership was much more suspicious of big business and privatization than was their party's leadership. In the 2015 election, UKIP received the third-largest share of the popular vote at 12.9 percent, representing nearly four million votes. They took support from both the Conservatives and Labour, but because their vote was widely disbursed, they were only able to secure one seat in Parliament.

Tory supporters of Brexit like Gove and Johnson opportunistically embraced a populist message, although they had both emerged from the traditional social and political elite. They played on the same anxieties about immigration and resentment towards urban, cosmopolitan elites that UKIP did. Gove said while campaigning, "the British people have had enough of experts" and "the elites have done very well out of the EU, that's why they support it, but what about decent, ordinary people?" Both Leave campaigns relied heavily on emotional appeals rather than trying to counter the statistical arguments put forward by Remainers. Leave campaigners appealed to voter nostalgia about Britain's pre-EU past; to anger about Westminster's austerity policies since 2010; to resentment of political and intellectual elites and their perceived condescension towards the masses; and to fear, particularly of outsiders. This contrasted directly with the expert-opinion-driven approach of the Remain campaign. As Arron Banks, the major financial backer of UKIP and the Leave. EU campaign, stated immediately after the referendum: "Facts don't work for winning votes. The Remain campaign featured fact, fact, fact, fact, fact. It just doesn't work. You have to connect with people emotionally."

A small number of Labour MPs joined the Leave campaign. Had he not been the Labour leader, Jeremy Corbyn might have done so himself. Against the wishes of most Labour MPs, Corbyn had been elected leader by the party's membership after their disappointing showing in the 2015 election. He had been an outsider within the party after Blair and Brown had remade it, but he was popular with Labour youth and, channelling discontent about the status quo, aimed to move Labour to the left again, much as Bernie Sanders was attempting to do with the American Democratic Party. On a personal level, he was highly ambivalent about the referendum and was roundly criticized by Labour Remainers for his half-hearted approach. In fact, Corbyn had long been a Euroskeptic who had voted against Britain's membership in the European Economic Community in 1975, the Maastricht Treaty in 1993 and the Lisbon Treaty in 2008. Indeed, Corbyn refused to confirm that he had voted to remain in 2016.

The referendum campaign debates in the spring and early summer of 2016 were vigorous and often heated. The competing claims of both sides coalesced around certain issues. On trade the Remain side pointed to the fact that 45 percent of British exports went to the EU, which meant that leaving would be disastrous to the British economy. The Leavers countered that a Britain outside the EU could negotiate similar trade terms with both the EU and non-EU countries while becoming free of EU laws and regulations. EU regulation was frequently invoked as a problem, with Leavers calling for a return of British sovereignty over employment, product standards, and health and safety laws. Remainers pointed out that most EU regulation collapsed twenty-eight different national standards and laws into one European-wide set, reducing red tape and making exports more economical for business.

The two most controversial Leave claims, however, revolved around immigration and the EU budget. On immigration, the Leave campaigns claimed that Britain could end the "out of control" system that offered an open door to the EU while blocking non-EU immigrants. Remainers countered that leaving the EU would not by itself reduce immigration and that British citizens benefitted from being able to travel, work, study and live freely across the EU. Remainers pointed out that the recent increase of concerns over immigration was due to refugees fleeing the Middle East and North Africa rather than internal EU migrants. In 2015, there had been a European-wide spike in claims of refugee status. Many of the refugees were fleeing war-torn Syria, while other migrants were fleeing desperate economic conditions in Africa and the Middle East. The Leave.EU campaign billboards controversially depicted long lines of Syrian refugees with the slogan "Breaking Point." This and other campaign materials were roundly criticized by Remainers as racist and deceptive. Britain could already deny non-EU citizens entry because it had never signed onto the Schengen Agreement (which allowed non-EU citizens the freedom to move around the EU once they had legally entered it), and responsibility to process refugees was based on international agreements unrelated to the EU. And despite the claims of Farage and others, Britain had accepted a very small proportion of the millions of refugees who had made it into Europe over the previous eighteen months, with Germany in particular taking a much larger share.

Other Leave claims that EU migrants, especially those from Eastern Europe, were "stealing" welfare benefits had been debunked during the 2015 election campaign, with statistics showing that less than 3 percent of EU migrants were in receipt of any form of working-age welfare benefit, compared to the national average of 14.5 percent. Leave campaigners, however, pointed to the total number of EU migrants per year (about 184,000) and the total number of EU citizens living in Britain (about three million) as evidence of a massive problem. The fact that 1.2 million British citizens lived elsewhere in Europe, or that the percentage of people living in Britain but born elsewhere was comparatively low at 9 percent (compared to 13 percent in the United States, 20 percent in Canada and 27 percent in Australia), made little dent in the emotional appeal to "take back control" of the border.

It was the issue of the EU budget and what Britain contributed to it, however, that led to the most controversial claim made by the Leave campaign. On the campaign tour bus in which Boris Johnson traveled around the country was plastered the claim that Britain sent £350 million to the EU each week, and that if Britain left the EU that money could be spent on the NHS instead. Britain had in fact never paid that amount because Margaret Thatcher had negotiated an annual rebate in the 1980s. Moreover, it did not take into account the large amount of money that came back to Britain from the EU in spending on "deprived areas" and other programs. In reality, the net amount that the UK paid to the Brussels for the functioning of the EU was around £164 million a week, still a large sum, but less than half of what was claimed by Johnson's bus. Immediately after the referendum, Leave leaders backtracked and claimed there had been no guarantee that any savings from leaving the EU would go towards the NHS.

As it progressed, the referendum campaign polarized the country, cutting across traditional partisan divides. Less than two weeks before the vote, the pro-Europe Labour MP Jo Cox was murdered in the street outside her Yorkshire constituency office. The right-wing extremist who cried out "Britain will always come first" as he stabbed her was later convicted using the UK's anti-terrorism provisions.

In striking similarity to the Scottish independence referendum, most politicians and pundits were confident to the point of complacency that the economic case for staying in the EU was so strong that a Remain outcome for the referendum was assured. Opinion polls in early June, however, showed that the referendum result was too close to call. Panic began to creep into the Remain ranks, resulting in some fairly desperate tactics. The chancellor of the Exchequer George Osborne released a statement indicating that if Britain left the EU, he would have to prepare an austerity budget far more sweeping in its spending cuts than any of those of the previous five years.

On the 23rd of June, the public went to the polls. The result was a surprise victory for the Leave side by 51.9 to 48.1 percent. About 72 percent of the eligible population voted. The demographic breakdown of the vote indicated sharp divisions nationally, regionally and by age. Sixty-two percent of Scots voted in favour of remaining in the EU, while Northern Ireland voted to stay by a smaller margin, with the vote there divided between Protestant areas, where a slim majority voted to leave, and Catholic areas, where there was a stronger vote to remain. Greater London, other large cities and university towns all voted to Remain, whereas rural areas and small towns in England and Wales generally voted to leave. Some of the biggest majorities for the Leave campaign were in the post-industrial small cities and towns of the Midlands and the North of England. Men were slightly more inclined to vote Leave than women, and the young were overwhelmingly more in favor of remaining than were older adults. Seventy-five percent of voters under the age of twenty-five wanted to stay, but 66 percent of those over the age of sixty-five voted to leave. The proportion of people who voted increased by age, so a much higher percentage of the older population voted than did their younger counterparts.

In the days following the vote, the implications of being the first country to ever leave the EU began to dawn on the public at large. David Cameron tendered his resignation, plunging his party and the government into a succession crisis. Labour MPs forced a no-confidence vote on their own leader, Jeremy Corbyn, who was judged to have failed to meet the challenge of the referendum. Much was made in the media of the fact that on the day after the vote the top trending questions on UK Google were "What does it mean to leave the EU?" and "What is the EU?" It is likely that those questions were driven by teachers getting their classes to understand what had just transpired, rather than proof that the electorate did not know what they were voting for, but the sense of uncertainty was palpable across a Britain that had collectively, if by a very narrow margin, taken a step into the unknown.

Conclusion

Between 1997 and 2016, Britain underwent major changes to its political structure and its social make-up. The Blair and Brown Labour governments brought about sweeping changes to the constitutional structure of Britain through devolution and the Northern Ireland peace process. After 2010, the Cameron-Clegg coalition approved a referendum that, had it passed, would have broken apart the three-century union of England and Wales with Scotland. Economically, Britain went from a period of rising affluence in the early 2000s through the crash of 2008 and into a period of austerity not seen since the early 1980s. Socially and culturally, Britain became more liberal and progressive, particularly in large urban areas, but at the same time a backlash against those changes also grew, especially in post-industrial areas. A multicultural and multiracial society was accepted by most Britons: the 2011 census revealed that there was a larger percentage of mixed-race families in Britain than anywhere else in Europe. New immigrants, however, were increasingly seen as unwelcome. All these developments provide context for perhaps the most divisive moment in Britain's postwar history: the referendum that would remove Britain from its forty-year membership in the European Economic Community and European Union.

Bibliography

Bale, Tim, *The Conservative Party: From Thatcher to Cameron* (2011)

Clarke, Harold, Matthew Goodwin, Paul Whiteley, *Brexit: Why Britain Voted to Leave the European Union* (2017)

Esler, Gavin, *How Britain Ends: English Nationalism and the Rebirth of Four Nations* (2021)

Gould, Philip, *The Unfinished Revolution: How New Labour Changed British Politics for Ever* (2011)

Harris, John, *Britpop!: Cool Britannia and the Spectacular Demise of English Rock* (2004)

Hayward, Katy, *The Irish Border* (2021)

Menon, Anand and Geoffrey Evans, *Brexit and British Politics* (2017)

O'Rourke, Kevin, *A Short History of Brexit* (2019)

Peele, Gillian and John Francis, eds., *David Cameron and Conservative Renewal* (2016)

Rawnsley, Andrew, *Servants of the People: The Inside Story of New Labour*, new edn (2001)

Rawnsley, Andrew, *The End of the Party: The Rise and Fall of New Labour* (2010)

Sardar, Ziauddin, *Balti Britain: A Provocative Journey through Asian Britain* (2008)

Shaw, Eric, *Losing Labour's Soul? New Labour and the Blair Government 1997–2007*, new edn (2008)

Snowden, Peter, *Back from the Brink: The Extraordinary Fall and Rise of the Conservative Party* (2010)

Sobolewska, Maria and Robert Ford, *Brexitland: Identity, Diversity and the Reshaping of British Politics* (2020)

Stephens, Philip, *Britain Alone: The Path from Suez to Brexit* (2021)

Wall, Stephen, *Reluctant European: Britain and the European Union from 1945 to Brexit* (2020)

16 Conclusion
Crisis and an Uncertain Future

Topics Covered

- The Brexit conundrums
- Return of coalition government, 2017
- Constitutional crisis and the Brexit election, 2019
- COVID-19
- The state of the United Kingdom in 2020

Timeline

2016	Theresa May replaces David Cameron as prime minister
2017	Britain formally submits to the European Union its intention to leave by March 2019
2017	Conservatives lose majority in election
2018	May faces leadership vote
2019	May's withdrawal agreement plans are defeated three times in Parliament
2019	Deadline to leave the European Union extended
2019	Boris Johnson replaces May as prime minister
2019	Johnson fights election on Brexit terms and Conservatives win a majority
2020	Britain leaves the European Union
2020	COVID-19 arrives in the United Kingdom

It is difficult to assess the very recent past in Britain, as the impact of the decisions and events of the past few years are not yet fully clear. What is evident is that the Brexit referendum of 2016 not only upended Britain's forty-year relationship with the project to integrate Europe, but also opened up a constitutional crisis, exposed polarizing fissures in the social fabric and overturned political norms and partisan divides that dated back almost a century. The longer-term results of Britain's departure from the European Union in 2020 can at present only be speculated on. Hard on the heels of the Brexit crisis came the global COVID-19 pandemic, which hit Britain particularly hard and has obscured the degree to which Brexit is already beginning to change Britain's economy and society. What is more certain is that Britain's exit from Europe and the political, social and economic issues that caused the people to vote for it have called into question many of the constitutional compromises worked out in the previous decades.

DOI: 10.4324/9781003284758-16

The Search for an Exit

David Cameron announced his resignation immediately after the Brexit referendum in June 2016, although he remained prime minister until a successor was chosen by the Conservative Party. In the subsequent leadership contest, Boris Johnson, who had campaigned so successfully for Brexit, was the obvious front-runner, but his erstwhile ally Michael Gove publicly declared that Johnson would be incapable of providing the leadership to take Britain out of the European Union. After Johnson announced he would not stand for election, the right-leaning *Daily Telegraph* called Gove's comments "the most spectacular political assassination in a generation." Gove himself then joined the election contest, along with four rivals, but in the end it was the home secretary, Theresa May, who prevailed and became Conservative leader and prime minister in July of 2016. May had been the longest serving home secretary since the 1940s and had been responsible for the "hostile environment" policy towards undocumented immigrants, which had sought to make life so difficult for them that they would "voluntarily leave" the UK. On most issues she sided with the Party's right wing, but she had been pro-EU prior to the referendum and had campaigned for the Remain campaign. When she announced her decision to seek the leadership of the Conservative Party, May declared that the public had spoken and the result of the referendum must be upheld. She made it clear that she was committed to seeing Britain leave the EU; in a phrase that she would often deploy later when asked about her plans for negotiating with the EU, she said, "Brexit means Brexit." As absolutely no planning for the possibility of a Leave result had been made by Cameron's government, once she took office May had to work out what Britain's position on the planned withdrawal would be.

Figure 16.1 Theresa May meets with European Commission president Jean-Claude Juncker in Brussels in December 2017 during the negotiations over the UK's departure from the EU.

Reproduced courtesy of Number 10.

While the Conservative government tried to figure out what it wanted from Brexit, the Labour Party was facing its own crisis. The day after the 2016 referendum, in which their leader, Jeremy Corbyn had – albeit unenthusiastically – campaigned for the Remain side, Labour saw a massive wave of resignations, as 172 Labour MPs declared they had no confidence in Corbyn as leader. But since it is the party members and not the MPs that choose the Labour leader, his discontented MPs had to watch impotently as the membership re-elected Corbyn as leader by an overwhelming margin. Brexit had created a major dilemma for Labour. While nationally two-thirds of the party's supporters and almost all its MPs were firmly in the Remain camp, the Labour supporters who wanted to leave were clustered in constituencies in the industrial Midlands and the North, where the majority of Labour's safe seats were located. Labour was therefore at risk of being wiped out electorally if they did not honor the Leave result. In an effort to appease both camps, Corbyn stressed that Labour would abide by the referendum result but would seek the best possible exit terms from the EU, including keeping Britain within the single market and customs union.

On the 29th of March 2017, May delivered to Brussels the formal notice of Britain's intention to leave the EU, which due to EU regulations meant that negotiations on the terms of the withdrawal had to be completed by the end of March 2019. Facing disagreements within her own caucus about the exit strategy and seeking to benefit from Labour's own internal discord, May called a snap general election in the summer of 2017. Labour and the Liberal Democrats supported her, as they saw it as an opportunity to get the public on side for their own positions. Because Labour was so divided on Brexit and Corbyn was generally unpopular, the opinion polls indicated that Labour would lose seats. May, on the other hand, fully expected that the Conservatives would gain a larger majority, which would give her more room to maneuver around her own backbenchers, who were making it difficult for her to produce a consensus regarding the negotiations with the EU. May, however, ran a poor campaign in which the Conservatives alienated older voters by reneging on promises regarding pensions and winter fuel benefits. Corbyn, meanwhile, largely ignored Brexit and focused on reversing the austerity policies of the previous seven years. Younger voters flocked to Labour in large numbers. The surprise election result saw May's government lose thirteen seats and Labour gain thirty.

Rather than getting the bigger majority May needed, the Tories no longer had a majority at all. To get a working majority, May had to find another party with at least eight MPs willing to support the Tories. She therefore agreed to a "confidence and supply" arrangement with the Democratic Unionist Party (DUP) of Northern Ireland. The DUP's main concern was to make sure the government supported the closest possible union between Northern Ireland and the rest of the United Kingdom, and they vowed to vote against any measures which might weaken that bond. This tactical agreement would severely complicate May's Brexit negotiations.

Over the next two years, May failed to build a consensus within her party and with the DUP about the terms of withdrawal. She tried to work around the lack of support amongst her caucus by having the government negotiate the withdrawal agreement without seeking the approval of Parliament and presenting the withdrawal agreement as a "done deal" like any other diplomatic negotiation, subject to questions and criticism in Parliament but not formal consultation or ratification. This plan was foiled by a case brought before Britain's Supreme Court by a private citizen, which resulted in a ruling that Parliament had to be consulted and vote on the deal. Finding it impossible to reach an agreement that garnered sufficient support from Tory MPs, May resorted to running down the clock, hoping that the fear of Britain "crashing out" (i.e., leaving without any agreement) of the EU after the

March 2019 deadline would convince the other parties in Parliament to accept her deal. Angry that she was not pursuing a tough enough line with the EU negotiators, the Brexit hardliners in the Tory ranks forced a vote on May's leadership in December 2018. She won the vote, with 200 MPs supporting her and 117 voting against, but only after indicating she would remain prime minister just until the Brexit negotiations were completed.

As alarming reports appeared in the press of possible food and medicine shortages and massive inflation if no deal with the EU was reached, May put her Brexit withdrawal agreement before Parliament in January 2019. It was rejected by 230 votes, in the largest parliamentary defeat for a government in British history. Modified versions of May's deal were voted down two more times in March. The Liberal Democrats, the Scottish National Party and some Labour MPs voted against May's withdrawal agreement because they were opposed to leaving entirely, while the Labour leadership did so because of perceived tactical political advantage. But May's deal was ultimately sunk by the DUP and the "hard Brexiteers" within the Conservative ranks who voted against their own government. The withdrawal agreement had included a payment of £39 billion by Britain to cover the costs of relocating and reconfiguring the EU institutions that had been established in the United Kingdom, as well as an arrangement that allowed a route to permanent resident status for EU citizens living in the United Kingdom and British citizens living in other EU countries. The "hard Brexiteers" did not want to pay the EU a penny and would have allowed Britain to crash out of the EU to avoid doing so; they were also unconcerned about the plight of EU nationals living in Britain.

The most controversial provision in May's withdrawal agreement, however, was the so-called Northern Irish "backstop," which reflected the way in which Brexit generated a particular problem for Northern Ireland. Britain's departure from the EU meant that the 310-mile-long border between Northern Ireland and the Republic of Ireland, which had been largely open and across which tens of thousands traveled every day without passport controls, would now also be a border between the United Kingdom and the EU. Customs and regulatory checks would therefore be required, since different trade rules would be in force on each side. This hardening of the border threatened to upset the terms of the peace process that had led to the Good Friday Agreement in 1998. That agreement and its rules and institution, including the right of those in Northern Ireland to claim British or Irish citizenship (or both), worked because the UK's and Ireland's membership in the EU allowed for free movement across the border. The reimposition of an actual physical border threatened not only serious economic disruption, but also to remind people of the difference between being a citizen of the Republic of Ireland and one of Northern Ireland. Neither side wanted the return of a hard border since that had been a major source of violence for paramilitaries during the Troubles and potentially might be again.

To protect the Good Friday settlement, in her initial withdrawal agreement proposals May suggested a "backstop": Northern Ireland would remain in the EU customs union and in "full regulatory alignment" with the European single market until alternative custom arrangements and border issues could be worked out, which might take many years. For all practical purposes, Northern Ireland would therefore remain in the EU while the rest of the United Kingdom would not. This was a major compromise on the part of the EU, but for the DUP this was an intolerable concession because it would create an economic frontier between Britain and Northern Ireland. They feared this would further erode the position of the Unionist community in Northern Ireland and ultimately lead to the unification of all Ireland. To secure support from the DUP, May's final withdrawal agreement proposal included all of the United Kingdom in the "backstop" during the transition period. This would have meant that the UK would effectively remain in the EU customs union and single market until the alternative border arrangements with Northern Ireland were worked out, but Britain would not have any say in Brussels about how those economic institutions were run. This idea enraged the hard Brexiteers, who feared that Britain might forever remain trapped in the EU's custom union if those alternative arrangements over the Irish border proved impossible to sort out.

The backstop issue destroyed May's chances of getting her deal through Parliament and ultimately her premiership. After her deal was defeated on its third attempt at the end of March 2019, a humiliated May was required to get an extension from the EU of the deadline by which Britain would leave. The delay further infuriated the hard Brexiteers. Amid concerns that another referendum might be needed on the terms of the deal, and as local Conservative associations petitioned for another vote of no confidence in May's leadership, May announced that she would resign as Conservative leader on the 7th of June 2019. A leadership contest followed, in which the party membership chose Boris Johnson, who took office in July.

Johnson is the most divisive political figure in Britain since Margaret Thatcher. Born in America into an Anglo-French family with Turkish ancestors and upper-class connections, Johnson moved to England a few months after his birth and was educated at Eton College and Oxford, where he cultivated his eccentric and outwardly bumbling persona. He became active in Conservative politics at Oxford, where he was a contemporary of David Cameron, Michael Gove and others who would become prominent figures in the Tory party. As a political commentator in various newspapers, he earned a reputation for his witty writing style but was criticized for perceived bigotry towards religious and ethnic minorities and the LGBT community. He also gained notoriety for his tendency to play fast and loose with the truth, especially about the EU. He was accused of fanning Euroskepticism in order to advance his career and was fired from the *Times* for fabricating a quotation.

While continuing his journalistic endeavors, Johnson became a Tory MP in 2001. Seven years later, he was elected mayor of London. In this role he seemed to become more politically liberal, as he introduced new double-decker buses, made London safer for bicyclists and aggressively promoted the 2012 London Olympics, which earned him a second term. In 2015, he returned to Parliament, where he quickly reverted to more right-wing views. He was appointed foreign secretary in 2016, which was widely seen as a tactic by May to weaken him as a rival, since he would have to be out of the country frequently. In 2018, Johnson resigned in protest of May's Brexit negotiations, which he regarded as insufficiently tough with the EU.

On becoming prime minister the following year, Johnson vowed that Britain would leave the EU by the 31st of October 2019 – the new deadline that Theresa May had negotiated – with or without a withdrawal agreement. He also promised to remove the controversial Irish backstop plan. Johnson then asked the Queen to prorogue Parliament (i.e., to end the current session) and suspend it from sitting between September 10 and October 14. This was a clear attempt to prevent Parliament from exercising oversight of the Brexit negotiations. Protests erupted across Britain, and a number of court cases were launched. On the 4th of September, Parliament passed the Benn Act, which blocked the government from allowing Britain to leave the EU without a withdrawal agreement. This was made possible by a number of centrist Tory MPs, furious at Johnson's hard line towards Brussels, who crossed the floor and joined other parties in voting for the measure. Some of them were thrown out of the Tory caucus by Johnson in consequence, including Kenneth Clarke, a prominent cabinet minister in the Thatcher years, and Nicholas Soames, the grandson of Winston Churchill.

By firing members of his own caucus who opposed his no-deal threat, Johnson eliminated his working majority in the Commons. He therefore demanded that a general election be called, but since under the Fixed Term Elections Act he needed two-thirds of the house to agree to the election, and this would only be granted once the possibility of a no-deal Brexit was ruled out, his request was denied. In another first in its history, Parliament was holding the government hostage: refusing to pass its legislation, but also refusing to allow its dissolution.

Soon afterwards, the Supreme Court decided unanimously that Johnson's prorogation of Parliament had been unlawful. Johnson was judged to have lied to Parliament, to the people and to the monarch about the purpose of the prorogation. Crucially, along with the earlier decision about Parliament's role in approving the withdrawal agreement, what the judges were deciding was not about the mechanics or justness of Brexit, but rather the existential constitutional question the whole Brexit saga had opened up: who holds supreme political power in the United Kingdom? Is it the people, Parliament or the government? May and Johnson, in differing ways, had both acted as if it was the government itself that had supreme authority. But the Supreme Court upheld the traditional view of Britain's unwritten constitution and rebuked Johnson (and May) for assuming that the government had authority beyond Parliament. On issues central to the constitutional arrangement of the United Kingdom, the Supreme Court ruled that Parliament, as the elected representatives of the people, must be consulted and ultimately decide.

As a consequence of the Supreme Court's decision, Johnson was forced to ask the EU for another extension of the deadline, which was now set at the end of January 2020. To the surprise of many, Johnson was able to revise the withdrawal agreement with the EU, with the main change being a new protocol on Northern Ireland to replace the "backstop." For the purposes of trade and tariffs, Northern Ireland would legally remain part of the United Kingdom, but the customs border between the United Kingdom and the EU would be between Northern Ireland and the rest of Britain in the Irish Sea, rather than at the land border between the Republic of Ireland and Northern Ireland. A further change was that, in contrast to the backstop, which was a fallback position in case further negotiations between the EU and Britain failed, the new protocol was the starting point of negotiations and would remain in effect for four years, after which the Northern Ireland Assembly could vote on whether to continue the arrangement.

Labour, the Liberal Democrats and the DUP all rejected the proposed deal and declared that getting the public's views in an election was now necessary. Johnson thus proposed and fast-tracked legislation that sidestepped the provisions of the Fixed Term Elections Act for an election to be held on the 12th of December 2019. After a campaign in which Johnson's main message was "getting Brexit done," the election produced a healthy majority for the Conservatives, while Labour suffered an historic loss. Areas that had consistently voted Labour for the previous century fell to the Conservatives; these losses were predominantly in areas where the electorate supported Brexit. The Conservatives emerged with their highest share of the popular vote since 1979 and their largest proportion of seats since 1987. Labour's seat total fell to 202, the lowest number they had held since 1935. The other big winner was the Scottish National Party, led by Nicola Sturgeon, which won forty-eight of the fifty-two seats in Scotland.

Armed with a majority of eighty in the Commons, Johnson was able to ram his withdrawal agreement through Parliament. The deal was then fast-tracked through the EU approval process, and the United Kingdom formally left the EU on the 30th of January 2020. This was not the end of the Brexit saga, however. Due to transportation disruptions and the exodus of some international businesses to cities on the continent, the British government still needed to resolve its long-term economic relationship with the EU, sort out the arrangements for the Northern Irish border and negotiate new trade deals with non-EU countries. At the time of writing, these processes are all still ongoing.

A New Crisis: COVID-19

Soon after the withdrawal agreement was passed, Johnson's government faced a new crisis, in the form of the COVID-19 pandemic. The novel corona virus was declared a health emergency of international concern by the World Health Organization in January 2020, and the first cases of the virus were detected in Britain in that same month. As case numbers rose over the course of February 2020, Johnson's government debated what its response should be. Mass gatherings were allowed to continue into March, while people who had traveled abroad or displayed symptoms were asked to self-isolate. Johnson was initially adverse to the mandatory lockdowns that some European countries – most notably hard-hit Italy – began imposing in February, suggesting such measures were not based on science and would lead to panic and economic ruin. The government was accused of pursuing a strategy in which the virus would be allowed to spread in order to reach "herd immunity." This led to a backlash from the British scientific and medical community, and Health Secretary Matt Hancock was forced to deny that herd immunity was an official plan. In mid-March 2020, the government announced it would introduce social distancing measures for older and health-compromised people. Then, as new cases and deaths surged, the government imposed a nationwide lockdown on the 23rd of March. Nonessential travel was forbidden, and stores selling nonessential goods, schools, playgrounds, libraries and places of worship were closed. Gatherings of more than two people in public were banned, with the sole exception of funerals. This first lockdown would last until the summer, with the restrictions lifted on a sector-by-sector and regional basis. There would be two more nationwide lockdowns over the course of the fall and winter of 2021.

The first wave of COVID in Britain produced some 26,000 deaths, giving Britain the dubious distinction at the time of having the most deaths from COVID-19 of any country in Europe. Boris Johnson himself contracted COVID in late March 2020 and spent a few days in an intensive-care unit. The second wave at the end of 2020 was worse, but by that time other countries around the world were faring no better. By the end of the third wave in 2021, the United Kingdom had registered 185,000 deaths, second only to Russia in Europe in total deaths, and the twentieth highest globally. A study of excess deaths (comparing the number of deaths from all causes during the pandemic to the average number of deaths in prior years), however, indicates that the British death rate was not significantly higher than other European countries. Instead, the United Kingdom was more aggressive in testing and in attributing death to COVID than other countries. Even so, the pandemic led to the largest fall in life expectancy since records began in 1981. There were also accusations of corruption and cronyism in the awarding of government contracts for personal protective equipment. The British government did, however, lead the world with its vaccination policy, using both vaccines obtained from overseas (Pfizer-BioNTech and Moderna) and the homegrown Oxford University-AstraZeneca vaccine in one of the fastest rollout of vaccines in the world. By 2022, 87 percent of the population over the age of twelve had received at least two doses of the COVID vaccine.

As it did around the world, the pandemic imposed social and economic hardships on the British people. Hundreds of thousands of people lost their jobs, and millions more were saved from unemployment only by the government's subsidy programs, most notably the

Coronavirus Job Retention Scheme, which paid employers 80 percent of workers' salaries (up to £2,500 per month) so that they could be given paid leave during lockdowns. Ultimately, some 8.4 million people received income through the scheme at a cost to the government of over £14 billon per month. Even with this help, the health, social and economic costs of the pandemic were immense, and their full impacts have yet to be calculated.

Britain Faces a New Future

During the period 2016 to 2020, political views within Britain became much more polarized, with many people telling pollsters that their views on Brexit determined which party they now supported, thereby splitting the population into two almost equally sized groups and making it clear that a major shift in traditional alignments has occurred. It is no exaggeration to say that the Brexit referendum result produced a constitutional crisis. Since 1688, the United Kingdom's constitutional system has increasingly transferred sovereignty to Parliament. The public votes for whom they want to represent them, and those representatives sit in Parliament as MPs. The government ultimately answers to the people through seeking support from Parliament in the firm of legislation passed by MPs. This has been complicated by the devolution of power to regional Parliaments in Scotland, Wales and Northern Ireland, with the consequences still not fully worked out. The vote to leave the European Union was not accomplished through representative democracy, however. Instead, it was an act of direct democracy. The referendum itself offered a democratic legitimacy that has energized many people who were fed up with politics as usual, wanted change and therefore voted for Leave. The vote, however, only required that Britain leave the EU with no details about how to achieve it. The populist United Kingdom Independence Party, led by Nigel Farage, the Conservative "hard Brexiteers" and the opportunistic Johnson all responded by claiming that they alone could interpret the referendum result and that they would enact the "will of the people." But Leave voters were not unanimous in what they wanted; neither, for that matter, were Remain voters. Brexit therefore brought into conflict different understandings of democracy in Britain. Only the actions of the British Supreme Court and the rebel Tory MPs prevented the government from asserting its claim that it could do what it wanted because it, rather than Parliament, "spoke for the people." In response, the justices of the Supreme Court were labeled the "enemies of the people" by the right-wing press. It is far from certain how the traditional constitutional system will adapt to meet the populist challenge unleashed by the Brexit referendum.

As the 2016 referendum result was so close, those people who opposed leaving the EU demanded a second referendum, arguing that many people had voted merely as a protest to Westminster's indifference to their concerns and that they had been misled by the claims of how easy and beneficial Brexit would be. Since they were better informed about what leaving actually meant, many who voted to leave the EU in 2016 might now vote to stay. Major protests were held in support of a second referendum, particularly in large urban areas. But the demands and counter-claims regarding a second referendum expose the problem of relying on referendums to solve important political issues in a parliamentary democracy.

The Brexit referendum was in no way legally binding on the government, but the Conservatives (and Labour as well) recognized that failure to act on the "will of the people" as directly expressed in the vote would be a disaster for them electorally and would possibly lead to a further erosion of public trust in government. Consequently, the leadership of both parties resisted calls for a second referendum. Public opinion polls indicated that four years after the referendum, those in favor of leaving remained around 50 percent of those polled, and so not much had changed from the time of the vote. Indeed, people's attitudes on the issue hardened as time went on and became less likely to change. To be sure, at certain points a second referendum might have produced a slight majority for staying in the EU, but the polarization of the population on the issue would have still been in place.

The Brexit crisis also confirmed an ongoing change in people's voting patterns. Regional cleavages are increasingly apparent. In England, the Conservatives have emerged as the dominant party, taking more seats there than the other parties in every election since 2001. In Scotland, the Scottish National Party has been dominant since 2010 and has almost entirely replaced Labour in national elections, although Labour still holds a significant number of seats in the Scottish Parliament. The Welsh nationalists have not had quite the same degree of success, as Plaid Cymru has been unable to reduce Labour's dominance. In Northern Ireland, the Nationalist and Unionist communities elect MPs from the relevant parties in roughly equal measure. Thus, with the partial exception of Wales, it is now the case that entirely different party alignments exist in each of the four nations within the United Kingdom.

The Labour Party's position in the 1990s and early 2000s of being the only party with wide representation in England, Scotland and Wales has ended. Most of their seats are now won in the big English cities and in South Wales. This points to an even deeper change in partisan loyalties and the most fundamental political realignment since the Second World War. The Conservatives, at least in England, can now claim to be the party of much of the working class, whilst Labour is increasingly the party of middle-class university graduates who live in urban areas. To be sure, there have long been working-class Tories, at least since the 1870s when Benjamin Disraeli began making serious efforts to woo workers to the Conservative tent. The imposition of the welfare state by Labour in the late 1940s, however, created a bond between industrial workers and the Labour Party, especially in the Midlands, the North of England, South Wales and Scotland, which persisted through the end of the 1970s. But deindustrialization, Thatcherism and the rise of and identity politics has significantly weakened those bonds. Ultimately, the decline of manufacturing in Britain fundamentally undermined the male, trade-union-based working-class identity on which Labour had depended since 1945.

The effects of this transformation have only come to be fully felt in recent years. Many white working-class men and women remained Labour supporters prior to 2000 even though they themselves were socially conservative. While young, well-educated and cosmopolitan-minded urbanites sought to make Labour a progressive party on cultural issues like multiculturalism and women's and gay rights, anxiety over mass migration from the EU and the admission of refugees to the UK became more prevalent among traditional working-class Labour voters. Fears that British society was changing too much and too fast led to the steady erosion of working-class support from Labour (and initially from the Conservatives as well) towards the populist United Kingdom Independence Party and the far right, white-supremacist groups such as the English Defence League (founded in 2009) and Britain First (2011). The Conservatives' promise that leaving EU would "take back control" of the borders and restore sovereignty to ordinary people resonated with many in the disaffected white working class. But after Leave's victory, many of these voters saw no reason to continue supporting UKIP and instead rewarded Johnson's administration for delivering Brexit. Tory MPs were elected in working-class constituencies in England where they had not won in many decades. The Tory electoral base, which had previously been reduced to the suburban and rural parts of England, was given a massive boost by the addition of working-class support in the Midlands and North. Class as a key factor in determining how people vote has not disappeared in Britain, but its effect on political alignment has shifted.

Race 8

The Removal of Edward Colston's Statue

On the 7th of June 2020, protestors from the Black Lives Matter movement, who were responding to the killing of George Floyd by police in the American city of Minneapolis, toppled a statue of the merchant Edward Colston that had stood in the city of Bristol in southwestern England since 1895. Once revered as a local philanthropist, Colston had been the focus of increasing controversy since the 1990s due to his role in the slave trade. In 2018, Bristol's City Council had authorized a new plaque that attempted to explain Colston's links to the slave trade, but it was rejected by Mayor Marvin Rees, who felt that it did not go far enough, and never installed. After the protestors toppled the statue, they sprayed it with graffiti and pushed it into Bristol Harbour. It was retrieved four days later and placed into storage; in June 2021 it was displayed in the city's local history museum, M Shed. The Colston statue became a focal point of discussion about what should happen to Britain's numerous statues of historical figures with ties to slavery and empire. Since 2015, a campaign called "Rhodes Must Fall" has been advocating for the removal of a statue of the African imperialist Cecil Rhodes from the exterior of Oriel College at the University of Oxford. Even Winston Churchill, one of Britain's most revered political leaders, has not escaped scrutiny. In 2020, Black Lives Matter protestors graffitied "was a racist" after his name on the plinth of his statue in London's Parliament Square;

Figure 16.2 Protestors throw the statue of Edward Colston into the River Avon in Bristol in June 2020.

Reproduced courtesy of PA Images/Alamy Stock Photo.

the government temporarily boarded up the statue to prevent further damage. So far Rhodes and Churchill are still standing, but various strategies have been adopted for dealing with other statues of Britain's slave-traders and imperialists. A statue of the Jamaican planter Robert Milligan was removed from outside the Museum of London Docklands in 2020, while explanatory plaques have been added to Rhodes's statue and that of Henry Dundas, a politician who delayed the abolition of the slave trade, in Edinburgh's St. Andrew Square.

Brexit also indicated the revival of a particular kind of English nationalism. A 2018 academic survey of residents in England indicated that 64 percent of those who understood their identity to be "English rather than British" supported Brexit, while only 28 percent of those who felt that they were "British, not English" were opposed to EU membership. The EU has been regarded as an enabler of the independence movement in Scotland, and by Nationalists (and Unionists) in Northern Ireland as an enabler of Irish unity, but in England it has been seen by some people as a threat to English identity. Devolution – giving more political power to Scotland, Wales and Northern Ireland – has not quelled any of this nationalism; in fact, it has led to calls for an English Parliament as well.

In Scotland, the Scottish National Party now dominates the Scottish seats at Westminster and runs the Scottish government at Holyrood. Because Scots were overwhelmingly in favor of staying in the EU, the Brexit result has led to demands for another independence referendum. In 2021, the Welsh nationalist party Plaid Cymru also indicated their intention to call for an independence referendum should they become the leading party in the Welsh Assembly, but in the ensuing election they fell to third place behind the Conservatives. Northern Ireland was at the center of the difficulties that Theresa May faced in getting her Brexit withdrawal agreement through Parliament. Johnson's solution of leaving the EU on terms that neither community in Northern Ireland wanted has merely delayed the reckoning that Brexit will necessitate there. Some violence, especially amongst the young, did re-erupt in Ulster during the negotiations, and the danger to the peace process is real. Only time will tell if the ultimate consequence of the "border in the Irish Sea" imposed by the Northern Ireland Protocol will be the reunification of Ireland.

Economically, Britain, much as in the United States and Canada, has seen rising income inequality since the early 2000s. Studies suggest that, although the country as a whole has become more affluent, household income is more unequally distributed in Britain than at any point since the early 1960s. This inequality underlies a deep-rooted skepticism about the country's recovery from the 2008 economic crisis. On the eve of the Brexit referendum, only 29 percent of people in England were optimistic about the economy. Embedded in this figure were important regional disparities. Only 24 percent of people in northern England were optimistic, compared to 30 percent in London and 34 percent in the southeast of England. It was not a coincidence that it was in the old industrial heartlands of the country, which had never fully recovered from their economic decline in the 1970s and 1980s, that the desire to leave Europe was most emphatic. In those places, working-class young men, who could once hope to obtain relatively high-paying manufacturing jobs, no longer have that option. An educational system that fails to provide them with the skills they need for the new economy has left many of them alienated, angry and likely to engage in self- and socially destructive behavior. Alcohol consumption has been on the rise for decades, while it has been declining in the United States, France and Germany; Britain in 2021 ranked fifth among twenty-two western nations in its per capita alcohol consumption. Britons tend to drink not as frequently as people do in other countries but to drink larger quantities when they do, leading to more disorder and violence.

But while some of Britain's social problems are real, others are more perceived than actual. A number of high-profile cases, such as the murder of two-year-old James Bulger by two ten-year-old boys in 1993, led to fears that British society was becoming more violent. In truth, crime rates in Britain have fallen consistently since 1995, and violent crime is at its lowest level since the early 1980s. In a society with strict gun-control laws, there has been much discussion of rising rates of knife violence, but the statistics show that any increase has been slight. Claims that the nature of the British family has changed significantly in recent decades are more valid. As in most of Europe, marriage is a declining institution: the number of couples opting to marry has fallen by half since the 1950s. Soon, more British children will be born to unmarried than married couples. And as marriage has declined, divorce has increased: Britain has one of the highest divorce rates in Europe.

The state remains a key determinant of people's welfare even if the free market now plays a much larger role. This change took place most dramatically under Thatcher's leadership in the 1980s, but it continued under New Labour and the Conservative administrations that followed. In his social and economic policies, Tony Blair emphasized the need for a "Third Way" which would represent a synthesis of policies from the left and right and which accepted many of the precepts of market-based capitalism. Labour has also accepted other Conservative policies such as privatization, lower taxes and means-testing for some welfare benefits. David Cameron pushed his "Big Society" idea to increase community and reduce government involvement in social welfare, as welfare spending was slashed in the "austerity" budgets between 2010 and 2015. But after a backlash from voters who flocked to Labour in the 2015 election, May relaxed some of the austerity measures. Faced with the pandemic, Johnson's government introduced budgets that massively increased government spending. This indicates that the Tories could and would be big spenders if circumstances demanded it, and despite the rightward lurch of the past decade, British society and government remains further to the left on most issues than is the United States. On average, Britons are more socially liberal than Americans, and they are willing to pay higher taxes in return for public services. The "postwar consensus," which related largely to the welfare state, has been seriously eroded since 1980, but it has not been completely overturned.

This is a history textbook, and so it is fitting to end on an historical note. Differing views of Britain's history have played a conspicuous part in political and cultural debates in recent years. Whether it was Scottish nationalists arguing for the return of their national sovereignty, Brexiteers calling for a return to the "buccaneering" spirit of the age of empire, or Jeremy Corbyn calling for a return to the relative equality of the 1970s, the past has been deployed in support of arguments about the present and plans for the future. This shows us how much history matters. It is impossible to assess the state of British society today without a discussion of the pivotal role of social class over the centuries. It is equally impossible to discuss the issues of immigration and multiculturalism without acknowledging the influence of the British Empire in determining the places from which many of those immigrants have come. The British past has clearly shaped the British present (and will shape its future), in ways that we hope this textbook helps to make clear.

Bibliography

Akala, *Natives: Race and Class in the Ruins of Empire* (2019)

Bogdanor, Vernon, *Beyond Brexit: Towards a British Constitution* (2019)

Eddo-Lodge, Reni, *Why I'm No Longer Talking to White People about Race* (2017)

Hudson, Kerry, *Lowborn: Growing Up, Getting Away and Returning to Britain's Poorest Towns* (2020)

McGarvey, Darren, *Poverty Safari: Understanding the Anger of Britain's Working Class* (2018)

Sangera, Sathnam, *Empireland: How Imperialism Has Shaped Modern Britain* (2021)

Surridge, Paula, Robert Ford, Tim Bale and Will Jennings, *The British General Election of 2019* (2021)

Glossary

Apartheid: South African government policy, enforced through legislation, from 1948 to 1994 which mandated racial separation between whites and those of other races (defined as "black," "coloured" and "Indian"). The policy, derived from an Afrikaans word meaning "separateness," discriminated against the African minority and was used to maintain white minority rule.

Ascendancy: The Protestant elite in eighteenth-century Ireland. The Ascendancy controlled both the Irish Parliament in Dublin and the vast majority of Irish land. The height of the Ascendancy's power came between 1782 and 1800, when the Irish Parliament had legislative independence. Also known as the "Protestant Ascendancy" or the "Anglo-Irish Ascendancy."

Backbencher: A Member of Parliament who does not hold government or shadow government office. The name derives from the fact that they do not sit on the front benches of the House of Commons with the government and opposition ministers, but rather on the back benches. They are sometimes referred to as "private members," and can introduce Private Members' Bills for consideration by Parliament. They have more freedom to speak and vote than front bench MPs, who must support the government, and thus can be a challenge to the party whips who are charged with ensuring that all the party's MPs vote together.

Bank Holiday: A public holiday in the United Kingdom on which banks and government offices are closed. Bank holidays were created by the 1871 Bank Holiday Act; the dates vary slightly among England, Wales, Scotland and Northern Ireland.

British-Indian: The British in India during the period of colonial rule. While "Anglo-Indian" was the term used historically, "British-Indian" reflects the reality that not only English, but Scottish, Welsh and Irish people comprised the British community in colonial India.

By-election: Election held to fill a vacancy (such as for a Parliamentary seat) between regularly scheduled elections. By-elections are normally held when an MP resigns or dies, although seats can also be declared vacant because of an MP's mental illness, bankruptcy, or conviction for a serious criminal offense.

Calico: Fabric made from unbleached cotton and typically printed with colorful designs. The name "calico" is derived from the city of Calicut in southwestern India, the place from which this fabric was originally exported to England.

Chancellor of the Exchequer: The chief financial officer in the British government, equivalent to the Secretary of the Treasury in the United States.

Church of England: Since 1534, the officially established church in England. Its adherents in England, Wales, Ireland, and what became the British Commonwealth were known as "Anglicans." It was affiliated with, but separate from, the Episcopal Church in Scotland.

Civil List: After 1689, an annual income granted by Parliament to the monarch to replace the duties on imports and exports that had previously made up most of the ruler's income.

Clan System: The primary means of governance in the Scottish Highlands prior to its near-eradication by the British government after the Jacobite Rebellion of 1745. A clan was a group of loosely related people, or of other people who accepted the clan's authority, who lived in the same vicinity and were headed by a chief. Clans also, however, recognized the authority of the Scottish monarchy, which distinguished them from tribal forms of political organization.

Conscription: The compulsory enlistment of individuals for military service and other forms of national service. Conscription was employed in Britain during both world wars and continued as National Service until 1962.

Constituency: A geographical and political division, the population of which elects one or more members to Parliament or other elected bodies. For the House of Commons, constituencies are divided into counties and boroughs (in Scotland burghs). Today, the difference between them is slight, but prior to the late nineteenth century they differed significantly in the size of their electorates and in their property qualifications for the franchise. There are currently 650 constituencies for the House of Commons.

Council Housing: Public rental accommodation provided by local government authorities, mainly by district and London borough councils. Legislation passed in the 1980s allowed tenants to purchase council flats (apartments) and houses.

Counter-insurgency: Military and political measures taken by governments to defeat opponents, typically guerillas or those practicing irregular warfare, seeking to overthrow them. Though there were earlier examples, the British use of counter-insurgency was greatest during the era of decolonization following the Second World War.

Coverture: A legal principle according to which the property of an unmarried woman (a *femme sole*) was controlled by her husband once she was married (and thus a *femme coverte*).

Decolonization: The achievement of independent rule by a colony, particularly in the period following the Second World War.

Devolution: The transfer of power and functions to local authorities by a central government. In the context of the United Kingdom, this specifically refers to the transfer of local governing authority to Northern Ireland, Scotland and Wales. Northern Ireland has had devolved government since its inception, and Scotland and Wales since 1999.

Disestablishment: The severing of links between church and state. Disestablishment became a political issue in nineteenth-century Britain because the Church of Ireland and the Church of England in Wales were both official state churches, supported by the payment of tithes, but were worshipped in by a minority of the population. The Church of Ireland was disestablished in 1869, while the Church of England in Wales was disestablished in 1920.

Dissenters: Protestants in England, Wales and Ireland who did not belong to the Church of England. Congregationalists, Presbyterians, Baptists, Quakers and later Methodists were the largest dissenting denominations. The Toleration Act of 1689 allowed Dissenters who accepted the doctrine of the Trinity to worship publicly, but did not allow them to hold public office. Dissenters were also known as "Nonconformists."

Dominion: A country within the British Empire prior to the Second World War which had substantial powers of self-government but still acknowledged the British monarch as head of state. The first dominion was Canada in 1867. "The dominions" was often used in this era to refer to the white settler colonies of the Empire such as Canada, Australia and New Zealand.

Enclosure: The fencing off by a landlord of common land in order to increase agricultural productivity. Enclosure was practiced in Britain as early as the Middle Ages, but was a particularly prominent feature of the eighteenth-century agricultural revolution.

Euroskeptic: Person, especially a politician, who objects to increasing the powers of the European Union and to the closer integration of the United Kingdom with the EU. Today, Euroskepticism is most commonly associated with the right wing of the Tory Party and with the United Kingdom Independence Party.

Excise: Taxes on goods such as tobacco, spirits and wine that were collected from retailers and passed on to consumers.

Fakir: A Muslim religious ascetic. The term is sometimes applied to Hindus as well.

First Lord of the Admiralty: Between 1708 and 1964, the Cabinet member with responsibility for the British Navy. The office was discontinued in 1964, and the Royal Navy is now administered by the Ministry of Defence.

First Past the Post: Electoral system used in United Kingdom parliamentary elections in which the candidate receiving the most votes in a constituency is the victor. Since the election of MPs is based on results in individual constituencies, under the first past the post system a party may win a majority of parliamentary seats without winning a plurality of votes (in other words, the most votes cast overall). The first past the post electoral system is generally seen as encouraging the growth of two major opposing parties within a political system, and lessening the influence of smaller parties. Also known as the single-ballot or single-member electoral system.

fiscal–Military State: A government that finances expanding armed forces through taxation and a national debt, necessitating the growth both of a bureaucracy and of powerful financial institutions both inside the state and outside of it.

Franchise: The right to vote, in British history usually in the context of elections for Members of Parliament.

Gaelic: A family of languages spoken by the indigenous Celts of Scotland and Ireland. Welsh and Cornish are also Celtic languages, but are not related to Gaelic.

Georgian: The name given to the period comprised of the reign of the first four Georges, from 1714 to 1830.

Grammar Schools: one of three types of secondary schools established under the 1944 Education Act. Grammar schools were the most academic and selective, while secondary modern schools and technical schools provided practical and technical education. Admission to grammar schools was by examinations taken by eleven-year-old students, known as the Eleven Plus. Beginning in the 1970s, grammar schools and other types of secondary institutions were replaced by comprehensive schools.

High Church: Before the middle of the nineteenth century, this term applied to a faction of the Church of England that advocated strict adherence to Anglican liturgy and hierarchy, and opposed the toleration of dissent. By the Victorian period, however, it increasingly denoted clergy and laity interested in recovering the Catholic roots of Anglicanism in ritual, vestments, music, and the decoration of churches.

Highlands: The rugged area north and west of the Highland Boundary Fault in Scotland. Historically distinct from the Lowlands because Gaelic was widely spoken there prior to the eighteenth century and because it was dominated by the clan system.

House of Commons: The "lower" house of Parliament, consisting of the elected representatives of counties and local boroughs.

House of Lords: The "upper" house of Parliament, consisting (until the twentieth century) of the hereditary peers of England and Wales (and later of small delegations of Scottish and Irish peers), senior bishops and archbishops of the Church of England, and high-ranking jurists known as the "law lords."

Hung Parliament: Situation in which no one party has a majority in the House of Commons following a general election. A hung parliament may result in the formation of a coalition government between two or more parties.

Indentured Servants: Servants in colonial America who worked a contract term (usually four to seven years) in exchange for their passage to America. Indentured servants typically received "freedom dues" of land and other benefits at the completion of their contract.

Inner Temple: One of four legal societies in London known as Inns of Court. One must be "called to the bar" by one of the four Inns of Court in order to practice as a barrister (a lawyer who appears in court as an advocate) in England and Wales.

Jacobites: Britons who continued to recognize the Stuart dynasty (James II, and subsequently his heirs), as the legitimate rulers of England, Scotland and Ireland after 1688.

Jingoism: Aggressive, warlike patriotism. The term originated in an 1878 music hall song, written at a time when Russia threatened the Ottoman capital of Constantinople, which Britain viewed as a threat to the Mediterranean and the Suez Canal route to India.

Joint Stock Company: Business entity owned by shareholders who share both the risk and the profits of the business relative to the amount they have invested.

Keynesian: Economic theory based on the ideas of the British economist John Maynard Keynes (1883–1946). Keynes argued for a greater government interventionist role in the economy, and in particular contended that governments had to stimulate aggregate demand in order to achieve full employment. Keynesianism formed the basis of economic policies in most western societies, including Britain, in the decades after the end of the Second World War.

Kirk: A Scottish word for "church," also used to refer to the Church of Scotland specifically. Prior to the seventeenth century, the official name for the established, Presbyterian Church in Scotland was the Kirk of Scotland; thereafter "the Kirk" remained in use as an informal term for the Church of Scotland.

Laissez-Faire: From the French term meaning "to let act," an economic philosophy in which markets are left to regulate themselves with little or no government intervention, in the belief that this will produce the greatest efficiency and wealth through competition and the promotion of self-reliance over dependence.

Life Peerage: A non-hereditary aristocratic title conferring membership for the life of the recipient in the House of Lords. Life peerages can be awarded to both men and women under the Life Peerages Act of 1958. Since the passage of the House of Lords Act of 1999, life peers form the vast majority of the members of the House of Lords.

Low Church: A faction of the Church of England that favored the acceptance and comprehension of protestant dissenters. From the Victorian period, however, the term applied to Anglicans who favored simpler and less ritualized worship, with an emphasis on preaching rather than the sacraments.

Lowlands: The part of Scotland that lies south and east of the Highland Boundary Line.

Maginot Line: System of defensive fortifications constructed by France along the German border in the interwar period, which was outflanked by the German Army during the 1940 blitzkrieg.

Means-Tested: The calculation of a welfare entitlement based on a person's income and financial assets.

Mercantilism: The dominant European economic and commercial philosophy in the seventeenth and eighteenth centuries. Mercantilism emphasized the possession of gold reserves as vital to a nation's economic health. Mercantilist policies attempted to maintain a positive trade balance through trade restrictions such as tariffs (or taxes on imported goods). The Navigation Acts, which stipulated that trade with English (later British) colonies to be conducted in English ships, are an example of a mercantilist policy.

Metropolis: A term used by historians of empire to refer to the imperial center in relation to the colonial periphery. (In the case of the British Empire, "metropolis" refers to Britain.)

Middle England: Refers to the middle classes outside of London, a group traditionally considered to hold provincial attitudes and conservative political views.

Neoclassical: In architecture, a style of building that imitated ancient Greek and Roman models, especially those discovered in the later eighteenth century through the new field of archaeology.

Nonconformists: see "Dissenters."

Old Pretender: James Edward Stuart, the eldest son of the exiled James II. After his father's death in 1701, he claimed to be King of England, Scotland and Ireland. His son, Charles Edward Stuart, was called the Young Pretender after 1766, because he like his deceased father "pretended" to the throne.

Oxbridge: A conflation of the universities of Oxford and Cambridge. The term "Oxbridge" is often used to connote elite status within British society (for example, in reference to someone with an "Oxbridge education").

Patronage: The power to control appointments to political office, often used as a reward for electoral support; also, the ability to provide financial support to an artist, writer or musician.

Penal Laws: Discriminatory legislation enacted against Roman Catholics, forbidding them to hold services, marry protestants, hold public office, serve in the armed forces or possess firearms, and requiring them to practice partible inheritance and pay double taxation on any land that they owned. The penal laws were gradually repealed between 1778 and 1829.

Pocket Borough: A borough constituency for the House of Commons that was in the control of a single person or family.

Poll Tax: A uniform tax on all adult individuals that is imposed without reference to income. While poll taxes were collected in medieval England, in the modern era poll tax refers to the Conservative government's introduction in 1989 (in Scotland) and 1990 (in the rest of the UK) of a poll tax, known as community charge, in place of rates (taxes levied on the value of property).

Postcolonialism: Academic field that analyzes the impact of imperialism on the cultures of both the colonizer and colonized and its continuing influence in the contemporary world.

Prime Minister: The head of the British government, nominally appointed by the monarch, but actually chosen by the political party or parties in control of Parliament. "Prime Minister" was originally a term of disparagement, and to this day, it is an informal title; technically, the PM (as the title is abbreviated) is the "Lord Treasurer."

Privatization: The transfer of ownership of public services, businesses and agencies from the public sector (government) to the private sector (business). Under Margaret Thatcher's Conservative government from 1979 to 1990, numerous government enterprises were privatized, including British Airways, British Steel, and British Telecom.

Privy Council: "The Private Council," so-called to distinguish it from the "Great Council," or Parliament. Before 1689, this body of high-ranking royal and courtly officials was critically important, as the monarch ruled through its agency when Parliament was not sitting. It was later eclipsed in importance by the Cabinet, whose members answer to the Prime Minister.

Public School: A private secondary school requiring the payment of tuition rather than a school run by local government. The term "public school" was first used in the eighteenth century to reflect the fact that these schools accepted boarding students whose parents could afford to pay their fees, as opposed to purely local schools. Although today most public schools are co-educational and accept day students, they were traditionally boarding institutions that educated the sons of the upper and upper-middle classes. Still elite institutions today, they are also known as "independent schools."

Queen's Speech (or King's Speech): The royal address that begins the new session of Parliament each year. It is the focal point of the ceremonial state opening of Parliament; in it, the current monarch sets the legislative agenda. Today, the speech's content is determined by a Cabinet committee, with the Prime Minister the final arbiter, but it was once written by the monarch himself or herself and his or her advisers.

Raj: Derived from the Hindi word "raj" meaning "rule" or "reign," the Raj refers to the British colonial government in India, particularly in the era from the establishment of the Government of India in 1858 to the end of colonial rule in 1947.

Redbrick Universities: British universities founded in late-nineteenth- and early-twentieth-century British provincial cities. The description of these new universities as constructed out of "red bricks" was intended to contrast them with the centuries-old stonework of the elite Oxbridge colleges.

Republicanism: In Irish history, an ideology advocating that all of Ireland should be an independent republic, rather than under British rule.

Rotten Borough: A borough constituency for the House of Commons that had very few voters in it, thereby making it susceptible to bribery and corruption.

Royal Society: Learned society for the promotion of scientific knowledge founded in 1660, and which received the patronage of Charles II in the following year.

Shadow Cabinet: A group of the leading opposition politicians who form an alternative government to the one in power. Each member of the Shadow Cabinet is given a "shadow" position that parallels a position in the real Cabinet. The Shadow Cabinet offers criticisms of government policies as well as alternative policies of its own.

Shilling: A currency denomination formerly used in Britain. Before decimalization in 1971, there were twenty shillings in a pound and twelve pence in a shilling.

Sinecure: A salaried position with few responsibilities, if any, attached. *Sine cure* means "without care" in Latin.

Sinking Fund: A fund created by Sir Robert Walpole to pay off, or "sink," a portion of the national debt every year.

Ska: Jamaican musical form popular in 1960s Britain. Rhythmic and syncopated, ska music prominently features bass and was popular among black youth in dance halls in British cities, and increasingly spread to white audiences following the hit single "My Boy Lollipop" by Millie Small in 1964.

Sterling: The currency of the United Kingdom. Also called "pound sterling." Up to 1971, the pound sterling was divided into 240 pence, or 20 shillings worth 12 pence each. Since 1971 sterling has been a decimal currency in which 100 pence equal one pound.

Tories: One of the two major political parties in Parliament; after 1846, the nickname of the Conservative Party. Initially, the Tories were associated with the Royalists of the English Civil War; they believed in the supremacy of the Church of England and of the monarchy, for which reason they opposed the exclusion of James II from the throne. They traditionally represented the interests of rural landowners. After free-trade Tories defected to the Whigs to repeal the Corn Laws in 1846, the Tories were officially known as the Conservative Party.

Underground: Public subway or metro system in the greater London area. Opened in 1863, it was the first underground railway in the world. Popularly known as "The Tube" after the circular train tunnels first dug in the late nineteenth century.

Westminster: Central London borough where the Palace of Westminster, which houses the United Kingdom Parliament, is located. As a result, "Westminster" is often used as a shorthand term to refer to Parliament.

Whigs: Until 1846, one of the two political parties in Parliament. Loosely associated with the parliamentarians or "roundheads" in the English Civil War, Whigs believed in the supremacy of parliament and the toleration of dissent, and generally supported the interests of commerce and trade. In the nineteenth century, they became advocates of free trade and the expansion of voting rights. In 1846, Whigs joined with free-trade Tories to become the Liberal Party.

Whitehall: A road in central London, the name of which is derived from the Palace of Whitehall that used to occupy the area but which burned in 1698. Because many of its departments and ministries are located along Whitehall, the term is often used to refer to the British government.

Index

Note: Page numbers in **bold** indicate text to be found in the text boxes throughout the book and those in *italics* indicate those referring to figures, pictures and photographs